Lecture Notes in Computer Science   10066

Commenced Publication in 1973
Founding and Former Series Editors:
Gerhard Goos, Juris Hartmanis, and Jan van Leeuwen

More information about this series at http://www.springer.com/series/7410

Guojun Wang · Indrakshi Ray
Jose M. Alcaraz Calero · Sabu M. Thampi (Eds.)

Security, Privacy, and Anonymity in Computation, Communication, and Storage

9th International Conference, SpaCCS 2016
Zhangjiajie, China, November 16–18, 2016
Proceedings

 Springer

Editors
Guojun Wang
Guangzhou University
Guangzhou
China

Jose M. Alcaraz Calero
University of the West of Scotland
Paisley, Glasgow
UK

Indrakshi Ray
Department of Computer Science
Colorado State University
Fort Collins, CO
USA

Sabu M. Thampi
Indian Institute of Information Technology
  and Management, Kerala (IIITMK)
Trivandrum, Kerala
India

ISSN 0302-9743   ISSN 1611-3349   (electronic)
Lecture Notes in Computer Science
ISBN 978-3-319-49147-9   ISBN 978-3-319-49148-6   (eBook)
DOI 10.1007/978-3-319-49148-6

Library of Congress Control Number: 2016957376

LNCS Sublibrary: SL4 – Security and Cryptology

Printed on acid-free paper

This Springer imprint is published by Springer Nature
The registered company is Springer International Publishing AG
The registered company address is: Gewerbestrasse 11, 6330 Cham, Switzerland

Preface

The 9th International Conference on Security, Privacy, and Anonymity in Computation, Communication and Storage (SpaCCS 2016) was held in Zhangjiajie, China, during November 16–18, 2016, and was jointly organized by Central South University, Guangzhou University, and Jishou University.

The SpaCCS conference series provides a forum for world-class researchers to gather and share their research achievements, emerging ideas, and trends in information security fields. Previous SpaCCS conferences were held in Helsinki, Finland (2015), Beijing, China (2014), Melbourne, Australia (2013), Liverpool, UK (2012), and Changsha, China (2011).

This year the conference received 110 submissions. All submissions received at least three reviews during a high-quality review process. According to the review results, 40 papers were selected for oral presentation at the conference and inclusion in this Springer volume, giving an acceptance rate of 36.4 %. Besides the regular paper presentations, the program included three interesting and insightful keynotes by Prof. Yang Xiao, the University of Alabama, USA, Prof. Indrakshi Ray, Colorado State University, USA, and Dr. Shui Yu, Deakin University, Australia. We are very grateful to the keynote speakers.

SpaCCS 2016 was made possible by the joint effort of numerous people and organizations worldwide. There is a long list of people who volunteered their time and energy to put together the conference and who deserve special thanks. First and foremost, we would like to offer our gratitude to Prof. Guojun Wang from Guangzhou University, China, and Prof. Gregorio Martinez from University of Murcia, Spain, the Steering Committee chairs, for guiding the whole process of the conference. We are also deeply grateful to all the Program Committee members for their great effort in reading, commenting, debating, and finally selecting the papers. We also wish to thank all the external reviewers for assisting the Program Committee in their particular areas of expertise.

We would like to offer our gratitude to the general chairs, Jianbin Li, Prof. Felix Gomez Marmol, and Prof. Juan E. Tapiador, for their great support and good suggestions contributing to the success of the conference. Thanks also go to the: workshop chairs, Dr. Raymond Choo, Dr. Mianxiong Dong, and Dr. Jin Li; publicity chairs, Prof. Carlos Becker Westphall, Dr. Scott Fowler, and Dr. Xiaofei Xing; publication chair, Shuhong Chen; organization chairs, Prof. Fang Qi, Dr. Xiaofei Xing and Prof. Qingping Zhou; registration chair, Ms. Pin Liu; conference secretariat, Dr. Sancheng Peng; and Webmaster, Mr. Binji Mo.

We would like to thank all the authors, participants, and session chairs for their valuable efforts, many of whom travelled long distances to attend this conference and make their valuable contributions.

November 2016

Indrakshi Ray
Jose M. Alcaraz Calero
Sabu M. Thampi

Organization

General Chairs

Jianbin Li	Central South University, China
Felix Gomez Marmol	NEC Laboratories Europe, Germany
Juan E. Tapiador	The University Carlos III of Madrid, Spain

Program Chairs

Indrakshi Ray	Colorado State University, USA
Jose M. Alcaraz Calero	University of the West of Scotland, UK
Sabu M. Thampi	Indian Institute of Information Technology and Management, India

Program Vice Chairs

Security Track

Javier Lopez	University of Malaga, Spain
Qin Liu	Hunan University, China

Privacy Track

Rinku Dewri	University of Denver, USA
Wenjun Jiang	Hunan University, China

Anonymity Track

Mario Freire	The University of Beira Interior, Portugal
Md. Zakirul Alam Bhuiyan	Temple University, USA

Program Committee

Afrand Agah	West Chester University of Pennsylvania, USA
Habtamu Abie	Norwegian Computing Center/Norsk Regnesentral, Norway
Hamid Ali Abed Al-asadi	Basra University, Iraq
Ricardo Marco Alaez	University of the West of Scotland, UK
Bruhadeshwar Bezawada	International Institute of Information Technology, India
Cataldo Basile	Politecnico di Torino, Italy
Simona Bernardi	Centro Universitario de la Defensa, Spain
Jorge Bernal Bernabe	University of Murcia, Spain
Saad Bani-Mohammad	Dean of IT College, Al al-Bayt University, Jordan

Salima Benbernou	Université Paris Descartes, France
Yan Bai	University of Washington Tacoma, USA
Miguel Pupo Correia	University of Lisbon, Portugal
Alfredo Cuzzocrea	University of Trieste and ICAR-CNR, Italy, Italy
Aniello Castiglione	University of Salerno, Italy
Anupam Chattopadhyay	Nanyang Technological University, Singapore
Christian Callegari	The University of Pisa, Italy
John A. Clark	University of York, UK
Lien-Wu Chen	Feng Chia University, Taiwan
Mauro Conti	University of Padua, Italy
Naveen Chilamkurti	La Trobe University, Australia
Sudip Chakraborty	Valdosta State University, USA
Josep Domingo-Ferrer	Universitat Rovira i Virgili, Catalonia
Sabrina De Capitani di Vimercati	Università degli Studi di Milano, Italy
Ying Dai	Temple University, USA
Yucong Duan	Hainan University, China
Zhihui Du	Tsinghua University, China
Oscar Esparza	Universitat Politècnica de Catalunya, Spain
Dieter Gollmann	Hamburg University of Technology, Germany
Dimitris Geneiatakis	Aristotle University of Thessaloniki, Greece
Liang Gu	Yale University, USA
Saurabh Kumar Garg	University of Tasmania, Australia
Yao Guo	Peking University, China
Ying Guo	Central South University, China
Ching-Hsien Hsu	Chung Hua University, Taiwan
Mohammad Mehedi Hassans	King Saud University, KSA
Ragib Hasan	University of Alabama, Birmingham, UK
Xiaojun Hei	School of Electronic Information and Communications, Huazhong University of Science and Technology, China
Xinyi Huang	Fujian Normal University, China
Pedro Inácio	University of Beira Interior, Portugal
Hai Jiang	Arkansas State University, USA
Murtuza Jadliwala	Wichita State University, USA
Young-Sik Jeong	Dongguk University, Korea
Gabor Kiss	Obuda University, Hungary
Ram Krishnan	University of Texas, USA
Ryan Ko	University of Waikato, New Zealand
Vana Kalogeraki	Athens University of Economics, Greece
Chi Lin	Dalian University of Technology, China
Giovanni Livraga	Università degli Studi di Milano, Italy
Haibing Lu	Santa Clara University, USA
Haitao Lang	University of Physics & Electronics, China
Jialin Liu	Lawrence Berkeley National Lab, USA

Rongxing Lu	Nanyang Technological University, Singapore
Xin Li	Nanjing University of Aeronautics and Astronautics, China
Xin Liao	Hunan University, China
Yingjiu Li	Singapore Management University, Singapore
Guerroumi Mohamed	University of Sciences and Technology Houari Boumediene, Algeria
Jose Andre Morales	Carnegie Mellon University-CERT, USA
Aleksandra Mileva	University Goce Delcev, Republic of Macedonia
Juan Pedro Munoz-Gea	Universidad Politécnica de Cartagena, Spain
Mirco Marchetti	University of Modena and Reggio Emilia, Italy
Renita Murimi	Oklahoma Baptist University, USA
Sheikh M. Habib	TU Darmstadt Germany, Germany
Subhomoy Maitra	ISI Calcutta, India
Wissam Mallouli	Montimage, France
Ben Niu	Lehigh University, USA
David Naccache	École normale supérieure, France
Pouya Ostovari	Temple University, USA
Rolf Oppliger	eSECURITY Technologies, Switzerland
Al-Sakib Khan Pathan	UAP and SEU, Bangladesh/Islamic University in Madinah, KSA
Carlos Perez-Conde	Universidad de Valencia, Spain
Günther Pernul	University of Regensburg, Germany
Joon S. Park	Syracuse University, USA
Risat Mahmud Pathan	Chalmers University of Technology, Sweden
Roberto Di Pietro	Nokia Bell Labs, France
Sancheng Peng	Guangdong University of Foreign Studies, China
Miguel Pardal	University of Lisbon, Portugal
Vincenzo Piuri	Università degli Studi di Milano, Italy
Zeeshan Pervez	University of the West of Scotland, UK
Bimal Roy	Indian Statistical Institute, India
Imed Romdhani	Edinburgh Napier University, UK
Indrajit Ray	Colorado State University, USA
Md. Abdur Razzaque	University of Dhaka, Bangladesh
Mubashir Husain Rehmani	COMSATS Institue of Information Technology, Pakistan
Altair Santin	Pontifical Catholic University of Parana, Brazil
Chang-ai Sun	University of Science and Technology Beijing, China
Chao Song	University of Electronic Science and Technology of China, China
Chunhua Su	School of Information Science, Japan
Dimitris E. Simos	SBA Research, Austria
Hossain Shahriar	Kennesaw State University, USA
Hung-Min Sun	National Tsing Hua University, Taiwan
Jun Shen	University of Wollongong, Australia

Junggab Son	North Carolina Central University, USA
Qiang Tang	University of Luxembourg, Luxembourg
Ramakrishna Thurimella	University of Denver, USA
Traian Marius Truta	Northern Kentucky University, USA
Eugene Y. Vasserman	Kansas State University, USA
Luis Javier Garcia Villalba	The Complutense University, Spain
Tam Vu	University of Colorado-De, USA
Hejun Wu	Sun Yat-Sen University, China
Mingzhong Wang	University of the Sunshine Coast, Australia
Yongdong Wu	Insitute for Infocomm Research, Singapore
Yunsheng Wang	Kettering University, USA
Xiaolong Xu	Nanjing University of Posts and Telecommunications, China
Baoliu Ye	Nanjing University, China
Chau Yuen	Singapore University of Technology and Design, Singapore
Yu Hua	Huazhong University of Science and Technology, China
Ilsun You	Soonchunhyang University, Republic of Korea
Lin Ye	Harbin Institute of Technology, China
Muneer Masadeh Bani Yassein	Jordan University of Science and Technology, Jordan
Shucheng Yu	University of Arkansas at Little Rock, USA
Xuanxia Yao	Universty of Science and Technology Beijing, China
Congxu Zhu	Central South University, China
David Zheng	Frostburg State University, USA
Huan Zhou	China Three Gorges University, China
Mingwu Zhang	Hubei University of Technology, China
Qingchen Zhang	St. Francis Xavier University, Canada
Sherali Zeadally	University of Kentucky, USA
Yaoxiong Zhao	Google Inc, USA
Youwen Zhu	Nanjing University of Aeronautics and Astronautics, China
Yun-Wei Zhao	Tilburg University, The Netherlands

Steering Committee Chairs

Guojun Wang	Guangzhou University, China
Gregorio Martinez	University of Murcia, Spain

Steering Committee

Jemal H. Abawajy	Deakin University, Australia
Jose M. Alcaraz Calero	University of the West of Scotland, UK
Jiannong Cao	Hong Kong Polytechnic University, Hong Kong, SAR China

Hsiao-Hwa Chen	National Cheng Kung University, Taiwan
Jinjun Chen	University of Technology, Sydney, Australia
Kim-Kwang Raymond Choo	University of Texas at San Antonio, USA
Robert Deng	Singapore Management University, Singapore
Mario Freire	The University of Beira Interior, Portugal
Minyi Guo	Shanghai Jiao Tong University, China
Weijia Jia	Shanghai Jiao Tong University, China
Wei Jie	University of West London, UK
Georgios Kambourakis	University of the Aegean, Greece
Ryan Ko	University of Waikato, New Zealand
Constantinos Kolias	George Mason University, USA
Jianbin Li	Central South University, China
Jie Li	University of Tsukuba, Japan
Jianhua Ma	Hosei University, Japan
Felix Gomez Marmol	NEC Laboratories Europe, Germany
Geyong Min	University of Exeter, UK
Peter Mueller	IBM Zurich Research Laboratory, Switzerland
Indrakshi Ray	Colorado State University, USA
Kouichi Sakurai	Kyushu University, Japan
Juan E. Tapiador	The University Carlos III of Madrid, Spain
Sabu M. Thampi	Indian Institute of Information Technology and Management, India
Jie Wu	Temple University, USA
Yang Xiao	The University of Alabama, USA
Yang Xiang	Deakin University, Australia
Zheng Yan	Aalto University, Finland
Laurence T. Yang	St. Francis Xavier University, Canada
Wanlei Zhou	Deakin University, Australia

Workshop Chairs

Kim-Kwang Raymond Choo	University of Texas at San Antonio, USA
Mianxiong Dong	Muroran Institute of Technology, Japan
Jin Li	Guangzhou University, China

Publicity Chairs

Carlos Becker Westphall	Federal University of Santa Catarina, Brazil
Scott Fowler	Linkoping University, Sweden
Xiaofei Xing	Guangzhou University, China

Publication Chair

| Shuhong Chen | Hunan Institute of Engineering, China |

Registration Chair

Pin Liu   Central South University, China

Local Chairs

Fang Qi   Central South University, China
Xiaofei Xing   Guangzhou University, China
Qingping Zhou   Jishou University, China

Conference Secretariat

Sancheng Peng   Guangdong University of Foreign Studies, China

Webmaster

Binji Mo   Central South University, China

SpaCCS 2016 Sponsors

Contents

A Lightweight RFID Authentication Protocol with Forward Security and Randomized Identifier

Zhicai Shi[(✉)], Fei Wu, Changzhi Wang, and Shitao Ren

School of Electronic and Electrical Engineering,
Shanghai University of Engineering Science, Shanghai 201620, China
szc1964@163.com

Abstract. The RFID tags only have limited computing and memory resources. This makes it difficult to solve their security and privacy problems. Authentication is considered as an effective approach to protect the security and privacy of RFID systems. Based on Hash function and the randomization of the tag's identifier, a lightweight authentication protocol is proposed. The protocol uses Hash function to ensure the anonymity and confidentiality of the RFID system. It uses a randomization function to randomize the tag's identifier to enhance the difficulty to reveal the secrecy of the RFID system. Time stamp and pseudorandom number generator are combined to prevent replay attack. It also completes the strong authentication of the backend server to the tag by twice authentication. The analysis shows that this protocol provides forward security and it can prevent eavesdropping, tracing, replay and de-synchronize attack. The protocol only uses Hash function and pseudorandom number generator. It is very suitable to the low-cost RFID system.

Keywords: RFID · Authentication protocol · Hash function · Security · Privacy

1 Introduction

With the development and application of the Internet of Things, Radio Frequency IDentification (RFID) technique gets the wide attention from various fields. RFID is a pervasive technology deployed to identify and trace some objects automatically. It uses radiowaves to communicate, without visible light and physical contact. It is considered as a supplementary or replacement technology for traditional barcode technology. Today, RFID systems have been successfully applied to manufacturing, supply chain, agriculture, transportation, health, e-payment, food safety tracing, and some other fields [1]. But the tags of RFID systems only have limited computing and memory resources and they use open wireless channel to communicate. It is easy for the adversary to eavesdrop the session information of an RFID system. Attackers can attack an RFID system by tracing, forging, spoofing, impersonating, tampering and de-synchronizing. So the privacy and security of RFID systems has become one of the main factors to hinder their wide application. Although some physical methods have been proposed to solve the security and privacy problems of RFID systems the research results show that it is the most flexible and effective method to use software encryption and authentication technique. The popular tags are some low-cost passive tags. They have very limited

© Springer International Publishing AG 2016
G. Wang et al. (Eds.): SpaCCS 2016, LNCS 10066, pp. 1–13, 2016.
DOI: 10.1007/978-3-319-49148-6_1

computing and memory resources. They may be limited to hundreds of bits of storage, roughly between 5000 and 10000 logic gates. Within these logic gates, only 250 to 3000 gates can be devoted to security purpose [2]. It is very difficult to implement public key cryptography, even symmetric encryption algorithms for the low-cost passive RFID tags. So some lightweight cryptographic authentication protocols were proposed to satisfy the special requirements of RFID systems. But they usually use some complicated encryption algorithms and they are not suitable for the low-cost RFID tags. Some protocols use Hash function to complete the authentication for RFID systems, but they have some flaws so that they cannot entirely solve the security and privacy of RFID systems [3, 4]. So it is very necessary to design some simple and feasible lightweight authentication protocols for RFID systems, especially for the low-cost RFID systems.

The contribution of this paper is that we use Hash function and pseudorandom number generator to construct a novel lightweight authentication protocol for the low-cost RFID systems. Otherwise, we propose another special function, which is called the randomizing selecting bit function. This function randomly selects some bits of the tag's identifier to generate each session between tag and reader. Hence, each session only includes the partial information of the tag's identifier so as to enhance the difficulty to reveal the secrecy of RFID systems. The protocol provides forward security. It also completes the strong authentication of the backend server to the tag by twice authentication. It can prevent the leakage of the secret information and it implements the anonymous and confidential communication between tag and backend server/reader.

The paper is organized as follows. In Sect. 2, an RFID system's components, its security and privacy are introduced briefly. In Sect. 3, some typical Hash-based lightweight authentication protocols are analyzed and their flaws are pointed out. In Sect. 4, Hash function, a pseudorandom number generator and a randomizing selecting bit function are combined to construct a mutual authentication protocol for the low-cost RFID systems. In Sect. 5, the proposed protocol is analyzed and its security and privacy is proved. The secure performance of the protocol is compared with other similar authentication protocols. In Sect. 6, conclusions are given and the advantages of the proposed protocol are pointed out.

2 The RFID System, Its Security and Privacy

An RFID system consists of three components: Radio Frequency (RF) tag, RF reader and backend server, as shown in Fig. 1. A tag is a silicon chip with antenna and a small storage. There are two types of tags: active tag and passive tag. Active tags include batteries. Passive tags don't have any battery and they are activated by the RF signal from the reader. So they only have limited electric energy to transmit signals over shorter distance. This kind of tags is very cheap and they are usually called the low-cost tags. A reader is a device capable of sending and receiving data in the form of radio frequency signal. This device communicates with tag and reads its identifier. It has electric power enough to transmit signals over longer distance. So the communication channels between reader and tag are asymmetric. The channel from reader to tag is called forward channel and the channel from tag to reader is called backward channel.

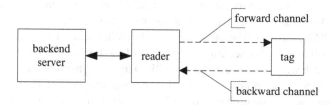

Fig. 1. The component of an RFID System

A backend server is used to store the detail information about the tagged objects, and it cooperates with reader to implement the authentication to tag. It searches the information about the tagged objects according to the tag's identifier and sends the information to the reader.

As an important component of the low-cost RFID system, the tag usually has very limited computing and memory resources and it uses the open wireless channel to communicate. It is difficult for a tag to implement some complicated cryptographic algorithms. So the channel between tag and reader is insecure. Most secure problems of RFID systems are resulted from the insecure wireless channel. But backend server and reader have abundant computing and storage resource. They can implement conventional cryptographic protocols. So the channel between backend server and reader is secure. They can be thought as one part of the RFID system, which is called the backend server/reader.

As a typical resource-constrained system, the low-cost RFID system is very vulnerable to some secure theats. An adversary can eavesdrop, intercept, tamper, block and replay each session between tag and backend sever/reader. It can impersonate a legitimate tag to cheat the backend server/reader. It can start de-synchronization attack by intercepting and blocking the sessions between tag and backend sever/reader. So a secure RFID system can resist against eavesdropping, tracing, replay and de-synchronization attack. Otherwise, it must satisfy forward security and anonymity.

3   Some Typical RFID Authentication Protocols

The cryptographic authentication protocols are thought as an important approach to ensure the privacy and security of RFID systems. They are divided into three categories: general authentication protocols, lightweight authentication protocols and ultra-lightweight authentication protocols. General authentication protocols are suitable for some situations with abundant computing and memory resources. They can use symmetric encryption algorithms, even public key cryptography. Lightweight authentication protocols use Hash function, CRC function, pseudorandom number generating function, bitwise operations. Ultra-lightweight authentication protocols only use pseudorandom number generating function and bitwise operations. The research results justify that the encryption strength is very limited for ultra-lightweight authentication protocols and they cannot protect the security and privacy of RFID systems. General authentication protocols need abundant computing and storing resources and they are not suitable for the low-cost RFID system. Therefore lightweight authentication protocols become a unique approach to solve the security and privacy of the low-cost RFID system.

Many research works have been done for RFID lightweight authentication in recent years. Some authentication protocols use the one-way property of Hash functions to solve the secure and private problems of RFID systems. But most of them have serious security problems or they are not suitable to the low-cost RFID system. These typical Hash-based authentication protocols are Hash-Lock protocol, Randomized Hash-Lock protocol, Hash-chain protocol, and so on.

Based on the difficulty of inverting to solve an one-way Hash function, S.A. Weis et al. [5] firstly proposed Hash-Lock protocol, which attempts to provide mutual authentication between tag and reader. The protocol uses the pseudonym of the tag, *MetaID*, to replace the actual tag's *ID* to ensure its privacy. During the authenticating process the plaintext of the tag's *ID* is transferred between tag and reader, and *MetaID* is fixed. So an adversary easily compromises mutual authentication by simply eavesdropping and replaying these exchanged sessions between tag and reader. Moreover, an adversary easily traces the tag's holder by the fixed *MetaID*.

In order to overcome the flaws of Hash-Lock protocol, S.A. Weis and S.E. Sarma et al. proposed randomized Hash-Lock protocol [5]. This protocol uses the pseudorandom number generator (PRNG) to randomize the transferred sessions between tag and reader. Tags respond to reader's queries by generating a random number r, then Hashing its *ID* and concatenating the result with r, and sending them to the reader. A legitimate reader identifies one of its tags by performing a brute-force search of its known *IDs*. Then the reader sends the identified tag's *ID* to the tag by plaintext. It is easy for an adversary to eavesdrop and obtain the identity information of the tag. Hence, it is vulnerable to spoofing and replay attack. Moreover, the tag's holder is easily traced and this protocol cannot satisfy forward security.

M. Ohkubo et al. firstly proposed Hash-chain protocol [6, 7]. The aim of their protocol is to provide better protection of the user's privacy by refreshing the identifier of the tag for each authentication. Different from Hash-Lock protocol, Hash-chain protocol uses two different Hash functions, $H()$ and $G()$. This protocol only provides one-way authentication, namely, the reader authenticates the tag while the tag does not authenticate the reader. To achieve forward security, this protocol uses the Hash chain technique to renew the secret information stored in the tag. But this protocol does not use a random number generator and it is vulnerable to spoofing and replay attack. Ohkubo et al.'s scheme has a complexity in terms of Hash computations of $m \times n$, where m is the given maximum limit on the Hash chain length and n is the total number of tags. Thus, when the number of tags n or the chain length m is large the computation becomes unimaginable for the low-cost RFID system. Another similar scheme was provided by Sang-Soo Yeo et al. [8]. The scheme gave a conceptually simple but elegant solution to defeat the tracing problem and ensure forward security. This scheme requires each tag to support 2 Hash functions. When the tag is queried by a reader, it sends the Hash value of its current identifier by a Hash function $G()$, and then renews its identity information using another different Hash function $H()$. These protocols use two different Hash functions and this makes it not suitable to the low-cost RFID system.

Yong Ki Lee et al. proposed a secure and low-cost authentication protocol for the RFID system, Semi-Randomized Access Control (SRAC) [9]. It also uses a pseudonym, *MetaID*, to replace the tag's *ID* like Hash-Lock protocol. It provides mutual authentication and forward security. It can protect RFID systems from many attacks, such as tracing, cloning and denial of service. However, it is vulnerable to replay attack. The adversary can simply eavesdrop and reuse *MetaID* to be authenticated successfully. Later, Su Mi Lee et al. used the challenge-response mechanism and proposed a low-cost RFID authentication protocol (LCAP) [10]. The aim of their effort is to solve the de-synchronized problem by maintaining a previous identifier in the backend server. This protocol provides mutual authentication and guarantees the location privacy of the tag's holder. It also provides untraceability by changing tag's identification dynamically. Nevertheless, it does not provide forward security, namely, an adversary can infer previous sessions about the tags after it reveals the present secret information of the tags.

Jung-Sik Cho et al. [11, 12] proposed a new Hash-based authentication protocol to solve the secure and private problems for the RFID system. However, Hyunsung Kim [13] demonstrated that this protocol is vulnerable to DOS attack. He pointed out that Jung-Sik Cho et al.'s protocol is vulnerable to traffic analysis and tag/reader imperso-nation attacks. More precisely, an adversary can impersonate a valid tag or reader with probability 1/4. Finally, an adversary can obtain some information about the secret values of the tag in the next session with probability 3/4. Therefore Hyunsung Kim proposed an improved protocol to offer protection against the attacks described above. But this enhanced version is as insecure as its predecessor. Walid I. Khedr [14] pointed out that an adversary can perform a de-synchronization attack by intercepting and tampering the transferred message. Further, Walid I. Khedr justified that Jung-Sik Cho et al.'s protocol cannot ensure forward security. Masoumeh Safkhani and Pedro Peris-Lopez et al. [15] also constructed three different attacks to demonstrate Jung-Sik Cho et al.'s protocol is vulnerable to de-synchronization attack and tag/reader imper-sonation attacks. Masoumeh Safkhani and Pedro Peris-Lopez et al. justified that the de-synchronization attack succeeds with probability 1 and the complexity of the attack is only one run of the protocol.

J.H. Ha and S.J. Moon et al. [16] proposed an RFID security protocol using the Hash-based functions and proved that their protocol can provide forward privacy. However, Da-Zhi Sun and Ji-Dong Zhong [17] pointed out that an attacker can track a target tag by observing previous unsuccessful sessions of the tag. Da-Zhi Sun et al. justified that J.H. Ha et al.'s protocol fails to provide forward privacy as they claimed and then they proposed another Hash-based authentication functions to overcome the weaknesses of J.H. Ha et al.'s protocol. But all these protocols use two different Hash functions and they are not suitable for the low-cost RFID system.

Liu Yang, Peng Yu et al. proposed an RFID secure authenticated protocol based on Hash function [18]. Their protocol ensures the privacy of the tag's secret information and realizes three party mutual authentications among tag, reader and backend server. But, for each authentication process of the protocol, the tag and the reader call Hash function more than five times respectively. So their proposed protocol is so complicated that it is not suitable to the low-cost RFID system.

By analysis as described above, it can be concluded that recent proposed RFID authentication protocols with Hash function failed to solve the security and privacy for the low-cost RFID systems. Especially, many Hash-based authentication protocols cannot ensure forward security, or they use two different Hash functions, which hinders their application to the low-cost RFID system.

4   A Secure Hash-Based Authentication Protocol with Randomized Identifier for the Low-Cost RFID System

Some low-cost tags like EPC Global Class1 Gen2 standard can provide Hash function, pseudorandom number generator and simple bitwise operations [19, 20]. Now, we use these on-chip functions and bitwise operations to complete the mutual authentication between tag and backend server/reader. Moreover, we construct a function to randomly select the tag's partial identifier so that each session only includes the partial secrecy of a tag.

Supposed ID is the identifier of a tag and it uniquely identifies the tag. pID is the pseudonym of a tag and $pID = PRNG(ID)$. $PRNG()$ is a pseudorandom number generator. The length of ID and pID is L bit and $L \in \{64, 96, 128\}$. ID and pID are stored in the tag. $curID, curpID, oldID$ and $oldpID$ are some other parameters, which are stored in the backend server. $curID$ and $curpID$ are the identifier and pseudonym of a tag used in the current authentication process. $oldID$ and $oldpID$ are the values of ID and pID used in the last successful authentication process. The purpose to store $oldID$ and $oldpID$ is to resist against de-synchronization attack. At the beginning of the authentication, the initial values of $curID$ and $oldID$ are set to the identifier of the tag. Namely, $curID = oldID = ID$ and $curpID = oldpID = PRNG(ID)$. The tag and the backend server share Hash function $Hash()$, pseudorandom number generator $PRNG()$ and a random selecting bit function $f(x, m, n)$. These three functions are defined as follows:

$$Hash():\{0, 1\} * \to \{0, 1\}^L$$

$$PRNG():\{0, 1\} * \to \{0, 1\}^L$$

$$f(x, m, n) = x_m x_{m+1} \cdots \cdots x_n$$

Where x is the tag's identifier and $x = x_0 x_1 \cdots \cdots x_{L-1}$, m and n are two random numbers generated by the pseudorandom number generator, $0 \leq m \leq L - 1$ and $0 \leq n \leq L - 1$.

The function $f(x, m, n)$ randomly selects the partial identifier of a tag and uses it to generate each session between tag and backend server/reader. Hence, each session only includes one part of the tag's identifier and this increases the difficulty to reveal the tag's secrecy. The one-way property of Hash function $Hash()$ is used to ensure the integrity of each session and the confidential transfer of the tag's secrecy. The pseudorandom number generator $PRNG()$ is used to keep the freshness of the sessions and to resist against tracing attack. Moreover, the time stamp of the backend server is used to resist against replay attack. The authentication protocol is shown in Fig. 2 and the symbols used by the protocol are described in Table 1.

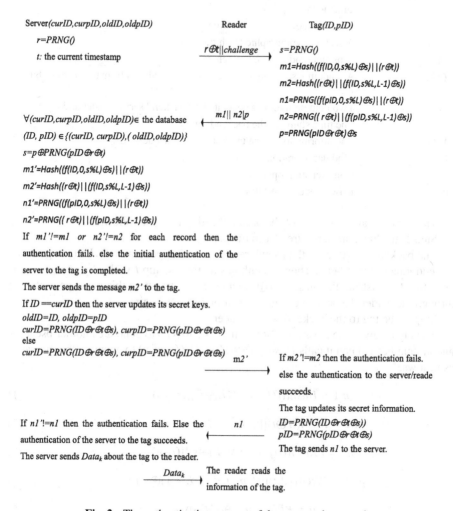

Fig. 2. The authentication process of the proposed protocol

Table 1. The symbols used in the proposed authentication protocol

Notation	Description
ID, pID	The tag's identifier and its pseudonym
curID and *curpID*	The tag's identifier and its pseudonym used for the current authentication process
oldID and *oldpID*	The tag's identifier and its pseudonym used for the prior successful authentication process
L	The length of the tag's identifier
Hash()	A secure cryptographic Hash function
PRNG()	A pseudorandom number generator
$f(x, m, n)$	A randomly selecting bit function and its value is from the mth to n^{th} bits of x
r, s	Two random numbers generated by backend server/reader and tag
t	The time stamp of the backend server
$DATA_k$	The information of the tag k stored in the backend server
%	Modular operation
‖	Concatenation operation
⊕	Bitwise exclusive-OR operation

The authentication process of the protocol is described as follows:

Step 1: the backend server/reader to the tag

The backend server calls the pseudorandom number generator *PRNG()* to generate a pseudorandom number r. Then it combines its time stamp t with r by exclusive-OR operation to construct the message $r \oplus t \| $ *challenge*. It transfers this message to the tag through the reader. Hence, a new authentication process begins.

Step 2: the tag to the backend server/reader

The tag receives the message $r \oplus t$ and it calls *PRNG()* to generate another pseudorandom number s. Then it calls *Hash()*, *PRNG()* and $f(x, m, n)$ to generate the messages as follows:

$$m1 = Hash((f(ID, 0, s\%L) \oplus s) \| (r \oplus t)) \tag{1}$$

$$m2 = Hash((r \oplus t) \| (f(ID, s\%L, L - 1) \oplus s)) \tag{2}$$

$$n1 = PRNG((f(pID, 0, s\%L) \oplus s) \| (r \oplus t)) \tag{3}$$

$$n2 = PRNG((r \oplus t) \| (f(pID, s\%L, L - 1) \oplus s)) \tag{4}$$

$$p = PRNG(pID \oplus r \oplus t) \oplus s \tag{5}$$

The tag constructs the message $m1 \| n2 \| p$ and it sends this message to the backend server through the reader.

Step 3: the backend server/reader to the tag

After the backend server receives the message $m1 \| n2 \| p$, it searches its backend database to get each record about the tags, (*curID, curpID, oldID, oldpID*). Firstly, it uses *curpID* of the current record to compute $p \oplus PRNG(curpID \oplus r \oplus t)$ and to abstract s.

Secondly, it uses *curID* and *curpID* of the current record to replace *ID* and *pID* in Eqs. (1) to (4) to compute $m1'$, $m2'$, $n1'$ and $n2'$. Then it compares $m1'$ and $n2'$ with $m1$ and $n2$ respectively. If one of them is not equal the backend server uses *oldID* and *oldpID* of the current record to repeat the above procedure to calculate s, $m1'$, $m2'$, $n1'$ and $n2'$ again. The backend server compares $m1'$ and $n2'$ with $m1$ and $n2$. If one of them is not equal yet then next record is picked up from the database to repeat the procedure described above until all records are processed. If $m1'$ does not equal $m1$ or $n2'$ does not equal $n2$ for all records, the authentication to the tag fails and the protocol exits. If there exists one record which satisfies that $m1'$ equals $m1$ and $n2'$ equals $n2$, the first authentication of the backend server to the tag succeeds. Then the backend server sends the message $m2'$ to the tag through the reader. The backend server begins to update its secret keys as follows.

If (*curID*, *curpID*) is used for the above successful authentication the backend server updates its secret keys as follows:

$$oldID = curID \tag{6}$$

$$oldpID = curpID \tag{7}$$

$$curID = PRNG(curID \oplus r \oplus t \oplus s) \tag{8}$$

$$curpID = PRNG(curpID \oplus r \oplus t \oplus s) \tag{9}$$

If (*oldID*, *oldpID*) is used for the above successful authentication the backend server holds its current *oldID* and *oldpID*. It only updates its partial secret keys as follows:

$$curID = PRNG(oldID \oplus r \oplus t \oplus s) \tag{10}$$

$$curpID = PRNG(oldpID \oplus r \oplus t \oplus s) \tag{11}$$

Step 4: the tag to the backend server/reader

After the tag receives the message $m2'$, it compares $m2'$ with $m2$. If they are not equal the authentication to the backend server/reader fails and the protocol exits. Otherwise the authentication to the backend server/reader succeeds. Then the tag begins to update its secret keys as follows:

$$ID = PRNG(ID \oplus r \oplus t \oplus s) \tag{12}$$

$$pID = PRNG(pID \oplus r \oplus t \oplus s) \tag{13}$$

The tag sends $n1$ to the backend server through the reader.

Step 5: the backend server to the reader

The backend server receives the message $n1$ from the tag and it compares $n1$ with $n1'$. If they are not equal the authentication fails and the protocol exits. Otherwise the second authentication to the tag is completed successfully.

Then the backend server gets the detail information about the tag, $DATA_k$, from its database and sends the information to the reader. After the reader receives $DATA_k$, it displays $DATA_k$ on its screen.

The procedure described above completes the mutual authentication between backend server/reader and tag. Meanwhile, it also completes the strong authentication of the backend server to the tag by twice authentication.

5 The Analysis to the Privacy and Security of the Proposed Protocol

The authentication process described above shows that the protocol uses the random selecting bit function to make the sessions unpredictable and this increases the difficulty to reveal the secret information of the tag. One-way property of Hash function ensures the integrity of the sessions and the confidential transfer of the secret information of the RFID system. A pseudorandom number generator randomizes the messages sent by the tag so that it is difficult for the adversary to trace and identify a tag. Meanwhile, the time stamp is used to resist against replay attack. The protocol provides forward security and it can also resist against de-synchronization attack.

- Forward security. After each authentication is completed the protocol updates the secrecy of the tag. Therefore the protocol uses some different secret keys to encrypt and generate the sessions for each authentication. There is not any relationship between the previous sessions and the current secret keys. Although an adversary reveals the current secrecy of the tag he cannot decrypt the previous session messages.
- De-synchronization attack. The protocol stores *curID*, *curpID*, *oldID*, and *oldpID* in the backend server. *oldID*, and *oldpID* are the values of *curID* and *curpID* for the last successful authentication. If the tag cannot synchronously update its secrecy with the backend server they can use *oldID*, and *oldpID* to complete the later authentication so as to resist against de-synchronization attack.
- Eavesdropping. For the whole authenticating process of the protocol, all session messages are processed by Hash function or the pseudorandom number generator. Although an adversary can eavesdrop all messages transferred between tag and backend server/reader he cannot reveal these message. So the protocol can effectively resist against the leakage of the secret information and it ensures the confidential and anonymous communication between backend server/reader and tag.
- Tracing attack. If a tag repeats to send the same message to the backend server/reader many times an adversary can easily trace and identify the tag. In order to resist against tracing attack, the tag generates a new pseudorandom number for each authentication and the pseudorandom number is used to randomize the session messages. Therefore the freshness of the session messages is ensured. For any different challenge from the backend server/reader the tag will give a different response. An adversary cannot judge which tag sends the session messages eavesdropped by him and it cannot distinguish two different tags. Therefore the protocol can resist against tracing attack.
- Replay attack. This attack means that an adversary re-sends the session messages intercepted by him so as to get the authentication of the RFID system. Because all session messages transferred between backend server/reader and tag are processed by the time stamp of the backend server. An adversary can intercept the session messages and re-sends them later. But these messages are out of time and they are

meaningless for the later authentication. So the protocol can resist against replay attack.

- Anonymity. The protocol uses Hash function and pseudorandom number generator to process the partial identifier of the tag and generate all sessions between tag and backend server/reader. Each session only includes the partial secret information of the tag. Although an adversary can intercept these sessions it is difficult for him to get the whole secrecy of the tag. Hash function is a one-way function. An adversary cannot get the plaintext of these sessions. So the protocol ensures the anonymity of the RFID system.

Compared with other similar protocols, our proposed protocol has many advantages, which are shown by Table 2.

Table 2. The comparison among the different authentication protocols

Protocols	Eaves dropping	Tracing attack	Replay attack	De-synchron-ized attack	Spoofing attack	Forward security
Hash-Lock	x	x	x	–	x	x
Random Hash-Lock	x	x	x	–	x	x
Hash chain	$\sqrt{}$	$\sqrt{}$	x	$\sqrt{}$	x	$\sqrt{}$
SRAC	$\sqrt{}$	$\sqrt{}$	x	$\sqrt{}$	x	$\sqrt{}$
LCAP	$\sqrt{}$	$\sqrt{}$	$\sqrt{}$	$\sqrt{}$	$\sqrt{}$	x
Our protocol	$\sqrt{}$	$\sqrt{}$	$\sqrt{}$	$\sqrt{}$	$\sqrt{}$	$\sqrt{}$

6   Conclusions

The privacy and security of the RFID system is one of the important factors to decide whether it can be applied widely. The current popular tags are some low-cost passive tags and they have very limited computing and storing resources. It is very difficult for these tags to complete some complicated cryptographic protocols. In order to ensure the security and privacy of the RFID systems with low-cost tags, we propose a strong light-weight authentication protocol. This protocol provides forward security and anonymity. It uses Hash function and random selecting bit function to process the session messages so as to increase the difficulty to reveal the secret information of the tag. Meanwhile, twice authentication to the tag also increases the secure strength of the protocol. The analysis to the proposed protocol proves that the protocol can provide forward security and it can resist against eavesdropping, tracing, replay and de-synchronization attacks. It completes the mutual authentication between tag and backend server/reader. The protocol only uses Hash function, pseudorandom number generator and some simple bitwise operations. So the protocol is very suitable to some resource-constrained environment like the low-cost RFID systems.

Acknowledgments. We are appreciated to anonymous reviewers for their constructive suggestion to this paper. The relative work about this paper is supported by National Natural Science Foundation of China (No. 61272097).

References

1. Chen, M., Luo, W., Mo, Z., Chen, S., Fang, Y.: An efficient tag search protocol in large-scale RFID systems with noisy channel. IEEE/ACM Trans. Netw. **24**(2), 703–716 (2016)
2. Peris-Lopez, P., Hernandez-Castro, J.C., Estevez-Tapiador, J.M., Ribagorda, A.: RFID systems: a survey on security threats and proposed solutions. In: Cuenca, P., Orozco-Barbosa, L. (eds.) PWC 2006. LNCS, vol. 4217, pp. 159–170. Springer, Heidelberg (2006). doi: 10.1007/11872153_14
3. Chikouche, N., Cherif, F., Cayrel, P.-L.: Weaknesses in two RFID authentication weaknesses. In: El Hajji, S., et al. (eds.) C2SI 2015, LNCS, vol. 9084, pp. 162–172. Springer, Heidelberg (2015)
4. Deng, R.H., Li, Y., Yung, M., Zhao, Y.: A new framework for RFID privacy. In: Gritzalis, D., Preneel, B., Theoharidou, M. (eds.) ESORICS 2010. LNCS, vol. 6345, pp. 1–18. Springer, Heidelberg (2010). doi:10.1007/978-3-642-15497-3_1
5. Weis, S.A., Sarma, S.E., Rivest, R.L., Engels, D.W.: Security and privacy aspects of low-cost radio frequency identification systems. In: Proceedings of the 1st International Conference on Security in Pervasive Computing, Boppard, Germany, pp. 201–212 (2003)
6. Ohkubo, M., Suzuki, K., Kinoshita, S.: Cryptographic approach to "Privacy-Friendly" tags. In: RFID Privacy Workshop. MIT Press, Cambridge (2003)
7. Ohkubo, M., Suzuki, K., Kinoshita, S.: Hash-chain based forward secure privacy protection scheme for low-cost RFID. In: Proceedings of the 2004 Symposium on Cryptography and Information Security, Sendai, Japan, pp. 719–724 (2004)
8. Yeo, S.-S., Kim, S.K.: Scalable and flexible privacy protection scheme for RFID systems. In: Molva, R., Tsudik, G., Westhoff, D. (eds.) ESAS 2005. LNCS, vol. 3813, pp. 153–163. Springer, Heidelberg (2005). doi:10.1007/11601494_13
9. Lee, Y.K., Verbauwhede, I.: Secure and low-cost RFID authentication protocols. In: Proceedings of the 2nd IEEE Workshop on Adaptive Wireless Networks, St. Louis, USA, pp. 1–5 (2005)
10. Lee, S.M., Hwang, Y.J., Lee, D.H., Lim, J.I.: Efficient authentication for low-cost RFID systems. In: Gervasi, O., Gavrilova, M.L., Kumar, V., Laganà, A., Lee, H.P., Mun, Y., Taniar, D., Tan, C.J.K. (eds.) ICCSA 2005. LNCS, vol. 3480, pp. 619–627. Springer, Heidelberg (2005). doi:10.1007/11424758_65
11. Cho, J.-S., Yeo, S.S., Kim, S.K.: Securing against brute-force attack: a hash-based RFID mutual authentication protocol using a secret value. Comput. Commun. **34**(3), 391–397 (2011)
12. Cho, J.-S., Jeong, Y.-S., Sang, O.-P.: Consideration on the brute-force attack cost and retrieval cost: a hash-based radio-frequency identification (RFID) tag mutual authentication protocol. Comput. Math. Appl. **3**, 1–8 (2012)
13. Kim, H.: Desynchronization attack on hash-based RFID mutual authentication protocol. J. Secur. Eng. **9**(4), 357–365 (2012)
14. Khedr, W.I.: SRFID: a hash-based secure scheme for low cost RFID systems. Egypt. Inf. J. **14**, 89–98 (2013)
15. Safkhani, M., Peris-Lopez, P., Hernandez-Castro, J.C., Bagheri, N.: Cryptanalysis of the Cho et al. protocol: a hash-based RFID tag mutual authentication protocol. J. Comput. Appl. Math. **259**, 571–577 (2014)

16. Ha, J., Moon, S., Zhou, J., Ha, J.: A new formal proof model for RFID location privacy. In: Jajodia, S., Lopez, J. (eds.) ESORICS 2008. LNCS, vol. 5283, pp. 267–281. Springer, Heidelberg (2008). doi:10.1007/978-3-540-88313-5_18

17. Sun, D.-Z., Zhong, J.-D.: A hash-based RFID security protocol for strong privacy protection. IEEE Trans. Consum. Electron. **58**(4), 1246–1252 (2012)

18. Yang, L., Yu, P., Bailing, W., Yun, Q., Xuefeng, B.: Hash-based RFID mutual authentication protocol. Int. J. Secur. Appl. **7**(3), 183–194 (2013)

19. Bogdanov, A., Knežević, M., Leander, G., Toz, D., Varıcı, K., Verbauwhede, I.: Spongent: a lightweight hash function. In: Preneel, B., Takagi, T. (eds.) CHES 2011. LNCS, vol. 6917, pp. 312–325. Springer, Heidelberg (2011). doi:10.1007/978-3-642-23951-9_21

20. Gao, S., Wang, H.: Forward private RFID authentication protocol based on universal hash function. J. Inf. Comput. Sci. **10**(11), 3477–3488 (2013)

A Security Proxy Scheme Based on Attribute Node Mapping for Cloud Storage

Huakang Li, Zhenyu Wang, Yitao Yang, and Guozi Sun(✉)

School of Computer Science and Technology, School of Software,
Institute of Computer Technology,
Nanjing University of Posts and Telecommunications, Nanjing 210023, China
{huakanglee,sun}@njupt.edu.cn

Abstract. Cloud storage provides convenient storage services with data leaking risk while the encryption and decryption keys are supported by cloud service. However, the traditional CP-ABE scheme cannot solve the problem of integrity of could service provider according to single attributes rules. In this paper, we design a prototype system for secure cloud storage which separates storage services and security service using Attribute node mapping based on CP-ABE scheme. The prototype system consists of four parts: a client, a key generation center, a security proxy and a storage system. We propose an innovative convergence encryption method and a shared access mechanism to improve the encryption against guessing attack. Hierarchical eliminate redundancy and parallel data access technologies are also proposed improving the data transmission efficiency.

Keywords: Cloud storage · Access control · Attribute-based Encryption · CP-ABE · Node mapping

1 Introduction

With the development of Internet and distributed computing in recent years, Could Computing has become an important technology for shared softwares and hardware resources. Cloud storage service is the most common and popular service (e.g. Google Drive, Dropbox, Huawei Cloud) for typical users. The bottleneck of limited storage space has become more and more significant, especially for mobile users while they take lots of pictures and videos.

Different with super computing system, inexpensive commodities are commonly used in cloud system due to the consideration of scalability [6]. The reliability issue of these systems is of particular relevance. To ensure the data reliability, redundancy scheme is a basic solution and has been extensively deployed [8]. With this scheme, the intuitive idea is to store copies of data objects over a set of network nodes for the successful recovery. At the same time, the cloud service provider could remove the extra redundancy data copies from data storage.

We also bear the risk of cloud storage, such as efficacy and security [7,11] while we enjoy the convenience of cloud storage. One problem of cloud service

© Springer International Publishing AG 2016
G. Wang et al. (Eds.): SpaCCS 2016, LNCS 10066, pp. 14–25, 2016.
DOI: 10.1007/978-3-319-49148-6_2

is verifying the integrity of the data since users cannot know how to handel their data in the cloud storage. Many researches introduced various systems and security models [1,10,16] to solve the problems of data integrity verification in the cloud storage. Private auditability [19], which is one efficient verifier, implies the data owner directly verifying data in the cloud storage service. However, the data owner could not verify the data frequently depending on the business requirements and spare time. Therefore, public auditability [20], which is another important verifier, implies the data owner allowing others to verify the owned data.

According to the basic requirements of security and performance, the existing scheme of security evaluation can be classified as follows:

- Blockless Verification: User can modify the data blocks to avoid retrieving all audited data blocks in cloud storage.
- Batch Auditing: User can verify the data from different client at the same time with a special token.
- Dynamic Data: The data can be continuously modified by competent users.
- Privacy Presenting: User can't access the delegated data in the cloud storage service.

In this paper, we propose a scheme for cloud storage combined with the security proxy and stochastic storage strategy to separate storage service and security service. The prototype system contains four parts: a client, a key generation center, a security proxy and a storage system. In the uploading process, client cuts the file into blocks with fixed size to calculate the hash fingerprints and sent to the security proxy. The security proxy compares the hash fingerprint to establish whether the data are redundant. Secret keys and random storage tables generated by the hash value and partial quantity value, are sent back to the client. The client uses the secret key to encrypt the data and upload to cloud storage with random storage table. In the downloading process, users need to pass the verification of access structure tree to achieve the secret key for decoding and random storage table when they are required to access the data. The client accesses the storage nodes according to the random storage table to decode the data block and reconstruct the data after the legitimate authentication. The method proposed under this paper solves the contradiction between data encryption and data redundancy. At the same time, it also can prevent the illegal use and data privacy from cloud storage service providers.

The article consists of the following parts: Sect. 2 introduces the related works of data encryption and data redundancy. The system design and improved ABE scheme are introduced in Sect. 3. Section 4 shows the access control scheme design. The experimental results of system performance are illustrated in Sect. 5. Section 6 concludes the main jobs and feature works.

2   Related Work

2.1   Data Redundancy

In cloud storage system, it's very straightforward to use redundancy scheme to achieve data reliability. Distributed data copy is the commonly used method to cope with data failure or missing. Research communities [14,23] introduce redundancy schemes for the system performance. Generally, redundancy scheme can be classified into two types: replication [21] and erasure code [13].

Cloud storage service providers utilize data redundancy to ensure the reliability of data while they hope to reduce the repeated data copies to save the storage costs. Whole File Detection (WFD) technologies [9] use the hash value of the whole file to estimate the comparing fingerprint to implement the data repetition. Fixed-sized partition (FSP) [3] cuts the files into data blocks with fixed size to calculate the hash fingerprint. Content-defined chunking method [17] uses a dynamic sliding window to calculate the Robin fingerprint value. Sliding block method [12] uses Rsync sum function and fixed block sliding window to calculate the calibration value of cross data block in the file. Comparable data detection technology contrasts data one by one to eliminate duplicate data in the system. However, the high computational complexity problem is existed for these methods.

2.2   Data Encryption

Wang et al. [20] proposed the scheme to support public verification and fully dynamic data instead of modifying or deleting data files. The definition of public auditability which implies public verification is delegated by a trusted third party auditor (TPA) to verify. Li et al. [10] proposed a public auditability scheme in resource-constrained devices using third party auditor for data uploading and audit delegating. After that Wang et al. [19] proposed a privacy protection scheme which is considered user's data privacy in the public auditability.

Attribute-based Encryption (ABE), which is one of public key encryption systems, is proposed by Sahai [15] firstly. This method is based on fuzzy identity-based encryption and can achieve the fine-grained access control issues. ABE uses the user access policies set of users attributes and data together. The system enables users to access data only if users access property structures match the access control policy. It is ideal for cloud storage that data are shared among users. In the cloud area, many researchers [18,24,25] have applied the ABE to achieve a more fine-grained access control and data sharing goals.

In recent years, researchers have proposed a number of ABE schemes. Waters [22] and Daza [4] proposed ABE schemes independently, whose cipher text lengths are $n + (1)$ and $2(n - t) + (1)$, using threshold-based access control policy. However, effects of these ABE schemes are very low for mobile agents. A fixed length of the cipher text ABE encryption scheme [5] was proposed while the users private key attribute must be fully consistent. This significant limitation made the established policy properties cipher text cannot be widely promoted.

Bethencourt [2] proposed the Cipher Text-polity Attribute-based Encryption scheme (CP-ABE). The attribute set is a direct result of the user's private key, and access structure is related with the cipher text. If a user's set of attributes satisfy the cipher text access structure tree, the user can decrypt the cipher text. The sender can set the access structure to identify which users can access the appropriate data cipher text. This type of CP-ABE scheme is ideal for a distributed and share-based computing environment, especially for cloud storage.

3   Design of Cloud CP-ABE Scheme

3.1   Design of System Model

When the CP-ABE scheme is used in secure cloud storage environment, one problem is the fundamental structure of CP-ABE scheme supports attribute sets only constructed by single property in accordance of a certain number of rules. And it does not support the attributes of third-party, such as authorization center. Therefore we designed a new CP-ABE scheme (Fig. 1) for cloud storage with Key Generation Center and Security Proxy.

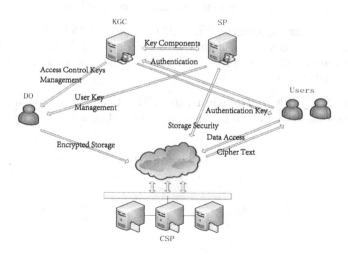

Fig. 1. System structure of cloud CP-ABE scheme.

– Key Generation Center (KGC): KGC is mainly responsible for the system to generate public and private keys. KGC is also responsible for the distribution of their corresponding properties of the component for different users with different access rights. In our work, KGC is deemed to be semi-credible (honest but curious) that the KGC will analyze users private information beside the default services.

- Security proxy (SP): SP is designed to separate the users security services from the cloud storage. It is responsible to store the fingerprint database and distribute the secret attributes. Also, SP is semi-credible.
- Cloud storage provider (CSP): CSP provides storage services for users, and control the data access according to the authentication of private key structure from users. Also, CSP is semi-credible.
- Data owner (DO): In order to reduce storage costs, data owners use the storage service from CSP, and upload their private data. DO are responsible for defining access control policy, and encrypt data before uploading to prevent illegal use of CSP.
- User: Users can get the data from CSP. If one user satisfies the access control policy with attribute structure, he can access the shared resources.

3.2 Sharing Degree-Based Authentication

We suppose that one file F is divided into N shared pieces stored on the cloud server. The server would reduce the redundancy blocks according to the data repetition and build an Access Structure Tree (AST) (Fig. 2) based on historic access frequency. Therefore, we have the definition as follows:

Definition 1: Sharing Degree (SD): If each piece data is shared by several documents, the SD can be estimated with the deeps of AST. The SD of leaf nodes which are on the bottom lay is [1 10], and the root node has the largest SD, such as $(1000 \, \infty)$;

Definition 2: Children Relationship (CR): CR presents the relationship between child nodes data blocks. Therefore, the CR of a leaf node amounts to

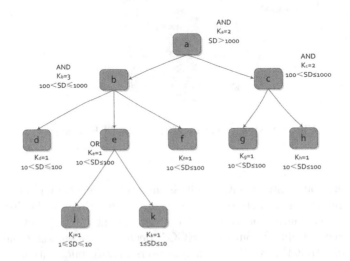

Fig. 2. A simple structure of sharing degree-based access tree.

Null. The CR of other nodes is defined as *AND* or *OR* or n/m, where m is the number of child nodes and $1 \leq n \leq m$.

Definition 3: Threshold Value (TV): TV is used to quantify the relation between child nodes. Therefore the TV (k_x) of a leaf node is 1 and the k_x of other nodes is $0 \leq k_x \leq m$.

When the owner gains access to the file F, the client applies the access structure λ which matches the access tree T generated by security proxy. In order to meet $T(\lambda) = 1$, we should satisfy the condition that $T_x(\lambda) = 1$ $(x = 1, ..., m)$, where T_x is the sub-tree of the AST.

3.3 ABE Scheme with SA

In order to import the CP for key management, we add Secret Attribute (SA) into the set for attribute keys (Fig. 3). Each user includes this property, and the values are very different for different data. Root of access structure tree must be AND gate, and the child node of the root must be a mapping node which including expiration and secret attributes. The operation (such as attribute addition and deletion) of attribute sets is not contained by these two attributes. So adversary cannot have all the users private key when update the key regardless of in cloud server of third-party security proxy.

3.4 Mapping Node

For the mapping node, a mapping function $e : \{SA, E\} \rightarrow \{\rho\lambda\}$ with Expiration (E) and Secret Attribute (SA). λ is SA set submitted by user. And the new key structure $S^{new}\{\rho\lambda, \rho i, \rho j, \rho k, ...\}$, $\rho\lambda \in U - S$ is generated synchronously by the key generation center.

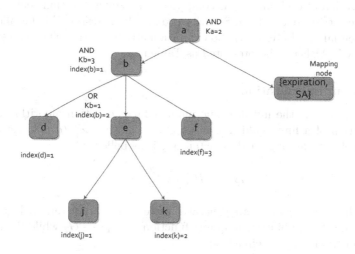

Fig. 3. A simple structure of access structure tree with SA.

Table 1. The Symbol descriptions of Cloud CP-ABE

Symbol	Description
KGC	Key generation center
SP	Security proxy
SA	Security attribute
EXPIRATION	Expiration attribute
PK	Public key
MK	Main key
SK	Private key
U	Attribute set
M	User data
CT	Cipher text

For the cloud service, if x is a leaf node, and key attribute set $|x| \in S^{new}$, $T_x(\lambda)$ will return value 1. If x is a non-leaf node, the value of $T_x(\lambda)$ will be calculated with its child nodes $\{y\}$. If x is a mapping node and the attribute of x satisfies $S_x \neq \phi$, S_x will be transformed to $\rho\lambda$ with the mapping function e. The mapping node becomes a leaf node and performs the leaf node matching operation.

4   Access Control Design

To accommodate de-duplication technology in cloud storage and reduce the calculate pressure of re-encryption by security agents. We firstly use the file division to cut files into a number of blocks of fixed size. The hash value and convergent encryption of each block was computed. The key generation center (KGC) assigns the attribute keys to n. Security proxy (SP) is responsible for allocating the confidential attributes (SA) and expiration attributes (E). The main symbols for Cloud CP-ABE can be presented as Table 1.

4.1   System Initialization

Assuming that q is the initial prime number for encryption algorithm and Z_p^* is a collection of a finite field. For any $i \in Z_p^*$, and $a \in Z_p^*$ (a is in set S), the definition of the Lagrangian Parameter $\Delta_{i,s}$ is as bellows:

$$\Delta_{i,s} = \Pi_{j \in S, j \neq i} \frac{x-j}{i-j} \tag{1}$$

The bilinear group $\{G_x\}$ are generated by security parameters with generator g. We can define the bilinear mapping function $e : G_1* \rightarrow G_2$ while the pseudorandom function can be defined as:

$$\Upsilon(x) = g_2^{x^n} \Pi_{i=1}^{n+1} t_i^{\Delta_{i,s}} \tag{2}$$

Therefore, Υ can be simplified as $g_2^{x^n} g^{h(x)}$, where $h(x)$ is a polynomial of degree n.

Attribute set U can be defined as $U = \{u_1, u_2, u_3, \ldots, u_n, sa*, expiration\}$. Here $sa*$ is secret attribute associated with a specific data block, $expiration$ is key attribute generated by security proxy. For any property $u_i \in U$ is associated with $\Upsilon(u_i)$. Randomly selected $y \in Z_p^*$, the system public key parameter PK is generated as:

$$T_1 = g^{t_1}, \ldots, T|u| = g^{t|u|}, Y = e(g,g)y \tag{3}$$

here, the main system secret key MK is $\{s_i : t_1, \ldots, t|u|, y\}$.

4.2   Encryption Algorithm

The encryption algorithm proceeds from the root node r of the access tree T. We choose a polynomial P_x for each node x from root to leaf. For the root node, $P_r(0) = s$ where $s \in Z_p^*$ is randomly selected. For the non-leaf node, $P_x(0) = P_{parent}(x)(index(x))$. The final cipher text (CT) can be written as:

$$CT = \{M \cdot e(g,g)\alpha s, C = hs, \forall y \in L, C_y = H(|y|)P_y(0)\} \tag{4}$$

where M is input data, α is the source unit in Z_p^*, and L is the set of all leaf nodes of AST.

4.3   Authentication

When user accesses file F, security proxy will extract d ($d \le f$) data blocks randomly to generate the access control tree Π. Here the original file F is divided into f blocks. The user must provide the full attribute set Π, otherwise its an illegal access from the current user.

4.4   Private Key Generation

For the PKG, the users private key SK is generated by attribute set U, primary key MK and public parameters PK.

$$SK = (D = g(\alpha + \gamma)/\beta, \forall j \in S : D_j = g\gamma \cdot H(j), D_j = g\gamma j) \tag{5}$$

here $\alpha, \beta, \gamma \in Z_p^*$ and $j \in S$ are selected randomly.

4.5   Decryption of Cipher Text

If and only if the attribute set meets the access tree, cipher text can be decrypted to plain-text. For the leaf-node x, we use $i = |x|$ and $i \in S$ to calculate as follows,

$$
\begin{aligned}
Decrypt(CT, SK, x) &= \frac{e(D_i, C_x)}{e(D_i', C_x')} \\
&= \frac{e(g^\gamma \cdot H(i)^{\gamma_i}, g^{P_x(0)})}{e(g^{\gamma_i}, H(i)^{P_x(0)})} \\
&= e(g,g)^{\gamma \cdot P_x(0)}
\end{aligned}
\tag{6}
$$

If $i \notin S$, $Decrpyt(CT, SK, x) = \perp$. For the non-leaf node x, we can use the return value of F_λ from its child node λ, then recursively calculate the F_x by polynomial interpolation:

$$F_x = \sum_{\lambda \in S_x} F_\lambda^{\Delta_{i,S_x}(0)} = e(g,g)^{s,P_x(0)} \tag{7}$$

S_x is a set of k_x child nodes, which make $F_\lambda \neq 0$, and $i = index(\lambda)$, $S_x' = \{index(\lambda) : \lambda \in S\}$, and

$$\Delta_{i,s}(x) = \Pi_{j \in s, j \neq i} \frac{x-j}{i-j} \tag{8}$$

According to this method, we can recursive the root node to restore the blind factor

$$A = e(g,g)^{\gamma q_\gamma(0)} = e(g,g)^{\gamma^S} \tag{9}$$

Finally, plain text can be decrypted from the cipher text with:

$$C * /(e(C,D)/A) = C * /(e(h^S, g^{\alpha+\gamma/\beta})/e(g,g)^{\gamma^S}) = M \tag{10}$$

5   System Performance

The confidentialities of access structure and data in this paper can be evidenced by the security issue of cipher text of encryption key according to symmetric key encryption algorithm (such as DES, AES, etc.). Therefore, in this section we just discuss the time cost for system performance. Table 2 shows that we used a computer with 2.5 GHz CPU and $4G$ $Memory$. The system is $Ubuntu$ 12.04 with JDK 1.7. We used the standard library $PCB-0.5.14$ from Stanford University. The encrypt data are generated randomly with [20 50] child nodes. The number of users attribute set is 10 uniformly. We calculated attribute set using KEK function. The finite field was set at 512, and 160 bit elliptic curve functions ($y^2 = x^3 + x$) for decryption were used from PBC library.

Table 2. System parameters for experiments

System environment		Experiment parameters	
CUP	2.5G	leaf nodes	[20 50]
Memory	4G	Attribute set	10
System	Ubuntu 12.04	$SK_{Eq.5}$	KEK
SDK	JDK 1.7.0	Z_p^*	512
Lib	PBC-0.5.14	$Decrypt_{Eq.6}$	$\{y^2 = x^3 + x\}$

Figures 4 and 5 show the encryption and decryption times with CP-ABE and our Cloud CP-ABE algorithm. Encryption times of the two schemes are significantly linear relationship with leaf nodes. The average time of our scheme

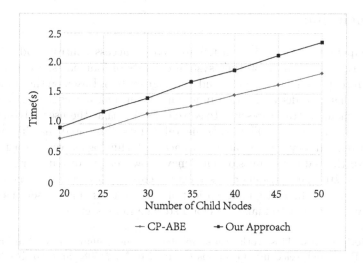

Fig. 4. Encryption time results for CP-ABE and our approach.

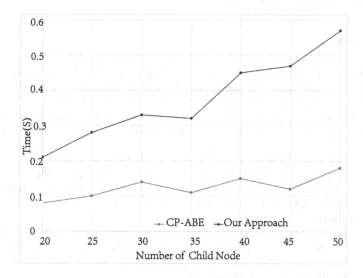

Fig. 5. Decryption time results for CP-ABE and our approach.

is 0.36 s more than the basic CP-ABE. The average time consuming of the basic CP-ABE program is 0.126 s, and the average time for our scheme is 0.376 s for decryption. Compared with the basic CP-ABE scheme, the time consuming is added within the acceptable range.

6 Conclusion

In this paper, we proposed an attributed-based access control model for the encryption scheme. The prototype system consists of four parts: a client, a key generation center, a security proxy and a storage system. Based on the traditional CP-ABE scheme, a de-duplication function, which makes access control tree of CP-ABE scheme more expressive, to solve defection that the user attribute sets must come from the user. The experimental results illustrated that hierarchical eliminate redundancy and parallel data access technologies were in a position to improve the data transmission efficiency. However, all of our work is based on the cloud storage providers and security agents are separated. In the feature, we could consider the mutual authentication mechanisms among user, agent and cloud service provider to make the cloud storage more secure.

Acknowledgments. This work was supported by the Foundation of Nanjing University of Posts and Telecommunications (Grant No. NY213085 and No. NY214069), the NSFC (No. 61502247, 11501302, 61502243), Natural Science Foundation of Jiangsu Province (BK20140895, BK20130417).

References

1. Ateniese, G., Di Pietro, R., Mancini, L.V., Tsudik, G.: Scalable and efficient provable data possession. In: Proceedings of the 4th International Conference on Security and Privacy in Communication Netowrks, p. 9. ACM (2008)
2. Bethencourt, J., Sahai, A., Waters, B.: Ciphertext-policy attribute-based encryption. In: IEEE Symposium on Security and Privacy, SP 2007, pp. 321–334. IEEE (2007)
3. Bobbarjung, D.R., Jagannathan, S., Dubnicki, C.: Improving duplicate elimination in storage systems. ACM Trans. Storage (TOS) **2**(4), 424–448 (2006)
4. Daza, V., Herranz, J., Morillo, P., Ràfols, C.: Extensions of access structures and their cryptographic applications. Appl. Algebra Eng. Commun. Comput. **21**(4), 257–284 (2010)
5. Emura, K., Miyaji, A., Nomura, A., Omote, K., Soshi, M.: A ciphertext-policy attribute-based encryption scheme with constant ciphertext length. In: Bao, F., Li, H., Wang, G. (eds.) ISPEC 2009. LNCS, vol. 5451, pp. 13–23. Springer, Heidelberg (2009). doi:10.1007/978-3-642-00843-6_2
6. Ford, D., Labelle, F., Popovici, F.I., Stokely, M., Truong, V.A., Barroso, L., Grimes, C., Quinlan, S.: Availability in globally distributed storage systems. In: OSDI, pp. 61–74 (2010)
7. Hashem, I.A.T., Yaqoob, I., Anuar, N.B., Mokhtar, S., Gani, A., Khan, S.U.: The rise of big data on cloud computing: review and open research issues. Inf. Syst. **47**, 98–115 (2015)
8. Hwang, G.H., Lin, H.F., Sy, C.C., Chang, C.Y., et al.: The design and implementation of appointed file prefetching for distributed file systems. J. Res. Pract. Inf. Technol. **40**(2), 91 (2008)
9. Khasnabish, B., Jin, W., Li, M.: Content de-duplication for CDNI optimization. Internet-Draft (2013)

10. Li, J., Tan, X., Chen, X., Wong, D., Xhafa, F.: OPoR: enabling proof of retrievability in cloud computing with resource-constrained devices. IEEE Trans. Cloud Comput. **3**(2), 195–205 (2015)
11. Liu, C., Yang, C., Zhang, X., Chen, J.: External integrity verification for outsourced big data in cloud and IoT: a big picture. Future Gener. Comput. Syst. **49**, 58–67 (2015)
12. Policroniades, C., Pratt, I.: Alternatives for detecting redundancy in storage systems data. In: USENIX Annual Technical Conference, General Track, pp. 73–86 (2004)
13. Reed, I.S., Solomon, G.: Polynomial codes over certain finite fields. J. Soc. Ind. Appl. Math. **8**(2), 300–304 (1960)
14. Rodrigues, R., Liskov, B.: High availability in DHTs: erasure coding vs. replication. In: Castro, M., Renesse, R. (eds.) IPTPS 2005. LNCS, vol. 3640, pp. 226–239. Springer, Heidelberg (2005). doi:10.1007/11558989_21
15. Sahai, A., Waters, B.: Fuzzy identity-based encryption. In: Cramer, R. (ed.) EUROCRYPT 2005. LNCS, vol. 3494, pp. 457–473. Springer, Heidelberg (2005). doi:10.1007/11426639_27
16. Singh, R., Kumar, S., Agrahari, S.K.: Ensuring data storage security in cloud computing. Int. J. Eng. Comput. **2**(12), 17–21 (2012)
17. Ungureanu, C., Atkin, B., Aranya, A., Gokhale, S., Rago, S., Calkowski, G., Dubnicki, C., Bohra, A.: Hydrafs: a high-throughput file system for the hydrastor content-addressable storage system. In: FAST, pp. 225–238 (2010)
18. Wan, Z., Liu, J., Deng, R.H.: Hasbe: a hierarchical attribute-based solution for flexible and scalable access control in cloud computing. IEEE Trans. Inf. Forensics Secur. **7**(2), 743–754 (2012)
19. Wang, C., Wang, Q., Ren, K., Lou, W.: Privacy-preserving public auditing for data storage security in cloud computing. In: 2010 IEEE Proceedings of INFOCOM, pp. 1–9. IEEE (2010)
20. Wang, Q., Wang, C., Ren, K., Lou, W., Li, J.: Enabling public auditability and data dynamics for storage security in cloud computing. IEEE Trans. Parallel Distrib. Syst. **22**(5), 847–859 (2011)
21. Wang, Y., Li, S.: Research and performance evaluation of data replication technology in distributed storage systems. Comput. Math. Appl. **51**(11), 1625–1632 (2006)
22. Waters, B.: Ciphertext-policy attribute-based encryption: an expressive, efficient, and provably secure realization. In: Catalano, D., Fazio, N., Gennaro, R., Nicolosi, A. (eds.) PKC 2011. LNCS, vol. 6571, pp. 53–70. Springer, Heidelberg (2011). doi:10.1007/978-3-642-19379-8_4
23. Weatherspoon, H., Kubiatowicz, J.D.: Erasure coding vs. replication: a quantitative comparison. In: Druschel, P., Kaashoek, F., Rowstron, A. (eds.) IPTPS 2002. LNCS, vol. 2429, pp. 328–337. Springer, Heidelberg (2002). doi:10.1007/3-540-45748-8_31
24. Yang, K., Jia, X., Ren, K.: Attribute-based fine-grained access control with efficient revocation in cloud storage systems. In: Proceedings of the 8th ACM SIGSAC Symposium on Information, Computer and Communications Security, pp. 523–528. ACM (2013)
25. Yu, S., Wang, C., Ren, K., Lou, W.: Achieving secure, scalable, and fine-grained data access control in cloud computing. In: 2010 IEEE Proceedings INFOCOM, pp. 1–9. IEEE (2010)

Privacy Preserving Scheme
for Location and Content Protection
in Location-Based Services

Tao Peng[1], Qin Liu[2], Guojun Wang[3(✉)], and Yang Xiang[4]

[1] School of Information Science and Engineering,
Central South University, Changsha 410083, China
[2] School of Information Science and Engineering,
Hunan University, Changsha 410082, China
[3] School of Computer Science and Educational Software,
Guangzhou University, Guangzhou 510006, China
csgjwang@gmail.com
[4] School of Information Technology, Deakin University,
221 Burwood Highway Burwood, Melbourne, VIC 3125, Australia

Abstract. Location-Based Services (LBSs) have been facilitating and enriching people's daily lives. While users enjoy plenty of conveniences, privacy disclosure in terms of both location information and query contents is common. Most of the existing solutions mainly focus on location privacy and adopt K-anonymity principle to preserve user's privacy. However, these methods are vulnerable to protect user's query content. In this paper, we propose a Privacy Preserving and Content Protection (PPCP) scheme for LBSs users. Unlike most of researches requiring a trusted third party (TTP), our scheme is based on a semi-trusted middle entity, which is unaware of both the exact location information about issuer and query content in the user's requirement. We utilize space filling curve to transform user location and protect user query content based on encryption technology, so that the proposed scheme can provide enhanced location privacy and query privacy protection in both snapshot and continuous LBSs.

Keywords: Location-Based Service (LBS) · Hilbert curve · Location privacy · Query privacy · Continuous query

1 Introduction

The proliferation of location-aware devices and rapid development of wireless communication have fostered various Location-Based Service (LBS) applications. According to a new research report [1] from the analyst firm Berg Insight, the global market for mobile LBSs is forecasted to increase from 10.3 billion Euro in 2014 at a compound annual growth rate (CAGR) of 22.5 % to 34.8 billion Euro in 2020. Searching for points of interests (POIs) based on a user's location is one

G. Wang et al. (Eds.): SpaCCS 2016, LNCS 10066, pp. 26–38, 2016.
DOI: 10.1007/978-3-319-49148-6_3

of the most popular applications in LBSs. Users can enjoy the service by issuing *snapshot* or *continuous* LBS queries [2] to a Location Service Provider (LSP) anytime and anywhere. Typical snapshot LBS requirements include k-Nearest Neighbor *(kNN) query* (e.g., "Get top-5 nearest hotels around me"), and *range query* (e.g., "Find all hospitals within the scope of 1 km"). Continuous query can be like "Continuously send me the nearest restaurant on my road every 5 min", or "Continuously report me real time traffic information on my road". For all these queries, users should submit their current locations and requirement contents (e.g., types of POI) to the remote LSPs to activate the LBSs. While users get great benefits from LBS, they may put the sensitive information in jeopardy. The adversary can collect user data in various ways to infer some privacy information of users, such as user's identity, home location, hobbies, and even health condition and religious affiliation, etc. Generally, privacy concerns in LBSs exist in two aspects [3, 4]: *location privacy* and *query privacy*. The former is related to the disclosure and misuse of user's location information, the latter, on the other hand, is related to disclosure of the service content. Although distinct, these two types are closely related. There is possibility that compromising one of them may lead to the failure of the other.

Existing researches mainly focus on location privacy and adopt popular K-anonymity principle [5, 6] for privacy protection: A user satisfies K-anonymity if the location information sent to the LSP is made indistinguishable from those of at least other K-1 users. To achieve location K-anonymity, a trusted third party (TTP), called the Anonymizer, is introduced acting as an intermediate tier between the users and the LSPs. The Anonymizer blurs exact location of a user into an anonymizing spatial region (ASR or K-ASR) and then transmits the query to the LSP. Even if the adversary knows there are K users in the region, he cannot learn the exact position of each user with a probability larger than $1/K$. However, the trusted Anonymizer has knowledge about all users' locations, which will lead it to be an attractive attack target. Once it is compromised by the adversary, the privacy of users or even the security of whole system will be under threat. Moreover, in practice, it is a tricky thing to find a third party that can be fully trusted by all users.

Another challenging issue to location K-anonymity arises from the *correlation* feature of continuous LBS. When a user sends continuous queries as he moves, a time-series sequence of the corresponding cloaking areas may be tracked and associated to refine the users location, which is called query association attack [7]. For example, assume three users, a, b, and c are located at different positions. User a issues two continuous queries in his trip. The simple K-anonymity (e.g., $K = 2$) approach used to generate an anonymity set (a, b) for the first query and an anonymity set (a, c) for the second query. The attacker can infer user a is the original sender by intersecting these two sets.

In this paper, we propose a Privacy Preserving and Content Protection (PPCP) Scheme for snapshot or continuous LBSs, in which both of location privacy and query privacy are preserved without any fully trusted entities. The key idea is to place a semi-trusted server, called Semi-Anonymizer, between the user and the LSP. By semi-trusted we mean that the server has no knowledge about a user's real location and query content, while it is honest to respond to all messages and process required operations in the scheme, i.e., it will be able to blur user's exact location and to perform the results matching operations with some transformed and shifted location information of users. The main contributions of proposed scheme are shown as follows:

1. We utilize a space filling curve to perform location transformation on the user and LSP side. The unauthorized entity (includes the Semi-Anonymizer), without the encrypted transforming parameters, is unable to infer any knowledge about a user's real location.
2. We use the public key encryption technique to protect query content so that the query privacy of user is preserved in our scheme.
3. We consider the problem of privacy leakage in the continuous LBSs, and enable the Semi-Anonymizer to cache all of candidate POIs within the whole querying area, so as to reduce the number of queries sent to the LSP. It not only greatly saves the overhead on the Semi-Anonymizer, but also reduces the risk of private information exposure to the LSP or the adversary.
4. Without compromising real locations, the Semi-Anonymizer still has ability to correctly match accurate results for each issuer, hence the user in our scheme can obtain desired answers at low communication, while privacy is preserved.

The remainder of this paper is organized as follows. We introduce technical preliminaries in Sect. 2, and describe the proposed PPCP scheme in Sect. 3. Then, we analyze the performance of our scheme in Sect. 4. Finally, we conclude this paper and present the future work in Sect. 5.

2   Preliminaries

In this section, we first present our system architecture of PPCP scheme, then provide the attacker model and the security requirements. Next, we give an overview for the Hilbert curves and location transformation method, which serve as the technical basis of our work.

2.1   LBS Query

Given a set of static objects $S = (o_1, o_2...o_n)$ in 2-dimension (2-D) space, each object has a *type* attribute, $type = TP_{poi}, TP_{poi} \in \{restaurant, hospital, hotel...\}$. A typical LBS user u enjoys the service involving two types of queries:

Definition 1. Snapshot LBS query. The user u with a query location *loc* issues a kNN query trying to find top k POIs from S where $type = TP_{poi}$. The query answer returned by the LPS is set $S' \subset S$ of k objects, where for any object $o \in S'$, and $o' \in S - S'$, $D(o, loc) \leqslant D(o', loc)$, D is the Euclidean distance function.

In case it is a range query (e.g., $1\,\mathrm{km}$), the returned answer is set S', where for any object $o \in S'$, $D(o, loc) \leqslant 1\,\mathrm{km}$. Since k or *range* is a pre-determined parameter, we can represent the query as a 4-tuple $< ID, loc, TP_{poi}, t_i >$, where t_i is the timestamp when the query issues.

Definition 2. Continuous LBS query. A continuous LBS requirement Q includes of a sequence of 4-tuples $q_1 :< ID, loc_1, TP_{poi}, t_1 >, q_2 :< ID, loc_2, TP_{poi}, t_2 >$ $,...q_n :< ID, loc_n, TP_{poi}, t_n >, \forall i \in [1, n-1], t_{i+1} > t_i$.

2.2   System Architecture

Figure 1 illustrates the system architecture of proposed scheme. We employ three roles, the mobile user, the Semi-Anonymizer and the LSP in our system.

Fig. 1. System architecture of our PPCP scheme

Mobile user: A mobile user carries location-aware (e.g., GPS) devices loaded with LBS applications. The user can determine his current location information by the GPS, and transforms his location and encrypts related information with the pre-process modules of the application. Then, he can enjoy the service by submitting the kNN or range LBS query to a specified LSP by the Semi-Anonymizer, which can be snapshot or continuous queries, for instance "Report me the top-5 nearest hotels", or "Continuously send me the restaurants within 1 mile of my current location every 5 minutes". The user concerns about location privacy and query privacy preserving when he seeks desired information from LSP.

Semi-Anonymizer: It is a semi-trusted party, acting as an intermediate tier between the mobile user and LSP. Semi-trusted in the context means that, on the one hand, it will honestly and correctly carry out all the required operations in the scheme, and will not arbitrarily modify or tamper with any messages, as well as falsifies fake messages; on the other hand, it is curious, and may attempt to locate a query sender and determine his identity based on what it has "see". While, without the transformation parameters and encryption keys, it has no knowledge about the user's real location and service content, as long as it does not collude with LSP. The main jobs of the Semi-Anonymizer in our system are as follows: (i) it processes the queries when receiving users' LBS requests, such as storing user information and forwarding encrypted data to the user-specified LSP. (ii) After getting response from LSP, it conducts result match operations under the rule of PPCP, pruning false points from the set of candidate POIs, and then returns the exact answers to query issuer.

In practice, the Semi-Anonymizer is analogous to a proxy server maintained by network carriers or other organization. It can be deployed on the network access points or intermediate nodes in different network environments (e.g., base station or gateway) and can be configured based on different policies. For example, in previous research [8,9] the Access Point (AP)-based approach has been used for LBSs in mobile environments. For ease of explanation, in this paper, we only use a single Semi-Anonymizer, but multiple Semi-Anonymizers should be deployed as necessary in reality.

LSP: The online location-based service provider, (e.g., Google Maps or Four Square), employs location-based database servers. They store map resources and the information of POIs (hotel, restaurants and bank, and so on), and other service information as well. As shown in the Fig. 1, LSP does not directly communicate with mobiles users, instead, it provides service via the Semi-Anonymizer. Upon receiving request, LSP searches desired information in its database and returns potential POIs to the Semi-Anonymizer. From the security and privacy aspects, like most researches assumed, LSP is always considered to be an untrusted entity. It has ability to collect all location or content information included in the queries to infer some sensitive data of users, also it may release valuable information to other third parties for monetary reason.

2.3   Threat Model

In our scheme, attackers collect information in various ways, trying to infer the exact location or service content of an LBS issuer. They are assumed to have the following capabilities:

- The location information in the query. This assumption states that either the Semi-Anonymizer is not trusted, or the communication channel between users and the Semi-Anonymiezer is not secure.
- The querying areas of user, and all positions of POIs within this area. This assumption implies that the LSP is untrustworthy. In the worst case the attacker is the LSP itself. The attacker has the knowledge about the map, the POIs in the querying areas, and also has the ability to collect all users' snapshot queries, or keep the history of continuous queries.
- The algorithms or methods that are used to offer privacy in the LBS. This assumption is common in the most security literatures due to the privacy algorithms are usually publicly available.

In our scheme, we also assume that the Semi-Anonymizer will not collude with LSPs. Collusion between the Semi-Anonymizer and some malicious LSP could lead to privacy disclosure. This assumption has also been made in many researches in the field of system security and privacy protection [10,11], in which the server is assumed to not collude with other entity to ensure the security of whole system.

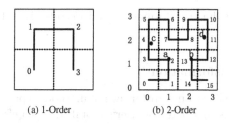

(a) 1-Order   (b) 2-Order

Fig. 2. Hilbert curve in two dimensions. (a) *1*-order. (b) *2*-order

2.4   Hilbert Curve

Hilbert curve [12] is one of the space-filling curves, which traverses through all cells in a two-dimension or multidimensional space once and only once. A N order Hilbert curve in 2-D space is a line which goes through every cell in a square where is separated into $2^N * 2^N$ equal-sized cells. Each cell is assigned by an integer value, named Hilbert value (denoted as H-value), according to the sequence when the curve traverses. Figure 2 shows the first two steps of production of the Hilbert curve in two dimensions. Figure 2(a) is a 1-order curve, where the square is divided into $2^1 * 2^1$ cells and the curve orderly passes through their center points to generate H-values of these cells. The Fig. 2(b) shows a 2-order Hilbert curve, which orderly passes through each center point of $2^2 * 2^2$ cells. In the square space, if we use the grid coordinates to denote very cell as $< i, j >$, the corresponding Hilbert value of each cell based on the space-filling curve order can be determined. This process can be defined as encoding and its inverse operation is decoding.

Definition 1: The H-value of a cell s, $< i_s, j_s >$, in the grid coordinate system can be transformed as

$$H(s) = \dot{f}(< i_s, j_s >) \tag{1}$$

where $0 \leqslant i_s, j_s < 2^N$, $0 \leqslant H(s) < 2^{2N}$, and $\dot{f}$ is the spatial transformation function, which transforms the 2-D grid coordinate into a 1-D H-value by a Hilbert curve. Given a curve setting parameter, the curve is determined, and the H-value mapping to each grid cell is assigned. We term this parameter as spacial transformation parameter (STP), and $STP = \{(X_o, Y_o), N, \Gamma, \Theta\}$, where (X_o, Y_o) is the curve's starting point, N is the curve order, Γ is curve orientation, and Θ is curve scale factor. For example, in the Fig. 2(b), the users *a, b, c, d* have the grid coordinates of $< 1, 1 >, < 2, 1 >, < 0, 2 >, < 3, 2 >$. When the 2-order Hilbert curve orderly passes each cell, the H-values of these users are 2, 13, 4 and 11, respectively. The Hilbert curve is suitable for our scheme due to its important property, that is the spatial transformation $\dot{f}$ is one-way function if the STP is not known [13,14]. The procedure of encoding the 2-D space and generating 1-D H-value by such a one-way function can be regarded as encrypting the elements of the original space, and STP is the key of this encryption. Any malicious attacker, without this key, is computationally impossible to reverse the transformation and decode the 1-D H-value back to the original space.

2.5 Location Transformation

In our scheme, we use location transformation method to preserve user's location privacy. This process is conducted on user's mobile device before user submits the LBS query. Mobile user determines his current location, loc, by location-aware device. We assume it is a point and is identified by two values, for instance, its latitude and longitude. Without loss of generality, we define the coordinate (x, y) as to the spatial position of the mobile node in the 2-D space (i.e., x- and y-axes). User has to first specify a STP of space-filling curve to transform the point, since the PPCP scheme use the Hilbert method to perform transformation. Specifically, referring to the curve scale factor, Θ, user can freely choose an area, e.g., a city or a region. According to the irregular spatial region specified by the user, the system will generate a minimum bounding rectangle to contain it as the transformation square space, and we denote it by the coordinates of left bottom vertex (x_l, y_l) and right top vertex (x_r, y_r). Then, the space scale is divided into $m * m$ equal-sized cells to construct a grid system, here $m = 2^N$, N is the order of Hilbert curve specified by the user. We define the unit length of each cell in this square space as $Unit$, and $Unit = (x_r - x_l)/m$. A user u with a 2-D point coordinate of (x_u, y_u) can be presented by the grid coordinate $< i_u, j_u >$.

$$< i_u, j_u > = < \left\lfloor \frac{x_u - x_l}{Unit} \right\rfloor, \left\lfloor \frac{y_u - y_l}{Unit} \right\rfloor > \tag{2}$$

In the cell user located, if we set the left bottom vertex as the origin of coordinates in this cell space, the user's relative location (relative offset to the origin of coordinate) can be presented by $(x_{u\_o}, y_{u\_o})'$.

$$(x_{cl}, y_{cl}) = (Unit * i_u, Unit * j_u) \tag{3}$$

$$(x_{u\_o}, y_{u\_o})' = (x_u - x_{cl}, y_u - y_{cl}) \tag{4}$$

Thus, a user u with a point coordinate of (x_u, y_u) transforms his location as the grid coordinate $< i_u, j_u >$ and his relative offset location in the corresponding grid, $(x_{u\_o}, y_{u\_o})'$. This process is to prepare for the Hilbert encoding.

With the specified STP, using Eq. 1, we can generate a Hilbert curve, and transform the user's grid coordinate $< i_u, j_u >$ to Hilbert value.

$$H(u) = \dot{f}(< i_u, j_u >) \tag{5}$$

Therefore, the user with a 2-D point of $loc : (x_u, y_u)$ can transform his location to 1-D H-value $H(u)$ and a relative position (x_{u_o}', y_{u_o}'). We denote the transformed location as loc'. The Fig. 2(b) illustrates examples of location transformation. In this figure, we assume the $Unit$ of each cell is 10. The users a, b, c, d have locations of (15,15), (25,15), (6,23), (34,26). After transforming, they can be presented as $\{2,(5,5)'\}$, $\{13,(5,5)'\}$, $\{4,(6,3)'\}$, $\{11,(4,6)'\}$. Notice that, in our scheme we view the cell user located as his querying area. In case the area is too small to preserve the location privacy, user can designate the smallest size of querying cell with a minimum value of *Unit*, where the user can accept to reveal the fact that he is in somewhere within this area without any concerns.

3   Privacy Preserving and Content Protection Scheme

In this section, we will present the details of PPCP scheme, which mainly consists by five steps: Step 1. query issue; Step 2. request processing; Step 3. POI search; Step 4. results match and Step 5. results transformation.

3.1   Query Issue

In order to preserve his privacy, the user has to perform some pre-process before issuing the LBS query. First of all, the user should specify a STP, and transforms his location (loc) to the encoded (loc') using the Hilbert curve as described in Sect. 2.5, which is

$$loc : (x_u, y_u) \rightarrow loc' : \{H(u), (x_{u\_o}, y_{u\_o})'\} \tag{6}$$

We take the user a in the Fig. 2(b) for example, after transforming, his location is $loc : (15, 15) \rightarrow loc' : \{2, (5, 5)'\}$. Then in order to preserve the query privacy, user a encrypts related information in his query, which includes two parts: the type of POI and the STP:

$$C = E^*_{pk}(TP_{poi}, STP) \tag{7}$$

where $E^*_{pk}(\cdot)$ is an asymmetric encryption algorithm under the public key [15] of the LSP. Along these information, the user sends a requirement to the Semi-Anonymizer. Message from user to the Semi-Anonymizer is

$$MSG_{U2A} = q : \{ID, loc', C, t_i\} \tag{8}$$

where ID refers to the identity of user (the user can also use a pseudonym to hide his real identity), loc' is the transformed location of the user, C is the encrypted information in Eq. 7, t_i is the timestamp when the request issued.

While user roams, there is possibility the movement trajectory of user may go out of the scope of one cell, which means the user may have different H-values included in his continuous queries.

Figure 3 shows the continuous query processing in PPCP scheme. In this figure, the red line shows trajectory of user a, the stars ($L_1 - L_4$) are footprints at times $t_1 - t_4$. If we use the Hilbert curve in the Fig. 2(b) to transform user location, the user traverses two Hilbert cells, for instance, 2 and 13. Thus, the transformation of a can be represented as: $loc_1 : (15, 15) \rightarrow loc'_1 : \{2, (5, 5)'\}$; $loc_2 : (18, 15) \rightarrow loc'_2 : \{2, (8, 5)'\}$; $loc_3 : (24, 15) \rightarrow loc'_3 : \{13, (4, 5)'\}$;

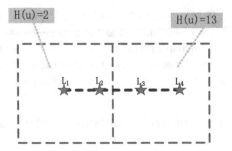

Fig. 3. Example of continuous LBS query processing in PPCP (Color figure online)

$loc_4 : (27, 15) \rightarrow loc'_4 : \{13, (7, 5)'\}$. In the continuous LBS query, messages from the user to the Semi-Anonymizer are sequence requests:

$$MSG_{U2A} = q_1 : \{ID, loc'_1, C_1, t_1\}...$$
$$q_4 : \{ID, loc'_4, C_4, t_4\} \tag{9}$$

3.2 Request Processing

Upon receiving the message from user, the Semi-Anonymizer extracts the ID and transformed location, loc'. According to different conditions, it will process the request under following 3 cases:

Case 1: It is an initial (or a snapshot) query, for example, the request, q_1, issued from user a when he is located on L_1, the Semi-Anonymizer stores the ID and location information, and forwards the encrypted query to the specified LSP.

Case 2: It is not an initial LBS query. While the H-value included in this request is just as the same as previous one, which means the user roams in the same cell. For example, the request q_2 and q_4 issued from user a when he is located on L_2 and L_4. Because the Semi-Anonymizer already cached the POIs within the whole cell from the previous answer, it does not need to contact LSP to get the update request results. Instead, the Semi-Anonymizer can skip Step 3, directly executes the results match in Step 4.

Case 3: It is not an initial LBS query. While the H-value in this request is as different as previous one, which means the user moves to other cells. For example, the request q_3 issued from user a when he is located on L_3. The Semi-Anonymizer stores new location information of user, and enlists LSP for help to find a update query answer. In case 1 and case 3, message from the Semi-Anonymizer to the LSP is

$$MSG_{A2L} = \{C, H(u)\} \tag{10}$$

3.3 POI Search

LSP decrypts the message with its private key and retrieves query which includes: the POI-type, the STP and H-value generated by the user in Step 1. With

STP and $H(u)$, LSP can decode the cell user located, and then computes the coordinate values of this cell, which can be presented by left bottom vertex (x_{cl}, y_{cl}) and right top vertex (x_{cr}, y_{cr}). LSP finds all of POIs, which match the required TPpoi in the cell from its database. For each selected POI P_i with a location (x_i, y_i) from the set of Pe', LSP transforms its real location into the relative offset coordinate, $(x_i, y_i)'$, to the left bottom vertex of the cell by

$$(x_i, y_i)' = (x_i - x_{cl}, y_i - y_{cl}) \tag{11}$$

Finally, LSP returns the set of transformed POIs, Pe' to the Semi-Anonymizer.

$$MSG_{L2A} = \{Pe'\} \tag{12}$$

3.4   Results Match

The Anonymizer obtains candidate POIs, which may potentially be the answers for the range of the entire querying cell. The Semi-Anonymizer caches these all POIs in order to handle the request in the case 2 of Step 2. Then, it finds out the exact results for the query sender. Since the position of user and corresponding candidate POIs are transformed by the same STP, they have the same H-value, which means that their relative offset locations are shifted by the same origin of coordinates (x_{cl}, y_{cl}). Hence, the Semi-Anonymizer can obtain distances between user and each POI, and exactly find out the desired result set, Re', from all candidate POIs according to the requirement of user. Then, the Semi-Anonymizer will return the accurate results to query sender. The message from the Semi-Anonymizer to user is:

$$MSG_{A2U} = \{Re', Re' \subset Pe'\} \tag{13}$$

3.5   Results Transformation

The user obtains exact POIs from the Semi-Anonymizer, but the locations of them are transformed ones. The task of the results transformation is to compute the real locations of the POIs. Notice that when user conducts the location transformation in Step 1, he already has got the origin of coordinates of the cell (x_{cl}, y_{cl}) by Eq. 3, and the POIs got from the Semi-Anonymizer are shifted based on the origin of the cell user located. Therefore, the user can easily transform POIs to the real location by Eq. 11 and finally gets the accurate answers for his LBS query.

4   Performance Analysis

In this part, we analysis the performance of our proposed PPCP scheme regarding computation and communication costs on the user side, the Semi-Anonymizer side and the LSP side respectively.

Computational Cost: First of all, we consider the computational overhead on the mobile user, who conducts *Query issue* (Step 1) and *Results transformation* (Step 5) of the PPCP scheme. The running time of *Query issue* is mainly on the pre-process of query, which includes two parts: location transformation and content encryption. The job of former is to transform the 2-D spatial point into a encoded location by a Hilbert curve, whose computational complexity is $O(N^2)$ [16], where N is the order of Hilbert curve. Generally it is a small constant less than 16. To clarify, the location transformation requires N exponentiations and several multiplications. Here, we only consider the cost of exponential operations due to the its computational overhead is 1000 times that of multiplications. The task of latter is to encrypt the data in Eq. 7 with asymmetric cryptographic algorithm (e.g., RSA). Its computational complexity is $O(1)$, since the encrypted information, type of POIs and STP, have a fixed small size. In terms of the *Results transformation*, its main task is to inverse the transformed POIs to the real places. The expression of transformed POIs are relative offset from the origin of coordinates of the cell, (x_{cl}, y_{cl}), which are already got when the user conducts location transformation in Step 1. Thus user can easily perform *Results transformation* only by several addition operations, and the computational time of it can be neglectful.

Next, we consider the computational overhead on the Semi-Anonymizer, who conducts *Request processing* (Step 2) and *Results match* (Step 4) of the PPCP scheme. The running time of *Request processing* is negligible, since it only needs to simply execute operations of data storage and message forwarding. The *Results match* is to compute distance between each candidate POI to the user, and to select requested results from the all candidate POIs within the whole query area. It depends on the number of POIs, d, and the computational complexity is $O(d)$.

Finally, we consider the computational overhead on the LSP, who conducts *POI search* (Step 3) of the PPCP scheme. The running time of *POI search* is mainly on the following three parts: (1) decode the H-value to the cell user located; (2) search for POIs in the area; and (3) transform the coordinate of candidate POIs. Computational cost of the first part is similar to the procedure of location transformation on the user side, which is $O(N^2)$, and N is a small constant. The running time of the second part is mainly on the number of POIs in the cell, the computational overhead is $O(d)$. The running time of the third part can be ignored, due to this part can be accomplished by several addition operations. Therefore, the computational overhead on the LSP is $O(N^2 + d)$.

Communication Cost: We first consider the communication cost between the user and the Semi-Anonymizer. The transfer-out message on the user side is LBS requirement, presented by MSG_{U2A} in Eq. 8, which has s small constant size. The message returned from Semi-Anonymizer is precise answers of his LBS requirement, presented by MSG_{A2U} in Eq. 13. If we consider pre-determined parameters in the requirement specified by the user (e.g., scope in the range query or top-k in the kNN query) as a fix constant, the communication cost between the user and the Semi-Anonymizer is $O(1)$.

Table 1. Performance analysis

Entity	Computational cost	Communication cost
User	$O(N^2)$	$O(1)$
Semi-Anonymizer	$O(d)$	$O(d)$
LSP	$O(N^2 + d)$	$O(d)$

Next, we consider the communication cost between the Anonymizer and LSP. The transfer-in message of LSP is encrypted data, presented by MSG_{A2L} in Eq. 11, whose size is a small constant. The message Semi-Anonymizer got from LSP, presented by MSG_{L2A} in Eq. 12, is the set of candidate POIs in the whole cell. Its size varies with the number of POIs, d, and the communication cost is $O(d)$. We summarize the computational and the communication overhead at the user, the Semi-Anonymizer, and the LSP, respectively, as shown in Table 1.

5   Conclusion

In this paper, we proposed Privacy Preserving and Content Protection (PPCP) scheme to protect user privacy in snapshot and continuous LBS. The main merit of our scheme is that both of location privacy and query privacy are preserved, which is rarely considered in other related approaches. Our scheme does not require any fully-trusted third party (TTP), instead, user privacy is preserved by technologies of location transformation and content encryption. The middle entity, Semi-Anonymizer, is semi-trusted, which has no knowledge of both query content and location information about mobile user. While it still has the ability to match results from the candidate POIs returned by the specified LSP, so that accurate answers can be forwarded to each issuer. Specifically, in continuous LBSs, the Semi-Anonymizer can contact LSP only once and cache all candidate POIs in the whole query area. In the following query processing, it may locally search for answers from the cached POIs and directly replies query user without the participation of LSP. In this way, the communication and computation overhead on the Semi-Anonymizer can greatly reduced. Moreover, the spatio-temporal correlation of continuous queries on the LSP side can be broken, which can enhance the security of whole scheme.

Acknowledgments. This work is supported in part by the National Natural Science Foundation of China under Grant Numbers 61632009, 61472451, 61272151 and 61502163, High Level Talents Program of Higher Education in Guangdong Province under Funding Support Number 2016ZJ01, and Hunan Provincial Natural Science Foundation of China under Grant Number 2016JJ3051.

References

1. Malm, A.: Mobile location-based services. Berg Insights LBS Research Series (2016). http://www.berginsight.com/ReportPDF/ProductSheet/bi-lbs9-ps.pdf
2. Hwang, R.H., Hsueh, Y.L., Chung, H.W.: A novel time-obfuscated algorithm for trajectory privacy protection. IEEE Trans. Serv. Comput. **7**(2), 126–139 (2014)
3. Shin, K.G., Ju, X., Chen, Z., Hu, X.: Privacy protection for users of location-based services. IEEE Wirel. Commun. **19**(1), 30–39 (2012)
4. Pingley, A., Zhang, N., Fu, X., Choi, H.A., Subramaniam, S., Zhao, W.: Protection of query privacy for continuous location based services. In: 2011 IEEE Proceedings of INFOCOM, pp. 1710–1718. IEEE (2011)
5. Gruteser, M., Grunwald, D.: Anonymous usage of location-based services through spatial and temporal cloaking. In: Proceedings of the 1st International Conference on Mobile Systems, Applications and Services, pp. 31–42. ACM (2003)
6. Pan, X., Xu, J., Meng, X.: Protecting location privacy against location-dependent attacks in mobile services. IEEE Trans. Knowl. Data Eng. **24**(8), 1506–1519 (2012)
7. Dewri, R., Ray, I., Whitley, D.: Query m-invariance: preventing query disclosures in continuous location-based services. In: 2010 Eleventh International Conference on Mobile Data Management (MDM), pp. 95–104. IEEE (2010)
8. Luo, W., Hengartner, U.: Veriplace: a privacy-aware location proof architecture. In: Proceedings of the 18th SIGSPATIAL International Conference on Advances in Geographic Information Systems, pp. 23–32. ACM (2010)
9. Niu, B., Li, Q., Zhu, X., Cao, G., Li, H.: Achieving k-anonymity in privacy-aware location-based services. In: 2014-IEEE Conference on Computer Communications, IEEE INFOCOM, pp. 754–762. IEEE (2014)
10. Liu, Q., Tan, C.C., Wu, J., Wang, G.: Cooperative private searching in clouds. J. Parallel Distrib. Comput. **72**(8), 1019–1031 (2012)
11. Xiao, M., Wu, J., Huang, L.: Home-based zero-knowledge multi-copy routing in mobile social networks. IEEE Trans. Parallel Distrib. Syst. **26**(5), 1238–1250 (2015)
12. Hilbert, D.: Ueber die stetige abbilding einer line auf ein flächenstück. Math. Ann. **38**(3), 459–460 (1891)
13. Khoshgozaran, A., Shahabi, C.: Blind evaluation of nearest neighbor queries using space transformation to preserve location privacy. In: Papadias, D., Zhang, D., Kollios, G. (eds.) SSTD 2007. LNCS, vol. 4605, pp. 239–257. Springer, Heidelberg (2007). doi:10.1007/978-3-540-73540-3_14
14. Peng, T., Liu, Q., Wang, G.: Enhanced location privacy preserving scheme in location-based services. IEEE Syst. J. **3**(2), 1–12 (2014)
15. ElGamal, T.: A public key cryptosystem and a signature scheme based on discrete logarithms. In: Blakley, G.R., Chaum, D. (eds.) CRYPTO 1984. LNCS, vol. 196, pp. 10–18. Springer, Heidelberg (1985). doi:10.1007/3-540-39568-7_2
16. Liu, X., Schrack, G.: Encoding and decoding the Hilbert order. Softw. Pract. Experience **26**(12), 1335–1346 (1996)

An Improved Asymmetric Searchable Encryption Scheme

Qi Wu[✉]

School of Information Technology,
Jiangxi University of Finance and Economics, Nanchang 330032, China
wuqiocjzd@126.com

Abstract. Data to be uploaded on the cloud storage system will often be encrypted for security reasons. No classic encryption & decryption algorithms however provide any search function. To increase user efficiency, an asymmetric searchable encryption scheme is designed in this paper. This improved scheme aims at fixing such flaws as "trapdoors that can be generated by anyone", "ciphertexts that are tampered with at discretion", "key pairs generated by users", "identities encrypted" and "a useless component". Findings suggest that the proposed scheme, while maintaining the established framework, perfectly resolves all the aforementioned flaws in the previous scheme.

Keywords: Cloud server · Searchable encryption · Asymmetric searchable encryption · Key pair · Trapdoor

1 Introduction

With the data volume growing fast, an increasing number of users now upload and store their data on the cloud servers to reduce local storage pressure. Different from previous C/S(Client/Server) mode, cloud servers are usually deemed "semi-trusted" because there exists a fear that the users' data may be hacked. Therefore, encryption is often used to protect the users' data privacy. Traditional encryption & decryption algorithms, such as DES [1], AES [2], and RSA [3], do not support search over encrypted data. When the data volume is huge, storage or bandwidth will not allow cloud users to retrieve all their stored data and then decrypt them to extract the required parts. It is then necessary to design schemes that support search over ciphertexts. Song et al. [4] initially discussed security properties such as controlled searching, provable secrecy, query isolation, and hidden queries, and then constructed the corresponding searchable encryption schemes. Searchable encryption has ever since attracted wide academic interests. In the light of whether index generation and queries use the same key or not, searchable encryption could be categorized into symmetric searchable encryption and asymmetric searchable encryption [5]. Here, only the latter is concerned.

Taking email systems as an example, Boneh et al. [6] constructed PEKS (Public Key Encryption with Keyword Search) model, designed a scheme based on BDH (Bilinear Diffie-Hellman) assumption and trapdoor permutations respectively, and also proposed a construction using Jacobi symbols. Abdalla et al. [7] analyzed the consistency of

© Springer International Publishing AG 2016
G. Wang et al. (Eds.): SpaCCS 2016, LNCS 10066, pp. 39–44, 2016.
DOI: 10.1007/978-3-319-49148-6_4

PEKS in detail, and proved that schemes proposed in [6] are computationally consistent. They successfully built a different statistically-consistent scheme, providing an approach to converting anonymous IBE (Identity Based Encryption) schemes to secure PEKS ones. Khader [8] constructed a PEKS scheme based on K-resilient IBE, which proved IND-CKA (Semantic Security against Adaptive Chosen Keyword Attack) secure under the standard model. Crescenzo et al. [9] proposed a PEKS scheme based on QRP (Quadratic Residuosity Problem). Hwang et al. [10] constructed the PECK (Public key Encryption with Conjunctive Keyword search) model, and then designed a scheme based on DLDH (Decisional Linear Diffie-Hellman) assumption. Compared with previous schemes, the ciphertext and private key of the new scheme proved to be the shortest. Then the model and scheme are extended to the multi-user circumstances. Baek et al. [11] proposed an improved scheme aiming at three issues such as "refreshing keywords", "removing secure channel", and "processing multiple keywords", which are left unconcerned by schemes proposed in [6]. Rhee et al. [12] pointed out that the capability of adversary in the scheme proposed in [11] is too limited, and instead constructed a reinforced secure model and its corresponding improved scheme. Zhao et al. [13] proposed trapdoor-indistinguishable PEKS. Yang et al. [14] proposed a variant aiming at making up missing computational consistency in the scheme proposed in [8], and promoted the efficiency dramatically. Luo et al. [15] proposed a PEKS scheme to tackle the IF (Integer Factorization) problem. Since users vary frequently under mobile cloud storage, Xia et al. [16] designed a PEKS scheme capable of data sharing and ciphertext modification. Shao et al. [17] designed a PEKS scheme in light of the "uni-sender multi-receiver" circumstance in the medical care area, resolving the problem that ciphertext is too long in previous schemes.

Using Elgamal algorithm, Liu et al. [18] fulfilled a PEKS scheme that provided the function of verifying retrieved data in asymmetric searchable encryption. Many flaws however are found in this scheme through our analyses. This paper thus attempts to fixe these flaws one by one as to obtain an improved scheme.

2   Verifiable Public Key Searchable Encryption Scheme

There are 3 principals in the scheme proposed in [18], namely, data uploader Alice, data retriever Bob and the cloud server. There are 5 algorithms in the scheme proposed in [18], namely, parameter generation, generation of the keyword and encrypted files, trapdoor generation, check, and verification, shown as follows.

(1) Parameter generation

Alice selects a big prime p_1 and a generator g_1 in $Z_{p_1}^*$. Alice selects a random integer x_1 ($0 \leq x_1 \leq p - 2$), calculates $y_1 = g_1^{x_1}$, sets her public key to (p_1, g_1, y_1) and private key to x_1. Similarly, Alice selects a generator g_2 in $Z_{p_2}^*$ and a generator g in Z_p^*, then sets the public key of Bob to (p_2, g_2, y_2) and his private key to x_2, sets the public key of the server to (p, g, y) and its private key to x. Alice selects a hash function $H : \{0, 1\}^* \to Z_p^*$ and sets the encryption algorithm and signature algorithm to Elgamal.

(2) Generation of encrypted files

Suppose Alice wants to send a file M including keyword W to Bob. Alice calculates $H(W)$, selects $r_1, r_2 \in_R Z_p^*$, computes $S_1 = r_1 r_2^{H(W)} \bmod p$, $S_2 = r_1^{H(W)^{-1}} r_2 \bmod p$, sets $S = <S_1, S_2>$.

Alice encrypts M with Bob's public key to obtain ciphertext $C_1 = <y_{11}, y_{12}>$.

Alice signs $H(W)$ with x_1 to obtain $sig = <H(W), r, s>$.

Alice encrypts its identity ID_A with Bob's public key to acquire ciphertext $C_2 = <y_{21}, y_{22}>$.

Alice uploads $S = <S_1, S_2>$ and $D = <C_1, sig, C_2>$ to the server.

(3) Trapdoor generation

When Bob wants to retrieve files including keyword W_1, he computes $H(W_1)$, which is encrypted with the server's public key to acquire $T_w = <y_{31}, y_{32}>$. Then, Bob sends T_w to the server.

(4) Check

After receiving T_w, the server decrypts it to obtain $H(W_1)$. Afterwards, the server checks each $S = <S_1, S_2>$ one by one. Once it satisfies that $S_1 = S_2^{H(W_1)}$, the server sends the corresponding $D = <C_1, sig, C_2>$ to Bob.

(5) Verification

After receiving D, first, Bob decrypts C_2 to acquire the identity of the sender. Then, Bob verifies sig with the public key of the sender. If the verification succeeds, Bob decrypts C_1. Otherwise, Bob discards.

Through our analyses, there are several flaws in the scheme, shown as follows.

(1) Trapdoors could be generated by anybody. From the description above, we could see, the trapdoor generation algorithm only uses $H(.)$ and the public key of the server. These two are known by every principal, which implies that anybody could generate the trapdoor. Usually, whether in symmetric searchable encryption or in its asymmetric counterpart, trapdoor generation should be the exclusive ability of the search requester. Otherwise, any principal could launch a search, which will greatly aggravate the burden of the server. Thus, the trapdoor generation algorithm should use the private key of the search requester.

(2) The adversary could replace C_1 with any ciphertext of M' other than M without being noticed. For example, he/she could replace $C_1 = <y_{11}, y_{12}>$ with $C_1' = <y_{11}', y_{12}'>$, in which C_1' is the outcome of encrypting M' other than M with Bob's public key. Thus, the adversary could easily cause misunderstanding between Alice and Bob. For this, we should prevent C_1 from being tampered with, such as using hash functions or digital signature.

(3) All key pairs are generated by Alice. Usually, both the knowledge for security and the computing power of users are rather limited. Therefore, there might be various flaws in the generated key pairs, such as weak pseudorandomness, short length, and apparent semantics, etc. Therefore, in cryptographic schemes, key pairs are usually generated by Key Generator. Moreover, each principal computes under its own field, which incurs extra difficulty for the implementation of the scheme. Usually, for most cryptographic schemes, all computations could be done under just one field.

(4) Identities are encrypted. Generally speaking, all the identities are public. For an adversary capable of monitoring the whole communication, the sender and the receiver of the message could be known easily. Hence, it is unnecessary to encrypt identities.

(5) S is absolutely useless. In Check phase, after obtaining $H(W_1)$, the server does not need to check $S_1 = S_2^{H(W_1)}$. It could just compare $H(W_1)$ with $H(W)$ in sig. If $H(W_1) = H(W)$, it sends the corresponding D to Bob.

3 The Proposed Scheme

The proposed scheme contains 3 principals and 5 algorithms as well, shown as follows.

(1) Parameter generation

KG (Key Generator) selects a big prime p and a generator g of Z_p^* (All computations are done under this field, if unspecified.). KG selects a hash function $H : \{0,1\}^* \rightarrow Z_p^*$. KG generates key pairs $(sk_A, pk_A = g^{sk_A})$, $(sk_B, pk_B = g^{sk_B})$, $(sk_C, pk_C = g^{sk_C})$ for Alice, Bob and the server, respectively. KG sets the algorithm for encryption and signature to Elgamal.

(2) File sending

Alice computes $H(W)$ and $S = pk_B \cdot g^{H(W)}$.

Alice computes $C = Enc_{pk_B}(M) = <y_1, y_2>$.

Alice computes $sig = Sig_{sk_A}(H(M)) = <H(M), r, s>$.

Alice sends S and $<C, sig, ID_A>$ to the server.

(3) Trapdoor generation

Bob sends $s = sk_B + H(W_1)$ to the server.

(4) File retrieving

The server computes $S' = g^s$, compares each S with S', and sends all $<C, sig, ID_A>$ where $S = S'$ to Bob.

(5) Verification

Bob fetches the public key pk_A corresponding to ID_A, which will be used to verify sig. If the verification succeeds, Bob decrypts C with sk_B to obtain M'. Bob computes $H(M')$ and discards once $H(M') \neq H(M)$.

4 Analyses of the Proposed Scheme

Apparently, the proposed scheme has perfectly fixed the aforementioned five flaws, shown as follows.

(1) Only the search requester could generate the trapdoor. From the trapdoor generation phase we could see, the private key of Bob, namely sk_B, is required, which is only possessed by Bob himself. Therefore, only the search requester is capable of generating the trapdoor.

(2) The adversary couldn't replace C with the ciphertext of M' other than M without being noticed. Suppose the adversary replaces C with $C' = Enc_{pk_B}(M') = <y_1', y_2'>$, let's discuss two cases below:

1) If the adversary replaces the 1st element in sig with $H(M')$, as he/she has no knowledge of the private key of Alice, namely sk_A, due to the unforgeability of Elgamal signature, he/she couldn't replace the 2nd and 3rd elements with Alice's legal signature r', s' on $H(M')$. Thus, in Verification phase, Bob definitely discards after verifying sig with Alice's public key pk_A.

2) If the adversary does not modify sig at all, then, in Verification phase, Bob will succeed when verifying sig. Then, after decrypting C' with sk_B, Bob will obtain M'. Due to collision resistance of $H(.)$, the probability of $H(M') = H(M)$ is negligible, which implies Bob will discard.

In a word, now the adversary could not cause any misunderstanding between Alice and Bob, which means the semantics of both principals is maintained.

(3) All key pairs are generated by KG, which ensures the security. All the computations are under the field Z_p^*, which avoids unnecessary troubles.

(4) Encryption of identities is removed. The identities of all principals are transmitted in the plaintext form, which avoids the overhead of encryption.

(5) There is a clear purpose for each component of the proposed scheme. None of them is useless, obviously.

5   Conclusion

This paper proposes an improved scheme aiming at fixing 5 flaws in the scheme proposed in [18]. Analyses show that the proposed scheme has well made up for the deficiency of the previous scheme and proves quite practical as well. In the future, we plan to design searchable encryption algorithms under more complicated application background, studying the issues including dynamic user group, single sender and multiple receivers, untrusted server, etc.

Acknowledgments. This research is financially supported by the Natural Science Foundation of China (No. 61462033). Thanks go to my supervisors Changxuan Wan & Zuowen Tan.

References

1. National Bureau of Standards. Data Encryption Standard, FIPS-Pub. 46. National Bureau of Standards, U. S. Department of Commerce, Washington D.C. (1977)
2. Daemon, J., Rijmen, V.: The Design of Rijndael: AES – The Advanced Encryption Standard. Springer, Heidelberg (2002)
3. Rivest, R., Shamir, A., Adleman, L.: A method for obtaining digital signatures and public-key cryptosystems. Commun. ACM **21**(2), 120–126 (1978)
4. Song, XD., Wagner, D., Perrig, A.: Practical techniques for searches on encrypted data. In: Proceedings of IEEE Symposium on Security and Privacy, Oakland, USA, pp. 44–55. IEEE (2000)
5. Fang, L.: Research on Public Key Encryption with Keyword Search. Nanjing University of Aeronautics and Astronautics, Nanjing (2012)

6. Boneh, D., Crescenzo, G., Ostrovsky, R., Persiano, G.: Public key encryption with keyword search. In: Cachin, C., Camenisch, J.L. (eds.) EUROCRYPT 2004. LNCS, vol. 3027, pp. 506–522. Springer, Heidelberg (2004). doi:10.1007/978-3-540-24676-3_30

7. Abdalla, M., Bellare, M., Catalano, D., et al.: Searchable encryption revisited: consistency properties, relation to anonymous IBE, and extensions. J. Cryptology **21**(3), 350–391 (2008)

8. Khader, D.: Public key encryption with keyword search based on k-resilient IBE. In: Gavrilova, M., Gervasi, O., Kumar, V., Tan, C.J.K., Taniar, D., Laganá, A., Mun, Y., Choo, H. (eds.) ICCSA 2006. LNCS, vol. 3982, pp. 298–308. Springer, Heidelberg (2006). doi:10. 1007/11751595_33

9. Crescenzo, G., Saraswat, V.: Public key encryption with searchable keywords based on jacobi symbols. In: Srinathan, K., Rangan, C.,Pandu, Yung, M. (eds.) INDOCRYPT 2007. LNCS, vol. 4859, pp. 282–296. Springer, Heidelberg (2007). doi:10.1007/978-3-540-77026-8_21

10. Hwang, Y.H., Lee, P.J.: Public key encryption with conjunctive keyword search and its extension to a multi-user system. In: Takagi, T., Okamoto, T., Okamoto, E., Okamoto, T. (eds.) Pairing 2007. LNCS, vol. 4575, pp. 2–22. Springer, Heidelberg (2007). doi:10.1007/978-3-540-73489-5_2

11. Baek, J., Safavi-Naini, R., Susilo, W.: Public key encryption with keyword search revisited. In: Gervasi, O., Murgante, B., Laganà, A., Taniar, D., Mun, Y., Gavrilova, Marina, L. (eds.) ICCSA 2008. LNCS, vol. 5072, pp. 1249–1259. Springer, Heidelberg (2008). doi:10.1007/978-3-540-69839-5_96

12. Rhee, H.S, Park, J.H, Susilo, W., et al.: Improved searchable public key encryption with designated tester. In: Proceedings of the 4th International Symposium on Information, Computer, and Communications Security, Sydney, Australia, pp. 376–379. ACM (2009)

13. Zhao, Y., Chen, X., Ma, H., et al.: A new trapdoor-indistinguishable public key encryption with keyword search. J. Wirel. Mobile Netw. Ubiquit. Comput. Dependable Appl. **3**(1/2), 72–81 (2012)

14. Yang, H., Xu, C., Zhao, H.: An efficient public key encryption with keyword scheme not using pairing. In: Proceedings of the 1st International Conference on Instrumentation, Measurement, Computer, Communication and Control, Beijing, China, pp. 900–904. IEEE (2011)

15. Luo, W., Tan, J.: Public key encryption with keyword search based on factoring. In: Proceedings of the 2nd International Conference on Cloud Computing and Intelligent Systems, Hangzhou, China, pp. 1245–1247. IEEE (2012)

16. Xia, Q., Ni, J., Kanpogninge, A., et al.: Searchable public-key encryption with data sharing in dynamic groups for mobile cloud storage. J. Univ. Comput. Sci. **21**(3), 440–453 (2015)

17. Shao, Z., Yang, B., Zhang, W., et al.: Secure medical information sharing in cloud computing. Technol. Health Care **23**, S133–S137 (2015)

18. Liu, P., Zu, L., Bai, C., et al.: A verifiable public key searchable encryption scheme. Comput. Eng. **40**(11), 118–120 (2014)

Recommendation Systems in Real Applications: Algorithm and Parallel Architecture

Mengxian Li, Wenjun Jiang$^{(\boxtimes)}$, and Kenli Li

School of Information Science and Engineering, Hunan University,
Changsha 410082, China
Jiangwenjun@hnu.edu.cn

Abstract. Recommendation systems are popular both in business and in academia. A series of works have been reported. In this paper, we briefly introduce the background and some basic concepts of recommendation systems, especially the applications in mainstream websites, most of them built upon parallel processing systems. However, how the recommendation algorithm works in real applications? We investigate (1) the key ideas of recommendation algorithms that are being used in real applications and (2) the parallel architecture in those real recommendation systems. In addition, the performance of recommendation system for those sites are also being analyzed and compared. We also analyze their features and compare their performances. Finally, we outline the challenges and opportunities that all recommendation systems are facing. It is anticipated that the present review will deepen people's understanding of the field and hence contribute to guide the future research of recommendation systems. Our work can help people to better understand the literature and guide the future directions.

Keywords: Recommendation system · Real application · Parallel architecture · Google news · Netflix · Meituan · Facebook

1 Introduction

With the development of the internet and information technology, we have entered the era of great explosion of the information. This phenomenon leads to big challenges for both resource consumers and providers. Recommendation system is mainly composed of three parts: the input (e.g., user preference), recommendation process (i.e., finding out the information or commodity user may be interested in) and the output (i.e., showing the recommendation result). In this article, we focus on investigating recommendation algorithms which are actually running in business applications, mainly from two aspects: the key idea of the algorithm and the parallel architecture of the real system.

At the year of 1992, Goldberg et al. [1] proposed the idea of collaborative filtering in the Tapestry system of Palo Alto Research Center for the first time. In 1994, Resnick et al. [2] first proposed the use of collaborative filtering algorithm

© Springer International Publishing AG 2016
G. Wang et al. (Eds.): SpaCCS 2016, LNCS 10066, pp. 45–58, 2016.
DOI: 10.1007/978-3-319-49148-6_5

to filter Network News. Therefore, GroupLens become one of the first automated collaborative filtering recommendation system. In the end of 20th century, the e-commerce site which represented by Amazon appeared and promoted the development of the recommendation system. As a technology, recommendation system has been widely used in various disciplines. Therefore, techniques in recommendation systems are developing rapidly. They can be classified into several categories, including content-based recommendation [3,4], knowledge-based recommendation [5,6], collaborative filtering recommendation (CF) [7,8], etc. Meanwhile, in the wake of new technologies such as parallel computing [9], data mining [10] and so on, some other new methods are being developed, including trust-aware recommendation [11], location-based recommendation [12], time-dependant recommendation [13], and so on. Since each method has its own pros and cons, a more common way is to combine several methods to produce more effective results [14].

Recommendation system has been studied for more than twenty years with a lot of relevant reports. However, it lacks a comprehensive study on recommendation systems from the perspective of real application. This motivates our work in this paper. We strive to study recommendation systems that are actually running in business applications. Our contributions are threefold, as follows:

1. We selectively study several representative real applications in which recommendation algorithms run as key components. We investigate (1) the key ideas of recommendation algorithms that are being used in those applications and (2) the parallel architecture in those real recommendation systems.
2. We comprehensively compare the representative recommendation systems from multiple aspects. It helps us to better understand the literature and guide the future directions for both researchers and application designers.
3. Based on the above two works, we make a further step to point out the current research hotspots, the remaining open challenges, and the promising research directions of recommendation systems.

2   Related Work

As a project, which is popular in both commercially and in terms of the academic research, many scholars have proposed various researches on recommendation. On taxonomy of recommendation systems, in [15], Schafer et al. presented an explanation of how recommendation system help online retailers increase income. Based on six real world examples, they created a taxonomy of recommendation systems from several aspects. Two years later, they further created a new taxonomy of recommendation systems and published another survey [16] to introduce the additional knowledge required from the database, ways of recommendations presented, and different level of personalization. In addition, they identified five commonly used E-commerce recommendation application models. In 2014, Bao et al. [17] proposed three taxonomies according to data source, method, and objective. They also summarized the goals, contributions and comparative analysis for each category. Moreover, in 2016, Jiang et al. [18] present

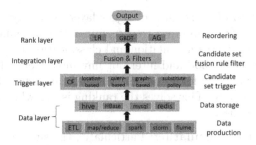

Fig. 1. The framework of Meituan

a comprehensive survey on graph-based trust evaluation models, in which trust-based recommendation is taken as an important application.

The implementation methods of parallel recommendation can be categorize as the distributed implementation, the parallel implementation, the platform-based implementation and the heterogeneous implementation of memory-based, model-based and hybrid recommendation systems [19]. Liang et al. [20] proposed a parallel user profiling approach, employing the advanced cloud computing techniques, Hadoop, MapReduce and Cascading. Christou et al. introduced a parallel multi-threaded implementation of collaborative filtering combined with a custom content-based algorithm in [21], which outperformed state-of-the-art implementations of similar algorithms.

3 Representative Recommendation Systems in Real Applications

Nowadays, many real applications are taking advantage of recommendation algorithms. In this section, we focus on key ideas and parallel architectures of the recommendation systems in real applications.

3.1 E-commerce Application: Meituan.com (2015)

Meituan is the first Groupon e-commerce site in China. It helps consumers find the most trustworthy businesses and low discount products. In 2015, the technology team of Meituan.com published an article in their official website[1], describing some of the practices about how they build and enhance their recommendation system.

Key idea: Figure 1 illustrates the framework of Meituan's recommendation system. There are mainly four layers: the data layer, the trigger layer, the integration layer, and the rank layer.

Details: As the name suggests, the data layer generates and stores the data. The trigger layer explores several triggering policies to produce recommendation candidate set, according to historical behavior, real-time behavior, location

---

[1] http://tech.meituan.com/mt-recommend-practice.html.

and other information of users. In the trigger layer, a variety of algorithms are explored simultaneously to improve the recommendation quality. After this, in the integration layer, it uses modulation and classification to fuse the results of each recommendation method and filter out unwanted items. In the last layer, it uses machine learning model to reorder the candidate sets, which are selected by the trigger layer before. This solves the ranking issues when fusing candidate set of different strategies.

Details of similarity calculating: Particularly, the similarity in the collaborative filtering, is calculated by loglikelihood ratio, which is used as an similarity calculation method in mahout. Assume that there are two events, A and B, making statistics with their occurring frequency. Make $K_{1,1}$ represent the frequency of A and B occurred at same time, $K_{1,2}$ represent the frequency of B occurs but A doesn't, and so on for $K_{2,1}$ and $K_{2,2}$. Then, the loglikelihood ratio can be calculated by Formula 1.

$$Ratio = 2 * (matrixEn - rowEn - columnEn) \tag{1}$$

Here, $matrixEn$, $rowEn$ and $columnEn$ are calculated by employing Formula 2. Entropy here means the shannon entropy of the system composed of several elements.

$$\begin{cases} matrixEn = entropy(k_{1,1}, k_{1,2}, k_{2,1}, k_{2,2}) \\ rowEn = entropy(k_{1,1}, k_{1,2}) + entropy(k_{2,1}, k_{2,2}) \\ columnEn = entropy(k_{1,1}, k_{2,1}) + entropy(k_{1,2}, k_{2,2}) \end{cases} \tag{2}$$

Parallel approach: In order to provide real-time computing for a large amount of users, Meituan.com adopts technologies of parallel computing, load balancing, and real-time streaming data processing (by a speech of Hao Cao, the senior technical experts of Meituan.com). For example, they designed a FeatureLoader module[2], which accesses and computes features in parallel. In real applications, the average response time in parallel is about 20 ms faster than that in serial.

3.2   Social Network Application: Facebook (2015)

The friend recommendation function, as a very popular and practical personalized service in social network, aims to recommend new friends to users according to their history. Facebook is an online social network site which has its headquarter in USA. In addition to text messages, users can send pictures, videos, sound media messages and other types of files to their friends by loading Facebook. Facebook announced the principles, performance and usage of its recommendation system[3] in their official website.

---

[2] http://tech.meituan.com/meituan-search-rank.html.
[3] https://code.facebook.com/posts/861999383875667/recommending-items-to-more-than-a-billion-people/.

Key idea: Facebook uses a distributed iterative image processing platform–Apache Giraph[4]. It is able to support large-scale data, and thus is taken as the basis of its recommendation system. The training models take the combination of data parallel and model parallel.

Key problem: As introduced in their official website, recommendation system of Facebook uses CF and Matrix Factorization (MF). Stochastic gradient descent (SGD) [22,23], alternating least squares (ALS) [24] and other iterative algorithms are implemented to reduce the time and space complexity. To take advantages of these algorithms, standard method of Giraph[5] need to be improved. The standard method processes users and items as vertices and the rating as the edge weight between two vertices. The iteration process of SGD or ALS is to traverse all edges, and send feature vectors of vertices to each vertex, then update these feature vectors partially. However, there are several serious issues in this method. First, the iterative process will bring a huge network traffic load. Second, the different popularity of items could result in an uneven distribution of the node degrees, which may lead to insufficient memory or processing bottlenecks.

Solution: To address the above issues, Facebook invents an efficient and convenient method which explores work-to-work information transmission. It divides the original graph into N workers, which are linked end-to-end to form a worker circle. Each worker contains a collection of items and a number of users. At each step, the adjacent worker sends message (e.g., the updating information of items) clockwise to the next worker. Only the internal ratings of each worker are processed in each step, so that all ratings are processed after N steps. The traffic is independent with the number of ratings. Moreover, the second problem above does not exist any longer, because items are not represented by vertices any more. To further improve the performance, Facebook incorporates the two algorithms, ALS and SGD, and adopts a rotation hybrid solution.

Parallel approach: Facebook uses multi-GPU training parallel framework, and uses the combination of data parallel and model parallel training models. The multi-core architecture of GPU (Graphic Process Units) consists of thousands of stream processors, which operate in parallel and reduce the computation time dramatically. Data parallel means that it cut the training data into N parts, and train them by N-workers in parallel. Meanwhile, model parallel splits the model into several model units, which work together to complete the training.

Friend recommendation differs from other types of recommendation, in that users may not need the most popular users, but the ones who are more possible to be their friends. In other words, the cold-start effect is more serious than that in other types of recommendation. We suggest that the location-based recommendation and cross-platform recommendation can be incorporated to alleviate this problem.

---

[4] http://giraph.apache.org/.
[5] https://zh.wikipedia.org/zh-cn/Giraph.

3.3   News Recommendation: Google News Recommendation

The life cycle of news is very short, which means there are less useful ratings. So, how to recommend by such a few ratings in a short time? Google news is an online information portal site. It gathers thousands of news sources (after grouping the similar news) and displays them to users in a personalized manner.

Key idea: For the system which was published by Google news [25] in 2007, Google news employ a mixed algorithm of memory based and model based to generate recommendations. In 2010, Google news develops a content-based click pattern using a Bayesian framework [26], which can predict a user's current interest according to his own behavior and that of other users in the same region.

Details of Google news (2007): As the quantity of articles and users are very large and the expected response time is limited, pure memory-based recommendation is not applicable. Hence, Google uses a combination of model-based and memory-based technology in its system. The model-based part relies on two clustering techniques: probabilistic latent semantic indexing (PLSI) [27] and MinHash[6]. The basic idea of PLSI is similar to probabilistic clustering, which identify like-minded users and related articles, and cluster them together. Min-hash puts the candidate objects (browsed by two users) in the same hash bucket. In addition, the approach of memory-based part is named "Adjoint PageView". It refers to an article browsed by the same user in a pre-defined period of time. Each of these method assigns a numeric score to an article, then the recommending scores R of the article a are deciding by Formula 3. In this formula, w_s is the weight given to the algorithm s, and r_a^s represents the score to article a given by algorithm s.

$$R = \sum w_s r_a^s \qquad (3)$$

Details of Google news (2010): In the system released in 2010, they combined their existing system with an extra part, content-based recommendation. In this part, user's interest is divided into two parts: the interest of a user himself and the interest influenced by local news. The key method of generating forecast is as follows: At first, Google news uses all user's click history in different periods to predict user's real interests. Then, it integrates these predicted results together to obtain a more accurate results of user's real interest. Finally, it uses the user's real interest and the trend of local news to predict the user's current interests. Using $CR(s)$ represent the score calculated by the part of content-based algorithm for a candidate article, and $CF(s)$ the score calculated by Formula 3. These two scores are combined for new recommendation using Formula 4.

$$R = CR(s) \times CF(s) \qquad (4)$$

Parallel approach: Google news uses its own MapReduce technology to distribute computing tasks among several clusters. MapReduce is a tool for parallel

---

[6] https://en.wikipedia.org/wiki/MinHash.

operation of large data sets, which is implemented with C++ programming language. Its main function is to provide a simple and powerful interface, to make computation be concurrent and be executed distributed automatically. MapReduce resolved the problems of calculating and obtaining the specified data from these massive data quickly.

Comparing to other recommendations, most of news only accumulates a few feedback, on account of its short lifecycle. It is necessary to find valuable information in a very limited time, and then recommend it to proper readers who may be interested in.

3.4 Movie Recommendation: Netflix (2012)

Compared to the news, movies accumulate much more feedback. But if the recommendation system cannot predict users preference accurately, it is likely to recommend films that do not meet the users taste, resulting in customer churn. As a successful online movie rental provider, Netflix[7] predict a users preference accurately. Meanwhile, it ensures timely updating of recommendation lists.

Key idea: On March 27, 2012, two engineers of Netflix published an article[8] in their official blog to introduce the architecture of Netflix. The system is consist of three parts: off-line, on-line and near-line. Figure 2 shows a screen capture from the original article. Soon after that, they released another article in their technology blog[9], providing more details about their ranking model.

Details of architecture: Online computation is expected to be more responsive to recent events and user interaction. Meanwhile, it must be done timely. These limit the amount of processed data and complexity of algorithms, and it may not meet Service-Level Agreement (SLA) in a certain type of situation. For the off-line computation, it has less restriction for data volume, algorithm complexity, and less requirement of time, but the data of off-line model obsolete easily. Nearline computation is a combination of these two models. Its performance is similar to online calculation, but doesn't need to complete in real time and the results are temporarily stored together. These make it be asynchronous and with faster response. Nearline approach utilizes the flow calculation to get some intermediate, which can either be sent to the online part to update the real-time recommendation model, or be stored for backups.

Details of ranking: The sorting part is done by off-line calculation. Instead of using a single model, they select, train and test lots of machine learning approaches. They keep tracks of multiple dimensions of indexes when testing, especially the residence time and the time of user's video playback. Generally, a plurality of A/B tests can be run in parallel, so as to verify multiple methods simultaneously. They put 6 different algorithms into A/B test weekly, and assess

---

[7] https://www.netflix.com/.

[8] http://techblog.netflix.com/2013/03/system-architectures-for.html.

[9] http://techblog.netflix.com/2012/06/netflix-recommendations-beyond-5-stars.html.

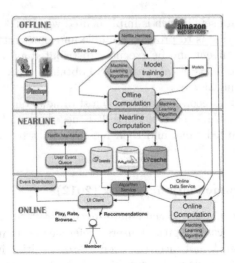

Fig. 2. The architecture of Netflix

offline and online indexes of these algorithms continuously. Then, the algorithm with excellent performance would be part of algorithm in their recommendation system.

Parallel approach: Amazon provides Hadoop PaaS platform to Netflix, and provides services to them through Elastic MapReduce (EMR). EMR provides apis and Hadoop cluster, where they can get one or more Hadoop jobs. Netflix has achieved Hadoop PaaS services (which is Genie (https://github.com/Netflix/gen-ie/wiki)). Genie could support thousands of concurrent jobs submit at the same time.

Summary: The above introduction of Google news and Netflix are the recommendation algorithms published before. Since they haven't disclosed their current system structures and main algorithms, we can only get the content published before, through either user interface or user experience speculate their operation.

4   Comparisons and Analyses

In this section, we analyze the mentioned systems above from seven aspects: the prediction accuracy, coverage, diversity, time complexity, cold-start, sparseness and personalization, as shown in Fig. 3. We can see that the performance of recommendation has been significantly improved during these years. It is worth noting that, in the following part, we will only compare the systems which have published the details on the specific aspects.

Accuracy: Accuracy is a measure of the ability of a recommendation system/algorithm on predicting users' behavior. Generally, it can be calculated from

	Accuracy	Coverage	Diversity	Instant-aneity	Cold-start	Sparsen-ess	Personaliz-ation
Google news(2007)	★★	★	★★	★★	★	★	E
Google news(2009)	★★★	★★	★★	★★	★★	★★	E
Netflix(2012)	★★★	★★★	★★	★★	★★	★★	E
Meituan(2015)	★★★★	★★★★	★★★★	★★★	★★★	★★★★	P
Facebook (2015)	★★★★	★★★★	★★★★	★★★★	★★★	★★★	P

Fig. 3. Comparison of systems (These comparision use the traditional recommendation system (each index are a star) as a benchmark for comparison. N, E, P in the column of "personality" represents non-personalization (we do not introduce non-personalization system in our paper), ephemeral personalization and persistent personalization respectively.)

the overlapping ratio of user's click behavior and recommendation list given by offline algorithms. The greater the overlapping ratio is, the higher the system accuracy is. The main purpose of recommendation system in real applications is to improve the prediction accuracy and obtain greater benefits. Therefore, each application uses a variety of methods to improve their accuracy. Among them, Meituan (2015) fuses data with multiple strategies, which improve prediction accuracy and thus ensure the accuracy of recommendation.

Coverage: The coverage metric describes the ability of a recommendation system to explore long tail goods [28] in a mass of goods. Which is generally defined as a ratio of recommended items to the total set of items. A Matthew effect is a developmental psychology phrase, it means the stronger are getting stronger and the small and weak are getting weaker. Google news (2007) can recommend a piece of news if and only if it has been clicked, there is a strong Matthew effect. In addition, it doesn't take the differences between users into account. Google news (2009) addresses those drawbacks by incorporating content-based method. In this way, the Matthew effect is reduced, and the coverage is increased. Query-based policy of Meituan (2015) helps to enhance the system's performance of exploring the long tail of goods and thus improves the coverage.

Diversity and noverty: The diversity metric describes the ability of a recommendation system in providing various recommendations, i.e., whether the recommendation results could override different interests of a specific user. Novelty means that the recommendation algorithm provides some novel items to a user, which he hasn't heard before and may not be similar to his historical records. Meituan (2015) takes multiple aspects into account and analyzes users' different interests comprehensively. These two policies both improve the diversity of the recommendation results. But most methods of Meituan (2015) are based on users' historical information, which leads to a low novelty.

Parallel and time complexity: It is worth noting that most of recommendation systems mentioned above are recommend by a variety of algorithms in parallel, improving the efficiency while ensuring the timeliness of the recommendation. Facebook (2015) uses multi-GPU training parallel framework and combining data parallel and model parallel to train models. Moreover, Facebook (2015) used iterative algorithms, SDG and ALS, to reduce the time complexity while work-to-work method could reduce the communication time effectively.

Cold-start: In recommendation systems, it is hard to make proper recommendations for new users, new items, and new systems, because there are none or very few ratings related to them. This leads to the cold-start problem. Google news (2009) introduces content-based method, making its results are not just rely on users' clicks. Meituan (2015) explores location-based policy to recommend items around users' location. These strategies can alleviate cold-start, to some extent.

Sparseness: Due to the fact that many users usually rate only a few items, most elements in the user-item matrix are zero. This phenomenon is called data sparsity. Location-based and query-based methods do not depend on the similarity matrix. Therefore, the impact brought by sparseness is limited in Meituan (2015). Furthermore, graph-based recommendation of Meituan (2015) uses transmissibility of similarity to obtain similar matrix more accurately and conveniently, which reduces the interference caused by sparseness.

Personalization: There are three categories about the degree of personalization [16], non-personalization, ephemeral personalization and persistent personalization. Non-personalization means that the recommendation results provided to each customer is identical. Ephemeral personalization is just simply making recommendations based on current browsing products or goods in a user's shopping cart. Persistent personalization means that the recommendations offered to different users are different even when they are looking at the same items.

5   Research Directions

In recent years, the developments of machine learning, large-scale network applications and high-performance computing have promoted recommendation system to a new upsurge. According to recent researches, particularly the achievements in ACM RecSys held in 2014[10] and 2015[11], we summarize some hotspots of recommendation system.

5.1   Hotspots for Long-Term

Context-aware recommendation systems (CARS): The utilization of context information alleviates sparsity and the decrease of recommendation accuracy caused by environmental changes, makes the system more intelligent and humanized. Hariri et al. [29] proposed an interactive recommendation system,

---

[10] http://recsys.acm.org/recsys14/.
[11] http://recsys.acm.org/recsys15/.

which uses the latest user behavior information to reconstruct model and to make recommendations, once the significant changes in the scene. Jiang et al. [30] propose a time-evolving rating prediction scheme in trust-based recommendation systems, using fluid dynamic theory.

Hybrid system: Hybrid a variety of recommendation methods makes the system access to their respective strengthes. For instance, the combination of collaborative filtering algorithm (CF) and content-based [31] or MP (Most Popular) ease cold start problem. Combining CF with social networks based method [32] alleviate problems caused by data sparseness.

Security issues: Security issues include the securities of system and user privacy. Seminario et al. [33] presents a strong program attack model (PIA) from the perspective of an attacker. It proves that attackers could attack collaborative recommendation systems based on SVD, user-based and item-based. Meanwhile, the experimental results of Frey et al. [34] show that in the case of CF, although the attacker forge a false identity to carry out attacks, the inherent similarities between real users protect the interests of users to some extent.

Social network: Social network covers all forms of network services around human society, and now becomes an indispensable part of human life. In fact, social networks are overlapping [35]. Making use of the overlapped identities of an user in different social networks can alleviate cold start problem and data sparseness problem. Furthermore, social networks are reflections of real life. People are more likely to be influenced by recommendation from friends. Jiang et al. [36] present the idea to evaluate trust by selecting proper recommenders.

In these research focus, security is a constant topic in the future for a long period, while both hybrid recommendation and CARS will be hot topics, until the "new darling" of the recommendation system appears.

5.2   Open Challenges

Cold-start: Cold-start problem exists even from the very beginning of recommendation system. There are many ways to partially solve the problem, but it is difficult to settle it. For instance, Ji and Shen [37] proposes a novel method to alleviate cold-start problem. They first build tag-keywords relation matrix based on the statistics, then select tags and extract keywords by a 3-factor matrix factorization model, and integrate the vectors at last. However, if a user has no record, the cold-start problem still exists.

Diversity and novelty: As we have mentioned in Sect. 4, many recommendation systems have a high prediction accuracy, but low variety and novelty. Vargas et al. [38] use backwards thinking to find users for items, which improves the diversity of recommendation successfully. However, there is still no effective way to ensure the novelty of recommended results while keeping high accuracy.

The directions above have troubled researchers for a long time, and these will persecute researchers in the future. Among them, diversity and novelty are contradict with accuracy in some degree. How to find a proper balance between them will also be the future research focus.

5.3 Meaningful Directions

Parallelization: As the volume of data growing, the effective integration of recommendation system and high-performance computing is becoming inevitable, for example, implementing the recommendation system [39] and processing data [40] on Hadoop. Well combination of recommendation system and high-performance computing can overwhelmingly improves computing performance and reduces computing time.

Interface display: The way of presenting recommendation results to users would affect their first impression on the system. Vanchinathan et al. [41] take advantage of the similarities between users or items to solve this problem. In addition, how to explain the recommendation result is also very important. Users often take a skeptical attitude towards recommendation results, so reasonable interpretation makes results more convincing.

How to do more tasks more efficiently? How to incorporate it into recommendation system? How to make users have more trust in our recommendation and take our advice? All the above aspects are worth further studies.

6 Conclusion

Recommendation system has been an effective tool to alleviate information overload. However, current recommendation systems still need to be improved to make the recommendation methods more effective in a broader range of applications, and make the results more in line with users' interests and needs.

In this paper, we introduce a range of representative recommendation applications and analyze the improvements in different periods. Based on this, we summarize the research focuses and open challenges as well as significant research directions. We also review the developments of the latest researches. Our work tries to provide some insights on future researches. In the real world, more factors should be considered than we have mentioned. Portability, scalability, robustness, and the ability to handle large data are issues we will take into account in future work. We believe that academic research should be able to guide the design of practical applications, that is why we choose to survey the real applications. We hope these issues we proposed in our paper can help to promote the developments of future applications of recommendation systems.

Acknowledgments. This work is supported by NSFC grants 61502161, 61472451, 61272151, the Chinese Fundamental Research Funds for the Central Universities 531107040845, and the National High-tech R&D Program of China 2014AA01A302 and 2015AA-015305.

References

1. Goldberg, D., Nichols, D., Oki, B.M., Terry, D.: Using collaborative filtering to weave an information tapestry. Commun. ACM **35**(12), 61–70 (1992)

2. Resnick, P., Iacovou, N., Suchak, M., Bergstrom, P., Riedl, J.: Grouplens: an open architecture for collaborative filtering of netnews. In: CSCW, pp. 175–186. ACM (1994)
3. Liu, L., Lecue, F., Mehandjiev, N.: Semantic content-based recommendation of software services using context. TWEB **7**(3), 17–36 (2013)
4. Di Noia, T., Mirizzi, R., Ostuni, V.C., Romito, D., Zanker, M.: Linked open data to support content-based recommender systems. In: I-SEMANTICS, pp. 1–8. ACM (2012)
5. Jung, G., Mukherjee, T., Kunde, S., Kim, H., Sharma, N., Goetz, F.: Cloudadvisor: a recommendation-as-a-service platform for cloud configuration and pricing. In: SERVICES, pp. 456–463. IEEE (2013)
6. Carrer-Neto, W., Hernández-Alcaraz, M.L., Valencia-García, R., García-Sánchez, F.: Social knowledge-based recommender system. Application to the movies domain. Expert Syst. Appl. **39**(12), 10990–11000 (2012)
7. Park, Y., Park, S., Jung, W., Lee, S.: Reversed CF: a fast collaborative filtering algorithm using a k-nearest neighbor graph. Expert Syst. Appl. **42**(8), 4022–4028 (2015)
8. Jiang, S., Qian, X., Shen, J., Fu, Y., Mei, T.: Author topic model based collaborative filtering for personalized POI recommendation. TMM **6**, 907–918 (2015)
9. Zhou, Y., Wilkinson, D., Schreiber, R., Pan, R.: Large-scale parallel collaborative filtering for the Netflix prize. In: Fleischer, R., Xu, J. (eds.) AAIM 2008. LNCS, vol. 5034, pp. 337–348. Springer, Heidelberg (2008). doi:10.1007/978-3-540-68880-8_32
10. Majid, A., Chen, L., Chen, G., Mirza, H.T., Hussain, I., Woodward, J.: A context-aware personalized travel recommendation system based on geotagged social media data mining. IJGIS **27**(4), 662–684 (2013)
11. Jamali, M., Ester, M., Trustwalker: a random walk model for combining trust-based and item-based recommendation. In: SIGKDD, pp. 397–406. ACM (2009)
12. Yin, H., Cui, B., Chen, L., Zhiting, H., Zhang, C.: Modeling location-based user rating profiles for personalized recommendation. TKDD **9**(3), 19 (2015)
13. Zhang, Y., Zhang, M., Zhang, Y., Lai, G., Liu, Y., Zhang, H., Ma, S.: Daily-aware personalized recommendation based on feature-level time series analysis. In: WWW, pp. 1373–1383. ACM (2015)
14. Debnath, S., Ganguly, N., Mitra, P.: Feature weighting in content based recommendation system using social network analysis. In: WWW, pp. 1041–1042. ACM (2008)
15. Ben Schafer, J., Konstan, J., Riedl, J.: Recommender systems in e-commerce. In: EC 1999, pp. 158–166. ACM (1999)
16. Ben Schafer, J., Konstan, J.A., Riedl, J.: E-commerce recommendation applications. In: Applications of Data Mining to Electronic Commerce, pp. 115–153. Springer (2001)
17. Bao, J., Zheng, Y., Wilkie, D., Mokbel, M.F.: A survey on recommendations in location-based social networks. GeoInformatica **19**(3), 525–565 (2014)
18. Jiang, W., Wang, G., Alam Bhuiyan, M., Wu, J.: Understanding graph-based trust evaluation in online social networks: methodologies and challenges. ACM Comput. Surv.**49**(1) (2016). Article 10
19. Karydi, E., Margaritis, K.G.: Parallel and distributed collaborative filtering: a survey. arXiv preprint arXiv:1409.2762 (2014)
20. Liang, H., Hogan, J., Yue, X.: Parallel user profiling based on folksonomy for large scaled recommender systems: an implimentation of cascading MapReduce. In: ICDMW, pp. 154–161. IEEE (2010)

21. Christou, I.T., Amolochitis, E., Tan, Z.-H.: Amore: design and implementation of a commercial-strength parallel hybrid movie recommendation engine. Knowl. Inf. Syst. **47**, 1–26 (2015)

22. Herbert, R., Monro, S.: A stochastic approximation method. Ann. Math. Stat. **22**(3), 400–407 (1951)

23. Jack, K., Wolfowitz, J.: Stochastic estimation of the maximum of a regression function. Ann. Math. Stat. **23**, 462–466 (1952)

24. Volinsky, C., Koren, Y., Bell, R.: Matrix factorization techniques for recommender systems. Computer **42**, 30–37 (2009)

25. Das, A.S., Datar, M., Garg, A., Rajaram, S.: Google news personalization: scalable online collaborative filtering. In: WWW, pp. 271–280. ACM (2007)

26. Liu, J., Dolan, P., Pedersen, E.: Personalized news recommendation based on click behavior. In: IUI, pp. 31–40. ACM (2010)

27. Hofmann, T.: Probabilistic latent semantic indexing. In: SIGIR, pp. 50–57. ACM (1999)

28. Anderson, C.: The long tail: why the future of business is selling more for less, Hyperion (2006)

29. Hariri, N., Mobasher, B., Burke, R.: Context adaptation in interactive recommender systems. In: ACM RecSys, pp. 41–48. ACM (2014)

30. Jiang, W., Wu, J., Wang, G., Zheng, H.: Forming opinions via trusted friends: time-evolving rating prediction using fluid dynamics. IEEE Trans. Comput. (2015). doi:10.1109/TC.2015.2444842

31. Saveski, M., Mantrach, A.: Item cold-start recommendations: learning local collective embeddings. In: ACM RecSys, pp. 89–96. ACM (2014)

32. Sedhain, S., Sanner, S., Braziunas, D., Xie, L., Christensen, J.: Social collaborative filtering for cold-start recommendations. In: ACM RecSys, pp. 345–348. ACM (2014)

33. Seminario, C.E., Wilson, D.C.: Attacking item-based recommender systems with power items. In: ACM RecSys, pp. 57–64. ACM (2014)

34. Frey, D., Guerraoui, R., Kermarrec, A.-M., Rault, A.: Collaborative filtering under a sybil attack: analysis of a privacy threat. In: EuroSec, p. 5. ACM (2015)

35. Rossi, L., Magnani, M.: The ML-model for multi-layer social networks. In: ASONAM, pp. 5–12. IEEE (2011)

36. Jiang, W., Wu, J., Wang, G.: On selecting recommenders for trust evaluation in online social networks. ACM Trans. Internet Technol. (TOIT) **15**(4) (2015). Article 14

37. Ji, K., Shen, H.: Addressing cold-start: scalable recommendation with tags and keywords. Knowl. Based Syst. **83**, 42–50 (2015)

38. Vargas, S., Castells, P.: Improving sales diversity by recommending users to items. In: ACM RecSys, pp. 145–152. ACM (2014)

39. Meng, S., Dou, W., Zhang, X., Chen, J.: Kasr: a keyword-aware service recommendation method on mapreduce for big data applications. TPDS **25**(12), 3221–3231 (2014)

40. Wang, C., Zheng, Z., Yang, Z.: The research of recommendation system based on Hadoop cloud platform. In: ICCSE, pp. 193–196. IEEE (2014)

41. Vanchinathan, H.P., Nikolic, I., De Bona, F., Krause, A.: Explore-exploit in top-n recommender systems via Gaussian processes. In: ACM RecSys, pp. 225–232. ACM (2014)

Big Data Security Analytic for Smart Grid with Fog Nodes

Wenlin Han and Yang Xiao[✉]

Department of Computer Science, The University of Alabama,
342 H.M. Comer, Box 870290, Tuscaloosa, AL 35487-0290, USA
whan2@crimson.ua.edu, yangxiao@ieee.org

Abstract. Big data throws big security challenges in Smart Grid. Fog computing emerges as a novel technology to bring the ability of Cloud and big data analytic (BDA) to the edge of the networks. However, we lack practice on how to utilize Fog, Cloud, and BDA to address big data security challenges in Smart Grid. In this paper, we propose a Mapreduce-style algorithm, named Mapreduce-style Fast Non-Technical Loss Fraud Detection scheme (Mapreduce-style FNFD), to detect Non-Technical Loss fraud in Smart Grid. Compared to its original version, FNFD, Mapreduce-style FNFD can utilize the ability of Cloud, Fog, and BDA, and thus can solve big data security issues.

Keywords: Smart Grid security · Big data · Non-Technical Loss · Fog computing

1 Introduction

Smart Grid [1,2] employs smart devices, such as smart meters, to provide advanced and efficient power services. The generation, transmission, distribution, and redistribution processes in Smart Grid are under intensive monitoring and are interactive. The devices in Smart Grid are electric and programmable. The novel framework of Smart Grid introduces environmental friendly energy resources to our daily lives and makes better use of current energy resources. Various security schemes have been proposed to enhance Smart Grid security including intrusion detection-based schemes [3,4], such as SCADA [5] and Amilyzer [6], and other schemes targeting some special security issues in Smart Grid [7–10].

With the fast growth of the number of smart meters installed globally, the data in Smart Grid becomes tremendously big. Big data in Smart Grid throws various challenges to the utility including big data storage, big data processing, and big data security. Big data storage and processing are widely studied, but there are only a few research works on big data security, especially in Smart Grid [11–13].

Cloud and Big Data Analytic (BDA) are often employed to address the big data security challenge, which we call Big Data Security Analytic (BDSA). However, there are two three problems of applying BDSA to Smart Grid. The first

© Springer International Publishing AG 2016
G. Wang et al. (Eds.): SpaCCS 2016, LNCS 10066, pp. 59–69, 2016.
DOI: 10.1007/978-3-319-49148-6_6

problem is availability. The limited resource of devices in Smart Grid often makes it difficult to access data in Cloud. The second problem is experience. There are only a few studies on BDSA in Smart Grid, and they only introduce BDSA at a high level. We lack experience and practice on how to analyze big data in Smart Grid for the security purpose. The last problem is feasibility. We have many traditional security algorithms but do not know whether they fit into BDSA and how.

Fog computing is an emerging technology that aims to bring Cloud and BDA closer to end-user devices. In this paper, we propose MapReduce-style FNFD, which is a BDSA algorithm for Smart Grid with the support of fog computing. MapReduce-style FNFD is built on a Non-Technical Loss (NTL) fraud [14] detector, FNFD [15]. FNFD is based on Recursive Least Square (RLS) [16]. We split the RLS problem into multiple sub-problems and parallel the problem-solving process, which is the basic idea behind MapReduce-style FNFD.

The main contributions of this paper include:

- We propose an algorithm for big data security analytic in Smart Grid;
- We study the feasibility of introducing fog computing into Smart Grid;
- Our study provides a concrete example on how to analyze big data in Smart Grid for the security purpose.

The rest of the paper is organized as follows: In Sect. 2, we introduce the background of this paper. In Sect. 3, we briefly introduce FNFD, a previously proposed NTL fraud detector. MapReduce-style FNFD is then presented in Sect. 4. We conclude the paper in Sect. 6.

2   Background

In this section, we will introduce the background of this paper, including big data, Cloud, Fog computing, big data security issues, and security analytic.

2.1   Big Data, Cloud and Fog Computing in Smart Grid

Smart Grid is the new generation of power grid, and it provides various advanced features including self-healing [17], real-time pricing and billing, distributed energy generation, real-time monitoring, renewable energy resources, smart home appliances, smart meters, etc. The communication flow is real time and two way in Smart Grid [18]. When smart home appliances connect with smart meters in a home, it is a Home Area Network (HAN). When homes in a community or neighborhood connect to each other, it is a Neighborhood Area Network (NAN) [19–22]. Factories have smart meters and other electric devices installed, and these form Industrial Area Networks (IAN). Vehicles are using electricity to replace gas and they can sell excess electricity back to the grid. The communication networks between these vehicles are Vehicle to Grid (V2G) networks [23,24].

However, with the growth of smart devices, applications, and networks in Smart Grid, the data are becoming tremendously big. Big data brings big challenges to the utility to deal with huge volume of data in Smart Grid. As a solution

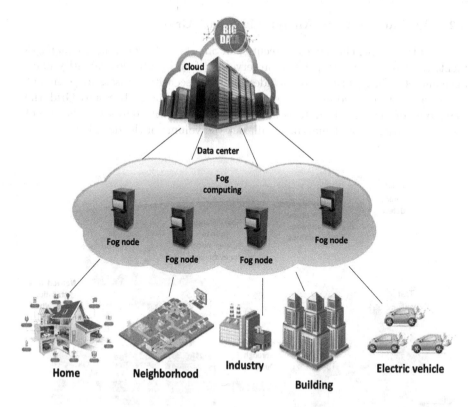

Fig. 1. The conceptual framework of Cloud and Fog computing in Smart Grid.

to big data problem, Cloud and big data analytic (BDA) often co-occur. Cloud utilizes the processing and storage capabilities of millions of servers to process or store data that a single server cannot handle. BDA is to employ Hadoop technologies, including MapReduce [25, 26], Hadoop distributed file system (HDFS), Hive, and Pig, to process and store big data. The main problem of Cloud in Smart Grid is bandwidth. Cloud has to process and store all the data in the data center, and the data center is often far from the devices in Smart Grid. Some networks in Smart Grid are wireless and highly dynamic, such as V2G networks. The bandwidth in these networks is slow.

Fog computing is an emerging technology that aims to address the above problem in Cloud. Instead of processing and storing data in the data center, fog computing brings processing and storage capability closer to the end-user devices. By the collaboration of multiple near-user devices, which we call fog nodes, fog computing can handle big data that a single device cannot process and can provide faster responses than Cloud. As shown in Fig. 1, it is the conceptual framework of Cloud and Fog computing in Smart Grid.

2.2   Big Data Security Analytic in Smart Grid

Big data throws big challenges to security in Smart Grid, including key management, trust management, privacy preservation, fraud protection, identity management, etc. Big security data includes single big security dataset, large amount of security datasets and big heterogeneous security data [27]. In Smart Grid, the main type of big security data is large amount of security datasets. The size of a single security dataset may be small, but the volume of the data is big.

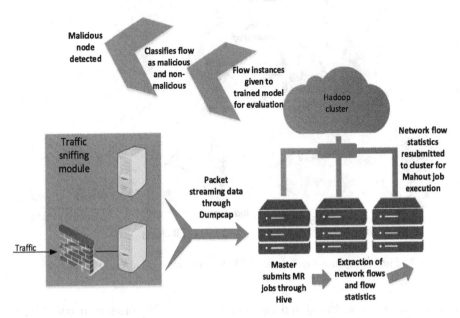

Fig. 2. A typical BDSA framework that uses a hadoop cluster to analyze network traffic and detect malicious nodes [27].

Big data security analytic (BDSA) is to use BDA tools or technologies to analyze security related data and make security related decisions. The traditional security solutions can handle these small datasets, however the speed is slow. Instead of analyzing the datasets one by one, BDSA parallelizes the process by using MapReduce-style algorithms. As shown in Fig. 2, it is a typical BDSA framework that uses a hadoop cluster to analyze network traffic and detect malicious nodes.

We propose MapReduce-style FNFD, which is a BDSA algorithm for Smart Grid. MapReduce-style FNFD is based on FNFD. FNFD is a algorithm that runs only at a single machine. MapReduce-style FNFD is a paralleled algorithm that runs collaboratively at fog nodes. Before introducing MapReduce-style FNFD, we briefly introduce FNFD and the problem it aims to solve in the following section.

3   Non-technical Loss Fraud and FNFD

In this section, we will briefly introduce FNFD and the problem it aims to solve.

3.1   Non-technical Loss Fraud

NTL fraud is a problem that harasses the utility for long. NTL fraud is where a fraudster tampers a smart meter so that·the meter reports less amount of electricity than the home/business consumed. The fraudster could be the customers who tampered their own meters or the attackers who hacked the meters remotely. The utility is the victim who suffers from economic loss.

3.2   FNFD

FNFD is a detection scheme that aims to detect NTL fraud in Smart Grid. The criterion that used to differentiate a normal meter and a tampered meter is the relationship between a coefficient a_i and two thresholds α_{min} and α_{max}. The coefficient a_i represents Meter i. If $a_i > \alpha_{max}$, the meter is tampered. If $\alpha_{min} \leq a_{ij} \leq \alpha_{max}$, it is a normal meter. A is the vector of all coefficients, denoted as:

$$A = (a_1, a_2, \ldots, a_n). \tag{1}$$

A is obtained from the function:

$$E = AX, \tag{2}$$

where X is the vector of the amount of electricity reported by the meters, and E is the vector of the amount of consumed electricity.

The problem is solved based on RLS. The basic idea is to get an estimation of A which satisfies:

$$\min_{\forall A} \|E - AX\|^2 \tag{3}$$

4   MapReduce-style FNFD

The basic idea of MapReduce-style FNFD is to divide the global problem, shown in Eq. 3, into several sub-problems, assign sub-problem to processes in fog nodes, and finally solve the global problem via local solutions of sub-problems. At each iteration, the processes communicate, exchange local solutions, and update their own local solutions for the next iteration. Since the sub-problems can be solved simultaneously, it saves a lot of time dealing with big data.

We partition matrix X into p blocks by columns, say:

$$X = (X_1, X_2, \ldots, X_p). \tag{4}$$

We have

$$AX = \sum_{i=1}^{p} A_i X_i. \tag{5}$$

Let's define $b_i(A)$ as:

$$b_i(A) = E - \sum_{j \neq i} A_j X_j \tag{6}$$

The global problem shown in Eq. 3 can be divided into p sub-problems, that is:

$$\min_{\forall y} \left\| b_i(A) - yX_i \right\|^2, \tag{7}$$

where $1 \leq i \leq p$.

Each sub-problem is also a RLS problem, thus it is a paralleled RLS problem [28]. Let's define the global solution at iteration k as:

$$A^k = (A_1^k, A_2^k, \ldots, A_p^k). \tag{8}$$

The global solution at iteration $k+1$, A^{k+1}, can be obtained by solving a local problem:

$$\min_{\forall y^{k+1}} \left\| b_i(A^k) - y^{k+1} X_i \right\|, \tag{9}$$

where $1 \leq i \leq p$.

Let's define $\tilde{A}^{k+1}$ as the updated local solution at iteration $k+1$, and $\tilde{A}^{k+1}$ can be obtained from local solutions of previous iterations, denoted as

$$\tilde{A}^{k+1} = (A_1^k, A_2^k, \ldots, A_{i-1}^k, y_i^{k+1}, A_{i+1}^k, \ldots, A_p^k). \tag{10}$$

The global solution at iteration $k+1$ is given by:

$$A^{k+1} = \sum_{i=1}^{p} \sigma_i^{k+1} \tilde{A}_i^{k+1}, \tag{11}$$

where $\sum_{i=1}^{p} \sigma_i^{k+1} = 1$.

The local solution at iteration $k+1$ is given by:

$$\begin{aligned}
A_i^{k+1} &= (\sigma_i^{k+1} \tilde{A}_i^{k+1})_i + \left(\sum_{\substack{j=1 \\ j \neq i}}^{p} \sigma_j^{k+1} \tilde{A}_j^{k+1} \right)_i \\
&= \sigma_i^{k+1} y_i^{k+1} + \sum_{\substack{j=1 \\ j \neq i}}^{p} \sigma_j^{k+1} A_i^k \\
&= \sigma_i^{k+1} y_i^{k+1} + (1 - \sigma_i^{k+1}) A_i^k \\
&= A_i^k + \sigma_i^{k+1} (y_i^{k+1} - A_i^k) \\
&= A_i^k + \sigma_i^{k+1} \xi_i^{k+1},
\end{aligned} \tag{12}$$

where $\xi_i^{k+1} = y_i^{k+1} - A_i^k$.

The local value $b_i(A)$ at iteration k can be obtained by:

$$b_i(A^{k+1}) = b_i(A^k) - \sum_{\substack{j=1 \\ j \neq i}}^{p} \sigma_j^{k+1} X_j \xi_j^{k+1}. \tag{13}$$

Let's define $B_j^{k+1} = X_j \xi_j^{k+1}$, and we get:

$$b_i(A^{k+1}) = b_i(A^k) - \sum_{\substack{j=1 \\ j \neq i}}^{p} \sigma_j^{k+1} B_j^{k+1}. \tag{14}$$

After getting the value of the vector A, we compare the value to α_{max} and α_{min}. If $a_i > \alpha_{max}$, the meter is tampered. If $\alpha_{min} \leq a_{ij} \leq \alpha_{max}$, it is a normal meter.

Algorithm 1. MapReduce-style FNFD algorithm at a slave node

1: Initiation: For all slave nodes i, $1 \leq i \leq p$, test linear independent of X_i. $b_i(A^{k+1}) = b$, $y_i^0 = A_i^0$, $k = 0$.
2: **repeat**
3:     calculate $B_i^{k+1} = X_i \xi_i^{k+1}$;
        global communication: B_i^{k+1} to all slave nodes;
        calculate $b_i(A^{k+1}) = b_i(A^k) - \sum_{\substack{j=1 \\ j \neq i}}^{p} \sigma_j^{k+1} B_j^{k+1}$;
        solve local least square $\min_{y^{k+1}} \left\| b_i(A^k) - y^{k+1} X_i \right\|$;
        $\xi_i^{k+1} = y_i^{k+1} - A_i^k$;
        $A_i^{k+1} = A_i^k + \sigma \xi_i^{k+1}$;
        test local convergence;
        global communication: convergence results;
        $k = k + 1$.
4: **until** converged
5: **for** each a_i in $\mathbf{A_i}$ **do**
6:     **if** $a_i > \alpha_{max}$ **then**
7:         identified as tampered
8:     **if** $\alpha_{min} \leq a_i \leq \alpha_{max}$ **then**
9:         identified as normal
10:     **else**
11:         report error

The algorithm of MapReduce-style FNFD can be divided into the master algorithm and the slave algorithm. The master algorithm runs at the master node. The main function is to split metrics A and X into p blocks by column. The slave algorithm runs at every slave node, shown in Algorithm 1. The matrix X has to be linear independent to have a solution. Testing liner independent can be carried out either at the master node or every slave node. Here, we let every slave node test liner independent individually.

Table 1. Registered electricity consumption (kWh) in the experiment: 3 m and 1 observer meter

Meter 1	Meter 2	Meter 3	Observer meter
3	4	1	10
2	3	1	8
1	2	3	12

Local convergence means that a given error, e, is satisfied when solving a local least square problem. When all the slave nodes get converged results, the global convergence is achieved and the detection process obtains a result.

5   A Case Study

In this section, we will use a simple case study to show the effectiveness of MapReduce-style FNFD.

As shown in Table 1 is the electricity consumption data of three smart meters and one observe meter. The data is collected every 15 min. The observer records the total unit supplied to these three meters. By simply adding these numbers, we can see that the total billed unit is less than the total unit supplied. Thus, some meter(s) are tampered.

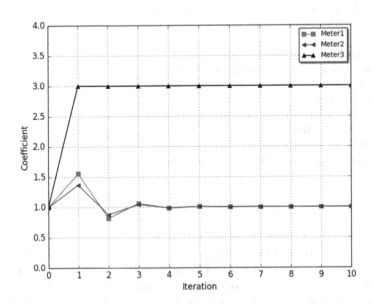

Fig. 3. The detection process of MapReduce-style FNFD. The coefficient of Meter 3 converges to 3 while the coefficients of other meters converge to 1. It shows that Meter 3 is tampered and Meter 1 and Meter 2 are normal.

In the previous work, we showed how to use FNFD, which runs at a single machine, to detect the tampered meter(s). Here, we split the global problem into three sub-problems and use four machines to detect the tampered meter(s), among which three machines are used as slave nodes. Thus, the value of p is 3. A_i^0 is set to a vector of 1 initially. The given error e is set to 10^{-5}.

The coefficient convergence process is shown in Fig. 3. The coefficient of Meter 3 converges to 3 while the coefficients of other meters converge to 1. It means that Meter 1 and Meter 2 are normal meters while Meter 3 is tampered. The simple case is only to illustrate how MapReduce-style FNFD works. It can work on large data sets and the performance is affected by coefficients p, e, σ and the size of the data sets, which will be introduced in the long and journal version of this paper.

6 Conclusion

In this paper, a big data analytic algorithm was proposed to address security issues in Smart Grid, which is named MapReduce-style FNFD. We introduced big data security challenges in Smart Grid and how Cloud, fog computing, and big data analytic can help to address these challenges. MapReduce-style FNFD is an algorithm built on an existing NTL fraud detector. Our study provides real practice of introducing big data security analytic into Smart Grid. As a future work, we will further test the performance and convergence of MapReduce-style FNFD in various aspects.

Acknowledgments. This work was supported in part by the National Natural Science Foundation of China under the Grant 61374200, and the National Science Foundation (NSF) under Grant CNS-1059265.

References

1. Liu, J., Xiao, Y., Li, S., Liang, W., Chen, C.L.P.: Cyber security, privacy issues in smart grids. IEEE Commun. Surv. Tutorials **14**(4), 981–997 (2012)
2. Kundur, D., Feng, X., Mashayekh, S., Liu, S., Zourntosand, T., Butler-Purry, K.L.: Towards modelling the impact of cyber attacks on a smart grid. Int. J. Secur. Netw. **6**, 2–13 (2011)
3. Han, W., Xiong, W., Xiao, Y., Ellabidy, M., Vasilakos, A.V., Xiong, N.: A class of non-statistical traffic anomaly detection in complex network systems. In: Proceedings of the 32nd International Conference on Distributed Computing Systems Workshops (ICDCSW 2012), pp. 640–646, June 2012
4. Kalogridis, G., Denic, S.Z., Lewis, T., Cepeda, R.: Privacy protection system and metrics for hiding electrical events. Int. J. Secur. Netw. **6**, 14–27 (2011)
5. Gao, J., Liu, J., Rajan, B., Nori, R., Fu, B., Xiao, Y., Liang, W., Chen, C.L.P.: SCADA communication and security issues. Secur. Commun. Netw. **7**(1), 175–194 (2014)
6. Berthier, R., Sanders, W.H.: Monitoring advanced metering infrastructures with amilyzer. In: Proceedings of C&ESAR: The Computer & Electronics Security Applications Rendez-vous, Cyber-security of SCADA & Industrial Control Systems, Rennes, France, 19-21 Nov. 2013, pp. 130–142 (2013)

7. Han, W., Xiao, Y., Combating, T.: Non-technical loss fraud targeting time-based pricing in smart grid. In: The 2nd International Conference on Cloud Computing and Security (ICCCS 2016), July 2016

8. Han, W., Xiao, Y.: NFD: a practical scheme to detect non-technical loss fraud in smart grid. In: Proceedings of the 2014 International Conference on Communications (ICC 2014), pp. 605–609, June 2014

9. Han, W., Xiao, Y.: CNFD: a novel scheme to detect colluded non-technical loss fraud in smart grid. In: Yang, Q., Yu, W., Challal, Y. (eds.) WASA 2016. LNCS, vol. 9798, pp. 47–55. Springer, Heidelberg (2016). doi:10.1007/978-3-319-42836-9_5

10. Zhang, J., Gunter, C.A.: Application-aware secure multicast for power grid communications. Int. J. Secur. Netw. **6**, 40–52 (2011)

11. IBM: Managing big data for smart grids and smart meters (2015). http://www-935.ibm.com/services/multimedia/Managing_big_data_for_smart_grids_and_smart_meters.pdf

12. Ray, P., Reed C., Gray, J., Agarwal, A., Seth, S.: Improving roi on big data through formal security and efficiency risk management for interoperating ot and it systems (2012). http://www.gridwiseac.org/pdfs/forum_papers12/ray_reed_gray_agarwal_seth_paper_gi12.pdf

13. Li, F., Luo, B., Liu, P.: Secure and privacy-preserving information aggregation for smart grids. Int. J. Secur. Netw. **6**, 28–39 (2011)

14. Han, W., Xiao, Y.: Non-technical loss fraud in advanced metering infrastructure in smart grid. In: The 2nd International Conference on Cloud Computing and Security (ICCCS 2016), July 2016

15. Han, W., Xiao, Y.: FNFD: a fast scheme to detect and verify non-technical loss fraud in smart grid. In: Proceedings of the International Workshop on Traffic Measurements for Cybersecurity (WTMC 2016), May–June 2016

16. Hayes, M.H.: Recursive least squares. In: Statistical Digital Signal Processing and Modeling, chap. 9.4, p. 154. Wiley (1996)

17. Mu, J., Song, W., Wang, W., Zhang, B.: Self-healing hierarchical architecture for ZigBee network in smart grid application. Int. J. Sens. Netw. **17**, 130–137 (2015)

18. Gao, J., Xiao, Y., Liu, J., Liang, W., Chen, C.L.P.: A survey of communication/networking in smart grids. Future Gener. Comput. Syst. **28**, 391–404 (2012). (Elsevier)

19. Xiao, Z., Xiao, Y., Du, D.: Exploring malicious meter inspection in neighborhood area smart grids. IEEE Trans. Smart Grid **4**(1), 214–226 (2013)

20. Xiao, Z., Xiao, Y., Du, D.: Non-repudiation in neighborhood area networks for smart grid. IEEE Commun. Mag. **51**(1), 18–26 (2013)

21. Xia, X., Liang, W., Xiao, Y., Zheng, M., Xiao, Z.: Difference-comparison-based approach for malicious meter inspection in neighborhood area smart grids. In: Proceedings of the 2015 International Conference on Communications (ICC 2015), pp. 802–807, June 2015

22. Xia, X., Liang, W., Xiao, Y., Zheng, M.: BCGI: a fast approach to detect malicious meters in neighborhood area smart grid. In: Proceedings of the 2015 International Conference on Communications (ICC 2015), pp. 7228–7233, June 2015

23. Han, W., Xiao, Y.: IP^{2}DM for V2G networks in smart grid. In: Proceedings of the 2015 International Conference on Communications (ICC 2015), pp. 782–787, June 2015

24. Han, W., Xiao, Y.: Privacy preserving for V2G networks in smart grid: a survey. Comput. Commun. **91–92**, 17–28 (2016)

25. Xiao, Z., Xiao, Y.: Accountable MapReduce in cloud computing. In: Proceedings of 2011 IEEE Conference on Computer Communications Workshops (INFOCOM WKSHPS), pp. 1082–1087 (2011)
26. Xiao, Z., Xiao, Y.: Achieving accountable mapreduce in cloud computing. Future Gener. Comput. Syst. **30**, 1–13 (2014). (Elsevier)
27. Han, W., Xiao, Y.: Cybersecurity in internet of things - big data analytics. In: Big Data Analytics for Cybersecurity. Taylor & Francis Group (2016, in press)
28. Renaut, R.A.: A parallel multisplitting solution of the least squares problem. Numer. Linear Algeba Appl. **5**, 11–31 (1998)

A Reduction Method of Analyzing Data-Liveness and Data-Boundedness for a Class of E-commerce Business Process Nets

Wangyang Yu[1,2,4], Guanjun Liu[3,4(✉)], and Leifeng He[3,4]

[1] Ministry of Education Key Laboratory for Modern Teaching Technology, Shaanxi Normal University, Xi'an 710119, China
ywy191@snnu.edu.cn
[2] School of Computer Science, Shaanxi Normal University, Xi'an 710062, China
[3] Department of Computer Science, Tongji University, Shanghai 201804, China
[4] The Key Laboratory of Embedded System and Service Computing, Ministry of Education, Tongji University, Shanghai 200092, China
liuguanjun@tongji.edu.cn

Abstract. E-commerce Business Process Nets (EBPNs for short) are a novel formal model of describing and verifying e-commerce business processes with multiple interactive parties. They can well reflect some behavior-security properties such as data-live and data-boundedness. However, the problem of effectively analyzing EBPNs remains largely open since data are considered in them. In this paper, a class of EBPNs called S-graph-Reducible EBPN (RENS for short) is defined. Some restrictions are set on the structure of a RENS and thus each RENS can be reduced to a marked S-graph. We prove that a RENS and the related marked S-graph are equivalent on behaviors. Thus, the properties of RENS such as data-liveness, data-boundedness, and reachability can be analyzed easily based on the methods applied in the marked S-graphs.

Keywords: Business process · E-commerce · Petri nets · Behavioural security

1 Introduction

E-commerce with multiple interactive parties has evolved worldwide, and become increasingly popular in global online economy [1,2]. The third-party payment platforms, e-commerce systems, banks, clients, and other applications together make up the entire trading process. As a distributed application on the web, e-commerce business processes are more complex and loosely coupled. This integration introduces new security challenges due to complex interactions among *Application Programming Interfaces* (APIs) of multiple interactive parties [3]. Research has shown that insufficient trust represents a key reason for many users to avoid making businesses over the Internet [3–6]. Online shopping systems are complex and thus it is difficult to be correctly designed. Design-level vulnerabilities are indeed a major source arising security issues [7–9].

© Springer International Publishing AG 2016
G. Wang et al. (Eds.): SpaCCS 2016, LNCS 10066, pp. 70–83, 2016.
DOI: 10.1007/978-3-319-49148-6_7

In order to deal with the security issues in e-commerce business process at both application-level and design-level, a formal model called *E-commerce Business Process Net* (EBPN) is proposed [10]. EBPNs are suitable for modeling and validating e-commerce business processes since they can ensure the integrity and reliability of e-commerce systems by revealing defects and logic errors in business processes through *Reachability Data State Graph* (RD) [10]. However, for RD, there may be the problem of state space explosion in some specific cases. For malicious behavior patterns, EBPNs can also be used to prove the expected security guarantees of e-commerce systems via specific modeling and verification methods [11]. Nevertheless, analysis methods of the EBPN properties remain unexplored currently. Due to the complex data factors, it is difficult to analyze EBPN directly by RD.

In order to enrich the EBPN analysis methods, this work introduces a reduction analysis technique for a class of EBPNs called S-graph-Reducible EBPN (RENS for short). A RENS can be reduced to a marked S-graph. Behavioral equivalence is proven to hold between a RENS and the related marked S-graph. Thus, the properties of any RENS can be analyzed by the existing methods for the marked S-graph.

The rest of this paper is organised as follows. Section 2 introduces the related work. Section 3 recalls some basic concepts such as EBPN, data-liveness, and data-boundedness. Section 4 defines RENS, presents a reduction method, proves the behavioral equivalence between RENSs and the reduced S-graphs, and gives algorithms to check behavior-security properties. Section 5 concludes this paper.

2   Related Work

As the new security challenges of online shopping business occur at the application-level, the sufficient protection of online shopping systems from attacks is beyond the capabilities of techniques taken in the network-level [12–14] and operating system-level such as cryptography, firewall, and intrusion detection. Since they lack the knowledge of application semantics, they cannot meet these new needs from todays distributed online shopping systems. Engineering software security is essential to incorporate the use of assurance techniques throughout development and operation [15]. Formal methods are mathematical techniques for specifying and verifying the correctness and trustworthiness of software systems. The US Department of Defense Trusted Computer System Evaluation criteria require that the highest-level of security classification (the A-class) should use the formal specification and verification techniques [16].

Petri net-based approaches [17,18] have been used to model and verify correctness and soundness of workflows [19]. A series of work have been done for cooperative systems and inter-organizational workflow based on Petri nets [20,21]. Some Petri net-based analyses have been carried out for the composition of web services [22–24]. However, most of the existing work concentrates on the soundness and correctness of behaviors of these systems. They do not involve the behavior security [11] related to the transaction and money. *Colored Petri nets*

(CPN) are a powerful tool for modeling concurrent systems, and a combination of Petri nets and programming language [25]. However, the non-determinacy of data states resulting from human factors such as tampering data cannot be depicted by CPN [10,11]. Many accidents in online shopping systems are caused by data errors and state inconsistency as exploited by malicious users. Thus, both data properties and data state non-determinacy must be well described [10,11].

Thus, EBPN [10,11] is proposed to address the above issues. It integrates both data and control flows based on Petri nets. Rationality and transaction consistency are defined and validated respectively to guarantee the structural correctness and transaction properties of an e-commerce business process. It offers a complete methodology for modeling and validating an e-commerce system with multiple interactive parties from the view point business processes. Data errors and non-determinacy of data states during the trading process can be depicted with the help of EBPNs [10]. They can help a designer identify errors in the conceptual model phase and thus these errors can be corrected before the deployment phase. If errors take place in an online execution phase, irreparable damage may be caused, and compensation for the errors and modification of the program are extremely costly. At the requirement analysis and design levels, an EBPN method for modeling and verification of online shopping business processes with malicious behavior patterns is presented in [11] to explicitly identify whether the online shopping systems are resistant to the possibly malicious behavior patterns [3,7]. It can analyze whether an online shopping business process is resistant to the known malicious behavior patterns and thus the difficulty and cost of modification for imperfect systems can be alleviated.

However, there are no sufficient analysis methods for EBPNs. Thus, this work focuses on a reduction analysis method for EBPN.

3   EBPN

The following Definitions 1–9 are from [10,11], and more details can be seen in the two references.

Definition 1 (EBPN). *An E-commerce Business Process Net (EBPN) is a 7-tuple* $EN = (P, T; F, D, W, S, G)$ *where*

1. *P is a finite set of* places;
2. *T is a finite set of* transitions T *such that* $P \cap T = \emptyset$ *and* $P \cup T \neq \emptyset$;
3. *$F \subseteq (P \times T) \cup (T \times P)$ is a set of* directed arcs;
4. *D is a finite, non-empty set of* symbol strings *denoting the types of tokens;*
5. *$W: F \rightarrow <a_1d_1, a_2d_2, a_3d_3, \cdots, a_ld_l>$, $a_l \in \{0, 1\}$, $d_l \in D$, and $l > 0$ is the number of* elements in D;
6. *$S \subseteq D$ denotes a set of* key token types;
7. *$G: T \rightarrow \Pi$ is a* predicate function *that assigns a predicate to each* transition $t \in T$ *where* Π *is the set of Boolean expressions on* D.

Definition 2 (Marking of EBPN). *A marking of an EBPN $EN = (P, T;$ $F, D, W, S, G)$ is $M: P \rightarrow\ <n_1 d_1, n_2 d_2, n_3 d_3, \cdots, n_l d_l>$, $n_l \in \mathbb{N} = \{0, 1, 2,$ $\cdots\}$; $d_l \in D$, and $l > 0$ is the number of data elements in D.*

The multi-set [25] of l-dimensional vector $M(p)$ is represented by $\widetilde{M}(p)$, and the data element set of $M(p)$ is represented by $\widehat{M}(p)$. The number of times that element $d \in D$ appears in is denoted by $\#(d, \widetilde{M}(p))$.

Definition 3 (Data state). *A pair $\Lambda = (M, \delta_D)$ is a data state of EN, if M is a marking of EN, and δ_D is called a data allocation which assigns a value $.\boldsymbol{T}.$ (true), or $.\boldsymbol{F}.$ (false) to each $d \in \{\widehat{M}(p)|p \in P\}$ such that $d \in (D - S) \rightarrow$ $\delta_D(d) = .\boldsymbol{T}.$, and $\delta_D : S \rightarrow \{.\boldsymbol{T}., .\boldsymbol{F}.\}$.*

Definition 4. (δ_G). *δ_G is a Boolean function that assigns a Boolean value $.\boldsymbol{T}.$ (true) or $.\boldsymbol{F}.$ (false) to each $G(t)$ such that $\delta_G: G(t) \rightarrow \{.\boldsymbol{T}., .\boldsymbol{F}.\}, t \in T$.*

Definition 5 (Firing conditions). *A transition $t \in T$ is enabled at a data state $\Lambda = (M, \delta_D)$ if*

1. $\forall p \in\ ^{\bullet} t$, $M(p) \geq W(p, t)$;
2. $\exists G(t): \delta_G(G(t)) = .\boldsymbol{T}..$

Definition 6 (Key transition). *Given $t \in T$, $^{\bullet}t = P'$, and $t^{\bullet} = P''$, t is called a key transition if*

1. $S \cap \{\widetilde{W}(t,p)|p \in P''\} \neq \emptyset$;
2. The token $s \in S \cap \{\widetilde{W}(t,p)|p \in P''\}$ is produced by $t \rightarrow \delta_D(s) \in \{.\boldsymbol{T}.,.\boldsymbol{F}.\}$.

In an EBPN, every arc has a vector. If $p \in P$, and $t \in T$, then the weight of an arc (p, t) or (t, p) is represented by $W(p, t)$ or $W(t, p)$, and the trading parameter set of k-dimensional vector $W(p,t)$ or $W(t,p)$ is represented by $\widetilde{W}(p,t)$ or $\widetilde{W}(t,p)$.

Definition 7 (Firing rules). *Let $EN = (P, T; F, D, W, S, G)$ be an EBPN, and $\Lambda = (M, \delta_D)$ be a data state of EN. A transition $t \in T$, which is enabled at (M, δ_D), can be fired under M (denoted as $M \xrightarrow{t}$), and a new marking M' (denoted as $M \xrightarrow{t} M'$) is yielded as follows, $\forall p \in P$:*

1. $p \in\ ^{\bullet}t \setminus t^{\bullet}$, $M'(p) = M(p) - W(p,t)$;
2. $p \in t^{\bullet} \setminus\ ^{\bullet} t$, $M'(p) = M(p) + W(t,p)$;
3. $p \in t^{\bullet} \cap\ ^{\bullet} t$, $M'(p) = M(p) - W(p,t) + W(t,p)$;
4. otherwise, $M'(p) = M(p)$.

If t is not a key transition, a new data state Λ' is $\Lambda' = (M', \delta'_D) = (M',$ $\forall d \in \{\widehat{M}(p)|p \in P\} \rightarrow \delta'_D(d) = \delta_D(d) \wedge \forall d \in \{\widehat{W}(t,p)|p \in t^{\bullet}\} - \{\widehat{M}(p)|p \in P\} \rightarrow \delta'_D(d) = .\boldsymbol{T}.);$

If t is a key transition, a new state set Γ is $\Gamma = \{(M', \delta'_D)|M \xrightarrow{t} M',$ $\forall s \in \{\widehat{W}(t,p)|p \in t^{\bullet}\} \cap S \rightarrow \delta'_D(s) \in \{.\boldsymbol{T}.,.\boldsymbol{F}.\}, \forall d \in \{\widehat{M}(p) - \{\widehat{W}(t,p)|p \in t^{\bullet}\} \cap S\} \rightarrow \delta'_D(d) = \delta_D(d)\}.$

Definition 8 (RD). *Let* $(M_0, \ \delta_{D_0})$ *be the initial data state of* $EN =$ $(P, T; F, D, W, S, G)$. *Its Reachability Data state graph (RD) can be defined as a 3-tuple* $RD(EN) = (N, E; L)$, *where*

1. N *is a set of nodes,* $N = R(M_0, \delta_{D_0})$;
2. E *is a set of arcs,* $E = \{(M_i, \delta_{D_i}), \ (M_j, \delta_{D_j}) | (M_i, \delta_{D_i}), (M_j, \delta_{D_j}) \in$ $R(M_O, \delta_{D_0}), \exists t_k \in T : (M_i, \delta_{D_i}) \overset{t_k}{\to} (M_j, \delta_{D_j})\}$;
3. $L: E \to T$, $L((M_i, \delta_{D_i}), (M_j, \delta_{D_j})) = t_k$ *if and only if* $(M_i, \delta_{D_i}) \overset{t_k}{\to} (M_j, \delta_{D_j})$, *and* t_k *is called the label of the arc between* (M_i, δ_{D_i}) *and* (M_j, δ_{D_j}). (M_j, δ_{D_j}) *is the successor (node) of* (M_i, δ_{D_i}), *and* (M_i, δ_{D_i}) *is the predecessor (node) of* (M_j, δ_{D_j}).

Definition 9 (Data-boundedness). *Let* $(M_0, \ \delta_{D_0})$ *be the initial data state of* $EN = (P, T; F, D, W, S, G)$. EN *is a data-bounded EBPN if* $\forall p \in P$, $\forall M \in R(M_0)$, $\forall d \in \widehat{M}(p)$: $\#(d, \widehat{M}(p)) \leq 1$.

Definition 10 (Data-liveness). *Let* $EN = (P, \ T; \ F, \ D, \ W, \ S, \ G)$ *be an EBPN,* $(M_0, \ \delta_{D_0})$ *be its initial data state, and* $t \in T$. *If* $\forall (M, \delta_D) \in R(M_0, \delta_{D_0})$, $\exists (M', \delta'_D) \in R(M, \delta_D)$, *such that* $(M', \delta'_D) \overset{t}{\to}$, *then* t *is data-live. If each* $t \in T$ *is data-live, then* EN *is data-live.*

4 Reduction and Analysis Methods

Due to the new characters, it is difficult to analyze an EBPN directly. Thus, we propose a class of subnets called RENS. First, some basic definitions are given.

Definition 11 (Marked S-graph [26]). *Let* $N = (P, \ T; \ F, \ M)$ *is an traditional marked Petri net, if* $\forall t \in T$: $|{}^{\bullet}t| = |t^{\bullet}| = 1$, *then it is called a marked S-graph.*

Definition 12 (RENS). *Let* $EN = (P, \ T; \ F, \ D, \ W, \ S, \ G, \ (M_0, \ \delta_{D_0}))$ *be an EBPN with an initial data state,* EN *is called a S-graph-Reducible EBPN (RENS for short) if*

1. $\forall t \in T$, $\exists p_i, \ p_j \in P$, ${}^{\bullet}t = \{p_i\}$ *and* $t^{\bullet} = \{p_j\}$, *where* $i, \ j \in \mathbb{N}^+$;
2. $\forall p \in P$, $\forall t_i \in {}^{\bullet} p$ *and* $\forall t_j \in p^{\bullet}$ *such that* $W(t_i, \ p) = W(p, \ t_j)$;
3. $M_0(p) = W(p, \ t)$, *where* $p \in P$, *and* p *is a marked place at* $(M_0, \ \delta_{D_0})$;
4. $d \in \{\widehat{M_0}(p) | p \in P\} \to \delta_{D_0}(d) = .T..$

It is a special class of EBPN with an initial data state, and has some restrictions on its basic structure. The first condition means that every transition has only one input place and one output place, just like the marked S-graph. The second one means that the weights on input and output arcs of every place are the same. The third one implies that every marked place that has tokens at (M_0, δ_{D_0}) satisfies the request of $W(p, t)$. The last condition means that every token is assigned by $.T.$ at $(M_0, \ \delta_{D_0})$.

We reduce an RENS to an equivalent traditional Petri net. Then, we can use the existing analysis methods of traditional petri net to analyze the reachability, date-boundedness, and data-liveness of RENS.

Figure 1(a) shows a business process fragment of Merchant derived from [11]. Its an RENS. The APIs are depicted by transitions. t_1 means the function Place an order. t_2 represents the function of confirming an order from TPP. t_3 and t_4 are control structures which are used to deal with abnormal events and rollback events respectively. There are three token types whose orders in a marking and weight are $<MIdle, orderID, SDone>$. The initial marking is $M_0 = [<MIdle, orderID, 0>, <0, 0, 0>, <0, 0, 0>]$, i.e., $M_0(p_1) = <MIdle, orderID, 0>$, $M_0(p_2) = M_0(p_3) = <0, 0, 0>$. This means that there are two tokens in p_1 with the types of MIdle and orderID respectively. In this paper, for simplicity, the expression of a marking is $M = [p_i(\lambda)|p_i$ is the place that has tokens, and $\lambda = \widetilde{M}(p_i)]$. Thus, the above initial marking can be simplified as $M_0 = [p_1(MIdle, orderID)]$. In order to facilitate graphic expression, the vector $<a_1d_1, a_2d_2, a_3d_3, \cdots, a_kd_k>$ would be simplified as a set on the arc. This is purely for graphical clarity, because an EBPN may have dozens of trading parameters, and the k-dimensional vector would be so long that it is impossible to represent it in a graph. On expression, the weights on arcs are also simplified according to the order. For example, in Fig. 1(a), $W(p_1, t_1) = <MIdle, orderID, 0>$ can be simplified as $\{MIdle, orderID\}$. At M_0, let $\delta_{D_0}(MIdle) = \delta_{D_0}(orderID) = .T..$

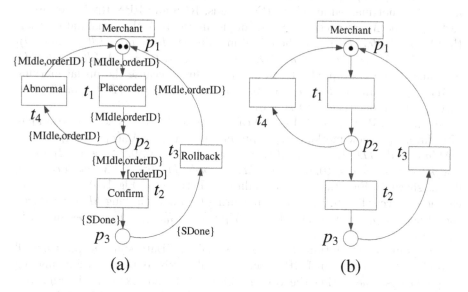

Fig. 1. Control flow of Merchant and its equivalent traditional Petri net

In this work, if $d \in \{\widetilde{M}|p \in P\} \cap S$ at a data state (M, δ_D), and $\delta_D(d) = .F.$, then we use notation dF to express its value. Otherwise, if $d \in D$, and $\delta_D(d) = .T.$, then its value would not be displayed for simplicity. The initial data state can be shown as $(M_0, \delta_{D_0}) = ([p_1(MIdle, orderID)])$. A predicate is added to t_2 for describing the validation criteria in this business process; t_1 is a key transition; orderID is the key token type.

4.1 Reduction and Equivalence

Definition 13 (RBN). *Let $RNS = (P, T; F, D, W, S, G, (M_0, \delta_{D_0}))$ be an RENS. The marked Petri net $RBN(RNS) = (P, T; F, M_0')$ is called* a Reduced Basic Net (RBN) *of RNS, where $M_0'(p) = 1$ if $p \in P$ is marked at M_0 in RNS; and $M_0'(p') = 0$ if $p' \in P$ is not marked at M_0 in RNS.*

RNS and RBN(RNS) have the same places, transitions and arcs. Every transition has only one input place and one output place. Figure 1(b) shows the RBN(RNS) corresponding to the RNS in Fig. 1(a). We call that RBN(RNS) and RNS are structurally equivalent. In fact, each RBN is a marked S-graph. For simplicity, the expression of a marking is denoted by $M = [p_i(n)|p_i$ is marked, and $n \in \mathbb{N}^+]$ in traditional Petri nets.

According to Definition 12, in RNS, $M_0(p) = W(p, t)$, where $p \in P$ is a marked place at (M_0, δ_{D_0}), and $d \in \{\widehat{M_0}(p)|p \in P\} \rightarrow \delta_{D_0}(d) = .T.$. For M_0 in RNS, there exists a marking M_0' in RBN(RNS) correspondingly, and the vector $W(p, t)$ in p that is marked at (M_0, δ_{D_0}) corresponds to a token in p that is marked at M_0', i.e., $M_0'(p) = 1$ if $p \in P$ is marked at M_0 in RNS; and $M_0'(p') = 0$ if $p' \in P$ is not marked at M_0 in RNS. Thus, RNS and RBN(RNS) can fire at (M_0, δ_{D_0}) and M_0' respectively. For example, in Fig. 1(a), the initial data state is $([p_1(MIdle, orderID)])$, and the initial marking is $M_0 = [p_1(MIdle, orderID)]$ where $M_0(p_1) = <MIdle, orderID, 0>$, and $W(p_1, t_1) = <MIdle, orderID, 0>$. Since there is no predicate on t_1, t_1 can fire. Because the initial marking is $M_0' = [p_1(1)]$ in Fig. 1(b), t_1 can also fire. $<MIdle, orderID, 0>$ of Fig. 1(a) corresponds to one token in Fig. 1(b).

In an RNS, $W(t_i, p)$ and $W(p, t_j)$ can be reduced to one token. For example, after firing t_1, a new marking M_1 is produced. $M_1(p_1) = M_0(p_1) - W(p_1, t_1) = <MIdle, orderID, 0> - <MIdle, orderID, 0> = <0, 0, 0>$, and $M_1(p_2) = M_0(p_2) + W(t_1, p_2) = <0, 0, 0> + <MIdle, orderID, 0> = <MIdle, orderID, 0>$, as shown in Fig. 2(a). Let the traditional Petri net in Fig. 1(b) execute synchronously according to Fig. 1(a). After firing t_1, a new marking M_1' is produced such that $M_1'(p_1) = M_0'(p_1) - 1 = 0$, $M_1'(p_2) = M_0'(p_2) + 1 = 1$, as shown in Fig. 2(b).

According to Definitions 3–7, the Reachability Data state graph show all possible data states of an EBPN, and there also exist data allocations making all predicates true during the running of an RNS. For example, in Fig. 1(a), $\delta_{D_0}(MIdle) = \delta_{D_0}(orderID) = .T.$, and t_1 is a key transition. After firing t_1, a new marking M_1 is produced, and a data state set is produced, i.e., $\Gamma = \{(M_1, \delta_{D_1}), (M_1, \delta_{D_1}')\} = \{([p_2(MIdle, orderID)]), ([p_2(MIdle, orderIDF)])\}$, in which $\delta_{D_1}(MIdle) = \delta_{D_1}(orderID) = .T.$ makes the predicate [orderID] true on t_2. Under (M_1, δ_{D_1}), t_2 can fire. As t_2 is not a key transition, a data state $(M_2, \delta_{D_2}) = ([p_3(SDone)])$ is produced, i.e., $M_2(p_2) = M_1(p_2) - W(p_2, t_2) = <0,$

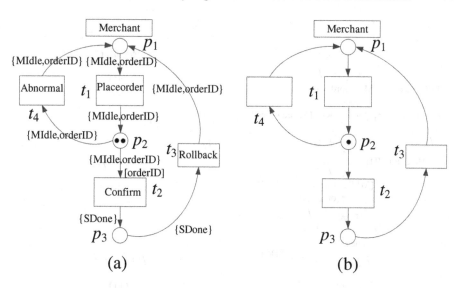

Fig. 2. The states after firing t_1

$0, 0>$, $M_2(p_2) = M_1(p_3) + W(t_2, p_3) = <0, 0, SDone>$, as shown in Fig. 3(a). Likewise, t_2 in Fig. 2(b) can also fire, and Fig. 3(b) shows the state reached by firing t_2. RD of the RNS in Fig. 1(a) is shown in Fig. 4, and the Reachability Marking Graph of Fig. 1(b) is shown in Fig. 5.

Lemma 1. *Let $RNS = (P, T; F, D, W, S, G, (M_0, \delta_{D_0}))$ be an RENS, and $RBN(RNS) = PN = (P, T; F, M_0')$. RNS is behaviorally equivalent to PN, and the follow conclusions hold:*

1. *If there exists a transition sequence $\sigma = t_{i_1}, t_{i_2}, \cdots, t_{i_k}$ such that $M_0' \xrightarrow{t_{i_1}} M_1' \xrightarrow{t_{i_2}} M_2', \cdots, M_{k-1}' \xrightarrow{t_{i_k}} M_k'$ in PN, $i_1, i_2, \cdots, i_k \in \mathbb{N}^+$, then there must exist the same transition sequence $\sigma = t_{i_1}, t_{i_2}, \cdots, t_{i_k}$ and a data state sequence $(M_0, \delta_{D_0}), (M_1, \delta_{D_1}), \cdots, (M_k, \delta_{D_k})$ such that $(M_0, \delta_{D_0}) \xrightarrow{t_{i_1}} (M_1, \delta_{D_1}) \xrightarrow{t_{i_2}} (M_2, \delta_{D_2}), \cdots, (M_{k-1}, \delta_{D_{k-1}}) \xrightarrow{t_{i_k}} (M_k, \delta_{D_k})$ in RNS;*
2. *If there exists a transition sequence $\sigma = t_{i_1}, t_{i_2}, \cdots, t_{i_k}$ such that $(M_0, \delta_{D_0}) \xrightarrow{t_{i_1}} (M_1, \delta_{D_1}) \xrightarrow{t_{i_2}} (M_2, \delta_{D_2}), \cdots, (M_{k-1}, \delta_{D_{k-1}}) \xrightarrow{t_{i_k}} (M_k, \delta_{D_k})$ in RNS, then there must exist the same transition sequence $\sigma = t_{i_1}, t_{i_2}, \cdots, t_{i_k}$ and a marking sequence $M_0', M_1', \cdots, M_k'$ such that $M_0' \xrightarrow{t_{i_1}} M_1' \xrightarrow{t_{i_2}} M_2', \cdots, M_{k-1}' \xrightarrow{t_{i_k}} M_k'$ in PN;*
3. *For M_α' in PN and M_α in RNS, $\alpha \in \mathbb{N}_k \cup \{0\}$, $\mathbb{N}_k = \{1, 2, \cdots, k\}$, if $M_\alpha'(p) = n$, $n \in \mathbb{N}$, $p \in P$, then in RNS, $M_\alpha(p) = nW(t, p)$, $\exists t \in {}^\bullet p$; and if $M_\alpha(p) = nW(t, p)$ in REN, $\exists t \in {}^\bullet p$, then in PN, $M_\alpha'(p) = n$.*

Proof: Based on the above statements and structural restrictions of RNS, S and predicates can be ignored when considering the equivalence among RNS

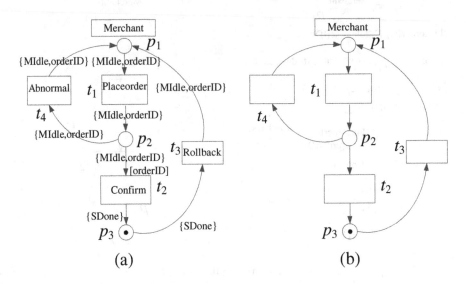

Fig. 3. The states after firing t_2

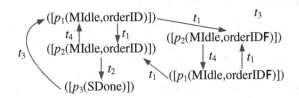

Fig. 4. RD of Fig. 1(b)

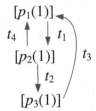

Fig. 5. Reachability Marking Graph of Fig. 1(b)

and PN. If there exists a transition sequence $\sigma = t_{i_1}, t_{i_2}, \cdots, t_{i_k}$ such that $(M_0, \delta_{D_0}) \xrightarrow{t_{i_1}} (M_1, \delta_{D_1}) \xrightarrow{t_{i_2}} (M_2, \delta_{D_2}), \cdots, (M_{k-1}, \delta_{D_{k-1}}) \xrightarrow{t_{i_k}} (M_k, \delta_{D_k})$. Then for $\forall (M_k, \delta_{D_k}) \in R(M_0, \delta_{D_0})$, $k \in \mathbb{N}^+$, $M_k(p) = M_{k-1}(p) - W(p, t_{i_k})$ where $p \in {}^\bullet t_{i_k} - t_{i_k}^\bullet$, and $M_k(p) = M_{k-1}(p) + W(t_{i_k}, p)$ where $p \in t_{i_k}^\bullet - {}^\bullet t_{i_k}$; Otherwise, $M_k(p) = M_{k-1}(p)$. Correspondingly, in PN, there exist dynamic behaviors from M_0' which correspond to (M_0, δ_{D_0}). First, $M_1'(p) = M_0'(p) - 1$ where $p \in {}^\bullet t_{i_1} - t_{i_1}^\bullet$; $M_1'(p) = M_0'(p) + 1$ where $p \in t_{i_1}^\bullet - {}^\bullet t_{i_1}$; Otherwise, $M_1'(p) = M_0'(p)$. Then, $M_2'(p) = M_1'(p) - 1$ where $p \in {}^\bullet t_{i_2} - t_{i_2}^\bullet$; $M_2'(p) = M_1'(p) + 1$ where $p \in t_{i_2}^\bullet - {}^\bullet t_{i_2}$; Otherwise, $M_2'(p) = M_1'(p)$. Until M_k', i.e., $M_k'(p) = M_{k-1}'(p) - 1$ where $p \in {}^\bullet t_{i_k} - t_{i_k}^\bullet$; $M_k'(p) = M_{k-1}'(p) + 1$ where $p \in t_{i_k}^\bullet - {}^\bullet t_{i_k}$; Otherwise, $M_k'(p) = M_{k-1}'(p)$. Thus, similarly, there exists a transition sequence $\sigma = t_i, t_j, \cdots, t_k$ such that $M_0' \xrightarrow{t_i} M_1' \xrightarrow{t_j} M_2', \cdots, M_{k-1}' \xrightarrow{t_k} M_k'$ in PN, and vice versa.

Let $M_\alpha' = M_0' \xrightarrow{\sigma'}$ in PN, then $\#({}^\bullet p, \sigma') - \#(p^\bullet, \sigma') = M_\alpha'(p) = n$. Similarly, in RNS, $(M_\alpha, \delta_{D_\alpha}) = (M_0, \delta_{D_0}) \xrightarrow{\sigma'}$, $M_\alpha(p) = \#({}^\bullet p, \sigma')W(t, p) - \#(p^\bullet, \sigma')W(p, t')$, $t \in {}^\bullet p$, $t' \in p^\bullet$. According to Definition 12, $W(t, p) = W(p, t')$, then $M_\alpha(p) = [\#({}^\bullet p, \sigma') - \#(p^\bullet, \sigma')]W(t, p) = nW(t, p)$, and vice versa. □

In Fig. 1(a), there is an enabled transition sequence $\sigma = t_1 t_2 t_3$, and the executing process is shown in Fig. 4. As t_1 is a key transition, orderID is the key token type. After firing t_3, a data state set is produced, i.e., $\Gamma = \{(M_1, \delta_{D_1}), (M_1, \delta_{D_1}')\} = \{([p_2(MIdle, orderID)]), ([p_2(MIdle, orderIDF)])\}$. From $([p_2(MIdle, orderID)])$, there is an executing process whose data allocations making all produced tokens $.T.$, i.e., $([p_2(MIdle, orderID)]) \xrightarrow{t_2} ([p_3(SDone)]) \xrightarrow{t_3} ([p_1(MIdle, orderID)])$. In this situation, the predicate on t_2 is true. The executing processes from $[p_2(MIdle, orderIDF)]$ cannot make predicate true. Thus, t_2 cannot fire. In the PN of Fig. 1(b), from $M_0' = [p_1(1)]$ which corresponds to $(M_0, \delta_{D_0}) = ([p_1(MIdle, orderID)])$, there is also an executable transition sequence $\sigma = t_1 t_2 t_3$ as shown in Fig. 5. As the Reachability Data state graph and the executing process of a transition sequence show all possible produced data states in RNS, we know that if there is an executable transition sequence $\sigma = t_1 t_2 t_3$ in PN, there also exists an executable transition sequence $\sigma = t_1 t_2 t_3$ in RNS such that there is a executing processes corresponding to Fig. 5, i.e., $([p_1(MIdle, orderID)]) \xrightarrow{t_1} ([p_2(MIdle, orderID)]) \xrightarrow{t_2} ([p_3(SDone)]) \xrightarrow{t_3} ([p_1(MIdle, orderID)])$, and every data state in the executing process corresponds to a marking in Fig. 5.

4.2   Data-Liveness and Data-Boundedness of RENS

Theorem 1. *Let* $RNS = (P, T; F, D, W, S, G, (M_0, \delta_{D_0}))$ *be an RENS. Under the initial data state* (M_0, δ_{D_0}), *RNS is data-live iff* $RBN(RNS)$ *is live.*

Proof: *(Sufficiency)* If $RBN(RNS) = (P, T; F, M_0')$ is live, i.e., $\forall t \in T, \exists M' \in R(M_0')$ and $\exists M'' \in R(M)$ such that $M'' \xrightarrow{t}$, then there must exist two transition sequences σ and σ' such that $M_0' \xrightarrow{\sigma} M' \xrightarrow{\sigma'} M''$ in $RBN(RNS)$. According to

Lemma 1, we know that for each $t \in T$ in RNS, there must exist two same transition sequences σ and σ' such that $(M_0, \delta_{D_0}) \xrightarrow{\sigma} (M, \delta_D) \xrightarrow{\sigma'} (M', \delta'_D)$, and $(M', \delta'_D) \xrightarrow{t}$. Thus, RNS is data-live.

(*Necessity*) If $RNS = (P, T; F, D, W, S, G, (M_0, \delta_{D_0}))$ is data-live, we have that $t \in T$, $\exists (M, \delta_D)$, $(M', \delta'_D) \in R(M_0, \delta_{D_0})$, and $(M', \delta'_D) \in R(M, \delta_D)$, such that $(M', \delta'_D) \xrightarrow{t}$. Then, there must exist two transition sequences σ and σ' such that $(M_0, \delta_{D_0}) \xrightarrow{\sigma} (M, \delta_D) \xrightarrow{\sigma'} (M', \delta'_D)$ in RBN(RNS). According to Lemma 1, in RBN(RNS), $\forall t \in T$, there must exist two same transition sequences σ and σ' such that $M'_0 \xrightarrow{\sigma} M' \xrightarrow{\sigma'} M''$, and $M'' \xrightarrow{t}$. Thus, RBN(RNS) is live. □

Theorem 2. *Let $RNS = (P, T; F, D, W, S, G, (M_0, \delta_{D_0}))$ be an RENS. Under the initial data state (M_0, δ_{D_0}), RNS is data-bounded iff RBN(RNS) is safe.*

Proof: (*Sufficiency*) If $RBN(RNS) = (P, T; F, M'_0)$ is safe, then we have that $\forall p \in P$, $\forall M'_\alpha \in R(M'_0)$, $M'_\alpha(p) \leq 1$. According to Lemma 1, there must exist a correspond marking M_α in RNS such that $M_\alpha(p) = W({}^\bullet p, p)$ or 0. Thus, according to Definitions 2 and 9, RNS is data-bounded.

(*Necessity*) If $RNS = (P, T; F, D, W, S, G, (M_0, \delta_{D_0}))$ is data-bounded, we have that $\forall p \in P$, $M \in R(M_0)$, $d \in \widehat{M}(p) \rightarrow \#(d, \widehat{M}(p)) \leq 1$. According to Lemma 1, there must exist a corresponding marking M'_α in RBN(RNS) such that $M'_\alpha(p) = 1$ or 0. Thus, RBN(RNS) is safe. □

In Fig. 1(b), the RBN(RNS) is actually a marked S-graph, and the determination of liveness and boundedness can be solved in polynomial time [27–31]. The RNS in Fig. 1(a) can be reduced and equivalent to the marked S-graph in Fig. 1(b). The properties of RNS in Fig. 1(a) can be analyzed by the methods for the latter. Thus, the determination of data-liveness and data-boundedness of the RNS can also be solved in polynomial time. According to Theorems 1 and 2, RNS in Fig. 1(a) is data-live and data-bounded because the RBN(RNS) in Fig. 1(b) is live and safe.

4.3   Reachability of RENS

The reachability of the RENS in Fig. 1(a) can be analyzed by the methods used for the marked S-graph in Fig. 1(b). In fact, the reachability of marked S-graph can all be decidable by algebraic methods (state equation) in polynomial time [32–35]. Thus, if an RENS can be reduced and equivalent to a marked S-graph, the reachability can be decidable.

Corollary 1. *Let $RNS = (P, T; F, D, W, S, G, (M_0, \delta_{D_0}))$ be an RENS, $RBN(RNS) = (P, T; F, M'_0)$. $\forall M'_\alpha \in R(M'_0) \rightarrow \exists (M_\alpha, \delta_{D_\alpha}) \in R(M_0, \delta_{D_0})$, and $\forall M'_\alpha \notin R(M'_0) \rightarrow \nexists (M_\alpha, \delta_{D_\alpha}) \in R(M_0, \delta_{D_0})$; if $M'_\alpha(p) = n$, $\alpha, n \in \mathbb{N}$, $p \in P$, then in RNS, $M_\alpha(p) = nW(t, p)$, $t \in {}^\bullet p$.*

According to Lemma 1, it is obvious that Corollary 1 holds. M'_α corresponds to M_α. If M'_α is not reachable in RBN(RNS), $(M_\alpha, \delta_{D_\alpha})$ is also not reachable in RNS. Otherwise, we can find a transition sequence σ such that $M'_0 \xrightarrow{\sigma} M'_\alpha$ in $RBN(RNS)$, and determine the reachability of $(M_\alpha, \delta_{D_\alpha})$ in RNS. Different from general Petri nets, marked S-graph can be easily analyzed, e.g., their reachability and legal firing sequence can both be decidable by algebraic methods in polynomial time [32–35]. If a RENS can be reduced to a marked S-graph, we can analyze it via the methods used in marked S-graph. Here, we give the specific procedure of determining the reachability of a data state in RENS.

Step 1: For an RENS $RNS = (P, T; F, D, W, S, G, (M_0, \delta_{D_0}))$, construct its Reduced Basic Net $RBN(RNS) = (P, T; F, M'_0)$;
Step 2: For a specific data state $(M_\alpha, \delta_{D_\alpha})$ in RNS, construct the corresponding marking M'_α in $RBN(RNS)$;
Step 3: Determine the reachability of M'_α in $RBN(RNS)$: if M'_α is reachable, execute Step 4, and otherwise, $(M_\alpha, \delta_{D_\alpha})$ is not reachable in RNS;
Step 4: Find a transition sequence σ such that $M'_0 \xrightarrow{\sigma} M'_\alpha$ in $RBN(RNS)$, execute σ in RNS, and determine the reachability of $(M_\alpha, \delta_{D_\alpha})$.

In Fig. 1(a), for the reachability of a given data state $(M_\alpha, \delta_{D_\alpha}) = ([p_3(SDone)])$, we can determine by analyzing the reachability of marking $M'_\alpha = [p_3(1)]$ in Fig. 1(b). By incidence matrix and state equation methods [26–29], it is easy to know that $M'_\alpha = M'_0 \xrightarrow{t_1} M'_1 \xrightarrow{t_2}$. Then, according to Corollary 1 and above steps, we can execute the transition sequence t_1, t_2 in Fig. 1(a). The executing steps are also shown in Fig. 4. Therefore, $(M_\alpha, \delta_{D_\alpha})$ is reachable from (M_0, δ_{D_0}).

5   Conclusion

EBPN is a formal model suitable for modeling and validating e-commerce business processes. Defects and errors in business processes can be revealed with the help of EBPN in a system design process. However, there are no sufficient methods to analyze the properties of EBPN. Due to the complex data elements, it is difficult to analyze EBPN directly. Thus, we propose a reduction method to analyze a class of EBPN. By this method, they can be analyzed through the existing methods for traditional Petri nets. The future work is to study other efficient analyzing methods such as invariant and matrix.

Acknowledgements. This paper is in part supported by the National Natural Science Foundation of China under Grants 41271387, 61572360, 61602289, 11372167 and 61303092, by the Fundamental Research Funds for the Central Universities of China under Grants GK201503061 and GK200902018, by the Natural Science Basic Research Plan in Shaanxi Province of China under Grants 2016JQ6056, by the Program of Key Science and Technology Innovation Team in Shaanxi Province under Grant 2014KTC-18, by the Postgraduate Education Reform Project of Shaanxi Normal University under grant GERP-15-12, by the Shanghai Education Development Foundation and Shanghai Municipal Education Commission (Shuguang Program).

References

1. iResearch: 2015 Q2 e-commerce market core data (2015). http://news.iresearch. cn/zt/256178.shtml
2. CNNIC: 36th China Internet development statistics report. China Internet Network Information Center, Beijing, China, July 2015
3. Wang, R., Chen, S., Wang, X.F., Qadeer, S.: How to shop for free online-security analysis of cashier-as-a-service based web stores. In: Proceedings of the 32nd IEEE Symposium Security Privacy, Berkeley, CA, pp. 465–480 (2011)
4. CNNIC: Q3 Chinese Internet security report. China Internet Network Information Center, Beijing, China, November 2015
5. Georgiadis, C.K., Pimenidis, E.: Web services enabling virtual enterprise transactions. In: Proceedings of IADIS International Conference on E-Commerce, Barcelona, Spain, pp. 297–302 (2006)
6. Pfitzmann, B., Waidner, M.: Properties of payment systems: general definition sketch and classification. IBM Research Division Research Report RZ 2823 (#90126), May 1996
7. Hoglund, G., McGraw, G.: Exploiting Software: How to Break Code. Pearson Education, India (2004)
8. Viega, G.: McGraw : Building Secure Software. Ohmsha, Tokyo (2006)
9. State of Application Security Report. https://www.securityinnovation.com/ company/news-and-events/press-releases/state-of-application-security-report. html
10. Yu, W.Y., Yan, C.G., Jiang, C.J., et al.: Modeling and validating e-commerce business process based on Petri nets. IEEE Trans. Syst. Man Cybern. Syst. **44**(3), 327–341 (2014)
11. Yu, W.Y., Yan, C.G., Jiang, C.J., et al.: Modeling and verification of online shopping business processes by considering malicious behavior patterns. IEEE Trans. Autom. Sci. Eng. **13**(2), 647–662 (2016)
12. Bhargavan, K., Fournet, C., Gordon, A.D.: Modular verification of security protocol code by typing. In: Proceedings of the 37th Annual ACM SIGPLAN-SIGACT Symposium Principles Programming Languages, New York, USA, pp. 445–456 (2010)
13. Ray, I., Natarajan, N.: An anonymous and failure resilient fair-exchange e-commerce protocol. Decis. Support Syst. **39**(3), 267–292 (2005)
14. Wang, Z.K.: Analyzing a fair exchange e-commerce protocol using CSP and FDR. In: Proceedings of the International Conference on E-Education, E-Business, E-Management, E-Learning, Sanya, China, pp. 303–307 (2010)
15. Neumann, P.: Principled assuredly trustworthy composable architectures. SRI International Computer Science Laboratory, Menlo Park, USA, Contract N66001–01-C-8040, December 2004
16. Latham, D.C.: Department of Defense Trusted Computer System Evaluation Criteria. US Department of Defense, vol. 5200.28-STD, ed (1985)
17. Hrz, B., Zhou, M.C.: Modeling and control of discrete-event dynamic systems. Springer, London (2007)
18. Liu, G.J., Jiang, C.J.: Net-structure-based conditions to decide compatibility and weak compatibility for a class of inter-organizational workflow nets. Sci. China Inf. Sci. **58**(7), 1–16 (2015). Article number 072103
19. van der Aalst, W.M.P., Lohmann, N., La Rosa, M.: Ensuring correctness during process configuration via partner synthesis. Inf. Syst. **37**(6), 574–592 (2012)

20. Du, Y.Y., Jiang, C.J., Zhou, M.C.: A Petri net-based model for verification of obligations and accountability in cooperative systems. IEEE Trans. Syst. Man Cybern. A Syst. Hum. **39**(2), 299–308 (2009)
21. Du, Y.Y., Jiang, C.J., Zhou, M.C., et al.: Modeling and monitoring of E-commerce workflows. Inf. Sci. **179**(7), 995–1006 (2009)
22. Du, Y.H., Li, X.T., Xiong, P.C.: A Petri net approach to mediation-aided composition of web services. IEEE Trans. Autom. Sci. Eng. **9**, 429–435 (2012)
23. Wang, S.G., Huang, L., Sun, L., et al.: Efficient and reliable service selection for heterogeneous distributes software systems. Future Gener. Comp. Syst. (2016, in press)
24. Wang, S.G., Hsu, C.H., Liang, Z.J., et al.: Multi-user web service selection based on multi-QoS prediction. Inf. Syst. Front. **16**(1), 143–152 (2014)
25. Jensen, K., Kristensen, L.M.: Coloured Petri Nets: Modeling and Validation of Concurrent Systems. Springer, New York (2009)
26. Wu, Z.H.: Introduction to Petri Nets. Machine Press, Beijing (2006)
27. Murata, T.: Petri nets: properties, analysis and applications. Proc. IEEE **77**(4), 541–580 (1989)
28. Zhou, M.C., Venkatesh, K.: Modeling, Simulation, and Control of Flexible Manufacturing Systems: A Petri Net Approach. World Scientific Publishing, Singapore (1999)
29. Wu, N.Q., Zhou, M.C.: System Modeling and Control with Resource-Oriented Petri Nets. CRC Press, New York (2010)
30. Liu, G.J., Jiang, C.J., Zhou, M.C., et al.: Interactive Petri nets. IEEE Trans. Syst. Man Cybern. A Syst. Hum. **43**(2), 291–302 (2013)
31. Liu, G.J., Jiang, C.J., Zhou, M.C.: Process nets with channels. IEEE Trans. Syst. Man Cybern. A Syst. Hum. **42**(1), 213–225 (2012)
32. Watanabe, T., Mizobataand, Y., Onaga, K.: Legal firing sequences and related problems of Petri nets. In: Proceedings of the 3rd International Workshop on Petri Nets and Performance Models (PNPM1989), pp. 277–286. IEEE Computer Society Press (1989)
33. Watanabe, T., Mizobataand, Y., Onaga, K.: Legal firing sequences and minimum initial markings for Petri nets. In: Proceedings of the 1989 IEEE International Symposium on Circuits and Systems, pp. 323–326 (1989)
34. Watanabe, T.: Time complexity of legal firing sequences and related problems of Petri nets. Trans. IEICE Jpn. **72**(12), 1400–1409 (1989)
35. Jiang, C.J.: Polynomial-time algorithm for the legal firing sequences problem of a type of synchronous composition Petri nets. Sci. China (Ser. F Inf. Sci.) **44**(3), 226–233 (2001)

Computation of Secure Consistency for Real Systems

Mimi Wang[1,2], Guanjun Liu[1,2(✉)], Changjun Jiang[1,2], and Chungang Yan[1,2]

[1] Department of Computer Science, Tongji University, Shanghai 201804, China
[2] Key Laboratory of Ministry of Education for Embedded System
and Service Computing, Tongji University, Shanghai 201804, China
wangmimi2013@hotmail.com, {liuguanjun,cjjiang,yanchungang}@tongji.edu.cn

Abstract. In real applications, many systems have the different security, but their securities are considered to be consistent. In other words, two workflow net systems with different security policies, are thought to be completely similar (i.e., their similarity degree is 1) by the formula proposed by Mendling et al. However, we find that their definition is not accurate. The reason is that the related definition does not accurately feature the relations of transitions. Therefore, this paper refines the relations of transitions based on event relations in the branching processes. And then to distinguish these two systems, we define the *security consistency* and *security consistency degree*, and propose a new formula to compute the security similarity degree of two nets. Additionally, this paper utilizes some examples to show these definitions, computation as well as the advantages.

Keywords: Secure consistency · Consistency degree · Workflow nets · Security · Behavioral relation

1 Introduction

With the development of network technology and computer, security is one of the most important topics for most of these networked systems. Workflow nets (WF-nets) have become one of the standard ways to model and analyze system [1].

We first use an example of two versions of a bank transfer system to illustrate this [2]. The two systems in [2] are sketched using two workflow nets as shown in Figs. 1(a) and (b). [2] has proved that different security policies can affect the interacting behaviors of a system. A good policy can ensure a system securer by these affections. However according to the method in [4], we find the consistency degree is 1, that is to say the two systems are completely consistent. Obviously the two systems are not completely consistent due to one with a security policy and another without. Then this paper focuses on the behavior secure consistency of two systems.

The consistency comparison of models is a basic operation when managing business process models [3]. This can help analysts to compare behaviors of

© Springer International Publishing AG 2016
G. Wang et al. (Eds.): SpaCCS 2016, LNCS 10066, pp. 84–97, 2016.
DOI: 10.1007/978-3-319-49148-6_8

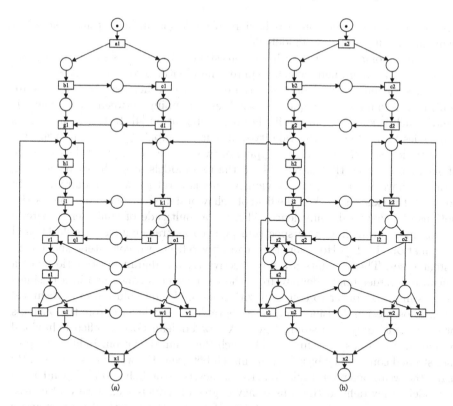

Fig. 1. Two workflow nets modeling bank transfer systems once: (a) logging in the system and receiving the verification information are operated in the same terminal device, (b) in two different ones [2].

models and accurately understand the differences among multiple variants in order to determine how to reconcile them. In the business process environment, it is important to transform business requirements into a system abstraction [4]. The main challenge of this work is that business analysts and systems analysts hold different views on the same real-world phenomenon, which leads to different models for the same system. Consistency of two models means that their semantics match each other, and this matching relation is usually built on the basis of a mapping between the graphical data. Therefore, consistency can reflect whether the mapping is effective or not [5].

There are three aspects featuring the consistency of models [6]: task labels, structure and behavior. Task labels or structure cannot meet the complex and fickle application requirements. For these environment, however, component interaction must consider the internal or external factors so that the interaction models cannot be implemented easily according to the expected behaviors. Behavior analysis is of important theoretical significance and practical value.

The consistency comparison of behaviors of models is an important topic when managing business process models [3].

There is some prior research on consistency. In [4] consistency is defined the basis of an alignment which requires the identification of *correspondences* of models. Given a correspondence, the question whether two data models are equivalent is similar to the question whether a mapping between data schema is valid, which is known from the field of data integration [4]. In this area, various properties for evaluating the validity of a schema mapping have been proposed. For instance, satisfiability of a mapping of two models [7] requires the existence of such single trace that is possible in the two models after the corresponding elements have been resolved. Obviously, this is a rather weak requirement. In contrast, the existing work in the field of behavioral models focuses on some strict notions of behavioral equivalence. There is a multitude of equivalence criteria in the linear branching time spectrum [8] such as trace equivalence [9–11] and bisimulation [12–14]. However, they can only reflect two consistent and inconsistent cases. These results are not effective for an alignment scenario since a software designer might deviate from the requirements concerned in a business process model in order to come up with a more elegant solution on a technical level. Those design decisions may be acceptable if they deviate from the business process model only to a small degree. A new boolean notion called behavioral profile [4,15–19] is successful to make such the small deviation. Behavioral profiles studied consistency based on the match between the two process models. By using the weak behavioral relations to characterize the behavioral dependencies of models, they defined the consistency degree of models, i.e., a ratio of consistent transitions to matching transitions. However, their method isn't accurate for two systems such as Fig. 1. That is because that their behavior relations aren't accurate. Therefore, this paper refines behavioral profiles based on events relations in the branching processes of models. And then we present the definition of *secure consistency*, and propose a new formula to compute the degree of *secure consistency degree* of two models. Examples show that the our definition and computation formula are more accurate than these in [4].

The paper is organized as follows: Section 2 introduces some basic concepts; Sect. 3 introduces secure consistency; Sect. 4 refines the behavioral profile and gives a new formula to compute secure consistency degree. Finally, we conclude this paper in Sect. 5.

2   Background

This section introduces Petri net and behavioral profiles. For more details, please refer to [4,5,15,17,20,21].

A net is a 3-tuple $N = (P, T, F)$ where P is a finite set of *places*, T is a finite set of *transitions*, $F \subseteq (P \times T) \cup (T \times P)$ is a set of *arcs*, and $P \cap T = \emptyset$.

A net may be thought of as a directed graph in which a circle represents a place and a box represents a transition.

Given a net $N = (P, T, F)$ and a node $x \in P \cup T$,

(i) $^\bullet x = \{y | (y, x) \in F\}$ is the *pre-set* of x; and *(ii)* $x^\bullet = \{y | (x, y) \in F\}$ is the *post-set* of x. If $X \subseteq P \cup T$, its pre-set and post-set are defined as follows: $^\bullet X = \cup_{x \in X} {}^\bullet x$ and $X^\bullet = \cup_{x \in X} x^\bullet$.

$\Sigma = (P, T, F, M_0)$ is a *Petri net* where

(1) $N = (P, T, F)$ is a *net*;
(2) M_0 is the *initial marking*;
(3) mapping $M : P \to \mathbb{N}$ is a *marking function* where $\mathbb{N} = \{0, 1, 2, \cdots\}$; and
(4) it has the following firing rules:
    (i) a transition $t \in T$ is *enabled* at M, denoted by $M[t\rangle$, if $\forall p \in {}^\bullet t : M(p) \geq 1$;
    (ii) if t is enabled, it can be *fired* and a new marking M' is generated and denoted by $M[t\rangle M'$, where

$$M'(p) = \begin{cases} M(p) + 1, & if \ p \in t^\bullet - {}^\bullet t \\ M(p) - 1, & if \ p \in {}^\bullet t - t^\bullet \\ M(p), & else \end{cases}$$

    (iii) if there exist transitions $t_1, t_2, \cdots, t_k$, and markings $M_1, M_2, \cdots, M_k$ such that $M[t_1\rangle M_1[t_2\rangle \cdots M_{k-1}[t_k\rangle M_k$, then M_k is *reachable* from M. All markings reachable from M are denoted by $R(M)$ and $M \in R(M)$.

The basic concepts of soundness and boundedness of WF-net can see [1, 22].

WF-nets have become one of the standard ways to model and analyze workflows [23–25] and are introduced as follows.

Definition 1 (WF-net). *A net $N = (P, T, F)$ is a WF-net if it has a source place $i \in P$ with $^\bullet i = \emptyset$, a sink place $o \in P$ with $o^\bullet = \emptyset$, and $N' = (P, T \cup \{t\}, F \cup \{(o, t), (t, i)\})$ is strongly connected where $t \notin T$.*

Let $\Sigma = (N, M_0) = (P, T, F, M_0)$ be a Petri net. The *unfolding* of Σ is the tuple $Unf(\Sigma) = (B, E, G, \rho)$, where (B, E, G) is an occurrence net, and a homomorphism $\rho : B \cup E \to P \cup T$, such that for every $e_1, e_2 \in E$, if $^\bullet e_1 = {}^\bullet e_2$ and $\rho(e_1) = \rho(e_2)$ then $e_1 = e_2$.

A *branching process* of a net system $\Sigma = (N, M_0)$ is a labeled occurrence net $\beta = (O, p) = (B, E, G, \rho)$ where the labeling function p satisfies the following properties:

(i) $p(B) \subseteq S$ and $p(E) \subseteq T$ (p preserves the nature of nodes);
(ii) for every $e \in E$, the restriction of p to $^\bullet e$ is a bijection between $^\bullet e$ (in Σ) and $^\bullet p(e)$ (in β), and similarly for $e^\bullet$ and $p(e)^\bullet$ (p preserves the environments of transitions);
(iii) the restriction of p to $Min(O)$ is a bijection between $Min(O)$ and M_0 (β starts at M_0);
(iv) for every $e_1, e_2 \in E$, if $^\bullet e_1 = {}^\bullet e_2$ and $p(e_1) = p(e_2)$ then $e_1 = e_2$ (β does not duplicate the transitions of Σ).

Branching process unfolding (BPU) is the *least upper bound* of the set of all branching process.

The relevant concepts and algorithms of branching process can refer to [26, 27]. We will use *BPU* to represent *branching process unfolding*.

There is a mapping function φ from Σ to its *BPU*. In Figs. 1(a) and 2(a), $\varphi(a_1) = e_{a1}$, $\varphi(b_1) = e_{b1}$, $\varphi(c_1) = e_{c1}$, $\varphi(d_1) = \{e_{d11}, e_{d12}\}$, $\varphi(e_1) = \{e_{e11}, e_{e12}\}$, $\varphi(f_1) = \{e_{f11}, e_{f12}\}$ and $\varphi(g_1) = \{e_{g11}, e_{g12}, e_{g13}, e_{g14}, \}$.

To study the behavior relation of WF-nets, the weak order relation and behavioral profiles were presented in [4]:

Let $(N, M_0) = (P, T, F, M_0)$ be a Petri net. A pair of transitions (x, y) is in *the weak order relation* over T, denoted as $x \succ y$, if there exists an enabled transition sequence $t_1 t_2 \cdots t_n$ such that $\exists j, k \in \{1, 2, \cdots, n\}: (j < k) \wedge (t_j = x) \wedge (t_k = y)$.

Based on the weak order relation, the following three relations are defined in [4]: A pair of transitions (x, y) is in

(1) the *strict order relation* $\rightsquigarrow$, if $x \succ y \wedge y \not\succ x$;
(2) the *exclusiveness relation* $+$, if $x \not\succ y \wedge y \not\succ x$;
(3) the *interleaving relation* $\|$, if $x \succ y \wedge y \succ x$.

$\mathbb{B} = \{\rightsquigarrow, +, \|\}$ is called the *behavioral profile*.

Let $\Sigma_1 = (P_1, T_1, F_1, M_1)$ and $\Sigma_2 = (P_2, T_2, F_2, M_2)$ be net systems.

(1) A *correspondence relation* $\sim \subseteq T_1 \times T_2$ associates correspondence transitions of the two systems. $T_1^\sim$ is defined as $\{t \mid \exists t' \in T_2 : (t, t') \in \sim\}$. Similarly, we can define $T_2^\sim$. For example of Figs. 1(a) and (b), $\sim = \{(a1, a2), (b1, b2), (c1, c2), (d1, d2), (e1, e2), (f1, f2), (g1, g2), (C, C2)\}$. $T_1^\sim = \{a1, b1, c1, d1, e1, f1, g1\}$ and $T_2^\sim = \{a2, b2, c2, d2, e2, f2, g2\}$.

Let $\Sigma_1 = (P_1, T_1, F_1, M_1)$ and $\Sigma_2 = (P_2, T_2, F_2, M_2)$ be two Petri nets, $\mathbb{B}_1 = \{\rightsquigarrow_1, +_1, \|_1\}$ and $\mathbb{B}_2 = \{\rightsquigarrow_2, +_2, \|_2\}$ be their behavioral profiles, and $\sim \subseteq T_1 \times T_2$ be a correspondence relation. Let $\mathbb{R}_1 \in \mathbb{B}_1 \cup \{\rightsquigarrow_1^{-1}\}$ and $\mathbb{R}_2 \in \mathbb{B}_2 \cup \{\rightsquigarrow_2^{-1}\}$. The set of *behavioral profile consistent transition pairs* $CT_1^\sim \subseteq (T_1^\sim \times T_1^\sim)$ for Σ_1 contains all pairs (t_x, t_y) such that:

(1) if $t_x = t_y$, then $\forall t_s \in T_2^\sim$ with $t_x \sim t_s: (t_x \mathbb{R}_1 t_x \wedge t_s \mathbb{R}_2 t_s) \Rightarrow \mathbb{R}_1 \simeq \mathbb{R}_2$,
(2) if $t_x \neq t_y$, then $\forall t_s, t_t \in T_2^\sim$ with $t_s \neq t_t \wedge t_x \sim t_s \wedge t_y \sim t_t, (t_x, t_y)$ fulfills:
   (i) $(t_x \mathbb{R}_1 t_y \wedge t_s \mathbb{R}_2 t_t) \Rightarrow \mathbb{R}_1 \simeq \mathbb{R}_2$; or
   (ii) $t_x \sim t_t \wedge t_y \sim t_s$.

The set $CT_2^\sim$ for Σ_2 is defined similarly.

Based on these, the behavioral profiles consistency degree is defined as follows $\Sigma_1 = (P_1, T_1, F_1, M_1)$ and $\Sigma_2 = (P_2, T_2, F_2, M_2)$ be two net systems, $\sim \subseteq T_1 \times T_2$ a correspondence relation, and $CT_1^\sim$ and $CT_2^\sim$ be their consistent transition pairs. The *degree of behavioral profile consistency* of $\sim$ is defined as:

$$\mathbb{PC}^\sim = \frac{|CT_1^\sim| + |CT_2^\sim|}{|(T_1^\sim \times T_1^\sim)| + |(T_2^\sim \times T_2^\sim)|} \tag{1}$$

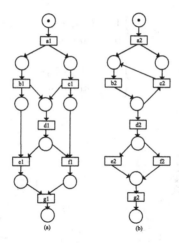

Fig. 2. Two WF-nets (a) and (b): (a) and (b) in a correspondence $x1 \sim x2$ ($x \in a, b, c, d, e, f, g$)

3 Secure Consistency

Here we consider an example of bounded WF-nets as shown in Figs. 2(a) and (b).

According to the concept of the behavioral profile, we know $b1 \succ c1$ and $c1 \succ b1$ in Fig. 2(a). That is to say, $b1$ and $c1$ are in the interleaving relation. $b2$ and $c2$ in Fig. 2(b) are in the interleaving relation since transition $b2$ and $c2$ are in a loop structure such that $b2 \succ c2$ and $c2 \succ b2$. But in fact, the two behavioral relations should be different since $b1$ and $c1$ may be fired concurrently but $b2$ and $c2$ can fired sequentially and concurrently. Therefore, we should refine the behavioral sequence relations.

Definition 2 (Behavioral Sequence Relations). *Let $\Sigma = (N, M_0) = (P, T, F, M_0)$ be a net system, and its unfolding of Σ is $Unf(\Sigma) = (B, E, G, \rho)$, where (B, E, G) is an occurrence net, and a homomorphism $\rho: B \cup E \to P \cup T$. Events pairs $(e_{t_i}, e_{t_j}) \in E \times E$ is in the following relation:*

(1) Selection Relation $\Diamond$ if $e_{t_i} \not\succ e_{t_j} \wedge e_{t_j} \not\succ e_{t_i}$.
(2) Order Relation $\triangle$ if $e_{t_i} \succ e_{t_j} \wedge e_{t_j} \not\succ e_{t_i}$.
(3) Concurrent Relation $\sharp$ if $e_{t_i} \succ e_{t_j} \wedge e_{t_j} \succ e_{t_i}$.
(4) Invertible Order Relation $\triangledown$ if $e_{t_i} \not\succ e_{t_j} \wedge e_{t_j} \succ e_{t_i}$.

Then the behavioral sequence relation of t_i and t_j is a four-tuple $BSR = [s_0, s_1, s_2, s_3]$ with:

$$s_0 = \begin{cases} 1 & \text{if } e_{t_i} \Diamond e_{t_j}, \\ 0 & \text{otherwise}. \end{cases}$$

$$s_1 = \begin{cases} 1 & \text{if } e_{t_i} \triangle e_{t_j}, \\ 0 & \text{otherwise}. \end{cases}$$

$$s_2 = \begin{cases} 1 & if\ e_{t_i} \sharp e_{t_j}, \\ 0 & otherwise. \end{cases}$$

$$s_3 = \begin{cases} 1 & if\ e_{t_i} \triangledown e_{t_j}, \\ 0 & otherwise. \end{cases}$$

$(t = 0, 1, 2, 3; i, j = 1, 2, \cdots, n)$

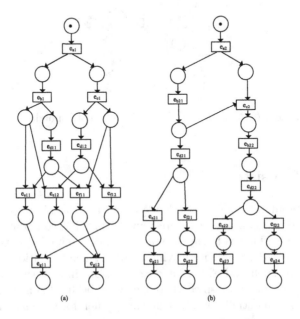

Fig. 3. BPU of Fig. 2

The events set corresponding to a transition t_i may have only one element when the number of $\rho^{-1}(t_i)$ is 1, and may more one elements when the number of $\rho^{-1}(t_i)$ greater than 1. We denote the set as E_i.

When the number of elements in E_i is greater than 1, we will compute the events relations of more than one pair. To obtain the behavioral sequence relation of a WF-net, we should obtain the event relations of its branching process. Algorithm 1 shows the process of computing the event relations. And Table 1 gives the introduction about event relation.

According to Definition 2, we can decide the behavioral sequence relation between two transitions using four kind of relations between events. To decide the relations between events, we must obtain the BPU. For a bounded WF-net, we can compute its BPU by the algorithms in [26] and [27]. For example, the BPUs of Figs. 2(a) and (b) are shown in Fig. 3.

Lemma 1. *The four events relations* $\diamondsuit, \triangle, \sharp, \triangledown$ *are mutually exclusive and they partition* $E \times E$.

Algorithm 1. Event Relation

Input: $\Sigma = (P, T, F, M_0)$, $E = \{e_{11}, e_{12}, \cdots, e_{1n}\}$, BPU.
Output: Event Relation ER.
$ER = \emptyset$;
for each e_{1i} and e_{1j} in BPU **do**
    if there is not any path from e_{1i} to e_{1j}, and a path from e_{1j} to e_{1i}
    then
        | $ER = \{\Diamond\}$;
    end
    if there is a path from e_{1i} to e_{1j}, and not a path from e_{1j} to e_{1i} **then**
        | $ER = \{\triangle\}$;
    end
    if there is a path from e_{1i} to e_{1j}, and a path from e_{1j} to e_{1i} **then**
        | $ER = \{\sharp\}$;
    end
    if there is not a path from e_{1i} to e_{1j}, and a path from e_{1j} to e_{1i} **then**
        | $ER = \{\triangledown\}$;
    end
end
return ER;

Table 1. Events relation introduction of Fig. 3

Event relation	Abbreviation	Symbol	$et_x\,et_y$	$et_y\,et_x$	Example
Selection Relation	SR	$\Diamond$	$et_i \not\succ et_y$	$et_y \not\succ et_x$	e_{e12} and e_{f12}
Order Relation	OR	$\triangle$	$et_x \succ et_y$	$et_y \not\succ et_x$	e_{b1} and e_{d11}
Concurrent Relation	CR	$\sharp$	$et_x \succ et_y$	$et_y \succ et_x$	e_{b1} and e_{c1}
Invertible Order Relation	IOR	$\triangledown$	$et_x \not\succ et_y$	$et_y \succ et_x$	e_{d11} and e_{b1}

According to Definition 2, it is easy to prove the lemma.

Based on Lemma 1 and Definition 2, we know that behavioral sequence relations are complete. The formal representation is as follows:

Theorem 1. *Given a WF-net N and its behavioral sequence relation BSR, then for $\forall x, y \in T$, $\exists R \in BSR$: xRy.*

We give some definitions in [5] to express the necessity of *secure consistency*.

Definition 3 (Weak Consistency [5]). *Let $S_1 = (N_1, M_1)$ and $S_2 = (N_2, M_2)$ be net systems with $N_1 = (P_1, T_1, F_1)$ and $N_2 = (P_2, T_2, F_2)$, and B_1 and B_2 their behavioral profiles. Let $R1 \in B1$ and $R2 \in B2$. A correspondence relation $T1 \sim\sim T2$ is weak behavioral profile consistent, if for all transition pairs $(t_x, t_y) \in (T_1^{\sim} \times T_1^{\sim})$, $t_x \neq t_y$, and transitions $t_s, t_t \in T_2^{\sim}$, $t_s \neq t_t$, $t_x \sim t_s$, $t_y \sim t_t$, it holds that either*

(1) $(t_x R_1 t_y \wedge t_s R_2 t_t) \Rightarrow R_1 \simeq R_2$;

(2) $t_x \sim t_t$ and $t_y \sim t_s$.

Definition 4 (Consistency [5]). *Let $S_1 = (N_1, M_1)$ and $S_2 = (N_2, M_2)$ be net systems with $N_1 = (P_1, T_1, F_1)$ and $N_2 = (P_2, T_2, F_2)$, and B_1 and B_2 their behavioral profiles. Let $R1 \in B1$ and $R2 \in B2$. A correspondence relation $T1 \sim\sim T2$ is behavioral profile consistent, if for all transition pairs $t_x \in T_1^\sim$, and $(t_s \in T_2^\sim$, $t_x \sim t_s$, it holds that $(t_x R_1 t_y \wedge t_s R_2 t_s) \Rightarrow R_1 \simeq R_2$.*

Definition 5 (Secure Consistency). *Let $S_1 = (N_1, M_1)$ and $S_2 = (N_2, M_2)$ be net systems with $N_1 = (P_1, T_1, F_1)$ and $N_2 = (P_2, T_2, F_2)$, and BSR_1 and BSR_2 their behavioral sequence relation set. A correspondence relation $T_1 \sim T_2$ is secure consistent, if for all transition pairs $t_x \in T_1$, $t_y \in T_2$, $t_x \sim t_y$, $(t_x, t_y) \in R_1$, and $(t_x, t_y) \in R_2$, it holds that $t_x R_1 t_y = t_x R_2 t_y$.*

Theorem 2. *Given two WF-nets N_1 and N_2, if they are secure consistent, then they must be behavioral profiles consistent.*

In fact, according to Theorem 1, we easily obtain the result. However, in turn this theorem is not established. In other word, if two nets are behavioral profiles consistent, they may be not secure consistent.

4   Consistency Degree Computing

For those consistency degree computation, the method in [4] is not too accurate for some cases. According to Eq. (1), the consistency degree between the nets in Figs. 2(a) and (b) is 1. However, (b) is sound but (a) is not. Obviously, they are not consistent. Therefore, we should improve the definition of consistency.

To introduce the case of exiting more than one ordered behavioral relation between transitions intuitively, a 4-bit matrix is defined as a tool to represent these relations.

Definition 6. *Let $N = (P, T, F)$ be a net and $T = \{a_1, a_2, \cdots, a_n\}$. 4-bit Relation Matrix is:*

$$M = \begin{pmatrix} a_{11} & a_{12} & \cdots & a_{1n} \\ a_{21} & a_{22} & \cdots & a_{2n} \\ \vdots & \vdots & \vdots & \vdots \\ a_{n1} & a_{n2} & \cdots & a_{nn}, \end{pmatrix} \tag{2}$$

Were a_{ij} expresses the behavior sequence relation of a_i and a_j, and $a_{ij} = (s_0, s_1, s_2, s_3)(s_k = \{0, 1\})(k = 0, 1, 2, 3).$

The M of Fig. 2 is shown in Fig. 4.

Definition 7 (Secure Consistency Degree). *Let $S_1 = (N_1, M_1)$ and $S_2 = (N_2, M_2)$ be two net systems, BPU_1, BPU_2 be their branching process unfolding*

$M_a =$

	a1	b1	c1	d1	e1	f1	g1
a1	[1,0,0,0]	[0,1,0,0]	[0,1,0,0]	[0,1,0,0]	[0,1,0,0]	[0,1,0,0]	[0,1,0,0]
b1	[0,0,0,1]	[1,0,0,0]	[0,0,1,0]	[0,1,1,0]	[0,1,0,0]	[0,1,1,0]	[0,1,0,0]
c1	[0,0,0,1]	[0,0,1,0]	[1,0,0,0]	[0,1,1,0]	[0,1,1,0]	[0,1,0,0]	[0,1,0,0]
d1	[0,0,0,1]	[0,0,1,1]	[0,0,1,1]	[1,0,1,0]	[0,1,1,0]	[0,1,1,0]	[0,1,0,0]
e1	[0,0,0,1]	[0,0,0,1]	[0,0,1,1]	[0,0,1,1]	[1,0,0,0]	[1,0,1,0]	[1,1,0,0]
f1	[0,0,0,1]	[0,0,1,1]	[0,0,0,1]	[0,0,1,1]	[1,0,1,0]	[1,0,0,0]	[1,1,0,0]
g1	[0,0,0,1]	[0,0,0,1]	[0,0,0,1]	[0,0,0,1]	[1,0,0,1]	[1,0,0,1]	[1,0,0,0]

$M_b =$

	a2	b2	c2	d2	e2	f2	g2
a2	[1,0,0,0]	[0,1,0,0]	[0,1,0,0]	[0,1,0,0]	[0,1,0,0]	[0,1,0,0]	[0,1,0,0]
b2	[0,0,0,1]	[1,1,0,1]	[0,1,0,1]	[1,1,0,0]	[1,1,0,0]	[1,1,0,0]	[1,1,0,0]
c2	[0,0,0,1]	[0,1,0,1]	[1,0,0,0]	[1,1,0,0]	[1,1,0,0]	[1,1,0,0]	[1,1,0,0]
d2	[0,0,0,1]	[1,0,0,1]	[1,0,0,1]	[1,0,0,0]	[1,1,0,0]	[1,1,0,0]	[1,1,0,0]
e2	[0,0,0,1]	[1,0,0,1]	[1,0,0,1]	[1,0,0,1]	[1,0,0,0]	[1,0,0,0]	[1,1,0,0]
f2	[0,0,0,1]	[1,0,0,1]	[1,0,0,1]	[1,0,0,1]	[1,0,0,0]	[1,0,0,0]	[1,1,0,0]
g2	[0,0,0,1]	[1,0,0,1]	[1,0,0,1]	[1,0,0,1]	[1,0,0,1]	[1,0,0,1]	[1,0,0,0]

Fig. 4. The 4-bit relation matrices of Figs. 2(a) and (b)

and M_1 and M_2 be their 4-bit relation matrices. Secure consistency degree based on M_1 and M_2 is defined as:

$$D_p = 1 - \frac{\sum_{i,j=1}^{n} a_{ij} \neq a'_{ij} | (a_{ij} \in M_1, a'_{ij} \in M_2, a_{ij} \sim a'_{ij}) |}{(\|M_1\| + \|M_2\|)} \qquad (3)$$

Where $\|M_1\|$ and $\|M_2\|$ express the number of M_1 and M_2, respectively.

Property 1. The following problem can be solved in $O(n^2)$ where n is the number of transitions and places of the system: for a bounded WF-net, to compute its 4-bit relation matrix M.

Proof. From the computing, we can compute the 4-bit relation matrix step-by-step. The first step should compute the diagonal elements of matrix M, which spends n times. The second step should compute the elements $a_{i,i+1}$ of matrix M, which spends $n - 1$ times. Then the third step compute the elements $a_{i,i+2}$, which spends $n - 2$ times. We do the similar thing until the element a_{1n}. The whole computing time is $\frac{n(n+1)}{2}$.

(a)

	a1	b1	c1	d1	g1	h1	j1	k1	l1	o1	q1	r1	s1	t1	v1	u1	w1	x1
a1	[1,0,0,0]	[0,1,0,0]	[0,1,0,0]	[0,1,0,0]	[0,1,0,0]	[0,1,0,0]	[0,1,0,0]	[0,1,0,0]	[0,1,0,0]	[0,1,0,0]	[0,1,0,0]	[0,1,0,0]	[0,1,0,0]	[0,1,0,0]	[0,1,0,0]	[0,1,0,0]	[0,1,0,0]	[0,1,0,0]
b1	[0,0,0,1]	[1,0,0,0]	[0,1,0,0]	[0,1,0,0]	[0,1,0,0]	[0,1,0,0]	[0,1,0,0]	[0,1,0,0]	[0,1,0,0]	[0,1,0,0]	[0,1,0,0]	[0,1,0,0]	[0,1,0,0]	[0,1,0,0]	[0,1,0,0]	[0,1,0,0]	[0,1,0,0]	[0,1,0,0]
c1	[0,0,0,1]	[0,0,0,1]	[1,0,0,0]	[0,1,0,0]	[0,1,0,0]	[0,1,0,0]	[0,1,0,0]	[0,1,0,0]	[0,1,0,0]	[0,1,0,0]	[0,1,0,0]	[0,1,0,0]	[0,1,0,0]	[0,1,0,0]	[0,1,0,0]	[0,1,0,0]	[0,1,0,0]	[0,1,0,0]
d1	[0,0,0,1]	[0,0,0,1]	[0,0,0,1]	[1,0,0,0]	[0,1,0,0]	[0,1,0,0]	[0,1,0,0]	[0,1,0,0]	[0,1,0,0]	[0,1,0,0]	[0,1,0,0]	[0,1,0,0]	[0,1,0,0]	[0,1,0,0]	[0,1,0,0]	[0,1,0,0]	[0,1,0,0]	[0,1,0,0]
g1	[0,0,0,1]	[0,0,0,1]	[0,0,0,1]	[0,0,0,1]	[1,0,0,0]	[0,1,0,0]	[0,1,0,0]	[0,1,0,0]	[0,1,0,0]	[0,1,0,0]	[0,1,0,0]	[0,1,0,0]	[0,1,0,0]	[0,1,0,0]	[0,1,0,0]	[0,1,0,0]	[0,1,0,0]	[0,1,0,0]
h1	[0,0,0,1]	[0,0,0,1]	[0,0,0,1]	[0,0,0,1]	[0,0,0,1]	[1,0,1,1]	[1,1,0,1]	[1,1,0,1]	[1,1,0,1]	[1,1,0,1]	[1,1,0,1]	[1,1,0,1]	[1,1,0,1]	[1,1,0,1]	[1,1,0,1]	[0,1,0,0]	[0,1,0,0]	[0,1,0,0]
j1	[0,0,0,1]	[0,0,0,1]	[0,0,0,1]	[0,0,0,1]	[0,0,0,1]	[1,1,0,1]	[1,0,1,1]	[1,1,0,1]	[1,1,0,1]	[1,1,0,1]	[1,1,0,1]	[1,1,0,1]	[1,1,0,1]	[1,1,0,1]	[1,1,0,1]	[0,1,0,0]	[0,1,0,0]	[0,1,0,0]
k1	[0,0,0,1]	[0,0,0,1]	[0,0,0,1]	[0,0,0,1]	[0,0,0,1]	[1,1,0,1]	[1,1,0,1]	[1,0,1,1]	[1,1,0,1]	[1,1,0,1]	[1,1,0,1]	[1,1,0,1]	[1,1,0,1]	[1,1,0,1]	[1,1,0,1]	[0,1,0,0]	[0,1,0,0]	[0,1,0,0]
l1	[0,0,0,1]	[0,0,0,1]	[0,0,0,1]	[0,0,0,1]	[0,0,0,1]	[1,1,0,1]	[1,1,0,1]	[1,1,0,1]	[1,0,1,1]	[1,0,1,1]	[1,1,0,1]	[1,1,0,1]	[1,1,0,1]	[1,1,0,1]	[1,1,0,1]	[0,1,0,0]	[0,1,0,0]	[0,1,0,0]
o1	[0,0,0,1]	[0,0,0,1]	[0,0,0,1]	[0,0,0,1]	[0,0,0,1]	[1,1,0,1]	[1,1,0,1]	[1,1,0,1]	[1,0,1,1]	[1,0,1,1]	[1,0,1,1]	[1,1,0,1]	[1,1,0,1]	[1,1,0,1]	[1,1,0,1]	[0,1,0,0]	[0,1,0,0]	[0,1,0,0]
q1	[0,0,0,1]	[0,0,0,1]	[0,0,0,1]	[0,0,0,1]	[0,0,0,1]	[1,1,0,1]	[1,1,0,1]	[1,1,0,1]	[1,1,0,1]	[1,0,1,1]	[1,0,1,1]	[1,1,0,1]	[1,1,0,1]	[1,1,0,1]	[1,1,0,1]	[0,1,0,0]	[0,1,0,0]	[0,1,0,0]
r1	[0,0,0,1]	[0,0,0,1]	[0,0,0,1]	[0,0,0,1]	[0,0,0,1]	[1,1,0,1]	[1,1,0,1]	[1,1,0,1]	[1,1,0,1]	[1,1,0,1]	[1,1,0,1]	[1,0,1,1]	[1,1,0,1]	[1,1,0,1]	[1,1,0,1]	[0,1,0,0]	[0,1,0,0]	[0,1,0,0]
s1	[0,0,0,1]	[0,0,0,1]	[0,0,0,1]	[0,0,0,1]	[0,0,0,1]	[1,1,0,1]	[1,1,0,1]	[1,1,0,1]	[1,1,0,1]	[1,1,0,1]	[1,1,0,1]	[1,1,0,1]	[1,0,1,1]	[1,1,0,1]	[1,1,0,1]	[0,1,0,0]	[0,1,0,0]	[0,1,0,0]
t1	[0,0,0,1]	[0,0,0,1]	[0,0,0,1]	[0,0,0,1]	[0,0,0,1]	[1,1,0,1]	[1,1,0,1]	[1,1,0,1]	[1,1,0,1]	[1,1,0,1]	[1,1,0,1]	[1,1,0,1]	[1,1,0,1]	[1,0,1,1]	[1,1,0,1]	[0,1,0,0]	[0,1,0,0]	[0,1,0,0]
v1	[0,0,0,1]	[0,0,0,1]	[0,0,0,1]	[0,0,0,1]	[0,0,0,1]	[1,1,0,1]	[1,1,0,1]	[1,1,0,1]	[1,1,0,1]	[1,1,0,1]	[1,1,0,1]	[1,1,0,1]	[1,1,0,1]	[1,1,0,1]	[1,0,1,1]	[0,1,0,0]	[0,1,0,0]	[0,1,0,0]
u1	[0,0,0,1]	[0,0,0,1]	[0,0,0,1]	[0,0,0,1]	[0,0,0,1]	[0,0,0,1]	[0,0,0,1]	[0,0,0,1]	[0,0,0,1]	[0,0,0,1]	[0,0,0,1]	[0,0,0,1]	[0,0,0,1]	[0,0,0,1]	[0,0,0,1]	[1,0,0,0]	[0,1,0,0]	[0,1,0,0]
w1	[0,0,0,1]	[0,0,0,1]	[0,0,0,1]	[0,0,0,1]	[0,0,0,1]	[0,0,0,1]	[0,0,0,1]	[0,0,0,1]	[0,0,0,1]	[0,0,0,1]	[0,0,0,1]	[0,0,0,1]	[0,0,0,1]	[0,0,0,1]	[0,0,0,1]	[0,0,0,1]	[1,0,0,0]	[0,1,0,0]
x1	[0,0,0,1]	[0,0,0,1]	[0,0,0,1]	[0,0,0,1]	[0,0,0,1]	[0,0,0,1]	[0,0,0,1]	[0,0,0,1]	[0,0,0,1]	[0,0,0,1]	[0,0,0,1]	[0,0,0,1]	[0,0,0,1]	[0,0,0,1]	[0,0,0,1]	[0,0,0,1]	[0,0,0,1]	[1,0,0,0]

	a2	b2	c2	d2	g2	h2	j2	k2	l2	o2	q2	r2	s2	t2	v2	u2	w2	x2
a2	[1,0,0,0]	[0,1,0,0]	[0,1,0,0]	[0,1,0,0]	[0,1,0,0]	[0,1,0,0]	[0,1,0,0]	[0,1,0,0]	[0,1,0,0]	[0,1,0,0]	[0,1,0,0]	[0,1,0,0]	[0,1,0,0]	[0,1,0,0]	[0,1,0,0]	[0,1,0,0]	[0,1,0,0]	[0,1,0,0]
b2	[0,0,0,1]	[1,0,0,0]	[0,1,0,0]	[0,1,0,0]	[0,1,0,0]	[0,1,0,0]	[0,1,0,0]	[0,1,0,0]	[0,1,0,0]	[0,1,0,0]	[0,1,0,0]	[0,1,0,0]	[0,1,0,0]	[0,1,0,0]	[0,1,0,0]	[0,1,0,0]	[0,1,0,0]	[0,1,0,0]
c2	[0,0,0,1]	[0,0,0,1]	[1,0,0,0]	[0,1,0,0]	[0,1,0,0]	[0,1,0,0]	[0,1,0,0]	[0,1,0,0]	[0,1,0,0]	[0,1,0,0]	[0,1,0,0]	[0,1,0,0]	[0,1,0,0]	[0,1,0,0]	[0,1,0,0]	[0,1,0,0]	[0,1,0,0]	[0,1,0,0]
d2	[0,0,0,1]	[0,0,0,1]	[0,0,0,1]	[1,0,0,0]	[0,1,0,0]	[0,1,0,0]	[0,1,0,0]	[0,1,0,0]	[0,1,0,0]	[0,1,0,0]	[0,1,0,0]	[0,1,0,0]	[0,1,0,0]	[0,1,0,0]	[0,1,0,0]	[0,1,0,0]	[0,1,0,0]	[0,1,0,0]
g2	[0,0,0,1]	[0,0,0,1]	[0,0,0,1]	[0,0,0,1]	[1,0,0,0]	[0,1,0,0]	[0,1,0,0]	[0,1,0,0]	[0,1,0,0]	[0,1,0,0]	[0,1,0,0]	[0,1,0,0]	[0,1,0,0]	[0,1,0,0]	[0,1,0,0]	[0,1,0,0]	[0,1,0,0]	[0,1,0,0]
h2	[0,0,0,1]	[0,0,0,1]	[0,0,0,1]	[0,0,0,1]	[0,0,0,1]	[1,0,1,1]	[1,1,0,1]	[1,1,0,1]	[1,1,0,1]	[1,1,0,1]	[1,1,0,1]	[1,1,0,1]	[1,1,0,1]	[1,1,0,1]	[1,1,0,1]	[0,1,0,0]	[0,1,0,0]	[0,1,0,0]
j2	[0,0,0,1]	[0,0,0,1]	[0,0,0,1]	[0,0,0,1]	[0,0,0,1]	[1,1,0,1]	[1,0,1,1]	[1,1,0,1]	[1,1,0,1]	[1,1,0,1]	[1,1,0,1]	[1,1,0,1]	[1,1,0,1]	[1,1,0,1]	[1,1,0,1]	[0,1,0,0]	[0,1,0,0]	[0,1,0,0]
k2	[0,0,0,1]	[0,0,0,1]	[0,0,0,1]	[0,0,0,1]	[0,0,0,1]	[1,1,0,1]	[1,1,0,1]	[1,0,1,1]	[1,1,0,1]	[1,1,0,1]	[1,1,0,1]	[1,1,0,1]	[1,1,0,1]	[1,1,0,1]	[1,1,0,1]	[0,1,0,0]	[0,1,0,0]	[0,1,0,0]
l2	[0,0,0,1]	[0,0,0,1]	[0,0,0,1]	[0,0,0,1]	[0,0,0,1]	[1,1,0,1]	[1,1,0,1]	[1,1,0,1]	[1,0,1,1]	[1,0,1,1]	[1,1,0,1]	[1,0,1,1]	[1,0,1,1]	[1,1,0,1]	[1,1,0,1]	[0,1,0,0]	[0,1,0,0]	[0,1,0,0]
o2	[0,0,0,1]	[0,0,0,1]	[0,0,0,1]	[0,0,0,1]	[0,0,0,1]	[1,1,0,1]	[1,1,0,1]	[1,1,0,1]	[1,0,1,1]	[1,0,1,1]	[1,0,1,1]	[1,1,0,1]	[1,1,0,1]	[1,1,0,1]	[1,1,0,1]	[0,1,0,0]	[0,1,0,0]	[0,1,0,0]
q2	[0,0,0,1]	[0,0,0,1]	[0,0,0,1]	[0,0,0,1]	[0,0,0,1]	[1,1,0,1]	[1,1,0,1]	[1,1,0,1]	[1,1,0,1]	[1,0,1,1]	[1,0,1,1]	[1,0,1,1]	[1,0,1,1]	[1,1,0,1]	[1,1,0,1]	[0,1,0,0]	[0,1,0,0]	[0,1,0,0]
r2	[0,0,0,1]	[0,0,0,1]	[0,0,0,1]	[0,0,0,1]	[0,0,0,1]	[1,1,0,1]	[1,1,0,1]	[1,1,0,1]	[1,0,1,1]	[1,1,0,1]	[1,0,1,1]	[1,0,1,1]	[1,1,0,1]	[1,1,0,1]	[1,1,0,1]	[0,1,0,0]	[0,1,0,0]	[0,1,0,0]
s2	[0,0,0,1]	[0,0,0,1]	[0,0,0,1]	[0,0,0,1]	[0,0,0,1]	[1,1,0,1]	[1,1,0,1]	[1,1,0,1]	[1,0,1,1]	[1,1,0,1]	[1,0,1,1]	[1,1,0,1]	[1,0,1,1]	[1,1,0,1]	[1,1,0,1]	[0,1,0,0]	[0,1,0,0]	[0,1,0,0]
t2	[0,0,0,1]	[0,0,0,1]	[0,0,0,1]	[0,0,0,1]	[0,0,0,1]	[1,1,0,1]	[1,1,0,1]	[1,1,0,1]	[1,1,0,1]	[1,1,0,1]	[1,1,0,1]	[1,1,0,1]	[1,1,0,1]	[1,0,1,1]	[1,1,0,1]	[0,1,0,0]	[0,1,0,0]	[0,1,0,0]
v2	[0,0,0,1]	[0,0,0,1]	[0,0,0,1]	[0,0,0,1]	[0,0,0,1]	[1,1,0,1]	[1,1,0,1]	[1,1,0,1]	[1,1,0,1]	[1,1,0,1]	[1,1,0,1]	[1,1,0,1]	[1,1,0,1]	[1,1,0,1]	[1,0,1,1]	[0,1,0,0]	[0,1,0,0]	[0,1,0,0]
u2	[0,0,0,1]	[0,0,0,1]	[0,0,0,1]	[0,0,0,1]	[0,0,0,1]	[0,0,0,1]	[0,0,0,1]	[0,0,0,1]	[0,0,0,1]	[0,0,0,1]	[0,0,0,1]	[0,0,0,1]	[0,0,0,1]	[0,0,0,1]	[0,0,0,1]	[1,0,0,0]	[0,1,0,0]	[0,1,0,0]
w2	[0,0,0,1]	[0,0,0,1]	[0,0,0,1]	[0,0,0,1]	[0,0,0,1]	[0,0,0,1]	[0,0,0,1]	[0,0,0,1]	[0,0,0,1]	[0,0,0,1]	[0,0,0,1]	[0,0,0,1]	[0,0,0,1]	[0,0,0,1]	[0,0,0,1]	[0,0,0,1]	[1,0,0,0]	[0,1,0,0]
x2	[0,0,0,1]	[0,0,0,1]	[0,0,0,1]	[0,0,0,1]	[0,0,0,1]	[0,0,0,1]	[0,0,0,1]	[0,0,0,1]	[0,0,0,1]	[0,0,0,1]	[0,0,0,1]	[0,0,0,1]	[0,0,0,1]	[0,0,0,1]	[0,0,0,1]	[0,0,0,1]	[0,0,0,1]	[1,0,0,0]

(b)

Fig. 5. The 4-bit relation matrices of Figs. 1(a) and (b): (a) M_a, (b) M_b.

Property 2. Every two WF-systems that are consistent based on 4-bit relation matrix M have the same behavioral profiles.

The property is drawn easily from the definition of behavioral sequence relation and 4-bit relation matrix, and its proof is omitted here.

The reverse of Property 3 is invalid. For example, Fig. 2 can both explain this issue.

Property 3. Every two WF-systems that are behavioral profiles consistent may not have the same 4-bit relation matrix.

Proof. The conclusion is obvious.

In fact, According to Eqs. (1) and (3), we can see that for two WF-systems whose behavioral profiles are consistent, their corresponding behavior pairs have the same behavior relations. However, their behavioral sequence relations may be different. Then at this time, they don't have the same 4-bit relation matrix.

Properties 2 and 3 mean that for two WF-nets, the value of our secure consistency degree computation method is less than or equal to behavioral profile's.

Based on the above conclusion, we can see that the secure consistency degree based on 4-bit relation matrix is effective to compute the secure consistency of two bounded WF-nets. In fact, when the correspondence relations are uncertain, there isn't effective methods to compute their secure consistency degree. We will be dedicated to do this research in the future.

Here we study the example given in Fig. 2. Firstly, we can obtain the BPU of net N_1 and N_2 as shown in Fig. 3. Then according to these behavioral sequence relations, we build a 4-bit relation matrix M_a and M_b as shown in Fig. 4. Finally, according to Eq. (3), the secure consistency degree of Figs. 2(a) and (b) is $D_p = 1 - \frac{28+28}{49+49} \approx 0.4286$. Similarly, we can obtain the 4-bit relation matrices of Fig. 1 as shown in Fig. 5. According to Eq. (3), the secure consistency degree of Figs. 1(a) and (b) is $D_p = 1 - \frac{8+8}{18 \times 18 + 18} \approx 0.9753$.

The Matthias' method cannot distinguish the relations which result in precisely two nets with different security, are thought to be completely consistent (i.e., their behavioral profiles consistency degree is 1). However, our method can distinguish the difference from two WF-nets with different security, and compute their secure consistency degree.

5   Conclusions

In this paper, we present a method of generating behavioral sequence relations based on branching processes and event relations. We refine behavioral sequence relations between two actions, and present a secure consistency measurement. Examples show that our result is better than the one in [4]. But there is also a lack of distinguishing the soundness between consistent models which are bounded.

In the future, we would like to focus on how to effectively prove the relation between soundness and consistency of bounded WF-net. Moreover, it is also one of our future works to study secure consistency of unbounded WF-net based on the process.

Acknowledgments. This paper is partially supported by the National Natural Science Foundation of China under grant Nos. 91218301 and 61572360.

References

1. van der Aalst, W.M., van Hee, K.M., ter Hofstede, A.H., Sidorova, N., Verbeek, H., Voorhoeve, M., Wynn, M.T.: Soundness of workflow nets: classification, decidability, and analysis. J. Formal Aspects Comput. **23**, 333–363 (2011)
2. Liu, G., Jiang, C.: Secure bisimulation for interactive systems. In: Wang, G., Zomaya, A., Perez, G.M., Li, K. (eds.) ICA3PP 2015. LNCS, vol. 9530, pp. 625–639. Springer, Heidelberg (2015). doi:10.1007/978-3-319-27137-8_45
3. Dijkman, R., Dumas, M., Van Dongen, B., Krik, R., Mendling, J.: Similarity of business process models: metrics and evaluation. J. Inf. Syst. **36**, 498–516 (2011)
4. Weidlich, M., Mendling, J., Weske, M.: Efficient consistency measurement based on behavioral profiles of process models. J. IEEE Trans. Softw. Eng. **37**, 410–429 (2011)
5. Weidlich, M.: Behavioural profiles: a relational approach to behaviour consistency. Ph.D. dissertation, Universitat Potsdam, Potsdam (2011)
6. Dumas, M., Garca-Bauelos, L., Dijkman, R.M.: Similarity search of business process models. J. IEEE Data Eng. Bull. **32**, 23–28 (2009)
7. Rull, G., Farr, C., Teniente, E., Urp Tubella, A.: Validation of mappings between schemas. J. Data Knowl. Eng. **63**, 414–437 (2008)
8. Glabbeek, R.J.: The linear time - branching time spectrum. In: Baeten, J.C.M., Klop, J.W. (eds.) CONCUR 1990. LNCS, vol. 458, pp. 278–297. Springer, Heidelberg (1990). doi:10.1007/BFb0039066
9. Cheval, V., Cortier, V., Delaune, S.: Deciding equivalence-based properties using constraint solving. J. Theor. Comput. Sci. **492**, 1–39 (2013)
10. Buchholz, P., Kriege, J., Scheftelowitsch, D.: Equivalence and minimization for model checking labeled Markov chains. In: 9th EAI International Conference on Performance Evaluation Methodologies and Tools, pp. 119–126. ICST (2016)
11. Ciancarini, P., Gorrieri, R., Zavattaro, G.: Towards a calculus for generative. J. Formal Methods Open Object Based Distrib. Syst. **1**, 283 (2016)
12. Fioriti, L.M.F., Hashemi, V., Hermanns, H., Turrini, A.: Deciding probabilistic automata weak bisimulation: theory and practice. Formal Aspects Comput. **28**, 109–143 (2016)
13. Sangiorgi, D., Vignudelli, V.: Environmental bisimulations for probabilistic higher-order languages. In: 43rd Annual ACM SIGPLAN-SIGACT Symposium on Principles of Programming Languages, pp. 595–607. ACM (2016)
14. Luttik, B.: Unique parallel decomposition in branching and weak bisimulation semantics. J. Theor. Comput. Sci. **612**, 29–44 (2016)
15. Polyvyanyy, A., Armas-Cervantes, A., Dumas, M., Garca-Banuelos, L.: On the expressive power of behavioral profiles. J. Formal Aspects Comput. **1**, 1–17 (2016)
16. Weidlich, M., Weske, M., Mendling, J.: Change propagation in process models using behavioural profiles. In: IEEE International Conference on Services Computing, pp. 33–40. IEEE (2009)
17. Weidlich, M., Polyvyanyy, A., Desai, N., Mendling, J., Weske, M.: Process compliance analysis based on behavioural profiles. J. Inf. Syst. **36**, 1009–1025 (2011)
18. Smirnov, S., Weidlich, M., Mendling, J.: Business process model abstraction based on synthesis from well-structured behavioral profiles. Int. J. Coop. Inf. Syst. **21**, 55–83 (2012)

19. Weidlich, M., Dijkman, R., Weske, M.: Behaviour equivalence and compatibility of business process models with complex correspondences. Comput. J. **55**, 1398–1418 (2012)
20. Murata, T.: Petri nets: properties, analysis and applications. Proc. IEEE **77**, 541–580 (1989)
21. Peterson, J.L.: Petri nets. J. ACM Comput. Surv. (CSUR) **9**, 223–252 (1977)
22. Wang, S., Gan, M., Zhou, M., You, D.: A reduced reachability tree for a class of unbounded Petri nets. IEEE/CAA J. Automatica Sin. **2**, 345–352 (2015)
23. Van Der Aalst, W.M.: WOFLAN: a Petri-net-based workflow analyzer. Syst. Anal. Model. Simul. **35**, 345–358 (1999)
24. Van der Aalst, W.M.: The application of Petri nets to workflow management. J. Circ. Syst. Comput. **8**, 21–66 (1998)
25. Aalst, W.M.P.: Verification of workflow nets. In: Azéma, P., Balbo, G. (eds.) ICATPN 1997. LNCS, vol. 1248, pp. 407–426. Springer, Heidelberg (1997). doi:10.1007/3-540-63139-9_48
26. Couvreur, J.-M., Poitrenaud, D., Weil, P.: Branching processes of general Petri nets. In: Kristensen, L.M., Petrucci, L. (eds.) PETRI NETS 2011. LNCS, vol. 6709, pp. 129–148. Springer, Heidelberg (2011). doi:10.1007/978-3-642-21834-7_8
27. Engelfriet, J.: Branching processes of Petri nets. J. Acta Informatica **28**, 575–591 (1991)

Study on Personalized Location Privacy Protection Algorithms for Continuous Queries in LBS

Jiayi Gan, Hongyun Xu, Mengzhen Xu, Kai Tian, Yaohui Zheng, and Yong Zhang[✉]

School of Computer Science and Engineering, South China University of Technology,
Guangzhou 510006, China
z.yoo@qq.com

Abstract. Privacy protection and quality of LBS is a pair of contradictions. How to improve quality of LBS while ensuring privacy requirements is worthy of study. In continuous queries, users may have different privacy requirements in different situations, so we propose two algorithms to address this problem, in which before satisfying privacy requirements, they expand cloaking area that contains least users according to the pyramid structure and user's moving trend respectively. Experimental results show that, the two algorithms both satisfy user's personalized privacy requirements, and reduce cloaking area, thus improve the query efficiency, especially the latter algorithm, where the cloaking area is nearly one sixth as large as that of the compared algorithms in the best situation.

Keywords: Personalized location privacy · Location-based service · Continuous queries · Intersection attack

1 Introduction

Location-based service (LBS) got great development in recent years. Based on user's location, LBSs provide services like location reminding, traffic condition tracking, path searching and targeted advertising. However while benefiting from LBS, the location privacy is under threat, attackers can obtain user's trajectory, and further mine user's occupation, address and even sensitive information like physical condition. Researchers have proposed plenty of approaches to protect location privacy, such as k-anonymity [1], pseudonymity [2], location obfuscation and so on. These approaches do protect location privacy to some extent, but they are not fit for reality sometimes since most of them assume the user has constant privacy requirements. In continuous LBS, privacy requirements can be differ depending on situations, for example, user's privacy requirements will be higher when he is at hospital than at park, if we use the requirement at park to deal with all the requests, it may cause privacy leaks when the user is at hospital.

Y. Wang et al. [3] notice this problem and propose to expand cloaking area according to pyramid structure and request sequence respectively before all cloaking areas can fulfill requirements. However these algorithms follow fixed rules in the pyramid structure and ignore user's actual situation, which may lead to many unnecessary expansions and cause large cloaking area which reduces quality of services. To address this problem, we propose our algorithms.

© Springer International Publishing AG 2016
G. Wang et al. (Eds.): SpaCCS 2016, LNCS 10066, pp. 98–108, 2016.
DOI: 10.1007/978-3-319-49148-6_9

Our contributions can be summarized as follows:

- We propose Least Users First Algorithm, which the expansion sequence of cloaking areas is decided on the number of users inside cloaking area.
- We propose Trend-based Algorithm, which expands cloaking area according to the user's moving trend.
- We simulate our algorithms based on the real map of Oldenburg, compare with other algorithms, and validate the efficacy of our algorithms.

The remainder of the paper will be organized as follows. Section 2 provides related work on location privacy. Section 3 introduces the models and metrics we use. The details of our algorithms are presented in Sect. 4. In Sect. 5, we show experiments and evaluations of our algorithms. Section 6 concludes the paper.

2 Related Work

For purpose of protecting location privacy in LBS, researchers have proposed a lot of approaches.

K-anonymity is widely used in many approaches. T. You et al. [4] propose to generate k-1 fake trajectories, mix them with user's trajectory and make more intersections among trajectories to confuse attackers. J.H. Um et al. [5] propose to use k-anonymity together with l-diversity, where l-diversity requires that there should be l different kinds of locations in cloaking area. Mohamed F. Mokbel et al. [6] propose Casper, a framework which contains a location anonymization server and a location-aware processor, and create cloaking areas using the pyramid structure. X-stars [7] hides query issuer through selecting cloaking star and constructing super-star, but it shows poor performance in high computation cost and low success rate, so A.A. Hossain et al. [8] propose to use Hilbert-order in network expansion. T. Xu et al. [9] propose two kinds of k-anonymity region (KAA) to protect privacy in continuous LBS, plain KAA and advanced KAA, both of them use entropy to calculate anonymity level. S. Mascetti et al. [10] formalize historical attack, and propose providentHider to defense it, which is effective under partial knowledge for reasonably long sequences of requests. H. Shin et al. [11] extend the notion of location k-anonymity to trajectory k-anonymity, and propose to optimally partition a continuous request into multiple LBS requests with shorter trajectories to enhance privacy. X. Zhang et al. [12] propose an adaptive spatial cloaking method based on semantic location for privacy protection in LBS, which uses asymmetric cloaking expand to help in fast computation. C. Lin et al. [13] propose a combined clustering algorithm, which applies an iterative k-means clustering method to group the user request into clusters for preserving location safety and utilizes a hierarchical clustering method for preserving the spatial privacy.

3   System Model

3.1   Attack Model

We assume attackers can obtain information (including geographic region and user information) sent to the service provider, so they can infer the issuer or narrow down the candidate set through computing common users of all the cloaking areas. For example, cloaking areas c_1, c_2 and c_3 contain users $\{u_1, u_2, u_3\}$, $\{u_2, u_3, u_4\}$ and $\{u_2, u_5, u_6\}$ respectively, the intersection set is $\{u_2\}$, so attacks can infer that u_2 is the query issuer. We call it intersection attack.

3.2   System Structure

Figure 1 shows the structure of our LBS system, which is comprised of three main components: mobile users, location privacy server and service provider. Privacy server is a layer between users and service provider, it receives continuous requests from user u_i, which includes location information (x_i, y_i), time information t_i and privacy require-ments r_i, we denote the request as $(u_i, x_i, y_i, t_i, r_i)$. Then privacy server creates cloaking area according to requirements, sends the transformed request to service provider. Finally privacy server receives candidate results and sends the accurate result to the user.

Fig. 1. System structure

3.3   Privacy Model

Figure 2 depicts the partition of geographic region [14]. We hierarchically decompose the region into several levels, a grid cell in level $h + 1$ is divided into smaller cells in level h recursively until the area of a bottom cell is less than the threshold value. Any cell contains the user can be used as a cloaking area.

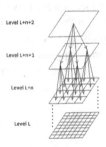

Fig. 2. Pyramid Quadtree structure

3.4 Privacy Metric

- Definition 1: K-anonymity privacy [15]:
  Let c represents a cloaking area and $U(c) = \{u_1, u_2,..., u_m\}$ represents the m users inside, these m users form the anonymity set of the cloaking area c. The k-anonymity privacy value pk(c) is the size of U(c), i.e.,

$$pk(c) = m \tag{1}$$

- Definition 2: Entropy-based privacy [16]:
  Let c represents a cloaking area, and $U(c) = \{u_1, u_2,..., u_m\}$ represents the m users inside based on the footprint database F. Let n_i represents the number of user u_i's footprints in c, and N represents the total number of footprints from the user set U(c).

$$N = \sum_{i=1}^{m} n_i \tag{2}$$

Then the entropy of c is

$$E(c) = -\sum_{i=1}^{m} \frac{n_i}{N} \log \frac{n_i}{N} \tag{3}$$

And the privacy value is

$$Pe(c) = 2E(c) \tag{4}$$

- Definition 3: Set of Common Users
  Let $c_1, c_2,..., c_m$ represent m cloaking areas, the common users among these m areas form the set of common users, we represent it as U'.

In this paper, we compute k-anonymity and entropy using U' instead of U, so as to ensure the algorithms can defense intersection attack.

4   Personalized Location Privacy Protection Algorithms

The purpose of personalized location privacy protection algorithms is: creating a series of cloaking areas, such that

- The user is contained in U'.
- All areas satisfy requirements with respect to U'.
- The total area of cloaking areas is minimized.

To achieve these goals, we propose two algorithms.

4.1 Least User First Algorithm

Least Users First Algorithm (LUF) starts with initializing all cloaking areas according to requirements respectively. Then check if the privacy values of all areas are greater than requirements, if not, the area which contains least users expands first, since this area is the most likely to cause disqualification; dealing with this area firstly may satisfy the requirement, and accordingly reduce unnecessary expansions and minimize cloaking area.

Algorithm 1. LUF

Input: a quadtree T, footprint database F, a series of m LBS requests $(u_i, x_i, y_i, t_i, r_i)$ of user u_i ($1 \le i \le m$).

Output: m cloaking areas c_i ($1 \le i \le m$).
1. Initialize cloaking areas $c_1, ..., c_m$ according to user's requirements respectively, and a candidate set $S_c = \{c_1, ..., c_m\}$.
2. Compute U' with respect to all cloaking areas, and privacy value $p(c_1), ..., p(c_m)$ of all areas with respect to U', if $p(c_1), ..., p(c_m)$ satisfy the requirements $r_1, r_2, ..., r_m$, then go to step 5.
3. Find the area c_i which contains least users from candidate set S_c and check its level, if it is on level 1, remove c_i from S_c, then repeat step 3.
4. Move c_i to be its direct parent in T, go to step 2.
5. Return $c_1, ..., c_m$.

As an example, assuming user u_1 has three requests and privacy requirements are 2, 6, 3 in k-anonymity respectively. As shown in Table 1, after initializing, the size of common users among areas c_1, c_2, c_3 is 2, requirements of c_2 and c_3 are not satisfied, so we expand c_1 which contains least users, after expanding, the size of common users becomes 4. Requirement of c_2 is not satisfied, in the same way, we expand c_3 and get 6 common users. The algorithm ends since all the requirements are satisfied. The whole process is shown in Fig. 3. It is worth mentioning that when an area is at the top of the pyramid, it should be removed from the candidate set since it can't be expanded. For a L-level pyramid structure, the time complexity of LUF is O(mL).

Table 1. An example of LUF

Operation	Users in c_1	Users in c_2	Users in c_3	Common users
Initialization	u_1,u_3	$u_1,u_2,u_3,u_4,u_6,u_8,u_9$	u_1,u_2,u_3,u_6	u_1,u_3
First expansion	$u_1,u_2,u_3,u_6,u_8,u_9,u_{10}$	$u_1,u_2,u_3,u_4,u_6,u_8,u_9$	u_1,u_2,u_3,u_6	u_1,u_2,u_3,u_6
Second expansion	$u_1,u_2,u_3,u_6,u_8,u_9,u_{10}$	$u_1,u_2,u_3,u_4,u_6,u_8,u_9$	$u_1,u_2,u_3,u_4,u_6,u_8,u_9,u_{10}$	u_1,u_2,u_3,u_6,u_8,u_9

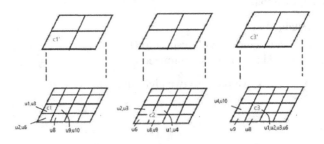

Fig. 3. Three cloaking areas of user u1

4.2 Trend-Based Algorithm

In the pyramid structure, expanding cloaking area is only relevant to user's current location, which is not beneficial for getting a larger size of common users set U'. In Fig. 4, assume user is moving from point A to point B, in the pyramid structure, the cloaking areas of point A and B are {11, 12, 15, 16} and {1, 2, 5, 6} respectively, the size of U' of these two cloaking areas may be small since there is no area overlap.

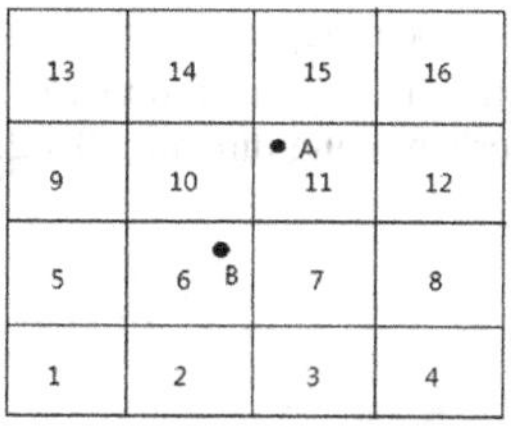

13	14	15	16
9	10	• A 11	12
5	6 • B	7	8
1	2	3	4

Fig. 4. The moving trend of user

Trend-Based algorithm (TB) changes the way to expand cloaking area, the location of cloaking area will shift following the trend of user's movements. In Fig. 5, assumes the user is at the red point, and user's moving direction can be classified as 0, 1, 2, and 3. In Fig. 4, user is moving from point A to point B, so his moving direction is 0, cloaking area shifts to the lower left and contains {6, 7, 10, 11} instead of {11, 12, 15, 16}. Figure 6 shows the cloaking areas of four directions respectively (the shadow cell is the location of the user, each cell may contain more cells), for the direction 0, user is moving towards the lower left, cloaking area shifts towards the lower left relative to the user following the trend of user's movement. So we can see user is at the top-right corner of the cloaking area. For a L-level pyramid structure, time complexity of TB is O(mL).

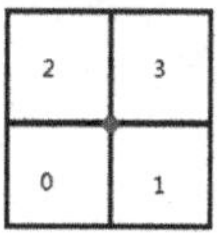

Fig. 5. Moving direction of A user

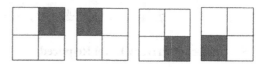

Fig. 6. Cloaking areas of four direction 0,1,2,3

Algorithm 2. TB

Input: a quadtree T, footprint database F, a series of m LBS requests $(u_i, x_i, y_i, t_i, r_i)$ of user $u_i(1 \le i \le m)$.
Output: m cloaking areas $c_i (1 \le i \le m)$.
1. Initialize cloaking areas $c_1, ..., c_m$ according to user's highest requirement respectively, and a candidate set $S_c = \{c_1, ..., c_m\}$.
2. Compute U' with respect to all cloaking areas, and privacy value $p(c_1), ..., p(c_m)$ of all cloaking areas with respect to U', if $p(c_1), ..., p(c_m)$ satisfy the requirements $r_1, r_2, ..., r_m$, then go to step 5.
3. Find the area c_i which contains least users from candidate set S_c and check the level of c_i, if it is on level 1, remove c_i from S_c, then repeat step 3;
4. Move c_i to be its direct parent in tree T and shift it towards the lower left, lower right, upper left and upper right according to user's moving direction 0,1,2,3 respectively, go to step 2.
5. Return $c_1, ..., c_m$.

5   Performance Study

In this section, we evaluate the performance of LUF and TB. We implement algorithm 2 (L2P2-1) and algorithm 3 (L2P2-2) in [3] for comparison. All algorithms are implemented in Java. And we use the Network-based Generator of Moving Objects [17] to simulate 1000 mobile users' movements in 1000 unit time, generate 35 K data as our footprint database. The input of the generator is the real map of Oldenburg, Germany, the area of which is about $16 \times 16 \, km^2$. We divide the region into smaller cells recursively until the smallest area has the size of $1 \times 1 \, km^2$. Then we choose users randomly, generate their requirements and apply all algorithms. Table 2 shows the parameters used in performance evaluation, Nr, Rk and Re represent the number of requests, k-anonymity and entropy value required by user respectively.

Table 2. Parameter Settings

Experiment	Nr	Rk	Re
1	20	5–10	NA
2	20	NA	5–20
3	10–50	7	NA
4	10–50	NA	12

5.1   Effect of Privacy Level Required

Figure 7 shows the performance under different k-anonymity requirements. In Fig. 7(a), L2P2-1 needs larger cloaking area compared with other algorithms, this is because L2P2-1 expands cloaking area according to the pyramid level, which may lead to unnecessary expansions and increase cloaking area. LUF needs smaller cloaking area than L2P2-2, this tells us that dealing with the area which contains the least users is efficient in term of reducing the average area. TB needs the smallest average area, which confirms our conjecture that more area overlap leads to more common users. And all algorithms maintain a stable value of average area when the requirement increases, the reason is shown in Fig. 7(b), we can see all algorithms provide higher privacy value than required, so a slight increase in requirements doesn't affect a lot.

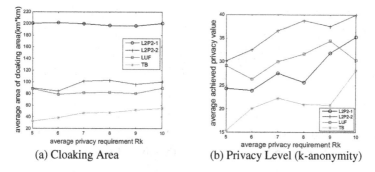

(a) Cloaking Area   (b) Privacy Level (k-anonymity)

Fig. 7. Result of different K-anonymity requirements

In Fig. 8, entropy is used as a metric. As for average cloaking area, when entropy requirement increases, the average area of L2P2-2, LUF and TB all increase. L2P2-1 still maintains a large and stable value of area because of its fixed expansion way. As for privacy level, on the basis of satisfying user's requirements, we can see privacy levels of all algorithms increase along with the increase of privacy requirements.

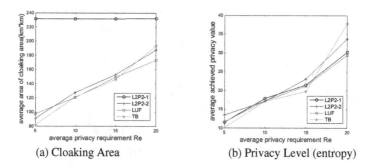

(a) Cloaking Area   (b) Privacy Level (entropy)

Fig. 8. Results of different entropy requirements

In conclusion, we can see different metrics have different influences on performance. Average area doesn't change a lot when k-anonymity requirement increases, it is because all algorithms can provide higher level privacy than required. But for entropy, average area and privacy level increase when entropy requirement increases, except that L2P2-1 always needs a large size of area.

5.2 Effect of Number of Requests

In Fig. 9, k-anonymity is used as a metric. When the number of requests increases, average area and privacy level of all algorithms increase. LUF and TB need smaller area than other algorithms, which shows that expanding according to actual situation improves efficiency and reduces unnecessary expansions, especially TB, shifting areas following the trend of moving direction increases the number of common users.

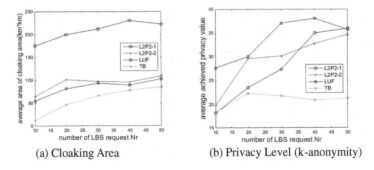

(a) Cloaking Area   (b) Privacy Level (k-anonymity)

Fig. 9. Results of different number of requests (k-anonymity)

The performance under different number of requests in entropy is shown in Fig. 10, except that L2P2-1 still needs a large area for cloaking, average cloaking area of other algorithms all increases along with the increase of the number of requests. In Fig. 10(b), we can't see a clear trend, this is because the size of common users set becomes volatile affected by a large number of requests.

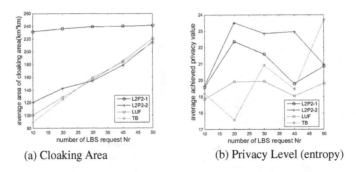

(a) Cloaking Area   (b) Privacy Level (entropy)

Fig. 10. Results of different number of requests (entropy)

In summary, when use k-anonymity as a metric, all algorithms can satisfy requirements, LUF and TB get better performance in reducing average cloaking area. And we find that it is hard to use entropy to evaluate the privacy level with respect to U', since entropy is mainly used to measure the distribution of users, but we can still prove that our algorithms can provide sufficient protection for users.

6   Conclusion

In this paper, we discuss issues about personalized location privacy protection for continuous queries, and propose two algorithms——LUF and TB. In our algorithms, before satisfying user's requirements, we expand cloaking area according to user's actual situation. And we evaluate our algorithms through a series of simulations, which show that our algorithms can protect personalized location privacy for continuous queries effectively, and reduce area of cloaking areas; when we use k-anonymity as a metric, cloaking area of TB is reduced to nearly one sixth the area of the compared algorithms in the best situation.

Acknowledgements. The work was partially supported by the Natural Science Foundation of China (No. 61272403), by the Fundamental Research Funds for the Central Universities (No. 10561201474).

References

1. Sweeney, L.: K-anonymity: a model for protecting privacy. Int. J. Uncertainty Fuzziness Knowl. Based Syst. **10**(5), 557–570 (2002)
2. Pfitzmann, A., Köhntopp, M.: Anonymity, unobservability, and pseudonymity — a proposal for terminology. In: Federrath, H. (ed.) Designing Privacy Enhancing Technologies. LNCS, vol. 2009, pp. 1–9. Springer, Heidelberg (2001). doi:10.1007/3-540-44702-4_1
3. Wang, Y., Xu, D., He, X., Zhang, C., Li, F., Xu, B.: L2P2: location-aware location privacy protection for location-based services. In: Proceedings of IEEE INFOCOM (2012)
4. You, T., Peng, W., Lee, W.: Protecting moving trajectories with dummies. In: Proceedings of the 2007 International Conference on Mobile Data Management (DMD 2007) (2007)
5. Um, J.H., Jang, M.Y., Jo, K.J., Chan, J.W.: A new cloaking method supporting both k-anonymity and l-diversity for privacy protection in location-based service. In: International Symposium on Parallel and Distributed Processing with Applications, (2009)
6. Mokbel, M.F., Chow, C.Y., Aref, W.G.: The new casper: query processing for location services without compromising privacy. In: Proceedings of the 32nd International Conference on Very Large Data Bases, Ser. VLDB 2006 (2006)
7. Wang, T., Liu, L.: Privacy-aware mobile services over road networks. In: VLDB, pp. 1042–1053 (2009)
8. Hossain, A.A., Hossain, A., Yoo, H.K., Chang, J.W.: H-star: Hilbert-order based star network expansion cloaking algorithm in of road networks. In: Proceedings of the IEEE 14th International Conference on Computational Science and Engineering, pp. 81–88 (2011)
9. Xu, T., Cai, Y.: Location anonymity in continuous location-based services. In: Proceedings of the 15th Annual ACM International Symposium on Advances in Geographic Information Systems (2007)
10. Mascetti, S., Bettini, C., Wang, X.S., Freni, D., Jajodia, S.: Providenthider: an algorithm to preserve historical k-anonymity in LBS. In: Proceedings of the International Conference on Mobile Data Management: Systems, Services and Middleware (2009)
11. Shin, H., Vaidya, J., Atluri, V., Choi, S.: Ensuring privacy and security for LBS through trajectory partitioning. In: Eleventh International Conference on Mobile Data Management (2010)
12. Zhang, X., Kim, G.B., Bae, H.Y.: An adaptive spatial cloaking method for privacy protection in location-based service. In: 2014 IEEE International Conference on Information and Communication Technology Convergence (ICTC), pp. 480–485 (2014)
13. Lin, C., Wu, G., Yu, C.W.: Protecting location privacy and query privacy: a combined clustering approach. Concurrency Comput. Pract. Experience **27**(12), 3021–3043 (2015)

14. Samet, H.: The Design and Analysis of Spatial Data Structures. Addison Wesley Longman Publishing Co. Inc., Boston (1990)
15. Gruteser, M., Grunwald, D.: Anonymous usage of location based services through spatial and temporal cloaking. In: Proceedings of the 1st International Conference on Mobile Systems, Applications and Services, San Francisco, California, pp. 31–42 (2003)
16. Xu, T., Cai, Y.: Feeling-based location privacy protection for location based services. In: Proceedings of ACM CCS 2009 (2009)
17. Brinkhoff, T.: A framework for generating network-based moving objects. GeoInformatica 6(2), 153–180 (2002)

A Novel Signature Generation Approach in Noisy Environments for Detecting Polymorphic Worm

Jie Wang[1(✉)] and Jie Wu[2]

[1] School of Information Science and Engineering,
Central South University, Changsha 410083, China
jwang@csu.edu.cn
[2] College of Science and Technology, Temple Unversity,
Philadelphia, PA 19122, USA
jiewu@temple.edu

Abstract. Polymorphic worms can change their patterns dynamically, that makes the generation of worm signatures a challenging task. In noisy environments the task is more difficult. In this paper, we propose a novel approach CGNRS to generate worm neighborhood-relation signatures (NRS) from suspicious flow pool with noisy sequences. CGNRS divides n sequences into m groups and each group contains 20 sequences. CGNRS identifies worm sequences for each group by adopting color coding and computing NRS. Then all identified worm sequences are used to generate NRS. We have carried out extensive experiments to evaluate the quality of signatures generated by CGNRS. In comparison with signatures generated by existing approaches, the experiment results show that NRS generated by our approaches can be used to detect effectively polymorphic worm when the suspicious flow pool contains noise sequences.

Keywords: Signature generation · Polymorphic worm detection · Neighborhood relation · Color coding · Intrusion detection

1 Introduction

Worms are self-replicating malicious programs and represent a major security threat for the Internet. They can infect and damage a large number of vulnerable hosts at timescales where human responses are unlikely to be effective [1]. According to an empirical study, a typical zero-day attack may last for 312 days on average [2]. Polymorphic worms are characterized by their ability to change their byte sequence when they replicate and propagate, and they can change their appearances with every instance. They have caused great damage to Internet in recent years.

In order to evade detection system, polymorphic worms use some techniques to remove any static signature which may be obtained from the payload.

© Springer International Publishing AG 2016
G. Wang et al. (Eds.): SpaCCS 2016, LNCS 10066, pp. 109–121, 2016.
DOI: 10.1007/978-3-319-49148-6_10

A polymorphic worm can be implemented by some methods such as instructions rearrangement, garbage-code insertion, register-reassignment, instruction-substitution and encryption [3–5]. No matter what method is used the worms produced can always be classified into two classes. The first class of worm signatures exhibits constant subsequences and we call these polymorphic worm PWCS (polymorphic worm with constant subsequences). The second class can not be identified based on constant subsequences but can be identified based on other kinds of regularities in the worm sequences, e.g. worm byte frequency distribution and the difference between adjacent bytes of the worm sequences. We call the second class of polymorphic worm PWVS (polymorphic worm with variant subsequences).

Polymorphic worm detection are mainly based on signature because of their simplicity and ability to operate online in real time [6]. However, most deployed worm signature based detection systems are ineffective to detect PWVS [7]. Generating high quality and accurate signatures based on the characteristic of polymorphic worm remains largely an open problem [8,9].

Additionally, suspicious flow pool, from which worm signatures are generated, often includes noise flows. Noise flows often are normal flow sequences or crafted worm-like flow sequences. These noise sequences can lead to existing signature generation methods to generate useless signature. For example, Fogla [10] introduced polymorphic blending attacks, which evade signature-based intrusion detection systems by blending lots of normal flow sequences with worm sequences. Perdisci [11] proposed an attack against worm signature generation systems. This attack uses deliberate noise injection and misleads these systems to generate useless signatures.

Because of the polymorphism of worm and noise problem in suspicious flow pool, existing work for defending against polymorphic worms and generating their signatures have inadequateness because they either can not handle noise well in the process of generating worm signature or can not generate worm signature to detect PWVS successfully. In this paper, for avoiding the situation that signature of polymorphic worms can not be generated when any static signature or invariant substring are removed from worms, we propose a neighborhood-relation signatures (NRS) to detect polymorphic worm. NRS is a collection of distance frequency distributions between neighbor byte. Moreover, for solving noise problem during generating worm signature, we propose CGNRS algorithm by combining color coding methods to generate NRS from suspicious flow pool with noise sequences. CGNRS divides n sequences into m groups and each group contains 20 sequences, and then identifies worm sequences for each group by adopting color coding. Finally, all identified worm sequences are clustered to generate NRS. The rest of the paper is organized as follows. Related works are introduced in Sect. 2. CGNRS algorithm is proposed in Sect. 3. Experimental results are illustrated in Sect. 4. Section 5 draws the conclusions.

2   Related Work

Anomaly-based detection is one of defending worm techniques. For example, a novel machine learning based framework is presented in [12] to detect known and newly emerging malware at a high precision using layer 3 and layer 4 network traffic features. This framework can detect Conficker worm successfully. Another technique for defending worm is signature-based detection. Signature-based detection techniques look for specific byte sequences (called attack signatures) that are known to appear in the attack traffic. Their efficiency of defending against worms depends on the quality of worm signatures that can be generated.

Recently, there have been many research efforts on generating signature for worms. Some of them only can detect single worms. For example, G. Portokalidis et al. [13] implemented SweetBait system, which automatically generates worm signatures. S. Ranjan et al. [14] presented DoWicher, which extracts the worm content signature via a LCS algorithm applied over the flow payload content of isolated flows. M. Cai et al. developed a collaborative worm signature generation system (WormShield) [15] that employs distributed fingerprint filtering. In these systems, a worm is assumed to have a long invariant substring used as a signature to detect the worm. However, many polymorphic worms do not contain a long enough common substring. Systems mentioned above are not applicable to detect polymorphic worms.

Some methods to generate worm signatures are more complicated than that based on LCS algorithm. For example, J. Newsome et al. [16] presented Polygraph, a signature generation system. Polygraph extracted multiple invariant substrings in all worm variants as worm signature. Z. Li et al. [17] developed the Hamsa, an improved system over Polygraph in terms of both speed and attack resilience. Hamsa takes the number of occurrences of a substring token into a part of signature. Lorenzo Cavallaro et al. [18] proposed LISABETH, an improved version of Hamsa, an automated content-based signature generation system for polymorphic worms that uses invariant bytes analysis of network traffic content. Burak Bayogle et al. [19] proposed Token-Pair Conjunction and Token-Pair Subsequence signature for detecting polymorphic worm threats. Y. Tang et al. [6] proposed Simplified Regular Expression (SRE) signature, and used multiple sequence alignment techniques to generate exploit-based signatures. A graph based classification framework of content based polymorphic worm signatures is presented in [20]. Based on the defined framework, a new polymorphic worm signature scheme, Conjunction of Combinational Motifs (CCM), is proposed. CCM utilizes common substrings of polymorphic worm copies and also the relation between those substrings through dependency analysis. Above these methods assumed that multiple invariant substrings must be present in all instances of polymorphic worm. They can not produce signature for PWVS because there is no same byte sequences exists in different copies of PWVS. In this paper, we propose the CGNRS algorithm to solve the noise problem by using color coding.

3 CGNRS Algorithm

3.1 Worm Signature

In this paper, we use NRS [21] as worm signature. $S = \{S_1, S_2, ..., S_n\}$ is a set of worm sequences, where $S_i = c_1 c_2 ... c_m$. There is at least a significant region in worms, which infects victim. Suppose $a_1, a_2, ..., a_n$ are the starting positions of significant region in n sequences, and the width of significant region is w. The number of worm sequences, in which neighbor distance of position p in the significant regions is d, is denoted as $count(p, d)$. Neighbor distance distribution $f_p(d)$ is as follows.

$$f_p(d) = \frac{count1(p, d)}{n} \qquad (1)$$

where $\sum_{d \in [0...255]} f_p(d) = 1$, and $p = 1, 2, ..., w-1$. NRS signature of n sequences is defined as $(f_1, f_2, ..., f_{w-1})$. The process of computing NRS (GNRS) was described in [21].

3.2 Process of Identifying Worm Sequences from 20 Sequences by Applying Color Coding

Consider an n-size suspicious flow pool with k worm sequences, CGNRS is designed to generate worm signature from the pool. The suspicious flow pool comprises of worm sequences and noise sequences. Worm sequences are PWCS, PWVS or both of them. Noise sequences contain normal flow sequences from real network and sequences generated by using special methods discussed in [11]. Since the position of worm sequence is unknown, we have to extract signature from each k-combinations of n sequences. In other words, procedure of extracting signature will be run C_n^k times. However, when the number of sequences in suspicious flow pool is very large, for example, when n=2000, C_n^k is too large to run for extracting signature. In this paper, we use divide-and-conquer method. n sequences are divided into m g-sequences, and $g = \lfloor \frac{n}{m} \rfloor$. Then we identify worm sequences by running identification procedure for each u-combinations sequences of g-sequences. Here the identification procedure is run mC_g^u times. If g is too large, so is C_g^u, and if g is too small, it is difficult to distinguish worm sequences. From above analysis we can see that the larger the value of g is, the easier distinguishing worm sequences will be, and the greater complexity of computation is. Assuming $g = 20$, $C_{20}^{15} = 15504$, $C_{20}^{14} = 38760$, $C_{20}^{13} = 77520$, $C_{20}^{12} = 15504$, and $C_{20}^{11} = 167960$. From these data, it can be seen that computation complexity is still large when $g = 20$. Therefore, we adopt color coding to reduce the number of times C_g^u of running identification procedure when $g = 20$. The detailed introduction about color coding was described in [8]. In this paper, $Coloring(20, u)(u = 11, 12, \cdots, 19)$ is used. Table 1 shows the comparison between the size of $Coloring(20, u)$ and the number of u-combinations of 20.

When the number of noise sequences in suspicious flow pool is larger than the number of worm sequences, it is hard to identify worm sequences. Therefore we

Table 1. Comparison between the size of $Coloring(20, u)$ and the number of u-combinations of 20

	$Coloring(20,u)$	u-combinations of 20
$u=19$	10	20
$u=18$	50	190
$u=17$	170	1140
$u=16$	403	4845
$u=15$	862	15504
$u=14$	1220	38760
$u=13$	2036	77520
$u=12$	2085	125970
$u=11$	3250	167960

only consider how to identify worm sequences when g-size suspicious flow pool includes $u(u > \frac{g}{2})$ worm sequences. The procedure of building $Coloring(g, u)$ is denoted as Build coloring(g,u). Assuming f is the number of (g, u)-colorings in the set $Coloring(g, u)$. For each (g, u)-coloring, sequences with the same color are merged. So g sequences are converted to u sequences. Then algorithm GNRS generates NRS_i signature for the u sequences. After NRS_i is generated, it is evaluated in one filter flow pool, which contains n normal sequences. We compute the matching score Θ_j of the jth sequence in the filter flow pool with NRS_i based on Eq. (1). If $\Theta_j > 0(1 \leq j \leq n)$, p_i adds 1. If $p_i/n < \varepsilon$, the u sequences used to generate NRS_i is considered as u worm sequences in the suspicious flow pool, where ε is a small predefined percentage. If all $NRS_i(1 \leq i \leq f)$ are not satisfied, u worm sequences are not identified. The process is described as GeWS algorithm, which is illustrated in Fig. 1.

In Fig. 1, $g = 20$ and $11 \leq u \leq 20$. Results returned by GeWS are u sequences. According to the method of color coding, the set $Coloring(g, u)$ can cover all u-combinations of g sequences. Therefore signatures generated from u sequences are the same as signatures extracted from each u-combinations of g sequences.

3.3   Description of Algorithm CGNRS

Given a suspicious flow pool with n sequences. Firstly, n sequences are divided into many groups, each of which includes 20 sequences. If the number of sequences in the last group is less than 20, copies of other sequences are put into the last group. Assuming that n sequences are divided into $m = \lceil \frac{n}{20} \rceil$ groups $G_1, G_2, ..., G_m$. Algorithm GeWS is applied to generate NRS signatures for each group, and returns u worm sequences or returns "can not identify worm sequences" for each group.

For group G_i, the parameter u of GeWS algorithm is 20. Assuming that NRS_i is signature generated by GeWS algorithm, and S_i' is u worm sequences

Algorithm GeWS(S_g, N, u)
Input: g sequences $S_g = \{y_1, \cdots, y_g\}$, n normal sequences $N = N_1, N_2, \cdots, N_n$, u, Width of signature w;
Output: u sequences S_u, NRS for g sequences;
Build $Coloring(g, u)$;
For each (g, u)-coloring of $Coloring(g, u)$
    $\{g$ sequences of S_g are colored with the (g, u)-coloring;
    $S_u = \{x_1, \cdots, x_u\}$ is generated by merging sequences with the same color
in S_u;
    $NRS_i \leftarrow GNRS(S_u, w)$;
    For $j = 1$ to n
        Computing the matching score Θ_j of N_j with NRS_i;
        If $(\Theta_j > 0)$ then $p_i + +$;
    If $p_i/n < \varepsilon$
        $NRS = NRS_i$; Flag="True"; break;
    Flag="False";
    $\}$
If(Flag=="True") then
    Return (S_u, NRS)
else return("can not identify worm sequences");

Fig. 1. Algorithm GeWS

returned by the algorithm. If NRS_i is not generated, CGNRS calls algorithm GeWS with $u = u - 1$ again until NRS_i is generated or $u < 11$. After dealing with all groups, CGNRS can obtain a set sequences S' by merging all not-null S'_i. Then CGNRS employs GNRS algorithm to generate NRS for S'. The CGNRS algorithm is illustrated in Fig. 2.

As shown in Fig. 2, the parameter a is set to be 20 and b is set to be 11 in CGNRS. GeWS algorithm aims to generate signatures when the number of worm sequences is larger than that of noise sequences in each group. If there is at least one group which generates signature and obtains the set of worm sequences, CGNRS can generate worm signature with probability 1.

4   Experiments and Results

Four kinds of worm are used in the experiments. They are MS Blaster worm, SQL Slammer worm, Apache-Knacker worm and Conficker worm. The MS Blaster worm exploits a vulnerability in Microsoft's DCOM RPC interface. Upon successful execution, the MS Blaster worm retrieves a copy of the file msblast.exe from a previously infected host [22]. SQL Slammer worm exploits a buffer overflow vulnerability in Microsoft's SQL Server. Apache-Knacker worm are based on the real world Apache-Knacker exploit. Conficker exploits a stack corruption vulnerability, the MS08-067 server service vulnerability, to introduce and

---

Algorithm CGNRS(S, N, w, a, b)
Input: n sequences $S = \{y_1, \cdots, y_n\}$, l normal sequences $N = N_1, N_2, \cdots, N_l$,
the width of signature w;
Output: worm signature NRS;
$S \rightarrow S_1, S_2, \cdots, S_m$;
For $i = 1$ to m
  $\{u = a$; $Flag = True$;
  While $(Flag == True)$
    $\{$GeWS(S_i, N, u, w);
    If NRS_i and S'_i are generated by algorithm GeWS, Then
      $\{Flag = FALSE$;
      Combining the set of sequences S' and S'_i;$\}$
    Else $\{u = u - 1$;
      If $(u < b)$ Then
        $\{S'_i = NULL$; $Flag = FALSE$;$\}\}\}$
If S' is not null, then
  $\{NRS \leftarrow GNRS(S', w)$;
  return (NRS);$\}$
Else return ("not generating signature");

Fig. 2. Algorithm CGNRS

execute shellcode on affected Windows system [23]. In our experiments, we apply polymorphism techniques to generate PWCS and PWVS for above 4 type worms.

4.1 Comparison of NRS and Other Signature Generated from Suspicious Flow Pool Without Noise Sequences

In the following experiments, NRS generated by algorithm CGNRS is compared with three worm signatures, PADS signature [24], token subsequence signature from Polygraph [16] and signature generated by using multiple sequence alignment algorithm (MSA) [6]. We use 200 MS Blaster worm variants and 200 SQL Slammer worm variants for generating signatures. Then we use 10000 correspondent worm sequences and 10000 normal flow sequences from real network as test variants. The false positive ratio and the false negative ratio are get respectively. The false positive ratio is defined as the number of normal flow sequences misclassified as worm variants divided by the total number of normal flow sequences. The false negative ratio is defined as the number of worm test variants misclassified as normal traffic divided by the total number of worm test variants. Experiments are run in the following two scenarios:

(1) Worm samples and worm test variants contain only PWCS. Since PWCS exhibits some constant subsequences, four kinds of worm signatures can all be generated. Because NRS with shorter signature length has better quality and so does PADS [24], the length of NRS and PADS is 10. The experi-

Table 2. The false positive ratio and the false negative ratio of different worm signatures when worm samples and test variants include PWVS variants

	Worm name	The false positive ratio	The false negative ratio
NRS	Blaster	0	0.0002
	Slammer	0	0
	Conficker	0	0
PADS	Blaster	0	0.2839
	Slammer	0	0.1346
	Conficker	0	0.0347
Polygraph	Blaster	None	None
	Slammer	None	None
	Conficker	None	None
MSA	Blaster	None	None
	Slammer	None	None
	Conficker	None	None

ment results show that these worm signatures are no false negative and false positive.

(2) Worm samples and worm test variants all contain PWVS. The experiment results are illustrated in Table 2.

It is easy to see from Table 2 that NRS and PADS can be generated when worm samples include PWVS. Since PWVS can not be identified by finding constant subsequences, Polygraph [16] and MSA [6] can not generate signature for PWVS. In Table 2, the false positive ratio of NRS and PADS is 0. NRS and PADS can distinguish the normal flow sequences well. The false negative ratio of NRS is lower than that of PADS. The reason is that PADS is based on bytes themselves. If polymorphic techniques, such as Encryption techniques, are used in worm variants, PADS will suffer from difficulties to detect such worms. NRS is based on neighbor relationship, and it is more flexibility.

4.2 Comparison of NRS and Other Signature Generated from Suspicious Flow Pool with Noise Sequences

In the experiments, the suspicious flow pool includes 200 worm samples. When the number of noise sequences is l, we randomly replace l worm sequences with l noise sequences in the suspicious flow pool. Here worm sequences belong to PWCS. Noise sequences are generated by method discussed in [11]. Every noise sequence has some common substrings with one worm sequence of the suspicious pool. There also have some common substrings among noise sequences and these common substrings come from normal flow sequences. But noise sequence does not contain the true invariant parts of the worm. NRS with different length are generated by CGNRS from the suspicious flow pool. Other kinds of worm

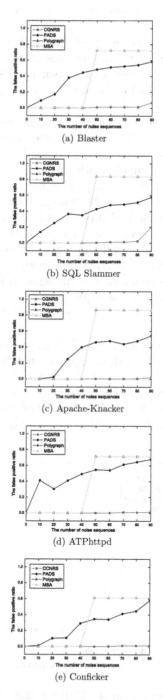

(a) Blaster

(b) SQL Slammer

(c) Apache-Knacker

(d) ATPhttpd

(e) Conficker

Fig. 3. The false positive ratio of CCNRS, PADS, Polygraph and MSA

signatures, including PADS, signatures of Polygraph and signatures of MSA, also are generated.

We use 10,000 worm variants and 10,000 normal flow sequences as test variants to measure NRS, where worm variants belong to PWCS. NRS is compared with other kinds of worm signatures. Comparison results of NRS and other kinds of signatures are illustrated in Figs. 3 and 4. In the experiments, the length of NRS and PADS is set to be 10.

From Fig. 3, it can be seen that when there are no noise sequences in suspicious flow pool, the false positive ratio of these worm signatures is 0. However, with the number of noise increasing gradually, the false positive ratio of PADS grows. PADS is collection of position-aware byte frequency distributions. If there are noise sequences in the suspicious flow pool, PADS will be generated by computing position-aware byte frequency of worm variants and noise sequences. Therefore, when the PADS is used to detect worms, PADS will classify some noise sequences into worm variants. When the number of noise adds to 50, signature generated by Polygraph and MSA also obtain higher false positive ratio. Because of the disturbance of craft noise, common substrings among noise sequences are extracted for composing worm signatures. If these signatures are used to detect noise sequences, noise sequences are considered as worm variants. Since CGNRS adopts color coding, NRS generated by CGNRS obtained lower false positive ratio.

Moreover, for signatures generated by Polygraph and MSA are common substrings of noise sequences, these signatures can not detect worm variants. So, the false negative ratio is 0 when they detect above 5 kind of worm variants. Since NRS and PADS are more flexible, they can detect correctly all worm variants. Therefore, we use one figure, Fig. 4, to show the false negative ratio of above 4 worm signatures in detecting different kind of worm variants. From the

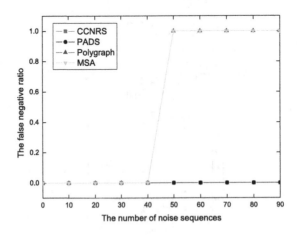

Fig. 4. The false positive ratio of CCNRS, PADS, Polygraph and MSA

Figs. 3 and 4, it can be seen that, compared with PADS, Polygraph and MSA, CGNRS is better in generating worm signature with high quality.

5 Conclusion

In this paper, we propose NRS signatures based on neighborhood relation for polymorphic worms. NRS are generated by GNRS algorithm based on distances between neighbor bytes. We perform extensive experiments to demonstrate the effectiveness of NRS. In order to deal with noise problem, we proposed a novel algorithm CGNRS by introducing color coding into our approaches. CGNRS is able to generate NRS signature automatically for polymorphic worms in the environments with noises. CGNRS are tested and compared with PADS, Polygraph and MSA. According to the results of comparison, we draw the following conclusions:

(1) If there are only PWCS in the suspicious flow pool without noise sequences, NRS, PADS, and signatures generated by Polygraph and MSA can be used to detect effectively polymorphic worm.
(2) When the suspicious flow pool without noise sequences contains PWVS, NRS can obtain lower the false negative ratio compared with PADS. Polygraph and MSA can not generate worm signature.
(3) When suspicious flow pool include noise sequences and PWCS, compared with PADS and signature generated by Polygraph and MSA, NRS by CGNRS can obtain lower false positive ratio and lower false negative ratio. Therefore, CGNRS is a better approach to generate signature for polymorphic worm.

Acknowledgment. This work is supported by National Natural Science Foundation of China under Grant No. 61202495 and No. 61573379.

References

1. Antonatos, S., Akritidis, P., Markatos, E.P., Anagnostakis, K.G.: Defending against hitlist worms using network address space randomization. Comput. Netw. **51**(12), 3471–3490 (2007). Elsevier
2. Bilge, L., Dumitras, T.: Before we knew it: an empirical study of zero-day attacks in the real world. In: Proceedings of ACM conference on Computer and communications security (CCS 2012), New Carolina, pp. 833–844, October 2012
3. Talbi, M., Mejri, M., Bouhoula, A.: Specification and evaluation of polymorphic shellcode properties using a new temporal logic. J. Comput. Virol. **5**(3), 171–186 (2009)
4. Stephenson, B., Sikdar, B.: A quasi-species approach for modeling the dynamics of polymorphic worm. In: IEEE Infocom, Barcelona, Catalunya, pp. 1–12 (2006)
5. Song, Y., Locasto, M.E., Stavrou, A., Keromytis, A.D., Stolfo, S.J.: On the infeasibility of modeling polymorphic shellcode. In: Proceedings of the 14th ACM Conference on Computer and Communications Security, Alexandria, Virginia, USA, pp. 541–551 (2007)

6. Tang, Y., Xiao, B., Lu, X.: Using a bioinformatics approach to generate accurate exploit-based signatures for polymorphic worms. Comput. Secur. **28**, 827–842 (2009). Elsevier, Available online 17 June 2009

7. Modi, C., Patel, D., Borisaniya, B., Patel, H., Patel, A., Rajarajan, M.: A survey of intrusion detection techniques in cloud. J. Netw. Comput. Appl. **36**(1), 42–57 (2013)

8. Wang, J., Wang, J.X., Chen, J.E., Zhang, X.: An automated signature generation approach for polymorphic worm based on color coding. In: IEEE ICC 2009, Dresden, Germany, pp. 1–6 (2009)

9. Tang, Y., Xiao, B., Lu, X.: Signature tree generation for polymorphic worms. IEEE Trans. Comput. **60**(4), 565–579 (2011)

10. Fogla, P., Sharif, M., Perdisci, R., Kolesnikov, O., Lee, W.: Polymorphic blending attacks. In: Proceedings of 15th USENix Security Symposium, Vancouver, B.C., Canada, pp. 241–256 (2006)

11. Perdisci, R., Dagon, D., Lee, W., Fogla, P., Sharif, M.: Misleading worm signature generators using deliberate noise injection. In: Proceedings of 2006 IEEE Symposium on Security and Privacy, Atlanta, GA, USA, pp. 17–31 (2006)

12. Comar, P.M., Liu, L., Saha, S., Tan, P.N., Nucci, A.: Combining supervised and unsupervised learning for zero-day malware detection. In: Proceedings of 32nd Annual IEEE International Conference on Computer Communications (INFOCOM 2013), Turin, Italy, pp. 2022–2030, April 2013

13. Portokalidis, G., Bos, H.: SweetBait: zero-hour worm detection and containment using low- and high-interaction honeypots. Comput. Netw. **51**(11), 1256–1274 (2007)

14. Ranjan, S., Shah, S., Nucci, A., Munafo, M., Cruz, R., Muthukrishnan, S.: DoWitcher: effective worm detection and containment in the internet core. In: IEEE Infocom, Anchorage, Alaska, pp. 2541–2545 (2007)

15. Cai, M., Hwang, K., Pan, J., Christos, P.: WormShield: fast worm signature generation with distributed fingerprint aggregation. IEEE Trans. Dependable Secure Comput. **5**(2), 88–104 (2007)

16. Newsome, J., Karp, B., Song, D.: Polygraph: automatically generation signatures for polymorphic worms. In: Proceedings of 2005 IEEE Symposium on Security and Privacy Symposium, Oakland, California, pp. 226–241 (2005)

17. Li, Z., Sanghi, M., Chen, Y., Kao, M., Chavez, B.: Hamsa: fast signature generation for zero-day polymorphic worms with provable attack resilience. In: Proceedings of IEEE Symposium on Security and Privacy, Washington, DC, pp. 32–47 (2006)

18. Cavallaro, L., Lanzi, A., Mayer, L., Monga, M.: LISABETH: automated content-based signature generator for zero-day polymorphic worms. In: Proceedings of the Fourth International Workshop on Software Engineering for Secure Systems, Leipzig, Germany, pp. 41–48 (2008)

19. Bayoglu, B., Sogukpinar, L.: Polymorphic worm detection using token-pair signatures. In: Proceedings of the 4th International Workshop on Security, Privacy and Trust in Pervasive and Ubiquitous Computing, Sorrento, Italy, pp. 7–12 (2008)

20. Bayoglu, B., Sogukpinar, L.: Graph based signature classes for detecting polymorphic worms via content analysis. Comput. Netw. **56**(2), 832–844 (2012)

21. Wang, J., Wang, J.X., Sheng, Y., Chen, J.E.: Polymorphic worm detection using signatures based on neighborhood relation. In: Proceedings of the 11th IEEE International Conference on High Performance Computing and Communications, pp. 347–353 (2009)

22. CERT Advisory CA-2003-20: W32/Blaster worm, Computer Emergency Response Team (2003). http://www.cert.org/advisories/CA-2003-20.html

23. Leder, F., Werner, T.: Know your enemy: containing conficker to tame a Malware. The Honeynet Project (2009). http://honeynet.org
24. Tang, Y., Chen, S.: An automated signature-based approach against polymorphic internet worms. IEEE Trans. Parallel Distrib. Syst. **18**, 879–892 (2007)

A User Authentication Scheme Based on Trusted Platform for Cloud Computing

Jiaqing Mo[1(✉)], Zhongwang Hu[1], and Yuhua Lin[2]

[1] School of Computer, Zhaoqing University, Zhaoqing 526061, China
{mojiaqing, huzhongwang}@126.com
[2] Education Technology and Computer Center, Zhaoqing University,
Zhaoqing 526061, China
183898054@qq.com

Abstract. Cloud Computing develops rapidly and has been widely used in recent years. Remote user security authentication plays an important role in Cloud Computing security mechanism. Some of remote authentication protocols have high computational cost, and they have much interaction rounds, the credibility of remote user's platform could not be guaranteed. In this paper, we put forward a user identity authentication scheme based on trusted platform for Cloud Computing. In this scheme, the cloud user registers in the trusted certificate authority (CA), and obtains the certificate issued by CA. Afterwards, the certificate is sent to the cloud server, and the cloud server verifies the validity of the remote user identity according to the certificate. At the same time, this scheme provides mutual authentication while it establishes communication key between the remote user and cloud server. The analysis shows that this scheme is secure against insider attack, replay attack, backward/forward attack, and forgery attack. Compared with the related work, the scheme has higher computing efficiency and less interaction rounds.

Keywords: Authentication · Trusted platform · Bilinear map · Key agreement · Cloud computing

1 Introduction

Cloud Computing is a kind of computing resource service model, which fulfills the need of the Internet users with flexible on-demand services. This model enables computing, storage, platforms, and services to be available to users on the Internet in an abstract, virtual, dynamic, extensible and manageable manner [1]. With the rapid development of the Internet and network technology, Cloud Computing has become the main environment for data storage and computing, and the impact is more and more extensive [2, 3].

However, the security problems caused by the openness, dynamic and large scale of the Cloud Computing also attract people's attention, which has become the main factor to hinder its further application. One of them is the authenticity of the user identity and the integrity and the forgery-resistance of the platform. Therefore, on the premise of ensuring the authenticity of the cloud user identity and the integrity of the platform,

© Springer International Publishing AG 2016
G. Wang et al. (Eds.): SpaCCS 2016, LNCS 10066, pp. 122–130, 2016.
DOI: 10.1007/978-3-319-49148-6_11

how can the cloud user access to the cloud server securely and efficiently has become a research hotspot [4–6].

Santos et al. [7] presented a trusted Cloud Computing platform (TCCP) protocol, the purpose is to use trusted computing to solve the problem of the credibility of the Cloud Computing platform. In this protocol, the trusted server first verifies the identity to the TC (Trusted Coordinator) with the EK (Endorsement Key) and the integrity measurement list. TC joined the node which was verified successfully to the list of trusted entities, while TC will participate in the protocol to ensure that the server was in the list of trusted entities. In this protocol, the user needs to trust the TC absolutely, and TC needs to participate in the protocol operation for many times. If TC is paralyzed, TCCP does not work properly; moreover, a large number of trusted cloud servers in the protocol need to interact with TC, which makes TC a performance and security bottleneck for the entire protocol. A robust Cloud Computing user authentication framework is proposed in [8], in which all users must login the cloud server through a strong validation of the legitimacy. This framework provides the functions of identity management, mutual authentication and session key establishment between the user and the server. According to the security analysis of this article, it can resist most of the network attacks. Nimmy et al. [9] proposed an cloud authentication scheme based on mutual authentication using secret sharing and steganography, in this scheme the user authentication process is divided into four phases which included register, login, authentication, and changing password. In order to prevent all attacks the user must pass the server's authentication before interacting with the cloud server. While Vorugunti et al. [10] has pointed out that scheme of [9] cannot resist the off-line password attack and denial of service attacks. At the same time, a new Cloud Computing scheme is proposed based on steganography [11]. This scheme introduced encrypted proxy in user identity authentication in the Cloud Computing, when the users access to the cloud servers, the server would verify their identities with the CUA (Cheat-Based user authentication agent), and then checks whether the user is registered with the MDHA (Modified Diffie-Hellman Agent). The users can access the cloud server via encrypted proxy only if they passed the checking. Chen [12] proposed a computing scheme of identity authentication based on one-way hash function and XOR operation for the cloud computing, the purpose of which is to reduce the computational cost. In addition, several literals [13–16] also put forward the identity based user authentication schemes. Some authentication schemes based on certificate have been proposed, but their computational efficiency and transmission efficiency have much room for improvement. Aiming at low efficiency of authentication scheme based on certificate, Zhang et al. [17] proposed a new user authentication protocol, the protocol used certificateless way to reduce computational time and also used temporary ID instead of its true identity in order to hide the true information. Although these schemes authenticate users in different ways, they do not ensure the credibility of the user's platform and the integrity of the platform.

We can see that in the process of remote user authentication in Cloud Computing, the following issues should be considered: (1) the credibility of their platform should be ensured while users accessing to the cloud computing; (2) at the same time, the users, as the protocol participants, computing capability of their platform is relatively weak, thus computation burden of them should be reduced; (3) in addition, the users as a remote party, have large communication time delay, the interaction round of the authentication protocol should be decreased.

According to the above considerations, this paper proposes a novel scheme of direct user identity authentication based on trusted platform in the Cloud Computing environment. In this scheme, the user first registers in the trusted third party CA, and obtains a certificate issued by CA, then the user proves the legitimacy of the identity according to the certificate which was sent to the cloud server to ensure user platform security. We show that this scheme reduces the computation burden of the user side in the authentication process and decreases the rounds of message exchanging, and improves the computational efficiency and security.

The reminder of this paper is organized as follows. Section 2 introduces the preliminaries. Section 3 proposes our authentication scheme in detail. Section 4 analyzes the security and efficiency of our proposed scheme. Finally, Sect. 5 concludes the paper.

2 Preliminaries

2.1 Bilinear Map

Let G_2 and G_1 be the additive and multiplicative cyclic groups respectively, and their prime order is q. If the mapping e: $G_1 \times G_1 \rightarrow G_2$ satisfies the following properties, it is called a bilinear map:

(1) Bilinearity: $e(aP, bQ) = e(P,Q)^{ab}$, for all $P,Q \in G_1$, and a, $b \in Z_q^*$;
(2) Non-degeneracy: there exists $P,Q \in G_1$, such that $e(P,Q) \neq 1$;
(3) Computability: for all $P,Q \in G_1$, there exists an efficient algorithm to compute $e(P,Q)$ in polynomial time.

2.2 Computational Problem

Discrete logarithm problem (DL): Let q ($q > 2^k$, k is a safe parameter) be a large prime number, and q is the order of cyclic group G with generator P, finding an integer $a \in Z_q^*$ such that $Q = aP \in G$ is hard.

Computational Diffie-Hellman Problem (CDH): G is a cyclic group with order of q and generator of P, given a, $b \in Z_q^*$ and aP, $bP \in G$, finding abP is hard.

3 Proposed Scheme

Figure 1 shows our proposed authentication scheme for Cloud Computing. This scheme involves the user U and trusted third-party CA, as well as Cloud Server (CS). CA is the certificate Issuer, publishes the relevant parameters and issues direct anonymous attention (DAA) certificate for the user; user U is the signer and his/her host is installed trusted platform module (TPM), obtains DAA certificate; CS is not anly a verifier but also a cloud service provider, and CS verifies the validity of DAA signature with CA's public key, at the same time CS verifies the authenticity of the platform by the validity of the signature.

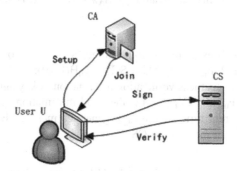

Fig. 1. Our Proposed Scheme

(1) Setup

CA selects the additive group G_1 and multiplicative group G_2 with the same order q which is big prime, the generator of G_1 is P. The bilinear map is defined as e: $G_1 \times G_1 \rightarrow G_2$, and one way strong collision-resistance hash function $H()$, the asymmetric encryption function $E()$ and decryption function $D()$ are selected, and the random number P_{ri_CA} is selected as the main key, and its public key $P_{ub\_CA} = P_{ri\_CA}P$. Later CA publishes the system parameter set CA_params = $\{G_1, G_2, e, q, P, H(), E(), D()\}$.

Cloud server also chooses random number $P_{ri\_s} \in Z_q^*$ as a master key and the public key Pub_S = $P_{ri\_s}P$, keeps P_{ri_s} secretly, publishes system parameter set S_params = $\{G_1, G_2, e, q, P, P_{ub\_S}, H(), E(), D()\}$;

(2) Join

TPM of user U chooses random number r_{u_1}, $n \in Z_q^*$, and uses his/her own identity ID_U to generate registration information $R_U = H(ID_U\|n)$ where $\|$ is a concatenation operation, computes $R_M = r_{u\_1}P$, generates message $M_{sg\_u} = E(P_{ub\_CA}\|ID_U\|R_U\|T_{u\_1})$ with local timestamp T_{u_1}, and send M_{sg_u} to CA via the secure channel.

CA verifies the message M_{sg_u} whether TPM is valid, if yes, the validity of user can be assured and CA performs subsequent operation; otherwise, aborts.

CA chooses a random number $r_{CA\_1} \in Z_q^*$, computes $R_{CA} = r_{CA\_1}P + R_M$, C = H $(ID_U\|R_{CA}\|R_U)$, as well as $R_{CA} = r_{CA\_1}P + R_M$, $L_{CA} = P_{ri\_CA}C + r_{CA\_1}$, thus (L_{CA}, R_{CA}) is the registration message generated by CA for user U.

CA chooses random number $r_{CA\_2} \in Z_q^*$, calculates the user's temporary ID information $ID_{U\_T} = H(ID_U\|r_{CA\_2})$, lets the certificate's expiration date be T_E, generates user's ID information $C_{ERT\_CA} = E(P_{ri\_CA}\|ID_{CA}\|ID_{U\_T}\|T_E)$, and sends the certificate to the TPM of user U in security channel. Meanwhile, CA adds user U to the register list.

User U decrypts C_{ERT_CA} from CA with public key P_{ub_CA} as he/she received the certificate, and then checks $R_M + L_{CA}P = P_{ub\_CA}C + R_{CA}$ whether is satisfied or not. If yes, the validity of certificate can be assured. At this time TPM computes $K = L_{CA} + r_{u\_1}$, thus user obtains certificate $C_{CA\_DAA} = (K, R_{CA}, H(ID_U \| R_{CA} \| R_U))$ issued by CA.

(3) Sign

TPM of User U chooses secret random number S_u, $y_u \in Z_q^*$, computes $X_u = S_u R_{CA}$, $Y_u = S_u CP$, $W_u = S_u KP$, $F_u = y_u P$, $M_u = S_u K + y_u H(F_u \| 0)$; Y_u is session negotiation parameters, M_u is the correctness verification information of key agreement parameters, $S_{ig\_u} = (X_u, Y_u, W_u, F_u, M_u, C_{ERT\_CA})$ is the valid information of the user's identity.

TPM reads the current time stamp T_{u_2}, generates message $E(ID_{CA} \| ID_{U\_T} \| S_{ig\_u} \| P_{ub\_u} \| T_{u\_2})$ and sends the message to CS.

(4) Verify

Upon receiving the information from CS, TPM decrypts the message using his/her own private key P_{ri_s}, after that TPM decrypts C_{ERT_CA} with public key of TPM and get the ID information of TPM and CA, that were denoted by ID_{U_T}' and ID_{CA}' respectively, and judges $ID_{U\_T}' = ID_{U\_T}$ and $ID_{CA}' = ID_{CA}$ whether are satisfied or not, if no, subsequent operation will be interrupted. Later, CS consults communication key with TPM. CS chooses secret random number $v \in Z_q^*$, computes $V = vP$, computes the communication key $KEY_{S-U} = H(vF_u \| 1) = H(vy_u P \| 1)$ between CS and TPM.

CS verifies $M_u P = H(F_u \| 0) \| + W_u$ and $e(Y_u, P_{ub\_CA}) = e(P, W_u - X_u)$ whether are satisfied or not, if yes, thus CS passes the legal authentication of TPM ID of user U, and user U is recognized as a valid user registered on the CA.

CS reads time stamp T_S, generates signature $L_S = Sig(P_{ri\_s} \| T_S \| V)$, sends message $(T_S \| V \| L_S)$ to user U. TPM checks the validity of identity of CS according to LS, and checks time stamp T_S whether is fresh or not, if two check hold, computes the communication key $KEY_{U-S} = H(y_u V \| 1) = H(vy_u P \| 1)$ between CS and TPM. Therefore the communication session key is established between TPM and CS.

4 Security Analysis

4.1 Correctness

In Join phase, because the equation $R_M + L_{CA}P = R_M + (P_{ri\_CA}C + r_{CA\_1})P = R_M + P_{ri\_CA}CP + r_{CA\_1}P = P_{ub\_CA}C + R_{CA}$, the user's TPM confirms that the certificate information generated by CA is legal.

In verify phase, $e(Y_u, P_{ub\_CA}) = e(S_u CP, P_{ri\_CA}P) = e(Su (r_{u\_1} + r_{CA\_1} + P_{ri\_CA}C) P - e(S_u (r_{u\_1} + r_{CA\_1})P, P) = e(W_u - X_u, P) = e(P, W_u - X_u)$, and $M_u P = H(F_u \| 0) \| + W_u$, CS confirms the validity of the certificate C_{ERT_CA} according to the decryption of the certificate, CS assures that the user U is the legal entity authenticated by CA finally.

4.2   Mutual Authentication and Key Agreement

In Verify phase, CS verifies the correctness with the user U's TPM valid message. The correctness of TPM valid information contains the certificate issued by the CA. In this way, CS will confirm that the user is legitimate one registered on the CA. At the same time, the user U confirmed the identity of the CS according to the CS signature information. The timestamp of the CS signature information also ensures the forgery-resistance of the signature information.

CS generates the secret communication key KEY_{S-U} according to the parameter F_u provided by the user U's TPM in Verify phase, as well as their own choice of secret random number v. Similarly, TPM establishes the same communication key with CS according to the signature information and the parameter v provided by CS, combined with his/her own secret parameter y_u.

Because the TPM sent F_u, which is the critical parameter in negotiating communication key, to CS by way of decryption, and CS sent parameter V to the user U by way of signature, the adversary cannot get the key agreement information. In addition, due to difficulty of DL problem, for the formula $V = vP$, users can't solve v according to the V and P; similarly, for the formula $F_u = y_uP$, CS can't solve the user's secret random number y_u according to F_u and P.

4.3   Anti-attack

(1) Anonymity

In the Join phase, CA generates temporary ID information $ID_{U\_T} = H(ID_U\|r_{CA\_2})$ for user U, and encrypts the temporary identity information in the certificate C_{ERT_CA}, and sends to CS, CS can judge the user's U identity is valid or not. Furthermore, when CA generated temporary identity for user, the selected number r_{CA_2} is different for different users, both CS and the adversary can't determine the true identity information of users U, so that the user anonymity of U is ensured.

(2) Resistance to insider attack

In Join phase, the user generates registered information with $R_U = H(ID_U \| n)$, If another user wants to get the value of the secret number n with the ID of the user U, but the H() is a strong strict one-way hash function, so this is not feasible. At the same time, it is not feasible that the adversary wants to obtain the secret value of r_{CA_2} by temporary identity information ID_{U_T}, also due to strong strict one-way hash function H().

(3) Resistance to replay attack

Assume that the adversary has intercepted messages that user U sends to CS in Sign phase, but he/she could not decrypt the messages, so that he/she is unable to get the user's identity information and temporary identity information, not even get the timestamp, so the adversary cannot initiate replay attack.

(4) Resistance to forward/backward attack

The implementation of forward/backward attack means that the adversary has access to the communication key, but in the process of authentication in this paper, the adversary cannot construct the communication key between TPM and CS. CS and TPM need to use their own secret random number in the process of generating communication keys, and each time the user login authentication CS used with different secret random number, and these number will not leak out. So the protocol in this paper can resist forward/backward attacks.

(5) Resistance to forgery attack

In Join phase, user U checks $R_M + L_{CA}P = P_{ub\_CA}C + R_{CA}$ whether is satisfied or not, and R_M contains secret random number r_{u_1} of user U, and L_{CA} contains the private key P_{ri_CA} of CA, these can not be faked by the adversary. In addition, CS need to verify $M_uP = H(F_u\|0) + Wu$ and $e(Y_u,P_{ub\_CA}) = e(P,W_u - X_u)$ in verify phase, in order to check whether the identity of the user U is valid or not. If the adversary wants to forge these information, he/she will face DL and CDH problems.

We compare our scheme with exist authentication schemes [15, 18, 19] in terms of functionality. Table 1 shows the result of the comparison.

Table 1. The functionality comparison between our scheme and the existing scheme

Comparison items	This paper	Tsai [18]	Chen [19]	Liao [15]
Single registration	Yes	Yes	No	No
Mutual authentication	Yes	Yes	No	Yes
Communication key agreement	Yes	Yes	No	Yes
User's anomymity	Yes	Yes	Yes	No
Resistance to insider attack	Yes	No	No	Yes
Resistance to replay attack	Yes	No	No	Yes
Resistance to forward/backward attack	Yes	No	No	No
Resistance to forgery attack	Yes	Yes	Yes	Yes

4.4   Computation Efficiency

In order to illustrate the computational efficiency of this protocol, we compare the computational cost of our proposal with other related schemes.

It is well known that time-consuming operation mainly include bilinear pairings computation, asymmetric encryption, signature and verification operations, exponentiation. Table 2 is comparison of computational cost in this scheme and other schemes. The various computing entities in the first four rows of this table are user U, CS, CA, and the last row is the rounds of interaction about U-CA, U-CS, CA-CS.

Table 2. Comparsions with other schemes in computing efficency

Comparison items	This paper	Tsai [18]	Chen [19]	Liao [15]
Bilinear pairings	0/2/0	1/4/0	2/2/1	7/2/5
Asymmetric encryption	1/2/0	N/A	N/A	N/A
Signature and verification	1/1/0	N/A	0/1/1	N/A
Exponentiation	N/A	1/2/0	18/4/16	2/0/1
Rounds of interaction	1/0/1	1/1/2	4/0/1	1/1/3

As can be seen from Table 2, in the process of implementing of this agreement, times of user U's executing the high computational complexity operations is 2, while Tsai [18], Chen [19], Liao [15] were 2, 20, 9 respectively. Since computing capability is limited on user side, this scheme shifts the computational burden to the powerful cloud server and reduces the computational cost required by the user side, improves the computational efficiency; moreover, as it is known to all, the bilinear pairing operation is more time-consuming than other operations, all entities in our scheme operates bilinear pairings 2 times in total, while schemes [15, 18, 19] reach 5, 5, 14 times respectively. In addition, from the table it also can be seen that the rounds of interaction is lower than other protocols, which reduces the communication delay, improves the efficiency of implementation.

Furthermore, the user's certificate C_{ERT_CA} issued by CA contains the expiration date T_E. If user U was authenticated successfully by CS once, he/she can login CS while skipping the Join phase, directly goes into the Sign and Verify phase for many times with certificate C_{CA_DAA}, as long as T_E is valid. This feature makes the calculation more efficient, and CA will not become the bottleneck of the agreement.

While improving the efficiency of execution, this paper utilizes the techniques such as signature and encryption to ensure the security of the remote user the Internet environment.

5 Conclusions

This paper proposes a user identity authentication scheme based on trusted platform for Cloud Computing which includes Setup, Join, Sign, Verify phases. The scheme uses the trusted third party CA for registered users to generate temporary identity ID. User and CA, users and the cloud server achieve mutual authentication. User of the proposed solution has a low computational complexity, high security features. And the entire agreement has fewer interaction rounds, and has lower communication delays too. Security analysis shows that computation efficiency of this scheme is higher than other schemes, and has better security.

References

1. Moghaddam, F.F., Ahmadi, M., Sarvari, S., et al.: Cloud computing challenges and opportunities: a survey. In: Proceedings of the 2015 1st International Conference on Telematics and Future Generation Networks (TAFGEN), pp. 34–38. IEEE(2015)
2. Lee, B., Awad, A., Awad, M.: Towards secure provenance in the cloud: a survey. In: Proceedings of the IEEE/ACM 8th International Conference on Utility and Cloud Computing (UCC), pp. 577–582. IEEE (2015)
3. Hussein, N.H., Khalid, A.: A survey of cloud computing security challenges and solutions. Int. J. Comput. Sci. Inf. Sec. **14**(1), 52 (2016)

4. Yassin, A.A., Jin, H., Ibrahim, A., et al.: Cloud authentication based on anonymous one-time password. In: Han, Y.H., Park, D.S., Jia, W.J., Yeo, S.S. (eds.) Ubiquitous Information Technologies and Applications. LNCS, vol. 214, pp. 423–431. Springer, Amsterdam (2013)
5. Gonzalez, N.M., Rojas, M.A.T., da Silva, M.V.M, et al.: A framework for authentication and authorization credentials in cloud computing. In: Proceedings of the 12th IEEE International Conference on Trust, Security and Privacy in Computing and Communications, pp. 509–516. IEEE (2013)
6. Jaidhar, C.D.: Enhanced mutual authentication scheme for cloud architecture. In: Proceedings of the 3rd International Conference on Advance Computing (IACC), pp. 70–75. IEEE (2013)
7. Santos, N., Gummadi, K.P., Rodrigues, R.: Towards trusted cloud computing. HotCloud **09** (9), 3 (2009)
8. Choudhury, A. J., Kumar, P., Sain, M., et al.: A strong user authentication framework for cloud computing. In: Proceeding of the IEEE Asia-Pacific on Services Computing Conference (APSCC), pp. 110–115. IEEE (2011)
9. Nimmy, K., Sethumadhavan, M.: Novel mutual authentication protocol for cloud computing using secret sharing and steganography. In: Proceedings of the Fifth International Conference on Applications of Digital Information and Web Technologies (ICADIWT), pp. 101–106. IEEE (2014)
10. Vorugunti, C., Sarvabhatla, M., Murugan, G.: A secure mutual authentication protocol for cloud computing using secret sharing and steganography. In: Proceedings of the Cloud Computing in Emerging Markets (CCEM), 2014 IEEE International Conference, pp. 1–8. IEEE (2014)
11. Moghaddam, F.F., Moghaddam, S.G., Rouzbeh, S., et al.: A scalable and efficient user authentication scheme for cloud computing environments. In: Proceedings on Region 10 Symposium, pp. 508–513. IEEE (2014)
12. Chen, T.H., Yeh, H., Shih, W. K.: An advanced ecc dynamic id-based remote mutual authentication scheme for cloud computing. In: Proceedings of the 5th FTRA International Conference on Multimedia and Ubiquitous Engineering (MUE), pp. 155–159. IEEE (2011)
13. Yang, J.H., Lin, P.Y.: An ID-based user authentication scheme for cloud computing. In: Proceedings of the Tenth International Conference on Intelligent Information Hiding and Multimedia Signal Processing (IIH-MSP), pp. 98–101. IEEE (2014)
14. Mnif, A., Cheikhrouhou, O., Jemaa, M. B.: An ID-based user authentication scheme for wireless sensor networks using ECC. In: ICM 2011 Proceeding, pp. 1–9. IEEE (2011)
15. Liao, Y.P., Hsiao, C.M.: The improvement of ID-based remote user authentication scheme using bilinear pairings. In: Proceedings of the International Conference on Consumer Electronics, Communications and Networks (CECNet), pp. 865–869. IEEE (2011)
16. Huang, H.F., Lin, P.H.: Enhancement of dynamic ID based user authentication for multi-server environment. In: Proceedings of the Sixth International Conference on Genetic and Evolutionary Computing (ICGEC), pp. 55–58. IEEE (2012)
17. Zhang, M., Zhang, Y.: Certificateless anonymous user authentication protocol for cloud computing. In: Proceedings of 2015 International Conference on Intelligent Transportation, Big Data and Smart City (ICITBS), pp. 200–203. IEEE (2015)
18. Tsai, J.L., Lo, N.W.: A privacy-aware authentication scheme for distributed mobile cloud computing services. IEEE Syst. J. **9**(3), 805–815 (2015)
19. Chen, X.F., Feng, D.G.: Direct anonymous attestation based on bilinear maps. J. Softw. **21** (8), 2070–2078 (2010)

ROP-Hunt: Detecting Return-Oriented Programming Attacks in Applications

Lu Si[✉], Jie Yu, Lei Luo, Jun Ma, Qingbo Wu, and Shasha Li

College of Computer, National University of Defense Technology,
Changsha 410073, China
{lusi,jackyu,luolei,majun,wuqingbo}@ubuntukylin.com,
shashali@nudt.edu.cn

Abstract. Return-oriented Programming (ROP) is a new exploitation technique that can perform arbitrary unintended operations by constructing a gadget chain reusing existing small code sequences. Although many defense mechanisms have been proposed, some new variants of ROP attack can easily circumvent them.

In this paper, we present a new tool, ROP-Hunt, that can defend against ROP attacks based on the differences between normal program and ROP malicious code. ROP-Hunt leverages instrumentation technique and detects ROP attack at runtime. In our experiment, ROP-Hunt can detect all types of ROP attack from real-world examples. We use several unmodified SPEC2006 benchmarks to test the performance and the result shows that it has a zero false positive rate and an acceptable overhead.

Keywords: Return-oriented Programming · Buffer overflow · Detection · Code reuse attack · Binary instrumentation

1 Introduction

Since the widespread adoption of data execution prevention (DEP) [1], which ensures that all writable pages in memory are non-executable, it's hard for attackers to redirect the hijacked control flow to their own injected malicious code. To bypass DEP mechanism, code reuse attack (CRA) techniques are proposed and have become attacker's powerful tools. Instead of injection code, they reuse instructions already residing in the attacked vulnerable process to induce malicious behaviors. Return-into-libc technique [37] is one simple practice of it, in which the attacker uses a buffer overflow to overwrite the return address stored in the stack to the address of the library function chosen to be executed. Traditional return-into-libc attack leverages libc functions and cannot support arbitrary computation on the victim machine.

Return-oriented Programming (ROP) is another code reuse attack technique, which executes short instruction sequences called gadgets instead of an entire function. ROP was first demonstrated by Shacham [35] for the ×86 platform,

© Springer International Publishing AG 2016
G. Wang et al. (Eds.): SpaCCS 2016, LNCS 10066, pp. 131–144, 2016.
DOI: 10.1007/978-3-319-49148-6_12

and was subsequently extended to other architectures [13,16,23,26]. It has been proved that ROP can perform Turing-complete computation [36]. Some tools have been developed that allow attackers to construct arbitrary malicious programs using ROP automatically [22,24,33,34].

In the last few years, a number of software and hardware defenses have been proposed to mitigate ROP-based attacks. For example, DROP [17] and DynIMA [20] will trigger an alarm if the small instruction sequences each ending with a *ret* instruction are executed consecutively. ROPdefender [21] maintains a shadow stack and verifies all return addresses. Li et al. [27] proposed a compiler for the ×86 platform that avoids issuing "$0 \times c3$" bytes that can be used as unintended return instructions. Further more, it replaces intended call and return instructions with an indirect call mechanism. However, these mechanisms only focus on the ROP gadgets ending with return instructions and can not defeat other types of ROP-like attacks that capture gadgets without return instructions. CFLocking [11] and G-Free [30] aim to defend against all types of ROP attacks, but they require the source code which is often unavailable to the end users in the real world. KBouncer [32] covers all ROP attack types, requires no side information and achieves good runtime efficiency. However, it only monitors the application execution flow on selected critical paths, e.g., system APIs. It inevitably misses the ROP attacks that do not use those paths.

ROP attack chains gadgets together to perform complex computations and has its own features: the length of gadget is short, contiguous gadgets are not in the same routine and they all execute system calls in somewhere. Based on these features, we design and implement a tool named ROP-Hunt, which dynamically detects all types of ROP attack by checking whether the execution behavior has these matched features. In ROP-Hunt, based on the hazard degree, we divide the ROP report into two categories: *Warning* and *Attack*.

In summary, the main contributions of our work are:

- We statistically analyze a number of normal applications and latest ROP malicious code, and extract features of the ROP attack.
- We propose a novel approach to protecting legacy applications from all types of ROP attacks without accessing to source code.
- We design and implement a prototype, ROP-Hunt, on ×86-based Linux platform and evaluate its security effectiveness and performance overhead.

The remainder of the paper is organized as follows: In Sects. 2 and 3, we describe the ROP attacks and analyze the features of them. The design and implementation of ROP-Hunt are illustrated at Sect. 4. Sections 5 and 6 discuss the parameter selections and delay gadget respectively. Section 7 presents the security and performance evaluation of ROP-Hunt. Section 8 examines its limitations. Finally, we conclude this paper and discuss the future work in Sect. 9.

2   ROP Attack

Without injecting new code into the programs address space, ROP attacks consist of short instruction sequences, which are called gadgets. Each gadget performs some small computation, such as adding two registers or loading a value to memory, and ends with return instruction. We can chain gadgets together and transfer the control flow from one gadget to another by writing appropriate values over the stack.

Figure 1 illustrates a general ROP attack workflow. In step 1, the attacker exploits a memory-related vulnerability of a specific program, e.g., a buffer over-flow, and moves the stack pointer (ESP) to the first return address. For example, Aleph in [31] uses stack smashing techniques to overwrite the return address of a function. Return address 1 is injected at the place where the original return address was located, and the value of ESP will be automatically changed to this point. In step 2, execution is redirected to the first gadget by popping return address 1 from the stack. The gadget is terminated by another return instruction which pops return address 2 from the stack (step 3) and redirects execution to the next gadget (step 4). Each gadget is executed one by one in this way until the attacker attains his goal.

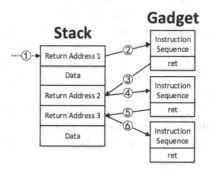

Fig. 1. A general ROP attack

Recently, some new variants of ROP attack without using *ret* instructions were proposed. Checkoway et al. [15] found it is possible to perform return-oriented programming by looking for a pop instruction followed by an indirect jump (e.g., *pop edx; jmp [edx]*). This instruction sequence behaves like returns, and can be used to chain useful gadgets together.

Jump-Oriented Programming (JOP) [12] is another variant of ROP attack which uses register-indirect jumps instead of returns. JOP uses a dispatcher table to hold gadget addresses. Each gadget must be followed by a dispatcher, which is an instruction sequence that can govern the control flow. The dispatcher is used as a virtual program counter and translates the control flow to an entry in the dispatch table, which is the address of a particular jump-oriented functional gadget. At the end of a functional gadget, the attacker uses an indirect jump back to the dispatcher. Then, the dispatcher advances the pointer to the next functional gadget. A simple case of dispatcher is *add edx, 4; jmp [edx]*.

Call Oriented Programming (COP) [14] was introduced by Nicholas Carlini and David Wagner in 2014. Instead of using gadgets that end in returns, the

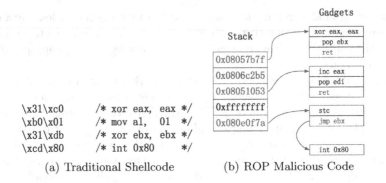

(a) Traditional Shellcode   (b) ROP Malicious Code

Fig. 2. A simple mixed ROP attack

attacker uses gadgets that end with indirect calls. COP attack does not require a dispatcher gadget and gadgets are chained together by pointing the memory-indirect locations to the next gadget in sequence.

To evade current protection mechanisms, attackers prefer to use combinational gadgets. Figure 2 shows a very simple mixed ROP attack constructed by only 4 short gadgets. It is derived from a traditional shellcode [3] which exits the running process on ×86 architecture. We used *exit(n)* (*n* represents a non-zero integer) system call instead of *exit(0)* for convenience. The system call number is stored in *eax* and the parameter is stored in *ebx*. DROP [17] and DynIMA [20] only detect contiguous ret-based gadgets and the attacker can leverage this simple ROP malicious code to evade these two defense mechanisms.

3   Features of ROP Attack

The key to ROP attack detection is finding the differences between ROP malicious code and normal programs. One of the important factors in ROP is the gadget length. [20] found that instruction sequences used in ROP attacks range from two to five instructions. DROP [17] found that the number of the instructions in the gadget is no more than 5. Kayaalp et al. [25] extracted gadgets from standard C library and conducted studies on average gadget lengths. The result showed that as the gadget length grew the number of side effects grew linearly making them increasingly more difficult to use.

There are also some other factors being considered in present detecting mechanisms. DynIMA [20] reports a ROP attack if three of small instruction sequences were executed one after another. Fan Yao et al. [38] found that it is relatively hard to find gadgets within short distances.

Based on the experience of writing ROP malicious code, we find out other two features. First, contiguous gadgets, no matter ending with jump or call instructions, do not locate in the same routine. Second, shellcodes always leverage system call to transfer the flow of control to the kernel mode.

In computer programming, routine is a sequence of code that is intended to be called and used repeatedly during the execution of a program. In high-level languages, many commonly-needed routines are packaged as functions. In the traditional ROP attacks, each gadget ends with the return instruction. At most time, they are not in the same routine except recursive returns. We extract gadgets from glibc by ROPGadget [8], which is an open source tool to search gadgets, and construct some JOP malicious code with the algorithm proposed by [12]. We find that it is extremely hard to use contiguous gadgets that are in the same routine.

ROP malicious code is the derivation of shellcode and bases on the traditional shellcode to construct gadgets. We analyze all 247 shellcodes from [5] and find that 212 of them invoke system call at least once. However, to evade the IDs detecting mechanisms, other shellcodes encrypt or self-modify payloads and do not use "$int\ 0 \times 80$" directly to avoid containing sensitive data (e.g., cd 80). But anyway they will invoke system call at runtime to get higher privilege. [2] invokes _kernel_vsyscall function that uses sysenter instruction to transfer the control flow from user mode running at privilege level 3 to operating system. However, sysenter instruction provides a fast entry to the kernel and also can be considered as another kind of system call.

We consider the (i) small gadget size, (ii) the execution of system call and (iii) contiguous candidate gadgets are not in the same routine as the ROP attack's most representative characteristics. Based on these three differences between ROP malicious code and normal programs, we develop a tool named ROP-Hunt, which dynamically detects ROP attack by checking whether the execution trace deviates from the normal execution route. We will show the design of ROP-Hunt in the next section.

4   ROP-Hunt Design and Implementation

Based on the features of ROP attack, we propose our approach to efficiently detect ROP attacks. Since we assume no access to source code, we make use of instrumentation technique that allows to add extra code to a program to observe and debug the program's behavior [29].

4.1   Assumptions and Definitions

In this paper, we define the number of instructions in a gadget as G_size. Candidate gadget refers to the gadget that G_size is greater than the threshold $T0$. The length of contiguous candidate gadget sequence is defined as S_length, and $Max(S\_length)$ represents the maximum values of S_length.

In order to simulate the real environment, we make the following assumptions:

1. We assume that the underlying system supports DEP [1] model that prohibits writing to executable memory. In this case, code injection based attacks are impossible. Modern processors and operating systems already enable DEP by default.

2. We assume that the attacker is able to perform a buffer overflow [19, 31, 39], a string formatting attack or a non-local jump buffer (using *setjmp* and *longjmp* [4]) to mount a ROP attack.
3. We assume that the attacker operates in the user mode and the vulnerability exploited to initiate the attack does not lead to a privilege escalation.
4. We assume that we have no access to source code.

4.2   System Overview

Figure 3 shows the flow chart of ROP-Hunt. According to the features of ROP that we have analyzed in Sect. 3, ROP-Hunt monitors the program dynamically, intercepts the system call instruction and three control flow sensitive instructions: *call*, *jmp* and *ret*. There are two categories of ROP report: *Warning* and *Attack*. *Warning* indicates that there is a serious risk that the process is under a ROP attack. Since it have not invoked a system call to visit the underlying system sources, we believe that it is not ready to do any meaningful attack. If the statistic values break the thresholds and a system call is being invoked, ROP-Hunt will kill the process appending with an *Attack* report.

- *Report Warning:* When ROP-Hunt recognizes these three instructions (call, indirect jump and return), it checks whether the length of instruction sequence is greater than $T0$. If not, it extracts the target address and the current instruction address. Especially for *ret* instruction, the target address will be popped from the stack. Then ROP-Hunt checks whether the two addresses locate in the same routine. If not, we record the instruction sequence as a candidate gadget. Next, we count the maximum length of contiguous candidate gadgets S_length. If S_length is less than or equal to $T1$, we will set the potential attack flag to *True* and raise a *Warning*.
- *Report Attack:* System call is the only way to transfer the flow of control from user space to kernel space. When a system call instruction is recognized, ROP-Hunt checks whether the potential attack flag is *True*. If the condition is satisfied, ROP-Hunt will report an *Attack* and terminate the process.

4.3   Implementation Details

To demonstrate the effectiveness and evaluate the performance of our approach, we have developed a prototype implementation for the ×86 32-bit version of Ubuntu 14.04 with kernel 3.19. For our prototype, ROP-Hunt, we used the binary instrumentation framework Pin [28] (version 2.14).

We incorporated ROP-Hunt directly into the Pin Framework. Pin is a tool for the instrumentation of programs and instruments all instructions that are actually executed. There are two kinds of working mode in Pin, probe mode and just-in-time (JIT) mode. In JIT mode, Pin can intercept each instruction before it is executed by the processor, even if the instruction was not intended by the programmer.

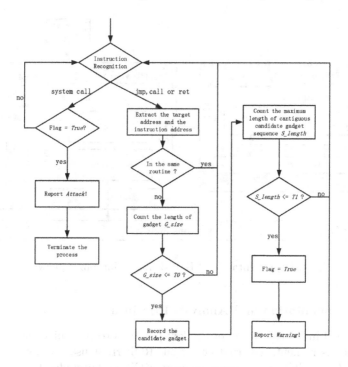

Fig. 3. Work flow of ROP-Hunt

To instrument a binary at runtime, we have to determine where code is inserted and what code to execute at insertion points. Pin provides instrumentation tools which are called Pintools. Pintools are written in the C/C++ programming language using Pin's rich API and allow to specify your own instrumentation code. We designed and implemented our own Pintool to detect ROP attacks in the Pin framework.

The overall architecture of the runtime system is depicted in Fig. 4. Our architecture consists of the Pin Framework and the Pintool ROP-Hunt. Pin is the engine that jits and instruments the program binary. Pin itself consists of a virtual machine (VM), a code cache, and instrumentation APIs invoked by Pintools. The VM consists of a JIT compiler, an emulator and a dispatcher. When a program is started, the JIT compiles and instruments instructions, which are then launched by the dispatcher. The compiled instructions are stored in the code cache in order to reduce performance overhead if code pieces are invoked multiple times. The emulator interprets instructions that cannot be executed directly.

Our Pintool, ROP-Hunt, consists of a record unit and a detection unit which contains instrumentation routines and analysis routines. The detection unit leverages instrumentation APIs to communicate with Pin and the record unit just stores the statistic values at runtime.

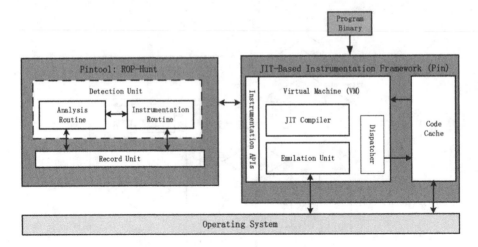

Fig. 4. Implementation of ROP-Hunt within pin framework

4.4   Instrumentation and Analysis Routines

As mentioned in Sect. 4.1, one of the key points is to recognize the instruction types. The instrumentation routines of our ROP-Hunt use the inspection functions *INS_IsSyscall(INS ins)*, *INS_IsSysenter(INS ins)* provided by the Pin APIs to determine whether the current instruction is a system call or a system enter, and use *INS_IsIndirectBranchOrCall(INS ins)* to determine whether the current instruction is a branch instruction. If the current instruction is an indirect jump, call or return instruction, then we invoke an analysis function that extracts the addresses of both the current instruction and the target.

POP-Hunt assigns each routine an ID. The ID is globally unique, i.e., an ID will not appear in two images. If the same routine name exists in two different images (i.e., they are in different addresses), each will have a different ID. If an image is unloaded and then reloaded, the routines within it will most likely have different IDs than before. ROP-Hunt leverages the function *PIN_InitSymbols()* to initialize the symbol table and read symbols from the binary. Since then, we can get the routine ID by the address.

The record unit allocates data space to each thread respectively. We use the thread local storage (TLS) from the Pin APIs to avoid that one thread accesses the record of another thread.

5   Parameter Selections

We have to determine the thresholds of the two factors which represent the features of ROP: the number of instructions in the gadget (*G_size*), the length of contiguous candidate gadget sequence (*S_length*).

The gadget size threshold (*T0*) affects the detection accuracy. Bigger threshold generally incurs higher false positive. To find *T0*, we used two well-know

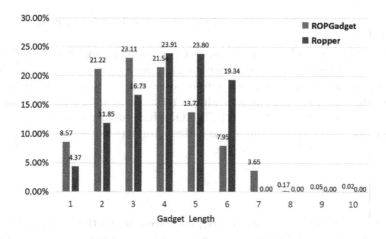

Fig. 5. The size of gadget measurement results

gadget search tools, ROPGadget [8] and Ropper [9], to measure the sizes of gadgets from many normal applications, which include 22 popular Linux tools (e.g., ls, grep, and find) under directory /bin and /usr/bin, and 3 large binaries (Apache web server httpd 2.4.20, mysql 5.6 and python 2.7). We collected 282341 gadgets totally, 125605 from ROPGadget and 156736 from Ropper. As shown in Fig. 5, the largest gadget size is 10 and nearly all gadgets size is less than 8. In the gadget set generated by Ropper, the largest size is 6. We also measured the ROP malicious code collected from the real world ROP attacks, and no gadget size is greater than 6. Based on the above results, we can safely choose 7 as the gadget size threshold ($T0$). If the length of an instruction sequence is not greater than 7, it will be treated as a candidate gadget by ROP-Hunt.

In ROP attack, the attacker chains a few gadgets together to complete an intended operation. To construct a system call operation, the attacker has to use at least 3 gadgets to place the correct parameters in the argument registers and jump to the system call entry. We believe an attacker can not do any meaningful attacks by just using 3 or less gadgets. So we set the $T1$ to 3, that is to say, ROP-Hunt checks whether there are more than 3 contiguous gadgets.

6   Delay Gadget

ROP-Hunt is effective under the assumption that usable gadgets are short allowing us to distinguish attacks from normal programs. However, smart attackers may be able to tolerate some of the side-effects in a long gadget and use it in the middle of the attack to evade the detection. Mehmet Kyaalp et al. [25] introduced delay gadget that was long enough to reset the gadget counter used by the signature detector. They made a call to a function that resulted in executing a larger number of instructions. By convention, when a function returns, many registers such as *ebx*, *esi*, *edi*, *esp*, and *ebp* are saved. That is to say, delay gadget can reduce side-effect greatly.

The purpose of a delay gadget is to avoid detection by signature-based detectors. It neither executes any part of the attack code or corrupts the machine state needed by the attack. It is impossible to conduct ROP attack only by delay gadgets. So when the previous gadget ending with a call invokes a function and the gadgets is longer than the threshold *T0*, ROP-Hunt just ignores this gadget and does not reset the counter. But if the gadget size does not break the threshold *T0*, the counter is still added by one.

7   Evaluation

In this section, we evaluated the security effectiveness and the performance overhead of ROP-Hunt. All experiments were performed on a computer with the following specifications: Intel Core i3 2370M CPU, 4 GB RAM, 32-bit Ubuntu with kernel version 3.19. For the security evaluation, we verify our approach with two real-world ROP attacks and a small program that has a simple stack buffer overflow triggered by a long input parameter. For the performance evaluation, we used 18 C and C++ SPEC CPU2006 [10] benchmarks for our experiments. The benchmarks were compiled using gcc-4.8.3 compiler.

7.1   Security Evaluation

In the first test, we evaluated the effectiveness of ROP-Hunt using two realistic programs: Hex-editer (2.0.20) and PHP (5.3.6). These two templates of ROP malicious code are available on the websites [6,7]. In the vulnerability exploitation of PHP, we inputted a long path name for a UNIX socket to trigger the buffer overflow and then transferred the control flow to the ROP payload. The ROP payload had 31 contiguous gadgets and the largest gadget contained 7 instructions (did not break the threshold *T0*). Therefore, ROP-Hunt raised a *Warning* and set the potential attack flag to *True*. The last gadget in the contiguous gadgets sequence invoked a system call to execute /bin/sh immediately. Hence, ROP-Hunt reported an *Attack* and terminated the process.

To further assess ROP-Hunt detection capabilities, we used a simple target program that had a *strcpy* vulnerability (demonstrated in [31]). The program were compiled by gcc-4.8.4 and linked with glibc-2.3.5. We used ROPGadget [8] to analyze the program and generate usable gadgets. We manually chained candidate gadgets together to rewrite 30 representative shellcode from the Shell-Storm Linux shellcode repository [5]. These shellcodes were composed of combinational gadgets which ending with *ret*, *jmp* or *call* instructions. Gadgets longer than 7 instructions were extremely difficult to incorporate due to side effects. The most simple attack required 4 gadgets (greater than *T1*). As we have analyzed in Sect. 3, all shellcodes used system calls to complete attacks. The experimental result showed that ROP-Hunt could detect all these ROP attacks without false positive.

7.2   Performance Overhead

We chose the benchmark tool SPEC CPU2006 benchmark suite [10] to measure the performance of ROP-Hunt. Specifically, we ran the testing suits with and without ROP-Hunt. The results are illustrated in Fig. 6, which shows that applications under protection of ROP-Hunt run on average 1.75×. The slowdown for benchmarks ranges from 1.05× to 2.41×. We compared ROP-Hunt with other ROP detectors based on instrumentation technique. According to the results in [17,21], applications running under ROPdefender and DROP are 2.17× and 5.3×. [18] causes an average slowdown of 3.5×.

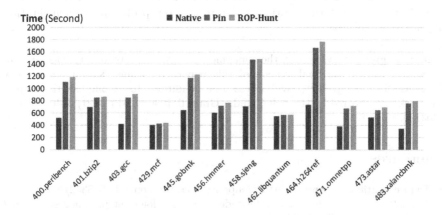

Fig. 6. SPEC CPU2006 benchmark results

The result shows that the Pin framework itself also induces an average slowdown of 1.66×. We believe the performance of ROP-Hunt will be continuously improved with the optimization of Pin Framework.

8   Discussion

We design and implement ROP-Hunt to detect ROP attacks at runtime, and currently ROP-Hunt is based on dynamic binary instrumentation tool Pin. Although ROP-Hunt is effective detecting ROP attacks, there are some limitations. First, ROP-Hunt only detects ROP malicious code on ×86 architecture. However, malicious code can be rewritten on other architectures by ROP technique. We believe that our approach can be deployed to other architectures. Second, ROP-Hunt detects ROP attack with the assumption that all ROP malicious codes meet the thresholds discussed in Sect. 5. Although it is extremely hard, there is a theoretical possibility that some ROP attacks may break this assumption. Finally, ROP-Hunt is implemented by using the jit-based binary instrumentation framework Pin and causes an average slowdown of 1.75×. The performance overhead may be unacceptable for some time-critical applications.

9   Conclusions

ROP is a very powerful exploitation technique used to bypass current security mechanisms. In this paper, we studied and extracted the features of the ROP malicious code. Based on the identification of distinctive attributes of ROP malicious code that are inherently exhibited during execution, we proposed a novel and practical approach for protecting against ROP attack without requiring access to source code. The experimental results showed that our prototype, ROP-Hunt, successfully detects all ROP attacks with no false positive. ROP-Hunt leverages instrumentation technique and adds a runtime overhead of 1.75× which is comparable to similar instrumentation-based ROP detection tools. As part of our future work, we plan to port our prototype implementation to other architectures.

Acknowledgments. We thank the anonymous reviewers for their constructive comments that guided the final version of this paper. We thank National University of Defense Technology for providing essential conditions to accomplish this paper. This work is supported by the NSFC under Grant 61103015, 61303191, 61402504 and 61303190.

References

1. Data execution prevention. http://support.microsoft.com/kb/875352/EN-US
2. Linux/×86 - /bin/sh sysenter Opcode Array Payload. http://shell-storm.org/shellcode/files/shellcode-236.php
3. Linux/×86 - sys exit(0). http://shell-storm.org/shellcode/files/shellcode-623.php
4. Setjmp - set jump point for a non-local goto. http://pubs.opengroup.org/onlinepubs/009695399/functions/setjmp.html
5. Shellcodes database for study cases. http://shell-storm.org/shellcode/
6. HT Editor 2.0.20 Buffer Overflow (ROP PoC). http://www.exploit-db.com/exploits/22683/
7. PHP 5.3.6 Buffer Overflow PoC. http://www.exploit-db.com/exploits/17486
8. ROPgadget - Gadgets finder and auto-roper. http://shell-storm.org/project/ROPgadget/
9. ROPPER - ROP GADGET FINDER AND BINARY INFORMATION TOOL. https://scoding.de/ropper/
10. Standard Performance Evaluation Corporation, SPEC CPU2006 Benchmarks. http://www.spec.org/osg/cpu2006/
11. Bletsch, T., Jiang, X., Freeh, V.: Mitigating code-reuse attacks with control-flow locking. In: Proceedings of the 27th Annual Computer Security Applications Conference, pp. 353–362. ACM (2011)
12. Bletsch, T., Jiang, X., Freeh, V.W., Liang, Z.: Jump-oriented programming: a new class of code-reuse attack. In: Proceedings of the 6th ACM Symposium on Information, Computer and Communications Security, pp. 30–40. ACM (2011)
13. Buchanan, E., Roemer, R., Shacham, H., Savage, S.: When good instructions go bad: generalizing return-oriented programming to risc. In: Proceedings of the 15th ACM Conference on Computer and Communications Security, pp. 27–38. ACM (2008)

14. Carlini, N., Wagner, D.: ROP is still dangerous: breaking modern defenses. In: 23rd USENIX Security Symposium (USENIX Security 2014), pp. 385–399 (2014)
15. Checkoway, S., Davi, L., Dmitrienko, A., Sadeghi, A.R., Shacham, H., Winandy, M.: Return-oriented programming without returns. In: Proceedings of the 17th ACM Conference on Computer and Communications Security, pp. 559–572. ACM (2010)
16. Checkoway, S., Feldman, A.J., Kantor, B., Halderman, J.A., Felten, E.W., Shacham, H.: Can DREs provide long-lasting security? The case of return-oriented programming and the AVC advantage. In: EVT/WOTE 2009 (2009)
17. Chen, P., Xiao, H., Shen, X., Yin, X., Mao, B., Xie, L.: DROP: detecting return-oriented programming malicious code. In: Prakash, A., Sen Gupta, I. (eds.) ICISS 2009. LNCS, vol. 5905, pp. 163–177. Springer, Heidelberg (2009). doi:10.1007/978-3-642-10772-6_13
18. Chen, P., Xing, X., Han, H., Mao, B., Xie, L.: Efficient detection of the return-oriented programming malicious code. In: Jha, S., Mathuria, A. (eds.) ICISS 2010. LNCS, vol. 6503, pp. 140–155. Springer, Heidelberg (2010). doi:10.1007/978-3-642-17714-9_11
19. Chen, S., Li, Z., Huang, Y., Xing, J.: Sat-based technique to detect buffer overflows in c source codes. J. Tsinghua Univ. (Science and Technology), S2 (2009)
20. Davi, L., Sadeghi, A.R., Winandy, M.: Dynamic integrity measurement and attestation: towards defense against return-oriented programming attacks. In: Proceedings of the 2009 ACM Workshop on Scalable Trusted Computing, pp. 49–54. ACM (2009)
21. Davi, L., Sadeghi, A.R., Winandy, M.: Ropdefender: adetection tool to defend against return-oriented programming attacks. In: Proceedings of the 6th ACM Symposium on Information, Computer and Communications Security, pp. 40–51. ACM (2011)
22. Dullien, T., Kornau, T., Weinmann, R.P.: A framework for automated architecture-independent gadget search. In: WOOT (2010)
23. Francillon, A., Castelluccia, C.: Code injection attacks on Harvard-architecture devices. In: Proceedings of the 15th ACM Conference on Computer and Communications Security, pp. 15–26. ACM (2008)
24. Hund, R., Holz, T., Freiling, F.C.: Return-oriented rootkits: bypassing kernel code integrity protection mechanisms. In: USENIX Security Symposium, pp. 383–398 (2009)
25. Kayaalp, M., Schmitt, T., Nomani, J., Ponomarev, D., Abu-Ghazaleh, N.: SCRAP: architecture for signature-based protection from code reuse attacks. In: 2013 IEEE 19th International Symposium on High Performance Computer Architecture (HPCA2013), pp. 258–269. IEEE (2013)
26. Kornau, T.: Return oriented programming for the ARM architecture. Ph.D. thesis, Masters thesis, Ruhr-Universität Bochum (2010)
27. Li, J., Wang, Z., Jiang, X., Grace, M., Bahram, S.: Defeating return-oriented rootkits with return-less kernels. In: Proceedings of the 5th European Conference on Computer Systems, pp. 195–208. ACM (2010)
28. Luk, C.K., Cohn, R., Muth, R., Patil, H., Klauser, A., Lowney, G., Wallace, S., Reddi, V.J., Hazelwood, K.: Pin: building customized program analysis tools with dynamic instrumentation. In: ACM Sigplan Notices, vol. 40, pp. 190–200. ACM (2005)
29. Nethercote, N.: Dynamic binary analysis and instrumentation (2004). http://valgrind.org/docs/phd2004.pdf

30. Onarlioglu, K., Bilge, L., Lanzi, A., Balzarotti, D., Kirda, E.: G-free: defeating return-oriented programming through gadget-less binaries. In: Proceedings of the 26th Annual Computer Security Applications Conference, pp. 49–58. ACM (2010)
31. One, A.: Smashing the stack for fun and profit. Phrack Mag. **7**(49), 14–16 (1996)
32. Pappas, V., Polychronakis, M., Keromytis, A.D.: Transparent ROP exploit mitigation using indirect branch tracing. In: Presented as Part of the 22nd USENIX Security Symposium (USENIX Security 2013), pp. 447–462 (2013)
33. Roemer, R.G.: Finding the bad in good code: automated return-oriented programming exploit discovery (2009)
34. Schwartz, E.J., Avgerinos, T., Brumley, D.: Q: Exploit hardening made easy. In: USENIX Security Symposium, pp. 25–41 (2011)
35. Shacham, H.: The geometry of innocent flesh on the bone: return-into-libc without function calls (on the $\times 86$). In: Proceedings of the 14th ACM Conference on Computer and Communications Security, pp. 552–561. ACM (2007)
36. Tran, M., Etheridge, M., Bletsch, T., Jiang, X., Freeh, V., Ning, P.: On the expressiveness of return-into-libc attacks. In: Sommer, R., Balzarotti, D., Maier, G. (eds.) RAID 2011. LNCS, vol. 6961, pp. 121–141. Springer, Heidelberg (2011). doi:10.1007/978-3-642-23644-0_7
37. Wojtczuk, R.: The advanced return-into-lib(c) exploits: PaX case study. Phrack Mag. **0x0b**(0x3a), Phile# 0x04 of 0x0e (2001)
38. Yao, F., Chen, J., Venkataramani, G.: Jop-alarm: detecting jump-oriented programming-based anomalies in applications. In: 2013 IEEE 31st International Conference on Computer Design (ICCD), pp. 467–470. IEEE (2013)
39. Zhang, M., Luo, J.: Pointer analysis algorithm in static buffer overflow analysis. Comput. Eng. **31**(18), 41–43 (2005)

On the Security of a Threshold Anonymous Authentication Protocol for VANETs

Jianhong Zhang[1]($\boxtimes$), Zhibin Sun[1], Shuai Liu[1], and Pengyan Liu[2]

[1] College of Sciences, North China University of Technology, Beijing 100144, China
jhzhangs@163.com
[2] Institute of Image Process and Pattern Recognition,
North China University of Technology, Beijing 100144, China
pengyanli@mail.edu.cn

Abstract. VANETs is a promising mobile ad hoc networks, it can significantly improve the traffic safety and efficiency. But it also raises some formidable challenges, where security assurance and privacy protection are two primary concerns. Without the security and privacy guarantees, attackers could track their interested vehicles by collecting and analyzing their traffic messages. Hence, anonymous message authentication is an essential requirement of VANETs. Recently, Shao *et al.* proposed a new threshold anonymous authentication protocol, and they claim that these protocol can achieve identity tracing of a malicious vehicle. Unfortunately, in this letter, we demonstrate that the protocol cannot satisfy traceability. A malicious vehicle is able to arbitrarily send the false without being traced by the group tracer in their scheme. Finally, we analyze the reason to produce and give the corresponding advise to fix this flaw.

Keywords: Anonymous authentication · Traceability · Security analysis · Group signature · VANETs

1 Introduction

As an intelligent transportation system, vehicular ad hoc networks (VANETs) [1] is a new-style mobile ad hoc networks. It is envisioned that each vehicle is equipped with wireless communication devices, called on-board units (OBUs), which allows vehicles to communicate with each other as well as with roadside units (RSUs) located at roadside or street intersection. Thus, VANET can be classified into two types: vehicle-to-infrastructure (V2I) communication or inter-vehicle (V2V) communication.

In VANET, each vehicle with OBUs periodically broadcasts information on their present states (e.g., the current time, position, direction, speed and traffic events) to other nearby vehicles and RSUs [2,11,13]. By this way, VANETs can collect traffic and road information from vehicles, and deliver road services including warnings and traffic information to users in the vehicles. The aim of VANET is to improve the road safety and avoid potential traffic accidents. It

© Springer International Publishing AG 2016
G. Wang et al. (Eds.): SpaCCS 2016, LNCS 10066, pp. 145–155, 2016.
DOI: 10.1007/978-3-319-49148-6_13

has also been envisioned to improve driving experiences by providing Internet services to the drivers and passengers and supporting possible e-commerce activities. However, VANETs is a double-edged sword, it can provide securer and more comfortable driving condition for drivers, at the same time, it also raises many security and privacy questions. Malicious cars can take advantage of VANET to disturb the whole system. For example, a compromised vehicle that forges messages to masquerade as an emergency vehicle could mislead other vehicles to pull over, or slow down; a tampered vehicle who masquerades as an RSU could mislead other vehicles to a particular location and cause traffic jam there. And the adversary in VANET can track the locations of the interested vehicles by collecting their routine traffic messages. Therefore, anonymous authentication becomes the fundamental technique for realizing the security of VANETs.

To ensure the security of VANETs and privacy of vehicles, many research efforts have recently been dedicated to design anonymous authentication for VANETs in [3–5,8–10,12]. According to the way of privacy-preserving, these schemes are divided into two types:pseudonymous certificate based schemes and group signature based schemes. In the pseudonymous certificate-based schemes, each vehicle is preloaded with a large number of anonymous public/private key pairs and the corresponding public key certificates. It makes that each vehicle needs a large storage capacity to save these key pairs and the corresponding certificates, and also incurs the high cost of message verification. To trace the identity of vehicle, the authority also needs to store all anonymous certificates of vehicles, which causes inefficiency for certificate management and is expensive for deployment. To overcome aforementioned problem, group signature-based anonymous authentication schemes [6,7,14] were proposed, In this type scheme, only a group public key and a private key are stored in the vehicle. And group public key is the same for all vehicles, and each vehicle's private key is different. Despite decreasing the overhead of pre-loading a large number of anonymous key materials in each vehicle, this type scheme increases a large computational cost through its requirement to maintain a certificate revocation list. In addition, to trace a malicious message, the authority has to exhaustedly look for in a huge database to find the real identity related with the compromised anonymous public key.

To increase traceability efficiency in the group signature-based anonymous authentication, recently, Shao et al.'s proposed a new conditional anonymous authentication scheme [1] by using a new group signature. And they shows that their scheme can realize conditional anonymity and the identity trace of the signer. Unfortunately, in this work, we show that their scheme cannot provide the traceability. This is to say, when a malicious vehicle sends a false message, the actual identity of the malicious vehicle cannot be revealed. Finally, we give the corresponding attack and indicates the reason to produce such attack.

2   Reviews of Shao et al.'s Threshold Anonymous Authentication Protocol for VANETs

Recently, to deal with distinguishability of message origin and traceability of malicious vehicle, Shao et al.'s proposed a novel anonymous authentication protocol for VANETs by using a new group signature scheme. It achieves traceability of malicious vehicle by including a group tracer. In the following, we briefly review Shao et al.'s new group signature scheme by using the same notation as [1], please the interested readers refer to [1] for detail.

2.1   Setup

Let $(\mathbb{G}_1, \mathbb{G}_2, \mathbb{G}_3, q, g_1, g_2, \tilde{g}_1, e, H_1, H_2)$ be system parameters, where $\mathbb{G}_1, \mathbb{G}_2, \mathbb{G}_3$ are three multiplicative cyclic groups with the same prime order q, $e : \mathbb{G}_1 \times \mathbb{G}_2 \to \mathbb{G}_3$ is a bilinear map, g_1 and g_2 are two generators of group $\mathbb{G}_1$, $\tilde{g}_1 \in \mathbb{G}_2$ is a generator of group $\mathbb{G}_2$, $H_1 : \{0,1\}^* \to \mathbb{G}_1$ is a hash function, and $H_2 : \{0,1\}^* \to Z_q$ is also a secure hash function. To simple representation, we use symbol "~" to denote the elements in $\mathbb{G}_2$.

The group manager randomly chooses $x_{gm1}, x_{gm2} \in Z_q^*$ to compute $y_{gm} = g_1^{x_{gm1}}$, $\tilde{y}_{gm1} = \tilde{g}_1^{x_{gm1}}$ and $\tilde{y}_{gm2} = \tilde{g}_1^{x_{gm2}}$. And it sets (x_{gm1}, x_{gm2}) as its private key, $(y_{gm}, \tilde{y}_{gm1}, \tilde{y}_{gm2})$ as the corresponding public key.

For the group tracer, it randomly chooses $r_{gt}, x_{gt1} \in Z_q^*$ to compute $\tilde{g}_2 = \tilde{g}_1^{r_{gt}}$ and $\tilde{y}_{gt} = \tilde{g}_1^{x_{gt1}} (= \tilde{g}_2^{x_{gt2}})$ where $x_{gt2} = x_{gt1}/r_{gt}$. Finally, the group tracer sets (x_{gt1}, x_{gt2}) and $(\tilde{g}_2, \tilde{y}_{gt})$ as its private key and public key, respectively.

For each group member, it chooses a random number $x_{mem} \in Z_q$ to compute $y_{mem} = g_1^{x_{mem}}$. Group member sets (x_{mem}, y_{mem}) as its public-private key pair.

2.2   CertGen

To join the group, a group member sends its public key y_{mem} to group manager, the group manager produces its group certificate (c_1, c_2) for this group member by using its private key (x_{gm1}, x_{gm2}).

$$c_1 = g_2^{x_{gm2}} \cdot (y_{mem}^{x_{gm1}})^{-r}, c_2 = g_1^r$$

where $r \in Z_q$ is a random number. Note that group certificate (c_1, c_2) should be kept secretely.

2.3   Sign

Given a message m, to produce a group signature on message m, the group member utilizes its private key x_{men} and its group certificate (c_1, c_2) to execute the following values:

$$\sigma_1 = c_1 \cdot (y_{gm}^{x_{mem}})^{-r'}, \quad \sigma_2 = c_2 \cdot g_1^{r'}$$

$$\sigma_3 = \tilde{g}_1^{\alpha}, \quad \tilde{\sigma}_4 = \tilde{g}_2^{\beta}$$

$$\tilde{\sigma}_5 = \tilde{g}_1^{x_{mem}} \cdot \tilde{y}_{gt}^{\alpha+\beta}, \quad \sigma_6 = \sigma_2^{x_{mem}}$$

$$\sigma_7 = \sigma_2^{\alpha}, \quad \sigma_8 = \sigma_2^{\beta}$$

$$\sigma_9 = H_1(m)^{x_{mem}},$$

$$\sigma_{10} = H_2(m||\sigma_1||\cdots||\sigma_9||\sigma_2^s||H_1(m)^s)$$

$$\sigma_{11} = s - \sigma_{10} \cdot x_{mem} \mod q$$

where r', α, β, s are random elements from Z_q. The resultant group signature is $(\sigma_1, \sigma_2, \tilde{\sigma}_3, \tilde{\sigma}_4, \tilde{\sigma}_5, \sigma_6, \sigma_7, \sigma_8, \sigma_9, \sigma_{10}, \sigma_{11})$.

2.4   Verify

Given a signature $(\sigma_1, \sigma_2, \tilde{\sigma}_3, \tilde{\sigma}_4, \tilde{\sigma}_5, \sigma_6, \sigma_7, \sigma_8, \sigma_9, \sigma_{10}, \sigma_{11})$ on message m, a verifier can use the public key $(y_g, \tilde{y}_{gm1}, \tilde{y}_{gm2})$ of group manager and the public key $\tilde{y}_{gt}$ of the group tracer to execute the following verification.

$$e(\sigma_1, \tilde{g}_1)e(\sigma_6, \tilde{y}_{gm1}) \overset{?}{=} e(g_2, \tilde{y}_{gm2}) \tag{1}$$

$$e(\sigma_2, \tilde{\sigma}_3) \overset{?}{=} e(\sigma_7, \tilde{g}_1), e(\sigma_2, \tilde{\sigma}_4) \overset{?}{=} e(\sigma_8, \tilde{g}_2)$$

$$e(\sigma_2, \tilde{\sigma}_5) \overset{?}{=} e(\sigma_6, \tilde{g}_1) \cdot e(\sigma_7 \cdot \sigma_8, \tilde{y}_{gt})$$

$$\sigma_{10} \overset{?}{=} H_2(m||\sigma_1|| \cdots ||\sigma_9||\sigma_2^{\sigma_{11}} \sigma_6^{\sigma_{10}}||H_1(m)^{\sigma_{11}} \sigma_9^{\sigma_{11}})$$

If all the above equations hold, then the signature is accepted; otherwise, it is rejected.

2.5   Open

If a signature $\sigma = (\sigma_1, \sigma_2, \tilde{\sigma}_3, \tilde{\sigma}_4, \tilde{\sigma}_5, \sigma_6, \sigma_7, \sigma_8, \sigma_9, \sigma_{10}, \sigma_{11})$ appears to dispute, group tracer can trace the actual identity of the signature's signer by the following steps:

1. First, it verifies the validity of signature σ.
2. Then, it computes $\tilde{g}_1^{x_{mem}} = \tilde{\sigma}_5/(\tilde{\sigma}_3^{x_{gt1}} \cdot \tilde{\sigma}_4^{x_{gt2}})$;
3. Finally, group tracer can trace the actual identity of signer by $\tilde{g}_1^{x_{mem}}$.

3   Cryptanalysis of Shao et al.'s Scheme

In this section, we give an attack on Shao et al.'s group signature. We show that any malicious group member can sign false message m and its identity can not be traced. It means that Shao et al.'s anonymous authentication for VANETs doesn't satisfy traceability since Shao et al.'s group signature is building block of its anonymous authentication protocol.

In the following, we give the corresponding attack. Let A be a malicious group member, supposed that its public-private key pair is $(x_{memA}, y_{memA} = g_1^{x_{memA}})$, its group certificate is (c_{1A}, c_{2A}), where $c_{1A} = g_2^{x_{gm2}}(y_{memA}^{x_{gm1}})^{-r}, c_{2A} = g_1^r$. Note that this malicious group member can forge a valid group signature by revising his private key, however, it honestly abides by the signing process in the forging phase.

In the open phase, group tracer traces the identity of group member by obtaining $\tilde{g}_1^{x_{mem}}$. As a result, to resist traceability of group tracer, the malicious group member A randomly chooses a number $k \in Z_q$ to blind $\tilde{g}_1^{x_{mem}}$ into

$(\tilde{g}_1^{x_{mem}})^k$. Therefore, it sets $x^*_{memA} = x_{memA}k$ and $y^*_{memA} = y^k_{memA}$ as its private key and public key. At the same time, the malicious group member with new public-private pair (x^*_{memA}, y^*_{memA}) computes its new group certificate as follows:

1. First, it lets

$$c^*_{1A} = c_{1A}$$
$$= g_2^{x_{gm2}} \cdot ((y^*_{memA})^{x_{gm1}})^{-rk^{-1}} \tag{2}$$

2. Then, it computes

$$c^*_{2A} = c_{2A}^{k^{-1}} = g_1^{rk^{-1}} \tag{3}$$

Let $r' = rk^{-1}$, then (c^*_{1A}, c^*_{2A}) can be represented as the form $c^*_{1A} = g_2^{x_{gm2}} \cdot ((y^*_{memA})^{x_{gm1}})^{r'}$ and $c^*_{2A} = g_1^{r'}$. Even though r' is unknown to the malicious group member A, it can compute new group certificate (c^*_{1A}, c^*_{2A}) by given group certificate (c_{1A}, c_{2A}). Note that (x^*_{memA}, y^*_{memA}) is the forged public-private key pair of the malicious group member A.

Let M be an arbitrary signed message, to produce a group signature, the malicious group member A uses its forged public-private pair (x^*_{memA}, y^*_{memA}) and its new group certificate (c^*_{1A}, c^*_{2A}) to compute as follows:

$$\sigma_1^* = c_1 \cdot (y_{gm}^{x^*_{memA}})^{-d}, \ \sigma_2^* = c^*_{2A} \cdot g_1^d$$
$$\sigma_3^* = \tilde{g}_1^\alpha, \ \tilde{\sigma}_4^* = \tilde{g}_2^\beta$$
$$\tilde{\sigma}_5^* = \tilde{g}_1^{x^*_{memA}} \cdot \tilde{y}_{gt}^{\alpha+\beta}, \ \sigma_6^* = \sigma_2^{* x^*_{memA}}$$
$$\sigma_7^* = \sigma_2^{*\alpha}, \ \sigma_8^* = \sigma_2^{*\beta}$$
$$\sigma_9^* = H_1(m)^{x^*_{memA}},$$
$$\sigma_{10}^* = H_2(M||\sigma_1^*||\cdots||\sigma_9^*||\sigma_2^{*s}||H_1(M)^s)$$
$$\sigma_{11}^* = s - \sigma_{10}^* \cdot x^*_{memA} \ \mod q$$

where d, α, β, s are random elements from Z_q. The resultant group signature on message M is $\sigma^* = (\sigma_1^*, \sigma_2^*, \tilde{\sigma}_3^*, \tilde{\sigma}_4^*, \tilde{\sigma}_5^*, \sigma_6^*, \sigma_7^*, \sigma_8^*, \sigma_9^*, \sigma_{10}^*, \sigma_{11}^*)$.

In the whole forgery process, the malicious group member A strictly follows the signing algorithm by its new group certificate (c^*_{1A}, c^*_{2A}) and its new public-private pair (x^*_{memA}, y^*_{memA}).

For group signature σ^*, it can pass all verification equations since

$$e(\sigma_1^*, \tilde{g}_1)e(\sigma_6^*, \tilde{y}_{gm1})$$
$$= e(g_2^{x_{gm2}} \cdot (y^*_{memA}{}^{x_{gm1}})^{-r'-d}, \tilde{g}_1) \cdot e(\sigma_2^*, \tilde{g}_1^{x_{gm1}})$$
$$= e(g_2^{x_{gm2}}, \tilde{g}_1)e(g_1^{x^*_{memA}x_{gm1}(-r'-d)}, \tilde{g}_1)$$
$$\cdot e(g_1^{x^*_{memA}(d+r')}, \tilde{g}_1^{x_{gm1}})$$
$$= e(g_2^{x_{gm2}}, \tilde{g}_1)$$

$$e(\sigma_2^*, \tilde{\sigma}_3) = e(\sigma_2^*, \tilde{g}^\alpha) = e(\sigma_2^{*\alpha}, \tilde{g}_1) = e(\sigma_7^*, \tilde{g}_1)$$
$$e(\sigma_2^*, \tilde{\sigma}_4) = e(\sigma_2^*, \tilde{g}^\beta) = e(\sigma_2^{*\beta}, \tilde{g}_1) = e(\sigma_8^*, \tilde{g}_1)$$

$$e(\sigma_2^*, \tilde{\sigma}_5) = e(\sigma_2^*, \tilde{g}_1^{x_{memA}^*} \cdot \tilde{y}_{gt}^{\alpha+\beta})$$
$$= e(\sigma_2^*, \tilde{g}_1^{x_{memA}^*}) \cdot e(\sigma_2^*, \tilde{y}_{gt}^{\alpha+\beta})$$
$$= e(\sigma_2^{*x_{memA}^*}, \tilde{g}_1) \cdot e(\sigma_2^{*\alpha+\beta}, \tilde{y}_{gt}) = e(\sigma_6^*, \tilde{g}_1)e(\sigma_7^*\sigma_8^*, \tilde{y}_{gt})$$

$$\sigma_2^{*s} = \sigma_2^{*\sigma_{11}^* + \sigma_{11}^* \cdot x_{memA}^*} = \sigma_2^{*\sigma_{11}^*} \cdot \sigma_6^{*\sigma_{10}^*}$$

$$H_1(M)^s = H_1(M)^{\sigma_{11}^* + \sigma_{11}^* \cdot x_{memA}^*} = H_1(M)^{\sigma_{11}^*} \cdot \sigma_9^{*\sigma_{10}^*}$$

It means that the produce group signature σ^* is valid. When group tracer wants to reveal the actual identity of the group member which produces group signature σ^*, it computes

$$\frac{\tilde{\sigma}_5^*}{\tilde{\sigma}_3^{x_{gt1}} \cdot \tilde{\sigma}_4^{x_{gt2}}} = \frac{\tilde{g}_1^{x_{memA}^*} \cdot \tilde{y}_{gt}^{\alpha+\beta}}{(\tilde{g}_1^\alpha)^{x_{gt1}} (\tilde{g}_2^\beta)^{x_{gt2}}}$$
$$= \tilde{g}_1^{x_{memA}^*}$$
$$= \tilde{g}_1^{k \cdot x_{memA}} = (\tilde{g}_1^{x_{memA}})^k$$

Thus, group tracer cannot reveal the actual identity of the malicious group member A which produces group signature σ^* since k is a random number and blinds the value $\tilde{g}_1^{x_{memA}}$. It means that Shao et al.'s scheme doesn't satisfy traceability.

Through the above analysis, it is known that Shao et al.'s conditional anonymous authentication scheme cannot satisfy traceability. The reason to such attack is that group certificate (c_1, c_2) of group member is malleable, any group member can produce a new group certificate (c_1', c_2') by its group certificate (c_1, c_2) and its private key x_{mem}. To resist such attack, we must ensure group certificate (c_1, c_2) to be non-malleable. Thus, we suggest including cryptographic hash function $H_3()$ to prevent the group certificate from being modified, namely, $(c_1 = g_2^{x_{gm2}} \cdot (y_{mem}^{x_{gm1}})^{-r}, c_2 = g_1^r)$ are revised into $(c_1 = g_2^{x_{gm2}} \cdot (y_{mem}^{x_{gm1}} \cdot H_3(\tilde{y}_{gt}))^{-r}, c_2 = g_1^r)$. It makes that group member cannot revise its group certificate, Therefore, our attack can be resisted.

4   The Improved Scheme

To our attack on Shao et al.'s scheme, the detail improved method is given in the following. Setup algorithm in our improved scheme is the same as that of Shao et al.'s scheme. The other algorithms are described as follows:

4.1 CertGen

In this phase, a group member first sends its public key y_{mem} to group manager, then group manager produces its group certificate (c_1, c_2, c_3) for this group member by using its private key (x_{gm1}, x_{gm2}). To resist the above attack, group certificate includes a hash function. The detail is as follows:

$$c_1 = g_2^{x_{gm2}} \cdot (y_{mem}^{x_{gm1}} \cdot H_3(\tilde{y}_{gt}))^{-r}, c_2 = g_1^r, c_3 = \tilde{g}_1^r$$

where $r \in Z_q$ is a random number. Here group certificate (c_1, c_2, c_3) should be kept secretely.

4.2 Sign

Given a message m, to produce a group signature on message m, the group member utilizes its private key x_{men} and its group certificate (c_1, c_2, c_3) to compute as follows:

$$\sigma_1 = c_1 \cdot (y_{gm}^{x_{mem}} \cdot H_3(\tilde{y}_{gt}))^{-r'}, \quad \sigma_2 = c_2 \cdot g_1^{r'}$$
$$\tilde{\sigma}_2 = c_3 \cdot \tilde{g}_1^{r'}$$
$$\sigma_3 = \tilde{g}_1^{\alpha}, \quad \tilde{\sigma}_4 = \tilde{g}_2^{\beta}$$
$$\tilde{\sigma}_5 = \tilde{g}_1^{x_{mem}} \cdot \tilde{y}_{gt}^{\alpha+\beta}, \quad \sigma_6 = \sigma_2^{x_{mem}}$$
$$\sigma_7 = \sigma_2^{\alpha}, \quad \sigma_8 = \sigma_2^{\beta}$$
$$\sigma_9 = H_1(m)^{x_{mem}},$$
$$\sigma_{10} = H_2(m||\sigma_1||\sigma_2||\tilde{\sigma}_2|| \cdots ||\sigma_9||\sigma_2^s||H_1(m)^s)$$
$$\sigma_{11} = s - \sigma_{10} \cdot x_{mem} \mod q$$

where r', α, β, s are random elements from Z_q. Then the resultant group signature is $(\sigma_1, \sigma_2, \tilde{\sigma}_2, \tilde{\sigma}_3, \tilde{\sigma}_4, \tilde{\sigma}_5, \sigma_6, \sigma_7, \sigma_8, \sigma_9, \sigma_{10}, \sigma_{11})$.

4.3 Verify

Given a group signature $(\sigma_1, \sigma_2, \tilde{\sigma}_2, \tilde{\sigma}_3, \tilde{\sigma}_4, \tilde{\sigma}_5, \sigma_6, \sigma_7, \sigma_8, \sigma_9, \sigma_{10}, \sigma_{11})$ on message m, a verifier can use the public key $(y_g, \tilde{y}_{gm1}, \tilde{y}_{gm2})$ of group manager and the public key $\tilde{y}_{gt}$ of the group tracer to execute the following verification.

$$e(\sigma_1, \tilde{g}_1)e(\sigma_6, \tilde{y}_{gm1})e(H_3(\tilde{y}_{gt}), \tilde{\sigma}_2) \overset{?}{=} e(g_2, \tilde{y}_{gm2}) \tag{4}$$
$$e(g_1, \tilde{\sigma}_2) = e(\sigma_2, \tilde{g}_1) \tag{5}$$

$$e(\sigma_2, \tilde{\sigma}_3) \overset{?}{=} e(\sigma_7, \tilde{g}_1), e(\sigma_2, \tilde{\sigma}_4) \overset{?}{=} e(\sigma_8, \tilde{g}_2)$$
$$e(\sigma_2, \tilde{\sigma}_5) \overset{?}{=} e(\sigma_6, \tilde{g}_1) \cdot e(\sigma_7 \cdot \sigma_8, \tilde{y}_{gt})$$
$$\sigma_{10} \overset{?}{=} H_2(m||\sigma_1||\sigma_2||\tilde{\sigma}_2|| \cdots ||\sigma_9||\sigma_2^{\sigma_{11}}\sigma_6^{\sigma_{10}}||H_1(m)^{\sigma_{11}}\sigma_9^{\sigma_{11}})$$

If all the above equations hold, then the group signature is accepted; otherwise, it is rejected.

4.4 Open

If a group signature $\sigma = (\sigma_1, \sigma_2, \tilde{\sigma}_2, \tilde{\sigma}_3, \tilde{\sigma}_4, \tilde{\sigma}_5, \sigma_6, \sigma_7, \sigma_8, \sigma_9, \sigma_{10}, \sigma_{11})$ appears to dispute, group tracer can trace the actual identity of the group member by the following steps:

1. First, it verifies the validity of signature σ.
2. Then, it computes $\tilde{g}_1^{x_{mem}} = \tilde{\sigma}_5/(\tilde{\sigma}_3^{x_{gt1}} \cdot \tilde{\sigma}_4^{x_{gt2}})$;
3. Finally, group tracer can trace the actual identity of signer by $\tilde{g}_1^{x_{mem}}$.

In the following, we show that our improved scheme is correct. In the verifying phase of our improved scheme, only Eqs. (4) and (5) are different from those of Shao et al.'s scheme. Then we only verify Eqs. (4) and (5).

$$
\begin{aligned}
&e(\sigma_1, \tilde{g}_1)e(\sigma_6, \tilde{y}_{gm1})e(H_3(\tilde{y}_{gt}), \tilde{\sigma}_2)\\
&= e(g_2^{x_{gm2}} \cdot (y_{mem}^{x_{gm1}} \cdot H_3(\tilde{y}_{gt}))^{-r-r'}, \tilde{g}_1) \cdot e(\sigma_2^{x_{men}}, \tilde{g}_1^{x_{gm1}})\\
&\quad \cdot e(H_3(\tilde{y}_{gt}), \tilde{g}_1^{-r-r'})\\
&= e(g_2^{x_{gm2}} \cdot (y_{mem}^{x_{gm1}} \cdot H_3(\tilde{y}_{gt}))^{-r-r'}, \tilde{g}_1) \cdot e((g_1^{r+r'})^{x_{men}}, \tilde{g}_1^{x_{gm1}})\\
&\quad \cdot e(H_3(\tilde{y}_{gt}), \tilde{g}_1^{-r-r'})\\
&= e(g_2, \tilde{y}_{gm2})
\end{aligned}
$$

$$
\begin{aligned}
e(\sigma_2, \tilde{g}_1) &= e(g_1^{r+r'}, \tilde{g}_1)\\
&= e(g_1, \tilde{g}_1^{r+r'})\\
&= e(g_1, \tilde{\sigma}_2)
\end{aligned}
$$

Obviously, our improved scheme is correct. If a group signature satisfies all verification equations, then it is a valid signature.

Theorem 1. Our improved group signature scheme satisfies unforgeability under the extended computational Diffie-Hellman assumption.

Proof. Here, we will show that if there exists an adversary $\mathcal{A}$ which could break our improved group signature scheme, then there exists another algorithm $\mathcal{B}$ can solve the extended computational Diffie-Hellman problem (eCDH) in group $\mathbb{G}_1$ and $\mathbb{G}_2$ by invoking $\mathcal{A}$. Let us recall eCDH problem, given five elements $(g_1, g_1^a, g_1^b, \tilde{g}_1, \tilde{g}_1^a)$, where $g_1 \in \mathbb{G}_1$ and $\tilde{g}_1 \in \mathbb{G}_1$, its goal is to output g_1^{ab}.

In the following, we will give the detail process.

To answer the different queries from the adversary $\mathcal{A}$, we need the challenger $\mathcal{B}$ to build the system parameters. Let $\mathbb{G}_1, \mathbb{G}_2$ and $\mathbb{G}_T$ be three cyclic groups with order p, and the eCDH problem holds in group $\mathbb{G}_1$. $e : \mathbb{G}_1 \times \mathbb{G}_2 \to \mathbb{G}_T$ is a bilinear pairing map. Let g_1, g_2 be the generators of group $\mathbb{G}_1$ and $\tilde{g}_1$ be an element of group $\mathbb{G}_2$. H_1, H_2 and H_3 are three hash functions. Finally, the challenger $\mathcal{B}$ sends the system parameters $Para = (\mathbb{G}_1, \mathbb{G}_2, e, H_3, H_1, H_2, g_1, g_2, \tilde{g}_1)$ to the adversary $\mathcal{A}$.

$\mathcal{B}$'s goal is to solve the eCDH problem, i.e. given $(g_1, g_1^a, g_1^b, \tilde{g}_1, \tilde{g}_1^a)$, $\mathcal{B}$ outputs g_1^{ab}. Therefore, $\mathcal{B}$ executes the following interaction with $\mathcal{A}$.

In SetUp phase, $\mathcal{B}$ generates all public keys of group manager and group tracer as the real execution.

Public Key Oracle. When the adversary $\mathcal{A}$ makes a query of a group member's public key, $\mathcal{B}$ randomly choose a $t_{men} \in Z_p$ to compute $y_{mem} = (g_1^a)^{t_{mem}}$ as public key of group member and return it to the adversary $\mathcal{A}$. Note that the private key of group member is $a \cdot t_{mem}$ which is unknown to $\mathcal{B}$.

H_1**−Oracle.** When the adversary $\mathcal{A}$ makes a query with message m, $\mathcal{B}$ first checks whether $(m, coin, r_1, R_1)$ exists in the H_1-list which is initially empty. It it exists, then $\mathcal{B}$ returns R_1; Otherwise, it tosses a coin with probability $Pr[coin = 1] = \zeta$ and randomly selects $r_1 \in Z_p$ to answer the following query.

1. if $coin = 0$, then $\mathcal{B}$ sets $R_1 = g_1^{r_1}$.
2. if $coin = 1$, then $\mathcal{B}$ sets $R_1 = (g_1^b)^{r_1}$.

Finally, $\mathcal{B}$ records $(m, coin, r_1, R_1)$ in the H_1-list.

H_2**−Oracle.** When an adversary makes a query with a string $m||\sigma_1||\sigma_2||\cdots$ $||\sigma_9||S_1||S_2$, $\mathcal{B}$ first checks wether $(m||\sigma_1||\sigma_2||\cdots||\sigma_9||S_1||S_2, r_2)$ exists in the H_2-list which is initially empty, if it exists, then r_2 is returned; otherwise, it randomly chooses $r_2 \in_R Z_p$ to set $r_2 = H_2(m||\sigma_1||\sigma_2||\cdots||\sigma_9||S_1||S_2)$ and returns r_2 to the adversary. At last, $(m||\sigma_1||\sigma_2||\cdots||\sigma_9||S_1||S_2, r_2)$ is recorded in the H_2-list.

CertGen Oracle. When an adversary $\mathcal{A}$ makes a query with a group member's public key y_{mem}, $\mathcal{B}$ executes as follows.

1. it randomly chooses $\hat{r}$ to compute

$$c_1 = g_2^{x_{gm2}}(y_{mem}^{y_{gm1}} \cdot H_3(\tilde{y}_{gt}))^{-\hat{r}}, c_2 = g_1^{\hat{r}}, c_3 = \tilde{g}_1^{\hat{r}}$$

2. It returns (c_1, c_2, c_3) to the adversary $\mathcal{A}$.

Signing Oracle. When an adversary $\mathcal{A}$ makes a signing query with message m and group member's public key y_{mem}, $\mathcal{B}$ randomly chooses $r, \alpha, \beta, \sigma_{10}, \sigma_{11} \in Z_p$ to compute the signature

$$\sigma_1 = g_2^{x_{gm2}}(y_{mem}^{y_{gm1}} \cdot H_3(\tilde{y}_{gt}))^{-r}, \sigma_2 = g_1^r, \tilde{\sigma}_2 = \tilde{g}_1^r$$

$$\tilde{\sigma}_3 = \tilde{g}_1^\alpha, \tilde{\sigma}_4 = \tilde{g}_1^\beta, \tilde{\sigma}_5 = (\tilde{g}_1^a)^{t_{mem}}\tilde{y}_{gt}^{\alpha+\beta}, \sigma_6 = (g_1)^{t_{mem}\cdot r}$$

$$\sigma_7 = \sigma_6^\alpha, \sigma_8 = \sigma_6^\beta, \sigma_9 = (g_1^a)^{r_1 t_{mem}}, S_1 = \sigma_2^{\sigma_{11}}\sigma_6^{\sigma_{10}}$$

$$S_2 = H_1(m)^{\sigma_{11}}\sigma_9^{\sigma_{10}}$$

Where t_{mem} responds to the value of $y_{mem} = g_1^{a \cdot t_{mem}}$, r_1 is the value in the H_1-list. And add $(m||\sigma_1||\cdots||\sigma_9||S_1||S_2, \sigma_{10})$ to the H_2-list. If such pair exists in the H_2-list, then $\mathcal{B}$ aborts it.

Opening Oracle. When the adversary $\mathcal{A}$ makes a query with message m and a group signature σ, $\mathcal{B}$ runs Open algorithm and returns the corresponding result.

Finally, $\mathcal{A}$ outputs a forged group signature $\sigma^* = (\sigma_1^*, \sigma_2^*, \tilde{\sigma}_2^*, \tilde{\sigma}_3^*, \tilde{\sigma}_4^*, \tilde{\sigma}_5^*, \sigma_6^*, \sigma_7^*, \sigma_8^*, \sigma_9^*, \sigma_{10}^*, \sigma_{11}^*)$ on message m^*. $\mathcal{A}$ wins this game if the following conditions hold.

1. m^* is not made signing query.
2. σ^* is a valid group signature.
3. m^* has been queried, and $coin$ of 4-tuple $(m^*, coin, *, *)$ in the H_1-list satisfies $coin = 1$.

According to the signing algorithm,

$$\sigma_9^* = H_1(m^*)^{x_{mem}^*} = ((g_1^b)^{r_1^*})^{a \cdot t_{mem}^*}$$

Thus, we can obtain the solution of eCDH problem

$$g_1^{ab} = (\sigma_9^*)^{\frac{1}{r^* t^*}}$$

where t^* is a value which satisfies $y_{mem}^* = (g_1^a)^{t^*}$. Obviously, it is in contradiction with the difficulty of solving eCDH problem.   □

5   Conclusion

In this letter, we revisited a threshold anonymous authentication protocol for VANETs in [1] and demonstrated that their scheme cannot achieve traceability, a malicious vehicle can send a false message but the actual identity of the vehicle cannot be revealed. After analyzing the reason to produce such attack, we also suggested an improved scheme to remedy this flaw. And we also show that our improved scheme can resist our attack way by analyzing the security of the improved scheme.

Acknowledgments. This work was supported by Beijing Municipal Natural Science Foundation (No: 4162020,4132056) and The importation and development of High-Caliber Talents project of Beijing municipal Institutions (CIT&TCD201304004).

References

1. Shao, J., Lin, X., Lu, R., Zuo, C.: A threshold anonymous authentication protocol for VANETs. IEEE Trans. Veh. Technol. **65**(3), 1711–1723 (2016)
2. Raya, M., Hubaux, J.P.: Securing vehicular ad hoc networks. J. Comput. Secur. Spec. Issue Secur. Ad Hoc Sens. Netw. **15**(1), 39–68 (2007)
3. Zhang, C., Lin, X., Lu, R., Ho, P.H., Shen, X.: An efficient message authentication scheme for vehicular communications. IEEE Trans. Veh. Technol. **57**(6), 3357–3368 (2008)
4. Lin, X., Chen, H.H.: A secure and efficient RSU-aided bundle forwarding protocol for vehicular delay tolerant networks. Wireless Commun. Mob. Comput. **11**(2), 187–195 (2011)
5. Lu, R., Lin, X., Zhu, H., Liang, X., Shen, X.: BECAN: a bandwidth-efficient cooperative authentication scheme for filtering injected false data in wireless sensor networks. IEEE Trans. Parallel Distrib. Syst. **23**(1), 32–43 (2012)
6. Guo, J., Baugh, J.P., Wang, S.: A group signature based secure and privacy-preserving vehicular communication framework. In: Proceedings Mobile Network Vehicular Environmental, pp. 103–108 (2007)

7. Xiong, H., Beznosov, K., Qin, Z, Ripeanu, M.: Efficient and spontaneous privacy-preserving protocol for secure vehicular communication. In: IEEE-ICC, pp. 1–6 (2010)
8. Babu, S., Patra, M., Murthy, C.S.R.: A novel context-aware variable interval MAC protocol to enhance event-driven message delivery in IEEE 802.11p/WAVE vehicular networks. Veh. Commun. **2**(3), 172–183 (2016)
9. Chen, L., Ng, S.-L., Wang, G.: Threshold anonymous announcement in VANETs. IEEE J. Sel. Areas Commun. **29**(3), 605–612 (2011)
10. Zhang, J., Mao, J.: Efficient multi-proxy signature scheme with short length in the standard model. J. Inf. Sci. Eng. **32**(4), 1097–1112 (2016)
11. Zhang, L., Wu, Q., Qin, B., Domingo-Ferrer, J.: APPA: aggregate privacy-preserving authentication in vehicular ad hoc networks. In: Lai, X., Zhou, J., Li, H. (eds.) ISC 2011. LNCS, vol. 7001, pp. 293–308. Springer, Heidelberg (2011). doi:10.1007/978-3-642-24861-0_20
12. Zhang, J., Yuwei, X.: Privacy-preserving authentication protocols with efficient verification in VANETs. Int. J. Commun. Syst. **27**(12), 3676–3692 (2014)
13. Lu, R., Lin, X., Liang, X., Shen, X.: A dynamic privacy-preserving key management scheme for location based services in VANETs. IEEE Trans. Intell. Transp. Syst. **13**(1), 127–139 (2012)
14. Zhang, J., Zhao, X., Mao, J.: Attack on Chen et al.'s certificateless aggregate signature scheme. Secur. Commun. Netw. **9**(1), 54–59 (2016)

The Encryption Scheme with Data Compression Based on QC-LDPC

Yiliang Han[1,2(✉)]

[1] School of Information Science and Technology,
Northwest University, Xi'an 710069, China
[2] Department of Electronic Technology,
Engineering University of PAP, Xi'an 710086, China
yilianghan@hotmail.com

Abstract. Aiming at the security issue of big data, a new encryption scheme with data compression was designed, which is based on the coding theory. Combining with the theory of compression, a compressed encryption scheme based on quasi-cyclic low density parity check code was proposed. Furthermore, the performance and security of the scheme are analyzed, and through analysis it demonstrates the superiority of the scheme for big data encryption.

Keywords: Big data · Compressed sensing · QC-LDPC code · Compressed encryption

1 Introduction

In the era of big data, owing to the huge amounts of data and the characteristics of high value, it is urgent to solve the problem of safety and privacy. Safety of big data, such as mass data encryption, integrity and authentication, becomes increasingly important [1, 2]. The traditional encryption method has caused great pressure on the capacity of the storage device, the bandwidth of the communication line and the processing speed of the computer. With the combination of encryption algorithm and compression, the requirements of fast encryption and storage of massive data can be realized. This makes it possible to deal with mass data in real time.

Code-based public key cryptography is a post quantum cryptography system based on the theory of information theory. In this paper, we combine the compressed sensing theory with cryptogram, and give a compressed encryption model, a logical process to achieve data compressed and encryption. This greatly reduces the computation and complexity of the data. Finally, we construct a data compressed encryption algorithm based on QC-LDPC (quasi-cyclic low density parity check) code. Specifically, the algorithm achieves strong security and excellent performance.

2 Preliminaries

2.1 Compressed Sensing

In recent years, Tao et al. [3] proposed a new compression sampling theory - compressed sensing, and successfully achieved the signal sampling and compression.

© Springer International Publishing AG 2016
G. Wang et al. (Eds.): SpaCCS 2016, LNCS 10066, pp. 156–163, 2016.
DOI: 10.1007/978-3-319-49148-6_14

Compressed sensing (also known as compressive sensing or compressive sampling) is a signal processing technique for efficiently acquiring and reconstructing a signal, by finding solutions to underdetermined linear systems. And the problem of low dimensional observation vector is able to reconstruct the original high dimensional signal accurately and accurately [4].The sampling rate of the compressed sensing is largely determined by the two basic criteria: sparsity and non-coherence. If the N dimension real signal $x \in R^{N \times 1}$ is expanded in a set of orthogonal basis $\{\psi_i\}_{i=1}^N$, and ψ_I is N vectors. That is,

$$x = \sum_{i=1}^{N} \theta_i \psi_i \tag{1}$$

Where expansion coefficient $\theta_i = \langle x, \psi_i \rangle = \psi_i^T \cdot x$. And its matrix form is expressed as $x = \Psi\theta$, where $\Psi = [\psi_1, \psi_2, \ldots, \psi_N] \in R^{N \times N}(\Psi\Psi^T = \Psi^T\Psi = I)$ is a matrix of orthogonal basis, and $\theta = [\theta_1, \theta_2, \ldots, \theta_N]^T$. Suppose θ is K-sparse, that is, the number of nonzero coefficients of θ is K << N. Select measurement matrix Φ sizes of M × N (M << N), which is non-coherent with Ψ. Perform a compressive measurement for signal x:

$$y = \Phi x. \tag{2}$$

We can get M-linear projection $y \in \mathbf{R}^M$, and this projection contains the information needed to reconstruct the signal x. Unknown number of abnormal state Eq. (2) is greater than the number of equations, and (2) have infinitely many solutions. But, when plug $x = \Psi\theta$ into (2), denoted $\Theta = \Phi\Psi$, we can see

$$y = \Phi\Psi\theta = \Theta\theta. \tag{3}$$

The sparse coefficients θ can greatly reduce the number of unknown, thus allowing the equation to be solved, and the signal reconstruction is possible.

2.2 Code-Based Cryptography

In the quantum cryptography era, code-based public key cryptography is one of the important research directions. In 1978, McEliece [5] proposed the first code-based public key cryptosystem, which used the NPC problem of the general linear decoding problem and fast decoding algorithm for Goppa codes. Then the Niederreiter public key cryptosystem based on error correcting codes is constructed [6]. At present, the research contents of the domestic and foreign are mainly about the improvement of the cipher system and searching for new construction codes. Some performance good codes research are also more and more full, such as QC-LDPC code, MDPC code, etc. And this aspect of the literature is mainly [7, 8] et al.

3   Compressed Encryption

3.1   Syntax of Compressed Encryption

Compressed encryption is a cryptographic algorithm, which can handle mass data. In the encryption phase, it is processed by the method of sampling, redundancy, and so on, which makes the encryption operation of the effective information. While the decryption phase, it can be completely or approximate to restore the original text by the text. Compressed encryption, which object is sparse or compressible, achieves high-speed real-time encryption and decryption on mass structural express. Compressed encryption system mainly has four processes, such as system initialization, message preprocessing, compression encryption and decryption. The algorithm is shown as follows (Fig. 1).

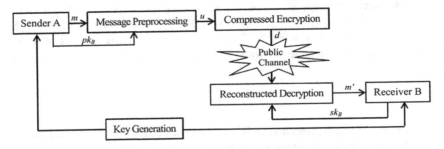

Fig. 1. Composition of compressed encryption algorithm

Setup. Input system parameters, the safety of the public parameters cp of system can be obtained.

KeyGen. Legal user U applies for service of key-generation to the system. After verifying the validity of the user's identity, the system generates a key pair $\{pk_U, sk_U\}$ for the user U according to the public parameters, and then transmits it to the user via a secret channel U.

Compressed Encryption. The user A send message m to users B, and the sender input $\{pk_B, m\}$. After deals with the message m, the sender compressed encrypts it. Get the cipher-text d at last.

Reconstructed Decryption. User B receives a message d which send by user A, and then input $\{sk_B, m\}$. Get the reconstructed message m', or reject the cipher-text d.

3.2 QC-LDPC Based Compressed Encryption Algorithm

Algorithm: QC-LDPC based compressed encryption

System Parameters: n, $t \in \mathbb{N}$, where $t \ll n$.

Key Generation: Given the parameters n, t generates the following matrices:

G: $k \times n$ generator matrix of code C in GF(2) of dimension k and minimum distance $d \geq 2t+1$, which can correct up to t errors. (Code C is a binary irreducible QC-LDPC code.)

H: $(n-k) \times n$ check matrix corresponding to G, which can correct up to t errors.

S: $k \times k$ random nonsingular perturbation quasi-cyclic matrix, which is a regular matrix of the $k_0 \times k_0$ block composition in $q \times q$ binary matrix.

Q: $n \times n$ w-weight cyclic transfer matrix, which is a regular matrix of the $n_0 \times n_0$ block composition in $q \times q$ binary matrix.

Then, compute the $k \times n$ matrix $G' = S^{-1} \cdot G \cdot Q^{-1}$.

Ψ: $\{\psi_i\}^{N}_{i=1}$ basis vectors in discrete information-space $\mathbf{R}^N$, that is, Ψ domain space.

Φ: $k' \times N$ measurement matrix, which size is v.

Then, compute $\Theta = \Phi \Psi$, which is $k' \times N$ information aggregating operators.

Decode( ): efficient syndrome decoding algorithm for QC-LDPC code.

Recovery( ): representing information reconstruction algorithm.

Public Key: (G', Φ, t)

Private Key: (H, S, Q)

Compressed Encryption. A message m is structural plaintext (except random data or noise, etc). And r is k bit random numbers. Choose a vector $e \in$ GF(2) of weight t randomly and compute the compressed ciphertext d as follows:

$m = \Psi \theta$,
$v = \Phi \Psi \theta = \Theta \theta$,
$u = v \oplus r$,
$c = u \cdot G' + e$,
$d \leftarrow (c, r)$

Reconstructed Decryption. To decrypt a compressed ciphertext d,

$c \cdot Q = u \cdot S^{-1} \cdot G \cdot Q^{-1} \cdot Q + e \cdot Q = u \cdot S^{-1} \cdot G + e \cdot Q$,
$u \cdot S^{-1} = \text{Decord}(c \cdot Q)$,
$u = u \cdot S^{-1} \cdot S$,
$v = u \oplus r$,
$m = \text{Recovery}(u)$.

3.3   Performance Analysis

The scheme above is based on the QC-LDPC code. Cyclic matrix has characteristics of representing a matrix with a row or column. This makes the storage of the key is greatly reduced. In this scheme, the public key G' is quasi cyclic matrix, that is, every block is a cyclic matrix ($k_0 \ll k$, $n_0 \ll n$). And the public key need to store is non-zero cyclic matrix and the number of cyclic shift position. So the public key sizes are $pk = q \times k_0 \times n_0 + v$.

Noncoherence compression perception theorem of sparse information indicates that noncoherent orthogonal basis pair meets a certain relationship. For sparse plaintext, we need $k \geq O(\mu^2(\Phi',\Psi) \cdot K log N)$ random compressive measurement data to approximate the exact reconstruction of the original information [8, 9]. When the orthogonal basis satisfies the maximum noncorrelation ($\mu(\Phi',\Psi) = 1$), we just need $k = O(K log N)$ random compressive measurement data. For compressible plaintext, $k \geq O(C \cdot \mu^2(\Phi',\Psi) \cdot K log N)$ (C is a certain constant) random compressive measurement data are needed to approximate the exact reconstruction of the original information [9]. Therefore, just only $q = O(2^{k/(c \cdot K)})$ data of plaintext, where $c = C \cdot \mu^2(\Phi',\Psi)$, are need in the phase of compressed encryption. And it's expressed as the following:

$$q = O(2^{k/(c \cdot K)})$$
$$= \begin{cases} O(2^{k/(\mu^2(\Phi',\Psi) \cdot K)}), & \text{when plaintexts are spare, } C = 1; \\ O(2^{k/(C \cdot \mu^2(\Phi',\Psi) \cdot K)}), & \text{when plaintexts are compressible, } C \text{ is a certain constant;} \end{cases}$$
$$(4)$$

The following table is the comparison of the new algorithm with the Goppa code and QC-LDPC code (Table 1).

Table 1. Algorithm comparison

Algorithm	Code(n, k)	Public key size	Input size	Output size
1 [5]	Goppa	$n \times k$	k	n
2 [6]	QC-LDPC	$q \times n_0 \times k_0$	$k = q \times k_0$	$n = q \times n_0$
Our algorithm	QC-LDPC	$q \times k_0 \times n_0 + v$	$O(2^{k/(c \cdot K)})$	n

From the above table, compared with the original Niederreiter scheme, the public key is only increased the size of the measurement matrix, and the size of plaintexts is up to $c \cdot K$, while ciphertexts remain unchanged. As $k = O(\mu^2(\Phi',\Psi) K log N)$ and $N \geq n$, we can get $O(2^{k/(c \cdot K)}) \geq n$. Given the QC-LDPC code of $n_0 = 3$, $k_0 = 2$, $q = 8192$, the coefficient vector Θ of sparsity coefficient $K = 2^8$, and the domain space Ψ of $N = 2^{15}$, we can get the change in sizes of plaintexts. In the case of different values of (Φ',Ψ), the change of plaintexts is shown as follows (Table 2).

We can know from above chart, compressed encryption algorithm can simplify the structured plaintext by compressive measurement and redundancy elimination, and can reconstructed decrypt the original text accurately. This greatly reduces data operand of

Table 2. The changing relation between measurement size and input size

Situation	$\mu\,(\Phi',\Psi)$	Sensing rate (Observe size/Input size)
Ideal situation	1	0.12
Situation^a	$\sqrt{2}$	0.23
Situation^b	2.2	0.57
Situation^c	2.9	0.99

[a] Φ is Noiselet function, Ψ is Harr Wavelet function;
[b] Φ is Noiselet function, Ψ is Daubechies D4 Wavelet function;
[c] Φ is Noiselet function, Ψ is Daubechies D8 Wavelet function.

encryption and decryption and memory capacitance of ciphertexts. That is to say, the new algorithm achieves real-time, fasten- and decryption of massive structured messages (Fig. 2).

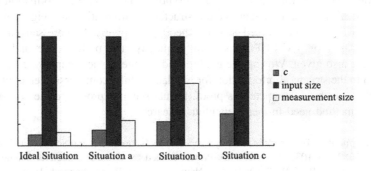

Fig. 2. The changing relation between measurement size and input size

In addition, the structure of QC-LDPC code makes information bits change greatly, and contributes to the low bit error rate. Characteristics of QC-LDPC code make the error correction ability enhanced, the retransmission probability reduced, and the information rate improved.

Remark. *Compressed sensing theory can't be applied to nonstructural messages such as random data, messy information or noise, neither can the new algorithm. In addition, the signal reconstruction of compressed sensing can be transformed into the non-convex optimization problem of minimize the L0 norm. However, it is a difficult problem for the combination of NP search. So we choose Lp(p > 0) for approximate substitute. Of cause, the completeness of the theory of information is reconstructed, which information reconstruction result is approximately exact.*

3.4   Security Analysis

The proof of security is that these security requirements are met provided the assumptions about the adversary's access to the system are satisfied and some clearly stated assumptions about the hardness of certain computational tasks hold. And the provable security of the new algorithm can directly reduce to the difficulty of solving the Syndrome Decoding Problem. The difficulty, which an adversary uses the ciphertext to recover the plaintext, directly determine the privacy of the encoding based public key system. In essence, the new algorithm is a QC-LDPC code based public key cryptosystem, so the analysis of attack method can be referred to [8, 9]. It is pointed out that the QC-LDPC code based public key cryptography is a method of resisting density reduction attacks, attacks to the dual code, information set decoding attacks, OTD attacks and countering OTD attacks. So the new algorithm also has high security.

4   Conclusions

We take the cryptography for big data as a starting point, and put forward a new encryption method, defined compressed encryption. Based on the information theory, compressed encryption is a method for structured information for big data. Then, combined with the compressed sensing theory, we give a compressed encryption algorithm based on QC-LDPC code. Subsequently, the performance and security analyses are also given. We can see the great advantage of the compressed encryption algorithm to the structural information for big data. While, compression encryption has the problems such as completeness proof, formal security proof,and the compression encryption method need further meticulous research.

Acknowledgments. This work is partially supported by National Natural Science Foundation of China (61572521, 61103231, 61272492), Project funded by China Postdoctoral Science Foundation (2014M562445, 2015T81047), and Natural Science Basic Research Plan in Shaanxi Province of China (2015JM6353).

References

1. Tankard, C.: Big data security. Netw. Secur. **2012**(7), 5–8 (2012)
2. Koushikaa, M., Habipriya, S., Aravinth, S.S., et al.: A public key cryptography security system for big data. Int. J. Innovative Res. Sci. Technol. **1**(6), 311–313 (2014)
3. Candès, E., Tao, T.: Near optimal signal recovery from random projections: Universal encoding strategies. IEEE Trans. Inf. Theory **52**(12), 5402–5425 (2006)
4. Wenze, S., Zhihui, W.: Advances and perspectives on compressed sensing theory. J. Image Graph. **17**(1), 1–12 (2012)
5. McEliece, R.J.: A public-key cryptosystem based on algebraic coding theory. DSN Prog. Rep. **42**(44), 114–116 (1978)
6. Niederreiter, H.: Knapsack-type cryptosystems and algebraic coding theory. Probl. Contr. Informat. Theory **15**, 159–166 (1986)

7. Gaborit, P., Ruatta, O., Schrek, J., Zémor, G.: RankSign: an efficient signature algorithm based on the rank metric. In: Mosca, M. (ed.) PQCrypto 2014. LNCS, vol. 8772, pp. 88–107. Springer, Heidelberg (2014). doi:10.1007/978-3-319-11659-4_6
8. Baldi, M.: QC-LDPC Code-Based Cryptosystems, pp. 91–117. Springer, Heidelberg (2014)
9. Baldi, M., Bianchi, M., Chiaraluce, F.: Security and complexity of the McEliece cryptosystem based on quasi-cyclic low-density parity-check codes. IET Inf. Secur. 7(3), 212–220 (2013)

Location Privacy Preserving Scheme Based on Attribute Encryption

Xi Lin, Yiliang Han[(⊠)], Yan Ke, and Xiaoyuan Yang

Department of Electronic Technology, Engineering University of Chinese
Armed Police Force, Xi'an 710086, China
hanyil@163.com

Abstract. There are only two modes, "public" or "private" to manage the user's location information in the social network. However, in some cases, users need to inform some people of their exact location, and the other people are only access to the inaccurate, maybe fuzzy location information. Therefore, we design a location privacy preserving scheme based on attribute encryption, which provides "precise", "more accurate", "fuzzy" and "private" four modes to manage the location information. The scheme based on the algorithm of WT-CP-ABE [1]. The location information is divided into three parts according to different ranks of intimacy, then we encrypt the key information and position information with attribute-based encryption and symmetric encryption respectively, and then issue the ciphertext to the social network. We analyze the security of the scheme, which shows that the scheme has the advantages of user attribute information confidentiality, data confidentiality and it can resist the collusion attack.

Keywords: Social network · Location · Privacy protection · Ranks of intimacy · Attribute-based encryption

1 Introduction

Mobile social networking is an online platform built on some certain social relations. In mobile social network, users can share their interests, hobbies, status and daily activities with friends and families to strengthen the contact each other and maintain the deep affection. Users can also use positioning technology on mobile phone or other intelligent devices to share their location information and get some sorts of location-based services (LBS).

However, as people enjoy the convenience brought by the positioning technology, personal location privacy is suffering serious threats [2]. To the protection of personal location privacy, there are mainly two kinds of methods, spatial cloaking and space twist [3, 4]. Location k-anonymity model [5] is the most commonly used among the technology of spatial cloaking. When users need to provide personal location information, it will collect and send location information of k users in a large enough area (hereinafter referred to as fuzzy area) to the Service Provider (SP). As a result, the server can't distinguish the location of the users'. Space twist is going to generate some false positions and then both the real positions and false positions will be sent to the

© Springer International Publishing AG 2016
G. Wang et al. (Eds.): SpaCCS 2016, LNCS 10066, pp. 164–177, 2016.
DOI: 10.1007/978-3-319-49148-6_15

server at the same time, therefore the user's location information will be hidden [3]. However, all these location privacy protection methods above assume the LBS provider as an attacker, and none of them think of the fact that the attacker may also be the user's "friends".

In fact, not all "friends" are credible and there may also be a potential attacker in the user's "friends list" [6]. Therefore, if the user publishes precise location indifferently to all friends in the network, it will inevitably cause the leakage of personal privacy and thereby users may suffer from security threats. In fact, when users post status, most of the social software, such as WeChat, Twitter provide the "visible" option, but they actually provide only "public" and "private" two options, therefore users are unable to show their precise location information to some close friends while showing fuzzy or not accurate location information to some good friends. Therefore, our paper contributes a location privacy preserving scheme based on attribute encryption. In our scheme, mobile social network users can choose "precise", "more accurate", "fuzzy" and "private" four modes for every friends according to the different ranks of intimacy, and friends in different ranks of intimacy can see different information of position. Besides, this scheme supports revocation of users' attributes, it can resist collusion attack and it is confidential in both users' attribute information and data.

2 Preliminary

2.1 Bilinear Maps

G1, G2 are two multiplicative cyclic groups of prime order p. If they satisfy the properties: (1) Bilinearity. For $\forall u, v \in G1$ and $\forall a, b \in Zp$, we have $e(u^a, v^b) = e(u, v)^{ab}$. (2) Non-degeneracy. $\exists u, v \in G1$, let $e(u, v) \neq 1$. (3) Calculability. $\forall u, v \in G1$, we can figure out $e(u, v)$ in a polynomial time. We call map e: $G1 \times G1 \to G2$ as the bilinear map [7].

2.2 Ciphertext-Policy Attribute-Based Encryption (CP-ABE)

In our paper, we use ciphertext-policy attribute-based (CP-ABE) to encrypt the information of key. We define A as the set of all the attributes {1, 2, ..., k}, S as the non-empty subset of A. P is the attribute strategy contributed by "AND" and "OR". The commonly used policy of CP-ABE to control the access is based on the access to the tree structure [8] or linear secret sharing [9, 10]. In our paper, we use linear secret sharing to make it and the concrete process is described as follows: (1) We use (M, ρ) to express the property strategy of P. M is a matrix of $l \times h$ and ρ is a one-way function. When i = 1, $\cdots$, 1, ρ(i) represents the ith line associated attributes of M. (2) When the set S satisfies the attribute strategy P, I = {i | P(i) ∈ S}, then we can thus calculate a constant coefficient group $\{\theta i \in Zp\}$ satisfying $\sum_{i \in I} \theta_i \vec{M}_i = \{1, 0, \ldots, 0\}$, and $\vec{M}_i$ is ith line vector of M. If S doesn't satisfy the attribute strategy P, there are no such group of constant coefficients. (3) Share the secret. We assume that s ∈ Zp is a secret need to share, then we randomly select h − 1 value, v2, v3, $\cdots$, vh ∈ Zp, contributing a vector of h dimensions $\vec{v} = (s, v_2, \cdots, v_h)$, and then we calculate $\lambda_i = \vec{M}_i \vec{v}(i = 1, 2, \ldots, 1)$, in which λ_i is the value of sharing secret. Only when the attribute set S satisfies the attribute strategy P can we figure out the secret $s = \sum_{i \in I} \theta_i \lambda_i$.

2.3   The Mechanism of Token Tree

A tree of tokens. Our scheme constructs a complete binary tree as a token tree whose depth is D. The maximum of nodes on each $1 \sim D-1$ floor is 2^{D-1}, and nodes in D are concentrated in the far left. Each edge of tree corresponds to a token, each node has the corresponding random key, and each leaf node corresponds to a user in the system. We define Φ_x as a set of the leaf nodes in token tree corresponding to users in attribute group G(x) and define Ψ_x as the minimum set of nodes which could cover Φ_x, then we call the set of all the random key corresponding to all the nodes in set Ψ_x as the minimum covering key set (MCKS) of attribute x, written as $MCKS_x$. If n_i presents a leaf node in the token tree, our scheme defines the set of all the random key corresponding to the nodes from n_i to the root node, including the root node and leaf nodes as the key chain set (KCS) of node n_i, written as KCS_i and defines the set of all the tokens it gets through from n_i to the root node as token chain set (TCS), written as TCS_i.

The mechanism of the token tree. Our scheme makes each leaf nodes in the token tree corresponds to a user u_t in the system and takes the random key of the leaf nodes as TDKey in users' private key. The security of the token mechanism in our scheme depends on three theorems in the token trees: (1) If you know the random key corresponds to the leaf node n_i and all tokens of all the edges it gets through on its way to the root node, then we can figure out the keychain set KCS_i corresponds to n_i. (2) If we only know the random key corresponds to the leaf node n_i, we can't get any random key corresponds to the nodes except for the nodes which get through from n_i to root node even if we get all the tokens in the token tree. (3) If the n_t represents the leaf node corresponds to user $u_t (1 \le t \le m)$, then there is only one element makes the KCS_i of n_t intersect the $MCKS_x$ of G(x) when $u_t \in G(x) (1 \le x \le k)$.

3   Our Construction

3.1   System Model

Privacy protection social network system (PPSNS) is shown in Fig. 1. Just like literature [11, 12], we assume attribute authority AA is credible, and AA is responsible for initialization of the system, generation and distribution of user private key and management of users' attributes. Social network service provider SNSP is responsible for storing the information of the location released by data owner DO and providing users with social network service. Data owner DO is responsible for generating and distributing his own master private key and designing the strategy of encryption for data. When visitors want to get access to the DO`s data, they need DO`s own master private key to update their private keys. If and only if the visitor's attributes satisfy the attribute strategy of encryption can visitors decrypt the data correctly.

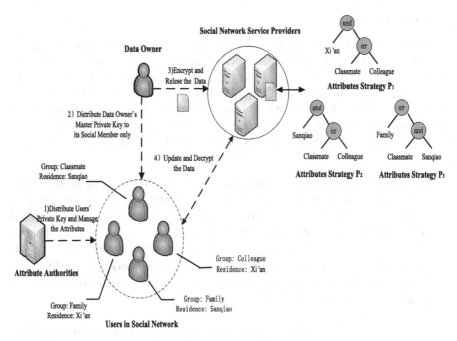

Fig. 1. Privacy protection social network system

3.2   Definitions

Definition 1. Attribute group. Users set $U = \{u_1, \cdots, u_m\}$, attribute set A = {1, 2, $\cdots$, k}, then we define the attribute group $G(x)$ is a set of all the users who have the attribute of x.

Definition 2. Attribute trapdoor. If there is always an attribute trapdoor for each attribute $x \in A$, if and only if the user $u_t \in G(x)$ can the user obtain the attribute trapdoor for attribute x.

Definition 3. Location information. We divide the location information m of DO into m_1, m_2, m_3, for example, divide m = "Qitian hotel, town of Sanqiao, Xi'an, Shaanxi province" into m_1 = "Xi'an, Shaanxi province", m_2 = "town of Sanqiao", m_3 = " Qitian hotel".

Definition 4. Rank of intimacy. According to user's relationship with the DO (strangers, ordinary, friendly and intimate), we can divide DO's friends into four ranks of intimacy, written as 0,1,2,3. And we design three kinds of attribute strategy P_1, P_2, P_3. If the user is in the rank of the "ordinary", then set the user's rank = 1 and user's attributes set S satisfies strategy P_1, If "friendly", then set rank = 2 and S satisfies strategy P_2, and if "intimate", then set rank = 3 and S satisfies strategy P_3.

3.3   Our Algorithm

In this paper, we divide data needs to encrypt into two parts, location information and key information. Then we use traditional symmetric encryption to encrypt the location information and use WT-CP-ABE [1] encryption algorithm to encrypt key information. WT-CP-ABE algorithm is based on CP-ABE. WT-CP-ABE let AA and DO complete the generation of key together, and add attribute trapdoors and attribute revocation function to CP-ABE. Our algorithm includes Setup (), KeyGen (), EncryptM (), EncryptK (), KeyUpdate (), DecryptK () and DecryptM () seven sub function.

(1) Setup (1^λ)

According to a given security parameter 1^λ, AA choose a multiplicative group whose order is p and generator is g, then there is a bilinear mapping $e : G_1 \times G_1 \rightarrow G_2$. We define attribute set in the system A = {1, 2, $\cdots$, k} and choose η_x and $TD_x \in Z_p$ randomly for attributes $x \in A$ $(1 \leq x \leq k)$, then we calculate $T_x = g^{\eta_x TD_x}$. Randomly select $\beta \in Z_p$, generate system master private key ASK = <β, {TD_x}>, and issue public key APK = <G_1, g, g^β, {T_x}$_{x \in A}$>. Finally, DO select $\alpha \in Z_p$ randomly, calculate users private key OSK = <g^α> and issue the users' public key OPK = <$e(g, g)^\alpha$>.

(2) KeyGen (ASK, S)

Use master private key ASK to generate private key corresponding to the attribute set. Randomly choose $t \in Z_p$, calculate D = $g^{\beta t}$, L = g^t. Calculate $D_x =$ = $g^{\eta_x t}$ for any attribute $x \in S$. Randomly select the trapdoor key TDKey, making up the user's private key SK = <D, L, {D_x}$_{x \in S}$, TDKey> . In order to avoid collusion attack, we add a random number t to D_x to randomize user's private key. Using the trapdoor key TDKey, we can restore the corresponding attributes trapdoor.

(3) EncryptM (m, k_1, k_2, k_3)

Use symmetric encryption to encrypt location information m. First of all, randomly choose three randomly generated symmetric key k_1, k_2, k_3, then divide location information m into m_1, m_2, m_3 according to the definitions in Sect. 3.2 and use k_1, k_2, k_3 to encrypt m_1, m_2, m_3. Then, we can get $E_{k_1}(m_1)$, $E_{k_2}(m_2)$ and $E_{k_3}(m_3)$. Output the cipher of location information CM :

$$CM = \langle E_{k_1}(m_1), E_{k_2}(m_2), E_{k_3}(m_3) \rangle$$

(4) EncryptK (APK, OPK, P_{rank}, K_{rank})

Use public key APK, OPK and attribute strategy P_{rank} to encrypt the information of symmetrical key K_{rank}. First of all, DO can design three attribute strategies P_1, P_2, P_3 according to the "ordinary", "friendly", "intimate" three ranks of intimacy. According to [9], we can get (M, ρ) representing the attribute strategy P_{rank}, rank $\in$ {1, 2, 3}. M is a matrix of $l \times h$, ρ is a one-way function. Then randomly select a vector of h dimensions $\vec{v} = (s, v_2, \cdots, v_h) \in Z_p$ and calculate $\tilde{C} = K_{rank} \cdot e(g, g)^{\alpha s}, C = g^s$. For any $i \in \{1, 2, \cdots, 1\}$, let $\vec{M}_i$ be the ith row vector of M and calculate $\lambda_i = \vec{M}_i \vec{v}$. Then, choose random numbers $r_1, \cdots, r_l \in Z_p$ and calculate $C_i = g^{\beta \lambda_i} T_{\rho(i)}^{-r_i}$, $C_i' = g^{r_i}$, Output the ciphertext CK_{rank}:

$$CK_{rank} = \left\langle (M, \rho), \tilde{C}, C, \{C_i, C_i'\}_{i\{1,2,\cdots,l\}} \right\rangle$$

In the ciphertext, each C_i can be figured out through $T_{\rho(i)}$, but only get the attribute trapdoor $TD_{\rho(i)}$ can we figure out $T_{\rho(i)}$. Therefore, if and only if get the attributes trapdoors $TD_{\rho(i)}$ can we get C_i and decrypt the ciphertext.

When rank = 1, 2, 3, we use attribute strategies P_1, P_2, P_3 to complete encryption. K_1, K_2 and K_3 represent k_1, $k_1 \| k_2$ and $k_1 \| k_2 \| k_3$ respectively. Then we can get CK_1, CK_2, CK_3 after the calculation, making up ciphertext of key:

$$CK = \langle CK_1, CK_2, CK_3 \rangle$$

(5) KeyUpdate (OSK, SK)

Use OSK to update private key SK. Get new *SK*:

$$SK = \left\langle D = g^\alpha g^{\beta t}, L, \{D_x\}_{x \in S}, TDKey \right\rangle$$

(6) DecryptK (SK, CK)

Decrypt the ciphertext of key CK_{rank}. If and only if the attribute set S of private key SK satisfies the attribute strategy P_{rank} adopted in encryption of CK_{rank} can users decrypt the ciphertext and get the key CK_{rank}. Let $I = \{i \mid \rho(i) \in S\}, W = \{\rho(i) \mid \rho(i) \in S\}$ and assume that we has figure out the attributes trapdoor $TD_{\rho(i)}$ for each attribute $\rho(i) \in W$ by using the trapdoor key TDKey.

First, use the method referred in literature [9] to figure out a set of constant coefficients $\{\theta_i\}_{i \in I}$ and let the $\sum_{i \in I} \theta_i \lambda_i = s$. Then, calculate

$$A = \prod_{i \in I} (e(C_i, L)e(C_i', D_{\rho(i)}^{TD_{\rho(i)}}))^{\theta_i}$$

$$= \prod_{i \in I} (e(g^{\beta \lambda_i} g^{-r_i \eta_{\rho(i)} TD_{\rho(i)}}, g^t) e(g^{r_i}, g^{\eta_{\rho(i)} t TD_{\rho(i)}}))^{\theta_i}$$

$$= e(g, g)^{t\beta \sum_{i \in I} \lambda_i \theta_i}$$

$$= e(g, g)^{t\beta s}$$

Finally, we can get

$$K_{rank} = \tilde{C}/(e(C, D)/A)$$

$$= \tilde{C}/(e(g^s, g^\alpha g^{\beta t})/e(g, g)^{t\beta s})$$

If the attribute set S of private key SK doesn't satisfy the strategies P_1, P_2, P_3 represented by (M, ρ) in CK_1, CK_2 or CK_3, we can't get K_{rank}; If the attribute set S of private key SK satisfies the strategy P_1 represented by (M, ρ) in CK_1, we can get K_1; If the attribute set S of private key SK satisfies the strategy P_2 represented by (M, ρ) in CK_2, we can get K_2; If the attribute set S of private key SK satisfies the strategy P_3 represented by (M, ρ) in CK_3, we can get K_3.

(7) DecryptM (K_{rank}, CM)

Use the symmetric key k_1, k_2, k_3 we get from K_{rank} to decrypt cipher CM. When we get K_1, due to $K_1 = k_1$, we can use k_1 to decrypt $E_{k_1}(m_1)$ in CM. $D_{k_1}(E_{k_1}(m_1))$ and we can get fuzzy location information m_1; When we get K_2, due to $K_2 = k_1 \| k_2$, we can use k_1, k_2 to decrypt $E_{k_1}(m_1)$ and $E_{k_2}(m_2)$ in CM. $D_{k_1}(E_{k_1}(m_1))$, $D_{k_2}(E_{k_2}(m_2))$ and we can get more accurate location information $m_1 \| m_2$; When we get K_3, due to $K_3 = k_1 \| k_2 \| k_3$, we can use k_1, k_2, k_3 to decrypt $E_{k_1}(m_1)$, $E_{k_2}(m_2)$ and $E_{k_3}(m_3)$ in CM. $D_{k_1}(E_{k_1}(m_1))$, $D_{k_2}(E_{k_2}(m_2))$, $D_{k_3}(E_{k_3}(m_3))$ and we can get precise location information $m_1 \| m_2 \| m_3$.

3.4   Our Scheme

System initialization. According to the security parameters 1^λ chosen, AA run $Setup(1^\lambda)$ to get the system's master private key ASK and public key APK. Then, each DO goes to generate his own master private key OSK and public key OPK together with AA.

New user registration. When new users u_t join social networks, AA generates the corresponding attribute set S according to the information of u_t and executes the KeyGen (ASK, S) to generate the private key SK associated with attribute set S, then distribute SK to u_t. In addition, the AA also need to build corresponding attribute group according to the user's attribute. If the attribute sets of users u_1, u_2, u_3 are respectively $\{1, 2\}, \{1, 2, 3\}, \{2, 3\}$, the corresponding attribute groups are $G(1) = \{u_1, u_2\}$, G $(2) = \{u_1, u_2, u_3\}$, $G(3) = \{u_2, u_3\}$.

Trapdoor information release. AA goes to build a token tree according to the method referred in Sect. 2.3. Each leaf node in the tree corresponds to a user in the system and the random keys of the leaf nodes are regarded as TDKey in user's private key. According to the attribute group G(x) corresponds to $x \in A(1 \leq x \leq k)$, we can determine the minimum cover key set $MCKS_x$ and then figure out the trapdoor information $TDM_x = \{E_{RK_j}(TD_x)\}_{RK_j \in MCKS_x}$. We define RK_j as the random key, define TD_x as the attribute trapdoor of x and define E as a fast symmetric encryption algorithm, such as exclusive or operation. Release the trapdoor information $TDM = \{TDM_x\}_{x \in A}$ and token chain $TCS = \{TCS_i\}_{i \in \{1,2,\cdots,m\}}$.

Establish social contact. DOs go to distribute their master private key OSK to their own social members through a security channel (such as SSL protocol).

Release private data. We only describe how data owner DO deals with single location information m here: (1) Use three groups of randomly generated symmetric key k_1, k_2, k_3 to encrypt the three parts m_1, m_2, m_3 of location information m and we can get $E_{k_1}(m_1)$, $E_{k_2}(m_2)$, $E_{k_3}(m_3)$ (E is a symmetric encryption algorithm), then they make up the ciphertext CM of the location information. (2) Run algorithm EncryptK (APK, OPK, P_{rank}, K_{rank}) to encrypt symmetric key information K_1, K_2, K_3 according to the three kinds of attribute strategies P_1, P_2, P_3 corresponding to the ranks of intimacy, then we can get CK_1, CK_2, CK_3 and they make up the ciphertext CK of key information. (3) Let $V = \{\rho(i) \mid 1 \leq i \leq l\}$, then calculate the trapdoor TDM_x for any attribute $x \in V$ to make up the trapdoor information $TDM_{DO} = \{TDM_x\}_{x \in V}$. (4) Release the location information file $ID_m \parallel ID_{DO} \parallel CM$ and key information file $ID_{DO} \parallel TDM_{DO} \parallel CK$ in the social network (ID_m is the unique number created for location information m and ID_{DO} is the unique number created for the data owner DO).

Data access. When user u_t wants to access location information file whose number is ID_m, SNSP goes to search for the corresponding key information file according to the number ID_{DO} and returns the location information CM, key information $TDM_{DO} \parallel CK$ and the user's token chain TCS_t. First, user u_t needs to decrypt TDM_{DO} to get the attribute trapdoor information, and then decrypt CK_{rank} in file CK with its own private key to SK and the attribute trapdoor got from the decryption of TDM_{DO}. After that, we can get the symmetric key K_{rank}. Then, we can decrypt location information file CM with symmetric key K_{rank} to get the location information. The process can be described as follow: (1) Decryption of TDM_{DO}. According to the first theorem of the token tree referred in Sect. 2.3, we can know that the key chain set KCS_t in token tree can be figured out with the trapdoor key TDKey in user u_t own private key SK and token chain set TCS_t. Obviously, if and only if the attribute set of user u_t own private key SK satisfies the attribute strategy represented by (M, ρ) can the user decrypts CK. It means that as for $W = \{\rho(i) \mid 1 \leq i \leq l \text{ and } \rho(i) \in S\}$, any attribute $x \in W$ and its corresponding attribute group $G(x)$, there must be a user $u_t \in G(x)$. According to the third theorem of the token tree referred in Sect. 2.3, we can know that as for the minimum cover key set $MCKS_x$ of $G(x)$, there must be a random key RK_y which could satisfy that $RK_y \in KCS_t$ and $RK_y \in MCKS_x$. It means that the user can use RK_y to decrypt TDM_x to get the corresponding attribute trapdoor TD_x of attribute x. Therefore, user u_t is able to get all the attribute trapdoors through the decryption of TDM_{DO} and then we can decrypt CK. (2) Decryption of CK. User u_t goes to run KeyUpdate (OSK, SK) to update the private key SK with owner's OSK, then run DecryptK (SK, CK) to decrypt CK to get K_{rank} with using the updated private key. (3) Decryption of CM. then, u_t runs DecryptM (K_{rank}, CM) to decrypt CM to get the corresponding location information with the K_{rank} we got.

Revocation of attributes. When it need to change user's attributes, AA goes to complete the revocation of attributes. We define the revocation set of attribute as R and the user whose attribute is revoked as u_t. The process of revocation is described as follow: (1) AA goes to update the attribute trapdoor information. As for any attribute $x \in R$, AA randomly generates new attribute trapdoor TD'_x and forms new attribute group $G(x)$ of attribute x. Obviously, as for the user u_t whose attribute is revoked, there must be $u_t \notin G(x)$. Then, rebuild the minimum cover key sets $MCKS'_x$, generate $TDM'_x = \{E_{RK_j}(TD'_x)\}_{RK_j \in MCKS'_x}$, and take TDM'_x in the place of the original TDM_x. (2) AA goes to update APK and ASK. For any attribute $x \in R$, AA goes to update the corresponding component in the APK

$$T'_x = T_x^{TD'_x/TD_x}$$

and take TD'_x in the place of TD_x in ASK. (3) DO encrypts the ciphertext of key information again. First of all, randomly generate three groups new symmetric encryption key k_1', k_2', k_3' and form K_1', K_2', K_3'. Execute EncryptK () three times to get CK_1', CK_2', CK_3' and form new CK' to take the place of the original CK. Then, update the information of attribute group. The process is described as follow: let the $V = \{\rho(i) \mid 1 \leq i \leq 1\}$, $VR = V \cap R$ (R is the set revocation set of attribute). If $VR = \emptyset$, it doesn't need to update; If the $VR \neq \emptyset$, then for any $x \in VR$, we calculate the corresponding TDM_x' of x and take it in the place of the original TDM_x, forming new trapdoor information

$$TDM_{DO}' = \{TDM_x'\}_{x \in V}$$

(4) Release the new key information file $ID_{DO} \parallel TDM_{DO}' \parallel CK'$ again.

4   Security Analysis

4.1   Confidentiality of Attributes

The revocation of attribute in literature [12, 13] inevitably reveal the attribute information of users. In this paper, AA generates users' private key and completes the management of users' attributes independently. Therefore, if we assume AA is fully trusted, then the information of users' attributes is confidential.

4.2   Confidentiality of Data

The confidentiality of data in this paper only depends on the ciphertext's confidentiality of the location information file and the ciphertext's confidentiality of key information file. Our scheme adopts the method of mixed encryption to encrypt files, therefore, if we assume the symmetric encryption algorithm used to encrypt location information file is secure, we can get that the confidentiality of data only depends on the security of attribute encryption algorithm used to encrypt key information file and the security of revocation. Our scheme uses the WT-CP-ABE encryption algorithm, which is based on CP-ABE and makes some changes: (1) Change its previous key generation model. In our scheme, users need to get data owner DO's master private key OSK and then use OSK to update their own private key, then they can decrypt the ciptertext correctly. (2) Add the mechanism of token tree. Our paper constructs a complete binary tree and introduce the mechanism of token tree to control users' access to the attribute trapdoor TD_x so as to realize the management of attributes. Use the random key in token tree to encrypt the attribute trapdoor TD_x, therefore, if the symmetric encryption algorithm and the length of the random key adopted satisfy the requirements of security, according to the first theorem and the second theorem of the token tree referred in Sect. 2.3, we can prove the mechanism of token tree to be secure. Because the CP-ABE [10] algorithm is judgmental PBDHE mathematical problems and proved to be secure under the standard model. Therefore, WT-CP-ABE encryption algorithm is also secure under the standard model.

Our scheme uses updating the information of trapdoor to realize the revocation of user's attributes. Among them, AA randomly generate new TD_x, then use symmetric encryption to encrypt TD_x with a new random key selected from the token tree. If we assume symmetric encryption is secure, the user whose attributes are revoked cannot decrypt and get the new TD_x. Therefore, the user whose attributes are revoked cannot decrypt the data, which guarantees the security of revocation of attributes.

4.3   Resist Collusion Attack

The collusion of SNSP and the user whose attributes are revoked is one of the most common attacks [12–15]. Our scheme adopts the mechanism of token tree, DO directly encrypts the ciphertext of key information when some attributes are revoked, therefore, even if the user whose attributes are revoked in collusion with the SNSP can't he gets the updated data.

The collusion attack from unauthorized users is another threat. If two users conspire, normally they can't decrypt the ciphertext because neither of the sets of attributes they have can satisfy the conditions of decryption. But they may get some unauthorized key information if they combine their private keys. Like the methods used in literature [8, 10], our scheme embeds the random numbers in each user's private key so that the co-conspirators cannot decrypt by combining their private keys. According to the process of decryption referred in the Sect. 3.3, we can know K_1, K_2, K_3 are tied together with $e(g, g)^{\alpha s}$, and if the attacker wants to get K_1, K_2, K_3, he must go to get $e(g, g)^{\alpha s}$ first. If someone wants to get $e(g, g)^{\alpha s}$, he need to calculate $(C, D)/e(g, g)^{t\beta s}$, namely calculate $e(g, g)^{t\beta s}$. As a result, as for any attribute $\rho(i)$ ($i \in I$), the attacker must calculate

$$e(C_i, L)e(C_i', D_{\rho(i)}^{TD_{\rho(i)}})$$

Our scheme embeds the users' unique random number t in L and D_i, so it cannot complete the above calculation through the combination of different user's private key. Therefore, the co-conspirators cannot get the information of symmetric key K_1, K_2, K_3.

5   Efficiency Analysis

In this section, we will compare our scheme with EASiER in [14]. We define OSKC, OSKS OENC, ODEC to represent the time complexity for DO to generate the private key, the space complexity to store the user's private key, time complexity for DO to encrypt data and time complexity for the user to decrypt data.

When it goes to generate the private key, DO in our scheme only need to generate OSK, thus OSKC is O(1). In EASiER, however, DO need to compute each user's private key, therefore OSKC is O(na), among them, n represents the average number of social members DO have and a represents the number of attributes associated with user's private key. When it goes to the storage of private keys, users in our scheme only need to keep their own private key SK and the OSK obtained from the DO, therefore, OSKS is $O(m) + O(a)$, among them, m represents the average number of users who build a relationship with DO. In EASiER, however, each DO need to distribute its private key SK to users and users have to store all of them, therefore, OSKS is $O(ma)$.

Both our scheme and EASiER adopt the method of mixed encryption, while our scheme need to use attribute encryption three times to encrypt the information file of symmetrical key. Therefore, in EASiER, OENC is $O(D) + O(b)$ and ODEC is $O(D) + O(c)$. OENC in our paper is $O(D) + O(3b)$ and ODEC is $O(D) + O(3c)$, among them, D, b, c respectively represents the size of location information file, the average number of the attributes associated with ciphertext when it encrypts and the average number of attributes needed for decryption.

From the Table 1, we can see though our scheme is greater in the time complexity of encryption and decryption process compared to the EASiER, we have obvious advantages in both the time complexity for DO to generate the private key and the space complexity to store the user's private key.

Table 1. Analysis of complexity

Scheme	OSKC	OSKS	OENC	ODEC
EASiER	$O(na)$	$O(ma)$	$O(D) + O(b)$	$O(D) + O(c)$
Our scheme	$O(1)$	$O(m) + O(a)$	$O(D) + O(3b)$	$O(D) + O(3c)$

From the Figs. 2, 3, 4 and 5, we can easily see the relationship between OSKC, OSKS, OENC, ODEC and n, m, D. When n, m is large, our scheme has more advantages in OSKC and OSKS compared with the EASiER. And with the increase in D, the increasing rate of OENC, ODEC in our scheme is the same to those in the EASiER.

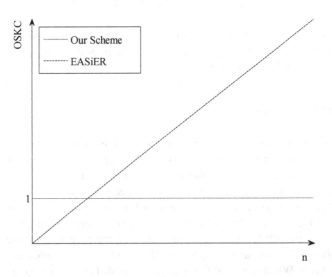

Fig. 2. Relation between OSKC and n

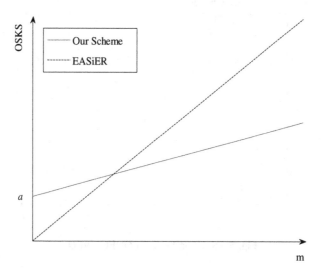

Fig. 3. Relation between OSKS and *m*

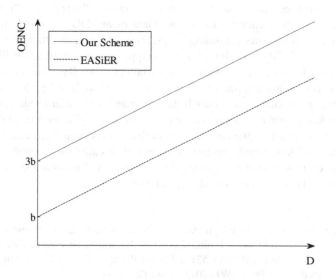

Fig. 4. Relation between OENC and *D*

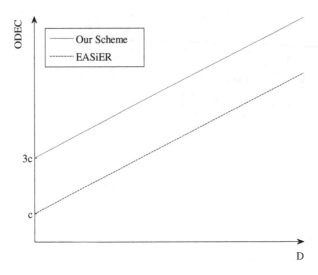

Fig. 5. Relation between ODEC and *D*

6 Conclusions

In our paper, we put forward a location privacy preserving scheme based on attribute encryption, which provides "precise", "more accurate", "fuzzy" and "private" four modes to manage the location information. Data owner DO can divide the location information into three parts according to the rank of intimacy, then use symmetric encryption and WT-CP-ABE algorithm to encrypt location information file and key information file, finally release ciphertext to social networks. By using the combination of symmetric encryption and public key encryption method, it makes the encryption of information more efficient. If and only if the key changes, the user needs to encrypt the ciphertext of key information again. However, in order to realize to decrypt the location information hierarchically, we need to use attribute encryption three times to encrypt the information of key, which increases the amount of calculation. Therefore, we will further study on how to combine symmetric encryption and attribute encryption better, reduce the tedious encryption procedures and improve the efficiency of our scheme in the future.

Acknowledgments. This work is supported by National Natural Science Foundation of China (61572521, 61272492, 61272468), Project funded by Natural Science Basic Research Plan in Shaanxi Province of China (2015JM6353) and Basic Research Plan of Engineering College of the Chinese Armed Police Force (WJY201523, WJY201613).

References

1. Lv, Z.Q., HONG, C., ZHANG, M., et al.: Privacy-perserving scheme for social networks. J. Commun. **35**(8), 23–32 (2014)
2. Chow, C.Y., Mokbel, M.F., Aref, W.G.: Casper*: query processing for location services without compromising privacy. In: Proceedings of the 32nd International Conference on Very Large Data Bases, VLDB Endowment, pp. 763–774 (2006)
3. Kido, H., Yanagisawa, Y., Satoh, T.: An anonymous communication technique using dummies for location-based services. In: Proceedings of the International Conference on Pervasive Services 2005, ICPS 2005, pp. 88–97 (2005)
4. Man, L.Y., Jensen, C.S., Huang, X., et al.: SpaceTwist: managing the trade-offs among location privacy, query performance, and query accuracy in mobile services. In: International Conference on Data Engineering, pp. 366–375 (2008)
5. Gruteser, M., Grunwald, D.: Anonymous usage of location-based services through spatial and temporal cloaking. In: International Conference on Mobile Systems, Applications, and Services, pp. 31–42 (2003)
6. Chen, W.H., Li, W.J., Zhu, J.: A model for protecting location privacy against attacks from friends in SNS. Comput. Eng. Sci. **37**(4), 692–698 (2015)
7. Boneh, D., Franklin, F.: Identity-based encryption from the Weil pairing. Adv. Cryptology **32**(3), 586–615 (2001). Crypt' 2001
8. Bethencourt, J.,Sahai, A.,Waters, B.: Ciphertext-policy attribute-based encryption. In: Proceedings of the 28th International Symposium on Security and Privacy (S&P 2007). Berkeley, CA, USA, 321–334 (2007)
9. Beimel, A.: Secure Schemes for Secret Sharing and Key Distribution. Ph.D thesis, Israel Institute of Technology, Technion, Haifa, Israel (1996)
10. Waters, B.: Ciphertext-policy attribute-based encryption: an expressive, efficient, and provably secure realization. In: Catalano, D., Fazio, N., Gennaro, R., Nicolosi, A. (eds.) PKC 2011. LNCS, vol. 6571, pp. 53–70. Springer, Heidelberg (2011). doi:10.1007/978-3-642-19379-8_4
11. Liang, X., Li, X., Lu, R., et al.: An efficient and secure user revocation scheme in mobile social networks. In: Global Telecommunications Conference (GLOBECOM 2011), pp. 1–5. IEEE (2011)
12. Hur, J., Noh, D.K.: Attribute-based access control with efficient revocation in data outsourcing systems. IEEE Trans. Parallel Distrib. Syst. **22**(7), 1214–1221 (2010)
13. Yu, S., Wang, C., Ren, K., et al.: Attribute based data sharing with attribute revocation. In: Proceedings of the 5th ACM Symposium on Information, Computer and Communications Security, ASIACCS 2010, Beijing, China, April 13–16, 2010, pp. 261–270 (2010)
14. Jahid, S., Mittal, P., Borisov, N.: EASiER: encryption-based access control in social networks with efficient revocation. In: ACM Symposium on Information, Computer and Communications Security, ASIACCS 2011, Hong Kong, China, March 2011, pp. 411–415 (2011)
15. Zhang, M., Lv, Z., Feng, D., et al.: A secure and efficient revocation scheme for fine-grained access control in cloud storage. In: 2012 IEEE 4th International Conference on Cloud Computing Technology and Science (CloudCom), pp. 545–550. IEEE (2012)

Attribute-Based Traceable Anonymous Proxy Signature Strategy for Mobile Healthcare

Dacheng Meng[1], Wenbo Wang[1], Entao Luo[1], and Guojun Wang[2(✉)]

[1] School of Information Science and Engineering,
Central South University, Changsha 410083, China
[2] School of Computer Science and Educational Software,
Guangzhou University, Guangzhou 510006, China
csgjwang@gmail.com

Abstract. In mobile healthcare, with the gradual development of the validity of electronic information, the use of electronic signatures as electronic prescriptions for medical users has gradually been adopted by various medical institutions. This electronic prescription can simplify the complex medical treatment of patients, while reducing the burden of healthcare providers, so the medical treatment process can be more standardized, rational, humane. Because of the importance of medical signatures, in order to solve the problem that doctors cannot provide a signature also needs to consider the case of proxy signature. For proxy signature, the legality and privacy disclosure of the agents need to be considered. In the existing signature system, proxy negotiation is wildly used to grant attorney, however, this authorization process is complex, which cannot provide fine-grained access control for the identity of the agent. In this paper, based on attribute-based encryption, we propose a traceable proxy signature scheme, only when the user's attributes satisfy the access policy, the user can decrypt the corresponding ciphertext to obtain the proxy signature right. The program can solve the signature issue in case of the doctors absence, while solving the problem of attorney abuse. Meanwhile, the authorization is completed in central authority, thus, the computational overhead is greatly reduced, a simple, safe and efficient proxy signature scheme can be achieved.

Keywords: Mobile healthcare · Digital signature · Anonymous proxy · Attribute-based encryption · Traceability

1 Introduction

With the rapid development of the Internet, mobile healthcare has gradually become a hot research topic. In mobile healthcare, doctors can directly using electronic signature to issue electronic prescription, so the patients do not need to get signed by a doctor to take medicine, and the patient also can have physical examination without getting signed by a doctor according to the electronic prescriptions. By using electronic prescriptions, electronic medical records and

G. Wang et al. (Eds.): SpaCCS 2016, LNCS 10066, pp. 178–189, 2016.
DOI: 10.1007/978-3-319-49148-6_16

electronic inspection report, facilitate the hospital staff and the difficulties of medical treatment of patients have been greatly reduced. In the mobile health-care system, the electronic medical records, electronic prescriptions, electronic inspection reports are called electronic medical documents, the medical documents record patients condition from medical treatment until the end of the diagnosis and the treatment of all the relevant condition changes, report check and the full course of treatment, and for a doctor, also record all the examination, judgment, treatment of the whole process, which contain personal privacy information. If the privacy is obtained by an attacker, patients' safety of life and property will be greatly impacted, so these privacy information can only be viewed or signed by professional doctors. However, in many cases, doctors can not personally carry out signatures, such as doctors are busy with surgery or business trip, then you need to find an agent to help doctors deal with these issues [1]. In the actual situation, many agents in order to protect their own privacy may be not willing to reveal his identity to the original signature. Therefore, agent identity anonymous is necessary. However, in the anonymous, the legitimacy of the agent should also be considered, if the agent uses the right of signature to make some illegal behavior, which needs timely tracking to the proxy to ensure efficiency of signature. Waters et al. proposes an identity-based encryption scheme [2], and on this basis a standard model of identity based signature scheme is given, but this method is relatively single, can not adapt to a variety of circumstances under the signature. To solve this problem, Kim et al. propose a proxy signature scheme [3], proxy signature can combine other signature technology to produce digital signature scheme. However, the signature of the agency privacy lack effective protection. Then Yu et al. propose a proved secure anonymous proxy signature scheme [4], the scheme combines proxy signature and ring signature, which realize the anonymity proxy signature and the protection of the proxy signature, but the program is not traceable and signature verification efficiency is low.

2   Preliminaries

In this section, some preliminaries related to bilinear maps, complexity assumptions and access structure are presented.

2.1   Bilinear Maps

Let G and G' be two multiplicative cyclic groups with big prime order p. Let g be a generator of G. Let be a bilinear map $e : G \times G \to G'$ with the following properties [5]:

(1) Bilinearity For all and the equation holds.
(2) Non-degeneracy $e(g, g) \neq 1$.
(3) Computability There exists an efficient algorithm to compute bilinear map $e : G \times G \to G'$.

2.2 Bilinear Diffie-Hellman Inversion Assumption

In order to prove the security of the ATAPS scheme, we introduce l-BDHI assumption used in [6]. The l-BDHI problem in G is as follows: Given g, h and g^{y^i} in G for $i = 1, 2, ..., l$ as input for some unknown random $y \in Z_p^*$, output $W \in G'$ to decide whether $W = e(g,g)^{y^{l+1}}$. We say that a polynomial-time adversary $\mathcal{A}$ has advantage ε in solving the decisional l-BDHI problem (G, G') if $|Pr[A(g, h, y, e(g, h)^{y^{l+1}}) = 0] - Pr[A(g, h, y, e(g, h)^{y^z}) = 0]| \geq \varepsilon$, Where the probability is taken over random y, z and the random bits consumed by $\mathcal{A}$.

Definition 1. *We say that the (t, ε)-l-BDHI assumption holds in (G, G') if no t-time algorithm has the probability at least ε in solving the l-BDHI problem for non-negligible ε [7].*

2.3 Access Structure and Access Tree

Definition 2 *(Access structure [8]). Let $\{P_1, P_2, ..., P_n\}$ be a set of parties. A collection $A \subseteq 2^{\{P_1, P_2, ..., P_n\}}$ is monotone if $\forall B, C$: if $B \in A$ and $B \in C$. An access structure (respectively, monotonic access structure) is a collection (respectively, monotone collection) A of non-empty subsets of $\{P_1, P_2, ..., P_n\}$, i.e. $A \subseteq 2^{\{P_1, P_2, ..., P_n\}} \backslash \{0\}$. The sets in A are called the authorized sets, and the sets not in A are called the unauthorized sets.*

2.4 Access Tree with Time-Specific Attributes

We denote γ as an access tree. Each non-leaf node of the tree represents a threshold gate, described by a threshold value and its children [9]. If num_x is the number of children of a node x and k_x is its threshold value, the $0 < k < num_x$ holds. The threshold gate is an OR gate when threshold value $k_x = 1$. If threshold value of node x of the tree is associated with a time instant t_x. If the t_x belongs to a time interval $[t_{L,x}, t_{R,x}]$, which is associated with the corresponding attribute x in the ciphertext, we let value $k_x = 1$.

Some functions are defined in order to facilitate dealing with γ. In γ, the function $parent(x)$ is represented as the parent of the node x. The component of attributes is associated with the leaf node x in γ, also defines an ordering between the children of a node which are numbered from 1 to num. The function $index(x)$ returns such a number associated with the node x, where the index values are uniquely allocated to nodes in γ for a given key [10].

In the following we will describe how to satisfy an access tree width attributes and time constraints. Let Γ be a with root r. Γ_x is represented as the subtree of Γ with the root node at x. For the root r of Γ, we denote Γ_r. If a set of attributes S satisfies Γ_x, we denote it as $\Gamma_x(S) = 1$. $\Gamma_x(S)$ is calculated recursively as follows: If x is a non-leaf node, evaluate $\Gamma_x(S)$ returns 1 if and only if at least k_x children return 1. If x is a node belongs to the last layer from bottom, then $\Gamma_x(S)$ returns 1 if and only if the current time instant t_x associated with leaf node (attribute) in the access tree belongs to time interval $[t_{L,x}, t_{R,x}]$ associated with the corresponding attribute x in the ciphertext, that is $t_x \in [t_{L,x}, t_{R,x}]$.

2.5   Security Model

In the model, an attacker can be preset to two categories:

(1) External attackers: the attacker $\mathcal{A}_1$ only knows public key of the original signer and the proxy signer;
(2) Internal attackers: the attacker $\mathcal{A}_2$ has access to the proxy signature key;

For the first attacker, now give a formal security game:

Setup: Challenger runs algorithm Setup and gives the public key PK to adversary.

Phase 1: Adversary repeatedly generates private keys of corresponding attributes set $S_1, S_2, ..., S_{q_1}$.

Challenge: Adversary offers two message M_0, M_1 with same length. Besides, attributes sets $S_1, S_2, ..., S_{q_1}$ provided by adversary cannot satisfy access policy A^*. Challenger randomly choose $b \in \{0, 1\}$, encrypt M_b under A^*, and send ciphertext CT^* to adversary.

Phase 2: Adversary provides attributes sets $S_{q_1+1}, S_{q_2+1}, ..., S_q$, and these sets cannot satisfy the access policy, repeat phase 1.

Guess: Adversary output the guess b' of b.

In the above game, the advantage of $\mathcal{A}_1$ is $Pr[b' = b] - \frac{1}{2}$. Note that this model can be used in phase 1 and phase 2 to allow the decryption of the adversary query to be extended to handle the case of chosen plaintext attack.

Definition 3. *In above security game, this scheme is secure if the adversary has the advantage that can be ignored in polynomial time.*

For the second attackers, game between the attacker $\mathcal{A}_2$ and the challenger $\mathcal{C}$ can be described as follows:

Setup: Challenger $\mathcal{C}$ runs algorithm Setup and sends public key PK to adversary. Next, challenger runs algorithm K to generate authorization key, and runs algorithm E to encrypt authorization certificate, then upload the ciphertext with access policy to the cloud.

Authorization asks: $\mathcal{A}_2$ ask the authorization of certificate for authority center. The authority runs algorithm V to verify the identity of attacker. When passing the verification, attacker obtains the certificate.

Proxy signature ask: $\mathcal{A}_2$ asks the proxy signature for any message $m \in \{0, 1\}^*$ from $\mathcal{C}$. If necessary, $\mathcal{C}$ firstly runs agent protocol (D, P) and generates the certificate of w. $\mathcal{C}$ runs proxy signature algorithm PS to generate the proxy signature $p\sigma$ about message $m \in \{0, 1\}^*$ with satisfying the certificate w, and then sends $p\sigma$ to $\mathcal{A}_2$.

Output: Game over, the adversary $\mathcal{A}_2$ outputs $m^*, w^*, p\sigma^*$. If the following conditions are established, then the attacker wins the game:

(1) Adversary does not query the authority of certificate w^*;
(2) Adversary does not query the proxy signature of m^*, po^*;
(3) $PV(m^*, po^*, y_A^*, y_B^*) = 1$.

The possibility to win the game is ε for adversary $\mathcal{A}_2$ within time t, after q_d times authority query and q_s times proxy signature query, $\mathcal{A}_2$ is called $(\varepsilon, t, q_d, q_s)$ attacker of proxy signature scheme. If the ε is negligible, the scheme is safe for the original signer.

3   Proposed Scheme

In this section, we propose an attribute-based anonymous proxy signature scheme and security analysis.

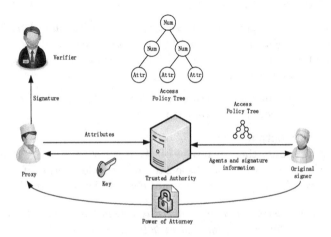

Fig. 1. System architecture model

3.1   Scheme Description

Suppose Alice is an origin signer, $\mu = \{\mu_1, \mu_2, ..., \mu_n\}$ is the collection of proxy signers, $\mu_i (1 \leq i \leq n)$ is a certain proxy signer. The scheme contains the following parts:

(1) Setup: G_0, G_1 are cyclic group with order p, bilinear mapping $e : G_0 \times G_0 \rightarrow G_1$ generator $g \in G_0$. randomly select security parameter κ this security parameter determines the scale of group. Meanwhile, this algorithm defines Lagrange coefficient $\Delta_{i,s} \in Z_p$, S is an element in Z_p: $\Delta_{i,s}(x) = \prod_{j \in S, j \neq i} \frac{x-j}{i-j}$. By hash function $H : \{0,1\}^* \rightarrow G_0$, any attribute of binary string description can be mapped to any random group. The encryption hash function is $H_0 : \{0,1\}^* \times G_0 \rightarrow Z_q^*$, $H_1 : \{0,1\}^* \rightarrow \{0,1\}^k$. Randomly selects $\alpha, \beta \in Z_p$ and generates system public key: $PK = \{G_0, g, h = g^\beta, e(g,g)^\alpha\}$, master key: $MK = \beta, g^\alpha$.

(2) Key Generation: Origin signer randomly selects $x_0 \in Z_q^*$ as the private key, and the public key is $Y_0 = x_0 \cdot g$. Similarly, each proxy signer selects $x_i \in Z_q^*$ as private key, the public key is $Y_0 = x_0 \cdot g$.

(3) Signature Stage: Before this phase, origin signer needs to encrypt authorization certificate and sends it with access policy to the authority. The authorization of signature is conducted by attributes, only when the agent satisfies the access policy designed by origin signer, he/she can be authorized.

(1) Construction of signature authorization certificate: Origin signer generates certificate m_w which contains the validate time of proxy signature authorization, identity of origin signer, the identity of all the proxy signer and the scope of the signing of the message. Selects a random number $\theta \in Z_q^*$ and computes $\Theta = \theta g, \lambda = \theta + x_0 H_0(m_w, \Theta) \bmod p$, then sends the $\{m_w, \Theta, \lambda\}$ to the authority center.

(2) Encryption algorithm: This algorithm encrypts m_w under the access structure τ. Algorithm firstly chooses a polynomial q_x for every node (including the leaf node) in τ. To begin with the root R. from top to the bottom, selects the polynomial. The degree d_x of the polynomial q_x of the node x is one less than the threshold k_x, which is $d_x = k_x - 1$.

The algorithm selects a random number $s \in Z_p$ from the root R and sets $q_R(0) = s$. Then, the algorithm selects d_R points from q_R to define q_R. As for other vertex x, sets $q_x(0) = q_{parent(x)}(index(x))$, randomly selects other d_x points to define q_x. Suppose Y is the collection of leaf nodes in τ, so we can get the ciphertext under the access tree τ:

$$CT = \{\tau, \tilde{C} = m_w \cdot e(g,g)^{\alpha s}, C = h^s, \forall y \in Y : C_y = g^{q_y(0)}, C_y' = H(att(y))^{q_y(0)}\}$$

(3) Access key generation algorithm: This algorithm inputs the attributes set S and outputs the secrete key denoted by S. Algorithm firstly selects a random number $r \in Z_p$, and for each randomly selects $j \in S$, then computes the private key:

$$SK = \{D = g^{(\alpha+r)/\beta}, \forall j \in S : D_j = g^r \cdot H(j)^{r_j}, D_j^* = g^{r_j}\}$$

(4) Decryption algorithm: Decryption algorithm is a recursive algorithm. For the sake of simplicity, we present the simplest form of decryption algorithm in this paper. Firstly, we define the recursive algorithm $Decrypt(PK, CT, x)$, ciphertext CT, the private key SK associated with attributes set S the node x in τ are the input. when x is the leaf node, set $i = att(x)$, if $iinS$, then

$$DecryptNode(CT, SK, x) = \frac{e(D_i, C_x)}{e(D_i', C_x')}$$

$$= \frac{e(g^r \cdot H(i)^{r_i}, g^{q_x(0)})}{e(g^{r_i}, H(i)^{q_x(0)})} = e(g,g)^{r q_x(0)} \tag{1}$$

if $i \notin S$, then $Decrypt(PK, CT, x) = \perp$.

Now consider the recursive case when x is not the leaf node. The working methods of the algorithm $Decrypt(PK, CT, x)$ are as follows: for all the leaf nodes z in x, calculates $F_z = Decrypt(PK, CT, z)$. Suppose S_x is the collection of leaf node z with size k_x and satisfying $F_z \neq \perp$. If there is no such collection, then the node is not satisfied, and the function returns $\perp$; otherwise calculates $F_x = \prod F_z^{\Delta_{i,s'_x}(0)}$, where $i = index(z)$, $S'_x = \{index(z) : z \in S_x\}$.

$$
\begin{aligned}
F_x &= \prod_{z \in S(x)} F_z^{\Delta_{i,s'_x}(0)} = \prod_{z \in S(x)} (e(g,g)^{r \cdot q_z(0)})^{\Delta_{i,s'_x}(0)} \\
&= \prod_{z \in S(x)} (e(g,g)^{r \cdot q_{parent(z)}(index(z))})^{\Delta_{i,s'_x}(0)} \\
&= \prod_{z \in S(x)} (e(g,g)^{r \cdot q_z(0) \cdot \Delta_{i,s'_x}(0)}) \\
&= e(g,g)^{r \cdot q_x(0)}
\end{aligned}
\tag{2}
$$

After defining function $DecryptNode$, we define decryption algorithm. This algorithm first runs $Decrypt(CT, SK, R)$, R is the root of tree τ. If the tree satisfies S, the algorithm sets:

$$
A = Decrypt(CT, SK, R) = e(g,g)^{r q_R(0)}
\tag{3}
$$

Decrypting by the following decryption algorithm:

$$
\tilde{C} \Big/ \frac{e(C,D)}{A} = \tilde{C} \Big/ \frac{e(h^s, g^{(\alpha+r)/\beta})}{e(g,g)^{rs}} = m_w
\tag{4}
$$

The signature authorization is carried out in the authority center, if the attributes of proxy signer match the access policy, she/he can decrypt the ciphertext $\tilde{C}$ to get m_w. The authority center randomly selects k_i and computes $PID_i = H_1(k_i, ID_i)$ as the identity of the proxy signer μ_i where ID_i is the real identity of μ_i. Then, the authority sends Θ, λ, PID_i to proxy signer through secure channel. When proxy signer receives Θ, λ, PID_i, the proxy μ_i verify the equation $\lambda g = \Theta + H_0(m_w, \Theta)Y_0$. If the equation is correct, the authority will accept authorization, or will reject it.

(4) Signature Phase: After obtaining the access authorization, the agent will calculate the proxy private key, and replace the original signature on file according to the definition of proxy authorization to.

(1) Generation of signature private key: After obtaining m_w, the signer randomly selects $k \in Z_p^*$ and calculates signature private key $psk_s = k(\lambda + x_s H_0(m_w, \Theta))$.

(2) Signing: The process is relatively simple, only needs to calculate the four signature components.

$$V = k \cdot H_0(m_w, \Theta)$$

$$\hat{Y} = k \sum_{i=1, i \neq s}^{n} (Y_0 + Y_i) \tag{5}$$

$$\sigma_s = psk_s^{-1} \cdot H(m_w \| m)$$

$$\Theta' = k\Theta$$

Signature can be obtained after calculating the above signature component

$$\sigma = \{\sigma_s, m, m_w, \Theta', \Theta, V, \hat{Y}, PID_s\}$$

(5) Validation Phase: After signing the documents, the verifier needs to verify the signature when viewing the file. According to the public key of proxy signer $Y_0, Y_1, ..., Y_n$ and the given anonymous proxy signature s, verifier verifies the following equation:

$$e(n\Theta' + v \sum_{i=1}^{n} (Y_0 + Y_1), \sigma_s) = e(g, H(m_w \| m))e((n-1)\Theta' + H_0(m_w, \Theta)\hat{Y}, \sigma_s) \tag{6}$$

If the equation is correct, verifier will accept signature, or will reject it.

3.2   Correctness Verification

In the description of the scheme in detail in section, an agent after the access to the agency that is able to file for the signature, this scheme for the validity of the signature can be directly by the following equation:

$$t_i g = (x_i h_0(m_w, K_i) + k_i)g = h_0(m_w, K_i)x_i g + k_i g = Y_i h_0(m_w, K_i) + K_i$$

$$\lambda g = (\theta + x_0 H_0(m_w, \Theta))g = \theta g + H_0(m_w, \Theta)x_0 g = \Theta + H_0(m_w, \Theta)Y_0$$

$$e(\sum_{i=1}^{n} (R' + V(Y_0 + Y_i)), \sigma_s)$$

$$= e(\sum_{i=1, i \neq s}^{n} \Theta' + V(Y_0 + Y_s), \sigma_s)e(\Theta' + V(Y_0 + Y_s), \sigma_s) \tag{7}$$

$$= e(\sum_{i=1, i \neq s}^{n} \Theta' + V(Y_0 + Y_s), \sigma_s)e(\Theta' + V(Y_0 + Y_s), psk^{-1}H(m_w \| m))$$

$$= e(P, H(m_w \| m))e((n-1)\Theta' + H_0(m_w, \Theta)\hat{Y}, \sigma_s)$$

3.3   Safety Analysis

Definition 4. *If in the polynomial time, the adversary can win the above game with negligible advantage, so the proposed scheme can achieve CPA security.*

Theorem 1. *If the adversary can break the security model, there is at least one polynomial time algorithm which can solve the DBDH problem without the negligible advantage.*

Proof. Suppose the adversary $\mathcal{A}$ can break the MHM-ABE algorithm with the nonnegligible advantage according to the security model, then we will prove the DBDH problem can be solved with the nonnegligible advantage $\frac{\varepsilon}{2}$.

Define the bilinear mapping $e : G_0 \times G_0 \to G_1$, G_0 is a multiply cyclic group with order p and generator g. First, the challenger of DBDH flips a coin b, and sets: $(g, A, B, C, Z) := \{(g, g^a, g^b, g^c, e(g,g)^{abc}), b = 0(g, g^a, g^b, g^c, e(g,g)^z), b = 1$, where $a, b, c, z \in Z_p$ are ransom numbers. Challenger then sends $(g, A, B, C, Z) = (g, g^a, g^b, g^c, Z)$ to simulator, in the following DBDH game, the simulator acts as the challenger.

(1) **System Initialization:** The adversary $\mathcal{A}$ chooses an access policy T^*.

(2) **System Setup:** Simulator $\mathcal{C}$ runs the parameter initialization algorithm in the proposed scheme, and generates the system public key

$$PK_0 = (G_0, g, h = g^\beta, f = g^{\frac{1}{\beta}}, e(g,g)^\alpha) \tag{8}$$

System master key $MK = (\beta, g^\alpha)$, $\mathcal{C}$ keeps MK_0, and sends PK_0 to adversary.

(3) **Query Phase 1:** The adversary requests the secrete key for the attribute sets $\{A_1, A_2, ..., A_q\}$, but any $A_i, 1 \leq i \leq q$ cannot satisfy the access tree T^*, simulator will call the secrete key construction method to calculate:

$$Du^{(k)} = g^{\frac{\alpha^{(k)}+ru^{(k)}}{\beta_{k,1}}},$$

$$Du_{i,j}^{(k)} = g^{ru_i^{(k)}} \cdot H(au_{i,j}^{(k)})^{ru_{i,j}^{(k)}}, \tag{9}$$

$$Du'_{i,j}^{(k)} = g^{ru_{i,j}^{(k)}}$$

then sends $SK_i, 1 \leq i \leq q$ to adversary.

(4) **Challenge Phase:** Adversary chooses the plaintext M_0, M_1 with the same length and sends them to $\mathcal{C}$, $\mathcal{C}$ flips a coin μ and $\mu \in \{0, 1\}$, then encrypts M_μ by T^*, finally sends the ciphertext CT^* to adversary.

$$CT^* = \{T^*, \tilde{C} = M_\mu \cdot Z, \{C^{(w)} = h_{w,1}^\theta, \bar{C}^{(w)} = h_{w,2}^\theta$$

$$\forall y^{(w)} \in Y^{(w)} : C_y^{(w)} = g^{q_y(0)}, C'_y^{(w)} = H(attr)^{q_y(0)}, \tag{10}$$

$$\forall x^{(w)} \in X^{(w)} : \hat{C}_x^{(w)} = h_{w,2}^{q_x(0)}\}_{w=1}^W\}$$

When $b = 0$, we defineand $Z = e(g,g)^{abc}$ set $c = \theta$, so the ciphertext CT^* is a ciphertext, because $\tilde{C} = M_\mu \cdot Z = M_\mu \cdot e(g,g)^{abc} = M_\mu \cdot e(g,g)^{a\theta}$. Otherwise, when $b = 1$, $Z = (g,g)^z$, $\tilde{C} = M_\mu \cdot Z = M_\mu \cdot e(g,g)^z$, Z is randomly chosen and dosen't relate to system, so $\tilde{C}$ is a random generator in G_0 and contains nothing about M_μ.

(5) **Query Phase 2:** Repeat the operation in query phase 1.

(6) **Guess:** Adversary outputs the guess of μ. If it is correct, which means $\mu = \mu'$, the simulator outputs $b' = 0$, which means the received tuple is DBDH tuple $(g, g^a, g^b, g^c, e(g, g)^{abc})$. Otherwise, the simulator outputs $b' = 1$, which means the received tuple is the random tuple $(g, g^a, g^b, g^c, e(g, g)^z)$.

In the above DBDH game, if $b = 1$, the adversary dosen't receive any information about M_μ, so $Pr[\mu' \neq \mu | b = 1] = \frac{1}{2}$. When $\mu' \neq \mu$, simulator guesses $b' = 1$, so $Pr[b' = b | b = 1] = \frac{1}{2}$.

If $b = 0$, the adversary can get the ciphertext M_μ, according to the definition, the adversary can break our scheme with the nonnegligible advantage, so $Pr[\mu' \neq \mu | b = 0] = \frac{1}{2} + \varepsilon$. When $\mu' = \mu$, simulator guesses $b' = 0$, so $Pr[\mu' \neq \mu | b = 1] = \frac{1}{2} + \varepsilon$.

Generally, the advantage that simulator in the above DBDH game can rightly guess $b' = b$ is:

$$
\begin{aligned}
Adv_c &= Pr[b' = b] - \frac{1}{2} \\
&= \frac{1}{2} Pr[b' = b | b = 1] + \frac{1}{2} Pr[b' = b | b = 0] - \frac{1}{2} \\
&= \frac{1}{2} \cdot \frac{1}{2} + \frac{1}{2} \cdot (\frac{1}{2} + \varepsilon) - \frac{1}{2} \\
&= \frac{\varepsilon}{2}
\end{aligned}
\tag{11}
$$

From the above analysis, if adversary $\mathcal{A}$ can break the security model with the nonnegligible advantage ε, then there exists an algorithm which can solve the DBDH problem with the advantage $\frac{\varepsilon}{2}$ in polynomial time.

Verifiability. In the signature $\sigma = \{\sigma_s, m, m_w, R', R, V, \hat{Y}, PID_s\}$, there is a proxy authorization m_w, and the participation of the original signer's public key is needed in the verification. Therefore, the verifier is convinced that the anonymous proxy signature by the original signer's authorization, which can meet the verifiability.

Traceability. In the case of disputes, the verifier will send the signature to the authorization server, the authorization server can reveal the identity of anonymous proxy signature. When receiving the proxy signature, the authorization server extracts PID_i from signature and searches corresponding ID_i from the stored information, so as to determine the identity of the proxy signature, so the traceability can be met.

3.4   Performance Analysis

In this section, the security and computing performance of the proposed scheme is compared with Yu. The comparison results are shown in Tables 1 and 2, e is bilinear mapping, P_a and P_b are the group multiplication and addition operations, respectively, n is the number of proxy signer, k represent a number of the property. Table 1 is the proposed scheme compared with Yu et al. on security,

Table 1. Safety comparison

Scheme	Anonymity	Unforgeability	Traceability
Yu	Yes	No	No
Our	Yes	Yes	Yes

Table 2. Performance comparison

Scheme	Keygen	Authorization	Signatures	Verification
Yu	Same	P_a	$(3n-2)P_a + (n+1)P_b$	$(n+1)e + nP_a + 2nP_a$
Our	Same	$ke + P_a$	$3P_a + (n-1)P_b$	$3e + 2P_a + 2nP_a$

Table 2 is compared with the proposed scheme and Yu et al. on computational cost.

From the table we can see that in the key generation phase, the two schemes have the same efficiency. During the delegation stage, the scheme in this paper has lower efficiency compared to Yu's scheme, but the authorization phase is completed in the trusted authority, which dose not occupy the signer and the proxys computing resource. In the signature generation and verification phase, when $n > 2$, the computational efficiency of the proposed scheme is higher than Yu's scheme, and with the increase of N, the efficiency advantages are more apparent. To implement anonymity, the number of the proxy signer is far greater than 2. Thus, the computational efficiency of the scheme in this paper is better than Yu's the anonymous signature scheme.

4   Conclusion

This paper mainly focuses on attribute-based access control, and how to apply this method to authorize to signature proxy in mobile healthcare. The privacy of proxy can be protected through anonymity and the malicious users can be traced when controversy occurred. Although some research results have been achieved, there are still some problems that need to be modified and concerned:

In the existing attribute-based schemes, the bilinear mapping is wildly used, because of its complexity, when attributes are large, the computational efficiency is not good enough. It needs further study that how to reduce time and computational overhead or design a new access structure to reduce the number of matching. Research on how to apply attribute-based encryption into medical signature is still in the primary stage, in real application, there are more actual demand, such as how to revoke without updating all the access policy when a malicious user is traced, meanwhile, the security and confidentiality can be guaranteed, which is the follow-up research work. In the proposed attribute-based proxy signature scheme, we suppose each user only has one key, which means he/she only has one attributes set. But in real application scenarios, users may have multiple identities, the agent may be also a doctor. How to cope with the multiple identities and prevent unauthorized illegal access also need to be addressed.

Acknowledgments. This work is supported in part by the National Natural Science Foundation of China under Grant Numbers 61632009, 61472451 and 61272151, and the High Level Talents Program of Higher Education in Guangdong Province under Funding Support Number 2016ZJ01. The Fundamental Research Funds for the Central Universities of Central South University 2016zzts339.

References

1. Santos-Pereira, C, Augusto, A.B, Cruz-Correia, R., et al.: A secure RBAC mobile agent access control model for healthcare institutions. In: Proceedings of the 26th IEEE International Symposium on Computer-Based Medical Systems, pp. 349–354. IEEE (2013)
2. Waters, B.: Efficient identity-based encryption without random oracles. In: Cramer, R. (ed.) EUROCRYPT 2005. LNCS, vol. 3494, pp. 114–127. Springer, Heidelberg (2005). doi:10.1007/11426639_7
3. Kim, Y.S., Chang, J.H.: Self proxy signature scheme. IJCSNS Int. J. Comput. Sci. Netw. Secur. **7**(2), 335–338 (2007)
4. Yu, Y., Xu, C., Huang, X., et al.: An efficient anonymous proxy signature scheme with provable security. Comput. Stan. Interfaces **31**(2), 348–353 (2009)
5. Zhou, J., Cao, Z., Dong, X., et al.: 4S: a secure and privacy-preserving key management scheme for cloud-assisted wireless body area network in m-healthcare social networks. Inf. Sci. **314**, 255–276 (2015)
6. Wang, G., Lu, R., Huang, C.: PSLP: Privacy-preserving single-layer perceptron learning for e-Healthcare. In 2015 10th International Conference on Information, Communications and Signal Processing (ICICS), pp. 1–5. IEEE (2015)
7. Son, J., Kim, J.D., Na, H.S., et al.: Dynamic access control model for privacy preserving personalized healthcare in cloud environment. Technol. Health Care **24**(S1), S123–S129 (2015)
8. Guo, F., Mu, Y., Susilo, W., et al.: CP-ABE with constant-size keys for lightweight devices. IEEE Trans. Inf. Forensics Secur. **9**(5), 763–771 (2014)
9. Bodong, C., et al.: A scheme supporting efficient attribute revocation for cloud storage based on CPABE. In: International Conference on Computer Science and Service System, pp. 736–740 (2014)
10. Schobel, J., Schickler, M., Pryss, R., Nienhaus, H., Reichert, M: Using vital sensors in mobile healthcare business applications: challenges, examples, lessons learned. In: International Conference on Web Information Systems and Technologies, pp. 509–518 (2013)
11. Yu, Y.C., Hou, T.W.: An efficient forward-secure group certificate digital signature scheme to enhance EMR authentication process. Med. BIol. Eng. Comput. **52**(5), 449–457 (2014)
12. Fadini, G.P., Albiero, M., Millioni, R., et al.: The molecular signature of impaired diabetic wound healing identifies serpinB3 as a healing biomarker. Diabetologia **57**(9), 1947–1956 (2014)
13. Rahman, F., Bhuiyan, M.Z.A., Ahamed, S.I.: A privacy preserving framework for RFID based healthcare systems. Future Gener. Comput. Syst. (2016). doi:10.1016/j.future.2016.06.001

A Privacy Preserving Friend Discovery Strategy Using Proxy Re-encryption in Mobile Social Networks

Entao Luo[1,3], Wenbo Wang[1], Dacheng Meng[1], and Guojun Wang[2(✉)]

[1] School of Information Science and Engineering,
Central South University, Changsha 410083, China
csgjwang@gmail.com
[2] School of Computer Science and Educational Software,
Guangzhou University, Guangzhou 510006, China
[3] School of Electronics and Information Engineering,
Hunan University of Science and Engineering, Yongzhou 425199, China

Abstract. In mobile social networks, based on secret sharing and CP-ABE, focusing on the security and privacy issues of friend discovery, we propose a matching scheme under different authorities and realize cross domain data access and sharing. By using proxy re-encryption technology, we hide users' access policy, which can guarantee the security and privacy in the friend making process. Because agents attend encryption and decryption, the privacy can be largely enhanced and the bottleneck of single authority also will be solved. Security and performance analysis show that the relationship of ciphertext's size and access policy is linear, which can resist collusion attack and meet CPA security, our scheme is superior to the existing schemes.

Keywords: Ciphertext-policy access control · Cross domain data access · Proxy re-encryption · Attribute-based encryption · Privacy preserving

1 Introduction

1.1 Background

With the rapid development of mobile social networks (MSN) and intelligent terminal equipment [1–4], users can share their emotions, photos, activities and hobbies to find new friends in MSN, many social applications can help enlarge the social scope (My Life Here, WeChat, etc.). Users can find friends with same interests or certain characteristics in cloud by comparing the personal attribute profile. But in this process, the cloud service provider (CSP) cannot be fully trusted, which may cause security risks of the stored data. For example, CSP may provide users' information to third parties without permission, which will affect users' data security. Hence, typically, users need to encrypt sensitive data to ensure the security and privacy.

© Springer International Publishing AG 2016
G. Wang et al. (Eds.): SpaCCS 2016, LNCS 10066, pp. 190–203, 2016.
DOI: 10.1007/978-3-319-49148-6_17

Attribute-based encryption scheme is a typical application of privacy protection in mobile social networks, including keyPolicy attribute based encryption (KP-ABE) [19–22] and ciphertext policy attribute based encryption (CP-ABE) [23–25]. In KP-ABE, the decryption key is related to the access policy, ciphertext is related to attributes set. If the attributes set in ciphertext can satisfy the access policy in secret key, the data visitor can decrypt the ciphertext. On the contrary, in CP-ABE, data owner can define special access policy depend on personal attribute profile. Secret keys are associated with attributes set, when and only when the attributes in secret keys can satisfy the access policy in ciphertext, users can obtain the plaintext, so data owners can control their data more directly. Hence, comparing to KP-ABE, CP-ABE is more suitable for friend discovery in mobile social networks.

In the system model and working mechanism, the existing modes always depend on single Trusted Authority ($\mathcal{TA}$) to distribute public keys and utilize the access tree generated from user's attribute to achieve access control to other users. But in this kind model, users are working in the same field, that is to say, the generation and distribution of all keys is generated by the same trusted authority.

Obviously, this model is not consistent with the actual application scenarios. For instance, in real dating system environment, data is stored in different clouds, when a data visitor expects to access data and exchange it, it is not possible to expect both data owner and visitor are in the same domain, inter cloud access needs to be taken into account. At the same time, in this model, the user's access control structure exists the risk of violent speculation by malicious attackers, once cracked successfully, it will directly threaten the data privacy. Therefore, single working domain scheme failed. Based on the above problems, this paper considers that users can share data in multi domains by introducing of proxy re encryption technology to ensure the data security.

1.2 Related Work

According to the research on security and privacy protection of friend discovery in the mobile social network, many researchers put forward their research results, literature [9–14] proposed a solution that does not rely on trusted authority, by calculating private set intersection (PSI) to ensure the user's privacy. The main method is: the two matching sides hold their own private attributes sets, by calculating the intersection or the intersection of the cardinal of the two sets to prevent the privacy leakage. Zhang et al. [15] improved the above methods, and proposed to distribute the different weight to the user's interest and calculate the similarity. In the follow-up work, Niu et al. [16] set the user's attributes with priority and improved it. Zhu et al. [17] proposed efficient confusion matrix transform algorithm to achieve a safe and efficient matching.

However, in the above schemes, users can only compare the number and weight of each attribute in the public collection, but do not consider the diversity of user attributes and access control. Therefore, the application range is limited. In the literature [5–8], the security and privacy in the process of making friends can be protected by the introducing the trusted authority and attribute encryption scheme, but in this model the problem of cross domain sharing of user data in the cloud cannot be solve. At the same time, it is a performance bottleneck to rely on single trusted authority. The literature [18] proposed the multi-authority attribute-based encryption scheme with access policy, the protocol using attributes to encrypt the message, and decrypts the message via trusted authority, and provide fine-grained access control to attributes matching and information sharing. But, in this scheme, there is violence speculation risk of access policy tree, once the access policy was successfully guessed, then the attacker can directly decrypt the stored data in a cloud, resulting in a security risk.

Therefore, in order to solve the problem of the performance bottlenecks and violent speculation of access policy, this paper intends to introduce the idea of multi-domain key sharing and proxy re-encryption technologies on the diversification of user management, to ensure the security and privacy of friend discovery in the mobile social networks. The symmetric encryption algorithm is adopted to encrypt the privacy sensitive data of the initiator, then utilize the CP-ABE algorithm to encrypt the symmetric key used in the symmetric encryption algorithm, finally get ciphertext of the key. When responder's attributes satisfy the access policy on initiator, the responder can decrypt the ciphertext of the key to get the decryption key, then decrypt the ciphertext downloaded from friend discovery center to obtain the plaintext. Further social activities can be carried out. The contributions of this paper are as follows:

(1) Based on secret sharing, an access control policy is proposed, ciphertext is associated with access policy, the ciphertext access control structure ensures that users can obtain the correct decryption key in accordance with the requirements of access control structure.
(2) We propose a proxy re-encryption based friend discovery scheme, using proxy re-encryption technology, the access control structure of data owner can be efficiently hided, and the user who satisfies the access control structure can correctly decrypt the encrypted data from the proxy user, which ensures that the friends of proxy user can be efficiently shared and guarantees the privacy of data owner.
(3) A multiple domain encryption scheme based on attributes is proposed, which can realize the data sharing among different domains, expand the scope of making friends, and improve the efficiency of the users.

2   Preliminaries

2.1   Mathematical Basis

Bilinear Mapping: Let $\mathbb{G}$ and $\mathbb{G}'$ be two multiplicative cyclic groups with big prime order p. Let g be a generator of $\mathbb{G}$. Let be a bilinear map $e : \mathbb{G} \times \mathbb{G} \rightarrow \mathbb{G}'$ with the following properties:

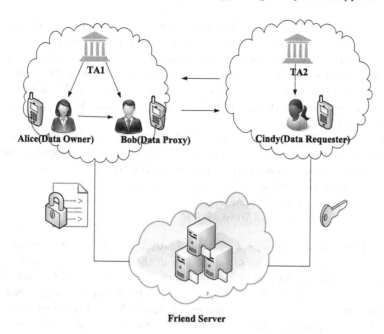

Fig. 1. Friend discovery scheme using proxy re-encryption

(1) Bilinearity: $e(P^a, Q^b) = e(P, Q)^{ab}, \forall P \in \mathbb{G}_0, Q \in \mathbb{G}_1$ and $a, b \in Z_q$.
(2) Non-degeneracy: The mapping will not map all pairs in $\mathbb{G}_0 \times \mathbb{G}_1$ to the identity in $\mathbb{G}_T$, because $\mathbb{G}_0, \mathbb{G}_1$ are groups of prime order, this means that if P and Q are generators of $\mathbb{G}_0$ and $\mathbb{G}_1$, respectively, then $e(P, Q)$ is the generator of $Z \in \mathbb{G}_T$.
(3) Computability: There exists an efficient algorithm to calculate $e(P, Q), \forall P \in \mathbb{G}_0, Q \in \mathbb{G}_1$.

2.2 System Model

The model in this paper mainly consists of the following components: Trusted Authority, Friend Server, Data Owner, Data Proxy, and Data Requester. The model assumes that Trusted Authority, is completely trustworthy and that Friend Server is honest and curious. That is, Friend Server will honestly comply with various system protocols but it will also do what it can to secretly access user files stored in it. Hence, the user should encrypt private files before uploading them to Friend Server. The general structure of the scheme is shown in Fig. 1.

(1) Trusted Authority ($\mathcal{TA}$): Responsible for initializing the system, generating the attribute keys of the region, distributing the keys, and for fine-granularity access control strategies.

(2) Friend Server ($\mathcal{FS}$): Responsible for storing the user's private cipher text, including personal photos, interests, contacts, identifies and private videos.

(3) Data Owner ($\mathcal{DO}$): Responsible for creating, modifying, deleting, encrypting files, and specifying access strategies. The encrypted files cannot be decrypted correctly unless the $\mathcal{DR}$'s property satisfies the $\mathcal{DO}$'s access control strategy before performing further communications. This paper supposes that Alice is $\mathcal{DO}$.

(4) Data Proxy ($\mathcal{DP}$): It is authorized by $\mathcal{DO}$ to re-encrypt $\mathcal{DO}$'s access control structure for the purpose of hiding $\mathcal{DO}$'s actual access control structure. Meanwhile, it can recommend its friends to $\mathcal{DR}$ to improve efficiency of the friend making mechanism. This paper assumes Bob as $\mathcal{DP}$.

(5) Data Requester ($\mathcal{DR}$): Responsible for submitting friend making request to $\mathcal{DP}$. This paper assumes Cindy as $\mathcal{DR}$.

First, $\mathcal{DO}$ uploads the access control strategy of a self-defined property to $\mathcal{TA}$. Each $\mathcal{TA}$ manages the set of properties in their respective domains, generates and distributes private keys for the set of properties owned by users in the domains. To ensure the safety of privacy during the friend making process, $\mathcal{DO}$ needs to encrypt the data to be shared and uploads the encrypted cipher text to $\mathcal{FS}$. During the friend making process, $\mathcal{DO}$ can grant authorization to the proxy, and $\mathcal{DP}$ can recommend friends to $\mathcal{DR}$ that satisfies the proxy's access control structure for the purpose of improving the friend making scope and efficiency of $\mathcal{DR}$, protecting the access control structure of $\mathcal{DO}$ from being intercepted by attackers, and ensuring privacy safety in the friend making process.

The access structure of sensitive data files is specified by $\mathcal{DO}$ or $\mathcal{DP}$. The cipher text of the sensitive data files can be accessed by other $\mathcal{DR}$ that satisfies the access structure. This enables $\mathcal{DO}$ and $\mathcal{DP}$ to flexibly control the access permission of other users.

The proposed scheme security validation relies on the security validation framework based on dual system encryption. The proposed scheme consists of five stages: system initialization phase, user private key generation phase, file encryption phase, cipher text proxy re-encryption phase, and file decryption phase.

3   Details of the Proposed Scheme

3.1   System Initialization Phase

$\mathcal{TA}$ chooses two cyclic groups $\mathbb{G}$ and $\mathbb{G}^{\mathrm{T}}$, whose order is the prime number p. It also randomly chooses elements $g, g_1 \in \mathbb{G}$, $a \in Z_p^*$. Let $e : \mathbb{G} \times \mathbb{G} \to \mathbb{G}_{\mathrm{T}}$ denote a bilinear mapping. The public parameter $GP = (p, g, \ g_1, g^a, \mathbb{G}, \mathbb{G}_{\mathrm{T}}, e)$, together with the Hash functions $H_1 : \{0,1\}^* \to \mathbb{G}$ and $H_2 : \mathbb{G}^{\mathrm{T}} \to Z_p^*$, are generated (Table 1).

Consider that the friend making system has multiple domains D_ϕ. For the TA_{ϕ_i} of any domain D_{ϕ_i}, it can execute the algorithm $setup(\ )$, randomly choose $\alpha_{\phi_i} \in Z_p^*$, generate the master key of the domain, $MSK_{\phi_i} = g^{\alpha_{\phi_i}}$, and the

Table 1. Summary of notations

Notation	Description
PK_{ϕ_i}, MSK_{ϕ_i}	Public key and master key
SK_S	Private key
KF	Symmetric key
CF	Data ciphertext
CT, CT'	Key ciphertext and re-encrypt key ciphertext
$DataFile$	Data plaintext
(M, ρ)	Data owner access control structure
(M', ρ')	Data proxy access control structure
$rk_{S \to (M', \rho')}$	Re-encrypt key
$Setup()$	System initializationfunction
$KeyGen()$	Key generation function
$Enc()$	Encryption function
$ReEnc()$	Re-encryption function
$ReKeyGen()$	Re-encrypt key generation function
$Dec()$	Decryption function

public key $PK_{\phi_i} = e(g,g)^{\alpha_{\phi_i}}$. The public parameter GP and the public key of the domain are public. The master key of the domain, MSK_{ϕ_i}, is stored by TA_{ϕ_i}.

3.2   User Private Key Generation Phase

The user who intends to join the network and participate in social activities, should first initiate the application on the smart terminal, and then chooses to register in a certain TA_{ϕ_i}. The registration process is as follows.

(1) The application of TA executes the algorithm $keyGen()$, chooses a random number $ts \in Z_p^*$ for the user, and generates the private key $SK_S = (K = g^{a \cdot ts} \cdot g^{\alpha_{\phi_i}}, L = g^{ts}, K_x = H_1(x)^{ts})$.
(2) TA_{ϕ_i} sends (PK_{ϕ_i}, SK_S) and the signature of this user in TA_{ϕ_i} to this user through the safe channels.

3.3   File Encryption Phase

The encryption process of DO is as follows:

(1) DO first chooses an unique document number FID randomly for the document, and randomly generates a symmetric key KF, which is then used to encrypt the plain text $DataFile$ for the purpose of obtaining the cipher text CF.

(2) $\mathcal{DO}$ runs the document encryption algorithm $Enc(\ )$, where (M, ρ) denotes the access control structure of $\mathcal{LSSS}$, M denotes the $l \times n$ matrix, ρ denotes the associated mapping from the rows of M to properties, $\{\rho(i)|1 \le i \le l\}$ denotes the property used in the access structure (M, ρ). $\mathcal{DO}$ randomly chooses a secret to be shared, $s \in Z_p^*$, and a vector $v = (s, y_2, ..., y_n), y_2, ..., y_n \in Z_p^*$. $\mathcal{DO}$ also sets $\lambda_i = v \cdot M_i$, where i ranges from i to l, M_i denotes the vector corresponding to the i_{th} row of M. We randomly choose $r_1, \ ... \ r_l \in Z_p^*$ to compute the cipher text:

$$A_1 = KFile \cdot e(g,g)^{\alpha \cdot s}, A_2 = g^s, A_3 = g_1^s;$$
$$B_1 = (g^a)^{\lambda_1} \cdot H_1(\rho(1))^{-r_1}, ..., B_l = (g^a)^{\lambda_l} \cdot H_1(\rho(l))^{-r_l}; \qquad (1)$$
$$C_1 = g^{r_1}, ..., C_l = g^{r_l};$$

The cipher text of the key can be expressed as:

$$CT = ((M, \rho), A_1, A_2, A_3, (B_1, C_1), ..., (B_l, C_l)) \qquad (2)$$

(3) $\mathcal{DO}$ sends (FID, CT, CF) and the signature to $\mathcal{FS}$, which will verify the signature after receiving it. If the signature is valid, (FID, CT, CF) will be stored.

3.4 Cipher Text Proxy Re-encryption Phase

The cipher text proxy re-encryption phase is as follows:

(1) Consider that the user Bob is a validly authorized proxy user that satisfies the access control structure (M, ρ) of $\mathcal{DO}$. Then, after receiving the permission from $\mathcal{DO}$, Bob will execute the algorithm $rekeyGen(\ )$.
Bob inputs the private key $SK = (K, L, K_x)$ and the set of properties S to generate a new access control structure (M', ρ'), where M' is the $l' \times n'$ matrix, ρ' is the associated mapping from the rows of M to properties. Let $\{\rho'(i)|1 \le i \le l'\}$ denote the properties used in the access structure (M', ρ').
(2) Bob randomly chooses $s' \in Z_p^*$ and the vector $v' = (s', y_2', ..., y_n'), y_2', ..., y_n' \in Z_p^*$. For i ranging from 1 to l', Bob sets $\lambda_i' = v' \cdot M_i'$, where M_i' is the vector corresponding to the i_{th} row of the matrix M'.
(3) If Bob and Cindy belong to the same $\mathcal{TA}$, D_{ϕ_i}, then Bob randomly chooses $\delta \in G_T$ to compute the cipher text.

$$A_1' = \delta \cdot e(g,g)^{\alpha_{\phi_i} \cdot s'}, A_2' = g^{s'};$$
$$B_1' = (g^a)^{\lambda_1'} \cdot H_1(\rho(1))^{-r_1'}, ..., B_l' = (g^a)^{\lambda_l'} \cdot H_1(\rho'(l'))^{-r_l'}; \qquad (3)$$
$$C_1' = g^{r_1'}, ..., C_{l'}' = g^{r_i'};$$

The cipher text can be expressed as:

$$C'_{(M', \ \rho')} = (A_1', A_2', B_1', C_1', ..., B_l', C_l') \qquad (4)$$

(4) If Bob and Cindy do not belong to the same $\mathcal{TA}$ (e.g., Bob belongs to D_{ϕ_i} and Cindy belongs to D_{ϕ_j}), Bob will apply for the public key $e(g,g)^{\alpha_{\phi_j}}$ of the domain D_{ϕ_j} and compute the cipher text.

$$A_1' = \delta \cdot e(g,g)^{\alpha_{\phi_j} \cdot s'}, A_2' = g^{s'};$$
$$B_1' = (g^a)^{\lambda_1'} \cdot H_1(\rho(1))^{-r_1'}, ..., B_l' = (g^a)^{\lambda_l'} \cdot H_1(\rho'(l'))^{-r_t'}; \tag{5}$$
$$C_1' = g^{r_1'}, ..., C_{l'}' = g^{r_l'};$$

The cipher text can be expressed as:

$$C_{(M', \ \rho')}' = (A_1', A_2', B_1', C_1', ..., B_{l_r}', C_l') \tag{6}$$

(5) Bob chooses $\theta \in Z_p^*$ and computes:

$$rk_1 = K^{H_2(\delta)} \cdot g_1^\theta = (g^{a \cdot ts} \cdot g^a)g_1^\theta, rk_2 = g^\theta, rk_3 = L^{H_2(\delta)},$$
$$\forall x \in S, rk_4 = C_{(M', \ \rho')}', R_x = K_x^{H_2(\delta)} \tag{7}$$

Bob outputs the re-encrypted key:

$$rk_{S \to (M', \ \rho')} = (S, rk_1, rk_2, rk_3, rk_4, R_x) \tag{8}$$

and sends $rk_{S \to (M', \ \rho')}$ to $\mathcal{FS}$.

(6) After receiving $rk_{S \to (M', \ \rho')}$, $\mathcal{FS}$ re-encrypts the cipher text of the key using the algorithm $reEnc(\ )$ and outputs the re-encrypted cipher text of the key, CT'. The calculation process is as follows:

If $I \subset \{1, ..., l\}$ is defined as $I = \{i : \rho(i) \in S\}$, $\{\lambda_i\}$ denotes the valid sharing of the secret s based on the matrix M, and S satisfies (M, ρ), then there exists a set of constants $\{\omega_i \in Z_p^*\}_{i \in I}$ which has $\sum_{i \in I} \omega_i \cdot \lambda_i = s$. Afterwards, we compute:

$$A_4 = \frac{e(A_2, rk_1)/e(A_3, rk_2)}{(\prod_{i \in I} (e(B_i, rk_3) \cdot e(C_i, R_{\rho(i)}))^{\omega_i})} \tag{9}$$

Output:

$$CT' = ((M', \ \rho'), A_1, A_3, (B_1, C_1), ..., (B_l, C_l), A_4, rk_4) \tag{10}$$

3.5   Document Decryption Phase

The document decryption phase is as follows:

Cindy issues a request to $\mathcal{FS}$ to access the encrypted document $\mathcal{CF}$ with a document number $\mathcal{FID}$. If the set of properties of Cindy, S, does not satisfy (M, ρ), then output the empty set $\perp$. If S satisfies $(M, \rho$, Cindy can download the encrypted $DataFile$ of $\mathcal{DO}$. Hence, Cindy needs to use the decryption algorithm $Desc(\ )$ to decrypt the cipher text of the key. The steps are as follows:

(1) If the cipher text of the key is the original cipher text CT:

Then define $I \subset \{1, ..., l\}$ as $I = \{i : \rho(i) \in S\}$. There exists a set of constants $\{w_i \in Z_p^*\}_{i \in I}$ which has $\sum_{i \in I} w_i \cdot \lambda_i = s$. Cindy computes:

$$
\begin{aligned}
A_4 &= \frac{e(A_2, rk_1)/e(A_3, rk_2)}{(\prod_{i \in I} (e(B_i, rk_3) \cdot e(C_i, R_{\rho(i)}))^{w_i})} \\
&= \frac{KF \cdot e(g,g)^{\alpha \cdot s} (\prod_{i \in I} (e(g^{\alpha \cdot \lambda_i} \cdot H_1(\rho(i))^{-r_i}, g^{ts}) \cdot e(g^{r_i}, H_1(\rho(i)^{ts}))^{w_i})}{e(g^s, g^{a \cdot ts} \cdot g^\alpha)} \\
&= \frac{KF \cdot e(g,g)^{\alpha \cdot s} e(g, g^{a \cdot ts})^{\sum_{i \in I} \lambda_i \cdot w_i}}{e(g^s, g^{a \cdot ts} \cdot g^\alpha)} \\
&= \frac{KF \cdot e(g,g)^{\alpha \cdot s} e(g, g^{a \cdot ts})^{\sum_{i \in I} \lambda_i \cdot w_i}}{e(g, g)^{\alpha \cdot s}} \\
&= KF
\end{aligned}
\tag{11}
$$

(2) Consider the case where the cipher text of the key is the re-encrypted cipher text of the key:

a. If $I' \subset \{1, ..., l'\}$ is defined as $I' = \{i : \rho'(i \in S'\}$ and $\{\lambda_1'\}$ is defined as the valid sharing of the secret s' based on M', then there exists a set of constants, $\{w_i' \in Z_p^*\}_{i \in I^*}$, which has $\sum_{i \in I} w_i' \cdot \lambda_i' = S'$. The user Cindy computes δ as:

$$
\delta = A_1'/e(A_2', K')/(\prod_{i \in I} (e(B_i', L') \cdot e(C_i', K_{\rho(i)}'))^{w_i'})
\tag{12}
$$

Correctness validation 1: If Cindy and Bob belong to the same domain D_{ϕ_i}:

$$
\begin{aligned}
&A_1'/e(A_2', K')/(\prod_{i \in I} (e(B_i', L') \cdot e(C_i', K_{\rho(i)}'))^{w_i'}) \\
&= \frac{\delta \cdot e(g,g)^{\alpha \phi_i \cdot S'} (\prod_{i \in I} (e(g^{a \cdot \lambda_i'} \cdot H_1(\rho'(i))^{-r_i'}, g^{ts'}) \cdot e(g^{r_i'}, H_1(\rho'(i))^{ts'}))^{w_i'})}{e(g^{S'}, g^{a \cdot t S'} \cdot g^{\alpha \phi_i})} \\
&= \delta
\end{aligned}
\tag{13}
$$

If Cindy and Bob does not belong to the same domain (e.g., Bog belongs to D_{ϕ_i} and C belongs to D_{ϕ_j}):

$$
\begin{aligned}
&A_1'/e(A_2', K')/(\prod_{i \in I} (e(B_i', L') \cdot e(C_i', K_{\rho(i)}'))^{w_i'}) \\
&= \frac{\delta \cdot e(g,g)^{\alpha \phi_j \cdot S'} (\prod_{i \in I} (e(g^{a \cdot \lambda_i'} \cdot H_1(\rho'(i))^{-r_i'}, g^{ts'}) \cdot e(g^{r_i'}, H_1(\rho'(i))^{ts'}))^{w_i'})}{e(g^{S'}, g^{a \cdot t S'} \cdot g^{\alpha \phi_j})} \\
&= \delta
\end{aligned}
\tag{14}
$$

b. Compute the cipher text of the key
$KF = A_1/(A_4)^{\frac{1}{H_2(\delta)}}$, and $A_4 = \frac{e(A_2, rk_1)/e(A_3, rk_2)}{(\prod_{i \in I} (e(B_i, rk_3) \cdot e(C_i, R_{\rho(i)}))^{w_i})}$.
Correctness validation 2:

$$A_4 = \frac{e(A_2, rk_1)/e(A_3, rk_2)}{\left(\prod_{i \in I} \left(e(B_i, rk_3) \cdot e(C_i, R_{\rho(i)})\right)^{w_i}\right)}$$

$$= \frac{e(g^S, (g^{a \cdot t_S} \cdot g^{\alpha_{\phi_i}})^{H_2(\delta)} \cdot g_1^\theta)/e(g_1^S, g^\theta)}{\left(\prod_{i \in I} \left(e((g^a)^{\lambda_i} \cdot H_1(\rho(i))^{-r_i}, (g^{t_S})^{H_2(\delta)}) \cdot e(g^{r_i}, H_1(\rho(i))^{t_S \cdot H_2(\delta)})\right)^{w_i}\right)} \tag{15}$$

$$= \frac{e(g^S, (g^{a \cdot t_S} \cdot g^{\alpha_{\phi_i}})^{H_2(\delta)})/e(g_1^S, g^{a \cdot t_S \cdot H_2(\delta)})}{e(g, g^{a \cdot t_S \cdot H_2(\delta)})^{\sum_{i \in I} \lambda_i \cdot w_i}}$$

$$= e(g^S, g^{a \cdot t_{\phi_i} \cdot H_2(\delta)})$$

$$A_1/(A_4)^{\frac{1}{H_2(\delta)}} = KF \cdot e(g, g)^{\alpha_{\phi_i} \cdot S}/e(g^S, g^{\alpha_{\phi_i}}) = KF \tag{16}$$

(3) Finally, Cindy can obtain the data document $DataFile$ by decrypting CF through KF in order to perform more profound communication. For example, Cindy can acquire DR's voice bands, videos, contacts and hobbies.

4   Security Analysis

Consider that the decidable $DBDH$ hypothesis is valid over (G, G_T), then no adversary A can conquer the proposed scheme using the access matrix (M^*, ρ^*) with a size of $\ell^* \times n^*(\ell^*, n^* \leq q)$.

Definition. Assume that an opponent A can conquer the proposed scheme in the CPA game by a margin of $\varepsilon = Adv_A$, then there is at least one polynomial time algorithm which can solve the $DBDH$ problem by an undeniable margin.

Proof: A challenger C is constructed for the decidable $DBDH$ hypothesis, determining $T = e(g, g)^{a^{q+1} \cdot S}$ or $T \in \mathbb{G}_T$.

C and A play the following CPA game: C inputs (p, g, G, G_T, e), $DBDH$ instance y and T, and then determine $T = e(g, g)^{a^{q+1} \cdot S}$ or $T \in \mathbb{G}_T$.

(1) **Initialization phase.** A delivers the access structure (M^*, ρ^*) to be challenged to C, where M^* is a matrix with a size of $\ell^* \times n^*$, ℓ^* is the number of rows, and n^* is the number of columns $(\ell^*, n^* \leq q)$.

(2) **Establishment phase.** If the property of the access control structure (M^*, ρ^*) belongs to the domain ϕ_i, then C chooses $\alpha_{\phi_i}, \gamma \in Z_p^*$, sets $g_1 = g^y$, and $e(g, g)^{\alpha_{\phi_i}} = e(g^\alpha, g^{\alpha^q}) \cdot e(g, g^{\alpha_{\phi_i}})$. Meanwhile, C chooses the Hash function H_1, H_2, sends the public parameter $GP = (p, g, G, G_T, e, g_1, g^\alpha, H_1, H_2)$ and the public key $PK = e(g, g)^{\alpha_{\phi_i}}$ to A.

A simulates fulfiment of the random prophecy $H_j(j \in \{1, 2\})$ by establishing the table $H_j^{List}(j \in \{1, 2\})$. And C answers the queries based on the following rules.

(a) H_1: C receives a query H_1 over $x \in U_{\phi_i}$. If the table H_1^{List} has contained the tuple $\{x, z_x, \delta_{2,x}, z_x \in Z_q^*, \delta_{2,x} \in G\}$, C returns the value $\delta_{2,x}$ in the tuple to A. Otherwise, C constructs $\delta_{2,x}$. Let X denote the set of labels $\rho^*(i) = x, (1 \leq i \leq \ell^*)$.

$\mathcal{C}$ chooses $z_x \in Z_q^*$, and sets: $\delta_{2,x} = g^{z_x} \cdot \prod_{i \in X}$
$g^{\alpha \cdot M_{i,1}^*/b_i + \alpha^2 \cdot M_{i,2}^*/b_i + \ldots + \alpha^{n^*} \cdot M_{i,n^*}^*/b_i}$.

If X is empty, then $\mathcal{C}$ sets $\delta_{2,x} = g^{z_x}$. $\mathcal{C}$ returns $\delta_{2,x}$ to $\mathcal{A}$ and adds the tuple $(x, z_x, \delta_{2,x})$ to the table H_1^{List}.

(b) H_2: $\mathcal{C}$ receives the query H_2 over $\delta \in G_T$. If H_2^{List} has included the tuple (δ, ξ), $\mathcal{C}$ sends the already included value $\xi \in Z_p^*$ to $\mathcal{A}$. Otherwise, $\mathcal{C}$ sets $H_2(\delta) = \xi$, returns ξ to $\mathcal{A}$, and adds the tuple (δ, ξ) to H_2^{List}.

(3) **Query phase 1.** $\mathcal{A}$ puts a series of queries to $\mathcal{C}$ and $\mathcal{C}$ answers based on the following rules.

(a) The private key extracts the query $O_{SK}(S)$: if $S \vdash (M^*, \rho^*)$, then $\mathcal{C}$ randomly chooses an output from 0,1 and then stops this game. Otherwise, $\mathcal{C}$ chooses a random value $r_S \in Z_p^*$, and finds $w = (w_1, w_2, \ldots, w_n) \in Z_p^*$, where $w_1 = -1$ and $w\dot{M}_i^* = 0$ when $\forall i, \rho^*(i) \in S$.

If S is in the domain D_{ϕ_i}, then $\mathcal{C}$ sets $L = g^{r_S} \cdot \prod_{i=1,\ldots,n} g^{a^{q+1-i} \cdot w_i} = g^{t_S}$. In this domain, t_S is easily defined as $t_S = r_S + w_1 \cdot a^q + \ldots + w_n \cdot a^{q-n+1}$. Next, based on this definition, $\mathcal{C}$ constructs $K = g^{\alpha \phi_j} \cdot g^{a \cdot r_S} \cdot \prod_{i=2,\ldots,n} g^{a^{q+2-i} \cdot w_i}$. Validation shows that $K = g^{\alpha \phi_j} \cdot g^{a^{q+1}} \cdot g^{-a^{q+1}} \cdot g^{a \cdot r_S} \cdot \prod_{i=2,\ldots,n} g^{a^{q+2-i} \cdot w_i} = g^{\alpha \phi_j} \cdot L^a = g^{\alpha \phi_j} \cdot g^{a \cdot t_S}$.

If $x \in S$ and $\rho^*(i) \neq x$ for all $i \in \{1, \ldots, \ell^*\}$, then let $K_x = L^{z_w} = \delta_{2,x}^{t_S} = H_1(x)^{t_S}$.

Otherwise,

$$K_x = L^{z_w} \cdot \prod_{i \in X} \prod_{j=1,\ldots,n} \left(g^{(a^j/b^j) \cdot r_S} \cdot \prod_{k=1,\ldots,n^*,k \neq j} \left(g^{a^{q+1+j-k}/b_j}\right)^{w_k}\right)^{M_{i,j}^*}$$
(17)

The equation above can prove validity of K_x by using the following equation.

$$K_x = L^{z_x} \cdot \prod_{i \in X} \prod_{j=1,\ldots,n} \left(g^{(a^j/b_i) \cdot r_S} \cdot \prod_{k=1,\ldots,n^*,k \neq j} \left(g^{a^{q+1+j-k}/b_i}\right)^{w_k}\right)^{M_{i,j}^*}$$

$$\cdot \prod_{i \in X} \prod_{j=1,\ldots,n} \left(g^{a^{q+1}/b_i}\right)^{w_j \cdot M_{i,j}^*}$$

$$= \left(g^{z_x} \cdot \prod_{i \in X} g^{a \cdot M_{i,1}^*/b_i + a^2 \cdot M_{i,2}^*/b_i + \ldots + a^{n^*} \cdot M_{i,n^*}^*/b_i}\right)^{(r_S + w_1 \cdot a^q + \ldots + w_{n^*} \cdot a^{q-n^*+1})}$$

$$= \delta_{2,x}^{(r_S + w_1 \cdot a^q + \ldots + w_{n^*} \cdot a^{q-n^*+1})}$$

$$= \delta_{2,x}^{t_S} = H_1(x)^{t_S}$$
(18)

where X is the set of i which has $\rho^*(i) = x$. If S does not satisfy (M^*, ρ^*), then we have $w \cdot M_i^* = 0$.

Hence,

$$\prod_{i \in X} \prod_{j=1,\ldots,n} \left(g^{a^{q+1}/b_i}\right)^{w_k \cdot M_{i,j}^*} = g^{a^{q+1} \cdot (\sum_{i \in X} \sum_{j=1,\ldots,n^*} w_j \cdot M_{i,j}^*/b_j)} = g^0 = 1$$
(19)

Finally, $\mathcal{C}$ adds the tuple (S, SK_S) to SK^{List}, and returns SK_S to $\mathcal{A}$.

(b) Re-encrypt the key to extract the query $O_{rk}(S, (M', \rho'))$: Use a property set S and an access structure (M', ρ') to query O_{rk}. According to the safety game, if S does not satisfy (M^*, ρ^*), $\mathcal{C}$ executes $O_{SK}(S)$ first to obtain the corresponding key (K, L, K_x), and then chooses $\theta, \sigma \in_R Z_p^*, \bar{K} \in_R G$. Compute the re-encryption key as $rk_1 = \bar{K} \cdot g_1^\theta, rk_2 = g^\theta, rk_4 = g^\sigma, R_X = \delta_{2,x}^\sigma$.

(4) **Challenge stage.** $\mathcal{A}$ outputs m_0, m_1 to $\mathcal{C}$. $\mathcal{C}$ chooses $b \in \{0,1\}$ and answers based on the following rules. For each row i in M^*, set $x^* = \rho^*(i)$ and query H_1 over x^* in order to obtain the tuple $(x^*, z_x, \delta_{2,x^*})$.
Choose $y_2', y_3', ..., y_{n^*}'$ and use the vector to share the secret $v = (s, s \cdot a + y_2', s \cdot a^2 + y_3', ..., s \cdot a^{n-1} + y_{n^*}') \in Z_p^{n^*}$. Choose $r_1', ..., r_{l^*}' \in Z_p^*$, and for all $i \in \{1, 2, ..., l^*\}$, R_i denotes the sets that have $i \neq k$ and $\rho^*(i) = \rho^*(k)$. We define that:

$$B_i^* = \delta_{2,x}^{-r_i} \cdot \left(\prod_{j=2,...,n} g^{a \cdot M_{i,j}^* \cdot y_j} \right) \cdot g^{b_i \cdot s \cdot (0 z_{x^*})} \cdot \left(\prod_{k \in R_i} \prod_{j=1,...,n^*} (g^{a^j \cdot s \cdot (b_i/b_k)})^{M_{k,j}^*} \right)^{-1}$$

(20)

$$C_i^* = g^{r_i^* + s \cdot b_i}$$

(21)

(a) $\mathcal{C}$ chooses $A_1^* \in \{0,1\}^{2k}$, defines $T \cdot e(g^s, g^{\alpha \phi_i}) = A_1^*/m_b$ in an implicit manner and sets $A_2^* = g^s, A_3^* = g_1^s$.
(b) Output the challenging cipher text:

$$CT^* = ((M^*, \rho^*), A^*, A_2^*, A_3^*, (B_1^*, C_1^*), ..., (B_{l^*}^*, C_{l^*}^*))$$

(22)

to $\mathcal{A}$. If $T = e(g, g)^{a^{q+1} \cdot s}$, then CT^* is a valid cipher text.

(5) **Query stage 2.** Query as in the first stage but the constraint in Definition 1 needs to be satisfied.

(6) **Prediction stage.** $\mathcal{A}$ outputs a predicted bit $b' \in \{0,1\}$. Then, $\mathcal{C}$ makes its prediction based on the prediction of $\mathcal{A}$. If $\mathcal{A}$ predicts correctly that $b' = b$, then $\mathcal{C}$ outputs the prediction $1(T = e(g,g)^{a^{q+1} \cdot s})$ in the challenge process of the game. Otherwise, $\mathcal{C}$ outputs $0(T \in G_T)$. The success probability of $\mathcal{C}$ can be computed follows.
If the output is 1, i.e. $T = e(g,g)^{a^{q+1} \cdot s}$, then what $\mathcal{A}$ obtains is a valid cipher text about m_b. According to the definition, $\mathcal{A}$ can correctly predict the result. Hence, $\Pr[b' \neq b | (y, T = e(g,g)^{a^{q+1} \cdot s}) = 0] = \frac{1}{2} + Adv_A$.
If the output is 0, i.e. $T \in G_T$, then $\mathcal{A}$ obtains no message on m_b. Hence, the prediction is right at a probability of $\Pr[b' \neq b | (y, T = R) = 0] = \frac{1}{2}$. In this case, $\mathcal{C}$ has an non-negligible advantage of $\frac{\varepsilon}{2}$ in the delidable$DBDH$ game.

5   Conclusion

In mobile social networks, maximizing the contact and communication between each other, while protecting the privacy of users is a research hotspot in privacy preserving field. Based on cryptography, we propose cross domain re-encryption protocol for privacy preserving. The scheme improves the efficiency of making friends in mobile social networks and enables users find friends satisfying the access policy with fine-grained access control. By using proxy re-encryption, the real access control structure is hidden. The security and privacy of friend discovery in mobile social networks is realized. Meanwhile, we introduce multi-authority, secret keys are generated from several authorities, which solves the bottleneck of single point and key management. From the security analysis, it is proved that the proposed scheme can meet CPA security.

Acknowledgments. This work is supported in part by the National Natural Science Foundation of China under Grant Numbers 61632009, 61472451, 61272151. Hunan Provincial Natural Science Foundation of China under Grant Numbers 2016JJ305. High Level Talents Program of Higher Education in Guangdong Province under Funding Support Number 2016ZJ01. The Fundamental Research Funds for the Central Universities of Central South University 2016zzts060. The Hunan Provincial Education Department of China under grant number 2015C0589.

References

1. Guo, L., Zhang, C., Sun, J., et al.: A privacy-preserving attribute-based authentication system for mobile health networks. IEEE Trans. Mob. Comput. **13**(9), 1927–1941 (2014)
2. Colman-Meixner, C., Develder, C., Tornatore, M., et al.: A survey on resiliency techniques in cloud computing infrastructures and applications. IEEE Commun. Surv. Tutorials **18**(3), 2244–2281 (2016)
3. Luo, E., Liu, Q., Wang, G.: Hierachical multi-authority and attribute-based encryption friend discovery scheme in mobile social networks. IEEE Commun. Lett. **20**(9), 1772–1775 (2016)
4. Xu, Q., Su, Z., Guo, S.: A game theoretical incentive scheme for relay selection services in mobile social networks. IEEE Trans. Veh. Technol. **65**(8), 6692–6702 (2015)
5. Salih, R.M., Lilien, L.T.: Protecting users' privacy in healthcare cloud computing with APB-TTP. In: IEEE International Conference on Pervasive Computing and Communication Workshops (PerCom Workshops), 2015, pp. 236–238 (2015)
6. Manweiler, J., Scudellari, R., Cox, L.P.: SMILE: encounter-based trust for mobile social services. In: Proceedings of the 16th ACM Conference on Computer and Communications Security, pp. 246–255 (2009)
7. Ge, A., Zhang, J., Zhang, R., et al.: Security analysis of a privacy-preserving decentralized key-policy attribute-based encryption scheme. IEEE Trans. Parallel Distrib. Syst. **24**(11), 2319–2321 (2013)
8. Dong, W., Dave, V., Qiu, L., et al.: Secure friend discovery in mobile social networks. In: Proceedings of IEEE INFOCOM 2011, pp. 1647–1655 (2011)
9. Freedman, M.J., Nissim, K., Pinkas, B.: Efficient private matching and set intersection. In: International Conference on the Theory and Applications of Cryptographic Techniques, pp. 1–19 (2004)
10. Kissner, L., Song, D.: Privacy-preserving set operations. In: Annual International Cryptology Conference, pp. 241–257 (2005)
11. Sang, Y., Shen, H.: Efficient and secure protocols for privacy-preserving set operations. ACM Trans. Inf. Syst. Secur. **13**(1), 315–326 (2009)

12. Cristofaro, E., Kim, J., Tsudik, G.: Linear-complexity private set intersection protocols secure in malicious model. In: Abe, M. (ed.) ASIACRYPT 2010. LNCS, vol. 6477, pp. 213–231. Springer, Heidelberg (2010). doi:10.1007/978-3-642-17373-8_13

13. Li, M., Cao, N., Yu, S., et al.: Findu: privacy-preserving personal profile matching in mobile social networks. In: Proceedings of IEEE INFOCOM 2011, pp. 2435–2443 (2011)

14. Guo, L., Liu, X., Fang, Y., et al.: User-centric private matching for ehealth networks-a social perspective. In: IEEE Global Communications Conference (GLOBECOM), pp. 732–737 (2012)

15. Zhang, R., Zhang, Y., Sun, J., et al.: Fine-grained private matching for proximity-based mobile social networking. In: Proceedings of IEEE INFOCOM 2012, pp. 1969–1977 (2012)

16. Niu, B., Zhu, X., Liu, J., et al.: Weight-aware private matching scheme for proximity-based mobile social networks. In: IEEE Global Communications Conference (GLOBECOM), pp. 3170–3175 (2013)

17. Zhu, X., Chen, Z., Chi, H., et al.: Two-party and multi-party private matching for proximity-based mobile social networks. In: IEEE 2014 International Conference on Communications (ICC), pp. 926–931 (2014)

18. Zhou, Z., Huang, D., Wang, Z.: Efficient privacy-preserving ciphertext-policy attribute based-encryption and broadcast encryption. IEEE Trans. Comput. 64(1), 126–138 (2015)

19. Wang, J., Lang, B.: An efficient KP-ABE scheme for content protection in information-centric networking. In: 2016 IEEE Symposium on Computers and Communication (ISCC), pp. 830–837 (2016)

20. Touati, L., Challal, Y.: Collaborative KP-ABE for cloud-based internet of things applications. In: 2016 IEEE International Conference on Communications ICC, pp. 1–7 (2016)

21. Liu, P., Wang, J., Ma, H., et al.: Efficient verifiable public key encryption with keyword search based on KP-ABE. In: 2014 Ninth International Conference on Broadband and Wireless Computing (BWCCA), pp. 584–589 (2014)

22. Okamoto, T., Takashima, K.: Fully secure functional encryption with general relations from the decisional linear assumption. In: Rabin, T. (ed.) CRYPTO 2010. LNCS, vol. 6223, pp. 191–208. Springer, Heidelberg (2010). doi:10.1007/978-3-642-14623-7_11

23. Waters, B.: Ciphertext-policy attribute-based encryption: an expressive, efficient, and provably secure realization. In: International Workshop on Public Key Cryptography, pp. 53–70 (2011)

24. Bethencourt, J., Sahai, A., Waters, B.: Ciphertext-policy attribute-based encryption. In: IEEE Symposium on Security and Privacy (SP 2007), pp. 321–334 (2007)

25. Ramesh, D., Priya, R.: Multi-authority scheme based CP-ABE with attribute revocation for cloud data storage. In: IEEE 2016 International Conference on Microelectronics, Computing and Communications (MicroCom), pp. 1–4 (2016)

Defect Analysis and Risk Assessment of Mainstream File Access Control Policies

Li Luo[✉], Hongjun He, and Jiao Zhu

School of Computer Science, National University of Defense Technology,
Changsha 410073, Hunan, China
li_luo@nudt.edu.cn

Abstract. Traditional research about file access control does not distinguish between user layer and application layer. This paper points out that file access control should include two layers, the first layer specifies file access rights the user has, and the second layer specifies file access rights of a program at current moment. Mainstream file access control policies can't meet the second layer requirements, and this is the very reason why current computer systems failed to against file attacking. At the same time, this paper proposes a quantitative risk assessment method, which is used to evaluate the mainstream policies, and the results show that there is no essential difference between these policies in terms of risk.

Keywords: File access control · File attack · The least privilege principle · Risk assessment

1 Introduction

File access control is an important mechanism to protect files stored on a computer, and mainstream file access control policy includes discretionary access control (DAC) [1], mandatory access control (MAC) [2], and role-based access control (RBAC) [3]. In theory, design of the mainstream policies follow the least privilege principle [4–6], as far as possible to reduce the attack surface of the file system. But in practice, the mainstream policies fail to against file attacking. In this paper, file attack is the act of reading, deleting, or modifying of a file without authorization.

In order to protect files on a computer system, the file access control needs two layers. The first layer specifies file access rights the user has, i.e. the set of files a user can access and access modes; the second layer specifies the set of files a program (the running state of a program is a process, conveniently the paper does not make distinction between program and process) can access and access modes at current time. Mainstream file access control policies meet the first layer requirements, but can't meet the second layer requirements. Correspondingly, the least privilege principle can be divided as the least privilege principle of user, and the least privilege principle of program. The former requires every user in a system is endowed with the least privilege set needs to finish

© Springer International Publishing AG 2016
G. Wang et al. (Eds.): SpaCCS 2016, LNCS 10066, pp. 204–212, 2016.
DOI: 10.1007/978-3-319-49148-6_18

the authorized task, and the later requires every program in a system is endowed with the least privilege set needs to execute the authorized task.

In order to accurately describe security of different access control policies, this paper proposes a quantitative risk assessment method, and evaluates risk of the policies.

In the second section, we put forward a quantitative risk assessment method of file access control policy, and point out that there is a limit of risk of any access control policy. Section 3 discusses the hierarchy of file access control requirements, and proposes to divide the least privilege principle as the least privilege principle of user, and the least privilege principle of program. Section 4 analyzes the defects of the main-stream file access control policies, points out that the defect is that the least privilege principle of program is not satisfied, and the risk of the policies are evaluated. Finally summarizes the full text.

2   Risk Assessment of File Access Control Policy

Security properties of different access control policies are different, and computer systems adopting them face different risk. This section presents a quantitative method, which measure risk of access control policy by the number of files that may be attacked successfully.

2.1   Basic Concepts

Definition. For a computer system adopting a certain access control policy, let R be the maximum number of files that may be attacked successfully at some moment, then R is the risk of this access control policy.

After defining the concept of risk, we need an assumption: under what circumstances a file may be attacked successfully? This assumption should be reasonable, that's to say, based on current condition of computer science and technology, there is no general algorithm to prevent all attacks under the assumption.

Risk Assumption. Files accessible to active programs may be attacked successfully.

Here are cases that a file f can be accessed by an active program p: (1) p already has the right to access f; (2) p needs no authorization to access f; (3) p needs to be authorized to access f, and p is authorized.

The "risk assumption" is reasonable for the following reason: At present, there is no proof whether a program has an intentional designed malicious, therefore, if an active program is malicious, it can attack files that it can access.

2.2   Risk Limit of Control Policy

Based on the risk assumption and the definition of risk, we can draw a conclusion directly: risk of an ideal access control policy must be dynamic, varies with number of active programs, and with number of files that active programs can access. This conclusion conforms with people's common sense, for more resources used, more risk a system faces.

According to the risk assumption and the definition of risk, in order to decrease risk of a policy, it is necessary to reduce the number of files that active programs can access. However, there is a limit to this reducing, which is a collection of files that the user needs to access at current moment. This can be represented by the following theorem.

Theorem (Risk Limit). *Risk of any access control policy is not less than the count of files that the user needs to access currently.*

3   File Access Control Requirements

The requirements of file access control are hierarchical, one layer is to control the user's rights, and the other is to control rights of a program. Therefore, the file access rights can be distinguished as the access right of user and the access right of program.

3.1   Hierarchy of Needs

"User" is an ambiguous concept, and there exist three different "users" while a computer running: (1) A person who operates a computer, namely the owner of data and programs stored in the computer. We call it master and denotes it U_M. (2) Logical user created and managed by operating system, it is on behalf of the master who is operating the computer. Denotes it U_A. (3) Running programs. When a user logs on the system, programs execute on behalf of the user. So a program is a user too, we denote it U_P. In summary, a person (U_M) may logs on as different agents (U_A), and a agent may run several applications (U_P) to fulfill his/her task.

Let SU_A be the set of files that U_A can access, and SU_P be the set of files that U_P can access. To protect files, computer system needs two control layers for file access: the first layer specifies file access rights of the user U_A, if U_A access a file outside of SU_A, it is illegal; the second layer specifies file access rights of the user U_P at current time, if U_P access a file outside of SU_P, it is illegal. According to "least privilege principle requires that each subject of a system is donated the least rights to finish its task" [6], SU_P should be the minimum set of files that U_P needs to access to fulfill U_M's command. Therefore SU_P must be a subset of SU_A (Fig. 1a).

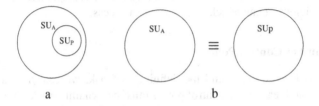

a   b

Fig. 1. Relationship between legal sets of accessible files

U_A is just an abstract concept in the computer system, the real running entity is the program, and all file operations the user does are through programs. File system is at the bottom of a computer system, it seems no need to distinguish an operation is issued by a U_A and a U_P. Therefore, for decades, computer system regards program's behavior as user's behavior when user logs on, so SU_A always equals to SU_P (Fig. 1b).

3.2 Access Right of User

"User" in this section and the following sections refers to a natural person. Access right of user refer to the file access rights owned by current user. According to the least privilege principle, we define the user's least privilege as follows.

Definition. *To perform his/her duty, user needs to access a minimum set of user files, and define this set as user's least privilege.*

Typically, user's position in an organization is stable, and accordingly his/her least privilege is stable. For a computer system adopting RBAC, a person can take several roles at the same time. However, in a specific period, the role types of system are fixed, and each role has fixed rights to access files. This can be expressed as the following property.

Property. *User's least privilege is static.*

According to the idea of the least privilege principle, we can present straightly the definition of the least privilege principle of user as follows.

Definition. *A security policy satisfies the least privilege principle of user, if the policy restricts a user's rights to user's least privilege.*

For a computer system satisfying the least privilege principle of user, if file access control mechanism is secure, no matter errors of operating system or applications, and malicious attacks, the possible damage of file system will be restricted to a minimum range, that is, the set of files that the current user can access.

However, the least privilege principle of user has no meaning for users, because all user files may be attacked successfully. Most of modern PCs adopt DAC, and theoretically all user files on it can be attacked by malware successfully.

Theorem (User's Least Privilege). *The least privilege principle of user has no meaning for protecting files, because malwares may sucessfully attack all files owned by current user.*

3.3 Access Right of Program

Access rights of program refer to the file access rights owned by a program. According to the least privilege principle, we define the program's least privilege as follows.

Definition. *To finish tasks assigned by the user, a program currently needs to access a minimum set of files, and define this set as program's least privilege.*

Program's least privilege issues with the assignment of a task, and disappears with completion of the task, and this is the nature distinction between program's least privilege and user's least privilege. For example, a user's task is to edit files f1 and f2 with program MS Word. The user edits file f1 at first, so the least privilege of MS Word is {read/write f1}; subsequently, user edits f2 and f1 at the same time, so the least privilege of MS Word is {read/write f1; read/write f2}; later, user closes f1, so the least privilege of MS Word is {read/write f2). This can be expressed as the following property.

Property. *Program's least privilege is dynamic, and it varies with the issuing and completing of tasks assigned by the user.*

According to the idea of the least privilege principle, we can present straightly the definition of the least privilege principle of program as the follow.

Definition. *A security policy satisfies the least privilege principle of program, if the policy restricts a program's rights to program's least privilege.*

A computer system makes good security performance if its security policy satisfies the least privilege principle of program.

Theorem (Program's Least Privilege). *If an access control policy adopted by a computer system satisfies the least privilege principle of program, then under normal circumstances, most of files in the computer system are immune to attack.*

Proof: *Let F_{Min} be set of files determined by programs' least privilege.*

• According to the idea of least privilege principle, the implementation of access control policy is reliable.

• Malware can only attack files in F_{Min} successfully.

Furthermore, according to the definition of program's least privilege,

Under normal circumstances, user' work needs to access a small number of user files.

That is, F_{Min} is much smaller than the set of entire files

• Most of files are immune to attack.

End of proof!

4　Defects of Mainstream File Access Control Policies

This section analyzes the defects of mainstream file access control policies, and evaluates the risk of policies using the method mentioned in Sect. 2. From the perspective of risk, there is no essential difference between the three policies.

4.1　DAC

Defect Analysis. DAC allows an object owner to design protecting strategies for objects [1, 7], that is, the principal (user) who have the power to grant certain access right can decide by themselves whether to grant a subset of access permissions to other subjects or revoke a subset of access permissions. Usually, DAC defines which subject can perform what operation for which object using the authorization list or access control lists (ACL). The advantage of DAC is user have great flexibility, which makes it suitable for many systems in real world and widely selected as the access control policy from variety of operating systems and applications.

DAC satisfies the least privilege principle of user, but it does not satisfy the least privilege principle of program. According to the least privilege principle of program, only when the user needs to access a file f, a corresponding program p can be authorized to access f, if the user need not to access f at current time, f is not accessible to p. The difficulty of the least privilege principle of program is that, only it is pre-known what files the user want to access in some future time, it is possible to permit the program to access a file in corresponding future moment. However in fact, it can't be accurately predicted what files a user wants to access in future moments.

Just because it is not predictable what files a user wants to access in a future certain time, for computer systems adopting DAC, a process automatically get the user's rights after creating. This means that a process can access all the files that the user can access.

Risk Assessment. For computer systems adopting DAC, programs are endowed the same file access rights as user's. According to the risk assumption and the definition of risk, the following conclusion can be directly drawn.

Theorem. *Let u be the current user, F_u be the set of files that u can access, $|F_u|$ be the count of files in F_u, and let R_{DAC} be risk value of DAC, then $R_{DAC} = |F_u|$.*

Proof. • *programs have the same file access rights of user.*
  • *F_u is the set of files that active programs can access.*
  According to risk assumption and definition of risk,

$$R_{DAC} >= |F_u|$$

Further, F_u is the set of files that user can access,

$$R_{DAC} <= |F_u|$$

  • *$R_{DAC} = |F_u|$*
  End of proof!

All current personal computer systems adopt DAC, therefore, files what the login user can access are likely to be successfully attacked. This is the root reason why existing computer systems have a file access control mechanism, but fail to against file attacking.

4.2 MAC

Defect Analysis. MAC [2, 7, 8, 16] is referred to that system assigns different security attributes to subjects and objects, and user can not change the security attributes of themselves and objects, that is, single user is not allowed to define access rights, only the system administrator can determine the access rights of user and user group. The system decide whether the subject can access the object by comparing the security attributes of objects and subjects.

The main advantage of MAC is that it guarantees better security performance than DAC, for it always makes information flows from entity with high level to entity with lower level, which ensures the confidentiality of information. BLP [2] is a model implemented MAC policy. However, such mandatory leads to poor usability, for it is difficult to manage authorization.

From the viewpoint of file protecting, MAC and DAC meet the least privilege principle of user, but not the least privilege principle of program. The reason analysis is similar as DAC.

Risk Assessment. For computer systems adopting MAC, security label of a process is the same as label of the login user, so the system grant a process the same file access rights of the login user. According to the risk assumption and the definition of risk, the following conclusion can be directly drawn.

Theorem. *Let u be the current user, F_u be the set of files that u can access, $| F_u |$ be the count of files in F_u, and let R_{MAC} be risk value of MAC, then $R_{MAC} = | F_u |$.*
The proof is similar to DAC.

4.3   RBAC

Defect Analysis. Compared with DAC, RBAC absorbs more interests of reaserchers in recent years [12–15]. The basic idea of RBAC [3, 9, 10] is to introduce the concept of role between the user and access rights, which will link users and roles, and to control users' access to system resources through the role of authorization.

Now RBAC has 4 different classifications: RBAC0, RBAC1, RBAC2, and RBAC3 [11]. The main advantage of RBAC is: it is similar to many systems in real world, and can be applied to many systems in reality; mean while, it also ensures the good security nature of them, and makes the problem of system license management easily be resolved as well.

However, RBAC does not precisely control the rights of executing subject. While executing, the subject can do what the role can do, but not the least privilege required for the particular task at hand.

From the viewpoint of file protecting, RBAC and DAC meet the least privilege principle of user, but not the least privilege principle of program. The reason analysis is similar as DAC.

Risk Assessment. For computer systems adopting RBAC, the system grant a process the same file access rights of the login user. According to the risk assumption and the definition of risk, the following conclusion can be directly obtained.

Theorem. *Let u be the current user, F_u be the set of files that u can access, $| F_u |$ be the count of files in F_u, and let R_{RBAC} be risk value of RBAC, then $R_{RBAC} = | F_u |$.*

The proof is similar to DAC.

A user may have multiple roles, when a malicious program attacks, only files what the current role can access may be attacked, rather than files what the user can access. This is RBAC better than DAC.

However, if different roles are regarded as different users, there is no essential difference between DAC and RBAC in terms of risk.

5   Summary

Contributions of this paper include:

(1) It needs two layers to control file accesses, the first layer specifies the file access rights the user has, and the second layer specifies the file access rights of a program at current time. Mainstream file access control policies meet the first layer requirements, but not the second layer requirements.

(2) Proposing a quantitative method of risk measurement for access control policies. The paper defines risk of an access control policy as the number of files that may be attacked, so different policies can be compared by their risks, and draw a conclusion that there is no policy whose risk is less than the number of files that the user want to access currently.

(3) Analyzing the defect of mainstream file access control policies, and points out the root reason why these policies fail to against file attacking.

References

1. NCSC-TG-003: A guide to understanding discretionary access control in trusted systems, National Computer Security Center, 30 September 1987
2. Bell, D.E., LaPadula, L.J.: Secure computer systems: a mathematical model. Technical report, ESD-TR-73-278, vol. 2, ESD/AFSC (1973)
3. Ferraiolo, D., Kuhn, R.: Role-based access control. In: Proceedings of 15th NIST–NCSC National Computer Security Conference, Baltimore, MD, pp. 554–563, October 1992
4. Saltzer, J.H.: Protection and the control of information sharing in multics. Comm. ACM 17(7), 388–402 (1974)
5. Saltzer, J.H., Schroeder, M.D.: The protection of information in computer systems. Proc. IEEE 63(9), 1278–1308 (1975)
6. DOD: Trusted Computer System Evaluation Criteria. DOD: DOD-5200.21-STD, December 1985
7. Sandhu, R.S., Samarati, P.: Access control: principles and practice. IEEE Comm. Mag. 32(9), 40–48 (1994)
8. Denning, D.E.: A lattice model of secure information flow. Comm. ACM 19(5), 236–243 (1976)
9. Ferraiolo, D.F., Barkley, J.F., Kuhn, R.: A role-based access control model and reference implementation within a corporate intranet. ACM Trans. Inf. Syst. Secur. 2(1), 34–64 (1999)
10. Ferraiolo, D.F., Sandhu, R., Gavrila, S., Kuhn, D.R., Chandramouli, R.: Proposed NIST standard for role-based access control. ACM Trans. Inf. Syst. Secur. 4(3), 224–274 (2001)

11. Sandhu, R., Coynek, E.J.: Role-based access control models. IEEE Comput. **29**(2), 38–47 (1996)
12. Jha, S., Li, N., Tripunitara, M., Wang, Q., Winsborough, W.H.: Toward formal verification of role-based access control policies. IEEE Trans. Dependable Secure Comput. **5**(4), 242–255 (2008)
13. Li, N., Tripunitara, M.V.: Security analysis in role-based access control. ACM Trans. Inf. Syst. Secur. **9**(4), 391–420 (2006)
14. Wei, Q., Crampton, J., Holloway, R., Beznosov, K., Ripeanu, M.: Authorization recycling in hierarchical RBAC systems. ACM Trans. Inf. Syst. Secur. **14**(1), 3–29 (2011)
15. Sun, Y., Wang, Q., Li, N., Bertino, E., Atallah, M.J.: On the complexity of authorization in RBAC under qualification and security constraints. IEEE Trans. Dependable Secure Comput. **8**(6), 883–897 (2011)
16. Shan, Z., Wang, X., Chiueh, T.: Enforcing mandatory access control in commodity OS to disable malware. IEEE Trans. Dependable Secure Comput. **9**(4), 541–555 (2012)

A Comprehensive Survey of Privacy-Preserving in Smart Grid

Guanlin Si[1], Zhitao Guan[1(✉)], Jing Li[1], Peng Liu[2], and Hong Yao[3]

[1] School of Control and Computer Engineering, North China Electric Power University, Beijing 102206, China
guanzhitao@126.com
[2] School of Computer Science, Hangzhou Dianzi University, Hangzhou 310018, China
[3] School of Computer Science, China University of Geosciences, Wuhan 430074, China

Abstract. As the next generation of power system, smart grid provides people with great convenience in efficiency and quality. It supports two-way communication and extremely improves the efficiency of utilization of energy resource. In order to dispatch accurately and support the dynamic price, a lot of smart meters are installed at users' house to collect the real-time data or power plan. Besides, many entities in smart grid need to share some necessary data. However, all these collected data are related to user privacy. In this paper, we make a comprehensive survey of privacy-preserving in smart grid, analyze the current privacy problems and list the corresponding solutions from a holistic angle. At last, we discuss the future work and make the conclusion.

Keywords: Privacy-preserving · Homomorphic encryption · Blind signature · Secret sharing scheme · Bilinear pairing · Smart grid

1 Introduction

As a new generation of energy network, smart grid is considered a useful way to solve the severe environment and resource problems. It is the product of the combination of energy network and information technology. Differing from the unidirectional centralized grid, the control mode of the smart grid is more flexible and reliable. It supports bidirectional power flow between the users and grid, that is to say, the user in smart grid is not only a consumer but also a generator. Smart grid can supply users with electricity, on the contrary, the users can also provide smart grid with their superfluous electricity which comes from their household energy. What's more, to realize the optimal scheduling, smart grid installs a smart meter at each house to collect the real-time electricity data, draw the real-time load curve, and create the plan for electricity generation. Not only that, smart grid also adopts many new service modes. For example, the dispatch center can make the dynamic price to encourage users to adjust their power consumption behaviors, collect the electricity consumption requirements and create the electricity generation plan in advance.

© Springer International Publishing AG 2016
G. Wang et al. (Eds.): SpaCCS 2016, LNCS 10066, pp. 213–223, 2016.
DOI: 10.1007/978-3-319-49148-6_19

Although smart grid has many advantages in those aspects, there also exist several risks which may disclose user privacy in some degree. An adversary can infer user's family behaviors through his real-time electricity data. For example, when you get up, when you go to work, when you take a shower and so on. Thus, user privacy can't be guaranteed even he is at his own home, and thieves may gain entry to user's house when they notice that there is nobody home. Therefore, the privacy-preserving in smart grid becomes an extremely important problem which can hamper the implement of smart grid.

For the privacy-preserving in smart grid, many scholars proposed various solutions. In this paper, we analyzed some correlative problems in smart grid which are related to user privacy. Later, we summarized the solutions for the privacy-preserving from a holistic angle. Privacy-preserving and authentication are two closely related issues in smart grid. We also analyzed correlative problems about authentication. What's more, we analyzed the flaws of the various solutions and pointed out our future work. The service model of smart grid is showed in Fig. 1.

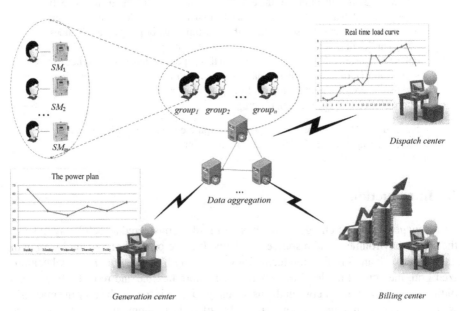

Fig. 1. The service model of smart grid

This paper is organized as follows. We showed the basic theory of the privacy-preserving in Sect. 2. Then, we described the privacy problems and protection strategies in smart grid in Sect. 3. Section 4 contained the main solutions to solve the privacy and authentication problems. Besides, we pointed out the future work in Sect. 5 and made a conclusion in Sect. 6.

2   Preliminaries

2.1   Homomorphic Encryption

Homomorphic encryption is a data aggregation encryption which can operate the cipher text to achieve ideal effect without knowing the plaintext. For example, there are three entities in our system: sender, intermediate, and receiver. All of the senders encrypt their own values and send them to the intermediate. The receiver wants to achieve the summary of the values from all the senders. In order to achieve this purpose, the intermediate can multiply these cipher texts and send the result to the receiver, thus, receiver can achieve the summary of the values coming from the senders while the intermediate provides the middle service without knowing the real values. We call this algorithm additive homomorphic encryption. Paillier encryption and Bone-Goh-Nission encryption are two common additive homomorphic algorithms.

2.2   Blind Signature and CL-Signature

A user times his data with a random number called blind factor and sends the result to the third party. Later, the third party authenticates the user's identity, signs the result with its private key and returns the signed data to the user. Thus, the user can obtain the right signature by multiplying the signed data with his inverse of the blind factor, while the third party doesn't know the content of the user's data. We call this algorithm blind signature.

The CL- Signature is similar to the blind signature, and it can realize that a user could obtain a signature while the signer has no information about the value. The detailed process is as follows:

Chooses two big primes p, q and calculates $n = pq$. $h, a, g_1 \ldots g_n$ are random numbers. Publish $(n, h, a, g_1 \ldots g_n)$ and keep p as the private key.

Users set their data $m_1 \ldots m_n$ as $g_1^{m_1} g_2^{m_2} \ldots g_n^{m_n}$ and send them to the signer. The signer calculates $l_r = l_m + l_n + l_s$ where l_m denotes the length of m_i and l_n denotes the length of n. l_s is a random number selected by signer. Then, the signer chooses a parameter e which satisfies $l_e > l_m + 2$. At last, calculates a parameter v through

$$v^e = ag_1^{m_1} g_2^{m_2} \ldots g_n^{m_n} h_r \bmod n \tag{1}$$

(e, v, r) is the CL- Signature and verifier can verify the signature by checking $v^e = ag_1^{m_1} g_2^{m_2} \ldots g_n^{m_n} h_r \bmod n$.

2.3   Secret Sharing Scheme

The secret sharing scheme is a scheme which splits a secret into n pieces and distributes these pieces with different valid members. If an adversary captures a member in the system, he can only get a piece of the secret. Only if the adversary gets at least k pieces of the secret, can he get the whole secret. We usually adopt the Shamir technique to realize this result.

The trusted party chooses a polynomial to split a secret denoted by s

$$f(x) = s + r_1 x + r_2 x^2 + \ldots r_{k-1} x^{k-1} \bmod p \tag{2}$$

(x_i, y_i) is the corresponding share. Remarkably, the Shamir secret sharing scheme is the fully homomorphic and can be designed as a better scheme to realize the data aggregation.

2.4 Bilinear Pairing

Let G be an additive group and P, Q are the generators of G. $e:G \times G = G_t$, where G_t is a multiply group. The bilinear pairing satisfies several properties:

$$e(P, Q)^x = e(P, Qx) = e(Px, Q) \tag{3}$$

$$e(P, Q)^{x_1} e(P, Q)^{x_2} = e(P, Q)^{x_1 + x_2} \tag{4}$$

$$e(P, P) \neq 1 \tag{5}$$

2.5 Commitment and BBS+ Signature

Commitment is a scheme which can commit verifier a value without revealing it. After a period of time, the sender reveals the value and the verifier can judge whether the value is the same as the previous one. Commitment is often used for verifying the message authenticity. A famous commitment scheme called Pedersen Commitment is created as follows: let g and h be the generator of a group. To commit a value m, the verifier chooses a random number r and computes $C = g^m h^r$ as the commitment.

BBS+ Signature is a partly blind signature based on the Pedersen Commitment. For a bilinear pairing: $e:G \times G = G_t$, let g, g_0, g_1 be generators of G. A sender chooses a random number r and computes $w = g^r$ as public key. To sign a message m, the signer computes $A = (g^c g_0^z g_1^m)^{1/(c+r)}$. While, c and z are random numbers chose by the signer. Then, (A, c, z) is the BBS+ signature and one can verify it by checking if

$$e(A, wg^c) = e(gg_0^z g_1^m, g) \tag{6}$$

3 Privacy Problems and Protection Strategies in Smart Grid

3.1 Privacy Problems

Smart grid can provide people with great efficiency and economy, while, it may disclose user privacy in some degree. We show the privacy-risks as follows:

- For dealing with the electrical fault which may happen at any time, smart grid needs to collect the real-time electricity data from all of the users to watch the status of the system. However, this may disclose user's real-time privacy. By analyzing the real-time electricity curve, user's family behavior would be disclosed easily.

- For saving power as much as possible, smart grid collects the power plan from all of the users in advance. Obviously, the power plan from users will disclose their behaviors for a period of time in the future. For example, smart grid can infer that your family will go on a trip if your power plan is closed to zero.
- There are many entities in smart grid such as power plant, transformer substation, control center and billing center. In order to achieve a better control, all the entities need to share some necessary data. However, the relationship of these entities is competitive and cooperative. Some important data are related to the core interests of an entity and should not be disclosed to any other entities. Therefore, all the entities in smart grid need to establish a security data sharing program to protect each entity's privacy.

As the first situation, the privacy-preserving scheme is related to real-time electricity data, so it may affect the dynamic price in smart grid. Therefore, when we need to establish a privacy-preserving scheme, we must ensure the scheme doesn't disturb the normal billing. For the second situation, there also exists a problem. A malicious user may send smart grid a wrong power plan which is much larger than its real consumption; thus, smart grid will produce much unnecessary electricity and lead to power waste. So, we need to authenticate all the users and ensure the validity of the power plan when we establish our privacy-preserving scheme.

3.2 Protection Strategies

To protect the privacy of users in smart grid, there exist three basic strategies currently.

We can protect the identity of each user. Even an adversary or dispatcher can obtain user's accurate data, but not knowing the identity of the user can still protect the user privacy.

We can protect the data of each user. Through some schemes such as data aggregation or obfuscation, we can ensure that the control center runs in a right way while has no information about any user's data.

We can protect the route between the sender and receiver. Thus, if an adversary captures a message through the network, he can't ensure the sender and receiver through the message.

Authentication is closely related to privacy in smart grid and it contains the following aspects. *a.* Message integrity
When the control center receives a message sent by smart meter, we must ensure the integrity of the message. Given the privacy-preserving, the best strategy is that the control center can guarantee the message integrity while has no information about the content.
  b. Validity of identity
When the control center receives a message from a user, we must ensure the identity of the user is validity and prevent the adversary from impersonating a legal user. Given

the privacy-preserving, the best strategy is that the control center can guarantee the validity of user's identity while has no information about user's real identity.

c. Message authenticity

Apart from the message integrity and the validity of user's identity, the message authenticity can't be ignored. For example, a malicious user may send a false power plan which is much larger than his real power consumption. Thus, smart grid will generate much unnecessary power, which causes a serious waste of energy. So, the best strategy is that smart grid can guarantee the authenticity of a message but has no information of the content or the sender's identity.

4   Countermeasures

Based on the aforementioned basic strategies, we can list the related solutions. We summarized some basic and classical solutions according to basic strategies at Table 1.

Table 1. Privacy strategies and major solutions

Privacy-strategies	Solutions
Mask identity	Virtual ring
	CL signature
	Blind signature
Mask data	Home battery
	BGN encryption
	Paillier encryption
	Data obfuscation
	Bilinear mappings
	Shamir secret sharing scheme
Mask route	Random re-transmission
Authentication	CL signature
	Blind signature
	BBS+ Signature
	Commitment

4.1   Privacy-Preserving by Masking the User's Identity

For masking the user's identity, a simple solution adopting a trusted- party to manage the identity list is proposed in [1]. However, finding a trusted-party is not easy. We have many better choices to select.

Some scholars proposed a scheme based on blind signature to solve the privacy-preserving and validity-authentication in [2]. The main idea of this scheme is as follows: a user times his data with a random number called blind factor and sends the result to the third party. Later, the third party authenticates the user's identity, signs the result with its private key and returns the signed data to the user. Thus, the user can obtain the right signature by multiplying the signed data with his inverse of the blind factor, while the third party doesn't know the content of the user's data. The downside of this scheme is that users should send their electricity data to the third party for authentication before communicating with the control center, which is against the real-time property of the power grid. Camenisch and Lysyanskaya proposed a scheme named CL -Signature scheme which is similar to the blind signature in [3]. It can ensure that a user can obtain a signature while the signer has no information about the value.

An effective scheme based on virtual ring is presented in [4]. It groups the users by their geographical positions and distributes each member in the same group with the same key. In this way, control center can obtain all of the users' data without knowing the senders' ID. Obviously, it's a good way to protect user privacy, but the validity-authentication can't be guaranteed because of the anonymity.

4.2 Privacy-Preserving by Masking the Real-Time Data

A solution using a battery to hide the real-time data is proposed in [5–7]. In these schemes, smart grid and the household battery provide users with electricity at the same time. When the household consumption curve goes high, the battery discharges. Otherwise, it charges. In this way, we can hide the user's real-time data to protect user privacy. The downside is that the effect depends on the battery capacity, besides, charging and discharging the battery frequently is detrimental to the battery life and may collide with dynamic electricity price.

A solution using the data aggregation is also popular in smart grid for privacy-preserving. It often uses homomorphic encryption and there are many algorithms which have the property of homomorphism, such as the Paillier and Bone-Goh-Nission encryption, secret sharing scheme, bilinear mapping and so on. Next, we will show them in details.

The Paillier encryption and Bone-Goh-Nission encryption are classical algorithms as the homomorphic encryption and they are used in many schemes such as [8–12]. However, the computational complexity of them can't be ignored. In [13], scholars try to group the members to realize a distributed authentication in order to reduce the complexity, but the effect is not very ideal. Thus, many scholars try to use other simple algorithms to substitute them.

Secret sharing scheme is proposed to realize the data aggregation. It adopts the Shamir technique to encrypt the electricity data [14]. As we mentioned in Sect. 2, users can choose the same argument x to create their shares like (x, y_i) and the shares have the homomorphic property. Of course, secret sharing scheme can be also applied into other aspects, such as the key management, but this property is not taken into our consideration.

The bilinear mapping is also a common solution for data aggregation. We usually use the formula (4) to create homomorphic encryption such as [16, 23, 25]. Remarkably, we usually use the formulas (3) and (4) to realize the key-exchange.

Besides those mentioned above, there are many algorithms to create the homomorphic encryption, such as [15]. It constructs an equation $C_i = M_i \bullet S + r$, where C_i and M_i stand for the cipher text and plaintext of the electricity data, and S is a common number which is shared by all the members. r is a random number. Smart grid can obtain the summary of M_i easily without disclosing user privacy. Obviously, this scheme does a good job in complexity, but it also has several flaws. To share the same parameter, all the smart meters have to communicate with each other and reach agreement on the S, which would increase the traffic in the network.

While, no matter which algorithm we choose to create the homomorphic encryption, there are always two problems to consider: error-tolerance and differential privacy. These two problems are discussed at [10].

Besides the homomorphic encryption, the data –obfuscation solution is also popular to realize the data aggregation for privacy-preserving. In [17], the author shows a scheme based on data obfuscation, which adds a random number to each electricity data to protect the real-time data from being disclosed by the adversary and control centre. But it will cause some large errors if the random numbers are not reasonable. If we consider the summary of random numbers is zero, then we have to face the problem about error-tolerance.

For the data sharing among different entities, a security data sharing program based on attribute has been presented in [18]. The main idea of this kind of scheme is as follows: the owner of a file sets some attributes in his file, and saves them in the data access centre. If someone wants to access a file, he must satisfy the attributes which are set by its owner. In [18], it not only encrypts a file based on attributes, but also encrypts the attributes themselves. In this way, each entity can set property attributes to protect their privacy during the common data sharing. Because the relationship of these entities is competitive and cooperative, some scholars devote into searching an approach to protect the sensitive information and solving the multi-party cooperation problem such as the optimal power flow in a shared computing platform [20].

4.3   Privacy-Preserving by Masking the Route Between Sender and Receiver

To mask the route between sender and receiver, we usually use the random re-trans-mission to mask the real route such as [21, 22]. Generally, we often use the topological matrix to achieve a better effect. There is no doubt that random re-transmission would increase the network traffic. Therefore, we need find some better solutions to mask the message route.

4.4   Privacy-Preserving and Authentication

Privacy-preserving and authentication are two closely related issues. As we analysed in Sect. 3, authentication in smart grid contains three aspects.

For the message integrity, there are many solutions to achieve a good effect, such as the message digest. If we want to realize the message integrity, while the verifier has no information about the content of the message, we can adopt the blind signature [2] or CL-signature [3] to achieve this effect.

For the validity of identity, we usually adopt asymmetric encryption to create digital signature. If we want to authenticate the validity of a user's identity, while the verifier has no information about the user's real identity, we can adopt commitment to create BBS+ Signature [23] and create a pseudonym to communicate with the control centre [24].

For the message authenticity, especially for the power plan, commitment is a good choice [19]. A sender firstly sends the control centre encrypted electricity data and a commitment. After a period of time, the sender has to send his real electricity data and the decryption key to the commitment. Thus, the verifier can easily verify whether the two electricity data are the same.

According to the above analysis, the zero-knowledge proof is widely adopted in the authentication related to privacy-preserving in smart grid.

5   Future Works

According to the analysis and aforementioned survey, there exist several disadvantages in current solutions to be solved in future.

As the solution which uses a battery to hide the real-time data, if we don't consider the capacity of the battery, that would be a good choice. But there also exists a severe problem which needs us to consider. The charging and discharging of the battery may conflict with the dynamic price, which would cause huge losses to consumer. That is to say, there is a tradeoff between the privacy-preserving and the dynamic price. Some papers have considered this problem and given some solutions like [11], but people maybe not satisfied with this tradeoff. So, finding a novel solution which can protect user privacy and doesn't damage his economy would be our future work.

As the homomorphic encryption and data-obfuscation, the main concerns are differential privacy and error-tolerance. For the differential privacy, many scholars proposed lots of novel solutions such as adding a random number in each electricity data, where the random number must obey some distribution (For example, it obeys the Laplace distribution) so that the whole aggregation can resist differential privacy [9]. For the error-tolerance, there are still some solutions to solve this problem. A representative solution is proposed by Zhiguo at [10], and it is a solution based on grouping to realize the error- tolerance. Although this solution has advantage in computational complexity to some extent, its accuracy isn't satisfied with our ideal requirement. Therefore, we should find a novel solution to realize the error-tolerance, which has an obvious advantage both in complexity and accuracy.

As we discussed before, we usually adopt Paillier encryption as homomorphic encryption to realize the data aggregation, but the complexity of the Paillier encryption cannot be ignored, which collides with the character of real-time in smart grid. Shamir secret scheme and bilinear mapping would be better choices, but there is not a perfect scheme to make the best of them. So, we had better find a solution to institute the Paillier encryption or create a novel solution which makes the best of the existing algorithms.

6   Conclusion

The current problem about privacy-preserving in smart grid has not been solved perfectly. Many solutions have been proposed, but there still exist some flaws such as complexity and the lack of feasibility. In this paper, we summarized the current privacy problems in smart grid from a holistic perspective and listed corresponding solutions currently. At last, we discussed the main flaws in the recent solutions and gave the advice for our future work. It's expected that the problem of privacy-preserving would be solved efficiently in the future.

Acknowledgments. This work is partially supported by Natural Science Foundation of China under grant 61402171, Central Government University Foundation under grant JB2016045.

References

1. Efthymiou, C., Kalogridis, G.: Smart grid privacy via anonymization of smart metering data. In: 2010 First IEEE International Conference on Smart Grid Communications (SmartGridComm). IEEE (2010)
2. Cheung, J.C.L., et al.: Credential-based privacy-preserving power request scheme for smart grid network. In: 2011 IEEE Global Telecommunications Conference (GLOBECOM 2011). IEEE (2011)
3. Diao, F., Zhang, F., Cheng, X.: A privacy-preserving smart metering scheme using linkable anonymous credential. IEEE Trans. Smart Grid $6(1)$, 461–467 (2015)
4. Badra, M., Zeadally, S.: Design and performance analysis of a virtual ring architecture for smart grid privacy. IEEE Trans. Inf. Forensics Secur. $9(2)$, 321–329 (2014)
5. McLaughlin, S., McDaniel, P., Aiello, W.: Protecting consumer privacy from electric load monitoring. In: Proceedings of the 18th ACM conference on Computer and communications security. ACM (2011)
6. Yao, J., Venkitasubramaniam, P.: The privacy analysis of battery control mechanisms in demand response: revealing state approach and rate distortion bounds. IEEE Trans. Smart Grid $6(5)$, 2417–2425 (2015)
7. Yang, L., et al.: Cost-effective and privacy-preserving energy management for smart meters. IEEE Trans. Smart Grid $6(1)$, 486–495 (2015)
8. Marmol, F.G., et al.: Do not snoop my habits: preserving privacy in the smart grid. IEEE Commun. Mag. $50(5)$, 166–172 (2012)
9. Bao, H., Rongxing, L.: A new differentially private data aggregation with fault tolerance for smart grid communications. Internet Things J. IEEE $2(3)$, 248–258 (2015)
10. Shi, Z., et al.: Diverse grouping-based aggregation protocol with error detection for smart grid communications. IEEE Trans. Smart Grid $6(6)$, 2856–2868 (2015)
11. Liang, X., et al.: UDP: usage-based dynamic pricing with privacy preservation for smart grid. IEEE Trans. Smart Grid $4(1)$, 141–150 (2013)
12. Chen, L., et al.: MuDA: multifunctional data aggregation in privacy-preserving smart grid communications. Peer-to-peer Netw. Appl. $8(5)$, 777–792 (2015)
13. Jo, H.J., Kim, I.S., Lee, D.H.: Efficient and privacy-preserving metering protocols for smart grid systems. IEEE Trans. Smart Grid $1(1)$, 65–75 (2015)
14. Barletta, A., et al.: Privacy preserving smart grid Communications by verifiable secret key sharing. In: 2015 International Conference on Computing and Network Communications (CoCoNet). IEEE (2015)
15. Dong, X., Zhou, J., Cao, Z.: Efficient privacy-preserving temporal and spacial data aggregation for smart grid communications. Concurrency Comput. Pract. Experience $50(9)$, 98–114 (2015)
16. Akula, P., et al.: Privacy-preserving and secure communication scheme for power injection in smart grid. In 2015 IEEE International Conference on Smart Grid Communications (SmartGridComm). IEEE (2015)

17. Beussink, A., et al.: Preserving consumer privacy on IEEE 802.11 s-based smart grid ami networks using data obfuscation. In: 2014 IEEE Conference on Computer Communications Workshops (INFOCOM WKSHPS). IEEE (2014)
18. Hur, J.: Attribute-based secure data sharing with hidden policies in smart grid. IEEE Trans. Parallel Distrib. Syst. **24**(11), 2171–2180 (2013)
19. Chim, T.W., et al.: PRGA: privacy-preserving recording & gateway-assisted authentication of power usage information for smart grid. IEEE Trans. Dependable Secur. Comput. **12**(1), 85–97 (2015)
20. Wu, D., et al.: Preserving privacy of AC optimal power flow models in multi-party electric grids. IEEE Trans. Smart Grid **7**(4), 2050–2060 (2016)
21. Nicanfar, H., et al.: Enhanced network coding to maintain privacy in smart grid communication. IEEE Trans. Emerg. Top. Comput. **1**(2), 286–296 (2013)
22. Rottondi, C., Verticale, G.: Privacy-friendly load scheduling of deferrable and interruptible domestic appliances in smart grids ☆. Comput. Commun. **58**(1), 29–39 (2014)
23. Gong, Y., et al.: A privacy-preserving scheme for incentive-based demand response in the smart grid. IEEE Trans. Smart Grid **7**(3), 1304–1313 (2016)
24. Tan, X., et al.: Pseudonym-based privacy-preserving scheme for data collection in smart grid. Int. J. Ad Hoc Ubiquit. Comput. **22**(2), 120–127 (2016)
25. Chen, J., Shi, J., Zhang, Y.: EPPDC: an efficient privacy-preserving scheme for data collection in smart grid. Int. J. Distrib. Sens. Netw. **11**, 1–12 (2015)

Ghost Train for Anonymous Communication

Przemysław Błaśkiewicz, Mirosław Kutyłowski, Jakub Lemiesz$^{(\boxtimes)}$, and Małgorzata Sulkowska

Faculty of Fundamental Problems of Technology,
Wroclaw University of Science and Technology, 50-370 Wrocław, Poland
`jakub.lemiesz@pwr.edu.pl`

Abstract. We study the problem of hiding communication: while it is easy to encrypt a message sent from Alice to Bob, it is hard to hide that such a communication takes place. Communiaction hiding is one of the fundamental privacy challenges, especially in case of an adversary having a complete view of the traffic and controlling a large number of nodes.

Following the Beimel-Dolev's buses concept and Young-Yung drunk motorcyclist protocol we propose a theoretical concept called *Ghost Train*. The ghost trains are travelling at random through the network just as drunk motorcyclists and one version of Beimel-Dolev buses. However, there are no assigned seats or motorcyclists holding a ciphertext. The trains are not generated by the senders, once created they travel forever, and hold messages in the way that the older messages gradually decay and are replaced by new messages inserted into the train. Each train route is random and stochastically independent from the existing sender-destination pairs, thus the protocol is fully oblivious. Additionally, it works for dynamic networks where the nodes can join and leave the network (unlike the Beimel-Dolev solution) and yet it is not possible to indicate the origin of any given package (unlike in the drunken motorcyclist protocol).

Our protocol is based on basic tools (Bloom filters, PRNGs) and a novel concept of inserting many ciphertexts on the same place and their decay.

Keywords: Anonymous communication · Traffic analysis · Random walk · Bloom filter · Shared keys · Probability

1 Introduction

Hiding Communication. Initially, confidentiality of communication has been understood in a narrow sense as hiding the message contents and securing it against manipulations. For this purpose it suffices to apply encryption and message authentication codes. However, in most network architectures we cannot encrypt the destination address and we do not automatically hide the route of a message, hence an observer may see which node is communicating with which. Moreover, in a standard case the (approximate) length of the plaintext message is visible as well. Even if the addresses and contents are hidden, traffic data

G. Wang et al. (Eds.): SpaCCS 2016, LNCS 10066, pp. 224–239, 2016.
DOI: 10.1007/978-3-319-49148-6_20

may indicate the sender and receiver of a message. Unfortunately, even the systems such as TOR (see [1]) provide only a limited protection against a powerful adversary having access to the traffic data.

The information "who-is-talking-with-whom" can be effectively used for deriving sensitive information. This is frequently used for computer forensics, but it can be misused as well for breaking privacy in ever growing ubiquitous networks. As "privacy-by-design" becomes now an important target, at least for European Union, there are expectations that the problem can be somehow solved on the technical grounds. However, this turns out to be a challenging problem having so far no ultimate solution even in theory.

Anonymous Communication Concepts. The very first solution to provide anonymous communication is to encrypt a message and flood the network with the ciphertext or to broadcast it over, say, a satellite. In this way the recipient of the message is perfectly hidden, as everybody can read the message. However, the overhead is high: flooding large scale ubiquitous networks would simply block the network. Broadcast channels may have a limited capacity. Finally, while the receiver is perfectly hidden, the sender is exposed to everybody.

For small networks, a fairly simple and effective folklore solution is a *token ring*: each message encrypted by the sender goes through the entire ring until it returns to the sender (see e.g. [7]). Apart from scalability issues, the protocol requires maintaining a communication ring and thus may be inconvenient for dynamic networks.

Onion routing [6] is a protocol designed for large networks, aiming to reduce the communication delay and the number of messages transmitted while preserving some degree of anonymity. A lot of work has been done in this area both on the practical side (e.g. TOR) and on the theoretical side (see e.g. [5]), however the anonymity guarantees are given only if the adversary has a limited view of the traffic data and under some additional assumptions (e.g. regarding the number of messages sent). The protocol does not hide the fact that a node is sending or receiving a message, the goal is to prevent linking the senders with the receivers.

The paper [4] presents a family of protocols extending the token ring protocol. The basic idea is that there is a so-called *bus* having some number of *seats* and travelling along a fixed Euler tour through all nodes. In the basic version, there is a dedicated seat for each (sender, receiver) pair so the size of the bus is quadratic in the number of nodes. A seat may contain either a ciphertext or a random dummy string pretending to be a ciphertext (some care is necessary when choosing the encryption method, as indicated in [8]). In the enhanced version there are less seats in the bus and a ciphertext is placed on a random seat (possibly overwriting completely an old message). Moreover, the route of a bus can be limited to a cluster with some exchange points between clusters so that we have multiple, intersecting token rings. In a yet another version of the protocol, in the scenario where the topology of the network is unknown or can change dynamically, the bus is travelling along a random route in the hope that eventually at least some of the encrypted messages arrive at the destination nodes.

More precisely, in each step a node holding the bus chooses uniformly at random one of its neighbors and sends there the bus. Note the expected delivery time of a message by using a random walk in an unknown graph with n nodes and m edges is $O(nm)$ and this bound is tight for some graphs (see [2]). In such a scenario not only the delivery time is high, but if the seats are taken randomly there is also a substantial risk of overwriting some ciphertexts (cf. Sect. 3.1.1. in [4]). Moreover, if the route is not known in advance we cannot use partial decryption for hiding a packet route. In this case all we can do is universal re-encryption or just transmitting the ciphertexts unmodified. However, re-encryption is computationally intensive, while forwarding a ciphertext without a change immediately reveals its origin. Finally, let us note that the bus protocol is not fully decentralized and communication could be easily blocked by an adversary.

Paper [8] presents the Drunk Motorcyclist Protocol in which buses are replaced by *motorcycles*, each having exactly one seat. A motorcyclist does not have a fixed route, but instead performs a random ride visiting a fixed number of network nodes. If drunk motorcyclists are sent repeatedly, eventually one of them passes through the destination node showing there the ciphertext. So in some sense the protocol follows the idea from Sect. 6.2 of [4] (random walk for buses), but on the other hand it is closely related to flooding the network. Its disadvantage is that the origin of any packet is not well hidden (the situation is somewhat better if the ciphertexts are re-encrypted, however, the time-to-live counter is public). Such an information does not break the sender anonymity provided that dummy messages are sent even if there is no message to be sent, but may ease some kind of a targeted attack. E.g. even in case of re-encryption an adversary may aim at isolating a node x and kill all messages leaving x with the highest "number of hops to go" (these are the messages sent by x – real and dummy ones). However, the main focus of the paper [8] is the choice of a public key cryptosystem in order to provide semantic security of communication. As it requires a lot of dummy encryption (to ensure anonymity and mitigate timing attacks) the solution is in fact a kind of continuous network flooding.

In this paper we change the encoding strategy. Instead of seats there is a homogeneous space with no boundaries between the ciphertexts of different messages in one packet. There are no packets devoted to a single ciphertext. Just as [8] and a version of the protocol from [4] we use random walks to hide sender-receiver pairs. However, the route never stops (as it eventually happens for a drunk motorcyclist) and is not predefined – it adjusts itself to the current state of the network.

The Model. As in [8] (where a packet "is sent to a peer vertex chosen uniformly at random from all peer vertices") we assume that communication is based on peer-to-peer interactions. More specifically, we follow the population model, where the nodes choose a match at random (or meet at random in the mobile setting) and exchange data pairwise (see e.g. [3]). Note that a possible solution providing an anonymous communication in the population model would be to exchange confidential (or dummy) data between two nodes only when they meet. However, in this case the adversary would know that there is no communication between A and B, if A and B do not meet.

The nodes themselves might have limited (or sometimes incompatible) computational resources, so we only demand that they are equipped with a secure pseudorandom generator – PRNG – which provides output indistinguishable from the random output. However, we assume that the communicating parties share a secret key and use the same PRNG. Note that traditionally PRNGs takes as input a single relatively short argument. However, for sake of readability, we may assume that the construction allows a few parameters of a fixed length. For protocol's security we have to assume that the output of PRNG is computationally indistinguishable from an output of a really random function. In our protocol each packet has a unique ID and holds an array of n bits. The content of the arrays changes over time as packets are performing an infinite random walk through the network. In accordance to the population model, a packet jumps to the node met by the current node. A correct packet should always be in equilibrium, namely its array contains exactly $\frac{n}{2}$ ones and $\frac{n}{2}$ zeros. If a node x wishes to anonymously send a bit of information to a node y, then it modifies a received packet in a certain way. Namely, the node A sets appropriate values in k pseudo-random positions determined by the key shared with the node y. Then, to restore the equilibrium state of the packet, the node x changes some other randomly chosen bits and forwards the packet to the next node. Finally, as in the Drunk Motorcyclist case, node x sends a packet to a random node. If x receives a packet and has no information to be sent, then (as in the Bus Protocol) it performs some dummy modifications on the packet.

Obviously, inserting a new data into a packet implies that some previous data can be destroyed. However, unlike in the Bus Protocol where the whole ciphertext is overwritten, in our solution overwriting some bits makes the secret message only less reliable. So one may consider a packet as a *ghost train* in which information gradually fade being replaced by the new data.

For comparison, let us consider the probability of overwriting a message in Beimel-Dolev's Bus Protocol in a bus with n seats. Assume that k ciphertexts are already in the bus. As we insert a new ciphertext into a random seat, the probability to destroy a given ciphertext is k/n. If all seats are already taken ($k = n$), then some ciphertext is destroyed for sure. In our protocol we encode a message within a bit string considered as a Bloom filter by setting a bit pattern determined by an encryption key. Obviously, as in a Bloom filter, a new message may overwrite some old content. However, if the positions encoding an old message and the positions used by the new message are not overlapping too much, it might be possible to recover the old message despite overlapping.

Paper Overview. In Sect. 2 we present the Ghost Train protocol. In Sect. 3 we provide a formal probabilistic analysis of the protocol which will allow us to choose the appropriate values of its parameters. In Sect. 4 we comment the security properties of the protocol - due to space limitation we skip a formal treatment, as it is a standard one and can be easily reconstructed by the reader.

2   Ghost Train Protocol

The pseudo-code of the Ghost Train protocol is given by Algorithms 1, 2, 3 and 4 (see pp. 5 and 6). The idea is as follows. We assume that time is divided into epochs and in each epoch there are T time slots. Each packet P holds a bit array $P.B$ of length n that can be treated as a Bloom filter. In a correct packet the array always contains exactly $\frac{n}{2}$ ones and $\frac{n}{2}$ zeroes. Each packet P holds its unique identifier $P.id$. The total number of packets in the network is (more or less) fixed and each packet should travel forever. When a packet arrives to any node it is processed and forwarded to another node chosen uniformly at random from the set of all nodes, independently of other choices. Assume that there are N nodes in the network. By the first moment method it can be easily verified that $\omega(N \log N)$ packets suffice to ensure in each time slot each node has at least one packet w.h.p.

Global Parameters: threshold f, subset size k, bit array length n,
epoch length T
Initialization: set list of known nodes L and stored packets U
1 **upon** *new epoch i*
2        $t \leftarrow 0$, $readStreams(i, L)$
3   **upon** *new slot $t \leq T$*
4   for each packet from U, move it to a node chosen independently at random, $U \leftarrow \emptyset$
5   **upon** *new packet P arrives*
6                    $packetDecoding(i, t, L, P)$
7                    $packetEncoding(i, t, L, P)$
8                    $U \leftarrow U \cup \{P\}$

Algorithm 1: The main procedure executed by a node x

Let us consider two nodes: x and y. The node x can communicate with y, if they share a secret key; let $x.K_y$ denote the key used to encode messages from x to y. By L we denote a list of nodes with whom a given node x can communicate. In order to encode information in a packet we use a keyed PRNG (cryptographic pseudorandom number generator) denoted by h. More precisely, we use h to determine a subset S of k positions to be set to the value of the bit to be transmitted (see Algorithm 2, line 3). If a node x wishes to send bit b to y in a packet P obtained in epoch i, then it encodes b by setting k bits of $P.B$ to b. The k positions in the array where the bits are set in this way are determined by $S = h(x.K_y, i, P.id)$.

Additionally, x changes the value of some other bits in $P.B$ to ensure that the number of ones and zeros in $P.B$ remains to be $\frac{n}{2}$. Positions of these bits are

---

Arguments: epoch index i, slot index t, list of destinations L, received
  packet P

1   inspect the history $P.H$ and determine node $y \in L$ for which packet P has
    not been used in epoch i and *bit* to be sent to y

2   **if** $y \neq null$ **then**

3   $\quad \lfloor \; S \leftarrow h(x.K_y, i, t, P.id)$

4   **else**

5   $\quad \lfloor \;$ choose S and *bit* at random

6   *ones* $\leftarrow$ the number of ones on positions S in $P.B$

7   set all positions from S in $P.B$ to *bit*

8   **if** *bit* $= 1$ **then**

9   $\quad \lfloor \;$ *ones* $\leftarrow k - $ *ones*;

10 **while** *ones* > 0 **do**

11 $\quad r \leftarrow rand[1, n]$

12 $\quad$ **if** $r \notin S \wedge P.B[r] = bit$ **then**

13 $\quad \quad \lceil \; P.B[r] \leftarrow 1 - bit$

14 $\quad \quad \lfloor \;$ *ones* $\leftarrow$ *ones* $- 1$

15 push$((x, t), P.H)$ /* push (x,t) to 1st position in $P.H$ */

Algorithm 2: *packetEncoding* procedure for node x

chosen at random. If node x has no message to be sent, then both the positions
as well as the value of bits are chosen at random (see Algorithm 2, line 6).

To ensure a high probability of a successful delivery, a node should encode a
bit b in more than a single packet. Namely, we assume that if node x has to send
bit b to y it encodes that bit on k positions in T different packets during one
epoch. Let node y receive s out of those T packets ($1 \leq s \leq T$) and find on the
all agreed positions altogether at least $f \cdot s \cdot k$ ones (or zeroes) for some constant
threshold $f \in (0.5, 1]$. Then y decodes a message from x as 1 (or 0 respectively),
see Algorithm 4, line 5–6.

Arguments: i, t, L, P

1   **foreach** *node* $y \in L$ **do**

2   $\quad$ **foreach** *position j of an entry (y, τ) in $P.H$* **do**

3   $\quad \quad$ **if** $j \geq t$ **then** $r \leftarrow 1$ **else** $r \leftarrow 2$

4   $\quad \quad S_r \leftarrow h(y.K_x, i - 2 + r, \tau, P.id)$

5   $\quad \quad y.X_r \leftarrow y.X_r +$ the number of ones in $P.B$ on positions from S_r

6   $\quad \quad y.b_r \leftarrow y.b_r + k$

Algorithm 3: *packetDecoding* procedure for node x – gathering data for trans-
missions received by node x

Arguments: i, L
1 **foreach** *node* y *in* L **do**
2      $y.stream[i-2] \leftarrow ?$
3   **if** $y.b_1 > 0$ **then**
4          $p \leftarrow y.X_1/y.b_1$
5   **if** $p > f$ **then** $y.stream[i-2] \leftarrow 1$
6   **else if** $p < 1 - f$ **then** $y.stream[i-2] \leftarrow 0$
7      $y.X_1 \leftarrow y.X_2 \,, \; y.X_2 \leftarrow 0$
8      $y.b_1 \leftarrow y.b_2 \,, \; y.b_2 \leftarrow 0$

Algorithm 4: *readStreams* procedure for node x, interpretation of the results from epoch $i - 2$ computed at epoch i

In order to ease decoding, each packet P holds a queue $P.H$ of length T storing the IDs of T most recently visited nodes. Additionally, to each ID we attach a slot number (within an epoch) that is used to randomize the output and defer replay attacks (sending the same packets to a node). In the last step of the encoding procedure a node pushes its own identifier to the first position of this queue. Thereby, the contents of $P.H$ is shifted and its last element is dropped. Notice that a packet from x to y can be encoded close to the end of a given epoch. To ensure each packet has T time slots to get to the destination, the decoding procedure (see Algorithm 3, line 3) uses the index of the current or the previous epoch. The decision which index to use is based on the position of a sender node in the packet history $P.H$. Namely, if this position is equal or greater than a current slot number t, then the previous epoch should be considered.

At the beginning of an epoch i there is no more information about epoch $i - 2$ in the history of any packet and we consider epoch $i - 2$ as completed. Then, in *readStreams* (see Algorithm 4) to learn a bit sent to x by y in epoch $i - 2$, node x compares the proportion p of 1's decoded in the completed epoch (variable $y.X_1$) and the total number of decoded bits $y.b_1$ with respect to some threshold f. The value of f needs to be carefully chosen to ensure unambiguous decryption (for details see the next section).

3   Protocol Analysis

If x tries to send y a message (a bit 0 or 1), then it encodes T packets and each such packet has at most T time slots to be delivered and correctly decoded by y. Since in each step a new message (or dummy data) is encoded in each packet, each carried message "decays" as the packet travels through the network. In this section we prove that the probability of delivering a legible message from x to y is high for appropriately chosen parameters T (the length of one epoch), n (the size of the packet), k (the number of agreed positions) and f (the message detection threshold).

3.1 Message Lifetime

Without loss of generality let us further assume that x sends to y a bit 1 (unless stated otherwise). By $\mathbb{X}$ we denote the number of ones that y finds on positions agreed with x in all s (out of T) packets obtained from x. In what follows we will find the relation between the parameters of our protocols which for a given $\delta \geq 0$ ensure that

$$\mathbb{P}[\mathbb{X} \geq f \cdot s \cdot k] \geq 1 - \delta \quad \text{and} \quad \mathbb{P}[\mathbb{X} \leq (1 - f) \cdot s \cdot k] \leq \delta .$$

Thereby we will prove that after T steps a message is still legible for the receiver w.h.p. and the probability that it decodes an incorrect value is sufficiently small.

Let us consider one particular packet P encoded by x to y at some step. Without loss of generality let us assume that k bits determined by the key shared between x and y are located at the beginning of the bit array $P.B$ (positions 1 to k) – it will simplify the notation but has no influence on the result. Let $X_t^{(i)}$ be the value of the ith bit in $P.B$ after P visits t next nodes and let $M_t \in \{0,1\}$ denote the message encoded in P at step t. Recall that in our algorithm each message is independently encoded on random positions (see Algorithm 2). Since x sends 1 at time $t = 0$, the ones are set at the positions from 1 to k and according to our notation we have $M_0 = 1$ and $X_0^{(1)} = X_0^{(2)} = \ldots = X_0^{(k)} = 1$.

Lemma 1. *The probability that a single bit in a packet remains unchanged after one step is $\mathbb{P}[X_{t+1}^{(i)} = b | X_t^{(i)} = b] = 1 - \frac{k}{n}$ no matter whether the message 0 or 1 has been encoded during this step.*

Proof. W.l.o.g. let $X_t^{(i)} = 1$. First, suppose that $M_{t+1} = 0$. Our bit will change if it is chosen as one of k positions on which bit 0 will be encoded at time $t+1$. This happens with probability $\binom{n-1}{k-1}/\binom{n}{k} = \frac{k}{n}$. Thus $\mathbb{P}[X_{t+1}^{(i)} = 1 | X_t^{(i)} = 1 \cap M_{t+1} = 0] = 1 - \frac{k}{n}$.

Our model of communication is symmetric, namely it does not favor neither ones nor zeroes. In each step in a packet l zeroes are turned to ones and l ones turned to zeros, where l may vary from 0 to k. Therefore, intuitively the above probability should not change if we assume $M_{t+1} = 1$ instead of $M_{t+1} = 0$. For clarity below we present the formal proof of this fact. Let Z denote the event $[X_t^{(i)} = 1 \cap M_{t+1} = 1]$. Let L be the number of "new" ones that appear in the packet when a one is encoded at time $t + 1$ (i.e. the number of bits such that $X_t^{(i)} = 0$ and $X_{t+1}^{(i)} = 1$). We get

$$\mathbb{P}[X_{t+1}^{(i)} = 1 | Z] = \sum_{l=0}^{k} \mathbb{P}[X_{t+1}^{(i)} = 1 | Z \cap L = l] \mathbb{P}[L = l | Z] = \sum_{l=0}^{k} \left(1 - \frac{l}{n/2}\right) \frac{\binom{n/2}{k-l}\binom{n/2}{l}}{\binom{n}{k}}$$

$$= 1 - \sum_{l=0}^{k} \frac{l}{n/2} \frac{\binom{n/2}{k-l}\binom{n/2}{l}}{\binom{n}{k}} = 1 - \frac{1}{\binom{n}{k}} \sum_{l=0}^{k-1} \binom{n/2}{k-l-1}\binom{n/2-1}{l} = 1 - \frac{\binom{n-1}{k-1}}{\binom{n}{k}} = 1 - \frac{k}{n}. \qquad \square$$

Lemma 2. *The probability distribution of a single bit b at time t, conditioned on being b at time 0 is defined by $\mathbb{P}[X_t^{(i)} = b | X_0^{(i)} = b] = \frac{1}{2}\left(1 - \frac{2k}{n}\right)^t + \frac{1}{2}$.*

Proof. For brevity let B denote the event $[X_0^{(i)} = b]$. For $t \geq 1$, by Lemma 1, we have that $\mathbb{P}[X_t^{(i)} = b|B]$ is equal to

$$\mathbb{P}[X_t^{(i)} = b|B \cap X_{t-1}^{(i)} = b] \cdot \mathbb{P}[X_{t-1}^{(i)} = b|B]$$
$$+ \mathbb{P}[X_t^{(i)} = b|B \cap X_{t-1}^{(i)} = 1 - b] \cdot \mathbb{P}[X_{t-1}^{(i)} = 1 - b|B]$$
$$= \left(1 - \tfrac{k}{n}\right) \mathbb{P}[X_{t-1}^{(i)} = b|B] + \tfrac{k}{n}\left(1 - \mathbb{P}[X_{t-1}^{(i)} = b|B]\right)$$
$$= \left(1 - \tfrac{2k}{n}\right) \mathbb{P}[X_{t-1}^{(i)} = b|B] + \tfrac{k}{n}.$$

Thus, we obtain a linear non-homogeneous recurrence relation: $\mathbb{P}[X_0^{(i)} = b|B] = 1$ for $t = 0$ and $\mathbb{P}[X_t^{(i)} = b|B] = \left(1 - \tfrac{2k}{n}\right) \mathbb{P}[X_{t-1}^{(i)} = b|B] + \tfrac{k}{n}$ for $t \geq 1$. The formula for $\mathbb{P}[X_t^{(i)} = b|B]$ stated in this lemma can be obtained in a standard way. For example, by setting $\mathbb{P}[X_t^{(i)} = b|B] = \mathbb{P}[X_{t-1}^{(i)} = b|B] = p^*$ we can find the steady state $p^* = \tfrac{1}{2}$ and rewrite non-homogeneous recurrence in homogeneous form $\left(\mathbb{P}[X_t^{(i)} = b|B] - p^*\right) = \left(1 - \tfrac{2k}{n}\right)\left(\mathbb{P}[X_{t-1}^{(i)} = b|B] - p^*\right)$ for which the solution of the form $c\left(1 - \tfrac{2k}{n}\right)^t$ is well known. Applying the boundary condition we get $c = \tfrac{1}{2}$ and $\left(\mathbb{P}[X_t^{(i)} = b|B] - p^*\right) = \tfrac{1}{2}\left(1 - \tfrac{2k}{n}\right)^t$. Note that when t increases probability $\mathbb{P}[X_t^{(i)} = b|B]$ approaches $\tfrac{1}{2}$ (i.e. information fades).   □

Definition 1. *Let* X_t *denote the number of correctly encoded bits (ones according our assumption) in packet* P *at positions 1 to* k *at time* t*, that is,* $X_t = \sum_{i=1}^{k} X_t^{(i)}$*.*

Corollary 1. *The expected number of ones at time* t *at positions from 1 to* k *is*

$$\mathbb{E}[X_t] = \tfrac{k}{2}\left(1 - \tfrac{2k}{n}\right)^t + \tfrac{k}{2}$$

and converges to $\tfrac{k}{2}$*, the mean of the binomial distribution* $B(k, \tfrac{1}{2})$*.*

Definition 2. *Let us define* $p_t = \mathbb{P}[X_t^{(1)} = 1|X_0^{(1)} = 1]$*.*

Remark 1. Note that for all $i \in \{1, \ldots, k\}$ the value of $\mathbb{P}[X_t^{(i)} = 1|X_0^{(i)} = 1]$ is the same thus we have $p_t = \mathbb{P}[X_t^{(i)} = 1|X_0^{(i)} = 1]$.

Corollary 2. *If* $\mathbb{X}$ *denotes the number of ones that* y *finds on positions agreed with* x *in all* s *($1 \leq s \leq T$) received packets, then we have* $\mathbb{E}[\mathbb{X}] \geq k \cdot s \cdot p_T$*.*

Proof. Note that $\mathbb{X}$ is the sum of s independent random variables which all have the distribution of X_t, however, the values of p_t may be different for different t's. Since $\mathbb{E}[X_t]$ is decreasing in t the expectation of each of them is at least $k \cdot p_T$.   □

Lemma 3. *The variance of the random variable* X_t *is 0 for* $t = 0$*. For* $t \geq 1$ *it equals*

$$\mathbb{V}ar[X_t] = k \cdot p_t \cdot \left(1 - p_t\left(1 + \tfrac{k(k-1)(2-1/p_t)}{(n-2k)(n-1)}\right)\right).$$

Proof. By our assumptions at $t = 0$ we have $X_0 = k$, thus $\mathbb{P}[X_0 = k] = 1$ and $\mathbb{V}ar[X_0] = 0$. Since $\mathbb{V}ar[X_t] = \mathbb{E}[X_t^2] - (\mathbb{E}X_t)^2$, let us find $\mathbb{E}[X_t^2]$ for $t \geq 1$. For any event A let us write $\mathbb{P}_1[A]$ instead of $\mathbb{P}[A|X_0^{(1)} = 1, X_0^{(2)} = 1]$. By the linearity of expectation, Corollary 1 and the fact that $X_t^{(i)}$ are equally distributed 0-1 random variables, we get

$$\mathbb{E}[X_t^2] = \sum_{i=0}^{k} \mathbb{E}[X_t^{(i)}] + k(k-1)\mathbb{E}[X_t^{(1)}X_t^{(2)}] = kp_t + k(k-1)\mathbb{P}_1[X_t^{(1)} = 1, X_t^{(2)} = 1]. \quad (1)$$

Note that $\mathbb{P}_1[X_t^{(1)} = 1, X_t^{(2)} = 1] = \mathbb{P}_1[X_t^{(1)} = 1|X_t^{(2)} = 1] \cdot \mathbb{P}_1[X_t^{(2)} = 1]$ and $\mathbb{P}_1[X_t^{(2)} = 1] = p_t$. Moreover, $\mathbb{P}_1[X_0^{(1)} = 1|X_0^{(2)} = 1] = 1$ and $\mathbb{P}_1[X_{t+1}^{(1)} = 1|X_t^{(1)} = 1, X_{t+1}^{(2)} = 1] = 1 - \frac{k}{n-1}$, which results from the reasoning analogous to the one in Lemma 1; one only has to remember about the condition that at time $t + 1$ there is already 1 at position 2 (therefore now we divide by $n - 1$ instead of n). Thus we have

$$\mathbb{P}_1[X_{t+1}^{(1)}=1|X_{t+1}^{(2)}=1] = \mathbb{P}_1[X_{t+1}^{(1)}=1|X_t^{(1)}=1, X_{t+1}^{(2)}=1] \cdot \mathbb{P}_1[X_t^{(1)}=1|X_{t+1}^{(2)}=1]$$
$$+ \mathbb{P}_1[X_{t+1}^{(1)}=1|X_t^{(1)}=0, X_{t+1}^{(2)}=1] \cdot \mathbb{P}_1[X_t^{(1)}=0|X_{t+1}^{(2)}=1] = \left(1 - \tfrac{k}{n-1}\right)p_t + \tfrac{k}{n-1}(1-p_t) \ .$$

By putting the above results together and applying to (1) we get $\mathbb{E}[X_t^2]$. Note that as t increases this variance approaches $\frac{k}{4}$, the variance of the binomial distribution $B(k, \frac{1}{2})$. $\qquad \square$

Corollary 3. *Recall that $\mathbb{X}$ is the number of ones that y finds on positions agreed with x in all s $(1 \leq s \leq T)$ packets obtained from x. We have $\mathbb{V}ar[\mathbb{X}] \leq s \cdot \mathbb{V}ar[X_T]$.*

Proof. Notice that $\mathbb{X}$ is the sum of s independent random variables which all have the distribution of X_t, however, the values of p_t may be different for different t's. Since $\mathbb{V}ar[X_t]$ is increasing in t, we may write that the variance of each of them is at most $\mathbb{V}ar[X_T]$. $\qquad \square$

Lemma 4. *Let $\hat{\varepsilon} \in (0, \frac{1}{2})$. Then $p_t \geq 1 - \hat{\varepsilon}$ if $\frac{k}{n} \leq \frac{1}{2}(1 - (1 - 2\hat{\varepsilon})^{1/t})$.*

Proof. The result follows from the fact that $p_t = \frac{1}{2}\left(\left(1 - \frac{2k}{n}\right)^t + 1\right)$.

Based on the above results let us now find the probability of the successful message delivery.

Theorem 1. *Let $f \in (\frac{1}{2}, 1]$ and $\hat{\varepsilon} \in (0, \frac{1}{2})$ be such that $p_T \geq 1 - \hat{\varepsilon} > f$ and let $\delta \in (0, 1)$. Recall that $\mathbb{X}$ is the number of ones that y finds on positions agreed with x in all s packets received from x. Then for $k \geq \frac{\hat{\varepsilon}(1-\hat{\varepsilon})}{\delta \cdot s \cdot (1-\hat{\varepsilon}-f)^2}$ we have*
$$\mathbb{P}[\mathbb{X} \geq f \cdot s \cdot k] \geq 1 - \delta \ .$$

Proof. Equivalently, we will show that $\mathbb{P}[\mathbb{X} \leq f \cdot s \cdot k] \leq \delta$. Let $\mathbb{Y} = s \cdot k - \mathbb{X}$. By Corollary 2 we have $\mathbb{E}[\mathbb{Y}] \leq s \cdot k(1 - p_T)$. Since $p_T > f$, $p_T > 1 - \hat{\varepsilon}$, and $k \geq \frac{\hat{\varepsilon}(1-\hat{\varepsilon})}{\delta s(1-\hat{\varepsilon}-f)^2}$, by Chebyshev's inequality and Corollary 3 we get

$$\mathbb{P}[\mathbb{X} \leq f \cdot s \cdot k] = \mathbb{P}[s \cdot k - \mathbb{X} \geq s \cdot k - f \cdot s \cdot k] = \mathbb{P}[\mathbb{Y} - \mathbb{E}[\mathbb{Y}] \geq s \cdot k - f \cdot s \cdot k - \mathbb{E}[\mathbb{Y}]]$$

$$\leq \mathbb{P}[|\mathbb{Y} - \mathbb{E}[\mathbb{Y}]| \geq s \cdot k \cdot (p_T - f)] \leq \frac{Var[\mathbb{Y}]}{(s \cdot k)^2 (p_T - f)^2} = \frac{Var[\mathbb{X}]}{(s \cdot k)^2 (p_T - f)^2}$$

$$\leq \frac{p_T \left(1 - p_T \left(1 + \frac{k(k-1)(2-1/p_T)}{(n-2k)(n-1)}\right)\right)}{s \cdot k(p_T - f)^2} \leq \frac{p_T(1 - p_T)}{s \cdot k(p_T - f)^2} \leq \frac{\hat{\varepsilon}(1 - \hat{\varepsilon})}{s \cdot k(1 - \hat{\varepsilon} - f)^2} \leq \delta. \quad \square$$

Remark 2. Since $f \in (\frac{1}{2}, 1]$, the inequality $\mathbb{P}[\mathbb{X} \leq fsk] \leq \delta$ implies $\mathbb{P}[\mathbb{X} \leq (1-f)sk] \leq \delta$, therefore we have proved both bounds postulated at the beginning of this section.

3.2   Packet Length

Let us now discuss what relations between n and k the above theorem enforces for $\delta \in (0,1)$, $f \in (\frac{1}{2}, 1]$ and for $\hat{\varepsilon} \in (0, \frac{1}{2})$ chosen such that $p_T \geq 1 - \hat{\varepsilon} > f$. Note that we do not know how many packets s will be delivered from x to y, so to use Theorem 1 we need to ensure sufficiently large k for any $s \in \{1, \ldots, T\}$. Therefore we will assume that $k \geq \frac{\hat{\varepsilon}(1-\hat{\varepsilon})}{\delta(1-\hat{\varepsilon}-f)^2}$. Thus in order to satisfy the assumptions of Theorem 1 for arbitrary s, the following inequalities need to be satisfied

$$\frac{\hat{\varepsilon}(1-\hat{\varepsilon})}{n\delta(1-\hat{\varepsilon}-f)^2} \leq \frac{k}{n} \leq \frac{1}{2}(1 - (1 - 2\hat{\varepsilon})^{1/T}),$$

where right-hand side comes from Lemma 4 and ensures that $p_T > 1 - \hat{\varepsilon}$. Since we need to ensure also $1 - \hat{\varepsilon} > f$, where f is some constant from the interval $(\frac{1}{2}, 1]$, we can think of $\hat{\varepsilon}$ as a function tending (with N) to 0 or a small constant, e.g. $\hat{\varepsilon} = (1 - f)/2$. Note that $1 - (1 - 2\hat{\varepsilon})^{1/T} \geq 2\hat{\varepsilon}/T$ and that this estimation is quite accurate for $\hat{\varepsilon}$ close to 0. Thus, instead of the above set of inequalities let us study

$$\frac{\hat{\varepsilon}(1-\hat{\varepsilon})}{n\delta(1-\hat{\varepsilon}-f)^2} \leq \frac{k}{n} \leq \frac{\hat{\varepsilon}}{T}.$$

For n we obtain the inequality $n \geq \frac{T(1-\hat{\varepsilon})}{\delta(1-\hat{\varepsilon}-f)^2}$. If we aim at having as short packets as possible we may decide to have

$$n = \Theta\left(\frac{T(1-\hat{\varepsilon})}{\delta(1-\hat{\varepsilon}-f)^2}\right) \quad \text{and consequently} \quad k = \Theta\left(\frac{\hat{\varepsilon}(1-\hat{\varepsilon})}{\delta(1-\hat{\varepsilon}-f)^2}\right). \quad (2)$$

3.3   Delivery Time

Let us finally investigate how long must be an epoch in terms of a network size N to guarantee that sufficient number of packets encoded from x to y reach their destination so that the probability of delivering a message successfully is high.

Theorem 2. *Let $f \in (\frac{1}{2}, 1]$ and $\hat{\varepsilon} \in (0, \frac{1}{2})$ such that $p_T \geq 1 - \hat{\varepsilon} > f$. Let M denote the event that the message is delivered successfully from x to y and let $\hat{\delta} = \frac{\hat{\varepsilon}(1-\hat{\varepsilon})}{k(1-\hat{\varepsilon}-f)^2}$. Then there exists a function $g(N)$ such that $\mathbb{P}[M] \geq g(N)$ and*

$$g(N) \sim 1 - e^{-T^2/N} - 2\hat{\delta}\left(\frac{1-e^{-T^2/N}}{T(1-e^{-T/N})} - e^{-T^2/N}\right),$$

where $g(N) \sim f(N)$ means that $g(N)/f(N) \to 1$ as $N \to \infty$.

Proof. Recall $\mathbb{X}$ is the number of ones that y finds on positions agreed with x in s $(1 \leq s \leq T)$ packets obtained from x. Let Z be the random variable denoting the number of packets delivered from x to y. Z has binomial distribution $B(T, q)$ where $q = 1 - (1 - 1/(N-1))^T$. Note that $\mathbb{P}[M] = \sum_{s=1}^{T}(\mathbb{P}[M|Z = s] \cdot \mathbb{P}[Z = s]) = \sum_{s=1}^{T}(\mathbb{P}[\mathbb{X} \geq f \cdot s \cdot k|Z = s] \cdot \mathbb{P}[Z = s])$. By Theorem 1 we obtain

$$\mathbb{P}[M] \geq \sum_{s=1}^{T}\left(1 - \frac{\hat{\varepsilon}(1-\hat{\varepsilon})}{sk(1-\hat{\varepsilon}-f)^2}\right)\mathbb{P}[Z = s]$$

$$= 1 - \mathbb{P}[Z = 0] - \frac{\hat{\varepsilon}(1-\hat{\varepsilon})}{k(1-\hat{\varepsilon}-f)^2}\sum_{s=1}^{T}\frac{1}{s}\binom{T}{s}q^s(1-q)^{T-s}$$

$$\geq 1 - (1-q)^T - 2\hat{\delta}\sum_{s=1}^{T}\frac{1}{s+1}\binom{T}{s}q^s(1-q)^{T-s}.$$

Finally, note that $\sum_{s=1}^{T}\frac{1}{s+1}\binom{T}{s}q^s(1-q)^{T-s} = \frac{1-(1-q)^T(1+Tq)}{q(T+1)} \sim \frac{1-e^{-T^2/N}}{T(1-e^{-T/N})} - e^{-T^2/N}$, where the last relation results from $(1-q)^T = (1 - 1/(N-1))^{T^2} \sim e^{-T^2/N}$. $\qquad\square$

Theorem 2 allows us to set the protocol parameters so that the probability $\mathbb{P}[M]$ of delivering the message successfully is arbitrarily close to one. Below we present two examples that show the correlation between the value of this probability, the length of the epoch T and the length of the packet n. If we want to obtain at least a constant probability $\mathbb{P}[M]$ we can not let the term $e^{-T^2/N}$, which refers to $\mathbb{P}[Z = 0]$, go to 1 with N tending to infinity. Therefore we always require that $T = \Omega(\sqrt{N})$.

Example 1. Suppose that we wish to have packets and epochs as short as possible and we will be satisfied with probability $\mathbb{P}[M]$ greater than some constant close to 1. We set $T = \lceil c\sqrt{N} \rceil$, where c is some positive constant, $\hat{\varepsilon} = \frac{1-f}{2}$ and $\hat{\delta} = \frac{1}{\log N}$. By (2) let us set $n = \lceil\frac{2(1+f)}{(1-f)^2}c\sqrt{N}\log N\rceil$ and $k = \lceil\frac{1+f}{1-f}\log N\rceil$. By Theorem 2 we obtain $\mathbb{P}[M] \geq g(N) \sim 1 - e^{-c^2}$. Note the bigger c and smaller δ, the bigger the probability $\mathbb{P}[M]$. However, bigger c means a longer epoch and packet and smaller δ means a longer packet.

Example 2. Suppose that one is ready to increase the length of an epoch and the length of a packet to have the probability $\mathbb{P}[M]$ asymptotically equal to 1. Let us set $\hat{\varepsilon} = (1 - f)/2$, $\hat{\delta} = 1/\log N$ and $T = \lceil\sqrt{N\log N}\rceil$. Then $n = \lceil\frac{2(1+f)}{(1-f)^2}\sqrt{N\log N}\log N\rceil$ and $k = \lceil\frac{1+f}{1-f}\log N\rceil$. Again by Theorem 2 we obtain $\mathbb{P}[M] \geq g(N) \sim 1 - \frac{1}{N}$.

4   Security Discussion

4.1   Traffic Analysis

In this section we discuss security properties of our protocol under the passive adversary model. The function h used by the Ghost Train protocol has to determine subsets in such a way that the selection process is indistinguishable from choosing subsets at random. More formally, we should consider the following three-phase game.

Definition 3 (Distinguishability Game).

1. *Setup Phase executed by the Challenger and Adversary:*
   - *the Challenger chooses key K uniformly at random,*
   - *the Adversary chooses $i_1, \ldots, i_l$, $t_1, \ldots, t_l$, $P_1, \ldots, P_l$ (where $i_1, \ldots, i_l$ stand for the epoch numbers, $t_1, \ldots, t_l$ for step indexes within the epochs, $P_1, \ldots, P_l$ for packet ID's). However, for no j, j' the Adversary can choose so that $(i_j, t_j) = (i_{j'}, t_{j'})$.*
2. *Challenge Phase:*
   - *the Challenger chooses a bit b at random,*
   - *if $b = 0$, the Challenger picks at random subsets $S_1, \ldots, S_l$ of $\{1, \ldots, n\}$, each of size k,*
   - *if $b = 1$, then for $j = 1, \ldots, l$ the Challenger sets $S_j \leftarrow h(K, i_j, t_j, P_j)$*
   - *the Challenger presents $S_1, \ldots, S_l$ to the Adversary.*
3. *Decision Phase: the Adversary responds with a bit $\hat{b}$. The Adversary wins, if $b = \hat{b}$.*

The function h used by the scheme should ensure that the probability to win the game by the Adversary is at most $\frac{1}{2} + \varepsilon$, where ε is a sufficiently small value. Although we do not indicate any specific function h to be used here, there are many constructions which are believed to be safe, i.e. for which Distinguishability Game cannot be won by the Adversary with probability substantially bigger than $\frac{1}{2}$.

Remark 3. Note that Distinguishability Game provides more data than an observer of Ghost Trains typically gets: first, some positions of the sets S_j remain unknown due to the fact that the corresponding positions already store correct bit values. Second, the adversary does not know which changes are due to encoding a bit value and which are due to maintaining equilibrium between the number of zeroes and ones.

Remark 4. Definition 3 concerns the case of all encodings created by a single secret key. One can easily extend it to the case of multiple keys. We skip such an extension for readability.

Once we assume that the function h has the above claimed properties, then we can transform the protocol to a version where:

(1) set S where bits are to be set at a given moment to encode a bit sent from a node x to a node y is chosen in advance uniformly at random and independently from other choices,
(2) the communicating nodes x and y are presented in advance the sets intended for them.

If the adversary analyzing the traffic could recognize any change of behavior, we could immediately conclude that there is a distinguisher that can be used by the Adversary to win the Distinguishability Game.

After the transformation, the behavior of a sender is stochastically independent from the choice of destinations. Therefore, the adversary cannot derive any information on the undergoing traffic. This concerns not only the destinations addresses but also the situation when no message is encoded at all. Therefore we get the theorem:

Theorem 3. *If for a function h the advantage of the Adversary in the Distinguishability Game is negligible, then a passive adversary analyzing the traffic has a negligible advantage over an adversary that sees no traffic data.*

4.2   Active Attacks

The first kind of an active attack would be to break communication anonymity. However, we have to note two facts:

(1) the encoding activity of a node does not depend on the incoming data, except that the packet ID, epoch number and the slot number are used as arguments for h during encoding procedure (*packetEncoding*),
(2) since the slot numbers and epoch numbers are never the same for a given (attacked) node, we are at the scenario of Distinguishability Game.

Thereby, the adversary cannot learn more about the state of a node than assumed for the Distinguishability Game. It follows immediately that an active attack against anonymity of communication would fail in this case just as described in the previous subsection for the passive case.

Another kind of active attacks against the Ghost Train might be denial of service. An attacker may intend to destroy the messages coming from a node x or the messages with destination y. Of course, simple boycotting a node in a network would be enough to achieve this goal. However, the adversary would have to assure that a substantial fraction of nodes in the network "ignore" the node x (respectively, y). However, such a coalition could be easily identified and declared as malicious.

Another option of an denial of service attack against a node x would be to overwrite the packets leaving a node x in a malicious way. It would suffice to falsify the packet route history and erase the entry concerning x and its slot number. In such a case, the recipient would normally not attempt to decrypt the bit from x. Moreover, in order to destroy the message contents (the recipients might be aware of the attack and would perform trial decryptions without looking at the routing information) the adversary may intentionally revert or randomize the contents of the bit array at the places where node x performed the changes. (Note that for this attack the adversary must know the packet state immediately before node x performs its encoding, but we cannot exclude that the adversary somehow gains this knowledge.) Fortunately, it is quite easy to detect such behavior by testing a node: node x sends a test message w to an alleged malicious node u, and interacts with all friends to find out whether u has forwarded the message w in a modified form, and whether the modification indicates an attack or not.

Conclusions. We have presented a generic method for anonymous communication based on random walks, Bloom filters and pseudorandomness with shared keys. Of course, the protocol is not aimed to replace TOR or any other systems that have to sacrifice strong anonymity for fair efficiency. However, our goal was to show a yet different way for achieving perfect communication anonymity and encoding hidden data in a nonstandard way. Last not least, in many situations replacing asymmetric cryptography by symmetric cryptography has many advantages. One of the reasons is that is might be much easier to create tailored encryption/decryption methods.

We have to observe that the encoding data used in the scheme substantially complicates cryptanalysis by an adversary that knows that Alice is trying to communicate with Bob. Namely, the adversary has problems to separate changes in the Ghost Train contents related to the encrypted data and the random changes used to keep balance. Moreover, at some positions the bits have already the right value, so no change is observed and therefore the adversary cannot locate them. This, for instance, substantially impedes brute force attacks.

Acknowledgments. The research was supported by the Polish National Science Centre, Decision DEC-2013/08/M/ST6/00928.

References

1. Tor: Anonymity online. www.torproject.org
2. Aleliunas, R., Karp, R.M., Lipton, R.J., Lovász, L., Rackoff, C.: Random walks, universal traversal sequences, and the complexity of maze problems. In: 20th FOCS, pp. 218–223 (1979)
3. Aspnes, J., Ruppert, E.: An introduction to population protocols. Bull. Eur. Assoc. Theor. Comput. Sci. **93**, 98–117 (2007)
4. Beimel, A., Dolev, S.: Buses for anonymous message delivery. J. Cryptology **16**(1), 25–39 (2003)
5. Berman, R., Fiat, A., Gomułkiewicz, M., Klonowski, M., Kutyłowski, M., Levinboim, T., Ta-Shma, A.: Provable unlinkability against traffic analysis with low message overhead. J. Cryptology **28**(3), 623–640 (2015)
6. Rackoff, C., Simon, D.R.: Cryptographic defense against traffic analysis. In: 25th ACM STOC, pp. 672–681. ACM (1993)

7. Sherwood, R., Bhattacharjee, B., Srinivasan, A.: P5: a protocol for scalable anonymous communication. In: 2002 IEEE Symposium on Security and Privacy, pp. 58–70 (2002)
8. Young, A., Yung, M.: The drunk motorcyclist protocol for anonymous communication. In: IEEE Conference on Communications and Network Security, pp. 157–165. IEEE (2014)

Efficient Detection Method for Data Integrity Attacks in Smart Grid

Peixiu An and Zhitao Guan[✉]

School of Control and Computer Engineering, North China Electric Power University,
Beijing 102206, China
{anpeixiu14717,guanzhitao}@126.com

Abstract. With the developing of the Smart Grid, false data injection attacks (FDIAs) as a typical data integrity attack successfully bypass the traditional bad data detection and identification, has a serious influence on the power system safe and reliable operation. State estimation, which is an important process in smart grid, is used in system monitoring to get optimally estimate the power grid state through analysis of the monitoring data. However, FDIAs compromising data integrity will lead to wrong decision makings in power dispatch or electric power market transactions. In this paper, focusing on the power property, we introduce an index to quantitatively measure the node voltage stability and reflect the influence of FDIAs on the power system. Then, we use an improved clustering algorithm to identify the node vulnerability level, which helps operators take measures and detect the false data injection attacks timely. Besides, one effective state forecasting detection method is proposed, which is meaningful for real-time detection of false data injection attacks. Finally, the simulation result verifies the effectiveness and performance of the proposed method.

Keywords: Smart grid · Voltage stability · False data injection attacks · Cyber security · State estimation

1 Introduction

In recent years, the industrial control system and the power system automation, intelligent level continuous improvement make the power system rapidly develop. It also makes the grid security defense face more severe challenges at the same time [1–3]. By tampering the estimated value of power system state estimation, the false data injection attacks (FDIAs) would mislead control center to make wrong decisions and consequently impact severely on the grid's stability and reliability. Unconsciously, the FDIAs become one of the focuses of current researchers [4–8]. For this serious vulnerability, how to detect and identify the FDIAs has attracted a lot of attention among researchers. Although there are lots of articles about the FDIAs, most of the existing FDIAs detection methods rarely consider the impact of false data injection attacks on the power system. They ignore the connection of the FDIAs and the power system physical properties. However, for the system operators, it is an effective way that analysis the physical properties of power system to improve the detection and protection ability for FDIAs.

© Springer International Publishing AG 2016
G. Wang et al. (Eds.): SpaCCS 2016, LNCS 10066, pp. 240–250, 2016.
DOI: 10.1007/978-3-319-49148-6_21

For a given initial operating condition, the voltage stability reflect the ability of power system that regaining state operating equilibrium after being subjected to a physical disturbance [9]. It is very convenient that system operators use fast, simple and correct methods to monitor the proximity of voltage collapse of a power system. Moreover, the node voltage stability can quantitatively measure the stability and reflect the impact of false data injection attacks on the power grid. So, we study and analyze this physical property of power system. We also construct the relationship between the false data injection attack and the node voltage stability to identify the vulnerability level of each node in the complex system, which can help power operators to targeted detection and take the corresponding protective measures timely.

In this paper, we present an efficient detection method against FDIAs. And the main contributions of this paper can be summarized as the following:

We study and analyze the physical property of power system and introduce an index to quantitatively measure the impact of false data injection attacks on the power system. We also construct the relationship between the false data injection attacks and the node voltage stability to identify the vulnerability of each node in the complex system;

According to the value of the node voltage stability, we use the improved clustering method to cluster the nodes into three different clusters. As the result of clustering, the nodes with similar vulnerability level get together for a cluster;

We use the effective state forecasting method to obtain state prediction and detect the false data injection attacks. Besides, we simulate the tests on the IEEE 30-bus systems to verify the effectiveness and performance of the proposed method.

2   Related Work

False data injection attacks (FDIAs), a new typical data integrity attack which is one of the most threatening cyber-attacks in smart grids, is presented firstly in [10]. For this serious vulnerability, many smart algorithms are applied to detect the FDIAs [11], such as geometrically designed residual filter, the generalized likelihood ratio test [4]. And the cumulative sum (CUSUM) test-based detection mechanism introduced in [12–14] is also designed for these stealth attacks. The researchers of [15] use the machine learning method to deal with the stealth false data. Moreover, how to economically deploy PMUs to facilitate the state estimator and detect the FDIAs has become an interesting problem [16, 17]. In [18], a detection method based on the PMU is proposed, the authors assume that the measuring of a portion in the system is absolute secure under the protection of the secure physical parts, and the attackers couldn't tamper the protected meters, otherwise it will be detected as an attack and carry on a limit to the attackers' behavior. Later, with the power systems increasingly interconnected in the smart grid, distributed state estimate (DSE) becomes an important alternative to centralized and hierarchical solutions [19, 20]. In [21], two new methods of distributed state estimation are proposed, one is using the incremental mode of cooperation, and the other is based on diffusive interaction pattern. The authors of [22, 23] apply the distributed state estimation (DSE) into the fully distributed power system for attack detection. In [24], a bad data detection method based on an extended distributed state estimation (EDSE) is presented. A power system is decomposed into several subsystems using graph partition algorithms. For each subsystem, buses are classified into three groups: internal bus, boundary bus and adjacent bus. Simulation results demonstrate that the detection accuracy of the EDSE-based method is much higher than the traditional method on average, and its computation complexity is significantly lowered.

Nowadays, various methods have been proposed to address the problems of false data injection attacks in Smart Grid. However, the study of the physical property and analyzing networks data to detect the false data injection attacks is very meager. So, we study the corresponding work in this paper.

The rest of this paper is organized as follows. In Sect. 3, the system model and background are discussed. The proposed node vulnerability level identification is shown in Sect. 4. The state forecasting method is discussed in Sect. 5. We simulate the test and the effectiveness and performance of the proposed model and detection method are evaluated in Sect. 6. Finally, the paper is concluded in Sect. 7.

3 System Model and Background

In this section, we briefly discuss the state estimation in power system and the node voltage stability index.

3.1 Notations

In order to check the convenience, some important notations used in our paper are listed in the Table 1.

3.2 Problem Formulation

In our work, we present a common formulation of the state estimation problem when using a DC power flow. The measurements vector z is an m × 1 vector in a power system such as power flows at transmission lines, and power injections and loads at buses. The power flow measurements can be taken at one or both ends of a transmission line. In the progress of state estimation, we are interested in using the collected set of measurements to estimate an n × 1 vector x of unknown state variables, where $m \geq n$. The unknown state variables are the voltage angles or voltage magnitudes at different nodes. H denotes the m × n measurements Jacobian matrix.

$$z = Hx + e \tag{1}$$

Where, the e is the measurement noise. And the noise is normally Gaussian distributed with zero mean, then the estimated state variables can be express as:

$$\hat{x} = (H^T W H)^{-1} H^T W z \tag{2}$$

Where the W is a diagonal matrix whose diagonal elements are given by $W_{ii} = \delta_i^{-2}$, and δ_i^2 is the variance of e_i, for $i = 1, 2, \ldots, n$.

Table 1. Some important notations

Notation	Description
z	The $m \times 1$ vector of measurements
x	The $n \times 1$ vector of state variables
H	The $m \times n$ Jacobian matrix denoting the power system topology
e	Random errors of measurements
m	The number of measurements
n	The number of state variables
$\hat{x}$	The estimated value of state variables
W	The diagonal matrix
z_f	The $m \times 1$ measurements vector with false data
a	The $m \times 1$ attacked vector
c	The $n \times 1$ vector of estimated errors
$\hat{x}_f$	The estimated value of state variables with false data
τ	The threshold
r	The measurement residuals
$NVSI(N_i)$	T the voltage stability index at the node i
U_j	The voltage magnitude of node j
R	The resistance of branch
X	The reactance of branch
P_i	The real power of node i
Q_i	The reactive power of node i
s	The population size of the CFPSO
K	The number of the centroids
F_{sum_dis}	The total sum of the distance of each particle to the centroid
G_{t-1}	The state transition matrix at time sample $t-1$
Q_{t-1}	The nonzero diagonal matrix at time sample $t-1$
$\widehat{z}_t$	The forecasting measurements at sample t

In the FDIAs, an adversary try his/her best to hack the readings of sensors such that the vector of measurement z is replaced by a compromised vector $z_f = z + a$, where the a is a $m \times 1$ attack vector. The attacker constructs the attacked vector a to be a linear combination of the rows in matrix H, i.e., $a = Hc$ for some arbitrary n $\times$ 1 vector c, then the traditional detection methods based on residue test will not be able to detect the attack since the injected false data will no longer affect the residue:

$$\begin{aligned} \| r \| &= \| z_f - H\hat{x}_f \| \\ &= \| z + a - H(\hat{x} + c) \| \\ &= \| (z - H\hat{x}) + (a - Hc) \| \\ &= \| z - H\hat{x} \| < \tau \end{aligned} \tag{3}$$

and

$$\hat{x}_f = \hat{x} + (H^T WH)^{-1} H^T WHc$$
$$= \hat{x} + c \tag{4}$$

By using the knowledge of the line admittances and the power topology, the adversary can successfully implement false data injection attacks which not be detected by the traditional detection methods. But the attacked vectors to the measurements cause the deviation of the state estimation, and this will lead to the grid power collapse or paralysis.

3.3 Node Voltage Stability Description

As we all know, many methods and techniques have been reported for voltage stability analysis and voltage collapse prediction. A number of static voltage stability index have been widely used for evaluating and predicting the proximity of the system to voltage stability. In our paper, we introduce the node voltage stability index (*NVSI*) presented by the authors in [25], as follows,

$$NVSI(N_i) = 4U_j^{-4}(RQ_i - XP_i)^2 - 4U_j^{-2}(XQ_i + RP_j) \tag{5}$$

where the $NVSI(N_i)$ is the voltage stability index at the node i, U_j is the voltage magnitude of node j. R and X are the resistance and reactance of branch respectively, which can be obtained from the power network electric topological database. Besides, P_i, Q_i are the summation of the real power and reactive power. After a successful power flow solution of system, all parameters of Eq. (5) are known, and the $NVSI(N_i)$ index of each node can be calculated. This index can provide important information about the proximity of the system stability, which enables us to set an index threshold to monitor and predict system stability on-line so that a proper action can be taken to prevent the system from collapse timely and detect the false data in smart grid.

4 Node Vulnerability Level Identification

For real-time or extended real-time operation, the electricity operator collects power data from the SCADA. If an attacker has access to any or all of the measurements, he will manipulate the power data by injecting false data. When the measurements under FDIAs, the corrupted real and reactive power measurements, P_i, Q_i and U_j will be changed. Any higher value of the *NVSI* indicates that the system is highly likely to voltage collapse. So, the system operators should become concerned about keeping the system with instability margin.

In the light of the *NVSI* values of all monitored nodes, we can identify the weakest nodes of the system. The *NVSI* at the weakest node will be very large when the system approaches its voltage collapse point. Therefore, a threshold of *NVSI* can be easily set up to trigger an emergency remedial action scheme to remind the operator to detect the FDIAs and take appropriate measures protecting the system from voltage collapse.

Clustering algorithms are often used to measure the similarity between different data sources and to classify the data sources into different clusters. K-means++ algorithm is an efficient and well know unsupervised clustering algorithm which has a wide range of applications. However, a major problem of K-means++ is that it may trap in one of the local minima algorithm. In our work, we use the CFPSO algorithm to optimize that imperfection. At the beginning, we set the K-means++ algorithm is replicated $s/2$ times, where s is the population size of the CFPSO. We obtain the cluster centroids from the replicated K-means++ algorithm and use them as half of the initial population of the swarm. Besides, the remaining half swarm population are initialized randomly based on the solution space. In this way, the remaining half input vectors of the swarm still be capable to produce enough diversity in the velocities of the particles to reach to a better solution. In order to identify the nodes vulnerability level, we set $K = 3$. So the nodes will be clustered into 3 clusters, which indicates three vulnerability levels, the most vulnerable level, the vulnerable level and the stable level separately. In our analysis, we formulate the total sum of the distance of each particle to the centroids considered as a objection function F_{sum_dis}.

At the beginning of identifying the nodes vulnerability level, it is a key problem that how to get the best quality clustering centroid. The step-by-step procedure of the proposed solution is described briefly in Fig. 1.

Then the following steps describe the vulnerability identification procedure:

Read the system data and calculate of each node;
Obtain the best quality clustering centroid from above progress, and cluster the nodes into three swarm according the value;
Identify the nodes vulnerability level of three swarms. The most vulnerability level, the vulnerability level and the stable level separately.

We simulate experiment at the IEEE 30-bus at one moment, and the result of node vulnerability level in Table 2.

Table 2. The node vulnerability level of IEEE 30-bus system

The number of swarm	Vulnerability level	The number of node
Swarm 1	The most vulnerability level	7, 8, 9, 10, 11, 12, 13, 14, 15, 16, 17, 18, 26, 27, 28, 29, 30
Swarm 2	The vulnerability level	4, 5, 6, 23, 24, 25
Swarm 3	The stable level	2, 3, 19, 20, 21, 22

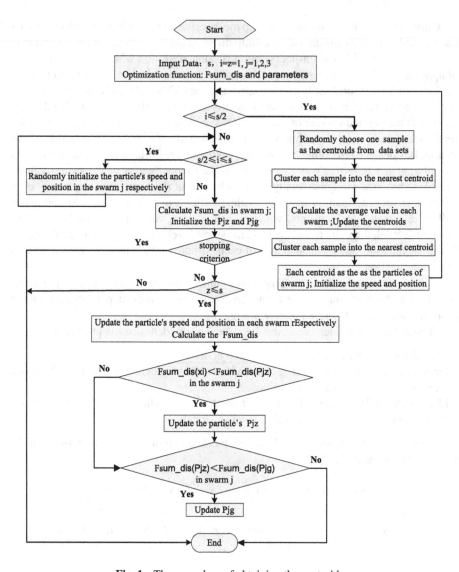

Fig. 1. The procedure of obtaining the centroids

5   State Forecasting Method

The main advantages of identifying the nodes vulnerability level are convenient in modeling and calculations, and ease in real time or on-line applications. The clustering results show that the nodes vulnerability level can reflect the weakest nodes causing system instability, but also help the operators detect the FDIAs. Combining this feature, we propose a new detection method considering two consecutive time frames from to forecast the state of power system and detect the FDIAs.

In the quasi steady state operation of the power system, we can obtain the prediction model by using the historical data and the state estimation. And the forecasting model is

$$x_t = G_{t-1}x_{t-1} + Q_{t-1} \tag{6}$$

Where G_{t-1} is state transition matrix, x_{t-1} is state estimated value at time sample $t-1$ and the Q_{t-1} is nonzero diagonal matrix. Sampling time is at $t-1$ and t separately. Hence, we can calculate the forecasting measurements as:

$$\widehat{z_t} = Hx_t \tag{7}$$

The measurement residuals at is

$$r = Hx - \widehat{z_t} = z - \widehat{z_t} \tag{8}$$

where z is estimated value at t, the $\widehat{z_t}$ is the forecasting measurements using the data at t. In order to simplify the complexity of the formula, we will omit time scale t in the following work.

6   Simulation

In this paper, the proposed method is tested on IEEE 30-bus. The experiment model is constructed in the MATPOWER [26], and the test data is obtained from it. We use the $J(x)$ detector and LNR detector with our power system physical property for detecting the FDIAs to prove the performance. We construct the attacked vectors using the similar way in [12, 13].

We compare the $J(x)$ detector and the LNR detector with our method to see the effectiveness at different false alarm. In the Fig. 2, the ROC shows the trade-off between the probability of attack detection at different probability of false alarms. In our method, if the historical state data is available, the state forecasting is performed.

From the Fig. 2, we can find that the detection rate is gradually increased with the change of false alarm. The $J(x)1$ indicates the detection rate of traditional detect method, and the $J(x)2$ shows the detection rate of our method. Similarly, $LNR1$ and $LNR2$ denote the traditional and our method respectively. On the other hand, we can see that the detection rate of the LNR detector is higher than the $J(x)$ detector.

In a word, according to the node voltage stability index, we can identify the node vulnerability level. After that, we focus on the most vulnerability level firstly, and it help operators take efficient measures timely. State forecasting make operators determine whether exist any false data at time sample t. Finally, the simulation result verifies that the proposed mechanism can effectively detect FDIAs in the smart grid.

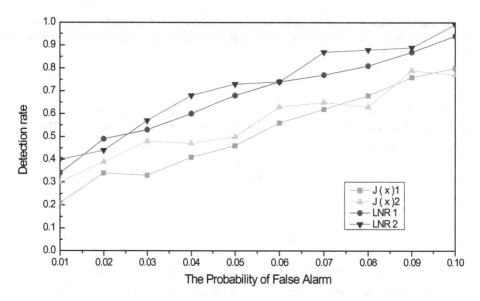

Fig. 2. The detecting results in IEEE 30-bus system

7   Conclusion

To deal with the problem of data integrity in smart grid, which may lead to wrong decision makings in power dispatch or electric power market operations, we propose an efficient FDIAs detection scheme based on power system physical property. Firstly, we analysis the power system and introduce the node voltage stability index to identify the vulnerability level of nodes in power system. As the result, we define three levels to cluster the system nodes into three swarms. In the progress of clustering, we use the improved cluster algorithm and realize the nodes clustering. This step help us to find the suspected false data injection points easily. Then we use the state forecasting method to obtain the states of power system. In addition, the and test methods are used to find the sensitive measurement vectors. In the simulation, we built different types of attack vectors, which makes an abundant experimental results. Finally, the simulation result verifies that the proposed mechanism can effectively detect FDIAs in the smart grid.

Acknowledgments.   This work is partially supported by Natural Science Foundation of China under grant 61402171, Central Government University Foundation under grant JB2016045.

References

1. Fang, X., Misra, S., Xue, G., et al.: Smart grid—the new and improved power grid: a survey. IEEE Commun. Surv. Tutorials **14**(4), 944–980 (2012)
2. Kayastha, N., Niyato, D., Hossain, E., et al.: Smart grid sensor data collection, communication, and networking: a tutorial. Wirel. Commun. Mob. Comput. **14**(11), 1055–1087 (2014)

3. Liu, T., Sun, Y., Liu, Y., et al.: Abnormal traffic-indexed state estimation: a cyber–physical fusion approach for Smart Grid attack detection. Future Gener. Comput. Syst. **49**, 94–103 (2015)
4. Pasqualetti, F., Dörfler, F., Bullo, F.: Cyber-physical attacks in power networks: models, fundamental limitations and monitor design. In: 2011 50th IEEE Conference on Decision and Control and European Control Conference (CDC-ECC), pp. 2195–2201. IEEE (2011)
5. Liu, Y., Ning, P., Reiter, M.K.: False data injection attacks against state estimation in electric power grids. In: ACM Conference on Computer and Communications Security, pp. 21–32. ACM (2009)
6. Guan, Z., An, P., Yang, T.: Matrix partition-based detection scheme for false data injection in smart grid. Int. J. Wirel. Mob. Comput. **9**(3), 250–256 (2015)
7. Guan, Z., Sun, N., Xu, Y., et al.: A comprehensive survey of false data injection in smart grid. Int. J. Wirel. Mob. Comput. **8**(1), 27–33 (2015)
8. Asada, E.N., Garcia, A.V., Romero, R.: Identifying multiple interacting bad data in power system state estimation. In: 2005 IEEE Power Engineering Society General Meeting, pp. 571–577. IEEE (2005)
9. Zabaiou, T., Dessaint, L.A., Kamwa, I.: Preventive control approach for voltage stability improvement using voltage stability constrained optimal power flow based on static line voltage stability indices. IET Gener. Transm. Distrib. **8**(5), 924–934 (2014)
10. Liu, Y., Ning, P., Reiter, M.K.: False data injection attacks against state estimation in electric power grids. ACM Trans. Inf. Syst. Secur. (TISSEC) **14**(1), 13 (2009)
11. Cui, S., Han, Z., Kar, S., et al.: Coordinated data-injection attack and detection in the smart grid: a detailed look at enriching detection solutions. Sig. Process. Mag. IEEE **29**(5), 106–115 (2012)
12. Kosut, O., Jia, L., Thomas, R.J., et al.: Malicious data attacks on the smart grid. IEEE Trans. Smart Grid **2**(4), 645–658 (2011)
13. Huang, Y., Esmalifalak, M., Nguyen, H., et al.: Bad data injection in smart grid: attack and defense mechanisms. IEEE Commun. Mag. **51**(1), 27–33 (2013)
14. Li, S., Yilmaz, Y., Wang, X.: Quickest detection of false data injection attack in wide-area smart grids. IEEE Trans. Smart Grid **6**(6), 2725–2735 (2015)
15. Esmalifalak, M., Nguyen, N.T., Zheng, R., et al.: Detecting stealthy false data injection using machine learning in smart grid. In: 2013 IEEE Global Communications Conference (GLOBECOM), pp. 808–813. IEEE, (2013)
16. Bi, S., Zhang, Y.J.: Graphical methods for defense against false-data injection attacks on power system state estimation. IEEE Trans. Smart Grid **5**(3), 1216–1227 (2014)
17. Bobba, R.B., Rogers, K.M., Wang, Q., et al.: Detecting false data injection attacks on dc state estimation. In: Preprints of the First Workshop on Secure Control Systems, CPSWEEK 2010 (2010)
18. Giani, A., Bitar, E., Garcia, M.A., et al.: Smart grid data integrity attacks. IEEE Trans. Smart Grid **4**(3), 1244–1253 (2013)
19. Kim, T.T., Poor, H.V.: Strategic protection against data injection attacks on power grids. IEEE Trans. Smart Grid **2**(2), 326–333 (2011)
20. Kekatos, V., Giannakis, G.: Distributed robust power system state estimation. IEEE Trans. Power Syst. **28**(2), 1617–1626 (2013)
21. Ozay, M., Esnaola, I., Vural, F.T.Y., et al.: Distributed models for sparse attack construction and state vector estimation in the smart grid. In: 2012 IEEE Third International Conference on Smart Grid Communications (SmartGridComm), pp. 306–311. IEEE (2012)

22. Yang, J., Yu, R., Liu, Y., et al.: A two-stage attacking scheme for low-sparsity unobservable attacks in smart grid. In: 2015 IEEE International Conference on Communications (ICC), pp. 7210–7215. IEEE (2015)
23. Gu, Y., Liu, T., Wang, D., et al.: Bad data detection method for smart grids based on distributed state estimation. In: 2013 IEEE International Conference on Communications (ICC), pp. 4483–4487. IEEE, (2013)
24. Cramer, M., Goergens, P., Schnettler, A.: Bad data detection and handling in distribution grid state estimation using artificial neural networks. In: 2015 IEEE Eindhoven PowerTech, pp. 1–6. IEEE (2015)
25. Jasmon, G.B., Lee, L.: New contingency ranking technique incorporating a voltage stability criterion. In: IEEE Proceedings of C-Generation, Transmission and Distribution, vol. 140, no. 2, pp. 87–90. IET (1993)
26. MATPOWER (2015). http://www.pserc.cornell.edu//matpower/

Fully Secure Unbounded Revocable Key-Policy Attribute-Based Encryption Scheme

Changji Wang[1(✉)], Jian Fang[2], and Jianguo Xie[1]

[1] Cisco School of Informatics, Collaborative Innovation Center for 21st-Century Maritime Silk Road Studies, Guangdong University of Foreign Studies, Guangzhou 510006, China
wchangji@gmail.com
[2] School of Data and Computer Science, Sun Yat-sen University, Guangzhou 510006, China

Abstract. Attribute-based encryption (ABE) is a promising cryptographic primitive which can provide fine-grained access control over encrypted data. Providing an efficient revocation mechanism for ABE scheme is crucial since users' credentials may be compromised or expired over time. Existing revocable ABE schemes in the literature are not satisfactory: (1) they are bounded in the sense that the size of the public parameters depends linearly on the size of the attribute universe; (2) they are only proved to be selectively secure in a prime order bilinear group setting or to be fully secure in a composite order bilinear group setting. In this paper, we present a unbounded revocable key-policy ABE scheme from prime order bilinear groups based on dual pairing vector space technique. The proposed scheme is proved to be fully secure under the DLIN and CDH assumptions in the standard model by adopting the dual system encryption methodology over dual pairing vector space. Compared with previous revocable key-policy ABE schemes, our proposed scheme is more efficient in terms of the size of ciphertext and private key, and the cost of encryption and decryption.

Keywords: Key-policy attribute-based encryption · Key revocation · Dual system encryption · Dual pairing vector space · Bilinear pairing · Full security

1 Introduction

With the development of the Internet and the distributed computing technology, there is a growing demand for remote data storage and sharing in an open distributed computing environment. As an emerging deployment and delivery model of computing resources, cloud computing can enable ubiquitous, on-demand access to a shared pool of configurable computing resources (e.g., networks, servers, storage, applications and services) with minimal management effort. Cloud computing has attracted an increasing number of individual and enterprise users to

© Springer International Publishing AG 2016
G. Wang et al. (Eds.): SpaCCS 2016, LNCS 10066, pp. 251–264, 2016.
DOI: 10.1007/978-3-319-49148-6_22

outsource their local data centers to remote cloud servers in recent years because of its cost effectiveness, flexibility and scalability [1].

Data security has been regarded as one of the greatest problems in the development of cloud computing [2]. To protect data security and privacy, encryption technology seems like an obvious solution. However, encryption functionality alone is not sufficient as data owners often have also to enforce fine-grained access control on the sensitive data for sharing. Traditional server-based access control methods are no longer suitable for cloud computing scenario because cloud server cannot be fully trusted by data owners. Traditional public key encryption and identity-based encryption [3] can not provide effective solution to the security challenges that arise in cloud computing, they only offer an all-or-nothing mechanism to data control.

To address the problem of secure and fine-grained data sharing and decentralized access control, Sahai and Waters [4] first introduced the concept of attribute-based encryption (ABE) with the name of fuzzy identity-based encryption, in which a user is able to decrypt the ciphertext if and only if at least a threshold number of attributes overlap between the ciphertext and user secret key. ABE is a promising cryptographic primitive that allows one-to-many encryption and enables access control over encrypted data using access policies and ascribed attributes associated with private keys and ciphertexts. ABE has drawn extensive attention from both academia and industry, a large number of ABE schemes have been proposed [5–10] and many cloud-based secure systems using ABE schemes have been developed [11–13]. Up to now, there are two main categories of ABE schemes: key-policy ABE (KP-ABE) [5] and ciphertext-policy ABE (CP-ABE) [6]. In a CP-ABE scheme, every user' private key is associated with a set of attributes, and a sender generates a ciphertext with an access policy specifying the attributes that the decryptors must have. In a KP-ABE scheme, the situation is reversed: users' secret keys are labeled with access policies and the sender specifies a set of attributes, only the users whose access policies match the attribute set can decrypt.

In practical application scenarios, a user's private key may might get compromised, and user might leave or be dismissed by an organization over time. An efficient user revocation mechanism is a crucial requirement in the context of ABE. The concept of revocable ABE was first introduced by Boldyreva et al. [14] in 2008. They combine the ciphertext and key with time period t_c and t_k respectively and the ciphertext can be decrypted by the key if and only if the attribute set satisfies the access policy as well as $t_c \leq t_k$. Later on, several revocable ABE schemes have been proposed in the literature [15–17]. However, existing revocable ABE schemes in the literature are not satisfactory. On the one hand, almost all previous revocable ABE constructions are bounded, in the sense that the public parameters *mpk* impose additional limitations on the parameters for encryption and decryption keys. On the other hand, almost all previous revocable ABE schemes were proved secure only in an unrealistic selective security model. Although [16] achieves full security, it is built on a composite order bilinear group setting under non-standard assumptions. From the efficiency and security view point, prime order bilinear groups are desirable compared to composite order ones [18].

In this paper, we present a new unbounded revocable KP-ABE scheme that is proved to be fully secure in the standard model under the DLIN assumption and the CDH assumption. The proposed scheme is built on a prime order bilinear group setting resulting in practical computation cost. Our construction follows the ABE construction of [19] based on dual pairing vector spaces (DPVS) technique. In this construction, the ciphertext components are generated by the bases of a DPVS and the keys are obtained by it's dual. For proving security of our proposed scheme, the main intricacy of this work, we utilize the dual system encryption methodology proposed by Waters [20] over DPVS, in a manner similar to that in [21].

This paper is organized as follows. We introduce some necessary preliminary work in Sect. 2. Then, we define the syntax and security model for revocable KP-ABE scheme in Sect. 3. We describe our revocable KP-ABE scheme in Sect. 4. Next, we present security and efficiency analysis of our revocable KP-ABE scheme in Sect. 5. Finally, we conclude our paper and discuss our future work in Sect. 6.

2 Preliminaries

In this section, we briefly review the basic concepts on linear secret sharing scheme, dual pairing vector spaces and some related complexity assumptions.

2.1 Notations

We denote by λ the system security parameter. When $\mathbf{S}$ is a set, $x \xleftarrow{\text{U}} \mathbf{S}$ denotes that x is uniformly picked from $\mathbf{S}$. When X is a random variable or distribution, $x \xleftarrow{\text{R}} X$ denotes that x is randomly selected from X according to its distribution. $x := y$ denotes that x is set, defined or substituted by y, and A^{T} denotes the transpose of matrix A. We denote by $\mathsf{GL}(n, \mathbf{F}_q)$ the general linear group of degree n over $\mathbf{F}_q$, and we express an attribute vector $\boldsymbol{x}$ by a pair of attribute index and value of attribute, i.e., $\boldsymbol{x} = \{(t, x_t) \mid t \in \{1, \ldots, n\} \wedge x_t \in \mathbf{F}_q\}$, where the size of attribute universe is n.

A bold face letter denotes an element of vector space $\mathbb{V}$, e.g., $\boldsymbol{x} \in \mathbb{V}$. When $\boldsymbol{b}_i \in \mathbb{V}$ for $i = 1, \ldots, n$, $\mathsf{span}\langle \boldsymbol{b}_1, \ldots, \boldsymbol{b}_n \rangle \subseteq \mathbb{V}$ denotes the subspace of $\mathbb{V}$ generated by $\boldsymbol{b}_1, \ldots, \boldsymbol{b}_n$. For bases $\mathbb{B} = (\boldsymbol{b}_1, \ldots, \boldsymbol{b}_n)$ and $\mathbb{B}^* = (\boldsymbol{b}_1^*, \ldots, \boldsymbol{b}_n^*)$, we define

$$(x_1, \ldots, x_n)_{\mathbb{B}} := \sum_{i=1}^{n} x_i \boldsymbol{b}_i \text{ and } (y_1, \ldots, y_n)_{\mathbb{B}^*} := \sum_{i=1}^{n} y_i \boldsymbol{b}_i^*.$$

2.2 Access Structure and Linear Secret Sharing Scheme

Let $\mathbf{P} = \{\mathcal{P}_1, \mathcal{P}_2, \ldots, \mathcal{P}_n\}$ be a set of parties, and denote by $2^{\mathbf{P}}$ its power set. A collection $\mathbb{A} \subseteq 2^{\mathbf{P}}$ is monotone if for every $\mathbf{B}$ and $\mathbf{C}$, if $\mathbf{B} \in \mathbb{A}$ and $\mathbf{B} \subseteq \mathbf{C}$

then $\mathbf{C} \in \mathbb{A}$. An access structure (respectively, monotone access structure) is a collection (respectively, monotone collection) $\mathbb{A}$ of non-empty subsets of $\mathbf{P}$, i.e. $\mathbf{P} \backslash \emptyset$. The sets in $\mathbb{A}$ are called the authorized sets, and the sets not in $\mathbb{A}$ are called the unauthorized sets [6].

Let $M_{\ell \times k}$ be a matrix, and $\rho : \{1, \ldots, \ell\} \to \mathbf{P}$ be a function that maps a row to a party for labeling. A secret sharing scheme for access structure $\mathbb{A}$ over $\mathbf{P}$ is linear secret-sharing scheme (LSSS) in $\mathbf{F}_q$ and is represented by $(M_{\ell \times k}, \rho)$ if it consists of two polynomial-time algorithms:

- Share$_{(M_{\ell \times k}, \rho)}$: The algorithm takes as input $s \in \mathbf{F}_q$ which is to be shared. It chooses $v_2, \ldots, v_k \overset{U}{\leftarrow} \mathbf{F}_q$ and let $v = (s, v_2, \ldots, v_k)$. It outputs $M_{\ell \times k} v$ as the vector of ℓ shares. The share $\phi_{\rho(i)} = M_i \cdot v$ belongs to party $\rho(i)$, where we denote M_i as the i-th row in $M_{\ell \times k}$.
- Recon$_{(M_{\ell \times k}, \rho)}$: The algorithm takes as input $\mathbf{S} \subseteq \mathbf{P}$ satisfies $\mathbb{A}$. Let $\mathbf{I} = \{i | \rho(i) \in \mathbf{S}\}$. It outputs reconstruction constants $\{(i, \nu_i)\}_{i \in \mathbf{I}}$ which has a linear reconstruction property, i.e., $\sum_{i \in \mathbf{I}} \nu_i \cdot \phi_{\rho(i)} = s$.

2.3   Dual Pairing Vector Spaces

Let $\mathcal{G}_{\mathsf{bpg}}$ be a probabilistic polynomial-time (PPT) algorithm that on input a security parameter λ and outputs a description of symmetric bilinear pairing groups $\mathsf{param}_{\mathbf{G}} := (q, \mathbf{G}, \mathbf{G}_T, P, \hat{e})$, where $\mathbf{G}$ is a cyclic additive group generated by P with prime order q, and $\mathbf{G}_T$ is a cyclic multiplicative group of the same order, $\hat{e} : \mathbf{G} \times \mathbf{G} \to \mathbf{G}_T$ is an efficiently computable map with the following properties:

- Bilinear: For $P, Q \overset{\$}{\leftarrow} \mathbf{G}$ and $a, b \overset{\$}{\leftarrow} \mathbf{Z}_q$, we have $\hat{e}(aP, bQ) = \hat{e}(P, Q)^{ab}$.
- Non-degenerate: There is an element $P \in \mathbf{G}$ such that $\hat{e}(P, P)$ has order q in $\mathbf{G}_T$.

Definition 1 (Dual Pairing Vector Spaces [19]). *A DPVS $(q, \mathbb{V}, \mathbf{G}_T, \mathbb{A}, \tilde{e})$ is a direct product over symmetric bilinear pairing groups $(q, \mathbf{G}, \mathbf{G}_T, P, \hat{e})$, where*

$$\mathbb{V} = \overbrace{\mathbf{G} \times \cdots \times \mathbf{G}}^{n}$$ *is a n-dimensional vector space over $\mathbf{F}_q$, $\mathbb{A} = (a_1, \ldots, a_n)$ is the canonical base of $\mathbb{V}$ with*

$$a_i = (\overbrace{0, \ldots, 0}^{i-1}, P, \overbrace{0, \ldots, 0}^{n-i}),$$

and pairing $\tilde{e} : \mathbb{V} \times \mathbb{V} \to \mathbf{G}_T$ is defined by

$$\tilde{e}(\boldsymbol{x}, \boldsymbol{y}) = \prod_{i=1}^{n} \hat{e}(x_i P, y_i P)$$
$$= \hat{e}(P, P)^{\sum_{i=1}^{n} x_i y_i} = \hat{e}(P, P)^{\boldsymbol{x} \cdot \boldsymbol{y}} \in \mathbf{G}_T$$

Here,

$$\boldsymbol{x} = (x_1 P, \ldots, x_n P) = x_1 \boldsymbol{a}_1 + \cdots + x_n \boldsymbol{a}_n \in \mathbb{V}$$
$$\boldsymbol{y} = (y_1 P, \ldots, y_n P) = y_1 \boldsymbol{a}_1 + \cdots + y_n \boldsymbol{a}_n \in \mathbb{V}.$$
$$\boldsymbol{x} := (x_1, \ldots, x_n) \in \mathbf{F}_q^n$$
$$\boldsymbol{y} := (y_1, \ldots, y_n) \in \mathbf{F}_q^n$$

Obviously, the pairing $\tilde{e}$ is non-degenerate bilinear, i.e.,

$$\tilde{e}(s\boldsymbol{x}, t\boldsymbol{y}) = \tilde{e}(\boldsymbol{x}, \boldsymbol{y})^{st}$$

for $\boldsymbol{x}, \boldsymbol{y} \xleftarrow{\$} \mathbb{V}$ and $s, t \xleftarrow{\$} \mathbf{Z}_q$, and if $\tilde{e}(\boldsymbol{x}, \boldsymbol{y}) = 1$ for all $\boldsymbol{y} \in \mathbb{V}$, then $\boldsymbol{x} = 0$. Let $\mathcal{G}_{\mathsf{dpvs}}$ be DPVS generation algorithm that takes input 1^λ, a dimension n and $\mathsf{param}_{\mathbf{G}}$, and outputs a description of $\mathsf{param}_{\mathbb{V}} = (q, \mathbb{V}, \mathbf{G}_T, \mathbb{A}, \hat{e})$.

To construct our revocable KP-ABE scheme based on DPVS, we need dual orthogonal bases for DPVS. We can apply a linear transformation $X = (\chi_{i,j}) \xleftarrow{\mathsf{U}} \mathrm{GL}(n, \mathbf{F}_q)$ on the canonical basis $\mathbb{A}$ to obtain a basis $\mathbb{B} = (\boldsymbol{b}_1, \ldots, \boldsymbol{b}_n)$ of $\mathbb{V}$, such that

$$\boldsymbol{b}_i = \sum_{j=1}^{n} \chi_{i,j} \boldsymbol{a}_j, \text{ where } i = 1, \ldots, n$$

$\mathbb{A}$ can also be transformed to a basis $\mathbb{B}^* = (\boldsymbol{b}_1^*, \ldots, \boldsymbol{b}_n^*)$ of $\mathbb{V}$ by applying a linear transformation $(\vartheta_{i,j}) = (X^{\mathsf{T}})^{-1}$, such that

$$\boldsymbol{b}_i^* = \sum_{j=1}^{n} \vartheta_{i,j} \boldsymbol{a}_j, \text{ where } i = 1, \ldots, n$$

We see that $\mathbb{B}$ and $\mathbb{B}^*$ are dual orthonormal bases of $\mathbb{V}$, i.e., $\tilde{e}(\boldsymbol{b}_i, \boldsymbol{b}_j^*) = \hat{e}(P, P)^{\delta_{i,j}}$, where $\delta_{i,j} = 1$ if $i = j$, and $\delta_{i,j} = 0$ if $i \neq j$.

We describe random dual orthonormal basis generator $\mathcal{G}_{\mathsf{ob}}$, which is used as a subroutine in our revocable KP-ABE scheme.

$\mathcal{G}_{\mathsf{ob}}(1^\lambda, n_0, n_1)$
    $\mathsf{param}_{\mathbf{G}} := (q, \mathbf{G}, \mathbf{G}_T, P, \hat{e}) \xleftarrow{\mathsf{R}} \mathcal{G}_{\mathsf{bpg}}(1^\lambda), \ \psi \xleftarrow{\mathsf{U}} \mathbf{F}_q^\times$
    for $t = 0, 1, \ \mathsf{param}_{\mathbb{V}_t} := (q, \mathbb{V}_t, \mathbf{G}_T, \mathbb{A}_t, \tilde{e}) \xleftarrow{\mathsf{R}} \mathcal{G}_{\mathsf{dpvs}}(1^\lambda, n_t, \mathsf{param}_{\mathbf{G}})$
    $X_t := (\chi_{t,i,j})_{i,j=1,\ldots,n_t} \xleftarrow{\mathsf{U}} \mathrm{GL}(n_t, \mathbf{F}_q), \ X_t^* := \psi \cdot (X_t^{\mathsf{T}})^{-1} := (\vartheta_{t,i,j})_{i,j=1,\ldots,n_t}$
    Denote by $\chi_{t,i}$ and $\vartheta_{t,i}$ the i-th rows of X_t and X_t^* for $i = 1, \ldots, n_t$.
    $\boldsymbol{b}_{t,i} := (\chi_{t,i})_{\mathbb{A}_t} = \sum_{j=1}^{n_t} \chi_{t,i,j} \boldsymbol{a}_{t,j}$ for $i = 1, \ldots, n_t, \quad \mathbb{B}_t := (\boldsymbol{b}_{t,1}, \ldots, \boldsymbol{b}_{t,n_t})$
    $\boldsymbol{b}_{t,i}^* := (\vartheta_{t,i})_{\mathbb{A}_t} = \sum_{j=1}^{n_t} \vartheta_{t,i,j} \boldsymbol{a}_{t,j}$ for $i = 1, \ldots, n_t, \quad \mathbb{B}_t^* := (\boldsymbol{b}_{t,1}^*, \ldots, \boldsymbol{b}_{t,n_t}^*)$.
    $g_T := \hat{e}(P, P)^\psi, \ \mathsf{param} := (\mathsf{param}_{\mathbb{V}_0}, \mathsf{param}_{\mathbb{V}_1}, g_T)$
    Output $(\mathsf{param}, \mathbb{B}_0, \mathbb{B}_0^*, \mathbb{B}_1, \mathbb{B}_1^*)$

2.4   Complexity Assumptions

Given $(P, aP, bP) \in \mathbf{G}^{(3)}$ where $a, b \xleftarrow{\text{R}} \mathbf{Z}_q^*$, the Computational Diffie-Hellman (CDH) problem is to compute abP. The advantage of an adversary $\mathcal{A}$ in breaking CDH problem is defined by

$$\mathsf{Adv}_{\mathcal{A}}^{\text{CDH}}(1^\lambda) = \Pr[\mathcal{A}(P, aP, bP) = abP].$$

Definition 2 (CDH Assumption). *We say that the CDH assumption holds if for any PPT adversary $\mathcal{A}$, the advantage $\mathsf{Adv}_{\mathcal{A}}^{CDH}(1^\lambda)$ is a negligible function in the security parameter 1^λ.*

Given a symmetric bilinear pairing groups $(q, \mathbf{G}, \mathbf{G}_T, P, \hat{e}) \xleftarrow{\text{R}} \mathcal{G}_{\text{bpg}}(1^\lambda)$ and $(\xi P, \kappa P, \delta \xi P, \sigma \kappa P, Y_b) \in \mathbf{G}^{(5)}$, where $\kappa, \delta, \xi, \sigma \xleftarrow{\text{U}} \mathbf{F}_q$, $b \xleftarrow{\text{U}} \{0, 1\}$, $Y_0 = (\delta + \sigma)P$, $Y_1 \xleftarrow{\text{U}} \mathbf{G}$, the Decisional Linear (DLIN) problem is to guess $b \in \{0, 1\}$. Let $D := (q, \mathbf{G}, \mathbf{G}_T, P, \hat{e}, \xi P, \kappa P, \delta \xi P, \sigma \kappa P)$, the advantage of an adversary $\mathcal{A}$ in breaking DLIN problem is defined by

$$\mathsf{Adv}_{\mathcal{A}}^{\text{DLIN}}(1^\lambda) = |\Pr[\mathcal{A}(D, Y_0) = 1] - \Pr[\mathcal{A}(D, Y_1) = 1]|.$$

Definition 3 (DLIN Assumption). *We say that the DLIN assumption holds if for every PPT adversary $\mathcal{A}$, the advantage $\mathsf{Adv}_{\mathcal{A}}^{DLIN}(1^\lambda)$ is a negligible function in the security parameter 1^λ.*

3   Revocable KP-ABE Scheme

In this section, we give syntax and security model for revocable KP-ABE scheme.

Syntax of Revocable KP-ABE Scheme. Let $\mathbf{U}$ and $\mathbf{\Omega}$ denote the set of all user identities and an attribute universe, respectively. A revocable KP-ABE scheme can be defined by the following five polynomial-time algorithms:

- **Setup:** The probabilistic setup algorithm is run by the PKG. It inputs a security parameter κ. It outputs the public system parameters mpk, the master secret key msk, an empty revocation list **RL**.
- **KeyGen:** The probabilistic private key generation algorithm is run by the PKG. It inputs the public parameters mpk, master secret key msk, an access structure $\mathbb{A} = (M_{\ell \times k}, \rho)$ and a user identity id. It outputs the corresponding private key $sk_{\mathbb{A}, \text{id}}$.
- **Encrypt:** The probabilistic encryption algorithm is run by a sender. It inputs the public parameters mpk, a message msg, a set $\Gamma \subseteq \mathbf{\Omega}$ of attributes and a legal user set $\mathbf{S} \subseteq \mathbf{U} \backslash \mathbf{RL}$. It outputs a ciphertext $ct_{\Gamma, \mathbf{S}}$.
- **Decrypt:** The deterministic decryption algorithm is run by a receiver. It inputs the public parameters mpk, ciphertext $ct_{\Gamma, \mathbf{S}}$, decryption key $sk_{\mathbb{A}, \text{id}}$. It outputs either plaintext msg or a reject symbol $\perp$.

– **Revoke:** The deterministic revocation algorithm is run by the PKG. It inputs the public parameters mpk, the user identity id to be revoked, current revocation lists $\mathbf{RL}$. It outputs the updated revocation lists $\mathbf{RL}'$ by setting $\mathbf{RL}' \leftarrow \{\text{id}\} \cup \mathbf{RL}$.

The set of algorithms must satisfy the following consistency requirement: For all $(\text{mpk}, \text{sk}) \overset{\mathrm{R}}{\leftarrow} \mathbf{Setup}(1^\kappa)$, all access structures $\mathbb{A}$, all decryption keys $sk_{\mathbb{A},\text{id}} \overset{\mathrm{R}}{\leftarrow} \mathbf{KeyGen}(\text{mpk}, \text{msk}, \mathbb{A}, \text{id})$, all messages msg, all sets Γ of attributes, all ciphertexts $ct_{\Gamma,\mathbf{S}} \overset{\mathrm{R}}{\leftarrow} \mathbf{Encrypt}(\text{mpk}, msg, \Gamma, \mathbf{S})$, it holds that

$$msg = \mathbf{Decrypt}(\text{mpk}, sk_{\mathbb{A},\text{id}}, ct_{\Gamma,\mathbf{S}})$$

with overwhelming probability, if $\mathbb{A}$ accepts Γ and $\text{id} \in \mathbf{S} \backslash \mathbf{RL}$.

Security Model of Revocable KP-ABE Scheme. The adaptive security model under chosen plaintext attack of revokable KP-ABE scheme is defined by the following game between an adversary $\mathcal{A}$ and a challenger $\mathcal{C}$.

– **Setup:** $\mathcal{C}$ runs the setup algorithm, $(\text{mpk}, \text{msk}) \overset{\mathrm{R}}{\leftarrow} \mathbf{Setup}(1^\kappa)$, and gives public parameters mpk to $\mathcal{A}$.
– **Phase 1:** $\mathcal{A}$ is allowed to adaptively issue a polynomial number of private key queries on access structure-user identity pairs $(\mathbb{A}_1, \text{id}_1), ..., (\mathbb{A}_{q_1}, \text{id}_{q_1})$. The challenger sends the corresponding private keys $\text{sk}_{\mathbb{A}_1,\text{id}_1}, ..., \text{sk}_{\mathbb{A}_{q_1},\text{id}_{q_1}}$ to $\mathcal{A}$ by running $\text{sk}_{\mathbb{A}_i,\text{id}_i} \overset{\mathrm{R}}{\leftarrow} \mathbf{KeyGen}(\text{mpk}, \text{msk}, \mathbb{A}_i, \text{id}_i)$ for $i = 1, \ldots, q_1$.
– **Challenge:** $\mathcal{A}$ submits two challenge messages (msg_0, msg_1) of equal length, a challenge set Γ^* of attributes and a challenge legal user set $\mathbf{S}^*$ with the following restriction: If a private key query on an access structure-user identity pair $(\mathbb{A}_i, \text{id}_i)$ such that $\mathbb{A}_i$ accepts Γ^* was requested, then $\text{id}_i \notin \mathbf{S}^*$. The challenger flips a random coin $b \in \{0,1\}$ and gives the challenge ciphertext ct^* to $\mathcal{A}$ by performing $ct^* \overset{\mathrm{R}}{\leftarrow} \mathbf{Encrypt}(\text{mpk}, msg_b, \Gamma^*, \mathbf{S}^*)$.
– **Phase 2:** $\mathcal{A}$ may continue to issue a polynomial number of additional private key queries on access structure-user identity pairs $(\mathbb{A}_{q_1+1}, \text{id}_{q_1+1}), ..., (\mathbb{A}_{q_k}, \text{id}_{q_k})$ subject to the same restriction in Phase 1, and $\mathcal{C}$ sends corresponding keys to $\mathcal{A}$.
– **Guess:** The adversary outputs a guess b' of b, and wins the game if $b' = b$.

The advantage of any PPT adversary $\mathcal{A}$ in the above game is defined as

$$\mathsf{Adv}_{\mathcal{A}}^{\text{Revocable KP-ABE}}(\kappa) = |\Pr[\mathcal{A} \text{ wins}] - 1/2|.$$

where the probability is taken over all the randomness of the game. A revocable KP-ABE scheme is adaptively secure under chosen plaintext attacks if all PPT adversaries have at most a negligible advantage in the above game. Note that the above security model can easily be extended to handle chosen-ciphertext attacks by allowing for decryption queries in Phase 1 and Phase 2.

4 Our Unbounded Revocable KP-ABE Construction

In this section, we propose a unbounded KP-ABE scheme supporting direct revocation based on KP-ABE scheme [19], where encryption is done using the bases of a DPVS and the keys are generated by it's dual. Our proposed scheme is described as follows.

- **Setup**$(1^\kappa, \text{Max})$: The PKG runs $\mathcal{G}_{ob}(1^\lambda, n_0 = 5, n_1 = 14)$ to get two groups of dual canonical basis $(\mathbb{B}_0, \mathbb{B}_0^*)$ and $(\mathbb{B}, \mathbb{B}^*)$, where

$$\hat{\mathbb{B}}_0 = (b_{0,1}, b_{0,3}, b_{0,5}), \quad \hat{\mathbb{B}} = (b_1, \ldots, b_4, b_{13}, b_{14}),$$
$$\hat{\mathbb{B}}_0^* = (b_{0,1}^*, b_{0,3}^*, b_{0,4}^*), \quad \hat{\mathbb{B}}^* = (b_1^*, \ldots, b_4^*, b_{11}^*, b_{12}^*).$$

Additionally, the PKG chooses a cryptographic hash function $H : \{0,1\} \to \mathbf{Z}_q^*$. It returns $\mathsf{mpk} = (\mathsf{param}, \hat{\mathbb{B}}_0, \hat{\mathbb{B}})$ and $\mathsf{msk} = (\hat{\mathbb{B}}_0^*, \hat{\mathbb{B}}^*)$.

- **KeyGen**$(\mathsf{mpk}, \mathsf{msk}, \mathbb{A} = (M_{\ell \times k}, \rho), \mathsf{id}_j)$: The PKG chooses $\delta, v_2, \ldots, v_k, \xleftarrow{\mathsf{U}} \mathbf{F}_q$, sets $v = ((1+\delta)H(\mathsf{id}_j), v_2, \ldots, v_k)$, computes $\phi_i = M_i v$ for $i = 1$ to ℓ. Then, the PKG performs the following steps:
  (1) Choose $\eta_{0,1}, \eta_{0,2} \xleftarrow{\mathsf{U}} \mathbf{F}_q$, set

$$k_{0,1}^* = (\delta H(\mathsf{id}_j), 0, 1, \eta_{0,1}, 0)_{\mathbb{B}_0^*}$$
$$k_{0,2}^* = (1, 0, 0, \eta_{0,2}, 0)_{\mathbb{B}_0^*}$$

  (2) For $i = 1, \ldots, \ell$, $\rho(i) = (t, \omega_i)$, choose $\mu_i, \theta_i, \eta_{i,1}, \eta_{i,2} \xleftarrow{\mathsf{U}} \mathbf{F}_q$, set

$$k_i^* = (\mu_i(t, -1), \theta_i \omega_i + \phi_i, -\theta_i, 0^6, \eta_{i,1}, \eta_{i,2}, 0^2)_{\mathbb{B}^*},$$

  Finally, the PKG outputs the private key $sk_{\mathbb{A}, \mathsf{id}_j} = (k_{0,1}^*, k_{0,2}^*, \{k_i^*\}_{i=1,\ldots,\ell})$.

- **Encrypt**$(\mathsf{mpk}, \Gamma := \{(t, x_t) \mid 1 \le t \le d, x_t \in \mathbf{Z}_q\}, \mathbf{S}, msg)$. The sender picks $\alpha, \zeta, \varphi_0 \xleftarrow{\mathsf{U}} \mathbf{F}_q$, computes $c = g_T^\zeta \cdot msg$, sets

$$c_0 = (\alpha, 0, \zeta + \alpha \sum_{\mathsf{id}_j \in \mathbf{S}} H(\mathsf{id}_j), 0, \varphi_0)_{\mathbb{B}_0},$$

For every $(t, x_t) \in \Gamma$, the sender chooses $\sigma_t, \varphi_{t,1}, \varphi_{t,2} \xleftarrow{\mathsf{U}} \mathbf{F}_q$, sets

$$c_t = (\sigma_t(1, t), \alpha(1, x_t), 0^6, 0^2, \varphi_{t,1}, \varphi_{t,2})_{\mathbb{B}},$$

Finally, the sender outputs the ciphertext $ct_{\Gamma, \mathbf{U}} = (c, c_0, \{c_t\}_{(t, x_t) \in \Gamma})$.

- **Decrypt**$(pk, ct_{\Gamma, \mathbf{U}}, sk_{\mathbb{A}, \mathsf{id}})$: Suppose that the attribute set Γ satisfies the access structure $\mathbb{A}$ and the user identity $\mathsf{id}_j \in \mathbf{S}$. Let $\mathbf{I} = \{i | \rho(i) \in \Gamma\}$. The receiver first calculates corresponding sets of reconstruction constants $\{(i, \nu_i)\}_{i \in \mathbf{I}} = \mathsf{Recon}_{(M_{\ell \times k}, \rho)}(\Gamma)$ and $L_{\mathsf{id}_j, \mathbf{S}} = \sum_{\mathsf{id}_i \in \mathbf{S} \setminus \{\mathsf{id}_j\}} H(\mathsf{id}_i)$. Then the receiver computes

$$c_{\mathsf{mask}} = \frac{\tilde{e}(c_0, k_{0,1}^*)}{\tilde{e}(c_0, k_{0,2}^*)^{L_{\mathsf{id}_j, \mathbf{S}}}} \cdot \prod_{i \in \mathbf{I} \wedge \rho(i) = (t, \omega_i)} \tilde{e}(c_t, k_i^*)^{\nu_i}$$

Finally, the receiver outputs the plaintext $msg = c/c_{\mathsf{mask}}$.

– **Revoke(RL, id)**: Once a user with index id is revoked, the PKG update the revocation list **RL** by setting $\mathbf{RL}' \leftarrow \{\mathsf{id}\} \cup \mathbf{RL}$. Finally, the PKG outputs the updated revocation list $\mathbf{RL}'$.

5 Security Proof and Efficiency Analysis

Theorem 1. *The proposed revocable KP-ABE scheme satisfies correctness.*

Proof. The correctness can be verified as follows.

$$
\begin{aligned}
c_{\mathsf{mask}} &= \frac{\tilde{e}(c_0, k_{0,1}^*)}{\tilde{e}(c_0, k_{0,2}^*)^{L_{\mathsf{id}_j,\mathbf{S}}}} \cdot \prod_{i \in \mathbf{I} \wedge \rho(i)=(t,\omega_i)} \tilde{e}(c_t, k_i^*)^{\nu_i} \\
&= \frac{g_T^{\alpha\delta H(\mathsf{id}_j)+\zeta+\alpha\sum_{\mathsf{id}_i \in \mathbf{S}} H(\mathsf{id}_i)}}{g_T^{\alpha\sum_{\mathsf{id}_i \in \mathbf{S}\setminus\{\mathsf{id}_j\}} H(\mathsf{id}_i)}} \cdot \prod_{i \in \mathbf{I} \wedge \rho(i)=(t,\omega_i)} g_T^{-\alpha\phi_i\nu_i} \\
&= g_T^{\alpha\delta H(\mathsf{id}_j)+\zeta+\alpha H(\mathsf{id}_j)} \cdot g_T^{-\alpha\sum_{i \in \mathbf{I} \wedge \rho(i)=(t,\omega_i)} \phi_i\nu_i} \\
&= g_T^{\alpha(1+\delta)H(\mathsf{id}_j)+\zeta} \cdot g_T^{-\alpha(1+\delta)H(\mathsf{id}_j)} = g_T^\zeta.
\end{aligned}
$$

Theorem 2. *The proposed revocable KP-ABE scheme is fully secure against chosen plaintext attacks under the DLIN assumption and CDH assumption.*

Proof. At the top level of strategy of the security proof, we adopt the dual system encryption methodology [20]. Consider the following $(3p+3)$ games.

– Game 0: It is the original game. The reply for access policy and user identity index pair $(\mathbb{A} = (M, \rho), \mathsf{id})$ is $\mathsf{sk}_{\mathbb{A},\mathsf{id}} = (k_{0,1}^*, k_{0,2}^*, \{k_i^*\}_{i=1,\ldots,\ell})$, where

$$
k_{0,1}^* = (\delta F(\mathsf{id}), 0, 1, \eta_{0,1}, 0)_{\mathbb{B}_0^*},
$$

$$
k_{0,2}^* = (1, 0, 0, \eta_{0,2}, 0)_{\mathbb{B}_0^*}, \quad \delta, \eta_{0,1}, \eta_{0,2} \xleftarrow{U} \mathbf{F}_q
$$

For $i = 1, \ldots, \ell$, $\rho(i) = (t, \omega_i)$, $y_2, \ldots, y_\kappa, \mu_i, \theta_i, \eta_{i,1}, \eta_{i,2} \xleftarrow{U} \mathbf{F}_q$. Let $y_1 = (1+\delta)F(\mathsf{id}) \in \mathbf{F}_q$ and $\mathbf{y} = (y_1, y_2, \ldots, y_\kappa)$, and set

$$
\phi_i = M_i \cdot y,
$$
$$
k_i^* = \left(\mu_i(t, -1), \theta_i\omega_i - \phi_i, -\theta_i, 0^6, \eta_{i,1}, \eta_{i,2}, 0^2\right)_{\mathbb{B}^*}.
$$

When adversary submits the challenge plaintext (m_0^*, m_1^*), a set of attributes $\Gamma^* = \{(t, x_t) | t \in [1, d]\}$ and user identity index set $\mathbf{U}^*$, the challenger will return ciphertext $\mathsf{ct}_{\Gamma^*, \mathbf{U}^*}^* = (c, c_0, \{c_t\}_{(t,x_t)\in\Gamma^*})$, where

$$
c = g_T^\zeta \cdot m_b^*,
$$

$$
c_0 = \left(\alpha, 0, \zeta + \alpha \sum_{j \in S^*} F(j), 0, \varphi_0\right)_{\mathbb{B}_0}
$$

where $\alpha, \zeta, \varphi_0 \xleftarrow{U} \mathbf{F}_q$, $b \in \{0,1\}$. For all $(t, x_t) \in \Gamma^*$, choose $\sigma_t, \varphi_{t,1}, \varphi_{t,2} \xleftarrow{U} \mathbf{F}_q$, then compute

$$\mathbf{c}_t = \left(\sigma_t(1,t), \alpha(1, x_t), 0^6, 0^2, \varphi_{t,1}, \varphi_{t,2}\right)_{\mathbb{B}}.$$

- Game 1: It is the same as Game 0 except that the challenge ciphertext is pre-semi-functional. The challenge ciphertext is computed as follows

$$c = g_T^\zeta \cdot m_b^*,$$

$$\mathbf{c}_0 = \left(\alpha, \tau, \zeta + \alpha \sum_{j \in S} F(j), 0, \varphi_0\right)_{\mathbb{B}_0}$$

for all $(t, x_t) \in \Gamma^*$,

$$\mathbf{c}_t = \left(\sigma_t(1,t), \alpha(1, x_t), \tau(1, x_t), 0^2, \tau(1, x_t) \cdot Z_t, 0^2, \varphi_{t,1}, \varphi_{t,2}\right)_{\mathbb{B}},$$

where $\tau \xleftarrow{U} \mathbf{F}_q^\times$, $Z_t \in \mathsf{GL}(2, \mathbf{F}_q)$.
- Game 2-h-1(h = 1, ..., p): Assume that the user only can issue p key query at most. The reply for the h-th key query is computed as follows.
  1. The challenger randomly chooses $\delta, \eta_{0,1} \xleftarrow{U} \mathbf{F}_q$ and $a_0 \xleftarrow{U} \mathbf{F}_q^\times$, then sets

  $$\mathbf{k}_{0,1}^* = \left(\delta F(\mathsf{id}), \; -a_0, \; 1, \; \eta_{0,1}, \; 0\right)_{\mathbb{B}_0^*},$$

  2. For $i = 1, \ldots, \ell$, $\rho(i) = (t, \omega_i)$, randomly chooses $z_2, \ldots, z_\kappa \xleftarrow{U} \mathbf{F}_q$, and lets $z_1 = a_0$ and $\mathbf{z} = (z_1, z_2, \ldots, z_\kappa)$, computes $a_i = \mathbf{M}_i \cdot \mathbf{z}$, and sets

  $$\mathbf{k}_i^* = \left(\mu_i(t, -1), \; \theta_i \omega_i - \phi_i, \; -\theta_i, \; 0^4, \; (a_i + b_i \omega_i, \; -b_i) \cdot U_t, \; \eta_{i,1}, \; \eta_{i,2}, \; 0^2\right)_{\mathbb{B}^*},$$

  where $\mu_i, \theta_i, b_i, \eta_{i,1}, \eta_{i,2} \xleftarrow{U} \mathbf{F}_q$, $Z_t \xleftarrow{U} \mathsf{GL}(2, \mathbf{F}_q)$, $U_t = (Z_t^{-1})^\intercal$.
- Game 2-h-2(h = 1, ..., p): It is the same as Game 2-h-1 except that the reply for the h-th key query is pse-semi-functional. The h-th key query for access policy and user identity index pair $(\mathbb{A} = (M, \rho), \mathsf{id})$ is computed as:

  $$\mathbf{k}_{0,1}^* = \left(\delta F(\mathsf{id}), \; \gamma, \; 1, \; \eta_{0,1}, \; 0\right)_{\mathbb{B}_0^*},$$

  where $\delta, \eta_{0,1} \xleftarrow{U} \mathbf{F}_q$, $\gamma \xleftarrow{U} \mathbf{F}_q^\times$.
- Game 2-h-3(h = 1, ..., p): It is the same as Game 2-h-2 except the reply for the h-th key query is semi-functional and the component $\mathbf{k}_i^*$ is computed as:

  $$\mathbf{k}_i^* = \left(\mu_i(t, -1), \; \theta_i \omega_i - \phi_i, \; -\theta_i, \; 0^4, \; 0^2, \; \eta_{i,1}, \; \eta_{i,2}, 0^2\right)_{\mathbb{B}^*},$$

  for $i = 1, \ldots, \ell$, $\rho(i) = (t, \omega_i)$, and $\mu_i, \theta_i, \eta_{i,1}, \eta_{i,2} \xleftarrow{U} \mathbf{F}_q$.
- Game 3: It is the same as Game 2-h-3 except the challenge ciphertext is semi-functional and the component $\mathbf{c}_0$ is computed as follows.

  $$\mathbf{c}_0 = \left(\delta F(\mathsf{id}), \; \tau, \; \zeta', \; 0, \; \varphi_0\right)_{\mathbb{B}_0}, \quad c = g_T^\zeta \cdot m_b^*,$$

  where $\delta, \zeta', \varphi_0 \xleftarrow{U} \mathbf{F}_q$ ane $\tau \xleftarrow{U} \mathbf{F}_q^\times$.

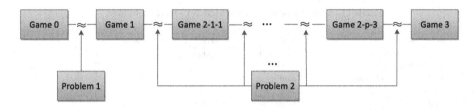

Fig. 1. The outline for the proof of our revocable KP-ABE scheme

Next, we will prove the indistinguishability of any two adjacent games. The outline of our proof is showed as Fig. 1.

Let $\mathsf{Adv}_{\mathcal{A}}^{(0)}(1^\lambda)$, $\mathsf{Adv}_{\mathcal{A}}^{(1)}(1^\lambda)$, $\mathsf{Adv}_{\mathcal{A}}^{(2\text{-}h\text{-}\iota)}(\lambda)$ where $h = 1,\dots,p$ and $\iota = 1,2,3$, and $\mathsf{Adv}_{\mathcal{A}}^{(3)}$ be the advantage of $\mathcal{A}$ in games Game 0, Game 1, Game 2-h-ι and Game 3, respectively. We can show that the indistinguishability of any two adjacent games for any PPT adversary is negligible. Therefore, we have

$$\mathsf{Adv}_{\mathcal{A}}^{\text{Revocable KP-ABE}}(1^\lambda) = \mathsf{Adv}_{\mathcal{A}}^{(0)}(1^\lambda)$$

$$\leq \left| \mathsf{Adv}_{\mathcal{A}}^{(0)}(1^\lambda) - \mathsf{Adv}_{\mathcal{A}}^{(1)}(1^\lambda) \right| + \sum_{h=1}^{p} \left[\left| \mathsf{Adv}_{\mathcal{A}}^{(2\text{-}(h-1)\text{-}3)}(1^\lambda) - \mathsf{Adv}_{\mathcal{A}}^{(2\text{-}h\text{-}1)}(1^\lambda) \right| \right.$$

$$\left. + \sum_{j=1}^{2} \left| \mathsf{Adv}_{\mathcal{A}}^{2\text{-}h\text{-}j}(1^\lambda) - \mathsf{Adv}_{\mathcal{A}}^{(2\text{-}h\text{-}(j+1))}(1^\lambda) \right| \right]$$

$$+ \left| \mathsf{Adv}_{\mathcal{A}}^{2\text{-}p\text{-}3}(1^\lambda) - \mathsf{Adv}_{\mathcal{A}}^{(3)}(1^\lambda) \right| + \mathsf{Adv}_{\mathcal{A}}^{3}(1^\lambda)$$

$$\leq \mathsf{Adv}_{\mathcal{B}_1}^{P_1}(1^\lambda) + \sum_{h=1}^{p} \left(\mathsf{Adv}_{\mathcal{B}_{2\text{-}h\text{-}1}}^{P_2}(1^\lambda) + \mathsf{Adv}_{\mathcal{B}_{2\text{-}h\text{-}2}}^{P_2}(1^\lambda) \right) + (4p+1)/q.$$

Due to space limitation, we will provide detailed security proof in the extended version.   □

Table 1 shows the efficiency and security comparison of revocable KP-ABE schemes. Compared to existing fully secure revocable KP-ABE schemes, our construction is more efficient in term of ciphertext size, private key size, encryption cost and decryption cost.

Here, we denote $|\mathbf{G}|$ and $|\mathbf{G}_T|$ by the bit-length of an element in group $\mathbf{G}$ and $\mathbf{G}_T$, respectively. We denote $|\Gamma|$ by the size of attribute set, ℓ by the row of access policy matrix M, and r and N by the number of revoked users and the maximum of users in the system, respectively. We denote n-BDHE by the Decision Bilinear Diffie-Hellman Exponent assumption, SGD by the Subgroup Decision assumption, DLIN by the Decision Linear assumption, and CDH by the Computable Diffie-Hellman assumption.

Table 1. Comparison of revocable KP-ABE schemes

Schemes	[15]	[16]	[17]	Ours
Bounded or unbounded	Bounded	Bounded	Unbounded	Unbounded
Security Model	Selective	Full	Full	Full
Order of $\mathbf{G}$	Prime	Composite	Prime	Prime
Complexity assumption	Decision n-BDHE	GSD	DLIN	DLIN & CDH
SK size	$2\ell|\mathbf{G}|$	$(2\ell + 2\log N)|\mathbf{G}|$	$[5 + 16(\ell + \log N + \log^2 N)]|\mathbf{G}|$	$(10 + 14\ell)|\mathbf{G}|$
CT size	$(|\Gamma| + 2)|\mathbf{G}| + |\mathbf{G}_T|$	$|\mathbf{G}_T| + [1 + |\Gamma| + r\log(N/r)]|\mathbf{G}|$	$|\mathbf{G}_T| + (16|\Gamma| + 64r - 27)|\mathbf{G}|$	$(5 + 14|\Gamma|)|\mathbf{G}| + |\mathbf{G}_T|$

6   Conclusions

In this paper, we presented an efficient unbounded revocable key-policy attribute-based encryption scheme in the prime order group setting, and proved the proposed scheme is full security by employing the dual system encryption methodology over dual pairing vector spaces. Compared to existing fully secure revocable KP-ABE schemes, our construction is more efficient in term of ciphertext size, private key size, encryption cost and decryption cost. In our future work, we will focus on constructing a fully secure attribute-based encryption scheme which can offer key revocation and ciphertext update functionalities simultaneously.

Acknowledgments. This research is funded by National Natural Science Foundation of China (Grant No. 61173189).

References

1. Sadiku, M.N.O., Musa, S.M., Momoh, O.D.: Cloud computing: opportunities and challenges. IEEE potentials **33**(1), 34–36 (2014)
2. Buchade, A.R., Ingle, R.: Key management for cloud data storage: Methods and comparisons. In: Fourth International Conference on Advanced Computing Communication Technologies, pp. 263–270. IEEE Press (2014)
3. Boneh, D., Franklin, M.: Identity-based encryption from the weil pairing. In: Kilian, J. (ed.) CRYPTO 2001. LNCS, vol. 2139, pp. 213–229. Springer, Heidelberg (2001). doi:10.1007/3-540-44647-8_13
4. Sahai, A., Waters, B.: Fuzzy identity-based encryption. In: Cramer, R. (ed.) EUROCRYPT 2005. LNCS, vol. 3494, pp. 457–473. Springer, Heidelberg (2005). doi:10.1007/11426639_27
5. Goyal, V., Pandey, O., Sahai, A., Waters, B.: Attribute based encryption for fine-grained access conrol of encrypted data. In: ACM Conference on Computer and Communications Security, pp. 89–98 (2006)

6. Bethencourt, J., Sahai, A., Waters, B.: Ciphertext-policy attribute-based encryption. In: IEEE Symposium on Security and Privacy, pp. 321–334. IEEE Press (2007)

7. Lewko, A., Okamoto, T., Sahai, A., Takashima, K., Waters, B.: Fully secure functional encryption: attribute-based encryption and (hierarchical) inner product encryption. In: Gilbert, H. (ed.) EUROCRYPT 2010. LNCS, vol. 6110, pp. 62–91. Springer, Heidelberg (2010). doi:10.1007/978-3-642-13190-5_4

8. Waters, B.: Ciphertext-policy attribute-based encryption: an expressive, efficient, and provably secure realization. In: Catalano, D., Fazio, N., Gennaro, R., Nicolosi, A. (eds.) PKC 2011. LNCS, vol. 6571, pp. 53–70. Springer, Heidelberg (2011). doi:10.1007/978-3-642-19379-8_4

9. Lewko, A., Waters, B.: Decentralizing attribute-based encryption. In: Paterson, K.G. (ed.) EUROCRYPT 2011. LNCS, vol. 6632, pp. 568–588. Springer, Heidelberg (2011). doi:10.1007/978-3-642-20465-4_31

10. Attrapadung, N., Libert, B., Panafieu, E.: Expressive key-policy attribute-based encryption with constant-size ciphertexts. In: Catalano, D., Fazio, N., Gennaro, R., Nicolosi, A. (eds.) PKC 2011. LNCS, vol. 6571, pp. 90–108. Springer, Heidelberg (2011). doi:10.1007/978-3-642-19379-8_6

11. Pirretti, M., Traynor, P., McDaniel, P., Waters, B.: Secure attribute-based systems. J. Comput. Secur. **18**(5), 799–837 (2010)

12. Li, M., Yu, S.C., Zheng, Y., Ren, K., Lou, W.J.: Scalable and secure sharing of personal health records in cloud computing using attribute-based encryption. IEEE Trans. Parallel Distrib. Syst. **24**(1), 131–143 (2013)

13. Wang, C.J., Xu, X.L., Shi, D.Y., Fang, J.: Privacy-preserving cloud-based personal health record system using attribute-based encryption and anonymous multi-receiver identity-based encryption. Informatica **39**(4), 375–382 (2015)

14. Boldyreva, A., Goyal, V., Kumar, V.: Identity-based encryption with efficient revocation. In: Proceedings of the 15th ACM Conference on Computer and Communications Security (CCS), pp. 417–426. ACM Press (2008)

15. Attrapadung, N., Imai, H.: Conjunctive broadcast and attribute-based encryption. In: Shacham, H., Waters, B. (eds.) Pairing 2009. LNCS, vol. 5671, pp. 248–265. Springer, Heidelberg (2009). doi:10.1007/978-3-642-03298-1_16

16. Qian, J.L., Dong, X.L.: Fully secure revocable attribute-based encryption. J. Shanghai Jiaotong Univ. (Sci.) **16**(4), 490–496 (2011)

17. Datta, P., Dutta, R., Mukhopadhyay, S.: Adaptively secure unrestricted attribute-based encryption with subset difference revocation in bilinear groups of prime order. In: Pointcheval, D., Nitaj, A., Rachidi, T. (eds.) AFRICACRYPT 2016. LNCS, vol. 9646, pp. 325–345. Springer, Heidelberg (2016). doi:10.1007/978-3-319-31517-1_17

18. Freeman, D.M.: Converting pairing-based cryptosystems from composite-order groups to prime-order groups. In: Gilbert, H. (ed.) EUROCRYPT 2010. LNCS, vol. 6110, pp. 44–61. Springer, Heidelberg (2010). doi:10.1007/978-3-642-13190-5_3

19. Okamoto, T., Takashima, K.: Fully secure unbounded inner-product and attribute-based encryption. In: Wang, X., Sako, K. (eds.) ASIACRYPT 2012. LNCS, vol. 7658, pp. 349–366. Springer, Heidelberg (2012). doi:10.1007/978-3-642-34961-4_22

20. Waters, B.: Dual system encryption: realizing fully secure IBE and HIBE under simple assumptions. In: Halevi, S. (ed.) CRYPTO 2009. LNCS, vol. 5677, pp. 619–636. Springer, Heidelberg (2009). doi:10.1007/978-3-642-03356-8_36

21. Okamoto, T., Takashima, K.: Fully secure functional encryption with general relations from the decisional linear assumption. In: Rabin, T. (ed.) CRYPTO 2010. LNCS, vol. 6223, pp. 191–208. Springer, Heidelberg (2010). doi:10.1007/978-3-642-14623-7_11

22. Attrapadung, N., Imai, H.: Attribute-based encryption supporting direct/indirect revocation modes. In: Parker, M.G. (ed.) IMACC 2009. LNCS, vol. 5921, pp. 278–300. Springer, Heidelberg (2009). doi:10.1007/978-3-642-10868-6_17

A Privacy-Preserving Hybrid Cooperative Searching Scheme over Outsourced Cloud Data

Qiang Zhang[1], Qin Liu[2], and Guojun Wang[3(✉)]

[1] School of Information Science and Engineering,
Central South University, Changsha 410083, China
[2] College of Computer Science and Electronic Engineering,
Hunan University, Changsha 410082, China
[3] School of Computer Science and Educational Software,
Guangzhou University, Guangzhou 510006, China
csgjwang@gmail.com

Abstract. With the progress of science and technology, cloud computing has attracted more and more attention. Individuals or companies use cloud computing to save money. The privacy problem has always been a stumbling block for the further development of cloud computing. A key problem is how to provide an efficient cloud service in a privacy-preserving way while preserving good user experience. In order to solve these problems, scientists have proposed several solutions. However these techniques either generate huge computation costs and bandwidth, or reduce the user experience. In this paper, we propose a Privacy-Preserving Hybrid Cooperative Searching (HCPS) scheme. Our scheme allows multiple users to combine their queries in order to reduce the query cost and at the same time to protect their privacy and have a good user experience.

Keywords: Cloud computing · Hybrid · Cooperative searching · Privacy-preserving · User experience

1 Introduction

Cloud computing is a model for enabling ubiquitous, convenient, on-demand network access to a shared pool of configurable computing resources (e.g.,networks, servers, storage, applications and services) that can be rapidly provisioned and released with minimal management effort or service provider interaction [1]. The benefits of utilizing the cloud (lower operating costs, elasticity, and so on) come with a tradeoff. Users will have to entrust their data to a potentially untrustworthy cloud provider. As a result, improving cloud security has become more and more important [2,3].

The potential privacy leakages may happen in the process of outsourcing data to the cloud. It is a big problem for application of cloud computing. For example, let us consider the application scenario as shown in Fig. 1. When users search for files, they will enter the exact keywords to the cloud. The cloud will compute

© Springer International Publishing AG 2016
G. Wang et al. (Eds.): SpaCCS 2016, LNCS 10066, pp. 265–278, 2016.
DOI: 10.1007/978-3-319-49148-6_23

these keywords and return the necessary files to the users. In the process, the cloud knows the users' query and interests. It is difficult to prevent the information leakage to the cloud, because the cloud has to know these information to return the appropriate files to the users.

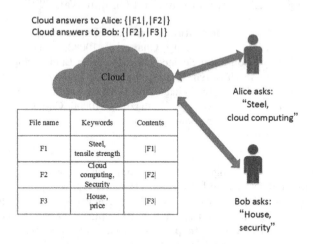

Fig. 1. Application scenario

Existing work, known as private searching protocols, have been proposed [4–8] to address this problem. In the private searching scheme, files stored in the cloud are in the clear forms. The user will send a special type of query that is encrypted under Paillier cryptography [9] to the cloud. By using the properties of Paillier cryptography, the cloud can return the right file to the user without knowing what keywords the users are searching for and which files have been returned.

However, in order to protect user privacy, a private searching scheme requires the cloud to process the encrypted query on every file in a collection. Therefore, when the cloud has to deal with hundreds of thousands of query services, this will be a performance bottlenecks for cloud service. If we are able to combine more than one queries together, we can save the overhead by reducing the number of queries.

Liu [10] proposes a new private searching scheme termed Cooperative Private Searching (COPS). This scheme reduces the computation and communication costs while providing similar privacy protection as in prior protocols. They introduce an aggregation and distribution layer (ADL)-a middleware layer between the users and the cloud. Users will first send their queries to the ADL, which will combine queries and query the cloud on the users behalf. Therefore, the cloud only needs to process a query and return the matched files to ADL. There are no redundant files will be returned to the ADL. Therefore, the communication cost will also be reduced. A key feature of the COPS scheme is that every users privacy is protected from the cloud, the ADL, as well as from other users.

However, the COPS scheme only suits to the medium or large organizations that outsource their data operations to a cloud. The more the number of queries combined at the ADL, the smaller the overhead incurred in the COPS scheme. The main drawback of the COPS scheme is that it requires the ADL to wait for a period of time to aggregate sufficient queries before querying the cloud. It will certainly reduce the user experience.

In this paper, we propose a new private searching scheme termed Hybrid Cooperative Private Searching (HCPS). This scheme can greatly reduce the computational costs and communication overhead while providing similar privacy protection as in prior protocols. The most importantly, HCPS scheme can provide a better user experience. Our solution introduces the two-level aggregation and distribution layers: the fog aggregation and distribution layer (FADL) and the Cloud aggregation and distribution layer (CADL)-two middleware layers between the users and the cloud. FADL-a fog middleware layer means a middleware layer closest to the user. CADL-a cloud middleware layer means a middleware layer closest to the cloud. Users will first send their queries to the FADL. The second step is that the FADLs send the combine queries to the CADL. In the third step, the CADLs will combine queries and query the cloud. In this way, the cloud needs to execute query only once to return files matching all users' queries to the CADL, which will return the files to the corresponding FADLs. Since each file needs to be returned only once, the communication cost will also be reduced. Because we have two middleware layers so that, we can speed less time to collect enough queries. Therefore, compare with the previous scheme, we can not only greatly reduce the computation and communication costs but also provide a better user experience.

The HCPS scheme can control degree of aggregating queries through a time-out mechanism to meet a given processing delay requirement. When the time-out is set to zero, this is degraded to the sequential queries. The number of searches will be very large, but there are two levels of aggregation and distribution layer, which can greatly reduce the waiting time and greatly reduce the cloud overhead.

The HCPS scheme allows us to provide the same privacy protection at a much lower cost and delivers a better user experience. We make the following contributions in this paper:

1. To the best of our knowledge, the HCPS scheme is the first cooperative private searching scheme that is not only at a much lower cost but also has a good user experience for a cloud environment. The proposed scheme outperforms existing private searching protocols while providing the same privacy protection as before.
2. Through analysis, merge similarity search can reduce the cloud overhead, HCPS scheme can merge more similarity search at the same time, so the cloud has low overhead than before scheme.

The following sections are arranged as bellow: In Sect. 2, we introduce the related work. In Sect. 3 we introduces the current technology. In Sect. 4, we describe the HCPS scheme in detail. Finally, we conclude this paper in Sect. 5.

2   Related Work

Our work is protecting user privacy while searching data on untrusted servers. User privacy can be classified into search privacy and access privacy [11].

Search privacy means that the servers do not know anything about what users are looking for, access privacy means that the cloud knows nothing about what documents returned to the user. There has been a lot of work conducted in this field including private searching [4–8,12,13],private information retrieval [14–16], and searchable encryption [17–22], where user privacy can be protected in private searching, but only search privacy can be protected in searchable encryption.

Ostrovsky and Skeith first proposed the retrieval privacy agreement [4] (also known as the Ostrovsky scheme), where data is stored in the clear form, and the query is encrypted with the Paillier cryptosystem [9,23] that exhibits the homomorphic properties. The server processes the encrypted query on each file and stores the encrypted file into a compact buffer, with which the user can successfully recover all wanted files with high probability. Since the query and the results are encrypted under the users public key, the server cannot know the users interests. The key merit of their work is that the buffer size depends on the number of files matching the query and is independent of the number of files stored on the server. Therefore, private searching can provide the same level of privacy as downloading entire database from the server while incurring significantly less communication costs. The work by Bethencourt et al. [5,12] proposed an improved scheme by solving a set of linear equations to recover data that reduced the communication cost. the work by Danezis and Diaz [6,13] presented an efficient decoding mechanism for private searching; the work by Adida and Wikstrom [7] applied private searching to achieve public shuffling. The main drawback of existing private searching protocols is that both the computation/communication cost will grow linearly with the number of users executing searches. In 2012, Liu [10] proposed the COPS scheme, in order to reduce costs, The COPS scheme have to allow the user to wait for a long time. But the users patience is limited, The longer waiting time for users, the poorer user experience. So we should not only consider the computation/communication cost, but also take into account the user waiting time.

PIR was first introduced in [14], where the data is viewed as an n-bit string $x = x1, x2, \ldots, xn$, and a user retrieves the bit xi while keeping the index i private from the database by accessing multiple replicated database copies. The work by Kushilevitz and Ostrovsky [15] provided a single-database PIR scheme to further reduce incurred communication costs. Recently, the work by Olumofin and Goldberg [16] applied the private information retrieval technique to a relational database by hiding sensitive constants contained in the predicates of a query. There are two main differences between PIR and private searching. First, the communication costs in existing PIR schemes depend on the size of the entire database other than the size of retrieved messages. Second, PIR is first proposed to let a user to retrieve a bit from a database without letting the database know which bit is retrieved. Although some work addressed the problem of retrieval files by keywords, none of them can support multi-keyword search.

Searchable encryption may be viewed as the flip side of private searching and PIR, where the user conducts searches on encrypted data. Searchable encryption was first proposed by Song et al. [17], where both the user query as well as the data is encrypted under a symmetric key setting. Therefore, only the users with the symmetric key can encrypt data and generate queries. The work by Boneh et al. [18] proposed the first public key-based searchable encryption scheme, where anyone with the public key can encrypt data, but only users with the private key can generate queries. The work by Goh [19] first used the Bloom filter to build an index of keywords for each file. The work by Chang and Mitzenmacher [20] also developed a similar per-file index scheme. The work by Wang et al. [21] encrypts files and queries with Order Preserving Symmetric Encryption (OPSE) [24] and utilizes keyword frequency to rank results; the later work by Cao et al. [16] uses the secure KNN technique [25] to rank results based on inner products. The main difference between all these work and ours is that in searchable encryption the cloud will know which files (file identifiers) are returned to each user, even if the file contents are encrypted. Thus, the cloud may deduce whether two users are interested in the same files.

Our scheme is built on above mentioned private searching technique and COPS scheme. We propose a scheme which can not only reduce computation and communication costs, but also have a good user experience by reducing the waiting time of user queries.

3   Preliminaries

In this section, we will first explain the problem for our work, and then provide the security requirements. Finally, we will outline the COPS scheme, which serves as a base of the HCPS scheme.

3.1   Problem Formulation

The users patience is limited, The longer waiting time for users, the poorer users experience. So we should not only consider the computation/communication cost, but also consider user time cost. Many unencrypted files are stored in a potentially untrusted cloud. The users can query the cloud to retrieve files that they are interested in. When the users do not want the cloud to know their interests, the private searching technique can be adopted to protect user query privacy.

Now suppose there are n users, where each user issues a query to the cloud using the private searching scheme. If each user independently requests the data from the cloud, the cloud needs to execute private searches n times, and return results to n users, respectively.

The COPS scheme that introduces an aggregation and distribution layer (ADL) that acts like an aggregator and distributor as shown in Fig. 2(a).

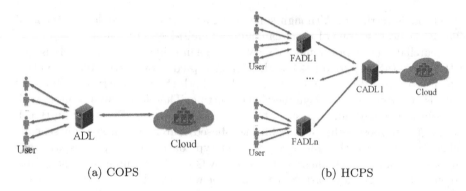

(a) COPS   (b) HCPS

Fig. 2. System model of COPS scheme and HCPS scheme

The users, who want to retrieve files that they are interested in form a group. Each user will first send query to the FADL and CADL, which will query the cloud in turn on the users' behalf and return the appropriate files to the user. In this way, the computational cost at the cloud will be largely reduced, since the cloud needs to execute the private search only once, no matter the number of users. The communication cost at the cloud will also be largely reduced, since all users conceivably have common interests and the number of files matching all users' queries will not grow linearly with the number of users. Figure 3 shows that cloud computation time and buffer size increase with the number of search. With the increase of the number of search, the advantage of COPS scheme is more and more obvious. But The more search shows that the longer waiting time for the query. And HCPS scheme will have much bigger number of users than COPS scheme under the same waiting time. In other words, when the number of users is the same, HCPS scheme with shorter waiting time than COPS scheme. Figure 3(b) shows that actual search times decrease with the increase of search similarity of users. Over a period of time, The more search have combined, the smaller average cloud overhead.

3.2   Security and Privacy Requirements

The HCPS scheme aims to search the data in the cloud while protecting the privacy of every user. The communication channels are assumed to be secured under existing security protocols such as SSL to protect user privacy during information transferring. There are four types of adversaries: the cloud, the FADL, the CADL, and other users. The cloud service providers may leak privacy for profit. The FADL collect user information may be a bigger target. The CADL collect FADLs information may be another target. In order to avoid information leakage, it must be protect the privacy of users from the FADL and protect the privacy of the FADL from the CADL, because the FADL contain the user privacy. A small number of malicious users may want to know other users' privacy.

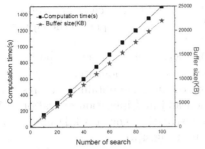
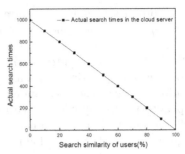

(a) Computation/communication vs Number of search.

(b) Actual search times vs Search similarity of users, the total number of search is 1000.

Fig. 3. The relationship between computation/communication costs and the number of search. The relationship between actual search times and search similarity of users. Each file is described by 1–5 keywords, and each user randomly chooses 1–5 keywords from a dictionary of 1000 keywords.

These adversaries are assumed to be honest but curious. That is, they will obey our scheme, but they still want to know some additional information.

Assume that the FADL do not collude with any other entities, but the CADL may collude with other entities. However, malicious users may either work together or collude with the cloud to know other users' interests. This assumption is reasonable, since the FADL, maintained by the organization, is reliable and independent, and thus has no incentive to collude with other entities during our scheme. This assumption has also been made in previous research by other researchers, e.g., the proxy reencryption systems [26,27], where the proxy server is assumed to not collude with other entity to ensure system-wide security.

We consider our scheme to fail if any of the following cases is true:

Case 1. The cloud knows keywords or file contents queried by any user.

Case 2. The FADL or CADL knows keywords or file contents queried by any user.

Case 3. The user knows keywords or file contents queried by other users.

3.3 Outline of the Ostrovsky Scheme and the COPS Scheme

The Ostrovsky scheme [4] relies on a public key cryptosystem, Paillier cryptosystem [9]. Let E(m) denote the encryption of a plaintext m. The Paillier cryptosystem has the following homomorphic properties:

$$E(a) \cdot E(b) = E(a + b)$$

$$E(a)^b = E(a \cdot b)$$

The homomorphic properties are achieved as follows: the ciphertexts of a and b can be considered as g^a and g^b, where g is a random generator. $g^a \cdot g^b = g^{a+b}$, i.e., the product of ciphertexts of a and b is equal to the ciphertext of a + b; $g^a \cdot g^b = g^{a+b}$, i.e., the ciphertext of a to the power of b is equal to the ciphertext of $a \cdot b$.

With the Paillier cryptosystem, the Ostrovsky scheme enables the cloud to perform certain operations, such as multiplication and exponentiation, on ciphertext directly. Given the resultant ciphertext, the user can obtain the corresponding plaintext that is processed with addition and multiplication operations. We briefly outline the working process of the Ostrovsky scheme while many users are querying data from the cloud, as shown in Fig. 4(a).

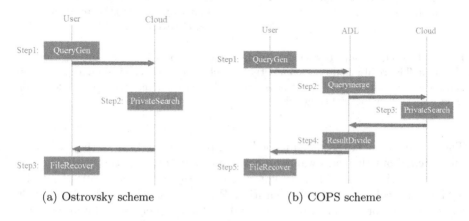

(a) Ostrovsky scheme   (b) COPS scheme

Fig. 4. Working processes of the Ostrovsky scheme and COPS scheme

Since the query and the results are encrypted under the users public key and the cloud processes each file similarly, the user can protect his/her query privacy from the cloud. This scheme also provides a collision–detection mechanism to let the user get rid of the conflicted file copies. We refer the readers to [4] for more details.

The main idea of COPS scheme is the introduction of an ADL is used to merge the user's query and distribute the right result to the user. The COPS scheme [12] consists of five steps (see Fig. 4(b)).

4   HCPS Scheme

In this section, we will first describe the HCPS scheme, and then describe how the system is set up. Finally, we will describe the working process of the HCPS scheme in detail.

4.1   System Setup

The system settings of the HCPS scheme is as follows: There are t files $F_1, \ldots, F_t$ stored in the cloud. Each file F_i can be described by keyword set W_i, where

$i \in 1, \ldots, t$ denotes a file index. Each keyword w exists in a public dictionary Dic that consists of an array of d keywords $<w1, \ldots, wd>$. Suppose n users constitute a group that shares a group public/private key pair (PKG, SKG). Let (PK_{FADL}, SK_{FADL}) PK_{CADL}, SK_{CADL} and (PK_{cloud}, SK_{cloud}) denote the public/private key pairs of the FADL, CADL and the cloud, respectively.

Then, we describe the properties of functions used in the HCPS scheme as follows. In summary, there are three kinds of functions can be only executed by the cloud and the user, i.e., shuffle function, pseudonym function, and obfuscate function. Each function has its own unique secret seed. Therefore, there are four secret seeds shared between the users and the cloud. Under the same FADL users in the same organization, the organization will manage and distribute the secrets. When a new user join in, the organization will distribute the secret seed to him off-line. This process can be analogous to an organization providing the password to a new user. The secret seed should be changed periodically. The rate of change is a system defined parameter which out the scope of this paper.

Dic is original dictionary, Dic' is shuffled dictionary.

Q_i is user i's original query, Q_i' is user i's shuffled query, Q is merged query.

Shuffle function $F1(s1, \rho_w)$ is used to shuffle a query or a dictionary.

w is keyword in the dictionary.

Pseudonym function $F2(s2, i)$ is used to calculate the pseudonym for a file.

Obfuscate functions $F3(s3, \eta_i)$ and $F4(s4, \eta_i)$ are used to calculate a obfuscate factor for the occurrence of user keywords in the file and a obfuscate factor for the file content, respectively.

Map functions $h_j(p'w)_{1 \leq j \leq log(k)}$ and $g_j(\eta_i)_{1 \leq j \leq log(f)}$ are used to determine the mapping locations of the file pseudonym in the file pseudonym buffer and the mapping locations of the obfuscated file content in the file content buffer, respectively.

4.2 Scheme Description

Our basic idea is to introduce FADL and CADL. FADL used to combine the users query and send the combine query to CADL, FADL also takes the query results from the CADL suitably and divide appropriate results to right user. CADL is responsible for combining FADLs queries and set to the cloud, CADL also divide appropriate results to FADLs. The users who want to retrieve files that they are interested in from a group, where each member shares a group public/private key pair. As in [4], we assume that the CADL and FADLs is able to estimate the number of files matching the query.

As illustrated previously, the main reason for introducing FADL and CADL to combine queries and divide results is to save both computation and communication costs while shorten the user's query waiting time so as to improve the user experience. We require the FADL to divide appropriate results to each user instead of simply returning everything to protect user privacy. For example, the results contain two files $|F1|$, $|F2|$, where $|F1|$ is wanted by Alice, and $|F2|$ is wanted by Bob. If the ADL directly passes $|F1|$, $|F2|$ to Alice and Bob, Alice will know Bob wants $|F2|$. The same case holds true for Bob. We also require

Table 1. Files stored in the cloud.

File *name*	File *keywords*	File *content*
F1	A, B	$|F1|$
F2	B, C	$|F2|$
F3	C, D	$|F3|$
F4	C	$|F4|$
F5	D	$|F5|$

the CADL to divide appropriate results to FADLs instead of simple returning everything to reduce communication overhead.

The HCPS scheme shown in Fig. 5 consists of seven steps. We use a simple example to illustrate its working process. The example assumes that the original dictionary Dic $= <A, B, C, D>$ and that the files stored in the cloud are as in Table 1, four users, Alice and Bob in FADL1 organization in wish to retrieve files with keywords A, B and A, C, respectively. Tom and Lisa in FADL2 organization in wish to retrieve files with keywords B, C and C, D, respectively.

Our scheme consists of seven steps (see Fig. 5):

Step 1: Each user runs the QueryGen algorithm to send a shuffled query to the FADL. The query is an array of 0s and 1s as in [4]. To protect each user's query from the FADL, our scheme requires each user to shuffle his query with a shuffle function. Since the FADL does not know the secret seed of the shuffle function, the FADL cannot deduce the unshuffled query to know what each user is searching for.

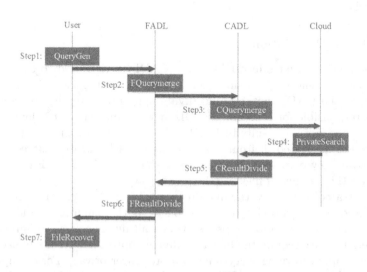

Fig. 5. Working processes of the HCPS scheme

If a keyword $w \in Dic$ is chosen by user i, then the corresponding entry in Q_i is set to 1, otherwise 0; then, Q_i is shuffled with F1. Actually, this process is equivalent to first shuffling the dictionary to Dic with F1, and then checking whether $w_j \in Dic'$ is chosen to determine the value (0 or 1) of $Q_i[j]$.

For example, Alices original query $Q_{Alice} = <1,1,0,0>$ and Bobs original query $Q_{Bob} = <1,0,1,0>$. Toms original query $Q_{Tom} = <0,1,1,0>$ and Lisas original query $Q_{Lisa} = <0,0,1,1>$, If the shuffle function F1(s1, 1) = 4, F1(s1, 2) = 1, F1(s1, 3) = 2, F1(s1, 4) = 3, then Alices shuffled query $Q_{Alice} = <1,0,0,1>$, and Bobs shuffled query $Q_{Bob} = <0,1,0,1>$, then Toms shuffled query $Q_{Tom} = <1,1,0,0>$, and Lisas shuffled query $Q_{Lisa} = <0,1,1,0>$.

Step 2: The FADL runs the FQueryMerge algorithm to send a combined query to the CADL. The FADL executes OR operations on user queries entry by entry to obtain a merged query. Since each user's query is an array of 0s and 1s, the merged query is also an array of 0s and 1s. Then, the FADL encrypts each entry of the merged query with the Paillier cryptosystem under its own public key. The encrypted query, the number of keywords in the merged query, and the estimated number of files matching the merged query will be sent to the CADL.

For example, the combined query $Q_1 = Q_{Alice} \vee Q_{Bob} = <1 \vee 0, 0 \vee 1, 0 \vee 0, 1 \vee 1> = <1, 1, 0, 1>$. The encrypted query is in the form of $Q_1 = <E(PK_{FADL}, 1), E(PK_{FADL}, 1), E(PK_{FADL}, 0), E(PK_{FADL}, 1)>$, the combined query $Q_2 = Q_{Tom} \vee Q_{Lisa} = <1 \vee 0, 1 \vee 1, 0 \vee 1, 0 \vee 0> = <1, 1, 1, 0>$. The encrypted query is in the form of $Q_1 = <E(PK_{FADL}, 1), E(PK_{FADL}, 1), E(PK_{FADL}, 1), E(PK_{FADL}, 0)>$. The FADLs also needs to estimate f, the number of files matching Q_1 or Q_2, and determine k, the number of keywords in Q_1 or Q_2, to determine buffer size and mapping times. Here, k is actually the number of 1s in Q_1 or Q_2.

Step 3: The CADL runs the CQueryMerge algorithm to send a combined query to the cloud. The CADL executes OR operations on FADL queries entry by entry to obtain a merged query. Since each FADLs query is an array of 0s and 1s, the merged query is also an array of 0s and 1s. Then, the CADL encrypts each entry of the merged query with the Paillier cryptosystem under its own public key. The encrypted query, the number of keywords in the merged query, and the estimated number of files matching the merged query will be sent to the cloud.

For example, the combined query $Q = Q_1 \vee Q_2 = <1 \vee 1, 1 \vee 1, 0 \vee 1, 1 \vee 0> = <1, 1, 1, 1>$. The encrypted query is in the form of $Q = <E(PK_{CADL}, 1), E(PK_{CADL}, 1), E(PK_{CADL}, 1), E(PK_{CADL}, 1)>$. The CADL also needs to estimate f, the number of files matching Q, and determine k, the number of keywords in Q, to determine buffer size and mapping times. Here, k is actually the number of 1s in Q.

Step 4: The cloud runs the PrivateSearch algorithm to return two compact buffers to the CADL. Since the merged query is encrypted under the CADLs public key, after processing the merged query on each file, each file is also encrypted under the CADLs public key. To protect file information from the CADL, we design a new mechanism as follows: The cloud uses a pseudonym function to replace the file name with the file pseudonym, and uses obfuscate functions to add some obfuscate factors to the file content. Without the secret seeds of these functions, the CADL cannot deduce the file names or the file contents. To enable the CADL to correctly distribute appropriate file pseudonyms and obfuscated file contents for each user, the cloud first shuffles the dictionary, and then constructs two buffers: file pseudonym buffer and file content buffer. The positions of the file pseudonym in the file pseudonym buffer are determined by a set of map functions and the positions of the file keywords in the shuffled dictionary. The positions of the obfuscated file content in the file content buffer are determined by another set of map functions and the file pseudonym. These map functions are publicly available.

Step 5: The CADL runs the CResultDivide algorithm to divide into two appropriate compact buffers to each FADLs. The CADL first decrypts each entry of the two buffers sequently using its private key. Given each FADLs shuffled query and a set of map functions, the CADL can find wanted by this FADL. For this type of map functions, the input is the location of the keyword in the shuffled query and output is the locations of file pseudonym buffer that store pseudonyms of files containing such a keyword. Then, given each file pseudonym and another set of map functions, the CADL can find obfuscated file contents desired by this FADL. For this type of map functions, the input is the file pseudonym and output is the locations of file content buffer that stores obfuscated file content with such a pseudonym.

Step 6: The FADL runs the FResultDivide algorithm to divide appropriate results to each user. Given each users shuffled query and a set of map functions, the FADL can find pseudonyms of files desired by this user. For this type of map functions, the input is the location of the keyword in the shuffled query and output is the locations of file pseudonym buffer that store pseudonyms of files containing such a keyword. Then, given each file pseudonym and another set of map functions, the FADL can find obfuscated file contents wanted by this user. For this type of map functions, the input is the file pseudonym and output is the locations of file content buffer that stores obfuscated file content with such a pseudonym.

Step 7: Each user runs the FileRecover algorithm to recover matched files. After obtaining the obfuscated file contents from the FADL, the user only needs to remove the obfuscate factors to recover the file contents.

5   Conclusion

We propose the HCPS scheme to achieve the efficient and sophisticated cloud services in a privacy-preserving way. To the best of our knowledge, the HCPS scheme is the first cooperative private searching scheme that not only has a low overhead but also has a good user experience for a cloud environment. There are two layers of ADL in the HCPS scheme. FADL-a fog aggregation and distribution layer that means a middleware layer closest to the user, which is located in the organization's internal and merges the searches from this organization. CADL-a cloud aggregation and distribution layer that means a middleware layer closest to the cloud, which is located in the organization's external and merges the searches from FADLs. Our future work is to make sure different people with different attributes have different access rights while enhancing the search efficiency.

Acknowledgments. This work is supported in part by the National Natural Science Foundation of China under Grant Numbers 61632009, 61472451, 61272151 and 61402161, and the High Level Talents Program of Higher Education in Guangdong Province under Funding Support Number 2016ZJ01, and the Hunan Provincial Natural Science Foundation of China (Grant No. 2015JJ3046).

References

1. Mell, P., Grance, T.: The NIST definition of cloud computing. Recommendations of the National Institute of Standards and Technology-Special Publication 800-145. NIST, Washington DC (2011). http://csrc.nist.gov/publications/nistpubs/800-145/SP800-145.pdf
2. Kaur, J., Garg, S.: Survey paper on security in cloud computing. Int. J. Appl. Stud. Prod. Manage. **1**, 27–32 (2015)
3. Chang, V., Kuo, Y.-H., Ramachandran, M.: Cloud computing adoption framework: a security framework for business clouds. Future Gener. Comput. Syst. **57**, 24–41 (2016)
4. Ostrovsky, R., Skeith, W.E.: Private searching on streaming data. In: Shoup, V. (ed.) CRYPTO 2005. LNCS, vol. 3621, pp. 223–240. Springer, Heidelberg (2005). doi:10.1007/11535218_14
5. Bethencourt, J., Song, D., Waters, B.: New constructions and practical applications for private stream searching. In: 2006 IEEE Symposium on Security and Privacy, p. 6. IEEE (2006)
6. Danezis, G., Diaz, C.: Improving the decoding efficiency of private search. In: Proceedings of Dagstuhl Seminar. Schloss Dagstuhl-Leibniz-Zentrum für Informatik (2006)
7. Adida, B., Wikström, D.: How to shuffle in public. In: Vadhan, S.P. (ed.) TCC 2007. LNCS, vol. 4392, pp. 555–574. Springer, Heidelberg (2007). doi:10.1007/978-3-540-70936-7_30
8. Yi, X., Bertino, E., Vaidya, J., Xing, C.: Private searching on streaming data based on keyword frequency. IEEE Trans. Dependable Secur. Comput. **11**(2), 155–167 (2014)
9. Damgård, I., Jurik, M.: A generalisation, a simplification and some applications of Paillier's probabilistic public-key system. In: Kim, K. (ed.) PKC 2001. LNCS, vol. 1992, pp. 119–136. Springer, Heidelberg (2001). doi:10.1007/3-540-44586-2_9
10. Liu, Q., Tan, C.C., Wu, J., Wang, G.: Cooperative private searching in clouds. J. Parallel Distrib. Comput. **72**(8), 1019–1031 (2012)
11. Curtmola, R., Garay, J., Kamara, S., Ostrovsky, R.: Searchable symmetric encryption: improved definitions and efficient constructions. In: Proceedings of the 13th ACM Conference on Computer and Communications Security, pp. 79–88. ACM (2006)
12. Bethencourt, J., Song, D., Waters, B.: New techniques for private stream searching. ACM Trans. Inf. Syst. Secur. (TISSEC) **12**(3), 16 (2009)

13. Danezis, G., Diaz, C.: Space-efficient private search with applications to rateless codes. In: Dietrich, S., Dhamija, R. (eds.) FC 2007. LNCS, vol. 4886, pp. 148–162. Springer, Heidelberg (2007). doi:10.1007/978-3-540-77366-5_15

14. Chor, B., Kushilevitz, E., Goldreich, O., Sudan, M.: Private information retrieval. J. ACM (JACM) **45**(6), 965–981 (1998)

15. Kushilevitz, E., Ostrovsky, R.: Replication is not needed: single database, computationally-private information retrieval. In: FOCS, p. 364. IEEE (1997)

16. Olumofin, F., Goldberg, I.: Privacy-preserving queries over relational databases. In: Atallah, M.J., Hopper, N.J. (eds.) PETS 2010. LNCS, vol. 6205, pp. 75–92. Springer, Heidelberg (2010). doi:10.1007/978-3-642-14527-8_5

17. Song, D.X., Wagner, D., Perrig, A.: Practical techniques for searches on encrypted data. In: Proceedings of the 2000 IEEE Symposium on Security and Privacy, S&P 2000, pp. 44–55. IEEE (2000)

18. Boneh, D., Crescenzo, G., Ostrovsky, R., Persiano, G.: Public key encryption with keyword search. In: Cachin, C., Camenisch, J.L. (eds.) EUROCRYPT 2004. LNCS, vol. 3027, pp. 506–522. Springer, Heidelberg (2004). doi:10.1007/978-3-540-24676-3_30

19. Goh, E.-J., et al.: Secure indexes. IACR Cryptology ePrint Archive, 2003:216 (2003)

20. Chang, Y.-C., Mitzenmacher, M.: Privacy preserving keyword searches on remote encrypted data. In: Ioannidis, J., Keromytis, A., Yung, M. (eds.) ACNS 2005. LNCS, vol. 3531, pp. 442–455. Springer, Heidelberg (2005). doi:10.1007/11496137_30

21. Wang, C., Cao, N., Li, J., Ren, K., Lou, W.: Secure ranked keyword search over encrypted cloud data. In: 2010 IEEE 30th International Conference on Distributed Computing Systems (ICDCS), pp. 253–262. IEEE (2010)

22. Changhui, H., Han, L., Yiu, S.M.: Efficient and secure multi-functional searchable symmetric encryption schemes. Secur. Commun. Netw. **9**(1), 34–42 (2016)

23. O'Keeffe, M.: The Paillier cryptosystem: a look into the cryptosystem and its potential application, College of New Jersey (2008)

24. Boldyreva, A., Chenette, N., Lee, Y., O'Neill, A.: Order-preserving symmetric encryption. In: Joux, A. (ed.) EUROCRYPT 2009. LNCS, vol. 5479, pp. 224–241. Springer, Heidelberg (2009). doi:10.1007/978-3-642-01001-9_13

25. Wong, W.K., Cheung, D.W., Kao, B., Mamoulis, N.: Secure KNN computation on encrypted databases. In: Proceedings of the 2009 ACM SIGMOD International Conference on Management of Data, pp. 139–152. ACM (2009)

26. Green, M., Ateniese, G.: Identity-based proxy re-encryption. In: Katz, J., Yung, M. (eds.) ACNS 2007. LNCS, vol. 4521, pp. 288–306. Springer, Heidelberg (2007). doi:10.1007/978-3-540-72738-5_19

27. Blaze, M., Bleumer, G., Strauss, M.: Divertible protocols and atomic proxy cryptography. In: Nyberg, K. (ed.) EUROCRYPT 1998. LNCS, vol. 1403, pp. 127–144. Springer, Heidelberg (1998). doi:10.1007/BFb0054122

Modeling and Propagation Analysis on Social Influence Using Social Big Data

Sancheng Peng[1], Shengyi Jiang[1(✉)], and Pengfei Yin[2(✉)]

[1] School of Informatics, Guangdong University of Foreign Studies,
Guangzhou 510420, China
jiangshengyi@163.com
[2] College of Information Science and Engineering, Jishou University,
Jishou 416000, Hunan, China
pppypf@163.com

Abstract. Although most existing models focus on the evaluation of social influence in online social networks, failing to characterize indirect influence. So we present a novel framework for modeling and propagation analysis on social influence using social big data. We design a method to transform the social big data into a social graph to characterize the connections between the social interaction and the spreading of short message service or multimedia messaging service (SMS/MMS) by using bidirectional weighted graph, and measure direct influence of individual by computing each node's strength, which includes the degree of node and the total number of SMS/MMS sent by each user to his/her friends. Then, we present an algorithm to construct an influence spreading tree for each node using the breadth first search algorithm, and measure indirect influence of individual by traversing the influence spreading tree. We extend the susceptible-infectious-recovery (SIR) model to characterize propagation dynamics process of social influence. Simulation results show that influence can spread easily in contact social network due to the good connectivity. The greater the degree of initial spread node is, the faster the influence spreads in social network.

Keywords: Social influence · Social big data · Influence evaluation · Influence propagation · Breadth first search · Propagation model

1 Introduction

Social networks [1] have been extensively used as an important communication media with exponential growth. Especially, 3G/4G and Web 2.0 technologies bring revolutionary changes to our daily lives in social networks. In the last decade, various social networks, such as Twitter, Facebook, LinkedIn, and smartphone-based 3G/4G communication networks, have emerged and tightly connected users all over the world. Users can use these networks to build their own friendship networks, and share their experiences, opinions, insights, information, and perspectives with each other. In addition, they can discover and

© Springer International Publishing AG 2016
G. Wang et al. (Eds.): SpaCCS 2016, LNCS 10066, pp. 279–291, 2016.
DOI: 10.1007/978-3-319-49148-6_24

propagate information by using various means, such as calls, messages, pictures, audios, and videos.

Social big data is a collection of very huge data sets of social networks with a great diversity (e.g., Twitter, Facebook, and LinkedIn). The 5V characteristics of social big data, including volume, velocity, variety, value, and veracity, make it difficult to handle such big data sets using traditional techniques, tools, and methods. Nowadays, the explosion of data in terms of high volume, high velocity, and high variety, fueled by stunning and exciting advances of the information technologies and web techniques, has become the focus of widespread attention. Applications of big data [2] lie in many scientific disciplines, such as biology, biogeochemistry, physics, medicine, astronomy, and so on.

Social influence [3] refers to the case that individuals change their behaviors under the influence of others. The strength of social influence depends on the relationship among individuals, the timing effect, the network distances, the characteristics of networks and individuals, etc. Lots of applications in real-world, such as viral marketing [4], online advertising and recommendation [5], can benefit from social influence by measuring quantitatively the influence of individuals or groups.

Social influence modeling and propagation analysis has become an important research topic in social networks. Thus, many efforts have been recently made to model social influence in social networks. Some schemes on social influence have been topic-oblivious [4,6–9]. In these models, social influence was measured either via the relative authority of individuals in their social network, or via the degree of information diffusion with the social network. Some schemes on evaluation of social influence have been topic-based [10–15]. In these models, social influence was measured by counting how much information related to a topic may be propagated in the network. In addition, some schemes are based on pairwise influence [5,16–20], which is defined on social ties and interactions between users.

It is still not well understood what fundamental rules the evaluation models for social influence must follow, although lots of existing methods for evaluation modeling and propagation analysis on social influence are available. Without a good answer to this question, the research for the evaluation modeling and propagation analysis on social influence is still not solid.

Motivated by this, we present a novel method for evaluation modeling and propagation analysis on social influence using social big data. First, we measure the direct influence of individual by computing each node's strength, which includes the degree of node and the total number of short message service or multimedia message service (SMS/MMS) sent by each user to his/her friends. Then, we use the breadth first search algorithm to construct an influence spreading tree for each node, and measure the indirect influence of individual by traversing the influence spreading tree. Our purpose is to develop a general method, which demonstrates the indirect influence of each individual on a given influence spreading tree. Our contributions are summarized as follows:

- We design a novel model to transform the social big data into a social graph, which represents the connections of social interaction and the spreading of short message service or multimedia messaging service (SMS/MMS). The social network graph is constructed using bidirectional weighted graph based on the real-world SMS/MMS-based big data set from people's daily lives for social interactions.
- We propose a new algorithm to measure social influence, includes both direct influence and indirect influence. The direct influence of individual is measured with the degree of node and the total number of SMS/MMS, and the indirect influence of individual is measured by traversing the influence spreading tree, which is constructed with the breadth first search algorithm.
- We also extend the susceptible-infectious-recovery (SIR) model to characterize propagation dynamics process of social influence under the selection of the top k influential nodes. Extensive experiments show that the greater the influence of initial spread node is, the more impact on the propagation of social influence in social networks.

The remainder of this paper is organized as follows: In Sect. 2, we provide a survey of related work, and provide evaluation modeling on social influence in Sect. 3. In Sect. 4, we provide an analysis of social influence propagation, and describe the experimental evaluation in Sect. 5. Finally, we conclude this paper and suggest future work in Sect. 6.

2   Related Work

In this section, we investigate related work in three dimensions. The first dimension is the topic-oblivious influence evaluation model; the second is related to the topic-based influence evaluation model; and the last is related to the pairwise-based influence evaluation model.

Domingos and Richardson [4] investigated social influence in the customer network. They proposed a model to identify customer's influence between each other in the customer network, and built a probabilistic model to mine the spread of influence for viral marketing. Li and Gillet [6] measured the academic influence of scholars based on the scientific impact of their publications using three different measures, and investigated their social influence using network centrality metrics. Sathanur and Jandhyala [7] investigated the information-theoretic measure called transfer entropy as a measure of directed causal influence in online social interactions. Wang et al. [8] presented a model, called dynamic social influence model, which simulates such social influencing processes that people dynamically change their attitudes when they communicate and exchange ideas with others. Ye et al. [9] presented a probabilistic generative model, namely social influenced selection, that explicitly quantifies and incorporates social influence from friends to a user.

Dietz et al. [10] presented a probabilistic topic model to explain the generation of documents. This model incorporated the aspects of topical innovation and topical inheritance via citations to predict the citation influences. Ding et al. [11] measured the influence of users using random walks on the multi-relational data (i.e. the retweet, the reply, the reintroduce, and the read) in Micro-blogging. Sang and Xu [12] presented a multimodal topic-sensitive influence model, which enables simultaneous extraction of node topic distribution, topic-sensitive edge strength, and the topic space. Tang et al. [13] studied a problem of conformity influence analysis in large social networks. They defined three major types of conformities to formulate the problem of conformity influence analysis. Cui et al. [14] presented a Hybrid Factor Non-Negative Matrix Factorization approach for modeling item-level social influence. Herzig et al. [15] presented an Author-Reader Influence model to evaluate the influence of various users on others by applying a retrospective analysis from an ordinary reader's point of view.

Peng et al. [16] introduced two factors to evaluate influence of each node. One factor is intimacy degree (ID), which is used to reflect the closeness between users. The other factor is activity degree (AD), which is used to determine which node is more active. Aral and Walker [17] presented a method by using vivo randomized experimentation to identify influence and susceptibility in networks. Su et al. [18] designed an algorithm based on the PageRank algorithm, called InfluentialRank, which calculates the influence of nodes based on the following relationship of users, retweet behaviours, and users' interests. Li et al. [19] presented a conductance eigenvector centrality model to measure peer influence in social networks. Phan et al. [20] presented the Topic-aware Community-level Physical Activity Propagation model, to capture the social influences of messages in the YesiWell study.

3   Evaluation Modeling on Social Influence

Social influence is a relationship established between two entities for a specific action. In particular, one entity influences the other to perform an action. For example, in a SMS/MMS-based social network, user u may influence v by sending SMS/MMS to v in daily social interactions. In this paper, the first entity is called the *influencer*, and the second one is called the *influencee*.

Definition 1 *[Direct Influence]: Given two individuals u and v in a SMS/MMS-based social network, who are directly connected each other in the network, u has the effect of change in the opinion of v in a direct way. Let $DI_u(t)$ denote the direct influence of user u on its one-hop friends.*

Definition 2 *[Indirect Influence]: Given two individuals u and v in a SMS/MMS-based social network, who are not directly connected in the network, u has a indirect impact on v. Let $II_{uv}(t)$ be the indirect influence of user u on v.*

Definition 3 *[Global Influence]: Given a SMS/MMS-based social network, u exerts the power over the whole network, $I_u(t)$ is defined as the global influence of u at time t, which represents the global influential strength of u over the whole network.*

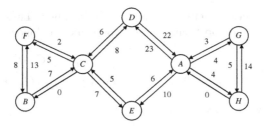

Fig. 1. A bidirectional weighted graph for social interactions in a week.

Table 1. The number of interactions between two cellular phone users in a week

Between two smartphones	The number of interactions	Between two smartphones	The number of interactions
$A \rightarrow D$	23	$D \rightarrow A$	22
$A \rightarrow E$	10	$D \rightarrow C$	6
$A \rightarrow G$	4	$E \rightarrow A$	6
$A \rightarrow H$	4	$E \rightarrow C$	5
$B \rightarrow C$	7	$F \rightarrow B$	8
$B \rightarrow F$	13	$F \rightarrow C$	2
$C \rightarrow B$	0	$G \rightarrow A$	3
$C \rightarrow D$	8	$G \rightarrow H$	5
$C \rightarrow E$	7	$H \rightarrow A$	0
$C \rightarrow F$	5	$H \rightarrow G$	14

3.1 Modeling on Smartphone Social Network

We model a mobile social network by a bidirectional weighted graph, $G(V, E_{ij}, W_{ij})$, where set V of vertices corresponds to the smartphones in cellular networks, set E_{ij} of directed edges corresponds to the traffic flow between any two cellular phones i to j, and set W_{ij} of weight values corresponds to the total number of SMS/MMS messages sent from cellular phone i to j in a given time period. In order to explain the idea of a smartphone social network, we take eight users from the data set and use them as an example. The data of this sample social network is listed in Table 1. According to Table 1, we treat each smartphone as a vertex, so a bidirectional directed, weighted social relationship graph can be obtained and is shown in Fig. 1.

3.2 Measuring Social Influence

(1) Computing direct influence

Let N be the total number of nodes in mobile phone based social networks, $N_i(t)$ be the number of one-hop friend nodes of node i in time t, and $C_{ij}(t)$ be the number of interactions between node i and k in time t. Thus, the total direct influence of i on its one-hop friend nodes is described as follows.

$$DI_i(t) = \omega_1 \frac{N_i(t)}{\max\{N_u(t)\}} + \omega_2 \frac{\sum_{k \in N_i(t)} C_{ik}(t)}{\max\{\sum_{v \in N_u(t)} C_{uv}(t)\}}, \tag{1}$$

where $i, k, u, v \in N$, $\omega_1 + \omega_2 = 1$.

(2) Constructing influence spreading tree

To characterize an individual exerting the power over the whole network, besides considering direct influence on its one-hop friend nodes, we also need to measure indirect influence on its two-hop friends or above. In this paper, we use the breadth first search algorithm to construct an influence spreading tree for each node for measuring the indirect influence of each individual by traversing the influence spreading tree.

To construct an influence spreading tree for each node, the each directed edge weight λ_{ik} is normalized as follows.

$$\lambda_{ik} = C_{ik}(t)/\max\{C_{uv}(t)\}, \tag{2}$$

where $i, k, u, v \in N$.

The construction algorithm of influence spreading tree is shown in Algorithm 1.

(3) Computing on indirect influence

According to Algorithm 1, the influence spreading tree of each node is obtained, and then we can measure the indirect influence of each nodes. For example, let r be the root node for a influence spreading tree. The influence of

---

Algorithm 1. Construction algorithm of influence spreading tree for all nodes.

Input: A social network $G(V, E, W)$ with total number of nodes N;
Output: A set of influence spreading trees T;
 1: Network initialization. Compute direct influence for each node i using Equation
    (1), and normalize each directed edge weight using Equation (2);
 2: **for** $i=1$ to N **do**
 3:     Add i into an empty queue Q_i;
 4:     Build influence spreading tree T_i for node i, set i as root node in T_i;
 5:     **while** Q_i is not empty **do**
 6:         Pull out a node v in Q_i, find node u through which can obtain a path p from
            root node to i, which has maximum $\prod_{e \in p} \lambda_e$ (λ_e is weight of edge e in p);
 7:         Add v into T_i under the corresponding parent node u;
 8:         Add all neighbors of node v into queue Q_i;
 9:     **end while**
10:     Add T_i into T;
11: **end for**
12: **return** T;

root node r on its child j in the tree is denoted by $RI_{rj}(t)$, which is described as follows.

$$RI_{rj}(t) = \begin{cases} \lambda_{rj}, \\ \text{if } j \text{ is a child of root node } r; \\ (RI_{ri}(t)/Br_i(t)) \times \lambda_{ij}, \\ \text{if } j \text{ is not a child of root node } r, \\ \text{but is a child of } i; \end{cases} \qquad (3)$$

where $RI_{ri}(t)$ denotes the influence of i on j, $Br_i(t)$ denotes the number of children of i, i and j belong to the same tree whose root node is r.

Thus, the indirect influence of r is described as follows.

$$II_r(t) = \sum_{j \in R_r(t)} RI_{rj}(t), \qquad (4)$$

where $R_r(t)$ denotes the set of non-direct reachable nodes of r in time t.

(4) Total influence of node

According to the above analysis, the total influence $I_i(t)$ of i is described as follows.

$$I_i(t) = \omega_3 DI_i(t) + \omega_4 II_i(t), \qquad (5)$$

where $\omega_3 + \omega_4 = 1$.

The complete computing process of influence for all nodes is shown in Algorithm 2.

Algorithm 2. Influence computing algorithm for all nodes.

Input: A social network $G(V, E, W)$ with total number of nodes N, a set of influence spreading trees T;
Output: Global influence of each node;
1: **for** $i=1$ to N **do**
2:    Compute direct influence for each node i using Equation (1);
3:    Access influence spreading tree T_i for node i, set $II_i(t) = 0$;
4:    Add root i into an empty queue Q_i;
5:    **while** Q_i is not empty **do**
6:       Pull out a node k in Q_i;
7:       **if** k is not a one-hop neighbor of i **then**
8:          Compute indirect influence $RI_{ik}(t)$ using Equation (4), $II_i(t) = II_i(t) + RI_{ik}(t)$;
9:       **end if**
10:    **end while**
11: **end for**
12: **return** The global influence of each node;

According to Algorithm 1, we can construct an influence spreading tree for each node. Let us take Fig. 1 as an example, the influence spreading tree of node E is shown in Fig. 2.

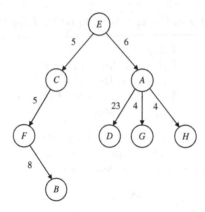

Fig. 2. Influence spreading tree of node E.

4   Analysis of Social Influence Propagation

According to the strength of social influence of individual, we use the minimum heap algorithm to select top k influential nodes. Then, we use SIR model to characterize propagation dynamics process of social influence under the immunization of the top k influential nodes in networks. The pseudo code of the mining algorithm for top k influential nodes is shown in Algorithm 3.

Algorithm 3.   Mining algorithm for top k influential nodes.

Input: A social network $G(V, E, W)$ with total number of nodes N, the number of k,
   $\mathbf{K} = \emptyset$;
Output: A set of top k influential nodes;
   1: Calls Algorithm 1 to build influence spreading tree for all nodes;
   2: Calls Algorithm 2 to compute social influence for each node;
   3: Selects the top k influential nodes by sorting the strength of social influence with
      minimum heap algorithm;
   4: Adds these nodes into $\mathbf{K}$;
   5: **return K**.

It is well known that the classical influence diffusion models [4] in social networks include linear threshold model (LTM), independent cascade model (ICM), and weighted cascade model (WCM). However, influence diffusion model can also be seen as a specific case of the traditional epidemic models. In [21], SIR model was described in detail. In this paper, we extend SIR model to conduct the analysis of social influence spreading. It is shown in Fig. 3.

According to the spread property of virus in mobile social networks, the epidemic state of a node is divided as follows:

(1) Susceptible state (S): nodes have not been infected by any virus in the network but are prone to infection.

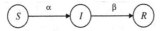

Fig. 3. SIR model.

(2) Infectious state (I): nodes have been infected by viruses in the network and they may infect nodes in state S.

(3) Recovered state (R): nodes that used to be infected by viruses have, and now recovered from the infection. Those nodes are cleaned and immune to the same type of cleaned viruses.

Due to that the SIR model can be mapped to the edge percolation process, many researchers use the SIR model to simulate the process of information and virus diffusion. In addition, the SIR model can be used to understand the influence propagation process and to obtain the exact solution for the theoretical analysis of the influence propagation process. In recent years, many researchers [22] have carried out a series of improvement and promotion of the SIR model, which makes it closer to the real propagation law, and more useful for the weighted directed graph. These analysis and studies have gained many new conclusions about the characteristics of dynamics propagation of information and virus.

Thus, we exploit the SIR model to evaluate the spreading ability of individual. In SIR epidemic model, we suppose a susceptible individual i (i.e. influencee), after successful contact with an infectious individual j (i.e. influencer), becomes infected. The above phenomenon shows that j influences i. Let α denote the probability with which a node in state S becomes a node in state I, β denote the probability with which a node in state I becomes a node in state R, and TT denote the transmission threshold through which a node i transforms from state S to state I. The rule for a node may change its states as follows.

(1) If an infected node u contacts with a susceptible node v, v may changes its state from S to I with probability α.

(2) If an infected node u contacts with a recovered node v, v may changes its state from I to R with probability β.

(3) The propagation process of infected nodes will not spread forever, and it will stop when these nodes change their states from I to R with a specific velocity V. According to the above transition rule of node state, the state transition algorithm is shown in Algorithm 4.

5   Performance Evaluation

To validate the effectiveness of the proposed model, we conduct extensive experiments using the message records collected by one of the largest cellular networks in China. In addition, we designed and developed a C# simulator to implement

---

Algorithm 4. State transition algorithm for all nodes.

Input: A social network $G(V, E, W)$ with total number of nodes N, a set of most
  influential k nodes;

Output: Influence spread in time t in a social network for a given set of most influential k nodes;

  1: Network initialization. Compute social influence for each node i using Algorithm
    2;
  2: Node state initialization. The most influential k nodes are selected, and their states
    are set to be state I, and the states of other nodes are set to be state S;
  3: Node i is accessed at time t, thus
  4: **while** $i \leq N$ **do**
  5:    **if** (The state of i is I) **then**
  6:       The 1-hop and multi-hop neighbor nodes of i are accessed according to the
         influence spreading path;
  7:       **while** $j \leq N_i$ **do**
  8:          **if** (The state of its friend node j is S) and ($I_j(t)$ is not smaller than TT)
            then
  9:             Node j changes its state from S to I with probability α;
  10:          **else**
  11:             Node j remains in its previous state;
  12:          **end if**
  13:       **end while**
  14:       Node i changes its state from I to R with probability β;
  15:    **end if**
  16: **end while**
  17: t equals to t plus Δt;

---

our proposed mechanism, which is an extension of the proposed model. Due to
the huge scale of the real-world big data set, we preprocessed the big data set
and took 119268 users (i.e., they are in same contact social network) for our
experiments, rather than including all the users.

The influence diffusion is a metric to measure how many users can be influenced by the most influential k specific users (or called seed nodes). To test the
influence spread, we use Algorithm 4 to propagate social influence. To obtain
the influence spread of each model, we first select top $k = (30, 50, 70, 90, 110)$
influential nodes as seeds, respectively. Besides degree centrality model, climb
greedy model, set cover model, influence evaluation model, we also implement a
random model as the benchmark, which selects seeds randomly.

Figure 4 shows the influence spread of the social influence evaluation model
with different k and different infected probability α at time t. As can be seen
from the results, as the value of k increases, the number of influence spread
increases. The reason is the higher the most influential nodes, the more nodes
can be influenced.

Figures 5 and 6 show the influence spread of different models with $k = 200$
influential nodes and $k = 300$ influential nodes, respectively, with infected probability $\alpha = 0.2$, at time t. From the results, it is can be seen that the influence

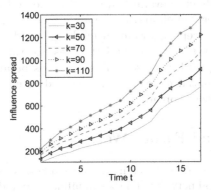

Fig. 4. A comparison of influence spread of the social influence evaluation model with different k influential nodes with infected probability ($\alpha = 0.2$).

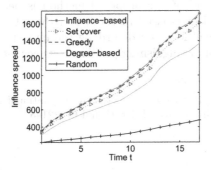

Fig. 5. A comparison of influence spread of different models with $k = 200$ influential nodes with infected probability ($\alpha = 0.2$).

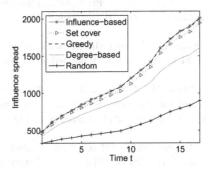

Fig. 6. A comparison of influence spread of different models with $k = 300$ influential nodes with infected probability ($\alpha = 0.2$).

spread of the social influence evaluation model is the best than the degree centrality model, set cover model, and the random model, and is approaching the climb greedy model. Except the random model, the influence spread increases slowly, as t changed from 1 to 10, and then, as the value of t increases, the number of influence spread increases quickly. This is because only the top 200 or 300 nodes are influential nodes and the succeeding nodes do not contribute to increasing the influence spread.

6   Conclusion and Future Work

In this paper, we present a novel method to quantify social influence in a smartphone-based social network. The social influence of individuals is measured through the analysis on the SMS/MMS-based communication behaviors among mobile users. In addition, we reveal and characterize the social relations among mobile users by analyzing the degree of node and the total number of SMS/MMS sent by each user to his/her friends. Extensive analytical results demonstrate that the influence spread of our proposed method is better than that of the random method, the degree-based method, and the set cover method. As for our further work, we will focus on describing the impact of casual relationship on social influence, and distinguishing positive influence, negative influence, and controversial influence.

Acknowledgments. This work is supported by the National Natural Science Foundation of China under Grant Nos. 61379041 and 61572145.

References

1. Peng, S., Wang, G., Xie, D.: Social influence analysis in social networking big data: opportunities and challenges. In: IEEE Network, pp. 12–18 (2016)
2. Chen, C.L.P., Zhang, C.: Data-intensive applications, challenges, techniques and technologies: a survey on big data. Inf. Sci. **275**, 314–347 (2014)
3. Wang, G., Jiang, W., Wu, J., Xiong, Z.: Fine-grained featurebased social influence evaluation in online social networks. IEEE Trans. Parallel Distrib. Syst. **25**(9), 286–2296 (2014)
4. Domingos, P., Riehardson, M.: Mining the network value of customers. In: Proceedings of the 7th ACM Conference on Knowledge Discovery and Data Mining, pp. 57–66 (2001)
5. Huang, J., Cheng, X., Shen, H., Zhou, T., Jin, X.: Exploring social influence via posterior effect of word-of-mouth recommendations. In: Proceedings of the Fifth ACM International Conference on Web Search and Data Mining, pp. 573–582 (2012)
6. Li, N., Gillet, D.: Identifying influential scholars in academic social media platforms. In: Proceedings of the 2013 IEEE/ACM International Conference on Advances in Social Networks Analysis and Mining, pp. 608–614 (2013)
7. Sathanur, A.V., Jandhyala, V.: An activity-based information-theoretic annotation of social graphs. In: Proceedings of the 2014 ACM Conference on Web Science, Bloomington, USA, pp. 187–191 (2014)

8. Wang, Z., Shinkuma, R., Takahashi, T.: Dynamic social influence modeling from perspective of gray-scale mixing process. In: Proceedings of the Eighth International Conference on Mobile Computing and Ubiquitous Networking, pp. 1–6 (2015)

9. Ye, M., Liu, X., Lee, W.-C.: Exploring social influence for recommendation: a generative model approach. In: Proceedings of the 35th International ACM SIGIR Conference on Research and Development in Information Retrieval, pp. 671–680 (2012)

10. Dietz, L., Bickel, S., Scheffer, T.: Unsupervised prediction of citation influences. In: Proceedings of the 24th International Conference on Machine Learning (ICML 2007) (2007)

11. Ding, Z., Jia, Y., Zhou, B., Han, Y.: Mining topical influencers based on the multi-relational network in micro-blogging sites. China Commun. **10**(1), 93–104 (2013)

12. Sang, J., Xu, C.: Social influence analysis and application on multimedia sharing websites. ACM Trans. Multimedia Comput. Commun. Appl. **9**(1s), 1–24 (2013)

13. Tang, J., Wu, S., Sun, J.: Confluence: conformity influence in large social networks. In: Proceeding of the 19th ACM SIGKDD International Conference on Knowledge Discovery and Data Mining (KDD 2013), pp. 347–355 (2013)

14. Cui, P., Wang, F., Liu, S., Ou, M., Yang, S., Sun, L.: Who should share what?: Item-level social influence prediction for users and postsranking. In: Proceedings of the 34th International ACM Conference on Research and Development in Information Retrieval (SIGIR 2011), pp. 185–194 (2011)

15. Herzig, J., Mass, Y., Roitman, H.: An author-reader influence model for detecting topic-based influencers in social media. In: Proceedings of the 25th ACM Conference on Hypertext and Social Media (HT 2014), pp. 46–55 (2014)

16. Peng, S., Wang, G., Yu, S.: Mining mechanism of top-k influential nodes based on voting algorithm in mobile social networks. In: Proceedings of the 11th IEEE/IFIP International Conference on Embedded and Ubiquitous Computing (EUC 2013), pp. 2194–2199 (2013)

17. Aral, S., Walker, D.: Identifying influential and susceptible members of social networks. Science **337**(6092), 337–341 (2012)

18. Su, C., Du, Y., Guan, X., Wu, C.: Maximizing topic propagation driven by multiple user nodes in micro-blogging. In: Proceedings of the 38th Annual IEEE Conference on Local Computer Networks, pp. 751–754 (2013)

19. Li, X., Liu, Y., Jiang, Y., Liu, X.: Identifying social influence in complex networks: a novel conductance eigenvector centrality model. Neurocomputing **210**, 141–154 (2016)

20. Phan, N., Ebrahimi, J., Kil, D., Piniewski, B., Dou, D.: Topic-aware physical activity propagation in a health social network. IEEE Intell. Syst. **31**, 5–14 (2016)

21. Peng, S., Yu, S., Yang, A.: Smartphone malware and its propagation modeling: a survey. IEEE Commun. Surv. Tutorials **16**(2), 925–941 (2014)

22. Yu, S., Gu, G., Barnawi, A., Guo, S., Stojmenovic, I.: Malware propagation in large-scale networks. IEEE Trans. Knowl. Data Eng. **27**(1), 170–179 (2015)

FASRP: A Fully Anonymous Security Routing Protocol in MANETs

Jun Pan[✉], Lin Ma, and Kai Yu

Broadband Wireless Communications Lab,
Shanghai Institute of Microsystem and Information Technology,
Chinese Academy of Sciences, Shanghai 200050, China
{jun.pan, lin.ma, kai.yu}@mail.sim.ac.cn

Abstract. The anonymous security in MANETs has drawn more attention in the military and commercial applications. Anonymous routing protocol is designed for avoiding node identity from being leaked by other nodes during communication and insuring the communication route not to be discovered. The anonymity goals of the protocol include identity anonymity, location anonymity and route anonymity. Although some anonymous routing protocols have been proposed, the requirement is not fully satisfied. In this paper, we propose a new anonymous routing protocol, i.e., fully anonymous security routing protocol (FASRP), to satisfy the requirement and defend against some potential attacks. We prove that it is an anonymous, effective and secure routing protocol. Through the simulation in NS-2, we demonstrate that FASRP has comparable network performance with the AODV and DSR routing protocols in some applications.

Keywords: Manets · Anonymity · Security · Onion routing · IBE

1 Introduction

DSR [7] and AODV [6] are two principal on-demand routing protocols in MANETs. However, they do not provide any security and anonymity protection, which make them vulnerable to a variety of security attacks. It is difficult to provide trusted and secure communications in adversarial environments, such as battlefields. Secure routing in MANETs has been studied extensively. All secure routing protocols focus on securing route discovery, route maintenance and defending against modification and fabrication of routing information. Anonymous communications are important for MANETs in adversarial environments, in which the node identities cannot be revealed to other nodes and the routes and traffic flows between the source and destination nodes cannot be recognized for protection purposed.

In the past decade many anonymous routing protocols are proposed to implement the anonymous communications in MANETs, which can be mainly classified into two categories: topology-based [1–5] and location-based routing protocol [11–14]. We focus on topology-based on-demand anonymous routing protocols, which are general for MANETs in adversarial environments. After examining these protocols, we find that the three goals of anonymity, including identity anonymity, location anonymity, and route anonymity are not fully satisfied.

© Springer International Publishing AG 2016
G. Wang et al. (Eds.): SpaCCS 2016, LNCS 10066, pp. 292–304, 2016.
DOI: 10.1007/978-3-319-49148-6_25

Some common security mechanisms are widely used in anonymous secure routing. The trapdoor, which is initiated by ANDOR [1] and adopted by later anonymous routing protocols such as AnonDSR [4], ASR [2] and SDDR [5], is used to hide the destination true ID. To avoid the public key time-cost and energy-cost operation in the trapdoor, they advise the correspondence nodes negotiate the symmetric key in the first route discovery by public key cryptosystem, and then the source node use the symmetric key to construct the trapdoor effectively in later route discovery phase for the same destination node. However, the traditional public key cryptosystem use certificate to distribute the public key and authenticate the public key. And the authentication through traditional CA will cost more network limited resources and may disclose either nodal ID or their party membership information. The MASK [3] introduce IBE cryptosystem which can avoid the public key directory maintenance and certificate exchange in traditional CA service. However, it is a contradiction that the correspondents' ID must be kept anonymously while IBE cryptosystem should use the ID as public key. The MASK use the pseudo ID to replace the correspondents true ID to promise the anonymous security. The private key generator (PKG) should furnish each node with a large set of pseudo ID and corresponding secret point set in advance. The first limitation is that it will cost more TA resources to generate collision-resistant sufficient pseudo ID in advance and require more memory to store the pseudo ID in the each node. The second is the node has to repeat the pseudo ID when it is used up, which will influence the node anonymity.

In this paper, we devise a fully anonymous security routing protocol (FASRP) for MANETs in adversarial environments. We propose a novel method based on IBE cryptosystem to negotiate the symmetric key, and construct the trapdoor using bilinear map to hide the destination ID, thus avoiding the complex public key management in the traditional CA. The nodes can generate the pseudo public key and corresponding pseudo private key by itself. We use onion routing [8] to protect the data and routing information during the after route discovery phase and data forwarding phase.

The rest of the paper is organized as follows. Section 2 presents the protocol preliminaries. In Sect. 3 FASRP protocol is described, which consists of symmetric key anonymous negotiation phase, anonymous route discovery phase and anonymous data forwarding phase. In Sect. 4 anonymity achievements and security analysis are given. In Sect. 5 performances is analyzed. Finally in Sect. 6 conclusion and future works are described.

2 Preliminaries

2.1 The Generation of Pseudo ID Public Key in IBE

In our protocol, the PKG should also generate the private key corresponding to each node real ID in advance. But the PKG needn't generate the large set of pseudo ID for each node. The pseudo ID public key of each node can be generated by each node randomly in secret. The method not only reduces the PKG computational overhead, but also prevents the PKG to overhear the communication between nodes in MANETs to some extent. The principle basis of the method is described as follows.

We assume the PKG master key $s \in Z_q^*$ and the system parameter $\{\hat{e}, G_1, G_2, q, P, P_{pub}, H_1, H_2\}$. When node i joins the MANETs, it will get the private key SK_{IDi} from the PKG, where $SK_{IDi} = sPK_{IDi} = sH_1(ID_i)$. Now the node i can generate its pseudo public key and corresponding pseudo private key by itself to protect its anonymous security. It selects a random $r \in Z_q^*$ and generates the temporal pseudonym public key $PK_{PIDi} = rPK_{IDi} = rH_1(ID_i)$. As a result, the corresponding private key is $SK_{PIDi} = rSK_{IDi}$. The derivation process is described as following equation: $SK_{PID_i} = sPK_{PID_i} = srH_1(ID_i) = rsH_1(ID_i) = rSK_{IDi}$.

Therefore each node can randomly generate its pseudo public key and corresponding pseudo private key by itself in secret.

2.2 Network Assumption and Attack Model

- We assume that all nodes are wishing to forward the packets according to the protocol and have enough computational ability to process the algorithms in our protocol.
- We assume that the adversaries have unbounded eavesdropping capability to overwhelm any practical security protocol but bounded computing and node intrusion capabilities.
- We assume that passive adversaries can communicate with each other through private and fast communication methods, either wireless or wired. They can collaborate with each other to monitor every radio transmission on every communication link. In addition, they may compromise any node in the target network to become an internal adversary.

3 Anonymous Route Protocol

3.1 Symmetric Key Anonymous Negotiation Phase

The IBE cryptography, in which the nodes ID can be used as public key, is more effective than RSA decryption algorithm due to admissible bilinear map based on elliptic curves. We introduce the pairing [10] to construct trapdoor in the protocol. In symmetric key anonymous negotiation phase, the communication sequence number and the corresponding symmetric key, which is used to construct the trapdoor in the later route discovery phase, are exchanged anonymously. It is mentioned that we use the broadcast mode in the whole phase to protect the anonymous security.

The follows depict how the source node Alice and destination node Bob negotiate the symmetric secret key. We denote their ID as ID_A and ID_B respectively. ID_A selects the random $r \in Z_q^*$ and generates the temporal pseudo public key and pseudo private key (PK_{PIDA}, SK_{PIDA}) (refer to Sect. 2.1. The source node broadcasts symmetric key anonymous negotiation packet (SKN_{AB}) described as follows:

$$< SKN, TR_{AB}, PK_{PIDA}, S\_INFO >$$

Where the detail parts is as follows:

$$PK_{IDB} = H_1(ID_B),$$
$$f_{AB} = \widehat{e}(SK_{PIDA}, PK_{IDB}),$$
$$TR_{AB} = H_2(f_{AB}),$$
$$K_{AB} = H_3(f_{AB}),$$

$$S\_INFO = E_{K_{AB}}(REQ, SOURCE\_ID, DEST\_ID, EXP\_TIME,$$
$$Sequence\_number, Shared\_symmetric\_key)$$

SKN denotes that it is a symmetric key negotiation packet. The source node calculates the bilinear map f_{AB} by its own temporal private key SK_{PIDA} and the destination node's public key PK_{IDB}. Then they can calculate the trapdoor TR_{AB} by hash function H_2 and the temporal symmetric key K_{AB} by hash function H_3 which is used to encrypt the S_INFO symmetrically. There are six parts in the S_INFO, which is explained in the following Table 1:

Table 1. S_INFO parameters

Parameters	Description
REQ	It indicates the packet is request packet for symmetric secret key negotiation
$SOURCE\_ID$	Source node identity
$DEST\_ID$	Destination node identity
EXP_TIME	It is timeout value for symmetric key and sequence_number valid period.
$Sequence\_number$	The communication sequence number, which is used for later route discovery phase and can be generated by hashing the source address and destination address through a collision resistant one-way function [9]. It should be global unique in the MANETs. The size of it is 128 bits. It is suggested that the sequence_number should be updated synchronously by hash function between the source node and destination node in the same manner.
$Shared\_symmetric\_key$	The shared symmetric key is corresponding to sequence_number one-to-one

When nodes receive the SKN packet, process as follows:

(a) Check if the packet has been received by comparing with PK_{PIDA}. If yes, discard it silently.

(b) If no, then calculate bilinear map by using its own private key and the source node temporal pseudo public key PK_{PIDA} and get the trapdoor TR_{iA} by hash function

H_2. We can determine the node is destination node if the trapdoor TR_{iA} is equal to TR_{AB}. The reason is showed as follows:

$$f_{BA} = \hat{e}(SK_{IDB}, PK_{PIDA}) = \hat{e}(sPK_{IDB}, PK_{PIDA}) = \hat{e}(PK_{IDB}, PK_{PIDA})^s$$
$$= \hat{e}(PK_{IDB}, sPK_{PIDA}) = \hat{e}(PK_{IDB}, SK_{PIDA}) = f_{AB}$$

$$TR_{BA} = H_2(f_{BA}) = H_2(f_{AB}) = TR_{AB}$$

When ID_B assures itself as destination node, it can calculate the K_{BA} by hash function H_3. And then it decrypts the S_INFO by K_{BA} and get the communication sequence number and the corresponding shared symmetric key. After checking the packet is integrity and non-repudiation by the S_INFO content, the destination node should reply the acknowledge packet to the source node. The packet format is depicted as follows:

$$< SKN\_ACK,\ Sequence\_number,\ SIGN_{AB} >$$
$$SIGN_{AB} = E_{K_{AB}}(ACK, SOURCE\_ID, DEST\_ID, Sequence\_number,$$
$$Shared\_symmetric\_key)$$

When source node receives the SKN_ACK packet by checking the Sequence_number in the packet, it will decrypt the $SIGN_{AB}$ by secret key K_{AB} and confirm the destination node has agreed on the sequence number and shared symmetric key. To reduce the forwarding delay due to the bilinear map calculation processed by each intermediate node, we suggest the nodes broadcast the SKN packet firstly and then calculate the trapdoor. It is also helpful to hide the destination node into the intermediate nodes and protect the destination ID. Although it also incurs packet flood in the MANETs, we think it doesn't matter due to the only one-time occurrence in the communication.

Through symmetric key anonymous negotiation phase, the correspondents will negotiate the communication sequence number and the corresponding shared symmetric key which are stored into the shared symmetric key table as follows. The timer column is used to store the timer threshold value they have negotiated in EXP_TIME which is existed in S_INFO. When the timer timeout the node could delete the corresponding row entry (Table 2).

Table 2. Shared symmetric key table

Target_node	Sequence_number	Shared_symmetric_key	Timer
Node A	SEQNUM_A	SSK_A	Timer_A
Node B	SEQNUM _B	SSK_B	Timer_B
...	...	...	...

3.2   Anonymous Route Discovery Phase

The route discovery phase consists two phases: the ARREQ phase (anonymous route request phase) and the ARREP phase (anonymous route reply phase).

ARREQ Phase. During the ARREQ phase, the source node broadcasts the ARREQ packet to the destination node. The ARREQ packet contains five parts as follows:

$$< ARREQ,\ SEQNUM_{tagt},\ PK_{temp},\ TR_{tagt},\ PDO >$$

ARREQ denotes the packet is anonymous route request packet. $SEQNUM_{tagt}$ is the global unique sequence number negotiated between source and destination node in the symmetric key anonymous negotiation phase. PK_{temp} is a temporally public key, and its corresponding private key SK_{temp} is stored in the trapdoor TR_{tagt}. Only the destination node can decrypt the trapdoor and get SK_{temp}. TR_{tagt} is the trapdoor encrypted by the symmetric key which is the shared symmetric key SSK_{tagt}. It is composed of the trapdoor sign, source ID, destination ID, and the temporal private key SK_{temp}.

$$TR_{tagt} = E_{SSK_{tagt}} \big(PDO\_SIGN, ID_{tagt}, ID_{src}, SK_{temp} \big)$$

PDO is similar to the route table in the RREQ of DSR protocol. It requires that any intermediate node forwarding the ARREQ should generate the temporal pseudo ID N_i and temporal symmetric session key K_i in advance. (N_i, K_i) should be a global unique pair in the whole MANETs. And then the intermediate nodes can asymmetrically encrypt the temporal session key K_i using the temporal public key PK_{temp}. At the same time, they also symmetrically encrypt the other information such as N_i, PDO_{i-1} and dummy pad by the temporal session key K_i. The ARREQ route is showed as follows. We assume the node A is source node and node E is destination node. The following figure depicts the route flow.

The *PDO* means it is a path discovery onion, and the *PRO* means a path reverse onion. The details of *PDO* is described as follows:

$$PDO_A = \{ E_{PK_{temp}}(K_A), E_{K_A}(N_A, ID_A, PK_A, PAD) \}$$
$$PDO_B = \{ E_{PK_{temp}}(K_B), E_{K_B}(N_B, PDO_A, PAD) \}$$
$$PDO_C = \{ E_{PK_{temp}}(K_C), E_{K_C}(N_C, PDO_B, PAD) \}$$
$$PDO_D = \{ E_{PK_{temp}}(K_D), E_{K_D}(N_D, PDO_C, PAD) \}$$

When node i receives the ARREQ packet, it processes as following steps:

(1) It checks whether the $SEQNUM_{tagt}$ is the first time to be received. It will drop the packet if it has received previously.
(2) It checks whether the $SEQNUM_{tagt}$ is stored in its shared_symmetric_key table. If yes the node is the destination node and will use SSK_{tagt} to decrypt the trapdoor TR_{tagt}.
(3) If the node is not intended destination node, then:

(a) Generates the randomly nonce and the session key (N_i and K_i) which can also be generated in advance;

(b) Encrypts the K_i using the temporal public key PK_{temp} and generates the new PDO_i by encrypting the N_i and PDO_{i-1} using K_i. To defend against the packet trace attack, it can pad the dummy message to the PDO_i;

(c) Broadcasts the new ARREQ packet to the neighbor nodes;

(d) Adds N_i and K_i to the route table which is described in following Table 3. The TIMER entry is used as overtime timer and will increase when the route entry is not used for a pre-defined period. When the timer expires, it will delete the corresponding row entry.

Table 3. Anonymous route table in the intermediate node

Communication sequence number	Temporal nonce	Temporal key	Timer
$SEQNUM_{tagt}$	N_i	K_i	$timer_i$
...	...	...	...

(4) If the node is the destination node, it will decrypt the trapdoor TR_{tagt} using symmetric key SSK_{tagt}, and extract ID_{tagt} and SK_{temp}. The ID_{tagt} is used to check the destination ID again. Then the receiver decrypts the PDO_i by private key SK_{temp} and gets the (K_i,N_i) information of all nodes en route which construct the complete anonymous route from source to destination. The whole route information is defined as PR_{route} which is $\{N_A, K_A, N_B, K_B, N_C, K_C, N_D, K_D\}$.

It is noted that there may exist multiple paths from source to destination node and the destination node can select the shortest path. The multi-path is also useful for anonymous security (Table 3).

ARREP Phase. The destination node will return the ARREP (anonymous route reply) packet after receiving the ARREQ. It sends ARREP packet on unicast mode which is different from the ARREQ broadcast mode. The destination node uses the whole route (K_i,N_i) to encrypt the PR_{route} information layer by layer as an onion, which is defined as PRO_i(path reverse onion). To prevent the adversary from detecting the route by tracing ARREP identifier, we use the same identifier as data payload to mix the ARREP packet into the data packet. To distinguish the ARREP from the true ADATA packet, we add RREP identifier in the each layer encryption.

The PRO_i flow is depicted as Fig. 1. The ARREP detail format is showed as follows:

$$<ADATA, N_D, PRO_D, PAD>$$
$$PRO_D = E_{K_D}(RREP, N_C, E_{K_B}(RREP, N_B, E_{K_B}(RREP, N_A, E_{K_A}(END, PRroute))))$$
$$PRroute = \{N_A, K_A, N_B, K_B, N_C, K_C, N_D, K_D\}$$

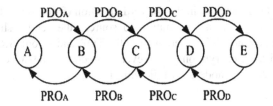

Fig. 1. Path discovery onion

PRO_D is the onion constructed by the destination node and encrypted symmetrically layered by the session key K_i corresponding to nodes en route. In the PRO_D, the RREP identifier represents the ARREP packet. When node D receives the ARREP packet, it checks whether N_D is exist in the anonymous route table. If yes it can peel off one layer by decrypting the PRO_D and get the next hop node's pseudo ID N_C. The PAD is dummy message which is used to prevent against the traffic analysis attack. Node D can also add new PAD to the new ARREP. The detail content is as follows:

$$<ADATA, N_C, PRO_C, PAD>$$
$$PRO_c = E_{k_c}(RREP, N_B, E_{k_B}(RREP, N_A, E_{k_B}(END, PRroute)))$$

The ARREP packet sent by node C is as follows:

$$<ADATA, N_B, PRO_B, PAD>$$
$$PRO_B = E_{K_B}(RREP, N_A, E_{K_A}(END, PRroute))$$

The ARREP packet sent by node B is as follows:

$$<ADATA, N_A, PRO_A, PAD>$$
$$PRO_A = E_{K_A}(END, PRroute)$$

At last the node A will get the ARREP packet according to N_A and decrypt the PRO_A. When it find the END identifier, it will know it is the destination of the packet and get the whole route information.

3.3 Anonymous Data Forwarding Phase

When source node, we assume node A, get the whole route, it can send data payload by using multi-layer encryption like TOR. To distinguish from the ARREP packet, we also introduce the PL identifier in the onion data (OD). The data packet format is described as follows:

$$<ADATA, N_i, OD_i>$$

It is mentioned that whether in the forward direction (from source to destination) or in the reverse direction (from destination to source) the sender should multi-layer encrypt the OD in advance. It is different from the TOR and AnonDSR method because they needn't multi-layer encryption in the reverse direction in advance. We describe the data flow from node A to node E as following Fig. 2:

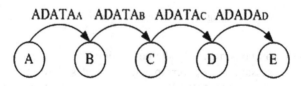

Fig. 2. Anonymous data forwarding

The data format in the different node is showed as follows:

$$ADATA_A = \{ADATA, N_B, OD_B = E_{K_B}(PL\_SIGN, N_C, OD_C), PAD\}$$
$$ADATA_B = \{ADATA, N_C, OD_C = E_{K_C}(PL\_SIGN, N_D, OD_D), PAD\}$$
$$ADATA_C = \{ADATA, N_D, OD_D = E_{K_D}(PL\_SIGN, N_E, OD_E), PAD\}$$
$$ADATA_D = \{ADATA, N_E, OD_E = E_{K_E}(PL\_END, data), PAD\}$$

The source node A firstly constructs the encrypted onion data as above and broadcasts the *ADATA* packets. The intermediate nodes check whether the N_i existed in its route table. If it is yes, it will decrypt the OD_i using the corresponding key in the route table. When the node see the *PL_SIGN* identifier, it will replace the N_i and OD_i with N_{i+1} and OD_{i+1} which are both extracted from the OD_i and construct the new $ADATA_{i+1}$. The process is repeated until the destination node receives the *PL_END* identifier.

4   Anonymity Achievement and Security Analysis

4.1   Identity Anonymity

During the symmetric key anonymous negotiation phase, we construct the trapdoor by using bilinear map and hash function. The adversary can't disclose the destination node ID with non-negligible probability. Meanwhile, the source node ID is replaced by the randomly pseudo public key and is also anonymous security.

During the anonymous route discovery phase, there are no node identity, including the source and the destination, exposed to the adversary due to the trapdoor information in ARREQ. The intermediate nodes identity is also protected by the onion encryption.

During the ARREP phase and the anonymous data forwarding phase, only the intermediate nodes' pseudo ID are exposed and ADATA packet is protected by the cryptographic onion method. So the identity anonymity is promised.

4.2   Location Anonymity

During the symmetric key anonymous negotiation phase, all packets are transferred on broadcast mode and the adversary can't locate the destination node and the source node by tracing the packet flow.

In the anonymous route discovery phase, the ARREQ is broadcast packet and the ARREP is hided in the ADATA flow. So the destination and source node are difficult to be located by tracing the ARREQ and ARREP packets.

The adversary may eavesdrop on ARREQ and ARREP packets and then deduce the distance from the source or the destination by checking the length of those packets. The method to address the problem is all packets can be padded to the same size.

4.3   Route Anonymity

During the route discovery phase, the packets are onion encrypted and their true IDs are replaced by the pseudo IDs. In addition, the discovery phase duration is not long. So it is difficult for adversary to find the route. We think the attack on the route anonymity always happen in the data forwarding phase. Of course, the adversary can't disclose the route from the packet content because the payload is onion encrypted by temporal public key.

However, the traffic analysis is a passive attack and hard to defend. One kind of traffic analysis is time analysis by monitoring the time of incoming packet and outgoing packet through some node. Refer to [9], we can buffer the incoming packet and send the buffered packet out of order. Moreover FASRP use CSMA/CD as MAC mechanism and the node may delay their packet transmission due to MAC channel collision. It also influences the time relationship between the incoming packets and outgoing packets. As a result, the adversary is difficult to find the route by timing analysis attack. The other kind of traffic analysis is packet length analysis which the adversary can trace the packet flow upon measuring the nodes input and output packet length. We introduce to pad dummy message to ADATA packet to change the packet length, and so the length information don't leak any information about packet flow.

4.4   Security Analysis

During the symmetric key anonymous negotiation phase, the trapdoor is based on bilinear map and the source node pseudo ID public key is generated in secret. So none adversary can decrypt the trapdoor and the source pseudo ID public key in polynomial time. In addition, the destination node can find whether the packet is modified by decrypting and checking the content.

S_INFO can also be helpful to resist the man-in-the-middle (MITM) attack. Although the attack can replace the pseudo public key of source ID and TR_{AB} in SKN packet by its own, the destination node can distinguish the forged packet by checking whether the S_INFO can be decrypted successfully because K_{AB} can't be forged.

During the route discovery phase, the communication sequence number and the shared symmetric key are only shared between the source and the node. And they are also updated periodically, so it is difficult for adversary to decrypt the packet and can thwart against the replay attack. In the route discovery and data forwarding phase, the intermediate nodes only use their temporal nonce and the payload are onion encrypted in advance, the adversary can't intercept the true content including route information in the packets and change the packet content.

5   Performance Evaluation

In this section, we evaluate FASRP and compare its network performance with MANET routing protocols (AODV, DSR) through the simulation. The cryptographic processing overhead evaluated in simulation is based on the [4, 9] testing results. In our simulation, we use RSA-2048 as the public key cryptosystem, AES/Rijndael (128 bit key) as the symmetric key cryptosystem, and SHA-1(160 bit) as the hash function.

The simulation is conducted within NS-2. 50 mobile nodes are randomly distributed with 1000 m-by-500 m. CBR sessions are used to generate network data traffic. For each session, data packets of 512 bytes are generated in a rate of 2 packets per second. The nodes maxim moving speed is 20 m/s. The ticks on x-axis represent the node pause time. The simulation lasts 100 s (Figs. 3, 4 and 5).

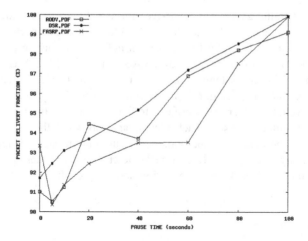

Fig. 3. Packet average delivery fraction (MAX CBR pair = 5)

The simulation results show that it is a trade-off between routing performance and anonymous security. To ensure the anonymous security, FASRP must introduce the excessive cryptographic process and lack all kinds of optimized process, which the DSR has, such as route cache, route packet snoop and Automatic Route Shortening.

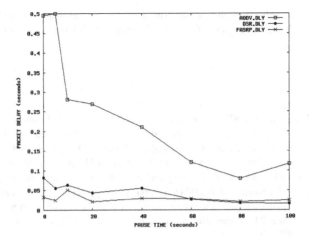

Fig. 4. Average end-to-end delay (MAX CBR pair = 5)

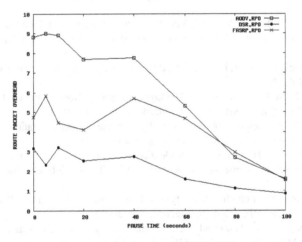

Fig. 5. Route pakcket overhead (MAX CBR pair = 5)

6 Conclusions

In order to provide an efficient, secure, and anonymous routing for MANETs in adversarial environments, we propose a novel protocol FASRP. It addresses the problems existing in other related anonymous routing protocols. Also we clarified the achievement of anonymity and security. FASRP ensures identity anonymity, location anonymity and route anonymity and strong against most known attacks. Meantime, FASRP can support multipath routing and unidirectional channel. This characteristic can strengthen the anonymous security and make FASRP more suitable for severe environment.

Acknowledgments. This research was supported in part by the National High Technology Research and Development Program of China (863 Program), SS2015AA011306.

References

1. Kong, J., Hong, X.: ANODR: anonymous on-demand routing with untraceable routes for mobile ad-hoc networks. In: Proceedings of the 4th ACM International Symposium on Mobile Ad Hoc Networking and Computing (MobiHoc 2003), pp. 291–302 (2003)
2. Zhu, B., Wan, Z., Kankanhalli, M.S., Bao, F., Deng, R.H.: Anonymous secure routing in mobile ad-hoc networks. In: Proceedings of the 29th IEEE International Conference on Local Computer Networks (LCN 2004), Tampa, USA, pp. 102–108, November 2004
3. Zhang, Y., Liu, W., Lou, W.: Anonymous communications in mobile ad hoc networks. In: Proceedings of the 24th International Conference of the IEEE Communications Society (INFOCOM 2005). IEEE (2005)
4. Song, R., Korba, L., Yee, G.: AnonDSR: efficient anonymous dynamic source routing for mobile ad-hoc networks. In: ACM Workshop on Security of Ad Hoc and Sensor Networks (SASN) (2005)
5. El-Khatib, K., Korba, L., Song, R., Yee, G.: Secure dynamic distributed routing algorithm for ad hoc wireless networks. In: Proceedings of ICPP Workshops, Kaohsiung, Taiwan, October 2003
6. Perkins, C., Belding-Royer, E., Das, S.: Ad hoc on-demand distance vector (AODV) routing, RFC 3561, July 2003
7. Johnson, D.B., Maltz, D.A., Hu, Y.: The Dynamic Source Routing Protocol for Mobile Ad Hoc Networks (DSR), April 2003. http://draft-ietf-manet-dsr-09.txt
8. Dingledine, R., Mathewson, N., Syverson, P.: Tor: the second-generation onion router. In Proceedings of the 13th USENIX Security Symposium, August 2004
9. Jiejun, K., Xiaoyan, H., Gerla, M.: An identity-free and on-demand routing scheme against anonymity threats in mobile ad hoc networks. IEEE Trans. Mob. Comput. **6**(8), 888–902 (2007)
10. D. Boneh and M. Franklin. Identify-based Encryption from The Weil Pairing. In: Proceedings of CRYPTO 2001, Springer-Verlag (2001)
11. Wu, X., Bhargava, B.: AO2P: ad hoc on-demand position-based private routing protocol. IEEE Trans. Mobile Comput. **4**(4), 335–348 (2005)
12. Defrawy, K.E., Tsudik, G.: Privacy-preserving location-based on demand routing in MANETs. IEEE J. Sel. Areas Commun. **29**(10), 1926–1934 (2011)
13. Shen, H., Zhao, L.: ALERT: an anonymous location-based efficient routing protocol in MANETs. IEEE Trans. Mob. Comput. **12**(6), 1079–1093 (2013)
14. Liu, W., Yu, M.: AASR: authenticated anonymous secure routing for MANETs in adversarial environments. IEEE Trans. Vehicular Tech. **63**(9), 4585–4593 (2014)

Privacy Protection in Mobile Recommender Systems: A Survey

Kun Xu[1] and Zheng Yan[1,2(✉)]

[1] The State Key Laboratory on Integrated Services Networks, School of Cyber Engineering,
Xidian University, Xi'an 710071, China
xidianxuk@163.com

[2] Department of Communications and Networking, Aalto University, 02150 Espoo, Finland
zyan@xidian.edu.cn

Abstract. A Mobile Recommender System (MRS) is a system that provides personalized recommendations for mobile users. It solves the problem of information overload in a mobile environment with the support of a smart mobile device. MRS has three fundamental characteristics relevant to the mobile Internet: mobility, portability and wireless connectivity. MRS aims to generate accurate recommendations by utilizing detailed personal data and extracting user preferences. However, collecting and processing personal data may intrude user privacy. The privacy issues in MRS are more complex than traditional recommender system due to its specific characteristics and various personal data collection. Privacy protection in MRS is a crucial research topic, which is widely studied in the literature, but it still lacks a comprehensive survey to summarize its current status and indicate open research issues for further investigation. This paper reviews existing work in MRS in terms of privacy protection. Challenges and future research directions are discussed based on the literature survey.

Keywords: Recommender systems · Mobile recommender systems · Privacy risks · Privacy protection · Mobile applications

1 Introduction

The wide popularity of mobile devices such as smart phones has led to huge increase of information. In the era of mobile Internet, this information can offer many services for mobile users. However, too much information in mobile Internet results in information overload, which makes mobile users become puzzled to choose what on earth they want. For example, Bob is planning a travel. After searching for "tourism" in Tuniu with his smart phone, Bob gets so many tourist sites with various positive or negative comments, so that he has no idea which one is the most suitable for him. In order to avoid such a situation, Bob needs a tool that can recommend the most suitable or interesting tourist sites for him, and this kind of tool is a recommender system.

Mobile recommender system (MRS) is a system that provides personalized recommendations for mobile users through a mobile device, thus solving the problem of information overload in mobile environments [1]. Concretely, MRS collects lots of personal

G. Wang et al. (Eds.): SpaCCS 2016, LNCS 10066, pp. 305–318, 2016.
DOI: 10.1007/978-3-319-49148-6_26

data of mobile users automatically, processes the collected data and offers useful information to target users. Compared to traditional online recommender systems based on PC desktop software, more personal data can be collected in MRS, because there are more sensors that can capture user's data in mobile devices, and there are more useful personal data can be collected in mobile environments due to mobility. These data may include demographic information such as age, gender, occupation, and social networking activities; Internet usage information such as browsing history, purchasing and rating records; context information such as location, time, and weather and so on. Then the collected data will be stored in different ways according to different system structures. By applying different recommendation methods, these personal data are processed to extract user preferences in different contexts, and the most suitable or interesting items will be recommended to the user. These recommendations are consistent with user's need or interests in different contexts. MRS can recommend various items to mobile users, such as foods, music, movies, books, friends, and tourist sites. These personalized recommendations are displayed usually in a form of list for the user to choose. Given the whole process of recommender system mentioned above, it is not difficult to find that there is so much sensitive information collected for generating recommendations, especially personalized recommendations. Moreover, the more the collected personal data are, the more accurate the recommendations. So, it seems to be a temptation for recommender systems to collect as many as possible personal data that is precious treasure in the era of big data. Unfortunately, the collection of these private data is usually carried without informing users with consent. Besides, users mostly worry about the process of their private data even though they allow data collection, and some casual displaying of recommendations for sensitive items can also make users disgusted. All above may result in privacy disclosure, so it is essential to protect the privacy of mobile users in MRS.

In this paper, we analyze the necessity and importance of researching privacy protection in MRS. We first present the definition and characteristics of MRS and review the methods adopted in MRS. Based on the analysis on the privacy risks in MRS, we propose evaluation criteria on privacy protection in MRS. We then review existing literature work by applying the criteria as a measure to comment pros and cons in order to disclose open problems and direct future research.

The rest of this paper is organized as follows. Section 2 gives a brief introduction on MRS and its specific characteristics. Section 3 proposes evaluation criteria on privacy protection in MRS based on the analysis on the privacy risks in MRS. In Sect. 4, we review the state-of-the-art in the literature by applying the criteria as an evaluation measure to comment each work's pros and cons. A further discussion about open issues and future research directions is presented in Sect. 5. A conclusion is given in the last section.

2   Mobile Recommender Systems

MRS plays an important role in obtaining a good service for providing the most interesting and suitable for mobile users. Compared to a traditional recommender system for PC users, MRS is more complicated and flexible due to the following reasons [1]: (1)

The limitation of mobile devices (e.g., screen size and computational ability), limitation of mobile environments (e.g., changeable network) and the behavior characteristics of mobile users (e.g., casual and changeable status, as well as mobility). (2) MRS features in location awareness and ubiquity, which is a big advantage compared to PC-based recommender system. MRS has three specific characteristics relevant to mobile Internet: mobility, portability and wireless connectivity.

Mobility means that mobile users and mobile devices can obtain information services at different locations and in different moving status. For example, Bob can get recommendations for restaurants and foods from MRS when he is on his way of travel. Portability focuses on mobile devices used for accessing MRS. These devices can be carried on with mobile users. Portability guarantees that MRS is able to quickly perceive the change of user contexts. Wireless connectivity means that mobile devices access MRS by means of a wireless technology such as Wi-Fi, UMTS, and Bluetooth. Wireless connectivity guarantees that mobile users can get recommendation services quickly at any time.

MRS aims to provide accurate recommendations for mobile users by collecting and processing their personal data with effective recommendation methods. There are many recommendation methods developed in these years [19, 23], e.g., traditional methods such as collaborative filtering, content-based filtering, demographic-based mechanisms, knowledge-based schemes, hybrid, and computational intelligence-based methods (e.g., Bayesian classifier, artificial neural networks, clustering, genetic algorithms, and fuzzy set theory, etc.). Recently developed advanced methods have a significant relationship with mobile Internet, which could be based on social networks, context awareness, and group recommendation [26]. Instead of discussing all methods mentioned above, this paper focuses on the recent advances of MRS, i.e., social network-based methods, context-based solutions, and group recommendations. Importantly, we can get clear sense of privacy issues in MRS by reviewing the recently developed methods.

Social network-based recommendation methods utilize users' social networks. More and more social software in smart phones make it easy for MRS to collect users' social information such as social relationships and hobbies. Rich personal data and tight social relationships guarantee that MRS can obtain more data that can be used for building up a graph-based model or a matrix-based model and further calculating user preferences for recommendation. However, there is no doubt that personal data, including some sensitive data, could be utilized by the MRS without vigilance.

Context-based methods utilize context information to enrich data and improve the accuracy of recommendation. Context information means any information that can be used to characterize the situation of an entity such as a person, a place, or any interactive objects [26]. In a mobile Internet environment, there are many context information data (e.g., location and weather) that can be collected by mobile devices and enrich user's personal data. It should be noted that user location is actually private information in many cases.

Group recommendation focuses on providing recommendation for group members. In the group recommendation, each user is inside in a certain group. The personal data of each user are generally aggregated and processed for generating recommendations for the group [26]. The group recommendation offers great applications to group members with common characters or hobbies in some specific items, such as music, movies, and games. Group recommendation can protect user's privacy to some extent by confusing privacy of personal data, but there is a risk that one user's privacy may be inferred from group recommendation results.

We notify that a recommender system is almost the same as personalization-based system [27]. On one hand, both of them can utilize user profile to provide personalized recommendation services by collecting and processing user personal data. Besides, the problem of privacy data protection exists in both of their process. On the other hand, there is a little difference between them, i.e., personalization-based system focuses more on personal preference and satisfies user's personal needs. A recommender system has more applications than providing personalized requirements. For example, a recommender system can also recommend one item that is most suitable for a user, even though this item is not what he or she favorites. Besides, a recommender system can provide recommendation for a group while personalization-based system targets on an individual person.

3   Privacy Protection in MRS

3.1   System Model

Figure 1 shows a model of MRS. In view of the procedure of MRS [1, 19, 25–27], MRS is divided into four modules: source data collection, data storage, recommendation generation, and result display. In the module of source data collection, data of mobile users and their device information can be collected by sensors, mobile applications, Internet services, communication services, and system services. These data may contain personal information such as social networking, location, SMS, contact list and so on. These collected data will then be stored in different way according to different storage schemes. Generally, there are C/S scheme, P2P scheme and distributed scheme such as

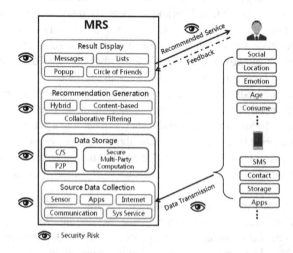

Fig. 1. A model of MRS with four modules and privacy risks marked as black eyes

security multi-party computation. And then in recommendation generation module, different recommendation methods could be adopted to process these data and generate recommendations. Finally, in result display module, the generated recommendations are provided or showed to mobile users in various ways, such as messages, popup windows, or lists.

3.2 Privacy Risks in MRS

The privacy risks arise because MRS needs to collect, store and process personal data of mobile users. Besides, casual displaying of private recommendations may also lead to privacy disclosure. Actually, personal data is the foundation for MRS to generate recommendations, and the amount, richness, and freshness of these data play important roles in the quality of the recommendations [19]. Moreover, when the system is collecting user personal data, a lot of related data will also be collected in many cases, which will result in a great danger if distrusted parties access these data. Therefore, it seems to be a contradiction that mobile users want to obtain accuracy and personalized recommendation while don't want to provide sufficient private information that is essential for generating such recommendations. This is also called "privacy-personalization trade-off".

In fact, privacy risks in MRS are, essentially, the threats of mobile user's personal data and sensitive information [27]. These threats exist in each module considering the system model of MRS. We analyze privacy risks in each module of MRS. In particular, privacy risks are classified into technology risks and policy risks according to the analysis and summarization of existing literatures [19, 23, 26, 27], as shown in Table 1.

Table 1. Privacy risks in MRS

Modules of MRS	Privacy risks	
	Technology risks	Policy risks
Data collection	Hacker attack on data transmission	Unconscious data provision
		Unauthorized data collection
		Data sharing
Data storage	Hacker attacks	Multi-cooperation
		Illegal data business
	Internal attacks on plaintext storage	Internal disclosure
Recommendation generation	Collaborative filtering analysis	Inference of sensitive information
	Machine learning	
Result display	Hacker attacks on display	Sensitive information disclosure
		Inference of recommendation outcome
		Improper display

Technology risk refers to the privacy risk caused by employing insecure technologies. In the process of data transmission, for example, hackers successfully capture user data because of the adoption of insecure protocol, thus leading to privacy disclosure. In data storage, DoS/DDoS attacks and internal attacks on plaintext storage could occur if the data center is not protected very well. During recommendation generation, the generation methods, such as collaborative filtering analysis and machine learning may discover potential private information. At recommendation result display, hackers could attack display to distort the results. Policy risk stands for the privacy risks caused by wrong execution of MRS. Some typical examples are unauthorized data collection, unconscious data provision, ineligible data sharing, multi-cooperation, illegal data trade, internal disclosure, inference of sensitive information, sensitive information disclosure, inference of recommendation outcome, and improper result display.

3.3   Evaluation Criteria

Privacy protection becomes crucially important due to the potential risks of privacy intrusion in MRS. Herein, we specify a number of criteria on privacy protection in order to measure the quality of a privacy protection scheme in MRS. Concrete criteria are described below.

(1) **Collection Security (CS)**. This requirement requests that source data collection for the purpose of recommendation generation should be secure. It is a bit vague if CS is considered as a unitary criterion. Thus, we specify the concrete requirements with regard to CS as follows:

- Transmission Security (TS_CS): personal data should be protected from being captured by adversaries during data collection [19], e.g., by applying data encryption and secure communication and transmission channel.
- Authorized Collection (AC_CS): This requirement guarantees that data collection is from a trusted source, thus support the security of data collection. To be specific, data must be collected with the permission of data owner. These personal data include unaware user-provided data, data automatically collected by a system [19, 27] and data shared among mobile applications in mobile environments.

(2) **Storage Security (SS)**. This requirement ensures that data storage is secure. Concrete requirements about SS are presented below.

- Storage Protection (SP_SS): collected personal data should be protected from divulging when they are stored in any storage media [19]. For example, hackers could attack on a server where lots of user personal data are stored, which definitely leads to privacy disclosure.
- Data Management (DM_SS): collected data access should be controlled and managed in a right way. Privacy data disclosure caused by, e.g., multi-cooperation [6, 11] and internal employees unauthorized access [19], should be avoided. Illegal data trade must be forbidden considering it is still a hard problem in practice [27]. It could be great if users can participate in this protection activity and control their collected data, instead of MRS alone.

(3) **Generation Security (GS)**. This requirement ensures that recommendation generation is secure. The main procedure of recommendation generation module is processing, calculating and generating recommendation by utilizing proper recommendation methods. So privacy protection in this module is mainly relevant to the security of data processing, analysis and mining, as described in details below.

- Processing Security (PS_GS): When generating recommendation using stored data, we should forbid inferring sensitive information from these data since this inference could cause privacy disclosure [19, 27]. Several recent studies have demonstrated that machine learning is able to discover sensitive and private personal information to some extent [19].

(4) **Display Security (DS)**. This requirement ensures that recommendation result display is secure. Concretely, it consists of two concrete requirements:

- Sensitivity Protection (SP_DS): The recommendation displaying should not leak any sensitive information of users. That is to say, when displaying recommendation, MRS should provide protective and implicit recommendation or ask user for explicit agreement. For example, explicit popup window of a recommendation for sex supplies may result in privacy disclosure if anyone else sees this recommendation.
- Resist Result Inference (RRI_DS): Public outputs of recommenders typically contain item similarity lists or cross-item correlations [19]. For instance, messages like "readers who bought this book also bought that book" are often occurred. In this case, an attacker with background knowledge on some items previously rated by a user could infer private information of the target user.

4 Solutions of Privacy Protection in MRS

Many surveys about privacy protection in recommender systems have been performed in these years [1, 2, 7, 19, 23, 26–28]. Some of them evaluated the solutions of privacy protection in recommender systems from different angles, such as information source [7, 8], policies [9, 11, 18, 28, 29] and data processing [17, 19, 20]. However, few work surveyed the literature on privacy protection in MRS. Due to the differences between traditional recommender system and MRS, it is essential to perform a survey on privacy preservation in MRS due to its specific characteristics since they may motivate new innovations and advance solutions. On the other hand, few existing surveys in the field of MRS discussed privacy protection from a bottom-up, procedure-oriented in a comprehensive way with an integral angle. Based on the procedure-oriented and bottom-up evaluation criteria proposed in Sect. 3, an overview of existing work about the solutions of privacy protection in MRS will be presented in this section. At the same time, the strengths and weakness of each solution will be discussed in a systematic and comprehensive way regarding each procedure in MRS. What's more, for the purpose of a systematic and clear survey, existing work are classified into three categories according to what specific theories and methods are applied in each solution, i.e., architecture and system design solutions, privacy-preserving algorithms and policy-based solutions.

After the discussion on the privacy and security of every solution, we compare all reviewed work in Table 2 based on the proposed criteria at the end of this section.

Table 2. Existing work comparison

Solutions	Methods	References	CS		SS		GS	DS	
			TS_CS	AC_CS	SP_SS	DM_SS	PS_GS	SP_DS	RRI_DS
Architecture and system design	Data stored in devices	[3]	–	N	Y	Y	N	N	N
		[12]	–	N	Y	Y	N	–	–
		[13]	–	Y	Y	Y	N	–	–
	C/S architecture	[8]	Y	–	Y	Y	N	–	–
	Distributed system and others	[6]	–	–	Y	N	Y	–	–
		[11]	N	Y	N	Y	N	N	N
Privacy-preserving algorithms	Anonymity algorithm	[20]	–	–	Y	N	Y	N	Y
		[16]	Y	Y	N	N	Y	N	Y
	Differential privacy	[5]	Y	Y	N	N	N	–	Y
		[4]	Y	Y	N	Y	Y	–	Y
		[7]	–	Y	N	N	Y	–	Y
		[15]	–	Y	N	N	Y	–	Y
	Cryptographic algorithm	[20]	Y	N	Y	Y	Y	N	N
		[17]	Y	–	Y	Y	Y	–	–
Policy-based solutions	Hierarchical privacy	[10]	–	Y	N	Y	N	–	Y
	Apps privacy	[21]	–	N	Y	Y	N	Y	Y
		[24]	–	N	Y	Y	N	Y	Y

4.1 Architecture and System Design Solutions

Some solutions mitigate privacy risks in MRS through architecture and system design. By assigning data and designing functions in different system modules, these solutions can achieve privacy protection.

In order to protect mobile users' private data, one straightforward approach is to store data in their own devices. In [3], the authors proposed Buying-net that is installed in a smart phone for purchase recommendations. The Buying-net is constructed by gathering all involved users and their purchase records. TS_CS wasn't mentioned in this scheme and violated AC_CS because of the automatic collection of purchase information while just informing users to select interests. Besides, SS, including SP_SS and DM_SS, was satisfied because user data were stored in their devices. PS_GS, SP_DS and RRI_DS were not satisfied because of direct and readable processing and recommending of purchase information. Storing data in user's mobile devices is also proposed in [12, 13]. In [12], a recommender system named Pythia was designed for tourism recommendation. Contextual personal data of user was automatically collected and stored in user-side, through a mobile application or desk software. And then, POI Collection Framework processes these data for providing tourism suggestions. The procedure of Pythia is similar to Buying-net, it supports SP_SS and DM_SS while AC_CS and PS_GS are not satisfied, and TS_CS, SP_DS and RRI_DS are not mentioned. Compared to [12], the difference of the proposed scheme in [13] is that mobile users are able to manage their private data and decide which information can be provided to the system, thus supporting AC_CS.

Another architecture is Client/Server structure. Magagna et al. proposed Context Aware Profile Packages (CA2P) architecture [8]. In this architecture, a client downloads all available packages from a server. All user data are stored in the client. These packages downloaded from server consist of event-vectors that are then used for matching with user-context-vectors collected from mobile users and generating personal recommendations. This scheme can protect privacy because no context information is sent from phone and the data transmission between client and server is secure, thus it supports TS_CS, SP_SS, DM_SS and PS_GS. However, how user data is collected, i.e., AC_CS is not mentioned, neither SP_DS nor RRI_DS. Besides, there is another drawback, i.e., this system is not able to update packages automatically.

Armknecht and Strufe proposed a distributed system that uses homomorphic encryption [6]. The homomorphic encryption scheme works based on real numbers, thus making it conceptually simple and more efficient to protect user data. This scheme can support SP_SS and PS_GS, while it cannot satisfy DM_SS considering privacy risks such as internal disclosure. With regard to other criteria, they were not mentioned. In [11], the authors presented the concept of trusted mobile alliance that supports DM_SS. By using a weighted road network and recommendation method based on ELECTRE III, the proposed scheme can protect mobile users' locations. The trusted mobile alliance is a third party used to communicate with a service provider and users, however, the mobile alliance is a hidden danger regarding single point attack, which makes the scheme hard to satisfy SP_SS.

4.2 Privacy-Preserving Algorithms

A number of algorithms were proposed to protect private information by converting or processing raw data. This research topic attracted much attention although current solutions are generally very complicated [19]. In general, many specific algorithms were developed for achieving anonymization, obfuscation, differential privacy and cryptographic solutions.

In [20], Clemente used k-anonymity to protect user identity. This was realized by utilizing an anonymizer installed in a user device, thus making user indistinguishable from other users. This algorithm supports SP_SS, PS_GS and RRI_DS. Another scheme using anonymity algorithm was presented in [16], which is based on DSMAS algorithm and can protect user location, identity and other sensitive information. However, a semi-trusted cloud is applied in this model, so it violates SP_SS and DM_SS.

Differential privacy provides protection by only allowing statistical queries on the data and adding noise to each response result [15]. In this way, an adversary can't learn any information about the existence of a certain user, so differential privacy can resist adversaries with background knowledge. In [5], the authors proposed a Client/Server architecture where the client is an app that sends requests and checks-in data in mobile phone while the server provides recommendations by adding noise to protect privacy. The limitation of this scheme is that the server knows all the plain data, thus this scheme cannot be deployed if the server cannot be fully trusted. Therefore, this scheme cannot support SP_SS, DM_SS and PS_GS. Other schemes proposed in [4, 7, 15] based on differential privacy can protect user privacy to some extent. However, all of them cannot fully support SS (including SP_SS and DM_SS) or hold the tradeoff between privacy and service quality.

Cryptographic solutions can mitigate privacy risks caused by the exposure of plain-text user data [19]. This exposure may include sharing data among multiple coopera-tions, inferring sensitive information, and system crash due to hacker attacks. In [20], a lightweight privacy preserving recommender system based on SMS was proposed for mobile users. In this scheme, addressable data in a user's phone such as call logs, contact lists, and SMS are transparently collected and encrypted, and then the encrypted data is sent randomly to other users for recommending new friends. The residual space in standard short messages was utilized to pad data. This scheme has little consideration on user permission for data usage, which violates AC_CS. Transmitting recommenda-tions via SMS makes it insecure considering SP_DS and RRI_DS. Besides, additive homomorphic encryption plays an important role in the area of cryptographic solutions. For example, the Paillier public-key cryptosystem is often adopted in privacy protection schemes. Erkin et al. proposed that private recommendations were generated efficiently by using homomorphic encryption and data packing [17]. Their proposed scheme intro-duces a semi-trusted privacy service provider (PSP), which is able to perform assigned tasks correctly. However, it is not allowed to observe private data because the data is encrypted, thus this scheme supports SP_SS, DM_SS and PS_GS. Besides, a protocol was also created for securing the communications between PSP and the service provider, and data packing was designed for the purpose of decreasing communication costs in order to support TS_CS. However, DS was not taken into consideration. In addition, data update and computation efficiency of this scheme can be further improved.

4.3 Policy-Based Solutions

Policy-based solutions focus on policy management in MRS. In [10], the authors proposed a hierarchical privacy architecture that provides anonymity, unlinkability, unobservability and pseudonymity to Instant Knowledge users. In this scheme, there is a 'distance' named 'proportional distance reservation', according to which users are grouped. This distance indicates the possibility that users are willing to share private information. That is to say, the far the distance between users, the less the possibility private information is shared. However, this architecture cannot guarantee SP_SS and PS_GS.

Another flourishing market is about applications of smart phones. Mobile app recommendation with security and privacy awareness was proposed in [21]. The authors developed a method based on an app-permission bipartite graph that establishes connec-tions between apps and permissions. By exploiting the requested permissions for each mobile App, potential security risks for each App can be detected automatically in the proposed scheme. Then, after striking a balance between the apps' popularity and mobile users' security concerns, the system recommends apps based on modern portfolio theory. The impact of different levels of privacy information on the performances of personalized app recommendations was further explored in [24]. The authors provided considerations about people's attitude on privacy and their behaviors on choosing apps. Knijnenburg and Kobsa described how users make information disclosure decisions in context-based recommender systems and demonstrated that satisfaction, trust, perceived threats and system-provided disclosure help were considered by users when they made information disclosure decisions [18]. All above shows that recommendations on mobile apps should be researched deeply in the running environment of apps with the concern on human privacy. Besides, some drawbacks of the above proposed scheme can be further improved, e.g., AC_CS and PS_GS are not supported in [21] and [24], because the usage information of an app is collected automatically.

4.4 A Comprehensive Comparison and Summarization

Y: supported; N: not supported; -: not mentioned

Based on the above literature overview and discussion, a comprehensive comparison and summarization of the existing literature is presented in Table 2 with regard to the evaluation criteria proposed in Sect. 3.3. As can be seen from Table 2, each kind of method is able to mitigate privacy risks in MRS to some extent, none of them, however, can satisfy all the criteria. SP_DS was seldom considered in most of work.

5 Open Research Issues and Future Research Directions

Based on the overview and analysis in Sect. 4, we can see that there are still a number of open issues and challenges in privacy protection in MRS. First, a universal and comprehensive security framework for privacy protection in MRS is missed in the literature. The existing work focused on some specific aspects of privacy and security. A comprehensive and bottom-up framework is still missed by considering the system model as described in Fig. 1. None of existing work solved the privacy risks in MRS with regard to all stages of data lifetime, i.e., data collection (including data transmission), data storage, recommendation generation, and result display, as well as user feedback. Solutions proposed in current work focus on solving some specific issue to preserve privacy in MRS. However, current research advance is not enough if we consider the whole data lifetime in MRS. It should be very promising if a solution can simultaneously satisfy CS, SS, GS and DS. Second, architecture design needs to consider solving the problem about how to guarantee the security on data storage and data process. Using Secure Multi-party Computation (SMC) to protect privacy data is a method, but we should consider resource cost and computational limitation of mobile devices. Although using distributional homomorphic encryption is a good way, its computation efficiency needs to be improved. Third, little existing researches in MRS or privacy protection in MRS took human aspects into consideration. Usable privacy preservation in MRS is an interesting research topic. Finally, there are few studies that considered DS, but it is very important issue in the design of privacy-preserving MRS.

With regard to future research direction, we think several promising research topics are worth our efforts to explore in the future. First, data collection with lightweight privacy preservation by user mobile devices should be further studied. We should innovate new solutions for MRS based on user network traffic analysis [9], social networking [14], and mobile context information [25]. Second, personalized recommendation based on mobile apps with privacy preservation is an attractive research topic since mobile smart phones are the most valuable user private data collector with unprecedented popularity. How to protect user privacy from mobile applications and recommend secure apps is a significant research topic. Third, user-centric data control in MRS with regard to the whole procedure of recommendation should be investigated. Mobile users should be able to supervise and control their own data, from data collection to scrapped data destruction and analytics.

6   Conclusion

This paper discussed the necessity and importance of privacy protection in MRS. It gave a brief survey on current literature of privacy protection in MRS based on the evaluation criteria proposed by analyzing potential privacy risks in MRS. Open issues and future research directions were also discussed to motivate future exploration.

Acknowledgments. This work is sponsored by the National Key Research and Development Program of China (grant 2016YFB0800704), the NSFC (grants 61672410 and U1536202), the 111 project (grants B08038 and B16037), the Ph.D. Programs Foundation of Ministry of Education of China (grant JY0300130104), the Project Supported by Natural Science Basic Research Plan in Shaanxi Province of China (Program No. 2016ZDJC-06), and Aalto University.

References

1. Ricci, F.: Mobile recommender systems. Inf. Technol. Tourism. **12**(3), 205–231 (2010)
2. Ackerman, M.S., Dong, T., Gifford, S., Kim, J., Newman, M.W., Prakash, A., Qidwai, S., García, D., Villegas, P., Cadenas, A., Sánchez-Esguevillas, A., Aguiar, J., Carro, B., Mailander, S., Schroeter, R., Foth, M., Bhattacharya, A., Dasgupta, P.: Location-aware computing virtual networks. IEEE Pervasive Comput. **8**(4), 28–32 (2009)
3. Kim, H.K., Kim, J.K., Ryu, Y.U.: Personalized recommendation over a customer network for ubiquitous shopping. IEEE Trans. Serv. Comput. **2**(2), 140–151 (2009)
4. Riboni, D., Bettini, C.: Differentially-private release of check-in data for venue recommendation. In: 2014 IEEE International Conference on Pervasive Computing and Communications (PerCom), pp. 190–198 (2014)
5. Riboni, D., Bettini, C.: A Platform for privacy-preserving geo-social recommendation of points of interest. In: 2013 IEEE 14th International Conference on Mobile Data Management, vol. 1, pp. 347–349 (2013)
6. Armknecht, F., Strufe, T.: An efficient distributed privacy-preserving recommendation system. In: 2011 The 10th IFIP Annual Mediterranean Ad Hoc Networking Workshop (Med-Hoc-Net), pp. 65–70 (2011)

7. Riboni, D., Bettini, C.: Private context-aware recommendation of points of interest: an initial investigation. In: 2012 IEEE International Conference on Pervasive Computing and Communications Workshops (PERCOM Workshops), pp. 584–589 (2012)

8. Magagna, F., Jaccomuthu, M., Sutanto, J.: CA2P: An approach for privacy-safe context-aware services for mobile phones. In: 2011 4th International Conference on Ubi-Media Computing (U-Media), pp. 89–94 (2011)

9. Su, X., Zhang, D., Li, W., Li, W.: Android app recommendation approach based on network traffic measurement and analysis. In: 2015 IEEE Symposium on Computers and Communication (ISCC), pp. 988–994 (2015)

10. Yau, P. W., Tomlinson, A.: Towards privacy in a context-aware social network based recommendation system. In: 2011 IEEE Third International Conference on Privacy, Security, Risk and Trust (PASSAT) and 2011 IEEE Third Inernational Conference on Social Computing (SocialCom), pp. 862–865 (2011)

11. Piao, C., Dong, S., Cui, L.: A novel scheme on service recommendation for mobile users based on location privacy protection. In: 2013 IEEE 10th International Conference on e-Business Engineering (ICEBE), pp. 300–305 (2013)

12. Drosatos, G., Efraimidis, P. S., Arampatzis, A., Stamatelatos, G., Athanasiadis, I. N.: Pythia: A privacy-enhanced personalized contextual suggestion system for tourism. In: 2015 IEEE 39th Annual Computer Software and Applications Conference (COMPSAC), vol. 2, pp. 822–827 (2015)

13. Jin, Hongxia., Saldamli, G., Chow, R., Knijnenburg, B. P.: Recommendations-based location privacy control. In: 2013 IEEE International Conference on Pervasive Computing and Communications Workshops (PERCOM Workshops), pp. 401–404 (2013)

14. Li, F., He, Y., Niu, B., Li, H., Wang, H.: Match-MORE: an efficient private matching scheme using friends-of-friends' recommendation. In: 2016 International Conference on Computing, Networking and Communications (ICNC), pp. 1–6 (2016)

15. Zhang, J. D., Ghinita, G., Chow, C. Y.: Differentially private location recommendations in geosocial networks. In: 2014 IEEE 15th International Conference on Mobile Data Management, vol. 1, pp. 59–68 (2014)

16. Piao, C., Li, X.: Privacy Preserving-based recommendation service model of mobile commerce and anonimity algorithm. In: 2015 IEEE 12th International Conference on e-Business Engineering (ICEBE), pp. 420–427 (2015)

17. Erkin, Z., Veugen, T., Toft, T., Lagendijk, R.L.: Generating private recommendations efficiently using homomorphic encryption and data packing. IEEE Trans. Inf. Forensics Secur. 7(3), 1053–1066 (2012)

18. Knijnenburg, B.P., Kobsa, A.: Making decisions about privacy: information disclosure in context-aware recommender systems. ACM Trans. Interact. Intell. Syst. (TiiS) 3(3), 20 (2013)

19. Ricci, F., Rokach, L., Shapira, B.: Recommender Systems Handbook, 2nd edn. Springer, Heidelberg (2015)

20. Clemente, F.J.G.: A privacy-preserving recommender system for mobile commerce. In: 2015 IEEE Conference on Communications and Network Security (CNS), pp. 725–726 (2015)

21. Zhu, H., Xiong, H., Ge, Y., Chen, E.: mobile app recommendations with security and privacy awareness. In: Proceedings of the 20th ACM SIGKDD International Conference on Knowledge Discovery and Data Mining, pp. 951–960 (2014)

22. Baglioni, E., Becchetti, L., Bergamini, L., Colesanti, U., Filipponi, L., Vitaletti, A., Persiano, G.: a lightweight privacy preserving SMS-based recommendation system for mobile users. In: Proceedings of the fourth ACM Conference on Recommender systems, pp. 191–198 (2010)

23. Cremonesi, P., Said, A., Tikk, D., Zhou, M. X.: Introduction to The Special Issue on Recommender System Benchmarking. ACM Trans. Intell. Syst. Technol. (TIST), 7(3), pp. 1–4 (2016)
24. Liu, B., Kong, D., Cen, L., Gong, N. Z., Jin, H., Xiong, H.: Personalized mobile app recommendation: reconciling app functionality and user privacy preference. In: Proceedings of the Eighth ACM International Conference on Web Search and Data Mining, pp. 315–324 (2015)
25. Zhu, H., Chen, E., Xiong, H., Yu, K., Cao, H., Tian, J.: Mining mobile user preferences for personalized context-aware recommendation. ACM Trans. Intell. Syst. Technol. (TIST) 5(4), 1–27 (2014)
26. Lu, J., Wu, D., Mao, M., Wang, W., Zhang, G.: Recommender system application developments: a survey. Decis. Support Syst. 74(C), 12–32 (2015)
27. Toch, E., Wang, Y., Cranor, L.F.: Personalization and privacy: a survey of privacy risks and remedies in personalization-based systems. User Model. User-Adap. Inter. 22(1–2), 203–220 (2012)
28. Reinhardt, D., Engelmann, F., Hollick, M.: Can i help you setting your privacy? a survey-based exploration of users' attitudes towards privacy suggestions. In: Proceedings of the 13th International Conference on Advances in Mobile Computing and Multimedia (MoMM 2015), pp. 347–356 (2015)
29. Zhang, B., Wang, N., Jin, H.: Privacy concerns in online recommender systems: influences of control and user data input. In: Symposium on Usable Privacy and Security (SOUPS), pp. 159–173 (2014)

Security in Software-Defined-Networking:
A Survey

Zhen Yao[1] and Zheng Yan[1,2(✉)]

[1] The State Key Laboratory on Integrated Services Networks,
School of Cyber Engineering, Xidian University, Xi'an 710071, China
zhenyaoxd@qq.com, zyan@xidian.edu.cn
[2] Department of Communications and Networking,
Aalto University, 02150 Espoo, Finland

Abstract. With the development of information and networking technologies, conventional network has been unable to meet the demands of practical applications and network users. A new network paradigm called Software-Defined Networking (SDN) was proposed and got public attention. By decoupling the forwarding and control planes and applying specific protocols, SDN greatly reduces the cost of network management. Moreover, SDN empowers network managers to program their networks with high flexibility. However, there are many network security issues with regard to SDN, which should be solved in order to ensure the final success of SDN. In this paper, we undertake an SDN security survey. We focus on analyzing SDN's security problems and reviewing existing countermeasures. Meanwhile, we identify the future research directions of SDN security.

Keywords: Software-Defined Networking · Network security · Network intrusion · Denial of Service · Network management

1 Introduction

With the development of information and networking technologies, conventional network has been unable to meet the demands of practical applications and network users [3]. In the era of information explosion, people have raised many demands on networks. They expect such networks with high efficiency, sound stability, good flexibility and advanced agility. Traditional network's routing devices integrate the function of routing control and data forwarding. This kind of working mechanism makes it hard to manage the network as a whole. Meanwhile, to realize a new desired network function, network operators have to configure each individual network device separately using low-level and often vendor-specific commands. This makes a traditional network hard to be upgraded. All of the above facts indicate that the traditional network is unable to meet practical demands at present. The traditional network mode should be improved urgently.

Software-Defined Networking (SDN) [1] makes it possible to break through the limitations of current network mode. A most prominent feature of SDN is that it physically separates the forwarding functionality of forwarding devices, known as a

G. Wang et al. (Eds.): SpaCCS 2016, LNCS 10066, pp. 319–332, 2016.
DOI: 10.1007/978-3-319-49148-6_27

data plane, from a control element, known as a control plane. The management of the entire network relies on the logically centralized control plane with no need to consider the type of the underlying devices (router, switch, firewall). This new kind of working mechanism ignores the difference between the underlying network devices, and gives the operators a very simple way to manage the network by only programing new network functions through Application Programming Interfaces (APIs).

SDN was born at Stanford University in 2006. Although it was originally used in academia to achieve the purpose of flexible control on network traffic, it also gained significant traction in industry with rapid development in these years [1]. Until now, major commercial switch vendors like Cisco, IBM, Dell, HuaWei have established research laboratories for studying SDN and manufactured some SDN based products, and others have announced intent to develop switching products to support OpenFlow [2]. The OpenFlow is a communication protocol that enables network controllers to determine the network packets' transmission paths between switches in forwarding planes. It originates from Stanford University's clean slate project. The goal of this project was to provide a platform to enable researchers to run experiments in operational networks, and the successful adoption of OpenFlow by both academia and industry has driven the development of SDN [4].

Security is obviously an important issue in developing a new Internet technology. SDN has a series of advantages when talking about security. For example, the controller in the SDN paradigm has a global network view, which helps it achieve intrusion detection quickly. The programmable features support SDN to realize many security goals in the future. But it is frustrating that SDN also faces many new security threats and attacks compared to the traditional network. Due to applying centralized control and using complicated flow tables, SDN has become a vulnerable target of Denial-of-Service (DoS) attacks. Apart from the above, how to manage numerous applications in an application plane to detect malicious and distrusted applications is still a big challenge in the SDN-based new network paradigm.

In the past few years, there are a series of researches performed to solve the security challenges of SDN. The objective of this paper is to summarize, analyze and evaluate them in order to identify future research directions. The paper is organized as follows. In Sect. 2, we introduce the architecture and characteristics of SDN in order to analyze SDN security issues and security requirements. In Sect. 3, we survey existing work about SDN security solutions, followed by open issues and future research directions discussed in Sect. 4. A conclusion is presented in the last section.

2 SDN Security

This section analyzes SDN security based on its architecture and specific characteristics. SDN is a revolutionary upgrade on the conventional networks. Its architecture is quite different from traditional ones. The specific characteristics of SDN introduce new security challenges.

2.1 SDN's Architecture and Characteristics

As is shown in Fig. 1, SDN's basic architecture [1] consists of three parts: Forwarding Plane, Control Plane and Application Plane. Since SDN's fundamental characteristic is that it decouples Control Plane and Forwarding Plane. Its architecture is enormously different from the traditional one. The forwarding plane is made up of simply inter-connected switches to form a physical network. These devices' function is forwarding packets based on control plane's routing policies.

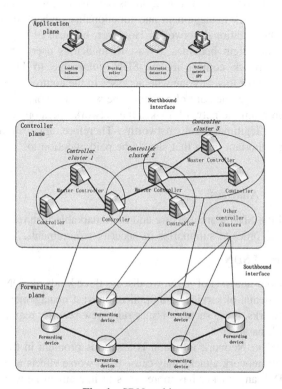

Fig. 1. SDN architecture

The control plane formulates the protocols that are used to update the forwarding tables of the forwarding plane devices. It works as the brain of the whole network. Its main task is to collect the running status of underlying devices, making routing policies and instructing the actions of forwarding devices. In a mature SDN architecture [21], a control plane is made up of controller clusters instead of a single controller. A controller cluster includes a master controller that is mainly responsible for the underlying plane's management task and some common controllers that assist the master controller to manage the whole network. What should be paid attention to is that these controller clusters are not isolated from each other. A controller can be a member of several controller clusters and a master controller may act as a common controller of other controller cluster.

The application plane is used to monitor the whole network and configure network functions. Network policies are generated in the application plane and embodied in the control plane. New network applications are also programmed in this plane, for instance, loading balance, intrusion detection and other network applications [20]. A northbound interface is responsible for the communications between the control plane and the application plane, while the forwarding plane connects the control plane with a southbound interface.

There are two most obvious characteristics of SDN [4]. The first one is the centralization of network control. The second one is the programmable feature. These two features make the network management and functionality update dramatically simplified compared to the traditional networks. However, because of these characteristics, this new network paradigm becomes a feast to malicious users and attackers. The centralization of network control makes SDN vulnerable to Denial of Services (DoS) attacks. Except for this, anyone who accesses to the controller or the application plane's host can easily get the control power of the whole network. The second feature that anyone can program the network makes the network operators hard to distinguish which application is legitimate and trustworthy. Therefore, application trust management becomes an important issue that should be paid attention to.

2.2   SDN Security Analyses

Having explained the SDN's architecture and its remarkable features, we now discuss its security issues in order to summarize its security requirements.

(1) Security Issues of SDN

Based on the previous analysis of SDN, we discuss three kinds of SDN security issues: network intrusion, denial of service, and application trust management. Different from the traditional networks, these security issues raise new security requirements on SDN based new network paradigms.

Network Intrusion: Network intrusion is a serious problem in the traditional networks. This kind of network attacks may cause even worse effects to SDN. Due to the architecture of SDN, an attacker has more ways to implement network intrusion. For example, it is quite easy for compromised controllers to access the forwarding plane, similarly, some malicious 3rd party applications may link to a pool of controllers. All of these malicious unauthorized accesses may cause data leakage. Effective security defense strategies aimed to this security issue include firewall, access control, intrusion detection and so on.

Denial of Service (DoS) and Distributed Denial of Service (DDoS): One of the biggest security weaknesses in SDN is DoS/DDoS attacks [22]. Compared to the traditional scenarios, this kind of attacks is even worse in SDN due to the logically centralized control. Given the limitation of current switches' storage capacity, their flow tables cannot contain all flows' forwarding policies. Once a switch cannot find a new incoming packet's matching rule, it will store the packet into its buffer and send a query to a controller asking for a suitable routing rule. This reactive caching mechanism makes switches and controllers vulnerable to a DoS attack. An attacker can flood a switch with packets of large payloads that belong to different flows. This switch's flow table and buffer will be filled up quickly, at this time, new legitimate incoming packets will be dropped. Meanwhile, controllers will exhaust its processing power to deal with the large amount meaningless queries causing the crash of the whole network. This attack has received extensive attention in academia. A lot of researches aimed to solve this issue. Concrete existing solutions will be reviewed in Sect. 3.

Application Trust Management: Another security problem in SDN is how to manage new network applications in the application plane. The programmable feature makes malicious applications easily embedded into the underlying network. As we known, controllers have no ability to distinguish these applications' legality and trustworthiness by themselves. Beyond that, a poorly designed or buggy application could unintentionally bring a series of new vulnerabilities to the SDN system. Therefore, how to manage the trust of a huge number of applications is an urgent problem that should be solved before a large-scale implementation of SDN. We will analyze this security issue based on the current work in the next section.

(2) Requirements of SDN Security

We summarize security requirements of SDN in order to overcome the above security issues. These requirements are criteria to protect the network, which are also used to evaluate the quality of SDN security solutions.

Confidentiality and Integrity (CI): Derived from network intrusion, *Confidentiality and Integrity* are the fundamental requirements to secure a system. In SDN, there are more network data and a variety of new applications compared to the traditional networks. An attacker can infer control policies by eavesdropping the data about network actions, so these data must be transmitted securely to prevent from malicious eavesdropping, modifying, leakage and network crash.

Authentication (Au): Authentication is an important criterion to guarantee the legitimacy of an identity in a network interaction. There are many data interactions in SDN. Some data about the control plane's routing instructions or applications' new network functionalities are even more crucial to the whole network. If these data are modified or delivered by attackers without applying any authentication methods, the network will be disordered. To sum up, authentication should be applied in SDN to ensure trustworthy interactions among network entities for supporting the resistance on network intrusions and managing the trust of network applications.

Fine-grained Access Control (FAC): FAC refers to subdividing objects in the SDN model and granting each object specific access rights. Due to the programmable feature, access control is related to more networking domains (e.g. a network programmer can access in switches and controllers) than traditional one. So we must give each network programmer a fine-grained access privilege to ensure the application's proper function in the first pass. This requirement is related to network intrusion and application trust management.

Self-healing (Sh): Aiming to mitigate the DoS attack and all kinds of applications bugs or crashes, self-healing is an essential and significant ability. Self-healing means network devices themselves can provide and maintain an acceptable level of service by making the network operate normally from an abnormal state. In order to realize self-healing in a given communication network, probable errors, faults, challenges and risks need to be identified by utilizing learning skills.

Revocability (Re): As mentioned above, the trustworthiness of an application must be guaranteed. In case an application performs maliciously, its privilege must be deprived. This requirement is an auxiliary to the application trust management.

Availability and Dependability (A\D): Availability and dependability ensure a network can operate normally and the users can enjoy the network service always. In order to realize this requirement, SDN should be able to resist any DoS or DDoS attacks. A\D should be taken into account in the security design of SDN.

3 SDN Security Countermeasures

Aiming to solve the security issues listed in Sect. 2, we survey the existing work about SDN security by applying the security requirements to evaluate its performance.

3.1 Network Intrusion

Dotcenko et al. proposed an algorithm to realize information security management. This algorithm is based on soft computing, which was implemented for intrusion detection in SDN [5]. Its prototype implementation consists of statistic collection, processing module and decision-making module, which are based on the Beacon controller in Java. The algorithm first collects and aggregates network statistical data. Then, it processes these statistical data and makes operation decisions, finally they train the decision-making module by applying machine learning techniques to adapt to a constantly changing environment. The intrusion detection was implemented based on the algorithms called TRW-CB and Rate Limit. Performance evaluation was performed with a mininet OpenFlow emulator. As a result, the proposed system was able to identify 95 % of tested attacks at 1.2 % false positives. By analyzing this work, we find this work does not consider FAC, but basically satisfies C/I and Au.

In [6], Klaedtke et al. presented an access control scheme for the southbound API of SDN controllers based on the OpenFlow model. This scheme designed based on three aspects: control access subjects and objects, permissions, and policies. In this scheme, four permissions are used, which are reading statistics, requesting information about an object, modifying an object's state, and subscription permissions. The access control scheme comprises a mandatory access control component managed by a network administrator and a discretionary one that allows subjects to delegate permissions to other subjects. This work satisfies FAC and Au and basically satisfies the C/I.

Hu et al. introduce FLOWGUARD [7], a comprehensive firewall framework that checks flow path spaces to detect firewall policy violations when OPENFLOW network states are updated. The core component of this framework is a new kind of violation detection and resolution method. The violation detection is based on flow path space analysis and firewall authorization space partition to discover the violation. Compared to the conventional firewalls that directly reject the flows violated a firewall policy, the new scheme's violation resolution is more refined by five different violation resolution strategies: flow rejecting, dependency breaking, update rejecting, flow removing and packet blocking. Their work evaluation shows that this work is more effective than the current firewall like Floodlight built-in firewall (FW) when a new flow rule is installed. Future direction of this work includes integrating the conflict detection and resolution solution into popular SDN controllers to test whether this solution is able to establish a robust security enforcement firewall for SDN controllers in a real environment. This work support Au, C/I, and FAC.

In Table 1, we summarize the above solutions against SDN network intrusions.

Table 1. Solutions against SDN network intrusions

Research work	Research goal	Proposed solution
An intrusion detection prototype [5]	Network data collection and intrusion detection	An information security management algorithm and implemented an intrusion detection prototype
Klaedtke's access control scheme [6]	Access control	A new access control scheme for SDN
FLOW-GUARD [7]	Firewall policy in dynamic OpenFlow network	A new violation detection method that tracks network flow paths and a refined violation resolution to build a robust firewall

3.2   Denial of Service (DoS) and Distributed Denial of Service (DDoS)

As DoS/DDoS is an obvious security threat to SDN, we survey the existing work to deal with this problem. In [9], the authors proposed a new DDoS blocking scheme against botnet-based attack, which was implemented in Python and run on the POX controller. The new scheme adds an additional module between switches and servers, which is called DBA (DDoS Blocking Application). When a botnet begins to launch DDoS attacks, the DBA will find it according to its action that it creates new entries flows' number exceeding a threshold. Then DBA provides a new IP address to the server. Once the server opens a new socket at a new redirect address, the DBA will provide any new incoming clients with this new address D' for a normal service, and tear down the connection from this botnet to avoid DDoS attacks. This new scheme has been tested on a real POX platform and Mininet emulation. The result shows that most of bots are blocked in an acceptable time. However, this work should pay attention to the size of a drop entries' table at perimeter switches to defend a large botnet-mounted attack. It basically satisfies A/D and Sh.

Lim et al. presented a new scheme to defend against DDoS attacks called "multiQ" [10]. As we known, controller is a vulnerable target to DDoS attacks due to the limitation of capability to handle the malicious large amount requests, so this paper's scheme is to improve the controller's processing capacity by a simple scheduling-based isolation of flow requests. Compared to a single request processing queue, the new scheme's controller is logically subdivided into k queues. This can reasonably use the processing resources of a controller. However how to divide the request queue, the specific algorithm remains future work. This work only basically satisfies A/D.

DDoS detection is an effective method to mitigate DDoS attacks. Through finding this kind of attack in its early stages, a network manager can make corresponding decisions to avoid potential network collapse. In [11], the authors proposed a lightweight solution to detect DDoS attacks in SDN. The concept of entropy was used in this method. As we known, the entropy is related to randomness, and the higher randomness is, the higher entropy is. If one or a number of hosts start to receive excessive incoming packets, the randomness decreases and the entropy drops. Once the entropy is lower than the threshold, a DDoS attack is checked out. And in order to work normally in a changing network environment, this threshold can be changed according to the statistics of the whole network in practice. This method only supports A/D.

Another DDoS detection method is proposed in [12]. In this paper, a new technique called Self Organizing Maps (SOM) was presented, which is an unsupervised artificial neural network that extracts features of interest with a low overhead. Utilizing this solution, they can detect DDoS attacks effectively. This DDoS detection scheme is made up of three parts: a flow collector, a feature extractor and a classifier module. It firstly collects flow information in each condition (normal and abnormal). Secondly it selects traffic features like the average of packets per flow, the average of duration per flow, etc. Finally it uses this traffic features to classify network traffic. This method only satisfies A/D.

In [13], Oktian et al. proposed a new application on the top of the Beacon controller to detect and react to DoS attacks dynamically. The application called Dossy has six features to mitigating DoS attacks: binding, location tracker, packets filtering, port and flow statistic queries, and port status. Through a proactive strategy, the controller binds the IP and MAC address of each port in the network at the network startup, and collects each port's statistics by flow statistic queries during network operation. Once a DoS attack is launched, the controller will position the specific port and drop malicious spoofed packets from it. Because this method is based on an IP and MAC address table, this paper also proposed solutions to prevent MAC and IP spoofing. This application satisfies A/D and basically satisfies Sh.

Loading balance is another way to mitigate the negative effects of DoS attacks. Belyaev et al. present a loading balance scheme for SDN DoS attack mitigation in [14]. Compared to the L7 that is a loading balance between computing nodes, they use L4 balancing between network equipment. Their guiding ideology is to find the shortest routes for a new incoming flow. Under DoS attacks, rapidly forwarding flow is a good way to guarantee an acceptable service. A loading balance algorithm was applied. However using Bellman-ford algorithm to find the shortest route is relatively inefficient. A more efficient algorithm can make this scheme mitigate DoS attacks more effectively. This scheme basically satisfies A/D.

Solutions reviewed above mostly solve the DoS problem via applying strategies, and designing detection algorithms. A survey in [15] listed a number of methods to mitigate DoS attacks through network device deployment and the hardware improvement suggestions. In Table 2, we summarize the solutions proposed for fighting against SDN DoS/DDoS attacks.

Table 2. Solutions proposed for fighting against SDN DoS/DDoS attacks

Research work	Research goal	Proposed solution
DBA [9]	DDoS attacks launched by botnet	A new scheme that adds DBA module between switches and servers to deal with DDoS attacks
MultiQ [10]	DDoS attacks to SDN controller	A request queue mechanism in controllers
Lightweight DDoS detection method [11]	DDoS attack detection	Use the concept of entropy to detect DDoS attacks
DDoS detection method based on SOM [12]	DDoS attack detection	A flow classification method based on SOM to detect malicious DDoS attack flows
Dossy [13]	DoS attack detection and mitigate	Based on a proactive strategy to detect and mitigate DoS attacks by IP and MAC addresses
Belyaev's loading balance scheme [14]	Use loading balance to mitigate DoS attacks	A loading balance algorithm to provide an acceptable service for SDN under DoS attacks

3.3 Application Trust Management

The programmable feature makes SDN face to a new challenge on how to manage the network applications to avoid maliciously utilizing this specific feature. In this subsection, we review some related work. Hayward et al. designed a scheme to allocate permissions to network applications, which sets limitations on application operations [16]. They defined a set of permissions to which application must subscribe during initialization with controllers and introduced an Operation Checkpoint that implements permission check prior to authorizing application commands. Three kinds of problems were indicated in this work: rule conflict detection and correction, application identification and priority enforcement, which are useful for malicious activity detection and mitigation. To summarize, this work satisfies FAC and Au, but does not take C/I, Re and Sh into account.

FRESCO [8] is a significance achievement for application development. It performs as a security application development platform, which combines with NOX OPENFLOW controller. The basic framework of FRESCO consists of an application layer and a security enforcement kernel. The application layer provides four main functions: (i) script-to-module translation, (ii) database management, (iii) event management, and (iv) instance execution. A security enforcement kernel was built up to avoid rule conflicts. The emergency of FRESCO makes it possible for a network manager to design or develop a security module rapidly with a script language. Implement examples were provided in [8]. The evaluation of FRESCO shows that it enables rapid creation of popular security functions with minimal overhead (over 90 % fewer lines of code). By evaluating on FRESCO, we find that it satisfies C/I, FAC and Au, however it does not support Re and Sh.

PermOF, a fine-grained permission system was presented in [17] to apply minimum privilege on applications. This system mainly considers two aspects: the most effective set of permissions and an isolation mechanism deployed to enforce the permission control. It gives a fine-grained action permission classification to each application, and an isolation mechanism to enforce the permissions at an API entry. This work only satisfies FAC and Au.

Application fault tolerance is also a big issue need to be dealt with in application management. Chandrasekaran et al. proposed a re-design of the controller architecture, which makes the controllers and network resilient to application failures [18]. They present LegoSDN that embodies described functions by providing AppVisor – an isolation layer between SDN's applications, and NetLog – a network-wide transaction system that supports atomic updates and efficient roll backs. In this architecture, each application is run in an isolated JVM (java virtual machine), and they are handled by NETLog intensively, once there are crashes in these applications, the NETLog will support the whole network back to the normal work station based on the concerned roll-back strategies. This is a wonderful work which satisfies RE, Au and Sh and basically satisfies C/I and FAC.

In [19], the authors made efforts to solve policy conflicts in a controller. They implemented a fully-functioning SDN controller called PANE that allows a network's administrator to safely delegate his authority using his APIs. Furthermore, they proposed a new algorithm for consolidating hierarchical policies, and utilized this algorithm to accomplish application policies conflict resolution. This work takes advantage of policy atom to run policy in an isolation environment, and uses the tree-structure to store controller requests. When a new request is coming, the controller will detect whether there will be a new conflict by checking the node to the root of this request's tree. This work does not take C/I into account and basically satisfies FAC, Re, Au and Sh. In Table 3, we summarized the work related to SDN application trust management.

Table 3. Solutions related to application trust management

Research work	Research goal	Proposed solution
Operation Checkpoint [16]	Application manage	A scheme to do application identification and priority enforcement
FRESCO [8]	Security application development	A security application development platform for SDN NOX controller
PermOF [17]	Applictaion permission authorization	A fine-grained permission system to apply minimum privilege on APPs
LegoSDN [18]	Application failure recovery	A system called LegoSDN containing AppVISOR to make applications running in an isolation environment and NETLog to support network roll-back
PANE [19]	Policy authentication and conflict resolution	A new SDN controller with a new algorithm based on policy atom and tree-structure to do authorization and conflict resolution

Table 4 shows the comparison of the existing work based on SDN security requirements. In Table 4, N represents not satisfied, BS represents basically satisfied and S represents satisfied.

Table 4. Comparison of existing work based on SDN security requirements

Research work		C/I	Au	FAC	Sh	Re	A/D
Network intrusion	An intrusion detection prototype [5]	BS	BS	N			
	Klaedtke's access control scheme [6]	BS	S	S			
	FLOW-GUARD [7]	S	S	S			
Denial of Service	DBA [9]				BS		BS
	MultiQ [10]				N		BS
	Lightweight DDoS detection method [11]				N		BS
	DDoS detection method based on SOM [12]				N		S
	Dossy [13]				BS		S
	Belyaev's loading balance scheme [14]				N		BS
Application management	Operation Checkpoint [16]	N	BS	S	N	N	
	FRESCO [8]	S	S	S	N	N	
	PermOF [17]	N	BS	BS	N	N	
	LegoSDN [18]	BS	S	BS	S	S	
	PANE [19]	N	S	S	N	S	

4 Open Issues and Future Research Directions

Based on the above literature survey, we discuss open issues in SDN security and aim to propose future research directions to motivate our future research.

4.1 Open Issues

Firstly, as shown in Table 4, most work related to DoS attacks have not taken self-healing into account or cannot mitigate this attack effectively. The existing work focused on how to detect DoS attacks. But how to make the SDN return quickly from a collapse state to a normal state once the attack is launched need study in particular.

Secondly, application trust management is a complex work in SDN. The existing work solved how to deal with the conflict between these applications and how to go back to a normal state in the case that the application crashes. However, these are far from perfect, for example, an attacker can install malicious applications to controllers. How to deal with these applications to make the network work normally and find the attackers' information from these malicious applications to deprive their privileges also need to be paid attention to.

Thirdly, most existing work focused on the security scheme implementation of the controller and the forwarding devices. But how to build a security connection channel between the controller and the application plane has not be well investigated.

4.2   Future Research Directions

The above open issues motivate some future research work. First, in order to overcome the attacks raised by malicious applications, a specific application trust management system for SDN should be explored. But in the context of SDN, such a trust management system is still missing in the literature. How to evaluate trust of the applications in the SDN application plane based on their performance and effects on networking security is still an open issue. How to establish an integrated and credible trust management system that can be used to manage a mass of applications in SDN is an interesting research direction.

Second, we have mentioned that it is necessary to establish a security communication channel between the controller and the application plane. In addition, a uniform SDN security architecture is needed. The existing work only focused on partial security issues in SDN. But whether there are conflicts between different security strategies, and how to deal with these conflicts to combine them to be an integrated system level security strategy need further study.

Finally, a lot of DoS detection and mitigate methods just stay on a theoretical level or only be tested under a small-scale network topology. This is far to meet the security requirements of a real network environment. The future research should pay a great attention to implementation of these solutions in order to evaluate them in a relatively reasonable and real environment to guarantee they can work effectively.

5   Conclusion

As a new technology, SDN has become a hot topic in the IT industry. The decoupling of forwarding and control planes makes this new scheme have great advantages for supporting network flexibility and management. However the widespread popularity of SDN needs to guarantee its security and credibility. In this paper, we presented an extensive survey on SDN security issues and countermeasures. We analyzed three types of security threats and summarized the existing works related to them. Except for this, we used the security requirements to evaluate the existing work. Based on the discussion on open issues found through our survey, we proposed some valuable future research directions of SDN security.

Acknowledgments. This work is sponsored by the National Key Research and Development Program of China (grant 2016YFB0800704), the NSFC (grants 61672410 and U1536202), the 111 project (grants B08038 and B16037), the Ph.D. Programs Foundation of Ministry of Education of China (grant JY0300130104), the Project Supported by Natural Science Basic Research Plan in Shaanxi Province of China (Program No. 2016ZDJC-06), and Aalto University.

References

1. Kreutz, D., Ramos, F.M., Verissimo, P.E., Rothenberg, C.E.: Software-defined networking: a comprehensive survey. Proc. IEEE **103**(1), 14–76 (2015)
2. Ali, S.T., Sivaraman, V., Radford, A., Jha, S.: A survey of securing networks using software defined networking. IEEE Trans. Reliab. **64**(3), 1086–1097 (2015)
3. Hawilo, H., Shami, A., Mirahmadi, M., Asal, R.: NFV: state of the art, challenges, and implementation in next generation mobile networks (vEPC). IEEE Netw. **28**(6), 18–26 (2014)
4. Scott-Hayward, S., Natarajan, S., Sezer, S.: A survey of security in software defined networks. IEEE Commun. Surv. Tutorials **18**(1), 623–654 (2016)
5. Dotcenko, S., Vladyko, A., Letenko, I.: A fuzzy logic-based information security management for software-defined networks. In: 16th International Conference on Advanced Communication Technology, pp. 167–171 (2014)
6. Klaedtke, F., Karame, G.O., Bifulco, R., Cui, H.: Access control for SDN controllers. In: 3rd Workshop on Hot Topics in Software Defined Networking, pp. 219–220 (2014)
7. Hu, H., Han, W., Ahn, G.J., Zhao, Z.: FLOWGUARD: building robust firewalls for software-defined networks. In: 3rd Workshop on Hot Topics in Software Defined Networking, pp. 97–102 (2014)
8. Shin, S., Porras, P.A., Yegneswaran, V., Fong, M.W., Gu, G., Tyson, M.: FRESCO: modular composable security services for software-defined networks. In: The ISOC Network and Distributed System Security Symposium, pp. 1–16 (2013)
9. Lim, S., Ha, J., Kim, H., Kim, Y., Yang, S.: A SDN-oriented DDoS blocking scheme for botnet-based attacks. In: Sixth International Conference on Ubiquitous and Future Networks, pp. 63–68 (2014)
10. Lim, S., Yang, S., Kim, Y., Yang, S., Kim, H.: Controller scheduling for continued SDN operation under DDoS attacks. Electron. Lett. **51**(16), 1259–1261 (2015)
11. Mousavi, S.M., St-Hilaire, M.: Early detection of DDoS attacks against SDN controllers. In: 2015 International Conference on Computing Networking and Communications (ICNC), pp. 77–81 (2015)
12. Braga, R., Mota, E., Passito, A.: Lightweight DDoS flooding attack detection using NOX/OpenFlow. In: 35th Annual IEEE Conference on Local Computer Networks, pp. 408–415 (2010)
13. Oktian, Y.E., Lee, S., Lee, H.: Mitigating denial of service (DoS) attacks in openflow networks. In: 2014 International Conference on Information and Communication Technology Convergence (ICTC), pp. 325–330 (2014)
14. Belyaev, M., Gaivoronski, S.: Towards load balancing in SDN-networks during DDoS-attacks. In: 2014 International Science and Technology Conference, pp. 1–6 (2014)
15. Dabbagh, M., Hamdaoui, B., Guizani, M., Rayes, A.: Software-defined networking security: pros and cons. IEEE Commun. Mag. **53**(6), 73–79 (2015)
16. Scott-Hayward, S., Kane, C., Sezer, S.: OperationCheckpoint: SDN application control. In: 2014 IEEE 22nd International Conference on Network Protocols, pp. 618–623 (2014)
17. Kreutz, D., Ramos, F., Verissimo, P.: Towards secure and dependable software-defined networks. In: 2nd ACM SIGCOMM Workshop on Hot Topics in Software Defined Networking, pp. 55–60 (2013)
18. Chandrasekaran, B., Benson, T.: Tolerating SDN application failures with LegoSDN. In: 13th ACM Workshop on Hot Topics in NetworYks, pp. 22–28 (2014)

19. Ferguson, A.D., Guha, A., Liang, C., Fonseca, R., Krishnamurthi, S.: Participatory networking: an API for application control of SDNs. ACM SIGCOMM Comput. Commun. Rev. **43**(4), 327–338 (2013)
20. Shin, M.K., Nam, K.H., Kim, H.J.: Software-defined networking (SDN): a reference architecture and open APIs. In: 2012 International Conference on ICT Convergence (ICTC), pp. 360–361 (2012)
21. Tootoonchian, A., Ganjali, Y.: HyperFlow: a distributed control plane for OpenFlow. In: 2010 Internet Network Management Conference on Research on Enterprise Networking, pp. 3–6 (2010)
22. Yan, Q., Yu, F.R.: Distributed denial of service attacks in software-defined networking with cloud computing. IEEE Commun. Mag. **53**(4), 52–59 (2015)

Building Root of Trust for Report with Virtual AIK and Virtual PCR Usage for Cloud

Qiang Huang[✉], Dehua Zhang, Le Chang, and Jinhua Zhao

Information Assurance Technology Laboratory, Beijing 100072, China
hqcc2007@163.com

Abstract. On the basis of analyzing difficulties and opportunities for attestation and comparison of TCG and trusted computing of China, a model of building root of trust for report with virtual AIK as VM identity which is derived from the concept of AIK within TCG specification and maintaining a set of individual virtual PCR value for each VM is proposed. Furthermore, certificate management mechanisms are proposed to support this model. At last, it is analyzed from several different management dimensions and compared with TCG's method. We conclude that it can build unambiguous identity for each VM and attest to verifier VM's integrity state as well as reduce complexity of verification procedure of VM.

Keywords: Trusted computing · Virtualization · Attestation · Certificate · Integrity report · Trusted cipher module

1   Introduction

Cloud computing infrastructure is built with a rapidly increasing speed as well as researchers are more and more concerning about security of virtualization platforms. The trusted computing ability of virtualization platform is exactly required for virtual platforms because trusted computing provide root of trust from hardware and build a trusted chain from bootstrap which makes a basic security assurance for not only legacy but also virtual platform. Trusted computing group (TCG) says that cloud and trusted computing is a natural match [1] then the first step is to build root of trust in cloud. The fundamental problem of trusted computing architecture, root of trust has not been solved practically in cloud computing environment not only in China but also worldwide because of the complexities and difficulties brought by virtualization to trusted computing platform (TCP). Although Trusted Platform Module (TPM) virtualization already has some realized solutions like TPM emulator or TPM simulator in normal virtual machine monitor (VMM) structures such as Xen or KVM/QEMU, the virtualization systems have not started to adopt them until very recently [2].

According to TCG specification, root of trust contains 3 key elements: root of trust for measurement, storage and report. The TPM hardware is the Root of Trust for Reporting (RTR) because it is trusted to perform measurements correctly [3]. Indeed, report is more complicated in these elements especially in cloud because it is logically concerned more on identity, infrastructure and application. The core idea behind is that

© Springer International Publishing AG 2016
G. Wang et al. (Eds.): SpaCCS 2016, LNCS 10066, pp. 333–342, 2016.
DOI: 10.1007/978-3-319-49148-6_28

TPM must be uniquely bound to a single platform with cipher mechanisms. So how we can do with cloud environment? In this thesis we concentrate on how to identify a Virtual Machine (VM) in the cloud, furthermore, from this basis, how to report its trustworthy state to a verifier. In another word, how to expand scheme of unambiguous identity and attestation of legacy host to cloud environment.

China has made gratifying development in trusted computing theory, technique and engineering [4–6], representing with Trusted Cipher Module (TCM)/Trusted Platform Control Module (TPCM) trusted computing hardware and trusted software base (TSB) architecture [7]. It is an inspiration of this thesis and where our scheme is aim at. So we compare TCG and trusted computing (TC) of China in Sect. 2 besides introducing the related works in this area.

Section 2.3 describes how virtual Attestation Identity Key (AIK) is derived and managed for identifying the VM. Section 3 introduces virtual Platform Configuration Registers (PCR) copying mechanism needed for VM integrity status reporting. Section 4 describes the overall architecture of trusted reporting we proposed. Section 4.3 makes the final conclusion.

2   Related Works

2.1   Difficulties and Opportunities for Attestation

Generally speaking, attestation is providing some evidence or proof of platform operation, value or process, raising visibility for trust [8]. According to TCG specification [9], Remote attestation is the concrete means for TCP to report its integrity state which is one of 3 important tenets that must be simultaneously true to achieve trust. It is minimally accomplished by at least 3 entities including TCP, trusted third-party and verifier, and concerns about at least 3 layers components of TCP architecture: TPM, TSS (trusted software stack) and application enforcing attestation client.

Report value is based on a set of PCR value in TPM extended as Eq. 1. This PCR extending action is done in TPM hardware, before the report, the PCR is signed with AIK also in TPM hardware.

$$PCR'_n = HASH\left(PCR_n \| new\,hash\right) \tag{1}$$

Although it is emphasized in TCG specification, attestation faces lots of difficulties in real world. Modern commonly used software has wide and deep dependency from graphical user interface to fundamental library like glibc. It requires not dozens of as now, but hundreds of PCR for a whole report (n in Eq. 1 must be large enough), and lots of signing procedures which cannot be accepted by the using time. [10] early argues that attestation of modern OS is infeasible because of the complexity and diversity. Researchers found property-based attestation [11] to overcome these shortcomings of binary attestation, but the main obstacle above still exists.

On the other hand, cloud and other new IT infrastructure like internet of things could have already found new uses and opportunities for attestation to fulfill new security demands such as multi-tenant property or work with new security equipments like asset tags and GEOTags. Obviously in cloud employment, remote challenger role change from optional third-party to cloud user interest concerned. A good example is as follows: [8, 12] take trusted compute pools based on the attestation ability of virtual TCP in datacenter as driving market factor. Trusted compute pool is a cloud subsystem that meets the specific and varying security policies of users. By attestation mechanism, a trusted host in trust compute pool can not only report increased and visible platform integrity and status to cloud user, but also make its data protected by enforcing higher levels of protection for their more critical and security-sensitive workloads.

Table 1. Function comparisons of two kinds of TC architectures

Entries	Similarities	Differences	
		TCG	TC of China
Root of trust	Based on trusted cipher module hardware	TPM	TCM/TPCM more emphasis on control ability to resources
Chain of trust	Based on Multi-entities enforcing verification composing a transitive chain of boot and verification	Concerned more on hardware and firmware	Emphasis on trusted computing base to be measured and measure upper layer software
TCP management	Relying on infrastructure and including key, policy management elements and so on	TPM-owner based	Tend to be centralized
Trusted measurement function	TCP's main function using hash algorithm to measure entities before loading.	Emphasizing on trusted boot and launch	Emphasizing on TSB verifying executable files
Trusted authentication function	Platform authentication based on X.509 certificates	Emphasis on privacy (like Direct Anonymous Attestation protocol usage)	Enhanced identity authentication feature (typically two-factor authentication with smart card)
Trusted storage function	Securing data at-rest with key protected by TPM/TCM	Sealing method to bind data to specific system state	Mainly encrypting sensitive data with TCM keys
Trusted report function	Based on AIK signed PCR value	As killer application of TC	Not so accepted by consumer
Typical TC service	Based on measurement and identity function	Attestation	TSB
Aim of protection	Malware and component replacement	Emphasis on data integrity	Emphasis on system integrity with TSB construction

2.2 TCG and TC of China Comparison

Because attestation is not a self-contained function of TCP, sometimes it is regarded as a main kind of trust service or trust infrastructure. It is why attestation is not accepted everywhere. Our analyzing results give an integrated view as Table 1 where we list and compare all acknowledged functions of TCP and important characters of TCP. We can see trusted measurement, authentication and TCP management are most related elements to trusted report. Main characters of two TC architectures are similar but application directions of TC are different. From our view, system integrity is a higher object than data integrity. And trust compute pool based on attestation makes efforts to report system integrity as well as TSB is engaged on building solid and broad system integrity.

2.3 AIK Identity Solution

AIK is a kind of TPM signature key for trusted reporting. The TPM can produce and store a number of AIK while EK (Endorsement Key) is the platform and TPM unique-ness. AIK is generated by the TPM Owner for preventing tracking of TPMs/platforms and used to attest to current platform configuration. In another word, the attester knows an AIK comes from A TPM but not WHICH TPM. AIK requires certification by Trusted Third Party (Privacy-CA in TCG Terminology) certifying that AIK comes from a TPM. In this process of obtaining an AIK from a CA, the TPM owner creates a request and TPM signs the request with its EK. The CA verifies the EK signature and then issues an AIK credential for the TCP. The generation of AIK credential is aimed to break the correlation property between EK and AIK. The authenticity of an integrity report as pertaining to a given platform with TPM hardware is achieved using the AIK credential. So there needs to be a way to link the AIK to the credentials such that the verifier knows the AIK represents a valid TPM. The AIK credential contains most information relative to the AIK, the TPM, and the platform. It does not contain any reference or indication of the EK [13]. TCG's AIK management mechanisms described above create a basic for using it in virtual environment.

2.4 AIK Usage in VM Environment

Virtual platform work group of TCG make its trusted virtualized platform architecture specification [14] that emphasis on deep attestation that report trustworthy evidence of multiple layers from VM, VMM to hardware of a virtualized TCP. Deep attestation is not yet applied by actual systems mainly because of its complexities. We focus on iden-tity of VM here. [14] also proposes that AIK credentials include an optional certificate field called rtmType that indicates information about the trusted platform. One of the values for the rtmType field could indicate whether the underlying platform (e.g. TPM) is physical or virtual. This value could enable the VM to assert its operating on a virtual trusted platform when it presents the AIK certificate to a Remote Challenger. And the lower layer's information (like IP address or a URI) could be encoded within the AIK certificate to provide to the remote attestation verifier.

Some researchers also have made efforts to specify the AIK function in virtual Trusted Platform. [15] presents a 2-AIK PCR signing method in which one AIK stands for physical TPM signing lower part of PCRs and another stands for virtual TPM signing upper part of PCRs. The AIK standing for VTPM is saved outside of TPM, which may result in expose risk.

Related works [15–17] also denote that virtual PCR attached to each VM should contain not only VM software character value but also the same physical devices and main board character value.

The main weak point of AIK usage in VM environment is as follows: In a physical trusted platform AIK and PCR value cannot be read from outside of a TPM. Only the authorized user can produce the PCR signed value as integrity proof for attestation. In a virtual trusted machine where VTPM run on software environment, it is possible for the attacker to get the AIK private key in the same running environment of VM or even in the lower level VMM environment.

We argue that building root of trusted report in virtual computing environment like cloud datacenter concerns about two key elements: (a) independent and separated identity for each VM in its life cycle; (b) protected and migratable storage of sensitive data such as PCR value and secret keys used in a VM. Our research is based on this opinion.

3   Building RTR Based on vAIK and vPCR

3.1   Model Assumptions

First, following the normal virtualization architecture, only VMM but no VM contain the physical TPM/TCM, on the other hand, users can only see and use the VMs on which their applications are running. So VMM and physical trusted cipher module has no need to report its state to verifier. We assign one unique vAIK for each VM and no AIK for the VMM.

Second, from trusted application's view, it runs in a virtualized environment identically to the way as if it was running natively on a physical platform, using the same interface including TSS, attestation protocols and so on. So only the AIK can represent for the VM, just like AIK represent application identity in TCG specification. It is the reason why we call vAIK is a specific kind of AIK, but not a new kind of key we invited.

We propose our TCP management principles as our model assumptions:

(a) Centralized TCP management

The management of vAIK for each TP cannot depend on the same way TCG described for AIK with management systems as Privacy CA. Privacy CA do not fit for the high security level IT environment. In cloud the VTPM owner is normally more concerned about security, manageable than privacy. Virtual TCP are most likely to be used in highly security-level environment like government where centralized management is enforced.

(a) Virtualization or non-virtualization united TP management

All the trusted platforms whether they are virtualized or not should be in the same management architecture. In the view of entities, only trusted platform manager knows the differences. In the view of data, only vAIK credential carries these differences.

3.2   Management Mechanism of vAIK

The management of vAIK has some new character to perform its function. We introduce the entity of TCP Manager that makes the keys and credentials for virtual TCP and maintain all the keys, policies and information of TCP.

TCP Manager representing Trusted Platforms' owner can put max VM amount of vAIKs into TCM in advance, and validate one vAIK for each VM exactly in the VM generation procedure. All of the AIK private keys reside in TCM and cannot be exposed to upper software. In runtime, vAIK is protected in hardware and cannot be revealed to software of VMM or VM layer, which makes it a reliable presentation of VM. So the hardware-based security advantage of trusted computing cannot be compromised in vAIK scheme.

The CA only contact with the TCP Manager. TCP Manager itself can be inline or offline. In TCG specification, anyone in the delivery chain can create the credentials for its benefit. On the contrary, only TCP Manager create credentials for TCP. Indeed, it produces and maintains all the information needed for TCP management (TCP database in Fig. 1), writing data fields in credentials and making request to CA to create credentials. In next step, it receives responses from CA and delivers corresponding credentials

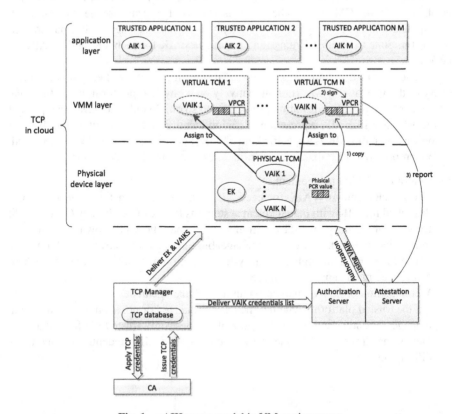

Fig. 1.   vAIK usage model in VM environment

to platforms and verifiers. Only verifier (like attestation server or authorization server in Fig. 1) determines if the evidence is correct or sufficient.

3.3 vPCR Value Copying Mechanism

PCR values dynamically represent the integrity state of host so it plays an important role for root of trusted report. It also applies to virtual situations. [14] denotes that once the VMM is operating, the platform TPM's PCRs MUST contain the extended (aggregate) set of measurements reflecting the operational state of the VMM in order to allow a remote challenger to attest the entire state of the platform.

As 2.4 said, virtual PCR attached to each VM should contain the VM private integrity state as well as the same physical devices and main board integrity state shared by the same physical platform. Normally speaking, the PCR that a VM reported should consist both the 'real' PCR value emerged from physical booting procedure and virtual PCR value recording VM software boot procedure. Because this model distinguishes the real hardware/BIOS integrity report value and VM software integrity report value with PCR and vPCR, we apply this model as well. So we develop a vPCR value copying mechanism, with which we can copy physical PCR values for each VM in its booting. This mechanism can be achieved in UEFI BIOS or VMM layer according to different architecture of platform.

4 The Overall Architecture

The overall architecture is show in Fig. 1. Every VM has its own vAIK to identify itself or its VTPM. From the verifiers standpoint the two vAIK in the same physical platform represent two different trusted platforms. All VMs belong to the same physical platform share the same EK and EK credential. VMM constructs every VM and corresponding VTPM, vAIK and vPCR at the same time and maintains them in VM lifecycle. TCP Manager is responsible for apply and deliver keys for not only the physical platform but also each VM. Users or Trusted applications running in VM can also apply their AIKs as usual following the TCG specification, which makes no conflict or confusion with vAIK usage.

The vAIK credential is used not only to verify the integrity report/status of VM in trusted virtual platforms but also directly verify VM identity. So this architecture can support authentication server with existing credential-based authentication mechanisms without any modification.

vPCR copying is denoted with 3 steps in Fig. 1 which requires physical TCM to record the physical boot state and fundamental software to perform copying action for each virtual TCM, at last, when attestation server asks for the integrity state of VM, VM signs its real and virtual combined PCR value with its vAIK and report it to the server to perform the attestation function.

4.1   vAIK Signing Method

vAIK signing function is performed following Eq. 2 below. VM report the signature results of Eq. 2 to the attestation server. In the equations below, {content} Sig(key) denote sign the content using key. To simplify the expression, we use one equation as a whole and do not distinguish every PCR index.

$$\{PCR\|vPCR\}Sig(vAIK) \tag{2}$$

To make a contrast, the PCR signing method and the integrity report value to attestation server in [15] can be summarized as Eq. 3.

$$\{PCR\}Sig(AIK1)\|\{vPCR\}Sig(AIK2) \tag{3}$$

We can conclude that the result from Eq. 2 is easier to produce and verify than the result from Eq. 3. And which makes it more complicated and time-consuming lies in virtual TCP must do signing two times and the attestation server must certificate 2 credentials (AIK1 credential and AIK2 credential) to verify the report value result from Eq. 3.

4.2   vAIK Binding Relationship

In TCG's specification, The EK credential contains information about the make, model and version of the TPM associated with the trusted platform [13]. The vAIK credential should contain information about the EK credential and hardware TCM/TPM associated with the VM. In our view, TCP Manager keeps the relationship between physical platform and its VM by binding unique information like TPM id in vAIK credential data fields. The vAIK credential may even contain EK signature if necessary so that attester can directly verify its belonging physical platform. These requirements can be satisfied because the trusted platform manager making vAIK credentials have all the information needed.

vAIK is the VM uniqueness. From the usage and management model's view, the vAIK and AIK can exist together and no logical or physical relationships bind to them. Given the VM's vAIK or vAIK credential, users can not detect whether an AIK from this VM.

4.3   Comparison and Conclusion

Beyond comparison we have made in 4.1, we compare our method with others from 2 management related respects: key tree which describes the key protection relationship and the key life cycle.

The comparison between key tree of TCG based method and our vAIK based method is as Fig. 2. The definitions of EK, SRK (Storage Root Key) and other user's keys are identical, the differences lie in that we do not apply a virtual SRK or virtual EK for each VTCM. We argue that one EK and one SRK is enough for each virtual TCM to complete its legacy functions and other special functions like migration.

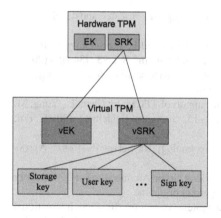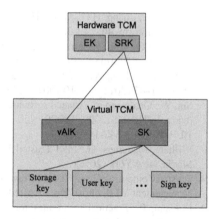

Fig. 2. Typical TCG key tree (left) and vAIK key tree (right) comparison

We contrast the vAIK & AIK responsible management entities in their life cycle as Table 2. We can conclude that our method is centralized and relying more on TCP Manager as well TCG method is more self-contained.

Table 2. The management entities and procedures of AIK & vAIK in key life-cycle

	Generation	Validate	Migration	Revoke
AIK	Privacy CA & TPM	In application requestion	Migration Controller	TPM
vAIK	TCP Manager	In VM generation	Migration Controller and TCP Manager	TCP Manager

5   Summary

A method for virtual TCP to identify itself with vAIK and provide its unique integrity state with vPCR value to verifiers like authenticator or attestation challenger is proposed. It keeps the advantage of trusted computing hardware-based security. At the next step, the security analysis of vAIK usage and management operation, the concrete vAIK verification protocols and the implementation of corresponding VM migration protocols should be made to continue this research.

References

1. Trusted Computing Group: Cloud Computing and Security – A Natural Match, April 2010. https://www.trustedcomputinggroup.org/home
2. Cucurull, J., Guasch, S.: Virtual TPM for a secure cloud: fallacy or reality? In: RECSI 2014, Alicante (2014)
3. Trusted Computing Group: TPM main part 1: design principles specification, version 1.2. https://www.trustedcomputinggroup.org/home

4. Shen, C.X., Zhang, H.G., Wang, H.M., et al.: Trusted computing research and development. Sci. Sin. Inform. **40**, 139–380 (2010). (in Chinese)
5. Zhang, H.G., Yan, F., Fu, J.M., et al.: Research on theory and key technology of trusted computing platform security testing and evaluation. Sci. China Inf. Sci. **53**, 434–453 (2010)
6. Zhang, H.G., Han, W.B., Lai, X.J., et al.: Surrey on cyberspace security. Sci. China Inf. Sci. **58**(11), 1–43 (2015). doi:10.1007/s11432-015-5433-4
7. Shi, W.: On design of a trusted software base with support of TPCM. In: Chen, L., Yung, M. (eds.) INTRUST 2009. LNCS, vol. 6163, pp. 1–15. Springer, Heidelberg (2010). doi: 10.1007/978-3-642-14597-1_1
8. William, F., James, G.: Intel Trusted Execution Technology for Server Platforms. Apress Media, New York (2013)
9. Trusted Computing Group: TCG Infrastructure Working Group Architecture Part II - Integrity Management V1.0. https://www.trustedcomputinggroup.org/home
10. England, P.: Practical techniques for operating system attestation. In: First International Conference on Trusted Computing and Trust in Information Technologies, TRUST 2008 Villach, Austria, 11–12 March 2008
11. Sadeghi, A.R., Stubl, C.: Property-based attestation for computing platforms: caring about properties, not mechanisms. In: Proceedings of the 2004 Workshop on New Security Paradigms (2004)
12. Yeluri, R., Castro-Leon, E.: Building the Infrastructure for Cloud Security. Apress Media, New York (2014)
13. Trusted Computing Group: TCG Credential Profile for v1.0, Specification Version 1.0, TCG Published, June 2005
14. Trusted Computing Group: Virtualized Trusted Platform Architecture Specification. TCG PUBLISHED. Ver 1.0 (2011)
15. Sun, Y.Q., Song, C., Xin, Y., et al.: Dual AIK signing mechanism on trusted virtualization platform. Comput. Eng. **37**(16), 114–116 (2011)
16. Berger, S., Cáceres, R., Goldman, K.A., et al.: vTPM: virtualizing the Trusted Platform Module. In: Proceedings of the 15th Conference on USENIX Security Symposium, vol. 15. USENIX Association, USA (2006)
17. Brohi, S.N., Bamiah, M.A., et al.: Identifying and analyzing security threats to virtualized cloud computing infrastructures. In: Proceedings of 2012 International of Cloud Computing, Technologies, Applications and Management, pp. 151–155 (2012)

On the Impact of Location Errors on Localization Attacks in Location-Based Social Network Services

Hanni Cheng[1], Shiling Mao[1], Minhui Xue[2,3], and Xiaojun Hei[1(✉)]

[1] Huazhong University of Science and Technology, Wuhan 430074, China
heixj@hust.edu.cn
[2] East China Normal University, Shanghai 200062, China
[3] NYU Shanghai, Shanghai 200122, China

Abstract. Location-based Social Network (LBSN) services, such as *People Nearby* in WeChat, enable users to discover users within the geographic proximity. Though contemporary LBSN services have adopted various obfuscation techniques to blur the location information, recent research has shown that based on the number theory, one can still accurately pinpoint user locations by strategically placing multiple virtual probes. In this paper, we conducted a comprehensive simulation study to examine the impact of location errors on localization attacks to track target users based on the number theory by using the LBSN services provided by WeChat. Our simulation experiments include four location error models including the exponential model, the Gaussian model, the uniform model, and the Rayleigh model. We improve the one-dimensional and two-dimensional localization algorithms where the location errors exit. Our simulation results demonstrate that the number theory based localization attacks remain effective and efficient in that target users can still be pinpointed with high accuracy.

Keywords: Privacy leakage · Localization attack · Error analysis · Location-based social network · WeChat

1 Introduction

The proliferation of smart phones has spawned the development of many popular pervasive location-based services (LBSs). In recent years, Location-Based Social Network (LBSN) services, enable users to discover their geographic neighbors and then communicate. For these services to function properly, the location of users have to be provided by the system; nevertheless, the integrity of user location privacy must be preserved. Otherwise, potential location privacy leakage may arise and users' location information may be misused by malicious attackers [1–4]. Some research has been conducted to study this new type of localization attacks and the defense schemes for mobile users against localization attacks [5,6].

© Springer International Publishing AG 2016
G. Wang et al. (Eds.): SpaCCS 2016, LNCS 10066, pp. 343–357, 2016.
DOI: 10.1007/978-3-319-49148-6_29

Among all the well-known LBSN applications, we focus our study on WeChat. With over 600 million registered users, WeChat has become the largest user group that provides an instant messaging service for intelligent terminals. WeChat also provides LBSN services by sharing instant data such as *"People Nearby,"* *"Shake,"* *"Circle of Friends,"* and *"Drift Bottles"* [7,8]. In [5], Xue et al. first conducted a theoretical study on the privacy leakage problem of online social applications and then proposed an effective approach to track target users in a simple one-dimensional case based on the number theory. In [9], Xue et al. extended a localization attack to a more general two-dimensional case. The theoretical analysis shows its effectiveness without considering the location errors. Peng et al. [10] developed a new two-dimensional algorithm in spite of location errors. In this paper, we first validate that the fundamental algorithm in [10] can work correctly; then we introduce four error models considering real-world location errors and improve the one-dimensional (1-D) algorithm and the two-dimensional (2-D) algorithm under the four error models.

The rest of the paper is organized as follows. In Sect. 2, we introduce the *"People Nearby"* service in Wechat and discuss the privacy-leakage problem due to this LBSN service. We also present the basic 1-D algorithm and the 2-D algorithm to determine the locations of users in practice. We then introduce four types of the error models in Sect. 3. Furthermore, we propose an improved 1-D algorithm in Sect. 4 and an improved 2-D algorithm in Sect. 5. Finally, we conclude the paper in Sect. 6.

2   Problem Statement

With the popularity of location-based services, improper use of user location information may bring privacy breaches. To defend against the trilateration-based localization attacks, contemporary LBSN applications have applied various obfuscation techniques to blur the location information. In the *"People Nearby"* service provided by WeChat, one obtains a list of user names and relative distances of people nearby when using *"People Nearby."* However, these relative distances are not so accurate; instead, WeChat only reports the relative distance in bands of 100 m or 1000 m. For example, two users, Alice and Bob, are using the *"People Nearby"* service. When WeChat shows to Bob that Alice is 800 m away from him, it means that Alice is located in a band centered at Bob's location with the radius ranging from 700 m to 800 m. Such a band-based approach to report a rough relative distance of nearby users, so that users are not able to obtain the accurate coordinates of target users directly. However, using the number theory, Xue et al. proved that one can pinpoint the location of a target user within a circle of radius no greater than 1 m theoretically [5]. We first examine two basic location attacks as follows.

2.1   1-D Algorithm

We first consider a special linear case. Assume that an attacker places multiple virtual probes on the line of a target user, while the probes can obtain the relative distances of the target using the *"People Nearby"* service. We summarize the notation introduced throughout this section in Table 1.

Table 1. Summary of notations for the 1-D algorithm

Symbol	Meaning
K	The length of band
x	The distance between one probe and any adjacent probe
r	The reported error generated by WeChat
d_i	The actual distance between the probe P_i and the target point
W_{p_i}	The reported distance between the probe P_i and the target point
D_{p1}	The estimated distance between the probe P_1 and the target point
$OneDim$	One-dimensional function
Z	The set of integers
$\gcd(\cdot,\cdot)$	The greatest common divisor

In Fig. 1, assuming that T is the target, a number of isometric probes are placed on the line. We can obtain the return values of the probes W_{p_i}. The relation between the reported relative distance W_{p_i} and the actual relative distance d_i can be determined following the basic 1-D algorithm in [10].

$$W_{p_i} = \left(\left\lfloor \frac{d_i}{K} \right\rfloor + 1\right) \times K, \tag{1}$$

where

$$K = \begin{cases} 100, & 0 \leq d < 1000, \\ 1000, & d \geq 1000. \end{cases} \tag{2}$$

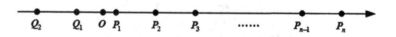

Fig. 1. Basic idea of the 1-D algorithm

In order to verify the correctness of the basic 1-D algorithm, we conducted simulation experiments using Matlab. Assume that the location error is 0, and the distances between probes are 11 m. Some representative simulation results of the 1-D algorithm are shown in Table 2.

By inspecting Table 2, we find that some errors are more than 1 m, which is unexpected. A deep examination shows for the point whose original location is already large enough since the coordinate of some probes will be exceeding 1,000 m. Based on the relationship between the actual distance and the reported distance by *"People Nearby,"* the reported distance will be 2,000 m (the band

Table 2. Some representative results of the 1-D algorithm

Actual distance (m)	Predicted distance (m)	Error (m)
322.43	322.50	0.07
555.16	555.50	0.34
804.52	833.50	8.97
24.41	24.50	0.09
371.51	371.50	0.01
491.87	491.50	0.37
466.05	466.50	0.45
41.71	41.50	0.21
617.00	622.50	5.50
578.03	578.50	0.47

will be 1,000 m). When the coordinate is too large, the 1-D algorithm is not able to work correctly. In Sect. 4, we will discuss how to reduce the errors by changing the location of the first probe. Although one is not able to locate the target within a circle of radius no greater than 1 m, over 90 % of the errors are less than 10 m. Therefore, the 1-D algorithm is sufficiently accurate for practice.

2.2   2-D Algorithm

Xue et al. developed a 2-D algorithm which can locate the target user very precisely for a triangle area [9]. Assume that the target user is in a triangle whose side length is X, as shown in Fig. 2.

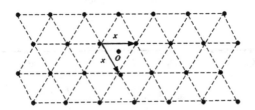

Fig. 2. Two-dimensional Lattice

The bar area is divided into several equilateral triangle whose side length is X. Xue et al. proved that one can pinpoint the target user with error no more than 1 m using the 2-D localization algorithm on all the sides of the triangle, as shown in Fig. 3.

The notation in the 2-D algorithm are shown in Table 3. We then introduce the basic principle of the 2-D algorithm. Take $\overrightarrow{X}$ direction in Fig. 3 as an example,

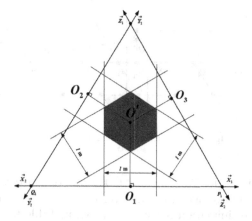

Fig. 3. An Illustration of the overlapping area

we place probe P_1 and Q_1 on the vertices of the equilateral triangle, and place p_i and q_i on the extension cord so that we can obtain the reported distance w_{p_i} and w_{q_i}, as shown in Fig. 4.

Table 3. Summary of notations for the 2-D algorithm

Symbol	Meaning
O'	The target point (the location of the user)
O_1	The first projection of the target point to a line of virtual probes
$d_{p_i} = \|O_1 P_i\|$	The actual distance from O_1 to the probe P_i
$d_{q_i} = \|O_1 Q_i\|$	The actual distance from O_1 to the probe Q_i
D_{p_i}	The estimated distance from O' to the probe P_i
D_{q_i}	The estimated distance from O' to the probe Q_i
w_{p_i}	The reported distance from O' to the probe P_i
w_{q_i}	The reported distance from O' to the probe Q_i

For the reported distance w_{p_i} and w_{q_i}, we run the 2-D algorithm to obtain the output D_{p_1} and D_{q_1}. The step $N = (\lfloor \frac{x}{K} \rfloor + 1) \times K + T \cdot s \pmod{K} + 1$ should be carefully selected; hence, we need more probes to ensure the precision if X is larger.

We conducted simulation experiments to evaluate the 2-D algorithm. If the algorithm works well in the given direction $\vec{X}$, the 2-D algorithm can pinpoint the target precisely. We place a few probes on the extension line of the triangle side in Fig. 4 and then we obtain the coordinates of the probes w_{p_i} and w_{q_i}. The parameter X is set as 99; hence, both the triangle side length and the interval of probes are 99. What we expect is that the target can be located quite precisely

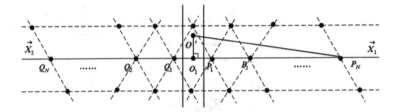

Fig. 4. Basic idea of the 2-D algorithm

in the equilateral triangle. We generate $1,000$ random targets for the tracking experiments, and the average tracking error of these $1,000$ targets is 25.15 m. Some representative simulation results are shown in Table 4.

Table 4. Some representative results of the 2-D algorithm

Actual distance (m)	Predicted distance (m)	Error (m)
42.37	49.50	7.13
84.43	49.50	34.92
22.40	49.50	27.10
63.22	49.50	13.72
9.00	49.50	40.50
77.59	49.50	28.10
69.25	49.50	19.75
66.66	49.50	17.16
46.15	49.50	3.34
27.14	49.50	22.36

These results show that most errors are much larger than what we expected. In the 2-D algorithm, if $X = 99$, we need 200 probes. As a result, most reported distances of the probes are more than $1,000$ m, so that K is $1,000$ m instead of 100 m which does not meet the assumptions of the 2-D algorithm. However, if we set X smaller, then the location range is too small that our algorithm is not practical. Therefore, we conclude that the basic 2-D algorithm should be improved. After we examine the 4 error models, we propose an improved 2-D algorithm in Sect. 5.

3   Error Models

In the previous section, we assume that the relationship between reported distance and the actual distance is determined based on Eq. (1). Nevertheless, the actual distance and the location distance reported by WeChat may not be the same. Note that the localization methods may incur errors during the positioning process. Besides, WeChat may intentionally introduce errors to the location distance in order to protect user's privacy. These location errors may differ significantly. There have been no reported studies on the system localization errors in WeChat. In this section, we assume some commonly-used error models to simulate the gap between the positioning distance and the actual distance. Based on the analysis of these error models, we aim to better understand the impact of localization errors on localization attacks in LBSN services.

3.1 Error Measurement

In order to understand the relationship between the actual relative distance and the distance reported by WeChat, we measured the total 42 sets of data points in the field. In the measurement process, we found that even at the same location, the measured distances at different time instants are not the same. Based on the analysis of these data, we conjecture that the errors follow two empirical rules:

1. The location error is relatively small comparing with the actual distance;
2. The location errors are roughly proportional to the actual distance.

3.2 Model Settings

We studied 4 commonly-used error models including the exponential distribution model, the Gauss distribution model, the uniform distribution model, and the Rayleigh distribution model. The parameters of these four models are configured following the observed empirical rules. We conducted simulate experiments with these 4 error models to evaluate the 1-D algorithm. Then, we further improve the 1-D and 2-D algorithms in spite of the location errors. To make the fair comparison, we ensure the same mean of each error model.

Exponential Error Model. Assume the exponential distribution model with the following parameter settings, in which the *exprnd* is an exponential distribution function, and the parameter is the mean value.

$$
r = \begin{cases}
0, & d \le 100, \\
\text{exprnd}(5), & 100 < d \le 200, \\
\text{exprnd}(10), & 200 < d \le 400, \\
\text{exprnd}(50), & 400 < d \le 800, \\
\text{exprnd}(100), & 800 < d \le 1200, \\
\text{exprnd}(150), & \text{otherwise.}
\end{cases}
$$

Gaussian Error Model. Assume the Gaussian distribution model with the following parameter settings, where *normrnd* is the Gauss distribution function, the first parameter is the mean, and the second parameter is the variance. Since the probability of points in range $(\mu - 3\sigma, \mu + 3\sigma)$ is 99.7%, we set $\sigma = \mu/3$ to ensure that the error is positive to match other error models.

$$
r = \begin{cases}
0, & d \leq 100, \\
\text{normrnd}(5,5/3), & 100 < d \leq 200, \\
\text{normrnd}(10,10/3), & 200 < d \leq 400, \\
\text{normrnd}(50,50/3), & 400 < d \leq 800, \\
\text{normrnd}(100,100/3), & 800 < d \leq 1200, \\
\text{normrnd}(150,150/3), & \text{otherwise.}
\end{cases}
$$

Uniform Error Model. Assume the uniform distribution model is configured with the following parameter settings, where $unifrnd$ is the uniform distribution function, the first parameter error is the maximum, and the second parameter is the minimum error.

$$
r = \begin{cases}
0, & d \leq 100, \\
\text{unifrnd}(0,10), & 100 < d \leq 200, \\
\text{unifrnd}(0,20), & 200 < d \leq 400, \\
\text{unifrnd}(0,100), & 400 < d \leq 800, \\
\text{unifrnd}(0,200), & 800 < d \leq 1200, \\
\text{unifrnd}(0,300), & \text{otherwise.}
\end{cases}
$$

Rayleigh Error Model. Note that the Rayleigh distribution meets the condition that $\mu(X) = \sigma\sqrt{\frac{\pi}{2}} \approx 1.253\sigma$. The parameter of the $raylrnd$ function in Matlab is the variance. In order to keep in line with the previous error models, the parameters are divided by the coefficient of 1.253.

$$
r = \begin{cases}
0, & d \leq 100, \\
\text{raylrnd}(5/1.253), & 100 < d \leq 200, \\
\text{raylrnd}(10/1.253), & 200 < d \leq 400, \\
\text{raylrnd}(50/1.253), & 400 < d \leq 800, \\
\text{raylrnd}(100/1.253), & 800 < d \leq 1200, \\
\text{raylrnd}(150/1.253), & \text{otherwise.}
\end{cases}
$$

3.3   Simulation Results

With the introduced location errors in the experiments, the simulation results show the degraded performance. Nevertheless, the accuracy of the location attacks still remain high as shown in Fig. 5. The performance trends with these four error model are similar, though. We will further improve the 1-D and 2-D algorithms in the next two sections.

4   Improving 1-D Algorithm

In this section, we propose to further reduce the errors by fine-tuning the position of the first probe.

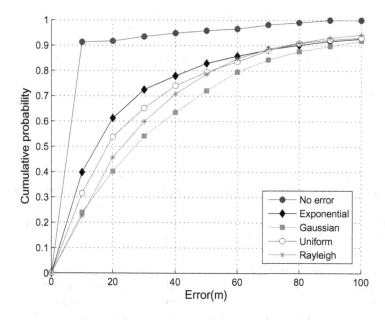

Fig. 5. Performance comparison by different error models

4.1 Basic Ideas

In Sect. 3, we assume that positioning error is proportional to the relative distance between two points. Therefore, we make preliminary positioning for the initialization of the 1-D algorithm. In the basic 1-D algorithm, probes are placed following Fig. 6. After determining the scope of 1,000 m, the first probe is placed on the origin point in the algorithm, and the rest probes are placed on the left side of the origin point in order. Eventually, the distance between the first probe and the target is used as the coordinate of the target. If the target point is far away from the origin point, the reported distance of all probes will also be very large. Hence, the error will be larger if the relative distance is large; besides, the error will increase greatly if the relative is even larger than 1,000 m.

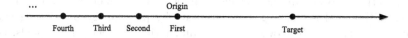

Fig. 6. Probe positioning in the 1-D algorithm

Since the distance band reported by *"People Nearby"* in WeChat is 100 m if the relative distance is less than 1,000 m, we can place 10 probes every 100 m to roughly determine the interval of the target point. Specifically, the preliminary positioning is as shown in Fig. 7.

Fig. 7. Preliminary probe positioning in the 1-D algorithm

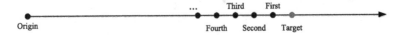

Fig. 8. Probe positioning in the improved 1-D algorithm

First of all, we place probes every 100 m within the determined 1,000 m, and we place 10 probes in total. Then, we can obtain the reported distances of the 10 probes $w_{p_i}, (1 \leq i \leq 10)$. At last we can obtain the i value corresponding to the minimum w_{p_i}. We may obtain two of i which replace the closest probes to the target point. In Fig. 6, i is 6 or 7. We want to choose the smaller one so that we set $i = 6$.

We place the first probe at coordinate $(i - 1) \times 100$, the following probes will be placed on the left side of the first probe with an equal interval as shown in Fig. 8. In this manner, the distance between all probes and the target will be smaller so that the error will decrease. The output of the 1-D algorithm is the distance between target and the first probe, so that the coordinate of the target is the output d_{p_i} added by $(i - 1) \times 100$. In summary, this improved 1-D algorithm is more accurate by reducing the distances between all the probes and the target. However, the time cost increases because the new 1-D algorithm is more complicated.

4.2   Simulation Results

We evaluate the new 1-D algorithm with the parameter $X = 11$ with the 4 error models. In Fig. 9, OneDim $v1$ is the original 1-D algorithm and OneDim $v2$ is the newly proposed 1-D algorithm. In Fig. 9, the results in four figures are very similar; the errors in OneDim $v2$ are much smaller than that in OneDim $v1$. Almost all the errors are less than 40 m in our new 1-D algorithm.

4.3   Summary

In this section, we evaluate the 1-D algorithm with 4 error models. The optimized 1-D algorithm makes tracking more accurate by preliminary positioning with these 4 error models. It shows that even under the different error models, the target can be located quite accurately using the new version, which indicates the location of users can still be tracked with high accuracy. Though the errors can be reduced, the complexity of this new 1-D algorithm increases.

5   Improving 2-D Algorithm

We have discussed that the tracking area should bounded in an equilateral triangle whose side length is upper-bounded. The 2-D algorithm cannot pinpoint

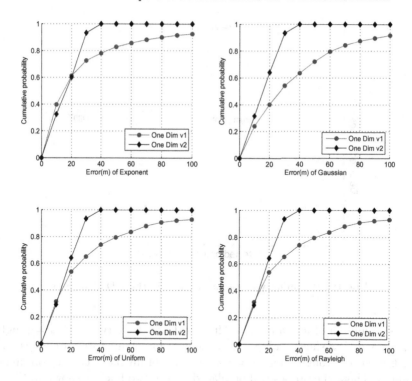

Fig. 9. Improving the 1-D algorithm to reduce errors

the target accurately if K is not 100 or extra errors exist. However, positioning errors are difficult to be neglected in practice. The tracking performance of the original 2-D algorithm is degraded with the inherent localization errors of the system. Another 2-D algorithm that can work well when extra error is added is proposed in [10]. The target user can be located precisely in an square area of $1,000 \times 1,000$. 1-D algorithm is carried out on both X axis and Y axis so that the coordinates of the target can be determined. In this section, we improve the 2-D algorithm in [10] and report our simulation results.

5.1   Basic Ideas

In Sect. 4, we notice that if the relative distances between the target and the probes are too large, the tracking results will be of less accurate. Thus, we follow the preliminary positioning idea to estimate a better initial location of the target before we use the 1-D algorithm to obtain more accurate coordinates.

First of all, we make preliminary positioning on both abscissa and ordinate as shown in Fig. 10. There is a target point in a square area of $1,000 \times 1,000$. We take the lower left corner of the square as the origin point, and place probes along the X axis and the Y axis every d m, then we obtain the reported distance w_{p_x} and w_{p_y}. P_x and P_y are the corresponding coordinates of the probe corresponding

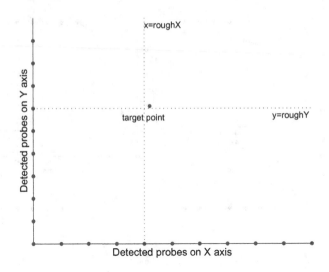

Fig. 10. Preliminary probe positioning in the 2-D algorithm

with the minimum of w_{p_x} and w_{p_y}. Afterwards, we have two lines: $x = \text{rough}X$ and $y = \text{rough}Y$ as shown in Fig. 10. In the next positioning step, we use the 1-D algorithm on $y = \text{rough}Y$ and $x = \text{rough}X$ to obtain the accurate coordinates of x and y. Then, the probes will be placed on the two lines as shown in Fig. 10.

We conduct some extra steps before by applying the 1-D algorithm. The analysis in Sects. 3 and 4 shows that larger relative distances between the probes cause larger tracking errors. As a result, if the target locates at the top right part of the square area far from the origin point, the positioning error may increase dramatically. The abnormal error may have a strong impact on the performance of the localization algorithm.

In order to reduce these above-mentioned abnormal errors, we attempt to partition the target area according to the distribution of localization errors as shown in Fig. 11. For the points on the right side of $x = M$, we still use the 1-D algorithm on $x = \text{rough}X$ and $y = \text{rough}Y$, but the first probe should be placed on the crossing point at $x = 500$ and $y = \text{rough}Y$ if we want to obtain the coordinate x. Similarly, for the points on the top side if $y = N$, the first probe should be put on the crossing of $y = 500$ and $x = \text{rough}X$ if we want to obtain the coordinate y. Figure 11 shows the detailed steps.

5.2   Simulation Results

At first we determine the values of M and N. Since the area is a square, M and N are considered to be the same. We expect that the error can be reduced to the minimum after M and N are carefully selected. The measurement of the performance is the number of points whose positioning error is more than $100\,\text{m}$, smaller n indicates better performance. For the 4 error models in Sect. 3, we start iterations from 501 to 1,000 to find the best M and N for each error model.

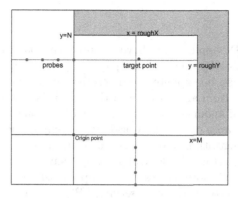

(a) 2-D probe positioning in white area

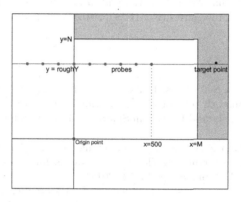

(b) 2-D probe positioning in blue area

Fig. 11. Localization steps in the 2-D algorithm (Color figure online)

The best M (or N) of the exponential model, the Gaussian model, the uniform model, and the Rayleigh Model are 512, 549, 503, and 520.

5.3 Summary

In this section, we examine the 2-D algorithm proposed in [10] with 4 error models. We can first determine the approximate location of the target user by preliminary positioning, then obtain the accurate coordinates by applying the 1-D algorithm on both X axis and Y axis. The simulation results show that the improved 2-D algorithm can still locate a target user quite accurately. Since the 2-D algorithm is more complicated, more time is needed for the tracking process. We emphasize again that the tradeoff between the accuracy and the overhead should be considered for effective attacks.

6   Conclusion

Contemporary LBSN applications have adopted the band-based approach to report distances of nearby users. In this paper, we show how the location-based feature of WeChat can be exploited to determine the user's location with great accuracy in any city from any location in the world. We examined the location algorithms developed in our previous work with 4 location error models to better evaluate the performance of the real-world attacks. Simulation results show that the improved 1-D algorithm and the 2-D algorithm still achieve good performance even under 4 error models. Our research may bring this serious privacy pertinent issue into the spotlight based on comprehensive experiment results and hopefully motivate better privacy-preserving LBSN designs.

Acknowledgments. This work was supported in part by the National Natural Science Foundation of China (No. 61370231), and in part by the Fundamental Research Funds for the Central Universities (No. HUST:2016YXMS303).

References

1. Ding, Y., Peddinti, S.T., Ross, K.W.: Beijing stalking from timbuktu: a generic measurement approach for exploiting location-based social discovery. In: ACM Workshop on Security and Privacy in Smartphones and Mobile Devices, pp. 75–80 (2014)
2. Li, M., Zhu, H., Gao, Z., Chen, S., Le, Y., Shangqian, H., Ren, K.: All your location are belong to us: breaking mobile social networks for automated user location tracking. In: ACM Mobihoc, pp. 43–52 (2014)
3. Polakis, I., Argyros, G., Petsios, T., Sivakorn, S., Keromytis, A.D.: Where's wally? Precise user discovery attacks in location proximity services. In: Proceedings of the 22nd ACM SIGSAC Conference on Computer and Communications Security, pp. 817–828. ACM (2015)
4. Xue, M., Ballard, C.L., Liu, K., Nemelka, C.L., Yanqiu, W., Ross, K.W., Qian, H.: You can yak but you can't hide: localizing anonymous social network users. In: Proceedings of the 2016 Conference on Internet Measurement Conference. ACM (2016)
5. Xue, M., Liu, Y., Ross, K.W., Qian, H.: I know where you are: thwarting privacy protection in location-based social discovery services. In: 2015 IEEE Conference on Computer Communications Workshops (INFOCOM WKSHPS), pp. 179–184 (2015)
6. Shokri, R., Theodorakopoulos, G., Papadimitratos, P., Kazemi, E., Hubaux, J.P.: Hiding in the mobile crowd: location privacy through collaboration. IEEE Trans. Dependable Secure Comput. **11**(3), 266–279 (2014)
7. Wang, R., Xue, M., Liu, K., Qian, H.: Data-driven privacy analytics: a WeChat case study in location-based social networks. In: Xu, K., Zhu, H. (eds.) WASA 2015. LNCS, vol. 9204, pp. 561–570. Springer, Heidelberg (2015). doi:10.1007/978-3-319-21837-3_55
8. Xue, M., Yang, L., Ross, K.W. et al.: Characterizing user behaviors in location-based find-and-flirt services: anonymity and demographics. Peer-to-Peer Netw. Appl. 1–11 (2016). doi:10.1007/s12083-016-0444-5

9. Xue, M., Liu, Y., Ross, K.W., Qian, H.: Thwarting location privacy protection in location-based social discovery services. Secur. Comm. Networks. **9**, 1496–1508 (2016). doi:10.1002/sec.1438
10. Peng, J., Meng, Y., Xue, M., Hei, X., Ross, K.W.: Attacks, defenses in location-based social networks: a heuristic number theory approach. In: International Symposium on Security and Privacy in Social Networks and Big Data (SocialSec), pp. 64–71, November 2015. doi:10.1109/SocialSec2015.19

Service-Oriented Workflow Executability
from a Security Perspective

Sardar Hussain[1]([✉]), Richard O. Sinnott[2], and Ron Poet[1]

[1] School of Computing Science, University of Glasgow, Glasgow G12 8QQ, UK
s.hussain.1@research.gla.ac.uk, ron.poet@glasgow.ac.uk
[2] Department of Computing and Information Systems, University of Melbourne,
Melbourne 3010, Australia
rsinnott@unimelb.edu.au

Abstract. Scientific workflows are composed of different services to support
scientific experiments. Often such services are provided by different organizations that can have their own autonomous access control policies. Workflows are
often shared and repurposed with the same and/or different datasets to repeat
scientific experiments, therefore, different users can require different privileges
to access different services to execute (enact) a given workflow. It can be the case
that a given user may not have sufficient privileges to access some of the services
of the workflow. As such, it needs to be ascertained whether a user (or enactment
engine acting on behalf of a user) with a given set of security credentials should
be allowed to enact a workflow and whether this will lead to runtime failure of
the workflow. Ideally it should be determined *a priori* whether a path exists from
the root node of the workflow graph to the leaf node, i.e. that it is possible for the
workflow to be fully executable or partially executable on the basis of the available credentials of the user. This paper presents an algorithm and its realization
that exploits existing workflow patterns to determine the structural path of the
workflow whilst checking the availability of credentials at different service points
in the workflow path.

Keywords: Workflow security · Scientific workflows · Workflow
executability · Workflow graph · Workflow path

1 Introduction

A workflow is a description of a process that typically contains a set of local and/or
distributed components (services) together with a description of how these components
can be coupled together to realise scientific objectives. One way of considering a workflow is as a set of possible execution flows and variables. The flow logic and components
interconnection are often represented in the form of a directed graph represented as G
(V, E) where G is the graph, V is the set of vertices (services) and E the set of edges
(dependencies/interactions/data flows between services). In business workflows, the
edges are mostly characterised by control-flow whilst in scientific/social science workflows, the edges are mostly characterised by data-flows [1].

© Springer International Publishing AG 2016
G. Wang et al. (Eds.): SpaCCS 2016, LNCS 10066, pp. 358–373, 2016.
DOI: 10.1007/978-3-319-49148-6_30

The dependencies between services in a workflow determine the execution paths and ordering relationships between them. In other words the components of workflows are interrelated such that the successful execution of one component is dependent on the successful completion of a previous (or number of other previous) workflow components. This ordering relationship can be realised in many different ways (patterns) as described in [2]. The actual execution can be undertaken in several ways: by an enactment engine responsible for centralized driving of the communications between services, or in a decentralised manner where workflows invoke one another directly. A workflow typically contains components and services that may either be executing locally, e.g. on the same resource as the enactment engine, or remotely. A workflow specification contains the "potential" execution and data transformations that can occur between a set of services when invoked (enacted). The internal execution mechanisms and the way such activities are interlinked are termed workflow patterns [2]. These patterns specify the flow of control amongst different activities and provide solutions to the design problems when modeling and analysing workflows. Workflow control flow patterns and their application in the business domain have been widely studied and a number of workflow languages exist that have implemented some of these patterns [3, 4]. Workflows in the scientific, data-intensive domain have also been extensively explored [5, 6].

The "actual" enactment of a workflow and the paths that are taken between services can depend on a great many factors: the run time information; service logic; and importantly here, the security information that a user or enactment engine provides. This area of security-oriented workflows has not been tackled successfully thus far, with the majority of approaches focusing on authentication-only security models [21, 22]. Finer-grained authorisation-oriented security has not been tackled and their importance in the scientific workflows was explored in our earlier work in [23, 24]. In a given workflow execution path (selected during execution), if a particular service fails to be executed either due to its unavailability or lack of sufficient credentials, the whole workflow process may fail to complete. To avoid/minimise such runtime workflow failures the required credentials to execute a given workflow should be used in advance to determine whether the workflow could be successfully enacted. To achieve this, an execution path based on the availability of credentials and security demands of individual services needs to be computed in advance. It makes no sense to execute a complex workflow involving many services if there is no way that the user provided security information will never allow that workflow to successfully complete.

The rest of the paper is organised as follows. Section 2 we discuss related work. In Sect. 3, we present an overview of workflow patterns and their security implications on successful workflow path execution. In Sect. 4 we provide the algorithm that determines whether a given workflow is executable or not from the security perspective. Section 5 discusses the application and implementation of the algorithm through a security-oriented workflow framework, and Sect. 6 presents its performance evaluation. Finally in Sect. 7 we draw some conclusions on the work as a whole and provide areas of future research.

2   Related Work

Workflows are graphs that interconnect web-services. These web services can be of many forms (SOAP, ReST etc.). Many graph algorithms exists that can be used to find the shortest paths [7, 8]. These include for example breadth first searches [9, 10] and depth first searches [11]. Researchers have worked to resolve the issue of deadlock and lack of synchronization in workflow specifications [12, 13]. Others have worked on workflow graph transformations, e.g. to calculate alternative graphs without compromising the workflow functionality [14, 15] and the identification of critical paths in a workflow graph [16]. They have, however, not considered the impact of security credentials in workflow path determination.

In [17], evaluation decisions before a workflow deployment are collected for a given workflow graph. However, in this approach the collection of evaluation decisions of individual service providers are made in the context of trust establishment at peer-to-peer level. Specifically, before deploying a business process, the engine makes sure that the services trust each other and are willing to collaborate. This model is concerned with deploying a business process from a trust perspective. It does not focus on whether a secure path exists with a given set of credentials to execute a secure workflow.

In a similar fashion, an access control consolidation approach comprising different web services in a workflow at an intra-organizational level was developed in [18]. Here the access control policies for individual services were used to consolidate an overall policy at the workflow level. In this approach the policies at the individual service level and their association with other services in the workflow path are considered to devise an overall workflow policy. Though this approach helps prevent a workflow from failure when the whole set of credentials for the complete set of services is not available, the approach is at a single organization level. This approach also requires that the security policies of each service are available before devising a consolidating policy at the workflow level. Demanding all credentials for all services is safe, i.e. the workflow can be successfully executed from a security perspective, but can be over-restricting in many cases, e.g. some paths may not be executed but the workflow can still (potentially) be successfully run to completion depending on the paths that are taken from the root node to final leaf node (first-last service). The focus of this research is to support this mechanism and allow greater flexibility and re-use of workflows by researchers with diverse security credentials. This requires analysing and checking the workflow graph to find executable workflow paths based on the availability of security credentials. The work also assumes that the credentials can be pushed to the services directly or pulled from remote attribute authorities as/when needed, i.e. it does not mandate a single approach.

3   Overview and Security Implications of Workflow Patterns

There are many features of workflows that are common across workflow languages. These aspects include structure/patterns of composition, data flow, constraints and logic amongst other features. In this research, the focus is primarily on workflow structure, since it affects many other aspects of the workflow process, e.g. the workflow path execution. Aalst et al. identified a number of workflow control patterns that are discussed in detail in [2]. These patterns were largely irrespective of implementation language. Motivation scenarios/examples of these patterns along with detailed explanation are also discussed in [2]. The basic workflow patterns are implemented in most workflow languages [11]. The formal semantics of these patterns are studied in other research work [19].

Here in this section an overview of basic workflow patterns that can affect execution of the workflow path is provided. As workflows may consist of many different services provided by different providers, the association amongst these services in the workflow graph is important since these patterns are of particular concern in workflow path determination and execution. As pointed out in the previous sections, determining whether a given workflow is executable (or not) from a security perspective depends on the availability and presentation of the credentials of the user (or the enactment engine) to access and use the services involved in the workflow graph. The aim here is to determine the impact of the availability of security credentials for services in a workflow and their association with successful workflow path determination from the security perspective. We present an overview of the basic patterns and their security implications.

3.1 Sequence Workflow Pattern

Two services in a workflow process are in sequence if the output of one service is consumed as input by the other (next) service in the workflow, i.e. the enactment of one service in a workflow process is enabled after the preceding service completes its execution. The graphical and corresponding XML representations for two services in sequence are shown in Fig. 1(a). With regard to security, this implies that the workflow can only be enacted if all credentials for all the services involved in the sequence path exist (and are held by the end user/enactment engine invoking the services).

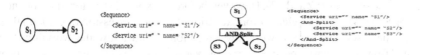

Fig. 1. (a) Sequence pattern (b) And-Split pattern

3.2 And-Split/Parallel-Split Workflow Patterns

AND-Split is used where the execution of a service is intended to cause the invocation of multiple services in parallel. In this pattern, the successful execution of all services involved in the split is necessary. Two services S2 and S3 split through And-Split are shown in Fig. 1(b). Services S2 and S3 will start concurrent execution after service S1 successfully completes. In the case of a secure workflow, enactment of such patterns requires a user/enactment engine to have credentials for all of the services to be executed.

3.3   And-Join Workflow Pattern (Synchronization)

The AND-Join pattern is used where multiple parallel executing services need to be joined into a single service in a workflow process synchronously. Three services that are synchronised through AND-Join are shown in Fig. 2(a) along with the XML representation. The execution order of the above workflow will be <S1 & S2 & S3> & S4, i.e. it leads to a single path of execution. The incoming service results for S1, S2 and S3 need to be synchronised before S4 can be executed. If any of the services in this pattern are missing or the credentials are not provided for all of the services involved, the whole workflow will fail to execute.

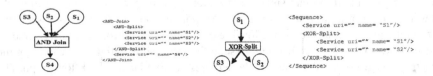

Fig. 2.   (a) AND-Join workflow pattern (b) XOR-Split pattern

3.4   XOR-Split Workflow Pattern (Exclusive Choice)

The XOR-Split is used when multiple services are called at a point in the workflow process, but where only one branch must be chosen for successful execution. The subsequent execution of one or more workflow service branches is typically based on the mechanism used in the workflow implementation (which in turn is based on the associated logic and conditions employed). A workflow path for XOR-Split may be non-deterministic. Two services S2 and S3 are shown with the XOR-Split pattern in Fig. 2(b) along with the corresponding XML representation.

   In the above scenario, S1 results in either S2 or S3 depending on the runtime decision, which is itself obtained by evaluating the logic used and/or the results obtained by executing S1. From a security perspective, it is not necessary to have credentials for both of these services (S2 and S3). However, before workflow execution, it is not known whether S2 or S3 will be selected for execution. Ideally, possession of credentials for both of these services before workflow execution would allow the workflow to be executed from any security perspective. However, possession of credentials for only one service split through XOR, may result in the workflow failing, e.g. if the logic requires the other services to be invoked as the next step in the workflow. For the services shown in Fig. 2(b), if credentials for S1 and any of S2 or S3 are available then this workflow is *potentially* executable from a security perspective.

3.5   XOR-Join/Asynchronous Join Workflow Pattern

In the XOR-Join, multiple parallel but mutually exclusive alternative services join into a single service without synchronizing in a workflow process. As such, this construct presents an opportunity to simplify a workflow process model by removing the need to explicitly replicate a sequence of tasks common to two or more branches. Instead, these branches can be joined with a merge construct and the common set of tasks needs only to be depicted once in the process model. The BPEL language supports this pattern by the *<switch>* or links within the *<flow>* construct.

This pattern is used for services previously split through the XOR-Split pattern. Three services joining through XOR-Join pattern are shown in Fig. 3(a). The execution order of the above workflow will be <S1& S4> XOR <S2 & S4> XOR <S3 & S4>. The incoming service results, namely: S1, S2 and S3, will be sequenced individually with S4. In this case it is not necessary to have credentials for all the preceding paths but just for one. Failure of a single service from S1, S2 and S3 will not lead to the failure of the whole workflow path. In the above case, three paths will be created. As discussed in the case of XOR-Split, it is not known before workflow execution, what service is enabled through the previous XOR-Split. Thus, if all the services in the XOR-Join have credentials available, then the workflow is executable from a security perspective. If at least one service in the XOR-Join has associated credentials available, then the workflow is potentially executable from a security perspective.

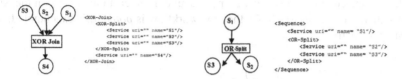

Fig. 3.   (a) XOR-Join pattern (b) OR-Split pattern

3.6   OR-Split Workflow Pattern (Multi Choice)

The OR-Split construct is used where the execution of a service leads to potentially multiple service paths that can be taken and executed. The selection of path is explicitly selected through some condition evaluation. Unlike XOR-Split where only one path out of many can be selected based on the condition evaluation, here the selection may include result in one or more paths. Two services split through OR-Split are shown in Fig. 3(b), along with the corresponding XML representation. From the security perspective, the behaviour of OR-Split is same as XOR-Split, since it is not known whether one path will be selected, or more than one path will be selected depending on the evaluation of the condition. It is not necessary that both the services must be available to pass this point in the workflow. Therefore, if all the services have their credentials available, then the workflow is executable from the security perspective. If credentials for at least one service are available and not for all, the workflow is *potentially* executable.

As argued in [2], the implementation of this pattern in workflow languages is not difficult, however, its corresponding merge/join is difficult to achieve, since the OR-Join depends on the future of the splitting of services through OR-Split. Thus, it will have to check how many and which services need to merge. Van der Aalst [2] discusses other issues in the implementation of this pattern where checking for dead-lock is required.

3.7 OR-Join Workflow Pattern

The OR-Join pattern is used to merge multiple services into one path with or without synchronization. It is used in association with the OR-Split pattern. If more than one service is selected in a previous OR-Split pattern, then they will be synchronised in the workflow process. However, if only one service is selected out of many, then the active service will be selected and workflow progresses without the need for synchronisation/joining of services. In this case it is not necessary to have all the incoming nodes available, i.e. the OR-Join will have to check the state of previous OR-Split services.

Three services combined through OR-Join are shown in Fig. 4 along with the XML representation. This workflow has many possible paths, such as: <S1 & S4>, <S2 & S4>, <S3 & S4>, <S1 & S2> & S4, <S1 & S3> & S4, <S2 & S3> & S4 and <S1 & S2 & S3> & S4, for example. The OR-Join pattern depends on the previous use of the OR-Split pattern. As discussed in the case of XOR-Split, it is not known before workflow execution, what service out of potentially many will be enabled through the OR-Split pattern. If all the services in the OR-Join have their credentials available, then the workflow is executable from a security perspective. If at least one service in the XOR-Join has their credentials available, then the workflow is *potentially* executable from a security perspective.

```
<OR-Join>
    <OR-Split>
        <Service uri="" name= "S1"/>
        <Service uri="" name= "S2"/>
        <Service uri="" name= "S3"/>
    </OR-Split>
    <Service uri="" name= "S4"/>
</OR-Join>
```

Fig. 4. OR-Join pattern

3.8 Workflow Path/Instance Construction

Many of the above patterns are part of the workflows languages. Migliorini et al. [11] evaluated major scientific and business workflows on the basis of the different patterns they support. Some of the patterns are supported via constructs in workflow languages, e.g. <*Switch*> and <*flow*> in BPEL for example, while other languages do not provide some of them and/or they are defined explicitly through the workflow logic. Thus Taverna does not support XOR-Split, however, it is possible to represent this behaviour through custom Beanshell scripts for example [20].

A successful workflow execution normally passes through every node of the workflow graph, except in the case of XOR-Split where exactly one branch is selected or in the case of OR-Split where a subset of the branches can be selected. Such an execution path through the workflow graph is called a workflow path or a workflow instance. A workflow can contain many paths depending on the OR-Split and XOR-Split branches that exist. However, before the workflow execution starts, one cannot always predict which path will be followed. If a workflow branch is split by the XOR-Split construct, i.e. any branch can be selected based on the run-time conditions evaluated, the input parameters and outputs produced within the workflow process can potentially lead to non-deterministic behaviour, e.g. both paths are possible but one is chosen (potentially) randomly. A complete workflow path is a collection of activities that lead to a successful workflow execution. Consider the following workflow graph shown in Fig. 5.

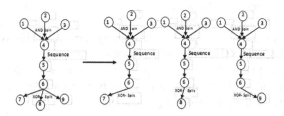

Fig. 5. Different workflow paths through workflow patterns

In this example, services 1, 2 and 3 will be synchronised with 4; services 4, 5 and 6 will be executed in sequence, whilst the last three services 7, 8 and 9 will only be executed after 6. Thus, the above graph gives us three workflow paths. Namely <1, 2, 3, 4, 5, 6, 7>, <1, 2, 3, 4, 5, 6, 8> and <1, 2, 3, 4, 5, 6, 9>. Thus, if we know in advance that any of the service from 1, 2, 3, 4, 5 and 6 is do not have their security credentials not available; then the whole workflow is not executable. However, if one or two of the three services 7, 8 and 9 have their security credentials available in the above graph, the workflow is potentially executable.

4   Finding Workflow Paths from Security Perspective

We assume that a given workflow graph exists comprised of services with security constraints, and that user credentials are available beforehand, i.e. before workflow enactment occurs. Each service policy needs to be evaluated based on the available credentials for each service to determine whether the user is entitled to execute that service as part of the workflow. For simplicity here, we do not deal with the constraints on whether a service is allowed to be a part of the workflow or whether a user is directly accessing the service or through an enactment engine.

To achieve the above goals, the workflow graph needs to be traversed, and the security credentials of each service needs to be evaluated along with the pattern in which the service is in relation to other services. The workflow graph itself is represented as an XML based workflow file, however, the workflow may be in any workflow language (e.g. Taverna and BPEL). The workflow includes the logic of the workflow and other variables involved in execution of the workflow. However, here the workflow graph provided will be in a XML format showing the services involved and the patterns used.

The different patterns discussed in Sect. 3 are represented in this XML format conformant to the XML schema available online at (https://github.com/aumidh) within the Analyser directly. The XML format is designed such that, the patterns themselves are shown as parent nodes/elements, whereas their associating services are shown as child nodes.

Consider the workflow graph shown in Fig. 6(a) and its corresponding XML representation. It is important to note that the Join pattern following the corresponding Split pattern is shown as parent in the workflow graph. For example, the workflow path is Split on Service B through OR-Split and Joined on service E. The OR-Join pattern is shown as the parent of the OR-Split and the Joining service E. This syntax is applied with all other Joins, e.g. XOR-join, and AND-Join. Similarly the services before the Split patterns are shown in the Sequence pattern and as parent nodes. The algorithm reads the XML based workflow file and recursively traverses the workflow services, checking them against the provided user credentials.

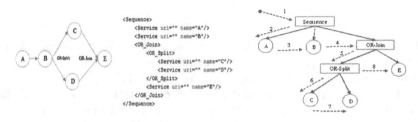

Fig. 6. (a) Workflow graph with XML representation (b) tree structure of workflow graph

Figure 6(b) depicts the corresponding graphical representation in a step-by-step execution order of the workflow graph and how the algorithm checks the XML graph for the availability of credentials. It is important to note that the services are always shown as leaf nodes, and the construct nodes are shown as parent nodes.

Algorithm 1. Executability of a Workflow from Security Perspective

```
 1: procedure GetWFExecutionStatus
 2:     N ← read workflow constructs
 3:     root ← first construct of N
 4:     wfExecStatus ← GetNodeExecutionStatus(root)
 5: end procedure
 6: procedure GetNodeExecutionStatus(node)          ▷ node is a WF construct
 7:     N ← get child constructs of node
 8:     isPE ← false , isNE ← false, isE ← false
 9:     for each childNode ∈ N do
10:         if typeof childNode is SERVICE then
11:             if execution credentials for SERVICE is available then
12:                 isE ← true
13:             else
14:                 isNE ← true
15:                 if typeof node is Or-Split or Xor-Split then
16:                     if isE or isPE is true then
17:                         return Potentially Executable
18:                     end if
19:                 else          ▷ i.e. And-Join, And-Split, Sequence, Or-Join, Xor-Join
20:                     return Not Executable
21:                 end if
22:             end if
23:         else
24:             execStatus ← GetNodeExecutionStatus(childNode)
25:             if execStatus is Not Executable then
26:                 isNE ← true
27:                 if typeof node is And-Join, And-Split or Sequence then
28:                     return Not Executable
29:                 else if typeof node is Or-Join or Xor-Join then
30:                     Continue
31:                 else                                     ▷ i.e. Or-Split or Xor-Split
32:                     if isE or isPE is true then
33:                         return Potentially Executable
34:                     end if
35:                 end if
36:             else if execStatus is Potentially Executable then
37:                 isPE ← true
38:             else
39:                 isE ← true
40:             end if
41:         end if
42:     end for
43:     if isE is true and isPE and isNE is false then
44:         return Executable                            ▷ node is fully executable
45:     else if isPE or isE is true then
46:         return Potentially Executable        ▷ node is Potentially executable
47:     else
48:         return Not Executable                     ▷ node is Not executable
49:     end if
50: end procedure
```

The algorithm 1 reads the next child node until it finds a service node (leaf node). A recursive approach is used for the implementation of this algorithm since it is not known in advance how many different services and workflow patterns are included in the workflow. The graph itself contains two types of nodes: a service node and a workflow pattern node. The credentials of the service node are checked and the corresponding parent node is assigned an execution status. The execution status of the parent node can either be executable, not executable or potentially executable. If the credentials of the service are available the service is denoted as executable, otherwise it is not executable. This evaluation takes place using a basic set of rules, which are designed specifically for this algorithm. These rules are based on the workflow patterns discussed in Sect. 3 and the availability of security credentials for child services (nodes). These rules determine the execution status of workflow patterns. The XML workflow itself is traversed from the root node.

The algorithm checks the current node status by evaluating the status of its child nodes. A child node can either be a service or another construct. As mentioned earlier the graph is recursively read until it finds a service node. The status of a current node is determined through the following rules.

Rule 1:
(a) If the current node is an AND-Split, AND-Join or Sequence, and if any of its child node statuses are identified as not executable, then the current node status is set as not executable, and returned without checking further child nodes;
(b) Otherwise, the current node is potentially executable, if any of its child status is potentially executable;
(c) Otherwise, the current node is executable. This will be the case where all of the child node statuses are executable and hence credentials are available.

Rule 2:
(a) The OR-Join and XOR-Join patterns are used for joining/merging previous OR-Split and XOR-Split services to a single service. Only one child of an OR-Join or an XOR-Join must be a service. If the joining service credentials are not available then the corresponding parent construct is also not executable, and will return without checking further child nodes.
(b) Otherwise, if any child nodes execution status is potentially executable, then the current node will be potentially executable.
(c) Otherwise, the current node is executable (in which case the statuses of all child constructs are executable).

Rule 3:
(a) If the current node is an OR-Split or XOR-Split, and if all the children are not executable, then the current node is not executable;
(b) Otherwise, the current node is executable, if all child nodes are executable;
(c) Otherwise, the current node is potentially executable, if any of the child nodes are potentially executable.

The algorithm 1 has been implemented on the basis of these rules. The algorithm itself consists of a recursive procedure that implements the rules. The root node of the workflow graph is passed to the recursive procedure, which will always be a construct node (workflow pattern). The end result of this algorithm will either be executable, potentially executable or not executable decision. Three flags are used in the pseudo code namely isPE, isE and isNE, which corresponds to the workflow being potentially executable, executable or not executable respectively. For each child node of the construct node (pattern node), two key conditions are provided based on the set of rules provided earlier and two further conditions. The first extra condition is the base condition (this starts from line No. 10 in the algorithm), and is used to check whether the current child is a service node or not. The second extra condition is the recursive condition (this starts from line No. 24 of the algorithm). This will call the procedure with the child node as a parameter to establish whether it is a service node. The base condition evaluates the rules to determine the execution status of the current node. It is here that the credentials of the child service are checked. The rules following the recursive condition (onward from line No. 24) are used to determine the execution status of the current node. The status of the current node will be one of the three execution statuses explained earlier. The final status for possibility of execution of a workflow is established when all child nodes are checked and their execution status established (from line No. 43). Since this is a recursive algorithm, the execution status of each node (parent construct) is evaluated on the basis of the execution status of the child constructs and services. Thus, the final execution status of the whole workflow will be the execution status from the root construct.

5   Application of the Algorithm in a Security-Oriented Workflow Framework

The algorithm presented in this research paper has been successfully implemented in a security-oriented workflow framework published in [25, 26]. This algorithm is realised as the *Analyser* component for workflow executability shown in Fig. 7. The code of the security-oriented workflow framework and its analyser component is available from (https://github.com/aumidh). Whilst the complete details of this framework are beyond the scope of this paper, however, we provide a brief overview and key components of the developed framework as shown in Fig. 7.

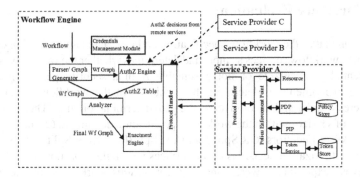

Fig. 7. Security-oriented workflow framework

The framework uses existing PEP, PDP and Policy Information Points (PIP) of available security solutions. The additional components added include: a *parser*, an *analyser*, an *authorization engine*, a *protocol handler*, a *credential management module*, and a *token service* that helps tackle the issues identified in the patterns discussed above. When a workflow is pushed for execution, the parser determines the workflow path based on the association of different services with each other and the workflows patterns [14]. The authorization engine then collects the authorization decisions from each individual participating web service, which is further used by the *analyser* to determine in advance whether the workflow is executable from the security perspective or not. This *analyser* is realized by implementing the algorithm presented in this research paper. The *analyser* determines this based on the available authorization decisions and the workflow graph pushed from the Parser. The algorithm developed in this research is used to determine the overall status of the workflow whether the workflow is executable, potentially executable or not executable. If the end result is either executable or at least potentially executable then workflow is pushactual ed for execution otherwise the user is asked for deficient credentials. This way the *analyser* helps in avoiding runtime workflow failure from the security perspective.

The credentials management module supports the *authorization engine* to provide the required credentials for the secure invocation of remote services. Whilst the authorization engine collects the authorization decision from each remote service, the *token service* keeps track of the issued authorization decisions. This further helps in maintaining session information of the authorization decisions issued by a PDP. This service is used when the workflow engine requests an authorization decision to be made. The Protocol Handler interacts with the *Token Service* by providing a *permit* authorization decision issued by the PDP along with the resource to be accessed. If the workflow is executable or potentially executable, the workflow is pushed to the engine for execution along with the collected authorization decisions. Otherwise the user is informed that the workflow cannot be executed. The details of this framework can be studied both in centralised [25] and decentralised [26] workflows execution context in our earlier research work.

6   Performance Evaluation

The *algorithm* takes the workflow specification and associated authorization decisions of individual workflow services as input and determines whether the workflow is executable, potentially executable or not executable from a security perspective. While conducting experiments to determine the efficiency of the workflow graph, various factors were considered that could affect the path determination time. These include (1) the number of services within the workflow specification document; (2) the number and type of workflow operators (OR Split/Join, And Split/Join, XOR Split/Join, Sequence), and (3) the authorization decisions of the services within the workflow.

Numerous experiments were conducted for various workflows to determine the efficiency of the algorithms. Each workflow shown in the graph was run 100 times to determine the time taken and their average as shown in Fig. 8. Since the values are small, the standard deviation is ignored and not shown in the graph. Increasing the number of services in a workflow slightly increases the workflow determination time (a fraction of a millisecond). However, the use of different operators or authorization decisions values has no major impact on the performance as shown in different figures. It should be noted that initially loading a workflow takes longer when the objects are created from the XML workflow file, however, here cold start values were discarded.

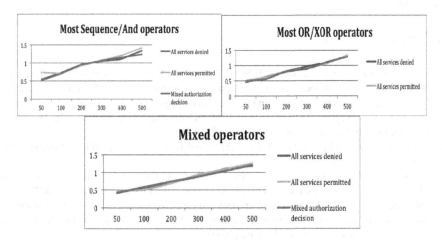

Fig. 8. Time taken by the algorithm for various workflows

The reason for this efficient performance is the workflow objects are created from the XML file. Subsequent checking of the workflow path on the basis of the authorization decision and/or an operator does not affect the majorly impact on the checking process. It should also be noted that this time does not include time taken for obtaining authorization decisions from remote services or policy evaluation. Rather the authorization decisions were directly provided to the algorithm and based on allow/deny values. It can be seen from the graphs that the workflow algorithm requires just a few milliseconds, and as such, its overheads on workflow enactment are negligible.

7   Conclusions and Future Work

This paper has highlighted the importance of patterns and security on the overall workflow execution status and workflow path construction. The other contribution of this paper is the development of a workflow executability algorithm to avoid runtime workflow failure from the security perspective. The algorithm determines whether a workflow is executable, potentially executable or not executable from a security perspective and uses both the basic workflow patterns and the credentials of the user. This helps to tackle the issue to avoid runtime workflow failure. This Algorithm is successfully exploited in a security-oriented workflow framework.

The algorithm focuses on the existence of a valid workflow path based on the security of the service providers. For many dynamic workflows the choices that are made depends on the data that is transferred from the previous workflows/services. Boolean operators based on returned data values are often used to determine the branches that a workflow takes. This has not been explored here and would be an area for future research and extensions. Using the security information to guide the enactment is also an area that can be directly supported. Thus in the case where non-deterministic choices can be made, these should be guided by knowledge of the successful paths that are possible through the workflow.

References

1. Bowers, S., Ludascher, B., Ngu, A.H.H., Critchlow, T.: Enabling scientific workflow reuse through structured composition of dataflow and control-flow. In: Proceedings of 22nd International Conference on Data Engineering Workshops, 2006, pp. 70–70 (2006)
2. Van Der Aalst, W.M.P., Ter Hofstede, A.H.M., Kiepuszewski, B., Barros, A.P.: Workflow patterns. Distrib. Parallel Databases **14**(1), 5–511 (2003)
3. Ter Hofstede, A.H.M., Van Der Aalst, W.M.: YAWL: yet another workflow language. Inf. Syst. **30**(4), 245–275 (2005)
4. Jordan, D., Evdemon, J., Alves, A., Arkin, A., Askary, S., Barreto, C., Bloch, B., et al.: Web services business process execution language version 2.0, OASIS Standard 11 (2007)
5. Fahringer, T., et al.: Askalon: a development and grid computing environment for scientific workflows. In: Taylor, I.J., Deelman, E., Gannon, D.B., Shields, M. (eds.) Workflows for e-Science, pp. 450–471. Springer, London (2007)
6. Taylor, I.J., Deelman, E., Gannon, D.B.: Workflows for e-Science: scientific workflows for grids (2006)
7. Johnson, D.B.: A note on Dijkstra's shortest path algorithm. J. ACM (JACM) **20**(3), 385–388 (1973)
8. Goldberg, A.V., Harrelson, C.: Computing the shortest path: a search meets graph theory. In: Proceedings of the Sixteenth Annual ACM-SIAM Symposium on Discrete Algorithms, pp. 156–165 (2005)
9. Xu, M., Cui, L., Wang, H., Bi, Y., Bian, J.: A data-intensive workflow scheduling algorithm for grid computing. In: ChinaGrid Annual Conference, 2009, ChinaGrid 2009, pp. 110–115 (2009)
10. Ludäscher, B., Lin, K., Bowers, S., Jaeger-Frank, E., Brodaric, B., Baru, C.: Managing scientific data: from data integration to scientific workflows. Geoinform. Data Knowl. 109 (2006)
11. Migliorini, S., Gambini, M., La Rosa, M., Ter Hofstede, A.H.M.: Pattern-based evaluation of scientific workflow management systems (2011)
12. Sadiq, W., Orlowska, M.E.: Applying graph reduction techniques for identifying structural conflicts in process models. In: Jarke, M., Oberweis, A. (eds.) CAiSE 1999. LNCS, vol. 1626, pp. 195–209. Springer, Heidelberg (1999). doi:10.1007/3-540-48738-7_15
13. Sadiq, W., Orlowska, M.E.: Analyzing process models using graph reduction techniques. Inf. Syst. **25**(2), 117–134 (2000)
14. Eder, J., Gruber, W., Pichler, H.: Transforming workflow graphs. In: Proceedings of the First International Conference on Interoperability of Enterprise Software and Applications (INTEROP-ESA 2005) (2005)
15. Vanhatalo, J., Völzer, H., Leymann, F., Moser, S.: Automatic workflow graph refactoring and completion. In: Bouguettaya, A., Krueger, I., Margaria, T. (eds.) ICSOC 2008. LNCS, vol. 5364, pp. 100–115. Springer, Heidelberg (2008). doi:10.1007/978-3-540-89652-4_11
16. Chang, D.-H., Son, J.H., Kim, M.H.: Critical path identification in the context of a workflow. Inf. Softw. Technol. **44**(7), 405–417 (2002)

17. Altunay, M., Brown, D., Byrd, G., Dean, R.: Trust-based secure workflow path construction. In: Benatallah, B., Casati, F., Traverso, P. (eds.) ICSOC 2005. LNCS, vol. 3826, pp. 382–395. Springer, Heidelberg (2005). doi:10.1007/11596141_29

18. Wimmer, M., Albutiu, M.-C., Kemper, A.: Optimized workflow authorization in service oriented architectures. In: Müller, G. (ed.) ETRICS 2006. LNCS, vol. 3995, pp. 30–44. Springer, Heidelberg (2006). doi:10.1007/11766155_3

19. Wong, P.Y.H., Gibbons, J.: A process-algebraic approach to workflow specification and refinement. In: Lumpe, M., Vanderperren, W. (eds.) SC 2007. LNCS, vol. 4829, pp. 51–65. Springer, Heidelberg (2007). doi:10.1007/978-3-540-77351-1_5

20. Li, P., Castrillo, J.I., Velarde, G., Wassink, I., Soiland-Reyes, S., Owen, S., Withers, D., et al.: Performing statistical analyses on quantitative data in Taverna workflows: an example using R and maxdBrowse to identify differentially-expressed genes from microarray data. BMC Bioinformatics 9(1), 334 (2008)

21. Tan, K.L.L., Turner, K.J.: Orchestrating grid services using BPEL and Globus Toolkit 4. In: 7th PGNet Symposium (2006)

22. Dornemann, T., Smith, M., Freisleben, B.: Composition and execution of secure workflows in wsrf-grids. In: 8th IEEE International Symposium on Cluster Computing and the Grid, 2008, CCGRID 2008, pp. 122–129 (2008)

23. Sinnott, R.O., Hussain, S.: Security-oriented workflows for the social sciences. In: 2010 4th International Conference on Network and System Security (NSS), pp. 152–159 (2010)

24. Sinnott, R.O., Hussain, S.: Architectural design patterns for security-oriented workflows in the social science domain. In: Conference on e-Social Science, Cologne, Germany, 24–26 June 2009 (2009)

25. Hussain, S., Sinnott, R.O., Poet, R.: A security-oriented workflow framework for collaborative environments. In: IEEE 15th International Conference on Trust, Security and Privacy in Computing and Communications (TrustCom), 2016 (2016, in press)

26. Hussain, S., Sinnott, R.O., Poet, R.: Security-enabled enactment of decentralized workflows. In: ACM 9th International Conference on Security of Information and Networks, 2016 (2016)

Distributed Multi-authority Attribute-Based Encryption for Secure Friend Discovery and Data Sharing in Mobile Social Networks

Fang Qi, Wenbo Wang, and Zhe Tang[✉]

School of Information Science and Engineering,
Central South University, Changsha 410083, China
{wb_wang,csqifang,tz}@csu.edu.cn

Abstract. With the rapid development of mobile social networks and cloud servers, more and more people will outsource their personal profiles for sharing in cloud. Compared to traditional web-based online social networks, the mobile social networks can assist users to easily discover and make new social interaction with others. To keep the shared data confidential against untrusted cloud service providers and solve the problem of single point failure as well as performance bottleneck, we propose a secure distributed multi-authority attribute-based encryption scheme without central authority, so as to provide not only fine-grained access control, but also high security and performance. By employing this scheme, users can achieve fine-grained access control and privacy preserving.

Keywords: Attribute-based encryption · Multi-authority · Mobile social networks · Friend discovery · Data sharing

1 Introduction

With the explosive growth of mobile social networks and cloud services, users can remotely access the data shared in cloud anytime and anywhere, using any device. Outsourcing data into the cloud provides great convenience to users for they do not need to consider the large investment in both the deployment and management of the hardware infrastructure. In mobile social networks, sharing data in cloud offers users opportunities to enjoy the online activities, for example, by sharing photos, users can appreciate the beauty of other places without actually being there. However, allowing the cloud servers to take part in the computation and communication processes, raises underlying security and privacy issues that will result in a series of unexpected consequences. For instance, the untrustworthy third parties may collude to get the confidential information about a user and sell it to make a profit. Hence, a natural way to keep sensitive data confidential is to store only the encrypted data in cloud.

Fang Qi and Wenbo Wang are co-first authors. These two authors contribute equally to this study.

© Springer International Publishing AG 2016
G. Wang et al. (Eds.): SpaCCS 2016, LNCS 10066, pp. 374–382, 2016.
DOI: 10.1007/978-3-319-49148-6_31

In recent years, many private matching schemes have been proposed to solve this problem. Among these schemes, some protect user's privacy based on trusted third party (TTP) [10,11,13,18], the other is TTP-free [8,14,17]. Although, this kind of approaches can achieve profile matching without the support of TTP, they have some disadvantages. The reliance on public-key crytosytem and homomorphic encryption [4,10,12,18] requires multiple rounds of interaction which causes high communication and computation overhead. Moreover, matched and unmatched users are all involved in the expensive computation and learn the matching result. Many schemes have been proposed to protect the privacy information. The technique of group signature [3,9] is widely used. In this kind of schemes, each visitor needs to be allocated a special group signature, which will cause huge amount of computation cost. Li et al. [8] propose a private matching scheme based on the common interests, which is not fine-grained. Zhang et al. [18] present a fine-grained private matching scheme but fail in considering the priority related to every attribute and they employ the homomorphic encryption which is resource consuming on mobile devices. Qi et al. [14] employ an asymmetric-scalar-production based on kNN query, but the presentation of interests is too single to get an accurate result. Moreover, the widely used technique of group signature [7,15] always costs huge volume of computational resources on users' hand-held devices, and the access control based on the key-policy attribute-based encryption [5] is not efficient enough. In addition, if any server or TTP is compromised, the confidentiality of the stored data may be compromised, too. Therefore, considering the powerful computational as well as storage ability of the TTP and cloud server, the main point of our work is to design an efficient privacy-preserving and fine-grained friend discovery system based on the combination of TTP and cloud server.

In this paper, the flexible encryption scheme, ciphertext-policy attribute-based encryption (CP-ABE) [2], is adopted to provide a fine-grained access control for the encrypted data. CP-ABE allows to encrypt data specifying an access policy over attribute, so that only users who satisfying the policy can decrypt the corresponding data [16]. For example, the access policy is designed as $(a_1 \wedge a_2) \vee a_3$ means that a user who has attribute a_1 and a_2 or a user with attribute a_3 can decrypt the data.

We design a distributed multi-authority scheme without central authority, the scheme can significantly relieve the users' trust on a single authority and is secure against collusion attack as well as chosen-plaintext attack. The applicability of system also has been increased. Our contributions are as follows:

· We propose a distributed multi-authority attribute-based encryption scheme without central authority, which can significantly reduce the risk of single point failure and performance bottleneck.
· The proposed scheme can achieve fine-grained access control, only the user who satisfies the access policy can decrypt the corresponding ciphertext.
· By combining the powerful computation and storage ability of cloud, the overhead on users' ends can be largely decreased.

The remainder of this paper is organized as follows. Preliminaries are introduced in Sect. 2. We propose our scheme in Sect. 3, followed by the performance evaluations in Sect. 4. Finally, we conclude our work.

2 Preliminaries

2.1 System Model

We assume that the system is composed of the following parts: the cloud servers, attribute authority (AA), data owner and visitor. The shared data which is outsourced in the encrypted form into the cloud by data owner, each visitor has a global identifier $gid \in GID$, where the GID is the identity set of all registered users. The cloud servers that store huge volumes of shared data and operate the computation process, and n attribute authorities $(AA_1, ..., AA_n)$ manage a set of attributes $U_i(U_i \cap U_j = \emptyset \wedge U = \cup_{i=1}^n U_i)$ $(i, j \in \{1, 2, ..., n\} \wedge i \neq j)$ and are responsible for generating keys for users. Each visitor with attribute set Λ will obtain their keys from the corresponding AA_n. We assume that all the authorities are run by different organizations and governed by the government. Figure 1 illustrates the system model.

2.2 Bilinear Mapping

Suppose p is a prime number, both $\mathbb{G}$ and $\mathbb{G}_T$ are multiplicative cyclic groups of the order p, g is the generator of $\mathbb{G}$. e is a bilinear map: $e : \mathbb{G} \times \mathbb{G} \to \mathbb{G}_T$. Bilinear mapping possesses the following characteristics:

1. bilinearity: $\forall x, y \in \mathbb{G}_1$ and $a, b \in Z_q$, there is $e(x^a, y^b) = e(x, y)^{ab}$
2. computability: $\forall u_1, u_2, v \in \mathbb{G}_T$, there exists a computable algorithm $e(x^a, y^b) = e(x, y)^{ab}$
3. non-degeneracy: for $g \in \mathbb{G}$, $e(g, g) \neq 1$

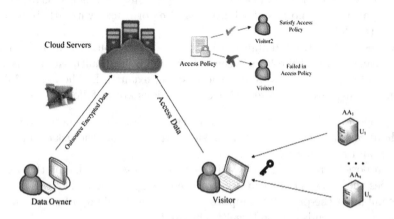

Fig. 1. Data sharing in mobile social networks

2.3 Adversary Model

In the profile matching process, there usually exist two main adversary models: honest but curious adversaries model [19] and malicious model [6].

The honest-but-curious adversary is a legitimate user who will honestly follow the protocol but will try to learn more information than allowed from legitimately received message. In this paper, we assume that the attacker is more interested in the private information of mobile social network users. At the same time, we suppose the data owner and visitor are honest-but-curious users.

The malicious adversary is a user who does not honestly obey the protocol and launch some active attacks to learn more information than allowed. These adversaries behave arbitrarily such as denial-of-service (DoS) and continuous fake-profile attacks.

In this paper, we mainly focus on the honest-but-curious adversaries; those active attacks are not in the scope of this paper.

3 Proposed Scheme

3.1 System Initialization

$\mathbb{G}$ and $\mathbb{G}_N$ are bilinear cyclic groups with the order $N = p_1 p_2$, where p_1, p_2 are distinct big prime numbers. $\mathbb{G}_{p_i}$ is the subgroup of $\mathbb{G}_N$ with order p_i, g_1 is the generator of $\mathbb{G}_{p_1}$ and g_2 is the generator of $\mathbb{G}_{p_2}$. On input the security parameter λ, the initialization algorithm randomly chooses $h \in_R \mathbb{G}_{p_1}$ and the global parameter is published as:

$$GP = (N, g_1, g_2, h) \tag{1}$$

For each AA_k, inputs GP, AA_k's index k and the attribute universe U_k belonging to AA_k. For each att in U_k, AA_k randomly selects $s_{att}, v_k, \alpha_k, a_k \in_R \mathbb{Z}_N$, then computes $T_{att} = g^{s_{att}}$ and $V_k = g^{v_k}$. The master key is:

$$MK_k = (v_k, \alpha_k, a_k, \{s_{att} | att \in U_k\}) \tag{2}$$

and the public key is published as:

$$PK_k = (V_k, g^{a_k}, e(g, g)^{\alpha_k}, \{T_{att} | att \in U_k\}) \tag{3}$$

where $e : \mathbb{G} \times \mathbb{G} \rightarrow \mathbb{G}_N$ is a bilinear map.

3.2 Encryption

This algorithm is performed on the data owner's end. The data owner designs the access policy that defines the special attributes that the visitors need to satisfy. The access policy is embedded in the ciphertext so that before decrypting the decryption can verify whether the visitor is qualified.

Data owner inputs GP, PK_k, the plaintext of data M and access policy $\mathbb{A} = (A, \rho)$. (A, ρ) a linear secret-sharing scheme (LSSS) [1] matrix, where A is a $l \times n$ matrix and ρ will map each row A_x in A to get an attribute $\rho(x)$. ρ is required that when mapping different row, the attribute must not be the same. Randomly chooses a vector $v = (s, v_2, ..., v_n) \in \mathbb{Z}_N^n$. These valuses will be used to share the encryption exponent s. For each $x \in \{1, 2, ..., l\}$, the algorithm randomly selects $r_x \in \mathbb{Z}_N$. The ciphertext is:

$$CT = (M \prod_{k=1}^{n} e(g, g)^{\alpha_k s}, C' = g^s, C_k'' = g^{\alpha_k s},$$

$$\forall x \in 1, 2, ..., l: \quad \{C_x = h^{A_x v} T_{\rho(x)}^{\frac{1}{r_x}}, C_x' = g^{r_x}\})$$

(4)

Along with the access policy $\mathbb{A}$, data owner outsources the ciphertext to the cloud.

3.3   Key Generation

Suppose a visitor wants to visit some data with certain characteristics, he/she will set up an attribute set Λ. To meet the security and efficiency requirements, all attributes in Λ will be split into n different shares and distributed to n different attribute authorities.

Visitor submits his/her identifier gid, attribute set Λ to the attribute authority AA_k for requesting a pair of secret keys $< SK_k^1, SK_k^2 >$. AA_k randomly selects $c_k \in \mathbb{Z}_N^*$, $r_k \in \mathbb{Z}_N$, $\beta_k, \beta_k', \beta_k'' \in \mathbb{G}_{p_2}$. Then it creates the SK_k^1 as:

$$SK_k^1 = (g^{\frac{a_k}{\alpha_k + c_k}} h_k^{r_k} \beta_k, c_k,$$

$$L_k = g_k^{r_k} \beta_k', L_k' = (g^{a_k})^{r_k} \beta_k'')$$

(5)

For each attribute $att \in U_k \cap \Lambda$, AA_k randomly chooses $\Gamma_k \in \mathbb{G}_{p_2}$, $\beta_{att}' \in \mathbb{G}_{p_2}$, AA_k computes

$$SK_{att,k} = (V_k^{(a_k + c_k) r_k} \Gamma_k)^{\frac{s_{att}}{v_k}} \beta_{att}'$$

$$= T_{att}^{(a_k + c_k) r_k} \Gamma_k^{\frac{s_{att,k}}{v_k}} \beta_{att}'$$

(6)

So the SK_k^2 is defined as:

$$SK_k^2 = (g^{\frac{\alpha_k - a_k}{\alpha_k + c_k}} h_k^{r_k} \beta_k, \{SK_{att,k} | att \in \Lambda\})$$

(7)

3.4   Decryption

When a visitor wants to visit certain data, first, he/she must satisfy the access policy designed by the data owner. If the visitor's attribute set Λ satisfies the access policy $\mathbb{A} = (A, \rho)$, which means there exists constants $\omega_x \in \mathbb{Z}_N$ and $\sum_{\rho(x) \in \Lambda} \omega_x A_x = (1, 0, ..., 0)$. If Λ fails in the access policy, the algorithm will output $\bot$, which means Λ dose not satisfy the access policy, the visitor cannot decrypt the ciphertext and continue the following steps.

If the verification is passed, then the visitor will input $< SK_k^1, SK_k^2 >$, then computes:

$$\frac{e((C')^{C_k}, g^{\frac{a_k}{\alpha_k + c_k}} h_k^{r_k} \beta_k)}{\prod_{\rho(x) \in \Lambda} (e(C_x, L_k^{C_k}) e(C'_x, SK_{\rho(x),k}))^{\omega_x}}$$

$$= \frac{e((g^s)^{C_k}, g^{\frac{a_k}{\alpha_k + c_k}} h_k^{r_k} \beta_k)}{\prod_{\rho(x) \in \Lambda} (e(h^{A_x} v T_{\rho(x)}^{\frac{1}{r_x}}, (g_k^{r_k} \beta'_k)^{C_k}) e(g^{r_x}, SK_{\rho(x),k}))^{\omega_x}} \quad (8)$$

$$= e(g, g)^{a_k s}$$

and computes

$$\frac{e((C')^{C_k}, g^{\frac{\alpha_k - a_k}{\alpha_k + c_k}} h_k^{r_k} \beta_k)}{\prod_{\rho(x) \in \Lambda} (e(C_x, L_k^{C_k}) e(C'_x, SK_{\rho(x),k}))^{\omega_x}}$$

$$= \frac{e((g^s)^{C_k}, g^{\frac{\alpha_k - a_k}{\alpha_k + c_k}} h_k^{r_k} \beta_k)}{\prod_{\rho(x) \in \Lambda} (e(h^{A_x} v T_{\rho(x)}^{\frac{1}{r_x}}, (g_k^{r_k} \beta'_k)^{C_k}) e(g^{r_x}, SK_{\rho(x),k}))^{\omega_x}} \quad (9)$$

$$= e(g, g)^{(\alpha_k - a_k)s}$$

Finally, the visitor can recover the plaintext:

$$M = \frac{CT}{\prod_{k=1}^{n} (e(g, g)^{a_k s} e(g, g)^{(\alpha_k - a_k)s})}$$

$$= \frac{M \prod_{k=1}^{n} e(g, g)^{\alpha_k s}}{\prod_{k=1}^{n} (e(g, g)^{a_k s} e(g, g)^{(\alpha_k - a_k)s})} \quad (10)$$

$$= M$$

4   Performance Analysis

In this section, we evaluate the proposed scheme with several existing works in terms of efficiency and practicability. Since the cloud is generally assumed to be resource abundant, we mainly focus on the computation and communication overhead loaded on both the data owner and visitor's ends.

We conduct the experiments on a laptop with 1.6 GHz processor and 2 GB RAM, and the simulation code was written in C++. We perform the comparisons between Boyen [3], Liang [9] and our scheme. The size of attributes set is fixed in 30 and n denotes the number of participated visitors.

Figure 2 represents the communication overhead comparison among Boney's scheme [3], Liang's scheme [9] and ours. It is obvious that the communication cost of Boney's and Liang's schemes sharply increase as the number of visitors grows from 50 to 500. However, the proposed scheme is significantly lower than Boney's and Liang's schemes. Moreover, with the increasing number of visitors,

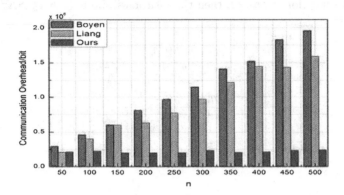

Fig. 2. Communication overhead

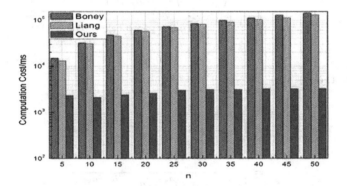

Fig. 3. Computation cost on data owner's end

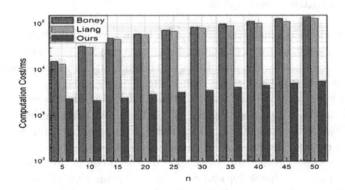

Fig. 4. Computation cost on visitor's end

the communication overhead keeps low and stable, which is really important in massive users enviroment.

Figure 3 illustrates the computation cost comparison among Boyen's scheme [3], Liang's scheme [9] and ours on the data owner's ends. From the curve, we can know that the computation cost in Boney's and Liang's schemes increases quickly as the number of visitors grows. Because the technique of group signatures is adopted, and to achieve privacy preserving, it is required for the data owner to generate one group signature for each visitor, which would bring about intolerable computation complexity on users' ends. Significantly from [3,9], our scheme requires no extra signature to protect privacy information.

Figure 4 shows the computation cost comparison among Boyen's shceme [3], Liang's scheme [9] and ours on the data's ends. It is obvious that the proposed scheme consumes less. When there are many visitors, each of them needs to wait for a special group signature, which is time-consuming. When $n = 50$, both Boyen [3] and Liang [9] need 129.07 ms to complete the computation processes on visitor's end. But in our scheme, the whole processes on visitor's end only consumes 5.54 ms.

From the above analysis, the proposed scheme is superior in both communication and computation overhead. With the increasing number of participated visitors, the system cost only grows slightly, especially in the massive users enviroment the communication overhead can be small and stable.

5   Conclusion

For the sake of enjoying a more comprehensive and high quality service, a distributed multi-authority attribute-based encryption is proposed for secure friend discovery and data sharing, which simultaneously achieves flexibility, high performance and security. The proposed scheme is collusion resistant and can decrease the work pressure and reliance on a single point. In the future work, we will design a more expressive encryption scheme to achieve better performance.

Acknowledgments. This work is supported by the National Natural Science Foundation of China under Grant No. 61632009 and Grant No. 31470028, and Fundamental Research Funds for the Central Universities of Central South University under Grant No. 2016zzts337.

References

1. Beimel, A., et al.: Secure schemes for secret sharing and key distribution. Int. J. Pure Appl. Math. **85**(5), 933–937 (1996)
2. Bethencourt, J., Sahai, A., Waters, B., et al.: Ciphertext-policy attribute-based encryption. In: Proceedings of the 2007 IEEE Symposium on Security and Privacy, SP 2007, no. 4, pp. 321–334 (2007)
3. Boyen, X., Waters, B., et al.: Full-domain subgroup hiding and constant-size group signatures. In: International Conference on Practice and Theory in Public-Key Cryptography, pp. 1–15 (2007)

4. Costantino, G., Martinelli, F., Santi, P., et al.: Privacy-preserving interest-casting in opportunistic networks. In: Proceedings of Wireless Communications and Networking Conference, pp. 2829–2834 (2012)

5. Goyal V, Pandey O, Sahai A, Waters B, et al.: Attribute-based encryption for fine-grained access control of encrypted data. In: Proceedings of the 13th ACM Conference on Computer, Communications Security, pp. 89–98 (2006). Observation of strains. Infect Dis. Ther. 3(1), 35–43 (2011)

6. Hazay, C., Toft, T.: Computationally secure pattern matching in the presence of malicious adversaries. In: Abe, M. (ed.) ASIACRYPT 2010. LNCS, vol. 6477, pp. 195–212. Springer, Heidelberg (2010). doi:10.1007/978-3-642-17373-8_12

7. Li, J., Au, M.H., Susilo, W., Xie, D., Ren, K., et al.: Attribute-based signature and its applications. In: Proceedings of the 5th ACM Symposium on Information, Computer and Communications Security, pp. 60–69 (2010)

8. Li, M., Cao, N., Yu, S., Lou, W., et al.: FindU: privacy-preserving personal profile matching in mobile social networks. In: Proceedings of IEEE INFOCOM, pp. 2435–2443 (2011)

9. Liang, X., Cao, Z., Shao, J., Lin, H., et al.: Short Group Signature Without Random Oracles. Springer, Heidelberg (2007)

10. Lu, R., Lin, X., Liang, X., Shen, X., et al.: A secure handshake scheme with symptoms-matching for mhealthcare social network. Mobile Netw. Appl. 16(6), 683–694 (2011)

11. Manweiler, J., Scudellari, R., Cox, L.P., et al.: Smile: encounter-based trust for mobile social services. In: Proceedings of the 16th ACM Conference on Computer and Communications Security, pp. 246–255 (2009)

12. Niu, B., Zhang, T., Zhu, X., Li, H., Lu, Z., et al.: Priority-aware private matching schemes for proximity-based mobile social networks. In: Computer Science, pp. 3170–3175 (2014)

13. Pietiläinen, A.K., Oliver, E., LeBrun, J., Varghese, G., Diot, C., Mobiclique, et al.: middleware for mobile social networking. In: Proceedings of the 2nd ACM Workshop on Online Social Networks, pp. 49–54 (2009)

14. Qi, F., Wang, W., et al.: Efficient private matching scheme for friend information exchange. In: Proceedings of Algorithms and Architectures for Parallel Processing, pp. 492–503 (2015)

15. Shahandashti, S.F., Safavi-Naini, R.: Threshold attribute-based signatures and their application to anonymous credential systems. In: Preneel, B. (ed.) AFRICACRYPT 2009. LNCS, vol. 5580, pp. 198–216. Springer, Heidelberg (2009). doi:10.1007/978-3-642-02384-2_13

16. Wang, G., Liu, Q., Wu, J., et al.: Hierarchical attribute-based encryption for fine-grained access control in cloud storage services. In: Proceedings of ACM Conference on Computer and Communications Security, pp. 735–737 (2010)

17. Zhang, L., Li, X.Y., Liu, Y., et al.: Message in a sealed bottle: privacy preserving friending in social networks. In: IEEE 33rd International Conference on Distributed Computing Systems (ICDCS), pp. 327–336 (2013)

18. Zhang, R., Zhang, R., Sun, J., Yan, U., et al.: Fine-grained private matching for proximity-based mobile social networking. In: Proceedings of IEEE INFOCOM, pp. 1969–1977 (2012)

19. Zhou, J., Cao, Z., Dong, X., Lin, X., Vasilakos, A.V., et al.: Securing m-healthcare social networks: challenges, countermeasures and future directions. Wirel. Commun. 20(4), 12–21 (2013)

Modeling Attack Process of Advanced Persistent Threat

Weina Niu[1], Xiaosong Zhan[1(✉)], Kenli Li[2], Guowu Yang[1], and Ruidong Chen[1]

[1] Center for Cyber Security, University of Electronic Science
and Technology of China, Chengdu 611731, China
niuweina1@126.com, {johnsonzxs,guowu}@uestc.edu.cn, crdchen@163.com
[2] Institute of Supercomputing and Cloud Computing,
Hunan University, Changsha 410082, China
lkl@hnu.edu.cn

Abstract. Advanced Persistent Threat (APT) with deep concealment has become one of the most serious network attacks. Modeling APT attack process can facilitate APT analysis and detection. However, existed modeling approaches neither reflects APT attack dynamically nor takes human factor into consideration. In order to achieve this, we propose a Targeted Complex Attack Network (TCAN) model for APT attack process. Compared with current models, our model addresses human factor by conducting two-layer network structure. Besides, our model introduces time domain to expand the traditional attack graph into dynamic attack network. Whats more, we propose dynamic evolution rules based on complex network theory and characteristics of the actual attack scenarios. Our simulation results show that the model can express the process of attack effectively.

Keywords: Attack process modeling · APT · TCAN · Human factor · Complex network theory

1 Introduction

Since Advanced Persistent Threat (APT) [1–3] coning as a new concept by the US Air Force in 2006 [4], it has flourished as a security marketing buzzword in network security. Nowadays, notion announced by the US National Institute of Standards and Technology [5] is widely acknowledged: an APT attack is launched by high-skilled and well-funded attackers. Such attack comprises multiple attack vectors used to exfiltrate information or sabotage the infrastructures. Explaining, detecting and predicting APT attacks are indispensable to model the procedure of APT attacks. Research of network attack modeling lasted for several years. Many models have been proposed so far, such as attack tree [6], attack graph [7] and attack net [8]. However, these traditional modeling methods present neither dynamic change of the actual APT attack nor consider the human factor.

The main goal of this paper is to identify the hosts that definitely involved in the attack process. To break current limitations, we propose a network-evolution-based approach to model the attack process of APT attacks. In our model, nodes

© Springer International Publishing AG 2016
G. Wang et al. (Eds.): SpaCCS 2016, LNCS 10066, pp. 383–391, 2016.
DOI: 10.1007/978-3-319-49148-6_32

and edges of traditional attack graph are redefined. Communication-contact network [9] is introduced to indicate the influence of social engineering since social engineering can be exploited in each APT case. In the simulated experiment, the free-scale network is used to express network structure. By analyzing the network formation, our approach can represent popular APT cases.

The remainder of this paper is organized as follows: Sect. 2 gives an overview of the related work; Sect. 3 represents how the TCAN is generated; Sect. 4 shows the preliminary experimental results; future work and conclusions are summarized in Sect. 5.

2   Related Work

In recent years, researches on modeling network attack have been proposed continually which bring about a number of models. However, few papers discussed APT attack modeling [10–14]. The attack pyramid model on attack tree proposed by Paul [10], which provide guidelines for detecting APT by the association of attributes and time. The attack kill chain model [12,13] can describe the phases of an APT attack based on the concept of intrusion kill chain [15], such as Chen et al. [12] divided APT attack into six stages. The impact on the target network caused by the next attack action can be measured using a probability. Thus, a novel Markov Multi-Phase Transferable Belief Model (MM-TBM) [13] was used to guide the network administrator to detect APT attack early. However, these three kinds of models lack the description of the state change.

Zhao et al. [11] proposed EPANM model combines attack scene, attack process, and state space by extending the structure of classical Petri net. However, EPANM model has poor adaptability because it limits attacks process to eight states. Thus, this model cannot reveal attack process dynamically. Fang et al. [14] use a game model to predict the optimal attack path of an attacker and the best-response strategies for a defender by quantifying rewards. However, this model did not consider the human factor.

3   Targeted Complex Attack Network

In this section, we give a detailed description of our network-evolution-based modeling approach [16]. At first, some definitions are shown; then the derivation of our model is described; the last part of this section expatiates the change of node state.

3.1   Definitions

Definition 1. A node is expressed by a three-tuple N = (description, host, status), which is used to indicate a device in the network.

The description is used to describe factors that affected nodes into connect-successful; represents node id, that is specified as an IP address; represents the node status, which is in one of the five states: susceptible, provide-information, attack-successful, active-propagation and removed.

Definition 2. An attack edge is expressed by a three-tuple $e = (n_i, n_j, R)$.

R represents relationships exploited by this attack behavior, which is subjected to $R = R^{Topology} \bigcup R^{Trust}$, indicated as T1, T2, where $R^{Topology}$ represents the topology relationship. If the value of R is R^{Trust}, this attack is going by social engineering. Thus, we take the human factor into consideration by using trust relationship to conduct an attack in the actual attack process.

Definition 3. The current attack situation is described by a complex attack network $CAN = (N, E)$ from the formalization perspective.

3.2   Model Derivation

According to the definition of a dynamic network [17], the dynamic attack network can be regarded as the attack sub-graph sequences over the series of consecutive time steps.

According to Definition 3, we define attack network at time t as $CAN_t = (N_t, E_t)$.

$N_t = \{n_i | i = 1, 2, ..., m_t\}$ represents the set of all nodes involved in the attack until time t, where n_i represents a node, indicated as "$\bigcirc$". $E_t = \{e_j | j = 1, 2, ..., s_t\}$, where e_j represents an attacking edge, indicated as "$\longrightarrow$".

Although the procedure of APT attack has a certain stability of time and space, with APT attack continues, there are new attack behaviors occurring. Thus, new nodes and edges need to join the attack network. If previous attacks failed, nodes and edges existed in the attack network need to be removed. However, most of the time attackers collect information about the target. This phenomenon is consistent with individual human mobility patterns, in other words, although most attack behaviors are placed soon after a previous attack behavior, occasionally there are long periods without any attack activity.

According to network evolution theory [16], APT attack process subjects the following steps:

1. Adding: Node and edges have characteristics of dynamic growth with the attack progress;
2. Removing: A node may become a failure node, once the previous attack behavior fails. For example, service as the prime attack target is shut down etc. before the attack succeeds.

Thus, the CAN at time t+1 can be expressed as $CAN_{t+1} = (N_{t+1}, E_{t+1})$, which meets the following conditions:

$$(1) N_{t+1} = (N_t \cup \{n_a^{t+1}\} - \{n_d^{t+1}\}),$$
$$(2) E_{t+1} = (E_t \cup \{e_a^{t+1}\} - \{e_d^{t+1}\}.$$

$\{n_a^{t+1}\}$ represents the new adding nodes. $\{n_d^{t+1}\}$ represents nodes set which needs to be removed from the attack network. $\{e_a^{t+1}\}$ represents the attack edges joining into the attack process. $\{e_d^{t+1}\}$ represents the attack edges removed from attack process once the target node is removed.

3.3 Change of Node State

In the target network, each node is in one of the five states: susceptible, provide-information, attack-successful, active-propagation and removed. In the beginning, we assume that all the devices in the network environment are susceptible and each device has a user. There are two layers in our multiplex network: communication network labelled A, contact network labelled B. A network and B network express trust relationship and topology relationship, respectively. There is no self-loops or repeated links in these two networks. Meanwhile, there is no correlation between the generated double-layer network. Each node in layer A is matched with that of layer B one-to-one.

The state of a device changes from susceptible to transitional in the following two situations: (1) this device has a connection to the active-propagation device, (2) the user of this device trusts the user of active-propagation device, that is to say, there is a trust relationship among the users of device changed status and device in active-propagation. A device changes stages from transitional to connect-successful, when this device in the selection region. After connecting with attackers successfully, this node will join into two statuses: provide-information and attack-successful. When a compromised node has been chosen as the stepping stone, the node is added to state active-propagation. Only this device is used as a stepping stone in the next attack step, it will infect other nodes. Moreover, the state transition from active-propagation to removed, attack-successful to removed in our model represent that the compromised computer is detected and fixed. Removed nodes will disconnect with the current active-propagation node in the target network. Nodes in provide-information state or nodes in the removed state are transformed into susceptible when these nodes connect to the current active-propagation node.

4 Experiments

4.1 Experiment Set-Up

To validate our models applicability to different attack scenarios, we choose the scale-free network and small-world network as the topology and trust relationship, respectively [17]. Experimental results reported below are the average of 100 repeated experiments. The measures of interest include the number of nodes in the attack-successful state, provide-information state, and remove state at the end of the attack, attack steps acquired by this attack. To jumpstart the APT attack progress, the initial number of active-propagation nodes is set to one. In other words, the statue of the attacker is active-propagation.

4.2   The Baseline Experiment

The first simulation is the baseline experiment. The number of topology size is set to 10. The topology and trust relationship of the target network is shown in Fig. 1. Node 5 is in active-propagation state. Node 9 is the target node. The parameter of probability provide-information is set to 0.8. The parameters of removal rate and failure rate are set to 0.1.

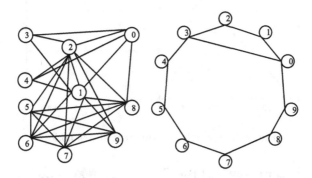

Fig. 1. Detection effect of flow-based and conversation-based features

Status of nodes in the target network at every attack step is shown in Fig. 2. Figure 3 presents the detailed attack path, where T1 is the topology relationship, and T2 is the trust relationship. PI, CI, A, P, R represent provide-information, collect-information, attack-successful, active-propagation, removed state, respectively. Meanwhile, they are described using cycle with different colors, like black cycle denotes attacker, yellow cycle node in provide-information state, blue cycle node in attack-successful, green cycle node in active-propagation state, the red cycle is target node.

4.3   The Baseline Experiment Analysis

In this simulated experiment, attacker collects information about target network from a public source, indicated as node 1, 2, 4, 6, 7, 9. Then attacker breaks into the node 8 through network infiltration method. Finally, the attacker controls the target node using social technologies. This attack pattern is similar to Operation Aurora [18]. Operation Aurora was a serious cyber attack caused by APT in 2009. In this attack, the user names and passwords of sensitive users accessed to google server were stolen. Its consequences led to the theft of important email information about these sensitive users.

The following analysis is implemented using the proposed TCAN on the background of Google Auraro.

1. The attacker collects information about staff in target network from open source.

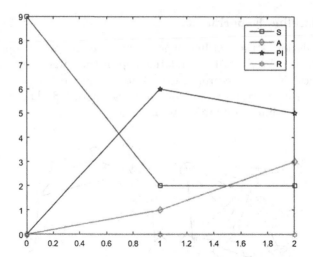

Fig. 2. The number of different states node

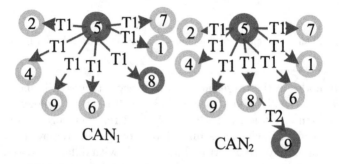

Fig. 3. A TCAN evolutionary process

2. A certain employee E is targeted. Then, the attacker collects information about this certain employee E from social network websites like Facebook, Twitter, and LinkedIn. Next, specific friend F who likes photograph is selected. Followed is that the attacker breaks into the host of friend F through network infiltration method.

3. The attacker pretends to be the friend E and sends an instant message to this employee in order to invite him to enjoy the latest photos. But the URL points to a web page loading shellcode and Javascript, which is managed by a Web server forged by an attacker. The employee E clicks the link to enter the malicious web site forged by the attacker, which can cause the overflow of IE browser with this specific employee in Google. The host of this specific employee executes FTP download program locally. The host of this specific employee downloads more programs to execute, such as Trojan. Then, the connection is established between target host and attacker host through SSL Tunnel.

Table 1. The attack steps to different probability of provide-information

The probability of provide-information	Attack steps
0.5	8
0.6	29
0.7	108
0.8	217
0.9	27

We found that there are many factors influencing attack choice. For example, the sometimes attacker chooses the sub-optimal attack path to escape detection. Thus, there are five kinds of nodes, including initial nodes, failure nodes, information nodes, immune nodes, and target nodes in our model. Failure nodes explain percolation phenomena in actual APT attacks. We cannot reconstruct the entire attack path when the failure nodes existing in this attack process. Immune nodes exist outside the attacking net in isolation, which reveals the herd immunity phenomena. There are no edges pointing to other nodes of information nodes, which illustrates cumulative advantage existing in the derivation of TCAN. At the same time, there is at least one node called target node, which does not have outing edges of the TCAN model. The TCAN model building completes after the target node added to the net.

4.4   Experiments of Different Probability Provide-Information

Table 1 shows the sensitivity of APT attack progress to different probability provide-information. It is obvious that the larger probability provide-information

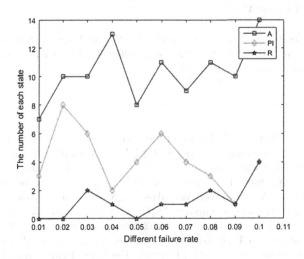

Fig. 4. The number of each state at the end of this attack to different failure rate

results in larger attack steps. The number of nodes involved in the attack progress increases with the probability provide-information as well. It can be seen that a serious fall in attack steps when the probability of provide-information increases to a certain size. Thus, we can make a conclusion that the more information about the target node collected by attackers, the faster, more cost-effective to reach their attack goal.

4.5   Experiments of Different Failure Rate

In the end of this section, we study the effect of failure rate on APT attack progress. It is obvious from Fig. 4 that different failure rates have their impacts on the attack progress. The anti-malware systems deployed in the target network defend network attacks at a fast-enough rate, then this APT attack can actually increase attack steps.

5   Conclusion

In this paper, a network-evolution-based attack network generating mechanism is introduced to express APT attack. A double-layer network is introduced to elucidate the effects of human interaction in layer A, topology link in layer B. Our proposed model focused on attack network that helps security analysts to understand APT attack mechanism. This work considers suspicious hosts involved in APT-related activities by social engineering and network penetration. Moreover, our model demonstrates the attack situation dynamically based on network evolution. In the simulated experiment, the free-scale network is used to express network structure.

Analysis methods of the dynamic network are still at its beginning the work focuses on studying the properties of TCAN model from the angle of the network is a meaningful future work.

Acknowledgments. This work is supported by National Natural Science Foundation of China (Grant Nos. 61572115, 61502086 and 61402080), Chinese Postdoctoral Science Foundation (Grant Nos. 2014M562307).

References

1. Li, F., Lai, A., Ddl, D.: Evidence of advanced persistent threat: a case study of malware for political espionage. In: 2011 6th International Conference on Malicious and Unwanted Software (MALWARE), pp. 102–109. IEEE (2011)
2. Jeun, I., Lee, Y., Won, D.: A practical study on advanced persistent threats. In: Kim, T., Stoica, A., Fang, W., Vasilakos, T., Villalba, J.G., Arnett, K.P., Khan, M.H., Kang, B.-H. (eds.) Computer Applications for Security, Control and System Engineering. CCIS, vol. 339, pp. 144–152. Springer, Heidelberg (2012)
3. Ask, M., Bondarenko, P., Rekdal, J.E., Nordbø, A., Bloemerus, P., Piatkivskyi, D.: Advanced persistent threat (APT) beyond the hype, Project report in IMT4582 NetworN security at GjoviN University College. Springer (2013)

4. Cloppert, M.: Security intelligence: Introduction (pt 1), SANS Digital Forensics and Incident Response Blog (2009)
5. Furlani, C.: Managing information security risk: organization, mission, and information system view (2011)
6. Schneier, B.: Attack trees. Dr. Dobbs J. **24**(12), 21–29 (1999)
7. Jajodia, S., Noel, S., OBerry, B.: Topological analysis of network attack vulnerability. In: Kumar, V., Srivastava, J., Lazarevic, A. (eds.) Managing Cyber Threats, pp. 247–266. Springer, Heidelberg (2005)
8. McDermott, J.P.: Attack net penetration testing. In: Proceedings of the 2000 Workshop on New Security Paradigms, pp. 15–21. ACM (2001)
9. Liu, Q.H., Wang, W., Tang, M., Zhang, H.F.: Impacts of complex behavioral responses on asymmetric interacting spreading dynamics in multiplex networks. Sci. Rep. **6** (2016)
10. Giura, P., Wang, W.: A context-based detection framework for advanced persistent threats. In: 2012 International Conference on Cyber Security (CyberSecurity), pp. 69–74. IEEE (2012)
11. Zhao, W., Wang, P., Zhang, F.: Extended petri net-based advanced persistent threat analysis model. In: Wong, W.E., Zhu, T. (eds.) Computer Engineering and Networking, pp. 1297–1305. Springer, Heidelberg (2014)
12. Bhatt, P., Yano, E.T., Gustavsson, P.: Towards a framework to detect multi-stage advanced persistent threats attacks. In: 2014 IEEE 8th International Symposium on Service Oriented System Engineering (SOSE), pp. 390–395. IEEE (2014)
13. Ioannou, G., Louvieris, P., Clewley, N., Powell, G.: A Markov multi-phase transferable belief model: an application for predicting data exfiltration APTs. In: 2013 16th International Conference on Information Fusion (FUSION), pp. 842–849. IEEE (2013)
14. Fang, X., Zhai, L., Jia, Z., Bai, W.: A game model for predicting the attack path of APT. In: 2014 IEEE 12th International Conference on Dependable, Autonomic and Secure Computing (DASC), pp. 491–495. IEEE (2014)
15. Hutchins, E.M., Cloppert, M.J., Amin, R.M.: Intelligence-driven computer network defense informed by analysis of adversary campaigns and intrusion kill chains. Lead. Issues Inf. Warfare Secur. Res. **1**, 80 (2011)
16. Skyrms, B., Pemantle, R.: A dynamic model of social network formation. In: Gross, T., Sayama, H. (eds.) Adaptive Networks, pp. 231–251. Springer, Heidelberg (2009)
17. May, R.M., Lloyd, A.L.: Infection dynamics on scale-free networks. Phys. Rev. E **64**(6), 066112 (2001)
18. Kurtz, G.: Operation "aurora" hit google, others, vol. 80 (2010). http://siblog.mcafee.com/cto/operation-%E2

A New Image Encryption Scheme Using a Hyperchaotic System

Chong Fu[1]([✉]), Ming Tie[2], Jian-lin Wang[2], Shao-ting Chen[1], and Hui-yan Jiang[3]

[1] School of Computer Science and Engineering, Northeastern University,
Shenyang 110004, China
fuchong@mail.neu.edu.cn
[2] Science and Technology on Space Physics Laboratory, Beijing 100076, China
[3] Software College, Northeastern University,
Shenyang 110004, China

Abstract. Recently, a number of chaos-based image encryption schemes with permutation-diffusion structure have been proposed. In those schemes, the permutation and diffusion are considered as two independent processes, both requiring iteration of a chaotic map/system. In this paper, we suggest a fast image encryption scheme where both processes are driven by a single hyperchaotic system. The permutation table and the diffusion keystream are generated from the same sequence extracted from the orbit of the employed system. The computational efficiency is improved as the total number of iterations is reduced by half. Moreover, the permutation table is created by a sorting mechanism that works on the chaotic sequence, and the strategy effectively avoid the flaw of periodicity that exists in discretized chaotic maps. The security of the proposed scheme is analyzed in detail, and the results demonstrate its satisfactory level of security.

Keywords: Image cipher · Hyperchaotic system · Permutation table · Diffusion keystream · Pseudorandom sequence sorting

1 Introduction

Nowadays, a tremendous amount of digital images are being stored on different media and transmitted over public networks, and consequently the security of image data has become a critical issue. As is known, the security of the renowned generic block ciphers, such as Triple-DES, AES and IDEA, crucially depends on their computational complexity, and thereby they are not suitable to handle bulky data, i.e., digital images, especially under the scenario of real-time communications. To meet this challenge, much research has been done over the past one and a half decades and substantial achievements have been made. Among those approaches, the chaos-based ones provide an optimal trade-off between security and performance. A simple but effective structure, permutation-diffusion, is widely adopted in chaos-based image encryption schemes. Under this structure, the pixels in the plain-image are firstly rearranged in a pseudorandom manner, which leads to a great reduction in the correlation among neighboring

© Springer International Publishing AG 2016
G. Wang et al. (Eds.): SpaCCS 2016, LNCS 10066, pp. 392–405, 2016.
DOI: 10.1007/978-3-319-49148-6_33

pixels. This can be generally accomplished by using one of the following three area-preserving invertible maps, i.e., the cat map, the baker map and the standard map. The control parameters of these chaotic maps serve as the permutation key. Next the pixel values are altered sequentially and the modification made to a particular pixel usually depends on the accumulated effect of all its previous pixel values. As a result, a minor change in one pixel of the original image may result in a totally different cipher image after several overall rounds of encryption. Various chaotic maps, such as the logistic and skew tent maps, and chaotic systems, such as the Lorenz and Chen systems, can be employed to generate diffusion keystreams with desired randomness. The initial condition(s) and sometimes the control parameter(s) of the employed chaotic map(s)/ system(s) serve as the diffusion key.

The early approaches usually employ a one-dimensional (1D) chaotic map to generate the diffusion keystream, and the most frequently used one is the logistic map. Those schemes have the advantage of high efficiency but suffer from the flaw of small key space. To address this issue, some improved image cryptosystems using more sophisticated chaotic systems or the combination of different chaotic systems are suggested. For instance, Behnia et al. [1] proposed an image cryptosystem using two cascaded chaotic maps, the keystream is generated by the nonlinear piecewise chaotic maps, whose probability parameter is determined by another chaotic map, i.e., the trigonometric chaotic map. The existence of two parameters of the trigonometric chaotic map, besides parameters of piecewise chaotic maps, has increased the size of key space. In another of their proposal [2], they suggested a way of improving the security of chaos-based cryptosystem by using hierarchy of one dimensional chaotic maps and their coupling, which can be viewed as a high dimensional dynamical system. In [3], Gao et al. reported an image encryption algorithm based on hyperchaos, whose states combinations are used to mask the original image. Compared with ordinary chaotic systems, hyperchaotic systems possess a greater number of state variables and positive Lyapunov exponents, which provide a larger key space and stronger unpredictability. In [4], spatial chaos system was used for high degree security image encryption. The basic idea is to encrypt the image in space with spatial chaos map pixel by pixel, and then the pixels are confused in multiple directions of space. In [5], Rhouma et al. proposed an OCML-based color image encryption scheme with a stream cipher structure. In this scheme, an external key of 192-bit length is chosen to generate the initial conditions and the parameters of the OCML by making some algebraic transformations so as to enhance the sensitivity to the change of any bit of the key. Two schemes with similar structures to [9] were suggested in [10, 11]. The differences are that the Coupled Nonlinear Chaotic Map (CNCM) and the Coupled Two-dimensional Piecewise Nonlinear Chaotic Map (CTPNCM) are employed to encrypt (color) images, and the key size is expended to 240-bit and 256-bit, respectively. Besides, to improve the robustness against chosen-plaintext attack, several schemes with plaintext-dependent keystream generation mechanisms have been proposed [6–8].

Apart from security considerations, performance is another fundamental issue for an image cryptosystem. Existing studies indicate that the diffusion procedure holds a substantial proportion of the whole execution time. This is because a considerable amount of computation load is needed to deal with the real number arithmetic operation and the subsequent quantization required by the keystream generation. Consequently, approaches on performance improvements are mainly focus on how to effectively reduce either the number of diffusion (overall) rounds or the computational complexity of diffusion operation without downgrading the security level. For instance, Xiang et al. [9] proposed a selective image encryption method that only masks the four higher bits of each pixel by the keystream generated from a one-way coupled map lattice. As only 50 % of the whole image data are encrypted, the execution time is reduced. In [10], Wong et al. suggested to introduce certain diffusion effect in the permutation stage by simple sequential add-and-shift operations. As the pixel value mixing effect is contributed by both stages, a lower number of overall rounds are needed to achieve a satisfactory level of security. In [11–13], bit-level permutation algorithms were suggested for the same purpose. In [14], Wong et al. proposed an efficient diffusion mechanism using simple table lookup and swapping techniques as a light-weight replacement of the 1-D chaotic map iteration. In [15], Wang et al. proposed a fast image encryption algorithm with combined permutation and diffusion. In their scheme, the image is firstly partitioned into blocks of pixels, and then, spatiotemporal chaos is employed to shuffle the blocks and, at the same time, to change the pixel values. In [7], Fu et al. introduced a bidirectional spreading mechanism to accelerate the diffusion process. Simulation results indicated that their scheme requires only one round of permutation and two rounds of diffusion to satisfy the plaintext sensitivity requirement.

In general, the permutation and diffusion are two independent processes. To generate the permutation table and diffusion keystream, the iterations of two chaotic map(s)/ system(s) are required and the number of iterations of each map/system typically equals to the original image. In the present paper, we suggest a fast image encryption scheme with a permutation-diffusion structure, where both processes are driven by a single hyperchaotic system. The permutation table and the diffusion keystream are generated from the same sequence extracted from the orbit of the employed system. As the total number of iterations is reduced by half, the computational efficiency is improved. Moreover, the permutation table is created by a sorting mechanism that works on the chaotic sequence, and the strategy effectively avoid the drawback of periodicity that exists in discretized chaotic maps.

The rest of this paper is organized as follows. Section 2 presents the architecture of the proposed scheme. The detailed encryption and decryption algorithms are described in Sect. 3. In Sect. 4, the security of the proposed scheme is analyzed in detail. Finally, conclusions are drawn in the last section.

2 Architecture of the Proposed Scheme

The architecture of the proposed scheme is illustrated by Fig. 1.

A 4-D hyperchaotic system is employed to produce a pseudorandom matrix of the same size as the original image. The four initial conditions of the employed system are used as the secret key. In the permutation stage, the pixels are shuffled according to two permutation tables, i.e., the row and column permutation tables. Both the tables are created by a sorting mechanism that works on the pseudorandom matrix. More

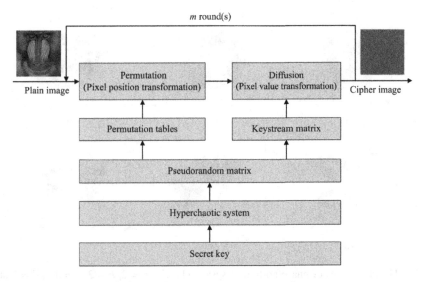

Fig. 1. Architecture of the proposed scheme.

specifically, the permutation tables record the permutation vectors obtained by sorting each row/column of the pseudorandom matrix. To ensure the randomness of the permutation vectors, the last 4 digits of the fractional part of the pseudorandom matrix elements are chosen for the sorting operation. In the diffusion stage, the shuffled image is mixed with a keystream matrix quantified from the pseudorandom matrix. To diffuse the influence of each pixel to the whole ciphered image, the pixel value is altered in a manner dependent on both the keystream element and its previously ciphered pixel. A minimum of two rounds of iteration of the whole permutation-diffusion operation is required to achieve a satisfactory level of security. The detailed implementation of the proposed scheme will be discussed next.

3   Image Encryption Based on Confusion-Diffusion Operations

In the present paper, a hyperchaotic system introduced by Liu et al. [16] is employed to generate the pseudorandom matrix for confusion and diffusion operations. Mathematically, the system is described by

$$
\begin{cases}
x_1 = ax_1 - x_2x_3, \\
x_2 = -bx_2 + x_1x_3 + ex_4, \\
x_3 = -cx_3 + x_1x_2, \\
x_4 = -dx_4 - x_1x_3,
\end{cases}
\tag{1}
$$

where a, b, c, d and e are positive constants with $b + c > a$. When $a = 2$, $b = 3$, $c = 1.5$, $d = 2$ and $2.55 < e < 3$, the system is mainly in its hyperchaotic state, and the projections of its phase portrait are shown in Fig. 2.

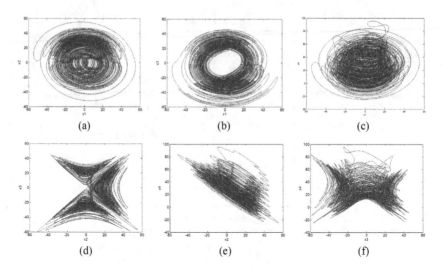

Fig. 2. The projections of phase portrait of system (1) with $a = 2$, $b = 3$, $c = 1.5$, $d = 2$ and $e = 2.7$. (a) x_1–x_2 plane. (b) x_1–x_3 plane. (c) x_1–x_4 plane. (d) x_2–x_3 plane. (e) x_2–x_4 plane. (f) x_3–x_4 plane.

3.1 Cipher Algorithm

Without loss of generality, we assume the image for protection is of $W \times H$ pixels. The detailed cipher process is described as follows:

Step 1: Pre-iterate system (1) for N_0 times to avoid the harmful effect of transitional procedure, where N_0 is a constant. The system can be numerically solved by using fourth-order Runge-Kutta method, as given by

$$\begin{cases} x_{1(n+1)} = x_{1(n)} + (h/6)\left(K_1 + 2K_2 + 2K_3 + K_4\right), \\ x_{2(n+1)} = x_{2(n)} + (h/6)\left(L_1 + 2L_2 + 2L_3 + L_4\right), \\ x_{3(n+1)} = x_{3(n)} + (h/6)\left(M_1 + 2M_2 + 2M_3 + M_4\right), \\ x_{4(n+1)} = x_{4(n)} + (h/6)\left(N_1 + 2N_2 + 2N_3 + N_4\right), \end{cases} \tag{2}$$

with

$$\begin{cases} K_j = ax_{1(n)} - x_{2(n)}x_{3(n)}, \\ L_j = -bx_{2(n)} + x_{1(n)}x_{3(n)} + ex_{4(n)}, \\ M_j = -cx_{3(n)} + x_{1(n)}x_{2(n)}, \\ N_j = -dx_{4n} - x_{1(n)}x_{3(n)}, \end{cases}$$

$$(j = 1)$$

$$\begin{cases} K_j = a(x_{1(n)} + hK_{j-1}/2) - (x_{2(n)} + hL_{j-1}/2)(x_{3(n)} + hM_{j-1}/2), \\ L_j = -b(x_{2(n)} + hL_{j-1}/2) + (x_{1(n)} + hK_{j-1}/2)(x_{3(n)} + hM_{j-1}/2) + e(x_{4(n)} + hN_{j-1}/2), \\ M_j = -c(x_{3(n)} + hM_{j-1}/2) + (x_{1(n)} + hK_{j-1}/2)(x_{2(n)} + hL_{j-1}/2), \\ N_j = -d(x_{4(n)} + hN_{j-1}/2) - (x_{1(n)} + hK_{j-1}/2)(x_{3(n)} + hM_{j-1}/2), \end{cases}$$

$(j = 2, 3)$

$$\begin{cases} K_j = a(x_{1(n)} + hK_{j-1}) + (x_{2(n)} + hL_{j-1})(x_{3(n)} + hM_{j-1}), \\ L_j = -b(x_{2(n)} + hL_{j-1}) + (x_{1(n)} + hK_{j-1})(x_{3(n)} + hM_{j-1}) + e(x_{4(n)} + hN_{j-1}), \\ M_j = -c(x_{3(n)} + hM_{j-1}) + (x_{1(n)} + hK_{j-1})(x_{2(n)} + hL_{j-1}), \\ N_j = -d(x_{4(n)} + hN_{j-1}) - (x_{1(n)} + hK_{j-1})(x_{3(n)} + hM_{j-1}), \end{cases}$$

$(j = 4)$

and the step size h is chosen as 0.0005.

Step 2: The system (1) is iterated continuously. For each iteration, append the four current state variables, $x_{1(n)} - x_{4(n)}$, to a pseudorandom matrix M_p of size M-by-N.

Step 3: Return to **Step 2** until M_p is fully filled. Obviously, the number of required iteration is $N_i = round(M \times N/4)$, where $round(\cdot)$ function rounds a number to its nearest integers.

Step 4: Create the row and column permutation tables, T_r and T_c. For this purpose, a new matrix, M_T, is constructed according to

$$M_T(i,j) = mod\left[round((abs(M_p(i,j)) - floor(abs(M_p(i,j)))) \times 10^{14}), 10^4\right], \tag{3}$$

where $mod(x, y)$ divides x by y and returns the remainder of the division, $abs(x)$ returns the absolute value of x, $floor(x)$ returns the value of x to the nearest integers less than or equal to x. Then each row of M_T is sorted in descending order and the resultant matrix is represented by M_T'. To ensure the computational efficiency, the "Quicksort" algorithm is suggested. Finally, the permutation vectors of each row of M_T, represented by $V_{row(i)} = \{V_{row(i,1)}, V_{row(i,2)}, \ldots, V_{row(i,w)}\}$ with $1 \le i \le H$, is recorded in the corresponding rows of T_r, such that $M_T(i,j) = M_T'(i, V_{row(i,j)})$, where $1 \le j \le W$. The column permutation table, T_c, can be created in a similar way.

Step 5: Rearrange the pixels of the plain-image row by row according to T_r, that is, move the pixel at position (i, j) to $(i, V_{row(i,j)})$. Similarly, the resultant image is shuffled column by column according to T_c.

Step 6: Construct the keystream matrix, K_m, by quantifying M_p according to

$$K_m(i,j) = mod\left[round((abs(M_p(i,j)) - floor(abs(M_p(i,j)))) \times 10^{14}), C_L\right], \tag{4}$$

where C_L is the color level (for a 256 gray-scale image, $C_L = 256$).

Step 7: Mask the pixels of the shuffled image according to Eq. (5).

$$C(i,j) = K_m(i,j) \oplus \{[S(i,j) + K_m(i,j)] \, mod \, C_L\} \oplus C_{-1}(i,j), \tag{5}$$

where $S(i, j)$ and $C(i, j)$ are the (i, j)th pixels of the shuffled image and output cipher image, respectively, $C_{-1}(i, j)$ is the previously ciphered pixels, and $\oplus$ performs bit-wise exclusive OR operation. The initial value of $C_{-1}(i, j)$, used as a seed for the diffusion procedure, may be set by the encipher as a constant.

Step 8: Perform the operations in **Steps** 2–7 for m ($m \geq 2$) rounds according to the security requirement.

The application of the proposed and three typical chaos-based image permutation methods are demonstrated in Fig. 3. Figure 3(a) shows the 512×512 pixels test image with 256 gray levels. Figure 3(b) shows the results of applying the proposed method once. Figure 3(c)–(e) show the results of applying the Arnold cat map, baker map and Chirikov standard map three times, respectively. As can be seen from Fig. 3, compared with those methods using chaotic area-preserving maps, the proposed method provides a better permutation effect with smaller rounds of operation.

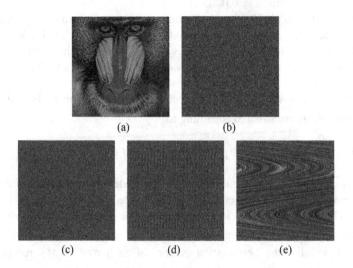

Fig. 3. The application of the proposed and three comparable permutation methods. (a) The test image 512×512 pixels with 256 gray levels. (b) The test image after applying the proposed permutation method once. (c)–(d) are the test images after applying the cat map, baker map and standard map three times, respectively.

3.2 Decipherment Algorithm

The decryption procedure is similar to that of the encryption process except that some steps are followed in a reversed order. As the proposed cryptosystem is a symmetric key cipher, the same secret key $(x_{1(0)}, x_{2(0)}, x_{3(0)}, x_{4(0)})$ and the initial value of $C_{-1}(i, j)$ should be used for decryption. The detailed decryption process is described as follows:

Steps 1 to **3** are the same as those of the encryption algorithm.

Step 4 is the same as **Step 6** of the encryption algorithm.

Step 5: Remove the effect of diffusion from the cipher image to obtain an intermediate image, i.e., the shuffled image. The detailed operations are the same as those described in **Step 7** in encryption, except that the inverse of Eq. (5) is applied, as given by

$$S(i,j) = [K_m(i,j) \oplus C(i,j) \oplus C_{-1}(i,j) + C_L - K_m(i,j)] \, mod \, C_L. \tag{6}$$

Step 6 is the same as **Step 4** of the encryption algorithm.

Step 7: Remove the effect of permutation from the shuffled image to recover the plain-image. This is done in reverse order of **Step 5** in encryption. The pixels in the shuffled image is firstly rearranged column by column according to T_c, that is, move the pixel at position $(V_{col(i,j)}, j)$ to (i, j). Then the resultant image is rearranged row by row according to T_r in a similar way.

4 Security Analysis

The fundamental requirement for an effective cipher is its capability to resist all kinds of known attacks. To demonstrate the robustness of the proposed scheme, thorough security analysis has been carried out in this section, as discussed in the following.

4.1 Brute-Force Attack

In cryptography, a brute-force attack is a cryptanalytic attack that can, in theory, be used against any encrypted data. It consists of systematically checking all possible keys until the correct one is found. Obviously, a cipher with a key length of n bits can be broken in a worst-case time proportional to 2^n and an average time of half that. A key should therefore be large enough that this line of attack is impractical – i.e., would take too long to execute. The key of the proposed cryptosystem consists of four floating point numbers, $(x_{1(0)}, x_{2(0)}, x_{3(0)}, x_{4(0)})$, which are independent of each other. In our scheme, all the variables are declared as 64-bit double-precision type, which gives 53 bits of precision according to the IEEE floating-point standard. Therefore, the key length of our proposed scheme is 212 bits. Generally, cryptographic algorithms use keys with a length greater than 100 bits are considered to be "computational security" as the number of operations required to try all possible 2^{100} keys is widely considered out of reach for conventional digital computing techniques for the foreseeable future. Therefore, the proposed scheme is secure against brute-force attack.

4.2 Key Sensitivity Analysis

Key sensitivity, one of the essential properties of cryptographic algorithms, ensures that no data can be reconstructed from the observed ciphertext by a partly correct guess of the key used for encryption. To evaluate the key sensitivity property of the proposed scheme, the test image (Fig. 3(a)) is firstly encrypted using a randomly selected key ($x_{1(0)} = 32.5889474557272$, $x_{2(0)} = 5.07947265174024$, $x_{3(0)} = -11.139928754\,6819$, $x_{4(0)} = 21.8752607681994$). Then the ciphered image is tried to be decrypted using five decryption keys, one of which is exactly the same as the one used for encryption and the other four have only 1-bit difference to it, as listed in Table 1. The resultant deci-phered images are shown in Figs. 4(a–e), respectively, from which we can see that no information about the plain-image is revealed even though there is only a slight differ-ence between the encryption and decryption keys. Therefore, it can be concluded that the proposed scheme fully satisfies the key sensitivity requirement.

Table 1. Keys used for key sensitivity test.

Figure	Decryption key
4(a)	$(x_{1(0)} = 32.5889474557272, x_{2(0)} = 5.07947265174024,$ $x_{3(0)} = -11.1399287546819, x_{4(0)} = 21.8752607681994)$
4(b)	$(\boldsymbol{x_{1(0)} = 32.5889474557273}, x_{2(0)} = 5.07947265174024,$ $x_{3(0)} = -11.1399287546819, x_{4(0)} = 21.8752607681994)$
4(c)	$(x_{1(0)} = 32.5889474557272, \boldsymbol{x_{2(0)} = 5.07947265174025},$ $x_{3(0)} = -11.1399287546819, x_{4(0)} = 21.8752607681994)$
4(d)	$(x_{1(0)} = 32.5889474557272, x_{2(0)} = 5.07947265174024,$ $\boldsymbol{x_{3(0)} = -11.1399287546818}, x_{4(0)} = 21.8752607681994)$
4(e)	$(x_{1(0)} = 32.5889474557272, x_{2(0)} = 5.07947265174024,$ $x_{3(0)} = -11.1399287546819, \boldsymbol{x_{4(0)} = 21.8752607681995})$

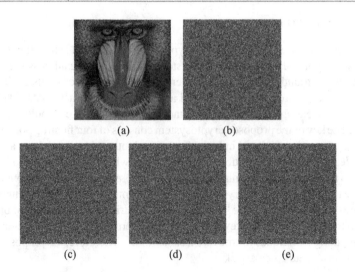

Fig. 4. Results of key sensitivity test.

4.3 Statistical Analysis

Frequency Distribution of Pixel Values. As is known, a good cipher should suffi-ciently mask the distribution of plaintext letters so as to make frequency analysis infea-sible. This is also true for an image cryptosystem except that the data unit is pixel rather than letter. That is, the redundancy of plain-image or the relationship between plain-image and cipher-image should not be observed from the cipher image as such information has the potential to be exploited in a statistical attack. The frequency distribution of pixel values in an image can be easily determined by using histogram analysis. An image histogram is a graph showing the number of pixels in an image at each different intensity value found in that image. Figures 5(b) and (d) show the histograms of the test image (Fig. 5(a)) and its output cipher image (Fig. 5(c)) produced by the proposed scheme, respectively. It's clear from Fig. 5(d) that the pixels in the cipher image are very well distributed across the grayscale, and therefore no information about the plain-image can be gathered through histogram analysis.

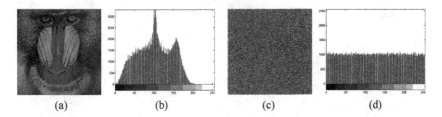

(a)   (b)   (c)   (d)

Fig. 5. Histogram analysis. (a) and (b) are the test image and its histogram. (c) and (d) are the output cipher image and its histogram.

To quantitatively compare the uniformity of gray level distributions between the plain-image and cipher-image, the information entropy is calculated. Information entropy, introduced by Claude E. Shannon in his classic paper "A Mathematical Theory of Communication", is a key measure of the randomness or unpredictability of the information. Information entropy is usually expressed by the average number of bits needed to store or communicate one symbol in a message, as described by

$$H(S) = -\sum_{i=1}^{N} P(s_i) \log_2 P(s_i), \tag{7}$$

where S is a random variable with N outcomes $\{s_1,..., s_N\}$ and $P(s_i)$ is the probability mass function of outcome s_i. It's obvious from Eq. (7) that the entropy for a random source emitting M symbols is $H(S) = \log_2 M$. Therefore, for a ciphered image with 256 gray levels, the entropy should ideally be $H(S) = 8$, otherwise there exists certain degree of predictability which threatens its security.

The entropies for the test image and its ciphered image are calculated according to Eq. (7), and the results are 4.923589 and 7.999212, respectively. Obviously, the entropy for the output cipher image is very close to the theoretical value of a random source. This means that the proposed cryptosystem can be regarded as a pseudorandom data generator and hence secure against statistical analysis.

Correlation Between Neighboring Pixels. To explore the correlation between neighboring pixels in an image, a scatter diagram is commonly employed. To plot a scatter diagram for image data, the following procedures are carried out. First, randomly select S_n pairs of neighboring pixels in each direction from the image. Then, the selected pairs is displayed as a collection of points, each having the value of one pixel determining the position on the horizontal axis and the value of the other pixel determining the position on the vertical axis. The scatter diagrams for horizontally, vertically and diagonally neighboring pixels in the test image (Fig. 5(a)) and its corresponding cipher image (Fig. 5(c)) with $S_n = 5000$ are shown in Figs. 6(a)–(c) and (d)–(f), respectively.

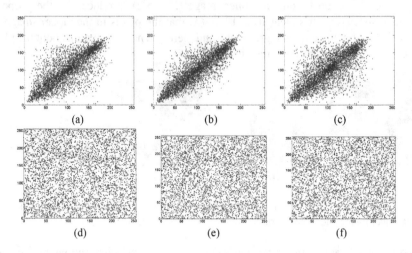

(a)   (b)   (c)

(d)   (e)   (f)

Fig. 6. Graphical analysis for correlation of neighboring pixels. (a)–(c) and (d)–(f) are scatter diagrams for horizontally, vertically and diagonally neighboring pixels in the test image and its output cipher image, respectively.

As can be seen from Figs. 6(a)–(c), most points are clustered around the main diagonal, which suggests a strong positive correlation between the pixels in the original image. In other words, knowing one pixel helps in predicting its neighbor. However, such a strong correlation is completely erased in the output cipher image as the points on Figs. 6(d)–(f) are fairly uniformly distributed.

To further quantitatively measure the correlation between neighboring pixels in an image, the correlation coefficients for the sampled pairs are calculated according to the following three formulas:

$$r_{xy} = \frac{\frac{1}{S_n} \sum_{i=1}^{S_n} (x_i - \bar{x})(y_i - \bar{y})}{\sqrt{\left(\frac{1}{S_n} \sum_{i=1}^{S_n} (x_i - \bar{x})^2\right)\left(\frac{1}{S_n} \sum_{i=1}^{S_n} (y_i - \bar{y})^2\right)}}, \tag{8}$$

$$\bar{x} = \frac{1}{S_n} \sum_{i=1}^{S_n} x_i, \tag{9}$$

$$\bar{y} = \frac{1}{S_n} \sum_{i=1}^{S_n} y_i, \tag{10}$$

where x_i and y_i form the ith pair of neighboring pixels.

Table 2 lists the results of the correlation coefficients for horizontally, vertically and diagonally neighboring pixels in the test image and its output cipher image. The data in Table 2 further proves the conclusion drawn from Fig. 6.

Table 2. Correlation coefficients for neighboring pixels in the test and its ciphered images.

Direction	Test image	Cipher image
Horizontal	0.7500	0.0134
Vertical	0.8575	0.0116
Diagonal	0.7131	–0.0103

4.4 Chosen-Plaintext Attack

In order to implement chosen-plaintext attack, an opponent may make a slight change, usually one bit, in the plain-image and observes the changes of corresponding cipher-image to find out some meaningful relationship between plain-image and cipher-image, which further facilitates in determining the secret key. Obviously, if a cryptosystem has the property of extreme sensitivity to plaintext, then such analysis may become impractical. The plaintext sensitivity property of an image cryptosystem is commonly measured by means of two criteria, i.e., *NPCR* (the number of pixel change rate) and *UACI* (the unified average changing intensity).

The *NPCR* is used to measure the percentage of different pixel numbers between two images. Let $P_1(i,j)$ and $P_2(i,j)$ be the (i,j) th pixel of two images P_1 and P_2, respectively, the *NPCR* can be defined as:

$$NPCR = \frac{\sum_{i=1}^{W}\sum_{j=1}^{H} D(i,j)}{W \times H} \times 100\,\%, \tag{11}$$

and $D(i,j)$ is defined as

$$D(i,j) = \begin{cases} 0 \text{ if } P_1(i,j) = P_2(i,j), \\ 1 \text{ if } P_1(i,j) \neq P_2(i,j). \end{cases} \tag{12}$$

The second criterion, *UACI* is used to measure the average intensity of differences between the two images. It is defined as

$$UACI = \frac{1}{W \times H}\left[\sum_{i=1}^{W}\sum_{j=1}^{H} \frac{|P_1(i,j) - P_2(i,j)|}{C_L - 1}\right] \times 100\,\%. \tag{13}$$

The *NPCR* and *UACI* values for two random images, which is an expected estimate for a good image cryptosystem, is given by

$$NPCR_{\exp ected} = \left(1 - \frac{1}{2^{\log_2 C_L}}\right) \times 100\,\% \tag{14}$$

and

$$UACI_{\exp ected} = \frac{1}{C_L^2}\left(\frac{\sum_{i=1}^{C_L-1} i(i+1)}{C_L - 1}\right) \times 100\,\%, \tag{15}$$

respectively. For instance, the expected *NPCR* and *UACI* for two random images with 256 gray levels are 99.609 % and 33.464 %, respectively.

To demonstrate the plaintext sensitivity of the proposed scheme, two test images with only 1-bit difference at the last, lower-right pixel are encrypted with the same key. This is the worst case as the diffusion operation is done from left to right and top to bottom. We obtain *NPCR* = 99.600 % and *UACI* = 33.495 %. The results indicate that the proposed scheme can effectively diffuse the influence of each pixel over the whole cipher image, and therefore is robust against chosen-plaintext attack.

5 Conclusions

This paper has suggested an efficient image encryption scheme with a permutation-diffusion structure. Unlike the existing schemes which consider the permutation and diffusion as two independent processes, we employed a single hyperchaotic system to drive both the processes. In the permutation stage, the original image is shuffled according to the row and column permutation tables, respectively. Both the tables are created by a sorting mechanism that works on a pseudorandom matrix generated by the employed hyperchaotic system. To ensure the randomness of the permutation vectors, the last 4 digits of the fractional part of the elements in the pseudorandom matrix are chosen for the sorting operation. In the diffusion stage, the shuffled image is mixed with a keystream matrix quantified from the same pseudorandom matrix. Compared with existing schemes, the suggested scheme only requires half the number of iterations of the chaotic map(s)/system(s), and thereby improving the computational efficiency. Moreover, the permutation mechanism introduced in our scheme effectively avoids the flaw of periodicity that exists in discretized chaotic maps. The results of security analysis have demonstrated the satisfactory level of security of our proposed scheme.

Acknowledgments. This work was supported by the National Natural Science Foundation of China (No. 61271350), the Fundamental Research Funds for the Central Universities (No. N150402004), and the Online Education Research Fund of MOE Research Center for Online Education (Qtone Education) (No. 2016YB123).

References

1. Behnia, S., Akhshani, A., Ahadpour, S., et al.: A fast chaotic encryption scheme based on piecewise nonlinear chaotic maps. Phys. Lett. A **366**, 391–396 (2007)
2. Behnia, S., Akhshani, A., Mahmodi, H., et al.: A novel algorithm for image encryption based on mixture of chaotic maps. Chaos Solitons Fractals **35**, 408–419 (2008)
3. Gao, T.G., Chen, Z.Q.: A new image encryption algorithm based on hyper-chaos. Phys. Lett. A **372**, 394–400 (2008)
4. Sun, F.Y., Liu, S.T., Li, Z.Q., et al.: A novel image encryption scheme based on spatial chaos map. Chaos Solitons Fractals **38**, 631–640 (2008)
5. Rhouma, R., Meherzi, S., Belghith, S.: OCML-based colour image encryption. Chaos Solitons Fractals **40**, 309–318 (2009)
6. Wang, Y., Wong, K.W., Liao, X.F., et al.: A chaos-based image encryption algorithm with variable control parameters. Chaos Solitons Fractals **41**, 1773–1783 (2009)
7. Fu, C., Chen, J.J., Zou, H., et al.: A chaos-based digital image encryption scheme with an improved diffusion strategy. Opt. Express **20**, 2363–2378 (2012)
8. Fu, C., Huang, J.B., Wang, N.N., et al.: A symmetric chaos-based image cipher with an improved bit-level permutation strategy. Entropy **16**, 770–788 (2014)
9. Xiang, T., Wong, K.W., Liao, X.F.: Selective image encryption using a spatiotemporal chaotic system. Chaos **17**, 023115 (2007)
10. Wong, K.W., Kwok, B.S.H., Law, W.S.: A fast image encryption scheme based on chaotic standard map. Phys. Lett. A **372**, 2645–2652 (2008)
11. Fu, C., Lin, B.B., Miao, Y.S., et al.: A novel chaos-based bit-level permutation scheme for digital image encryption. Opt. Commun. **284**, 5415–5423 (2011)
12. Zhang, W., Wong, K.W., Yu, H., et al.: An image encryption scheme using lightweight bit-level confusion and cascade cross circular diffusion. Opt. Commun. **285**, 2343–2354 (2012)
13. Fu, C., Meng, W.H., Zhan, Y.F., et al.: An efficient and secure medical image protection scheme based on chaotic maps. Comput. Biol. Med. **43**, 1000–1010 (2013)
14. Wong, K.W., Kwok, B.S.H., Yuen, C.H.: An efficient diffusion approach for chaos-based image encryption. Chaos Solitons Fractals **41**, 2652–2663 (2009)
15. Wang, Y., Wong, K.W., Liao, X.F.: A new chaos-based fast image encryption algorithm. Appl. Soft Comput. **11**, 514–522 (2011)
16. Liu, W.B., Tang, W.K.S., Chen, G.R.: Forming and implementing a hyperchaotic system with rich dynamics. Chin. Phys. B **20**, 090510 (2011)

Architectural Patterns for Security-Oriented Workflows in Collaborative Environments

Sardar Hussain[1(✉)], Richard O. Sinnott[2], and Ron Poet[1]

[1] School of Computing Science, University of Glasgow, Glasgow G12 8QQ, UK
s.hussain.1@research.gla.ac.uk, ron.poet@glasgow.ac.uk
[2] Department of Computing and Information Systems,
University of Melbourne, Melbourne 3010, Australia
rsinnott@unimelb.edu.au

Abstract. Scientific experiments often involve use of shared resources across organization boundaries in distributed collaborative environments. They are more often enabled through web services. A plethora of research is undertaken to protect individual web services. They include centralized security models wherein the main focus is on centralised Virtual Organization (VO) specific attribute authorities, e.g. VOMS, which can be used by collaborative service providers to make authorisation decisions. And a decentralized security model wherein each service provider themselves are responsible for the assignment of roles/privileges to the different members of collaborative environments. Workflows themselves can be orchestrated in centralized or decentralized orchestration models. In this research work we have identified a number of architectural design patterns for security-enabled workflows executions. These patterns are based on the different workflows execution and security models. The key issues in such patterns as well as a rationale of choice are provided. An overview of a security-oriented workflow framework is provided that can tackle some of the issues identified in these patterns.

Keywords: Workflows security · Workflow patterns · Access control · Service-oriented architecture · Centralised workflow · Decentralised workflow

1 Introduction

Security in e-Research is achieved through exploiting a number of technologies. Many of these solutions are based on utilising standard X.509 public key certificate-based PKIs [1] and attribute certificates based upon PMI [2, 3]. X.509 public key certificates are used for the authentication of users, i.e. where a user's identity is established and digitally signed attribute certificates are used for the authorization of users, e.g. to determine the level of access an individual may have to a resource. Authentication is typically augmented with authorisation. That is, authorization ensures that only after a user is authenticated should they have controlled access to the resources based on the privileges and access rights assigned to them by the VO and/or resource providers.

© Springer International Publishing AG 2016
G. Wang et al. (Eds.): SpaCCS 2016, LNCS 10066, pp. 406–421, 2016.
DOI: 10.1007/978-3-319-49148-6_34

Web services are often protected whilst using the PKI based or PMI based security solutions. Common implementations for authorization of web services are PERMIS [4] and XACML [5], amongst others. PERMIS is an RBAC [3] advanced authorisation infrastructure that uses role based policies and realises a scalable X.509 attribute certificate (AC) based PMI. XACML is a well known another implementation based on an XML schema for a general policy language, used to protect resources using both RBAC [3] and ABAC [6] based approaches. In their realisation the authorization credentials are often stored in an **Attribute Authority (AA)** – responsible to create and manage the attributes of the subjects, resources, and the environment. A **Policy Enforcement Point (PEP)** is used for the authorisation decisions based on resource owner policies and requirements applied to requesting entities. In implementing such mechanisms, the PEP is the first point of contact and must be able to intercept service (resource) requests between resource owners and consumers. Another key component is the **Policy Decision Point (PDP)** which is used for evaluating the policies defined by the resource provider and making the authorisation decisions (e.g. allow or deny).

Both push and pull model for credentials can be used for decision by a PEP/PDP. In the push model a user makes a request for a resource and passes (pushes) the credentials needed for authorization. In the pull model, the PDP pulls the user attributes from potentially remote attribute authorities. In this mode PDPs needs to be configured with remote AAs, i.e. it needs to know where to get the user's credentials from.

These authorization mechanisms can be implemented both in centralised and decentralised models. In the centralised model a centralised AA exists that is used by many different resource providers to get authorization credentials. VOMS [8] and CAS [9] are the common examples of such centralised models. Whereas in the decentralised models each resource provider is responsible for the management and provision of their own credentials. Shibboleth [10] is often exploited for such solutions.

Such secured services are often required to be part of a scientific workflow. Scientific workflows generally describe how multiple services can be collaboratively enacted as part of a scientific process. An individual service may have agreed to release and give access to its resources to an individual, but it is then after the job of a third service, i.e. an enactment engine to drive those services and do the actual specified job of enacting the services as a part of workflow process.

A plethora of research work has been undertaken regarding the protection of individual web services both from an authentication point of view and an authorization point of view [11]. To enable collaboration and enact such secured autonomous services in a workflow context is a challenge [20]. Whilst other approaches explored security of workflows [11, 12], however, their focus was mainly authentication-oriented, and/or considered the security of the whole workflow as a single process [13]. Such approaches mostly ignored the autonomy of individual service providers in terms of credentials provision and enforcing their own access control policies.

In this research a number of different security-oriented workflow patterns are identified. They are identified by investigating the existing security models used for the protection of individual web services and their combination with the execution models of workflows themselves. In other words these are not implemented directly; rather they represent theoretical approaches and frameworks for discussion using existing security models when applied for protection of workflows. These patterns provide a template that can be realised by enabling and further extending workflow technologies to exploit existing security mechanisms used in authorising access to web services through workflows. We provide a Name, Problem Domain, Description, Example Scenario and Issues/Challenges for these patterns.

Rest of the paper is organized as follows. In Sect. 2 we provide related work. In Sect. 3 the architectural patterns identified in this research are presented. In Sect. 4 we provide rational of choice and discussion. In Sect. 5 we present a brief overview of a security-oriented workflows framework that tackles some of the issues identified in these patterns. In Sect. 6 we provide conclusions and the future work.

2   Related Work

A pattern in general terms, abstractly describe a design problem in a specific context. It provides a general organization of key elements that can be used to solve a given problem. In this context, the specific problems of orchestrating secure services in workflows are described. Their realisation can be achieved using a range of security technologies. Other patterns in the workflow context are studied in a number of studies. (e.g. www.workflowpatterns.com). One example is the control flow patterns [14]. These patterns are primarily concerned with the flow of control during a workflow execution. These patterns are identified over a period of time by investigating business processes. They are constructed through providing a Name, Description, Example and Implementation for each pattern.

Design patterns were identified by Gamma et al. [15] with focus on object-oriented design patterns. There is no standard format for describing patterns; however, Gamma et al. [15] identified four essential elements of a pattern. Namely a pattern name which is used as a handle to describe the problem; a statement of when to apply the pattern; a description of important elements of the design such as relationships amongst participating elements, their role and responsibilities, and finally a consequences element describing the trade-offs in applying the pattern.

In business workflow systems, the authorization constraints associating tasks to participating people/agents are discussed as patterns in [16]. The elements that describe these patterns include a name, intent and classification which helps designers understand the goals of the pattern. This approach also includes a template part, which describes the pattern itself. The authorization patterns and rules of assigning/ensuring authorization constraints include the separation of duties pattern, binding of duties pattern and the number of roles pattern. The separation of duties pattern checks that no given two tasks are executed by a single agent/person in one workflow. The binding of duties pattern checks that a single agent/person is not executing two tasks in a given workflow. The number of roles pattern checks that a given number of minimum roles must be involved to enforce cooperation in a given workflow. These patterns are applied in the business workflow context with specific focus on task-oriented environments, where workflows are executed by multiple participants and where each individual is designated with a specific role to perform within a workflow in a given organization.

A number of attributes aggregation patterns in the context of secure access to protected resources are discussed in [17]. These patterns are namely Shibboleth-based Simple Attribute Aggregation, User-driven Privacy Preserving Attribute Aggregation and Provider-driven Privacy Preserving Attribute Aggregation. In the Shibboleth-based Simple Attribute Aggregation pattern attributes are simply aggregated from multiple attribute authorities for resource access through the Shibboleth software. In the User-driven Privacy Preserving Attribute Aggregation pattern users themselves aggregate their attributes from multiple authorities through a third service (ShinTau Linking Service) [18], by mapping (linking) between security-targeted service providers and their associated attribute authorities. In the Provider-driven Privacy Preserving Attribute Aggregation pattern the service providers themselves aggregate attributes from their trusted attribute authorities. These patterns are describe the different ways in which attributes for authorization can be provided to services for subsequent authorization and access control decisions.

The patterns identified in this research are based on the security provision mechanism and the workflow enactment models. The initial thoughts about such patterns were presented in [19]. In this research, however, we have further explored these patterns by providing them a specific format and a rationale of choice that explains where different workflow patterns are suited along with a proposed security-oriented workflow framework that tackles some of the issues identified in these patterns.

3 Architectural Patterns for Secure Workflows

3.1 Centralised Workflow Execution with Centralised Security Using Push Model

Problem: How to orchestrate distributed secure services in a workflow process, where the services themselves have delegated the credential definition and issuance to a centralised attribute authority as part of a VO?

Description: Various resource providers share their resources for a specific project through a VO using a centralised security model as typified in the VOMS scenario. Resources are often made available as web services suited for workflow orchestration. Well-established tools and clients exist to access protected individual resources by authorised clients/users (using VOMS and functionality such as voms-proxy-init). However, in the workflow context it is necessary for an EE to interact with multiple independent services in a workflow process. The push model can be used in this pattern, and hence the user is required to provide credentials to the EE, which will subsequently provide them to the workflow services.

Example Scenario: In the following centralized security scenarios for simplicity we focus upon a single VO that uses and trusts a single VO-specific attribute authority. This attribute authority is used to make local authorisation decisions based upon pre-agreed roles and privileges. It is also assumed that the services and data resources have been pre-deployed along with appropriate security policies recognising the roles issued by the centralised attribute authority. These steps would typically be part of the process involved in setting up the VO itself. In Fig. 1 we consider an EE acting as a central

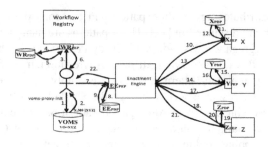

Fig. 1. Centralised workflow execution with centralised security using push model

service that orchestrates and interacts with distributed services X, Y and Z on behalf of a given user. Role "XYZ" is centrally defined and recognised by the service providers X, Y and Z.

Users with this role are able to access resources X, Y and Z. In this scenario, we consider that a user acquires their credentials role ("XYZ") from the centralised attribute authority, e.g. if this were VOMS then role XYZ would be acquired through running voms-proxy-init which creates an X.509 proxy certificate with role "XYZ" embedded as attribute certificate into the X.509 credential.

The workflow registry in this case is a secured repository that the participating organizations/providers use to publish their workflows. Since the services in the workflow are secured and protected, access to the workflow itself needs to be secured and hence not publically available (as in the case of myExperiment workflow repository for example). In this case it is assumed that the participants defining workflows have delegated the permission of accessing, browsing and downloading workflows to the centralised repository. The registry contains many workflows and enforces its own access control for access to the workflows. In this case, the "XYZ" attribute is extracted from the users proxy credential with the "XYZ" attribute embedded and uses this to make a local authorization decision through WRPEP and WRPDP (representing the policy enforcement and policy decision points for the registry itself). This extraction of VOMS credentials from X509 certificates and their usage for authorisation was realised in the JISC funded VPman project (http://sec.cs.kent.ac.uk/vpman).

We also note that the policy evaluation and actual enforcement itself can be realised in many different ways, e.g. using the PERMIS RBAC system [4] or XACML [5]. In this scenario the user submits the workflow to the EE for execution. The centralised EE itself is hosted on a server and protected to ensure that only authorised users are able to submit authorised workflows and as such it will not execute malicious workflows. The EE authenticates the user, e.g. through their X.509 proxy credential and extracts and uses the "XYZ" VOMS attribute certificate embedded within the proxy credentials for the authorization decision.

The workflow logic involves the invocation of three different secured services provided by different service providers. The EE enacts the workflow and invokes service X by forwarding the X.509 credential with role "XYZ" embedded. The policy enforcement point associated with service X (XPEP) extracts and passes the XYZ credentials to its local policy decision point (XPDP) which makes a local access control. After successful evaluation the PEP allows the invocation and service X is accessed and results returned to the EE, which continues with the enactment of the workflow. Subsequently and in a similar manner service Y is invoked and service Z is invoked. Finally service Z returns the final results for the workflow to the EE, which the user is then able to retrieve using their credentials (X509 proxy credential).

3.2 Centralised Workflow Execution with Centralised Security Using Pull Model

Problem: How do we orchestrate distributed secure services in a centralised fashion through a centralised attribute authority using a pull-based attribute aggregation model?

Description: In this model the services are protected through a centralised security model and invoked in a centralised fashion as discussed in the Description part of the pattern in Sect. 3.1. However, instead of using the EE to push the authorization credentials, the participating services themselves pull credentials from the central attribute authority. The EE is used to authenticate and forward the user's authentication credentials to the distributed services. The services themselves in turn use the user's authentication credentials and subsequently pull the authorization credentials from the centralised attribute authority to make their own access control decisions.

Example Scenario: In this scenario the PEPs pull credentials from the recognised and trusted attribute authorities. Pull models are used to counter the issues raised by transferring the VOMS credentials in direct service interactions. In this model the PEP is set up such that it can use the X.509 credentials alone without embedding attribute certificates and pull these attributes from the recognized (trusted) VOMS server itself. This requires that they ascertain the identity of the user (their DN) from the X509 proxy credential. In Fig. 2, this would mean that each PEP directly contacts the VOMS server and pulls the users "XYZ" attribute (identified by their DN) to make a local authorization decision. The typical interactions that take place in the pull model are shown in Fig. 2.

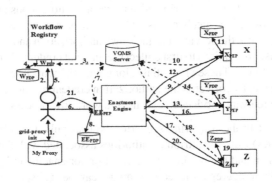

Fig. 2. Centralised workflow execution with centralised security using pull model

Issue 3.1: The primary issue here is to realise and implement the scenarios depicted in Figs. 1 and 2 using existing technologies. Given that the EE is responsible for invoking the workflow processes, it is necessary to extend the functionality of the EE to support both authentication and authorisation capabilities. This issue is common amongst all the coming patterns as well.

Issue 3.2: Workflow languages often do not have security credentials incorporated within a given workflow definition. The issue of concern here is, whether the workflow definition should also involve security information directly?

Issue 3.3: In the above scenarios we have only shown successful authentication and authorisation; what if a service Y or Z fail to allow access to their resource? Furthermore it may be the case that a workflow will consist of many more services, and the invocation and processing of each service themselves may take a longer time period to complete its processing. Failure of a service because of the non-availability of the user credentials will result in the whole workflow failing. In the above scenario, can we determine whether this will occur before service X is invoked? In other words, is it possible to know before workflow invocation whether a given workflow is completely executable from a security perspective?

Issue 3.4: The workflow definition is overly restrictive in the sense that only specific roles defined as part of a specific VO can execute the above workflow scenarios. However, there might be situations where the same service is offered through multiple VOs and/or where different sets of privileges are used to access the service. Is it possible to support heterogeneous set of credentials for workflows and what are the implications for multiple EEs and/or multiple VOs?

3.3 Centralised Workflow Enactment with Decentralised Security Using Push Model

Problem: How can a centralised workflow consisting of distributed and autonomous secure services be executed with each service having its own decentralised authorization and credentials issuing mechanisms realising the so called push model?

Description: In this pattern the distributed services are autonomous and use their own decentralised authorization mechanisms. The services are orchestrated through a centralised engine. Since the services use their own authorization and credentials issuing mechanisms, the user is required to first collect the relevant credentials for the individual services in the workflow. These credentials along with the workflow are pushed to the EE. The EE subsequently forwards the authorization credentials along with the invocation request to the relevant services to execute the workflow process.

Example Scenario: In the following scenario, the user pulls the relevant credentials (attribute certificates) from the attribute authorities associated with the workflow services and pushes them and the workflow specification for enactment by the EE. Such a decentralised attribute aggregation security model can be realised using the PERMIS RBAC infrastructure [4] and is supported through ShinTau [18] for example (Fig. 3).

Issues: The issues 3.1, 3.2, 3.3 and 3.4 also hold here.

Issue 3.5: In this scenario, the user collects (aggregates) authorisation credentials in advance and pushes them to the EE along with the workflow specification. The EE needs

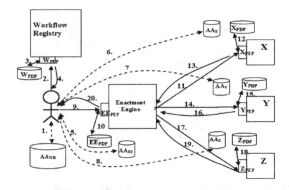

Fig. 3. Centralised workflow enactment with decentralised security using push model

to invoke the services by pushing them the relevant credentials. Implicit in this is how the engine differentiates which service needs, which credentials?

3.4 Centralised Workflow Enactment with Decentralised Security Using Pull Model

Problem: How can a centralised workflow consisting of distributed and autonomous secure services be executed where the services have their own decentralised authorization and credential issuing mechanisms - using the pull model?

Description: As discussed in the description part of pattern 3.3, this pattern also uses distributed and autonomous services having their own decentralised authorization mechanisms. However, here the authorization credentials of the user are pulled by the services themselves from their own trusted attribute authorities. Such services are orchestrated through a centralised EE. The EE is required to provide the authentication credentials of the user only and the services subsequently pull the authorization credentials through the user's authentication credentials (using the extracted DN from the X.509 certificate). The authentication credentials along with the workflow are pushed to the EE. The EE subsequently forwards the authentication credentials and initiates the execution of the workflow.

Example Scenario: As discussed in the beginning of this section, in the decentralised security models, multiple independent attribute authorities issuing their own attribute certificates may exist. Different services may trust different authorities. As such, a workflow that consists of many different services may require attributes from different authorities as shown in Fig. 4.

3.5 Decentralised Workflow with Centralised Security Using Push Model

Problem: How to compose and invoke distributed secure services in a decentralised fashion, where the services themselves have delegated the credential issuance to a centralised attribute authority as part of a VO using a push model?

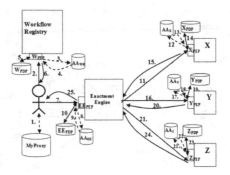

Fig. 4. Centralized enactment engine centralized security with attributes pull model

Description: This pattern is based on a decentralised workflow invocation with central-ised security model. In the decentralised enactment model of workflows scenario, serv-ices themselves are actually processes and interact with each other directly. The partic-ipating services are made aware of which next service to invoke in the workflow process through the workflow specification document. The workflow enactment itself passes from service to service in a decentralised fashion. In this pattern, the services themselves are protected by delegating the credentials issuing to a centralised authority with push-based security credentials, however, authorization decisions when accessing a service takes place at the service end. The user is required to collect the credentials needed for each service before invoking the workflow process. The credentials themselves are pushed to the first service in the workflow along with the workflow specification, which are forwarded onward to each participating service as the workflow is enacted.

Example Scenario: In the given scenario of workflow invocation shown in Fig. 5, the workflow itself is passed through to service X along with the proxy credential of the user. The PEP associated with service X uses its own local attribute authority (AAX) which passes the roles associated with that user (based on their DN) to make a local authorization decision. Once it is established that the invocation is allowed, the inter-action occurs and results are sent to service Y along with the proxy credentials of the initial invocation and the remaining workflow to be enacted, i.e. service Y and Z. Similar authorisation interactions with services Y and Z occur, where service Y forwards the remaining workflow to be enacted to service Z, and service Z sends the final data through to the end user upon completion (via the EE). In this decentralized workflow the activities are performed as shown in Fig. 5.

3.6 Decentralised Workflow with Centralised Security Using the Pull Model

Problem: How to realise a secure decentralised workflow comprised of secure distrib-uted services, where the services themselves have delegated their credentials issuance to a centralised attribute authority, as part of a VO using a pull model?

Description: This pattern is similar to pattern 3.5, wherein the workflow invocation model is decentralised and the security model of the participating services is centralised.

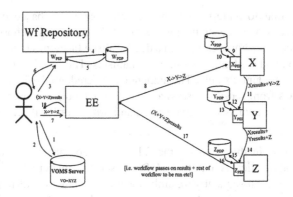

Fig. 5. Decentralised workflow with centralised security using push model

However, in this pattern the credentials are not provided by the user directly, rather, the participating services of the workflow themselves pull the authorization credentials of the user enacting the workflow. The user is required to pass in his/her authentication credentials to the participating services of the workflow process, which in turn are subsequently used to pull the security authorisation credentials from the centralised attribute authority by the services themselves as the workflow is enacted.

Example Scenario: In this scenario the service providers themselves pull the user's credentials from a centralised attribute authority, e.g. a VOMS server. The interactions in Fig. 6 illustrate the steps in realising this scenario.

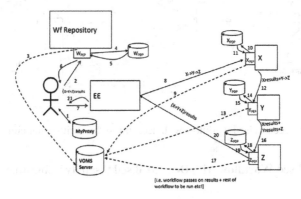

Fig. 6. Decentralised workflow with centralised security using pull model

3.7 Decentralised Workflow with Decentralised Security Using an Attribute Pull Model

Problem: How to execute a decentralised workflow consisting of distributed and autonomous services, each having their own decentralised authorization and credentials issuance mechanisms using a pull model?

Description: Similar to patterns 3.3 and 3.4, this pattern is based on autonomous distributed secured services, each having their own decentralised authorization mechanisms. The services are choreographed in a decentralised fashion. The services use their own authorization and credentials issuing mechanisms. The user is required to provide the authentication credentials only. The authentication credentials along with the workflow process flows from service to service. Each service pulls the user's authorization credentials from their own associated attribute authorities for local access control decisions.

Example Scenario: In this scenario the following steps are expected as shown in Fig. 7. The user authenticates, e.g. to a MyProxy service, that creates an X.509 proxy credentials to be used subsequently for authentication with the workflow repository and the service providers (steps 1, 2). An access request to the workflow repository is issued using the proxy credentials (step 3). The WF$_{PEP}$ authenticates the user and extracts their DN from X.509 credentials and uses this to pull the user's attributes certificates from its own attribute authority (steps 4, 5). The WF$_{PEP}$ submits the workflow request and the pulled attributes to the WF$_{PDP}$ for authorisation (step 6). The WF$_{PDP}$ performs authorisation checks and assuming the request is granted the workflow is released to the user (steps 7, 8).

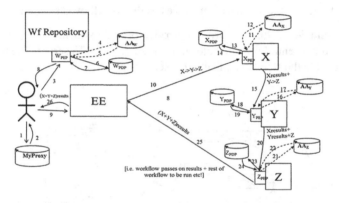

Fig. 7. Decentralised workflow with decentralised security using pull model

3.8 Decentralised Workflow with Decentralised Security Using an Attribute Push Model

Problem: How to orchestrate distributed and autonomous secure services in a decentralised fashion where the services have their own decentralised authorization and credentials issuance mechanisms using a push model?

Description: Similar to pattern 3.7, this pattern is based on distributed autonomous services, each having their own decentralised authorization mechanisms, orchestrated in a decentralised fashion. This pattern is, however, based on a push model of credential provision. The user is required to first collect the relevant credentials of the component services of the workflow. The authorization credentials of the component services of the workflow process are pushed with the service invocations for execution. The credentials along with the workflow process are forwarded from service to service during the execution of the workflow.

Example Scenario: In this scenario the user needs to collect the authorisation credentials for all the resource providers (including workflow providers and services providers) beforehand. There are many attribute authorities, and each service provider may well have their own attribute authority that they trust. The typical interactions in a decentralised workflow supporting decentralised security using an attribute push model are shown in Fig. 8 as follows.

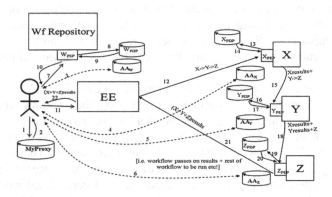

Fig. 8. Decentralise workflow with decentralised security using push model

Issue 3.6: In this scenario authentication, as well as, authorisation credentials are potentially passing from service to service within the workflow. As such the credentials are potentially exposed to each service. Their exposure can lead to privacy and security challenges, hence the model shown here creates attribute certificates in the local repositories (steps 4, 5, 6) - technologies such as PERMIS provide such capabilities.

4   Discussion and Rationale of Choice

These patterns are presented from the perspective whereby service providers are protected and securely enacted in given workflows. Whilst the service provider's will have their own requirements and access control priorities, it is the user's choice of selecting which model, either centralised or decentralise workflows to use. However, the service providers need to be willing to allow decentralised workflow orchestration. In the centralised workflow model service providers are unaware whether they are accessed in a workflow process or directly through a web service client. The security credential provision mechanisms need to be implemented on the workflow engine side.

Centralised and decentralised securities have their own advantages and disadvantages, which are outlined in [21]. The centralised security model restricts participants of a certain VO to agree upon a specific set of roles and their privileges before establishing the VO. It makes the definitions of roles/privileges less dynamic. In the decentralised security model on the other hand, roles are defined and privileges assigned by the participants service providers themselves. In this model service providers coordinate and collaborate at peer-to-peer level, i.e. they do not require to agree upon specific roles and privileges across the VO. This makes decentralised security models for VO's more scalable and dynamic. Centralised security models ideally suit static VOs where roles and privileges do not change frequently across the VO.

For large-scale collaborations encompassing a large number of organizations, it becomes unrealistic for a single VO administrator to have detailed knowledge about all end users at each participating site, and to assign them roles and privileges. Decentralised security models are more scalable in this respect and hence support more dynamic collaborations. Allowing users from different sites to access resources often requires delegating the task of assigning roles to users (delegation of authority). These advantages and disadvantages have a direct bearing on the secure workflow definition and execution, wherein the participant services in workflows can have centralised and decentralised security support.

Typically, centralised workflows have more control over the workflow processes, owing to the extended set of information available about the workflow process. They are, however, not suitable for large workflows that involves large datasets comprised of many inputs/outputs, since they can result in performance bottlenecks at the centralised EE. Decentralised workflows are, however, difficult to implement. They do, however, offer advantages when large and intensive data transactions takes place (Montage workflows, for example, http://pegasus.isi.edu/applications). Decentralised workflows are not easy to modify as they are themselves deployed across the participating service provider sites, and all providers need to decide on the workflow process definitions and their associated parameters. Centralised workflows on the other hand are more evolutionary in the sense that, parameters, can be changed, web services can be added and removed to modify the existing workflows for new set of experiments. Decentralised workflows also require having prior trust relationships amongst all of the participants before taking part in the workflow collaboration. In the case of centralised orchestration, however, it is the EE and the concerned web service that need to have a trust relationship. Other privacy policies may also be imposed by service providers, e.g. not to use/compose their datasets with data from other workflows.

Centralised workflows with centralised security (patterns 3.1 and 3.2) are suitable for less dynamic, VO-specific collaborative environments, i.e. the VO's are small and the credentials and their scope are defined at a VO-specific level. They are comparatively easy to implement, i.e. a single attribute authority can be used to define and assign roles and privileges. To enact a workflow, a user is required to have a specific role issued by the VO authority (push model) and forward this along with the workflow for execution. These are subsequently forwarded along with the service requests within the workflow execution. The pull model of credential provision in this case relieves the users from obtaining authorization credentials before workflow execution. The pull model also allows users to provide minimum credentials for workflow execution and the services themselves care for pulling further authorization credentials from the centralised authority.

Centralised workflow with decentralised security (patterns 3.3 and 3.4) leverage the advantages of both centralised workflow and decentralised security models. They are more scalable in terms of incorporating services from heterogeneous environments. The push model in this case, however, requires the user to keep track of the services, their associated credentials and the attribute authorities used. The pull model in this case is more scalable for workflows to add more services from different sites, and does not require that the user collect credentials before workflow execution.

Supporting decentralised workflows with centralised security (patterns 3.5 and 3.6) is easy to implement, i.e. by getting specific roles/credentials and forwarding them to the collaborative services of the workflow. The credentials flows along the workflow process execution from service to service. They are, however, only possible within a specific trust domain and specific VO. Services from outside of the VO collaboration are difficult to integrate in the workflow definition in this case. The pull model in this case, helps to minimise the exposure of the user's credentials and lessens the burden of keeping track of their attribute authorities.

Decentralised workflows with decentralised security (patterns 3.7 and 3.8) are arguably more suited to larger and more complex workflows. They are, however, difficult to implement owing to the exploratory nature and changing parameters of experiments in scientific workflows. Specific workflows that involve minor changes in their workflow definition are more suited to such implementations.

5 Security-Oriented Workflow Framework

To tackle some of the issues identified in these patterns a prototype of a security-oriented workflow framework (SOWF) has been realised [22, 23]. Whilst the complete details of this framework are beyond the scope of this paper, however, we provide a brief overview and key components of the proposed framework as shown in Fig. 9.

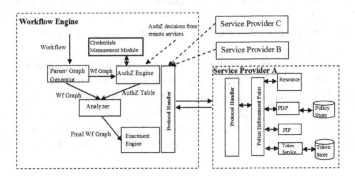

Fig. 9. Authorization-supported workflow architecture

The framework uses existing PEP, PDP and Policy Information Points (PIP) of available security solutions. The additional components added include: a *parser*, an *analyser*, an *authorization engine*, a *protocol handler*, a *credential management module*, and a *token service* that helps tackle the issues identified in the patterns discussed above. When a workflow is pushed for execution, the parser determines the workflow path based on the association of different services with each other and the workflows patterns [14].

The authorization engine then collects the authorization decisions from each individual participating web service, which is further used by the analyser to determine in advance whether the workflow is executable from the security perspective or not. The analyser determines this based on the available authorization decisions and the workflow graph pushed from the Parser. The credentials management module supports the *authorization engine* to provide the required credentials for the secure invocation of remote services. Whilst the authorization engine collects the authorization decision from each remote service, the *token service* keeps track of the issued authorization decisions. This further helps in maintaining session information of the authorization decisions issued by a PDP. This service is used when the workflow engine requests an authorization decision to be made. The Protocol Handler interacts with the *Token Service* by providing a *permit* authorization decision issued by the PDP along with the resource to be accessed. If the workflow is executable or potentially executable, the workflow is pushed to the engine for execution along with the collected authorization decisions. Otherwise the user is informed that the workflow cannot be executed. The detailed mechanism of this framework is beyond the scope of this paper. The implementation of this framework is available from Github at (https://github.com/aumidh).

6   Conclusions

The patterns identified and explored are based upon centralised and decentralised workflows with associated centralised and decentralised security models. It was shown that existing technologies could be used to realise these scenarios, e.g. MyProxy, PERMIS. However, a number of issues and challenges existed that need to be resolved. To enable collaboration, particularly in the scientific domain, the patterns identified in this paper provides a template that can be realised by enabling and further extending workflow technologies to exploit existing security mechanisms used in authorising access to web services through workflows.

The issues and challenges identified here are raised both in the context of the security of individual web services and the realisation of successful workflow execution. They describe models of provision of security credentials to protected web services. These patterns show how the design choices that can be made by existing resource providers in delivering secure services that can be enacted through workflows. An overview of one framework is provided that can tackle some of the issues identified in these patterns.

References

1. Housley, R., Polk, T.: Planning for PKI: Best Practices Guide for Deploying Public Key Infrastructure. Willey Computer Publishing, Chichester (2001)
2. Watt, J., Sinnott, R.O., Stell, A.J.: Dynamic privilege management infrastructures utilising secure attribute exchange (2005)

3. Chadwick, D.W.: An X.509 Role-based Privilege Management Infrastructure (2001)

4. Chadwick, D.W., Otenko, A.: The PERMIS X.509 role based privilege management infrastructure. Future Gener. Comput. Syst. **19**(2), 277–289 (2003)

5. OASIS eXtensible Access Control Markup Language (XACML) Version 2.0 [Specification] (2005)

6. Yuan, E., Tong, J.: Attributed based access control (ABAC) for web services. In: Proceedings of 2005 IEEE International Conference on Web Services, 2005, ICWS 2005 (2005)

7. Sinnott, R.O.: Grid Security: Practices, Middleware and Outlook. National e-Science Centre (2005)

8. Virtual Organization Management Service (VOMS). http://vdt.cs.wisc.edu/components/voms.html

9. Pearlman, L., Welch, V., Foster, I., Kesselman, C., Tuecke, S.: A community authorization service for group collaboration, pp. 50–59 (2002)

10. Internet2 Shibboleth technology (2009). http://shibboleth.internet2.edu

11. Dörnemann, T., Friese, T., Herdt, S., Juhnke, E., Freisleben, B.: Grid workflow modelling using grid-specific BPEL extensions. In: Proceedings of German e-Science Conference, vol. 2007, pp. 1–9 (2007)

12. Tan, K.L.L., Turner, K.J.: Orchestrating grid services using BPEL and Globus Toolkit 4. In: 7th PGNet Symposium (2006)

13. Paci, F., Bertino, E., Crampton, J.: An access-control framework for WS-BPEL. Int. J. Web Serv. Res. (IJWSR) **5**(3), 20–43 (2008)

14. van Der Aalst, W.M.P., Ter Hofstede, A.H.M., Kiepuszewski, B., Barros, A.P.: Workflow patterns. Distrib. Parallel Databases **14**(1), 5–51 (2003)

15. Vlissides, J., Helm, R., Johnson, R., Gamma, E.: Design Patterns: Elements of Reusable Object-Oriented Software, vol. 49, p. 120. Addison-Wesley, Reading (1995)

16. Castano, S., Fugini, M.G.: Rules and patterns for security in workflow systems. In: Jajodia, S. (ed.) Database Security XII, vol. 14, pp. 59–74. Springer, New York (1999)

17. Sinnott, R.O., Bayliss, C., Galang, G., Mannix, D., Tomko, M.: Security attribute aggregation models for e-research collaborations. In: 2012 IEEE 11th International Conference on Trust, Security and Privacy in Computing and Communications (TrustCom), pp. 342–349 (2012)

18. Shib-Grid Integrated Authorization (Shintau)

19. Sinnott, R.O., Hussain, S.: Architectural design patterns for security-oriented workflows in the social science domain. In: Conference on e-Social Science, Cologne, Germany, 24–26 June 2009 (2009)

20. Sinnott, R.O., Hussain, S.: Security-oriented workflows for the social sciences. In: 2010 4th International Conference on Network and System Security (NSS), pp. 152–159 (2010)

21. Sinnott, R.O., Chadwick, D.W., Doherty, T., Martin, D., Stell, A.J., Stewart, G., Su, L., Watt, J.: Advanced security for virtual organizations: the pros and cons of centralized vs decentralized security models, pp. 106–113 (2008)

22. Hussain, S., Sinnott, R.O.: A security-oriented workflow framework for collaborative environments. In: 2016 IEEE 15th International Conference on Trust, Security and Privacy in Computing and Communications (TrustCom) (in press)

23. Hussain, S., Sinnott, R.O., Poet, R.: Security-enabled enactment of decentralized workflows. In: ACM 9th International Conference on Security of Information and Networks, 2016 (2016)

Modeling and Vulnerable Points Analysis for E-commerce Transaction System with a Known Attack

Mimi Wang[1,2], Guanjun Liu[1,2(✉)], Chungang Yan[1,2], and Changjun Jiang[1,2]

[1] Department of Computer Science, Tongji University, Shanghai 201804, China
wangmimi2013@hotmail.com,
{liuguanjun,yanchungang,cjjiang}@tongji.edu.cn
[2] Key Laboratory of Ministry of Education for Embedded System
and Service Computing, Tongji University, Shanghai 201804, China

Abstract. With the rapid development of network and mobile terminal, online trading has become more and more widespread. However, E-commerce transaction systems aren't completely strong due to the openness of network. Some points of a system is vulnerable in the real world and thus they can be utilized by attackers and cheaters. We focus on E-commerce transaction systems with attacks, and propose a kind of Petri nets called VET-net (Vulnerable E-commerce Transaction nets) to model them. A VET-net considers both normal actions belonging to the related system and malicious actions ones such as tampering with a data. Based on VET-net, this paper proposes the concepts of vulnerable points and vulnerable levels in order to describe the cause and levels of vulnerability. And then it uses the dynamic sling method to locate the vulnerable points. A real example is used to illustrate the effectiveness and rationality of our concepts and method.

Keywords: E-commerce transaction · Vulnerable piont · Vulnerable level · Dynamic slicing · Petri nets · Known attack

1 Introduction

With E-commerce booming in China, online trading has become more and more widespread. Electronic payment (e-payment) has become an important trading activity in people's daily life. iResearch Consulting statistics show that the size of China's online-shopping market amounted to 16.4 trillion Yuan in 2014, and they have become an important force to promote the economy. The volume of online shopping with a third-party payment platform (TPP) reached 11.8 trillion Yuan in 2015, representing an increase of 46.9 % over 2014 [1].

However, e-payment is a new way of trade in recent years and still in a development process. There are some cases are shown that the system is under attack. We analyze the case and show the E-commerce system vulnerable to *combined attack*. The inherent vulnerability of the system to combined attack

© Springer International Publishing AG 2016
G. Wang et al. (Eds.): SpaCCS 2016, LNCS 10066, pp. 422–436, 2016.
DOI: 10.1007/978-3-319-49148-6_35

lies in the usage of the Trojan and fishing website in the pay process, which imperil the security and dependability of E-commerce system. In a E-commerce system, where processes are attacked, the challenge of finding vulnerabilities becomes more complicated and more pressing at the same time. For example, a company offering a vulnerable point to others will not only suffer locally from an internal defect, but might face penalties arising from, e.g., attack. [2] divides system vulnerability into two types: one is deadlock or internal defect of system itself, another is the vulnerability due to influence of external actions such as external attack. Vulnerability types have to be manually derived before tools can employ the corresponding vulnerability patterns for automated analyses.

Figure 1 shows a real case occurred in Mongolia. Criminal B buys a Trojan program through the QQ, and then obtains the buyers' IDs and the sellers' contact phone numbers from the TaoBao transaction records by using this Trojan program. B calls and tells seller C that he is a friend of buyer A and helps him to change the address. B calls to A and says that he is seller C and AliPay is upgrading now, and thus A should pay one yuan to activate this upgrade. B deliberately complicates activation process and then A cannot operate it. A has to ask for B to provide a remote assistance through QQ. B implants a Trojan program into the computer of A through QQ remote assistance. Then B steals the money from the net card of A and transfers them to account $a1$ of B. B uses this account to buy Unicode prepaid phone $CARDS$ and builds his own online shop on TaoBao. B asks his partner D to virtually buy card on online store, and then B transfers money from account $a1$ to account $a2$ of AliPay of B. In fact, Fig. 1 gives an attack process. And Fig. 3 illustrates this cheat process. In this case, we observe that a combination of both Trojan and fishing website would prevent the system from being vulnerable to the combined attack.

Technology today has a big impact on system, both in the manner of daily usage in our private lives and even more when it comes to business. For the vulnerability problem, it is different to define vulnerability and vulnerable points due to different concern objects and application scope. Krsul [12] first defined software vulnerabilities in his doctoral dissertation. Some weak points might only be some component defects, but most of the vulnerability stemmed from the operating system kernel, privilege processes, file systems, service process and the network system components. [13] gave the definition of security vulnerability of E-commerce: a security vulnerability is a weakness in a product that can allow an attacker to compromise the integrity, availability, or confidentiality of that product. However, in the real word, due to more and more attack forms such as Trojan, Fishing site attack, only to study the system itself' correctness or holes of designing system already cannot satisfy the needs of reality. We think that it is significant to consider the vulnerability under an attack. So the definition of vulnerability is based on an attack. We think that for the real E-commerce transaction system, the *vulnerability* is a weakness that induced the actions of some attack. In fact, for a unknown attack form, there isn't a good method to locate the *vulnerable region* (the vulnerable region can be considered to be some vulnerable points joined up to implement an attack)of system. As shown in Fig. 1, what we consider is the vulnerability due to external attacks. Fault/attack trees [7–9] and Failure Mode and Effects Analysis (FMEA) [10,11] are two prominent representatives of manual analysis methods. The strength of these methods is that they leave much room for the security expert to apply subjective skills and personal experience, enabling the discovery even of completely new types of vulnerabilities. However, given the vulnerabilities observed in real-world systems, the importance of searching for completely new types of vulnerabilities should not be overestimated. And these methods require much experience and provide little guidance during the analysis. So it has be a challenge foe us to analyze vulnerability in the absence of experience.

For a known attack form, we may try our best to find the *vulnerable region*. If we know the attack, it is more effective and credible to calculate the vulnerable parts.

According to the condition, we know that:

(1) the vulnerability type is the second one, i.e. the vulnerability of E-commence transaction system is caused by external attacks. At the same tine, attack process is known. In fact, Fig. 1 describes the attack process.
(2) the E-commerce transaction system itself is not strong. The attack process shows that for a E-commerce transaction system, attackers are likely to attack it. It shows that there are some safety loopholes in the system. For example, why the transaction record can be divulged. Whether the case will not or easily occur if the system has a verification process when the user uses activation process. Why there is no verification process when the user transfers money to account $a1$.
(3) there are some vulnerable regions. From the case, there are more than one points touched to the attacker' ultimate goal. Attacker uses more than one points to attack the system.

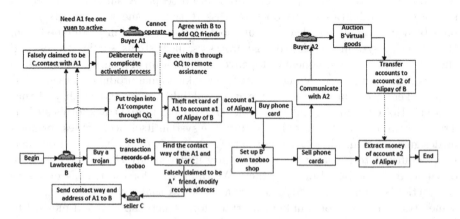

Fig. 1. A real case of E-commerce transaction system under an attack occurred in Mongolia

So based on the above, the questions are: how to use a formal method to locate the vulnerable points of a system with some given attacks and how to formally declare its vulnerable levels. This paper focuses on these questions and obtains the following results:

(1) We start from a real case of Alipay, and define *Vulnerable E-commerce Transaction net (VET-net)*. The VET-net is a labeled Petri net which can describe a real system considering malicious actions. The malicious actions are caused by some attacks.
(2) We propose the concept of *vulnerable points* that result in unpredictable states. And then we give three *vulnerable levels* to describe three different *vulnerable point sets* which express different safety levels.
(3) Based on the dynamic slicing algorithm, we further present a new method to locate the vulnerable points.

The structure of this paper is as follows: Sect. 2 reviews some basic knowledges. Section 3 defines VET-net. Section 4 defines vulnerable points and three vulnerable levels. Section 5 proposes a method to detect the vulnerable points, and conclusion is given in Sect. 6.

2   Background

This section recalls the basic concepts and definitions used in this paper. For more details, one can refer to [14,18].

Computing a net slice can be seen as a graph reachability problem. Program slicing is first defined by Weiser [17] in the context of program debugging. In particular, Weiser uses program slicing to isolate a program that contains a bug and thus it becomes easier for programmers to find this bug. In general, slicing extracts these statements that can affect some point of interest as the slicing criterion. The concepts of slicing criterion and slice can be found in [4,22,23].

Definition 1 (Slicing Criterion). *Let* $N = (P,T,F)$ *be a net. A slicing criterion of* N *is a pair* $\langle M_0, Q \rangle$ *where* M_0 *is an initial marking of* N *and* $Q \subseteq P$ *is a set of places.*

Definition 2 (Slice). *Let* $N = (P,T,F)$ *be a net and* $\langle M_0, Q \rangle$ *be a slicing criterion of* N. $N' = (P',T',F')$ *is a slice of* N *w.r.t.* $\langle M_0, Q \rangle$ *if the following conditions hold:*

(1) N' *is a subnet of* N*; and*
(2) for each firing sequence $\sigma = t_1 t_2 \cdots t_n$ *of* (N, M_0) *such that* $M_0 \xrightarrow{t_1} M_1 \xrightarrow{t_2}$
$\cdots \xrightarrow{t_n} M_n$ and $M_{n-1}(p) < M_n(p)$ *for some* $p \in Q$*, there exists a firing sequence* σ' *for* (N', M_0') *with* $M_0' = M_0 |_{P'}$*, such that*
(i) σ' *is the projection of* σ *over* T'*,*
(ii) $M_0' \xrightarrow{\sigma'} M_m'$*,* $m \leq n$*, and*
(iii) M_m' *covers* $M_n |_{P'}$ *(i.e.* $M_m' \geq M_n |_{P'}$*)*

For example in [23], Fig. 2(b) shows the slice N_1 considering the slicing criterion $\langle M_0, \{p_5, p_7, p_8\} \rangle$.

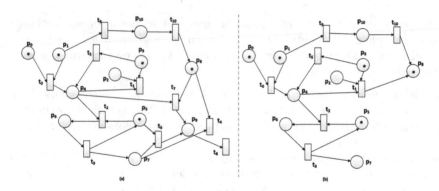

Fig. 2. An example introducing the slice: (a) an example from [23], (b) its slice.

3 Vulnerable E-commerce Transaction Net Under Attacks

In this section, we define Vulnerable E-commerce Transaction net (*VET*-net). We first recall *Attack*.

Definition 3 (Attack [20]). *An attack is a sequence of actions $a_1.a_2 \cdots a_n \in T$ such that there exists an elementary path from some initial state induced by $a_1 \cdots a_n$ and which reaches the set G. Let Attack(T) be the set of attacks in T; it is finite. G- the final states are the states where attackers hope to achieve.*

In our case of Fig. 3, the set G consists of state p_{b20} and p_{b23}.

Definition 4 (LPN [19]). *An LPN is a 6-tuple $\Sigma = (P, T, F, M_0, E, \lambda)$, where*

(1) (P, T, F, M_0) is a Petri net;
(2) E is a set of actions including unobservable action ε; and
(3) $\lambda : T \to E$ is a label function.

In order to describe and understand *VET*-net better, we first give the following two concepts.

Definition 5 (Malicious transition). *Given a net $N = (P, T, F)$, a malicious transition $t_Y \in T$ is a transition that is not a normal action of a transaction system (such as replaced or tampering with data).*

Definition 6 (Malicious place). *Given a net $N = (P, T, F)$, a maliciousplace $p_Y \in P$ is a place if it is associated with t_Y.*

In Fig. 3, the place p_{b20} and p_{b23} are two malicious ones since transition b_{19} is malicious. Our idea is to look for those source points leading to these malicious states.

Definition 7 (VET-net). *An VET-net is an 11-tuple $(P, T, F, M_0, p_I, p_F, A, I, O, \lambda)$, where:*

(1) (P, T, F, M_0) *is a Petri net;P is a finite set of places, $p_I \in P$ is the source place satisfying* $^\bullet p_I = \emptyset$ *and $p_F \in P$ is the sink place satisfying* $^\bullet p_F = \emptyset$;

(2) A *is a finite set of action;*

(3) $I = \{yo, no, \epsilon\}$ *is the set of input symbols;*

(4) $O = \{yf, nf, \epsilon\}$ *is the set of output symbols;*

(5) $\lambda : T \to (A \times I \times O)$ *is the label function.*

We know that $P = P_Y \bigcup P_N$ and $T = T_Y \bigcup T_N$, which P_Y is the *malicious place set* and T_Y is the *malicious transition set*.

We characterize the real case using VET-net such as Fig. 3, obtaining an initial and fuzzy model. Table 1 introduces the minings of transitions in Fig. 3. In Fig. 3, the transitions labeled by yo, yf mean that the actions aren't themselves' or tampered, the transitions labeled by no, yf mean that the actions aren't themselves' or tampered. In order to better describe the abnormal trading with tampered or replace behaviors in the electronic transaction process, we put forward a vulnerable points based on VET-net.

In real trading process, there may be some unmoral trading state, such as amount stolen, illegal trade. There are many reasons caused by malicious state, such as unsubstantial safety awareness of user itself, malicious attacks from the outside, the design problem of the system itself. We in addition to call for the user cautious in online transactions, mainly to find the system itself' vulnerable points. According to the real case in this section, we want to find the points which are not strong of system, in order to ensure that the similar situations don't occur.

4   Vulnerable Points and Vulnerable Levels

The Vulnerable points we considered are under attack. Firstly in this section, we recall the concept of attack. For more details one can refer to [20,21]

Definition 8 (Vulnerable Point). *An vulnerable point is a place that induced the actions of some attack.*

(Malicious state in Fig. 3 is the state p_{b20} that isn't the desired state of normal trading process).

For a reachability graph, maybe not only one path to the malicious state, and the same points that are in different path may not have the same vulnerability.

Flowing, from a computation view, we give some related concepts.

For the actual application needs, we give following three kinds of vulnerable points set.

Definition 9 (First-level Vulnerable Points Set (FVP)). *Let VET-net=* $(P, T, F, M_0, p_I, p_F, A, I, O, \lambda)$ *a vulnerable E-commerce Transaction net and with $i_i = t_{i1} t_{i2} \cdots t_{im}$. And for a state p_q, the first-level vulnerable points set FVP satisfy the following conditions:*

(1) $FVP \subseteq P$;

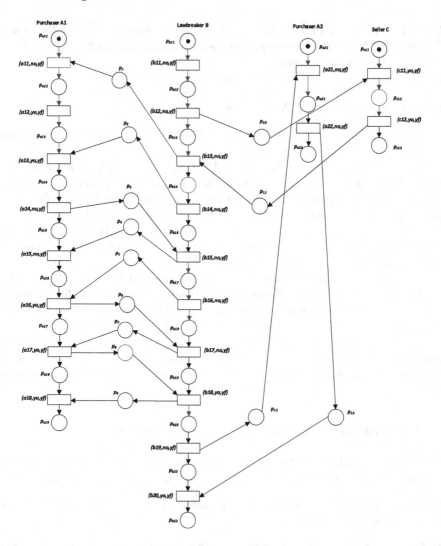

Fig. 3. VET-net model of Fig. 1

(2) $\sigma_1 \cap \sigma_2 \cap \cap \sigma_n \neq \emptyset$;

(3) $FVP = \{p_i \in^\bullet t_i \mid t_i \in (\sigma_1 \cap \sigma_2 \cap \cdots \sigma_n)\}$.

The path which leads to the first-level vulnerable points set is the public path. And these points in $FVP \backslash \{M_0\}$ is considered to be *Minimal Vulnerable Region*.

Definition 10 (Minimal Vulnerable Region(M_iVR)). *Let VET-net=$(P, T, F, M_0, p_I, p_F, A, I, O, \lambda)$ a vulnerable E-commerce Transaction net and with $\sigma_i = t_{i1}t_{i2}\cdots t_{im}$. And for a state p_q, the minimal vulnerable region M_iVP satisfy the following conditions:*

Table 1. Meaning of transitions in Fig. 3

Transitions in Fig. 3	Meaning
b_{11}	Query TaoBao transaction records, and get A1' and C' information
b_{12}	Falsely claimed to be A1' friend, contact with C
b_{13}	Contact with A1 and need A1 fee one yuan
b_{14}	Deliberately complicate activation process
b_{15}	Apply for A1 for QQ friends
b_{16}	Remote assistance through QQ
b_{17}	Put Trojan into A1' computer through QQ
b_{18}	Theft net card of A1 to account a1 of AliPay of B
b_{19}	Set up TaoBao shop to sell phone cards
b_{20}	Extract money of account a2 of AliPay
a_{11}	Receive B' call
a_{12}	Log on TaoBao
a_{13}	Fee the activation
a_{14}	Pay for failure
a_{15}	Agree with B to add as a QQ friend
a_{16}	Agree with B to remote assistance
a_{17}	Agree to pay 1 yuan for activation fee
a_{18}	Agree to transfer net silver to account a1 of AliPay
a_{21}	Auction B' virtual goods
a_{22}	Transfer accounts to account a2 of AliPay of B
c_{11}	Receive B' call
c_{12}	Send contact way and address of A1 to B

(1) $M_i VP \subseteq FVP$;
(2) $M_0 \notin M_i VP$.

Property 1. For a VET-net, if it exits a $M_i LR$, then the $M_i LR$ must be only one.

Definition 11 (Second-level Vulnerable Points Set(SVP)). *Let VET-net*$=(P, T, F, M_0, p_I, p_F, A, I, O, \lambda)$ *a vulnerable E-commerce Transaction net, with* $\sigma_i = t_{i1} t_{i2} \cdots t_{im}$. *And for a state* p_q, *the second-level vulnerable points set SVP satisfy the following conditions:*

(1) $SVP \subseteq P$;
(2) $\sigma_1 \cup \sigma_2 \cup \cdots \sigma_n \neq \emptyset$;
(3) $SVP = \{ p_i \in {}^\bullet t_i \mid t_i \in (\sigma_1 \cup \sigma_2 \cup \cdots \sigma_n) \}$.

The path which leads to the second-level vulnerable points set is the path only leading to malicious state. And these points in $SVP \setminus \{M_0\}$ is considered to be *Dimity Vulnerable Region*.

Definition 12 (Dimity Vulnerable Region (DVR)). *Let VET-net=$(P, T, F, M_0, p_I, p_F, A, I, O, \lambda)$ a vulnerable E-commerce Transaction net and with $\sigma_i = t_{i1} t_{i2} \cdots t_{im}$. And for a state p_q, the dimity vulnerable region DVR satisfies the following conditions:*

(1) $M_i VP \subseteq SVP$;
(2) $M_0 \notin M_i VP$.

We can see that for a VET-net, if it exits a $M_i LR$, then the $M_i LR$ may be more than one.

Definition 13 (Third-level Vulnerable Points Set (TVP)). *Let VET-net= $(P, T, F, M_0, p_I, p_F, A, I, O, \lambda)$ a vulnerable E-commerce Transaction net, with $\sigma_i = t_{i1} t_{i2} \cdots t_{im}$. And for a state p_q, the third-level vulnerable points set TVP satisfy the following conditions:*

(1) $TVP \subseteq P$;
(2) there isn't any state reached by firing sequence σ expect for state p_q;
(3) $TVP = \{p_i \in^\bullet t_i \mid t_i \in \sigma\}$.

The path which leads to the third-level vulnerable points set is all paths leading to malicious state. And these points in $TVP \setminus \{M_0\}$ is considered to be *Maximal Vulnerable Region*.

Definition 14 (Maximal Vulnerable Region ($M_a VR$)). *Let VET-net=$(P, T, F, M_0, p_I, p_F, A, I, O, \lambda)$ a vulnerable E-commerce Transaction net and with $\sigma_i = t_{i1} t_{i2} \cdots t_{im}$. And for a state p_q, the maximal vulnerable region ($M_a VP$) satisfies the following conditions:*

(1) $M_a VR \subseteq TVP$;
(2) $M_0 \notin M_a VR$.

According to three vulnerable points set, we can see that the vulnerable levels are similar to the dynamic slicing. So we can learn from the dynamic slicing computation.

The minimal vulnerable region, dimity vulnerable region, maximal vulnerable region are collectively called *Vulnerable Region*.

Property 2. For a VET-net, it must exit one and only one $M_a LR$.

Property 3. For a VET-net, if it exits $M_i LR$ and DVR, then it must hold that $M_i LR \subseteq DVR \subseteq M_a LR$.

In this section, we firstly give a brief introduction of Llorens's dynamic slicing algorithm. And then we give our improved algorithm based on Llorens'.

In a seminal paper [23], Llorens has proposed a new algorithm to obtain dynamic slicing. The algorithm is based on the traces, generally produces smaller slices by considering a particular firing sequence.

Definition 15 (Dynamic Slice [23]). *Let $N = (P, T, F)$ be a Petri net and let $\langle M_0, Q \rangle$ be a slicing criterion for N, with $\sigma = t_1 t_2 \cdots t_n$. Then, we compute a dynamic slice N' of N w.r.t. $\langle M_0, \sigma, Q \rangle$ as follows:*

(1) We have $N' = (P', T', F')$, where $M_0 \xrightarrow{t_1} M_1 \xrightarrow{t_2} \cdots \xrightarrow{t_n} M_n$, $P' \bigcup T' = slice(M_n, \sigma, Q)$, $P' \subseteq P$, $T' \subseteq T$, and $F' = F \mid_{(P', T')}$. Auxiliary function slice is defined as follows:

(2) The initial marking M_0' is the restriction of M_0 over P', i.e. $M_0' = M_0 \mid_{P'}$.

Trivially, given a marked Petri net (N, M_0), the complete net N is always a correct slice w.r.t. any slicing criterion. The challenge then is to produce a slice as small as possible.

Algorithm 1. Improved slice algorithm

Input: A PN, its reachability graph RG, a goal state set p_q.

Output: Slice S_W.

for *all firing sequences* $\sigma_1, \sigma_2, \cdots, \sigma_n$ *from* M_0 *to* P_q **do**
$\quad S_W = \emptyset;$
$\quad$**if** $\sigma_1 \cap \sigma_2 \cap \cdots \sigma_n = C \neq \emptyset$ **then**

$$S_W = \begin{cases} P_q, & if\ i = 0 \\ slice(M_{i-1}, C, P_q), & if \forall p \in P_q.M_{i-1}(p) \geq M_i(p) \\ \{t_i\} \cup slice(M_{i-1}, C, P_q \cup^\bullet t_i), & otherwise \end{cases}$$

$\quad$**end**
$\quad$**if** $\sigma_1 \cap \sigma_2 \cap \cdots \sigma_n = \emptyset$ *and there is a path* σ_i *such that there is not any other state expect for* P_q *from* σ_i **then**

$$S_W = \begin{cases} P_q, & if\ i = 0 \\ slice(M_{i-1}, \sigma_i, P_q), & if \forall p \in P_q.M_{i-1}(p) \geq M_i(p) \\ \{t_i\} \cup slice(M_{i-1}, \sigma_i, P_q \cup^\bullet t_i), & otherwise \end{cases}$$

$\quad$**else**

$$S_W = \begin{cases} W, & if\ i = 0 \\ slice(M_{i-1}, \bigcup_{i=1}^{n} \sigma_i, W), & if \forall p \in W.M_{i-1}(p) \geq M_i(p) \\ \{t_i\} \cup slice(M_{i-1}, \bigcup_{i=1}^{n} \sigma_i, W \cup^\bullet t_i), & otherwise \end{cases}$$

$\quad$**end**
end

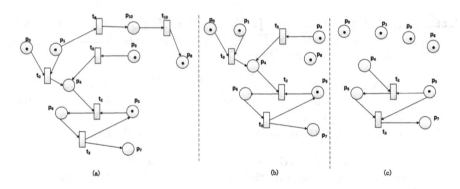

Fig. 4. The algorithm result for the example form [23]: (a) the results of Algorithm 1 in [23], (b) the results of Algorithm 2 in [22], (c) the results of our Algorithm.

Table 2. Algorithm comparison based on example in [23]

Algorithm	Required number of places	Required number of transitions
Algorithm from [22]	10	7
Algorithm 1 from [23]	9	6
Algorithm 2 from [23]	8	4
Our algorithm	8	2

We improve dynamic slicing method as shown in Algorithm 1.

For the example of Fig. 2(a) in [23]. It can get Fig. 4(a) by using the Llorens's algorithm 1, and Fig. 4(b) by using the Llorens's algorithm 2. Using our algorithm, it can get Fig. 4(c). We use the slice algorithm to get the vulnerable points, whose challenge is to produce a slice as small as possible. In fact, according to Table 2, we can see that our algorithm only uses the less points to reach the same state, which explains that our algorithm is better.

5   Vulnerability Analysis Method Based on Dynamic Slicing

To accurately find the vulnerable points of electronic trading system, we need to narrow vulnerable points down when ensuring that the system may result in malicious effect with less points, which need to study the following two questions: (1) in case of uncertain vulnerable points, how to find these vulnerable points; (2) when determining vulnerabilities, how to find lessees points to achieve the malicious state. So we rely on the Llorens's algorithm to lock preliminary points, and then use the improved algorithm to lock the less points.

In Sect. 4, we have introduced our computing method for dynamic slicing is more optimal than [22,23]. Then in this section, we firstly use the improved dynamic slicing to lock vulnerable regions, and secondly we solve the problem proposed in Sect. 1.

According to Algorithm 1, we can obtain the S_W, then for all transitions of S_W, we can get at least one firing sequence to the goal state P_q which may be one or more than one states. Then there are three conditions as follows:

(1) for all firing sequences $\sigma_1, \sigma_2, \cdots \sigma_n$, $\sigma_1 \cap \sigma_2 \cap \cdots \cap \sigma_n \neq \emptyset$;
(2) for all firing sequences $\sigma_1, \sigma_2, \cdots \sigma_n$, and exit a firing sequences such that there is not any other state expect for Pq;
(3) for all firing sequences $\sigma_1, \sigma_2, \cdots \sigma_n$, and don't exit any firing sequences such that there is not any other state expect for Pq;

So based on the improved dynamic slicing method, we can get the vulnerable regions as shown in Algorithm 2. We can get the reachability graph as shown in Fig. 5 of Fig. 3 using the tool $PIPE$. For the known malicious state $S20$, we can get the firing sequence which can reach the $S20$.

Algorithm 2. Locking vulnerable regions algorithm

Input: A VET-net, its reachability graph RG, a slice S_W derived from Algorithm 1.

Output: Minimum vulnerable region $M_i V R$, dimity vulnerable region DVR, and maximum vulnerable region $M_a V R$.

---

for all transitions of S_W, find a firing sequence σ_i of RG **do**
  $M_i V R = \emptyset$;
  $DVR = \emptyset$;
  $M_a V R = \emptyset$;
  if σ_i covers all transitions of S_W **then**
      Computer the triggered transitions t_i of σ_i;
      Computer the correspondence points ${}^\bullet t_i$ of PN, written as P_{mi};
      $M_i V R = P_{mi}$;
  end
  if find anther a firing sequence σ_j, and $\sigma = \sigma_i \cup \sigma_j$ **then**
      Computer the triggered transitions t_j of σ_j;
      Computer the correspondence points ${}^\bullet t_j$ of PN, written as P_{mj};
      $DVR = P_{mj}$;
  else
      find until the last firing sequence σ_n such that $\sigma = \sigma_1 \cup \sigma_2 \cup \cdots \cup \sigma_n$;
      Computer the triggered transitions t_m of σ;
      Computer the correspondence points ${}^\bullet t_m$ of PN, written as P_{mt};
      $M_a V R = P_{mt}$;
  end
end

According to Fig. 5, there are six firing sequences to reach the state $S20$ as follows:

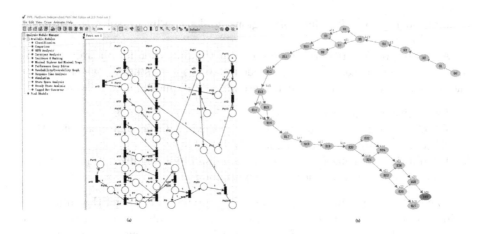

Fig. 5. PIPE implementation result of Reachability graph of Fig. 3: (a) Input Fig. 3, (b) output reachability graph of Fig. 3

(1) $\sigma_1 = b_{11}b_{12}c_{11}c_{12}b_{13}b_{14}a_{11}a_{12}a_{13}a_{14}b_{15}a_{15}b_{16}a_{16}b_{17}a_{17}b_{18}$;

(2) $\sigma_2 = b_{11}b_{12}c_{11}c_{12}b_{13}a_{11}a_{12}b_{14}a_{13}a_{14}b_{15}a_{15}b_{16}a_{16}b_{17}a_{17}b_{18}$;

(3) $\sigma_3 = b_{11}b_{12}c_{11}c_{12}b_{13}a_{11}b_{14}a_{12}a_{13}a_{14}b_{15}a_{15}b_{16}a_{16}b_{17}a_{17}b_{18}$;

(4) $\sigma_4 = b_{11}b_{12}c_{11}c_{12}b_{13}b_{14}a_{11}a_{12}a_{13}a_{14}b_{15}b_{16}a_{15}a_{16}b_{17}a_{17}b_{18}$;

(5) $\sigma_5 = b_{11}b_{12}c_{11}c_{12}b_{13}a_{11}a_{12}b_{14}a_{13}a_{14}b_{15}b_{16}a_{15}a_{16}b_{17}a_{17}b_{18}$;

(6) $\sigma_6 = b_{11}b_{12}c_{11}c_{12}b_{13}a_{11}b_{14}a_{12}a_{13}a_{14}b_{15}b_{16}a_{15}a_{16}b_{17}a_{17}b_{18}$.

Because $\sigma_1 \cap \sigma_2 \cap \cdots \sigma_6 \neq \emptyset$, according to Algorithm 2, it holds that $P_{mi} = \{p_{b1j}, p_{a1k}, p_s\}(j = 1, 2, \cdots, 18; k = 1, \cdots, 18; s = 1, 2, \cdots, 11)$, then $M_i VP = P_{mi} = \{p_{b1j}, p_{a1k}, p_s\}(j = 1, 2, \cdots, 18; k = 1, \cdots, 18; s = 1, 2, \cdots, 11)$. If any one of those points in $M_i VP$ don't happen, the real case will not happen. Back to real Electronic trading system, we need to avoid those vulnerable points happen. In fact, we should consider the real system without attack in real case. These points not from attacker such as those interactive points p_i are vulnerable. In fact, in real E-commerce tradition system also exits those points. In the future, we will protective these points.

6   Conclusion

In this paper, on the basis of previous study, we define VET-net for vulnerable E-commerce transaction system, and propose vulnerable points based on Petri net, and propose a method to lock vulnerable regions and so as to locate vulnerable points of E-commerce tradition system, last give the analysis for actual case of AliPay.

In future work, there are a lot of problems need to study. Such as preventing being attacked, and dealing with fault, adding the data flow information to lock the vulnerable points, and so on, are to be considered in future research.

Acknowledgments. This paper is partially supported by the National Natural Science Foundation of China under grant Nos. 91218301 and 61572360.

References

1. http://www.iresearch.com.cn/report
2. Lowis, L., Accorsi, R.: Vulnerability analysis in SOA-based business processes. J. IEEE Trans. Serv. Comput. **4**, 230–242 (2011)
3. Georgiadis, C.K., Pimenidis, E.: Web services enabling virtual enterprise transactions. In: Proceedings IADIS International Conference on e-Commerce, Barcelona, Spain, pp. 297–302 (2006)
4. Wang, R., Chen, S., Wang, X. F., et al.: How to shop for free online-security analysis of cashier-as-a-service based web stores. In: 2011 IEEE Symposium on Security and Privacy, pp. 465–480. IEEE Press, New York (2011)
5. Du, Y.Y., Jiang, C.J., Zhou, M.C.: A Petri net-based model for verification of obligations and accountability in cooperative systems. J. IEEE Trans. Syst. Man Cybern. A Syst. Hum. **39**, 299–308 (2009)
6. Yu, W.Y., Yan, C.G., Ding, Z.J., Jiang, C.J., Zhou, M.C.: Modeling and validating e-commerce business process based on Petri nets. J. IEEE Trans. Syst. Man Cybern. A Syst. Hum. **44**, 327–341 (2014)
7. Vesely, W.E., Goldberg, F.F., Roberts, N.H., Roberts, N.H.: Fault Tree Handbook. Nuclear Regulatory Commission, Washington DC (1981)
8. Schneier, B.: Attack trees. Dr. Dobb's J. **24**, 21–29 (1999)
9. Saini, V., Duan, Q., Paruchuri, V.: Threat modeling using attack trees. J. Comput. Sci. Coll. **23**, 124–131 (2008)
10. Ravi, S.N., Prabhu, B.S.: Modified approach for prioritization of failures in a system failure mode and effects analysis. J. Int. J. Qual. Reliab. Manage. **18**, 324–336 (2001)
11. Roseti, L., Serra, M., Bassi, A., et al.: Failure mode and effects analysis to reduce risks of errors in the good manufacturing practice production of engineered cartilage for autologous chondrocyte implantation. J. Curr. Pharm. Anal. **12**, 43–54 (2016)
12. Krsul, I.V.: Software vulnerability analysis. Ph.D. thesis, West Lafayette, IN, USA, Major Professor-Eugene H. Spafford (1998)
13. Dianxiang, X., Kendall, E.N.: Threat-driven modeling and verification of secure software using aspect-oriented Petri nets. J. IEEE Trans. Softw. Eng. **32**, 265–278 (2006)
14. Murata, T.: Petri nets: properties, analysis and applications. J. Proc. IEEE **1989**(77), 541–580 (1989)
15. Sun, H., Fu, X., Xie, S., Jiang, Y., Guan, G., Wang, B.: A novel slicing method for thin supercapacitor. J. Adv. Mater., Online press (2016)
16. Peterson, J.L.: Petri nets. J. ACM Comput. Surv. (CSUR) **9**, 223–252 (1997)
17. Weiser, M.: Program slicing. J. IEEE Trans. Soft. Eng. **10**, 352–357 (1984)
18. Yu, W., Ding, Z., Fang, X.: Dynamic slicing of Petri nets based on structural dependency graph and its application in system analysis. Asian J. Control **17**, 1403–1414 (2015)
19. Peterson, J.: Petri Net Theory and the Modeling of Systems. Prentice Hall, Upper Saddle River (1981)

20. Pinchinat, S., Acher, M., Vojtisek, D.: Towards synthesis of attack trees for supporting computer-aided risk analysis. In: Canal, C., Idani, A. (eds.) SEFM 2014. LNCS, vol. 8938, pp. 363–375. Springer, Heidelberg (2015). doi:10.1007/978-3-319-15201-1_24

21. Mauw, S., Oostdijk, M.: Foundations of attack trees. In: Won, D.H., Kim, S. (eds.) ICISC 2005. LNCS, vol. 3935, pp. 186–198. Springer, Heidelberg (2006). doi:10.1007/11734727_17

22. Rakow, A.: Slicing Petri nets with an application to workflow verification. In: Geffert, V., Karhumäki, J., Bertoni, A., Preneel, B., Návrat, P., Bieliková, M. (eds.) SOFSEM 2008. LNCS, vol. 4910, pp. 436–447. Springer, Heidelberg (2008). doi:10.1007/978-3-540-77566-9_38

23. Llorens, M., Oliver, J., Silva, J., Tamarit, S., Vidal, G.: Dynamic slicing techniques for Petri nets. J. Elec. Notes Theor. Comput. Sci. **223**, 153–165 (2008)

Authentication and Transaction Verification Using QR Codes with a Mobile Device

Yang-Wai Chow[1]($\boxtimes$), Willy Susilo[1], Guomin Yang[1],
Man Ho Au[2], and Cong Wang[3]

[1] School of Computing and Information Technology,
Centre for Computer and Information Security Research,
University of Wollongong, Wollongong, Australia
{caseyc,wsusilo,gyang}@uow.edu.au
[2] Department of Computing, The Hong Kong Polytechnic University,
Kowloon, Hong Kong
csallen@comp.polyu.edu.hk
[3] Department of Computer Science, City University Hong Kong,
Kowloon Tong, Hong Kong
congwang@cityu.edu.hk

Abstract. User authentication and the verification of online transactions that are performed on an untrusted computer or device is an important and challenging problem. This paper presents an approach to authentication and transaction verification using a trusted mobile device, equipped with a camera, in conjunction with QR codes. The mobile device does not require an active connection (e.g., Internet or cellular network), as the required information is obtained by the mobile device through its camera, i.e. solely via the visual channel. The proposed approach consists of an initial user authentication phase, which is followed by a transaction verification phase. The transaction verification phase provides a mechanism whereby important transactions have to be verified by both the user and the server. We describe the adversarial model to capture the possible attacks to the system. In addition, this paper analyzes the security of the propose scheme, and discusses the practical issues and mechanisms by which the scheme is able to circumvent a variety of security threats including password stealing, man-in-the-middle and man-in-the-browser attacks. We note that our technique is applicable to many practical applications ranging from standard user authentication implementations to protecting online banking transactions.

Keywords: Authentication · Mobile device · One-Time-Password (OTP) · QR code · Transaction-Authentication-Number (TAN) · Transaction integrity · Transaction verification

1 Introduction

User authentication and the verification of online transactions in Internet based services is an important issue that has received much attention by researchers and

© Springer International Publishing AG 2016
G. Wang et al. (Eds.): SpaCCS 2016, LNCS 10066, pp. 437–451, 2016.
DOI: 10.1007/978-3-319-49148-6_36

practitioners alike. Addressing the security concern surrounding user authentication and online transactions is essential considering the extensive use of computers and electronic devices in our everyday life. Moreover, with the increasing number and variety of malicious threats such as phishing, Trojans, key-loggers, etc. many transactions are conducted on untrustworthy computers or devices.

In addition, not only are the conventional approaches to authentication, like the traditional username and password login approach, susceptible to password stealing attacks, the increasing number of online services means that a person either has to remember a large number of different passwords or compromise on the security by using the same password for multiple services. As such, over the years a large variety of different authentication schemes have been proposed and studied [2,3]. For example, a number of schemes have proposed the use of One-Time-Passwords (OTPs) to prevent attacks like key-logging and phishing [14], Short-Message-Service (SMS) based OTP schemes [29], as well as others like two, or three, factor authentication [8,13].

However, while these schemes are useful, they are not necessarily secure. For instance, SMS-based OTP schemes rely on the security of the cellular network. Mulliner et al. [22] have contented that SMS OTP schemes cannot be considered to be secure, as researchers have shown several successful attacks against Global System for Mobile Communications (GSM) and 3G networks [1,12,19]. Furthermore, it has been argued that two, or three, factor authentication does not overcome man-in-the-middle and Trojan attacks [10,26,27].

This paper investigates the challenging problem of user authentication and transaction verification on an untrusted computer or device. We define transaction verification as encompassing both transaction authentication (i.e. the transaction was indeed performed by the user) and transaction integrity (i.e. the transaction has not been altered). In this paper, we present an approach that uses a personal trusted mobile device, with the requirement that the mobile device has a camera. This is a reasonable requirement that does not overburden the user, as nowadays personal mobile devices are common place and many individuals already own and use personal mobile devices like smartphones every day. Moreover, in our approach the user does not have to remember any passwords, except for the passcode used to login to the mobile device. In fact, some devices allow for other login methods like biometrics.

Unlike a number of other camera-based mobile phone approaches [11,20,23, 29], our approach *does not* require the mobile device to have an active connection (e.g., connection to the computer, cellular network, or Internet), all required information is obtained by the mobile device's camera via the visual channel using QR codes. As such, our approach does not suffer from lost of connection problems (e.g., losing Internet connection within a building, no roaming services when bringing the phone to another country, etc.) and does not require the user to establish a connection (e.g., Bluetooth) with, or install any special software on, the computer.

In principle, our approach does not specifically require the use of QR codes per se; any method of transferring the required data to the mobile device will suffice. We adopt the QR code approach as it is a convenient and widespread method of communication via the visual channel. One should also note that in our approach the device does not have to be a mobile phone; it can be any trusted mobile device with a camera, e.g., a tablet computer, or even a specialized security token.

Our Contributions. In this paper, we present the design of an authentication and verification approach for online transactions on untrusted devices, using a trusted camera-based mobile device in conjunction with QR codes. Our approach is separated into two phases; the user authentication phase and the transaction verification phase. In the user authentication phase, an OTP is obtained by the mobile device. The OTP is only valid for a single session, thus circumvent password stealing or replay attacks. After user authentication, important transactions are verified using a Transaction-Authentication-Number (TAN). The user can verify that the transaction information is accurate and the server can verify that the transaction came from the user. This is to prevent session hijacking attacks after user authentication. This paper analyzes the security and discusses the practical issues as well as the drawbacks of the proposed approach. The scheme described in this paper is applicable to many practical applications ranging from standard user authentication to protecting online banking transactions.

2   Related Work

Over the years, there has been a lot of work in the area of authentication and transaction verification. Researchers have proposed a variety of different schemes, that rely on diverse mechanisms to secure transactions. A number of key research efforts that are related to the scheme proposed in this paper are described in this section. We roughly organize them here into a number of categories; namely, SMS-based, token-based, connection-based, camera-based and QR code-based approaches. However, it should be noted that many of the approaches overlap and are not confined to a single category.

2.1   Authentication Methods

SMS-Based. Sun et al. [29] describe oPass, an SMS-based authentication method of using a cellphone. During the registration phase of this approach, a user registers an account ID and a phone number. The user will also setup a long-term password for generating a chain of OTPs for subsequent logins. To access an online service, the user enters his/her ID into an untrusted web browser. The user then opens the oPass program on his/her phone and enters the long-term password. The program will generate an OTP that is sent via SMS directly to the server, which verifies the user's identity based on the SMS. Similar approaches have also been proposed in other work [15] and there are numerous approaches where OTPs are sent to the user's cellphone via SMS [2,3].

Token-Based. The use of security tokens are another approach to authentication. Tokens can be in the form of a physical device like a smart card or even a mobile phone. For example, RSA SecurID [25] is a approach where a security token is used to generate authentication codes at certain time intervals based on an initial seed value. However, it has been highlighted that this approach does not defend against session hijacking or online phishing [11]. Li et al. [17] propose a low-cost hardware token based PIN/TAN system for protecting e-banking systems. This hardware takes the form of a physical USB token that has to be inserted into an untrusted computer to perform user/server/transaction authentication.

Connection-Based. MP-Auth [20] is an approach that relies on a trusted personal device to perform cryptographic computations. It requires a pre-established long-term password to be shared between the user and the server. To protect the password, password information is entered into the personal device instead of the untrusted terminal. For this to happen, MP-Auth needs a connection between the personal device and the computer, because cryptographic computations that are performed on the personal device are sent to the computer, which in turn forwards it to the server [20].

The Phoolproof phishing prevention system [23] is cellphone based approach that uses public key cryptography in conjunction with a username/password combination and an SSL connection. For the approach to work, a connection must be established between the trusted cellphone and the untrusted browser. A user who wishes to access an online account must always initiate the connection using a secure bookmark stored in the cellphone, and the cellphone will direct the browser to the associated URL [23].

Camera-Based. Clarke et al. [6] propose a camera-based authentication approach that requires a specialized device to perform constant monitoring of the user's interaction with an untrusted computer, by monitoring the information displayed on the computer's screen. The aim of the approach is to detect whether information displayed on the computer's screen has been tampered with. The required monitoring in this method can be rather computationally intensive.

Chow et al. [4] describe a visual OTP challenge-response authentication approach that is based on visual cryptography. The secret authentication message is split into two visual cryptography shares. Using the mobile device's camera, the user visual obtains the secret by overlaying one share on the mobile device's screen with the other share that is displayed on the computer's screen. Another method of authentication via the visual channel was demonstrated by McCune et al. [21]. Their approach is focused on authentication between two devices rather than an online service.

Cronto [7] is a commercial transaction authentication system for online banking transactions. The system uses a patented visual transaction signing approach in which a graphical cryptogram, a CrontoSign image, is displayed on a user's computer screen. The user uses a camera phone or a dedicated hardware device to capture the cryptogram. Transaction information can be securely decoded from the cryptogram if the image is untampered. The user is to check the transaction details and confirm that the transaction is genuine. An authentication code is then generated on the user's phone or device and the user has to pass this back to the bank's server to complete a transaction [7].

QR Code-Based. Snap2pass, and its extension Snap2pay, is a QR code-based approach which requires a camera cellphone to have an active connection [11]. To login to a website, the server sends a QR code, which encodes a cryptographic challenge, to the browser. The user is to take a picture of the QR code with his/her camera cellphone. After the cellphone performs the necessary cryptographic computations, it sends a cryptographic response directly back to the server. Upon receiving a valid response, the server then logs the user in through the browser.

Starnberger et al. [27] describe QR-TAN, a transaction authentication method based on QR codes and a trusted mobile device. In QR-TAN, a shared secret key must be pre-arranged between the mobile device and the server. In addition, it uses public key cryptography where the private key is stored in the mobile device and the untrusted computer has access to the public key. To perform a transaction, a nonce is requested from the server. The untrusted computer then encrypts transaction information and the nonce using the mobile device's public key and displayed the result as a QR code. The mobile device scans the QR code to obtain the encrypted information, which it is required to decrypt using its private key. It then computes a hash based on the transaction information, the nonce, and whether the user approves or rejects the transaction. Part of this hash is sent as a TAN to the server, which computes its own approve and reject hash values, and tries to match these with the value computed on the mobile device.

In addition to the approaches described above, there are various other proposed QR code authentication schemes [18,24,28,30].

2.2 The QR Code

The QR code is a two-dimensional code that was invented by the company Denso Wave [9]. Its widespread adoption in many different applications is due to its convenience and ease of use. Any device equipped with a camera and QR code reader can retrieve the information encoded within a QR code. Other than for authentication, QR codes have been used for a variety of security applications including secret sharing [5] and digital watermarking [16]. While our approach does not specifically require the use of QR codes, as any method that is able to pass data to the mobile device will suffice, we chose to adopt the QR code because of its intuitiveness.

3   System and Adversarial Models

In this section, we describe our system and adversarial models that will be used to analyze the security of our proposed scheme.

3.1   System Model

The system consists of the following entities: end users who are equipped with a mobile device that holds the user's long-term secret information such as passwords or cryptographic keys; a transaction server that the users will connect to for online transactions; and a public computer that will be used by the user to interact with the server via the Internet.

We assume that the mobile device is equipped with a camera but does not have any network connection (i.e., it is a stand alone device). The mobile device can only communicate with the computer via the visual channel using QR codes. The computer can connect to the transaction server through the Internet. In this paper, we assume that the computer is public such that any user, including malicious attackers, can access it and install any (possibly malicious) software on it. The transaction server will process any connection request from the Internet, including those initiated by malicious attackers.

Without losing generality, we also assume a Public Key Infrastructure (PKI) is in place where users and the transaction server can obtain Digital Certificates from a trusted Certification Authority (CA).

3.2   Adversarial Model

Based on the system model described above, we present our adversarial model. We assume that the transaction server and the mobile device of an honest user are trusted, which means attackers cannot access any secret information maintained by the mobile device or the transaction server. However, attackers can corrupt the public computer and install any software (e.g., key-logger) on it. In addition, an attacker can use the compromised computer to communicate with the mobile device via the visual channel and the transaction server through the Internet.

We also assume that an attacker, via the compromised computer, can access and record any user input from peripherals (such as keyboard, mouse, etc.) as well as any traffic generated in an online transaction between the user and the transaction server. Furthermore, during an online transaction, an attacker can modify the data exchanged between the user and the server through the compromised computer.

Security Goals. It is obvious that given an untrusted computer described above, we are unable to achieve security against certain attacks, such as the Denial of Service attack or the eavesdropping attack since we assume the attacker can directly control the network communication and monitor any transaction performed by the user. Therefore, in this paper we mainly focus on the security goals related to the integrity and authenticity of the online transactions. Specifically, we require the following security properties to be preserved with overwhelming probabilities.

- *User authentication.* We require that without the cooperation of the user (and the mobile device), an attacker who controls the compromised computer cannot successfully impersonate the user against the transaction server, given that the attacker can access all the previous user communication transcripts.
- *Transaction authentication.* Without the involvement of the user (and the mobile device), the attacker cannot successfully perform an online transaction with the server, given that the attacker can access all the previous user transactions.
- *Transaction integrity.* The attacker cannot modify any transaction data exchanged between the user and the transaction server without being detected.

4   The Proposed Scheme

The proposed approach addresses the problem of authenticating the user and verifying online transactions using two phases; namely, an initial user authentication phase and the transaction verification phase. During the user authentication phase the untrusted computer establishes an SSL connection with the server; information is exchanged between the server and the mobile device via the untrusted computer, and if certain conditions are met, the server will be able to authenticate that it is indeed communicating with the correct user.

After the user authentication phase, any important transactions made by the user will have to be verified by both the user and the server. This is to prevent any tampering by an attacker who manages to hijack the session after user authentication has already occurred, e.g., via a Trojan on the untrusted computer. Details of these two phases are described in the respective sections to follow.

4.1   User Authentication

During the user authentication phase, it is assumed that the user has already logged in to the mobile device and has opened the specific mobile application (app), which implements the proposed scheme. The mobile app will have access to the user's secret private key, k_{priv}, which is kept in a secure location on the mobile device. It is also assumed that given a user's identity, the server can obtain the user's public key from a PKI. Figure 1 presents an overview depicting the flow of required events during the user authentication phase.

The steps required for user authentication are described as follows. Let PKE.Enc($pk, \cdot$) denote public key encryption[1] of the parameter with public key

---

[1] In practice, we need to employ a CCA-secure public key encryption as part of the protocol.

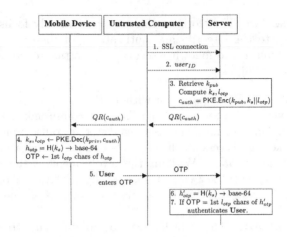

Fig. 1. Overview of the user authentication phase.

pk, and PKE.Dec($sk, \cdot$) represent public key decryption of the parameter with private key sk. In addition, let H be a collision free one-way hash function, and OTP denote a one-time-password.

1. User, U, enters URL into Browser, B, on an untrusted computer; B establishes an SSL connection with the Server, S.
2. U enters user identity, $user_{ID}$, into B; B sends $user_{ID}$ to S.
3. S:
    - uses $user_{ID}$ to retrieve U's public key, k_{pub};
    - computes two random numbers; namely, a random session key, k_s, and a random length, l_{otp}, which will be used as the length of OTP;
    - uses k_{pub} to compute an authentication ciphertext, c_{auth}, where $c_{auth} = $ PKE.Enc($k_{pub}, k_s || l_{otp}$)
    - encodes c_{auth} into a QR code, $QR(c_{auth})$;
    - sends $QR(c_{auth})$ to B.
4. B displays $QR(c_{auth})$; U uses Mobile Device, M; M:
    - scans $QR(c_{auth})$ and decodes it to obtain c_{auth};
    - obtains k_s and l_{otp} using U's private key, k_{priv}, via PKE.Dec(k_{priv}, c_{auth});
    - computes $h_{otp} = $ H(k_s);
    - converts h_{otp} into base-64 representation;
    - displays the first l_{otp} base-64 characters of h_{otp} to U. These characters will be used as OTP.
5. U enters the OTP into B; B sends this to S.
6. S:
    - computes $h'_{otp} = $ H(k_s);
    - converts the h'_{otp} into base-64 representation;
    - compares the first l_{otp} base-64 characters of h'_{otp} with OTP.
7. If the two character sequences match, then S authenticates U with $user_{ID}$.

4.2 Transaction Verification

After the user authentication phase, the user with $user_{ID}$ would have been authenticated. In addition, the mobile device and the server would have established a session key, k_s. Figure 2 illustrates the steps required for transaction verification.

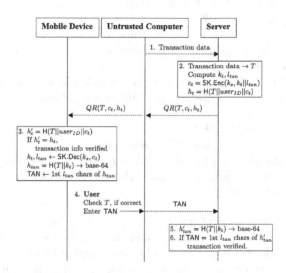

Fig. 2. Overview of the transaction verification steps.

The steps required for both the user and the server to verify the integrity of a transaction are described as follows. Let $SK.Enc(k, \cdot)$ and $SK.Dec(k, \cdot)$ denote symmetric key encryption and decryption, respectively, of the parameter with key k. Furthermore, let H represent a collision free one-way hash function, and TAN denote a transaction-authorization-number.

1. U confirms a transaction through B; B send the transaction data to S.
2. S:
   - converts the transaction data into a summarized form, T;
   - computes
     - two random numbers; namely, a random transaction key, k_t, and a random length, l_{tan}, which will be used as the length of TAN;
     - a transaction ciphertext, c_t, using k_s, where $c_t = SK.Enc(k_s, k_t || l_{tan})$;
     - a hash of the transaction information, h_t, where $h_t = H(T || user_{ID} || c_t)$;
   - encodes T, c_t and h_t into a QR code, $QR(T, c_t, h_t)$;
   - sends $QR(T, c_t, h_t)$ to B.
3. B displays $QR(T, c_t, h_t)$; U uses M; M:
   - scans $QR(T, c_t, h_t)$ and decodes it to obtain T, c_t and h_t;

- checks whether the QR code or the transaction information has been tamper with by
    - computing $h'_t = H(T||user_{ID}||c_t)$;
    - If $h'_t = h_t$, this verifies that the transaction information was sent from S, T has not been altered and the transaction was initiated by U with $user_{ID}$
- obtains k_t and l_{tan} via $SK.Dec(k_s, c_t)$;
- computes $h_{tan} = H(T||k_t)$;
- converts h_{tan} into base-64 representation;
- displays the first l_{tan} base-64 characters of h_{tan} to U. These characters will be used as TAN.

4. M presents T to U; U checks that the information in T is correct and authorizes the transaction by entering the TAN into B; B sends this to S.
5. S:
   - computes $h'_{tan} = H(T||k_t)$;
   - converts the h'_{tan} into base-64 representation;
   - compares the first l_{tan} base-64 characters of h'_{tan} with TAN.
6. If the two character sequences match, the server verifies the integrity of T and that U authorized T.

Note that the inclusion of $user_{ID}$ in $h_t = H(T||user_{ID}||c_t)$ is to provide additional assurance that the user initiated the transaction. It is not absolutely necessary to include this in the hash. The same applies to the inclusion of T in $h_{tan} = H(T||k_t)$, which provides added assurance that the user authorizes transaction T. The scheme can function without the inclusion of either parameter.

5   Analysis and Discussion

5.1   Practical Issues

In view of the fact that the proposed approach uses PKI, this means that this scheme can be used for multiple Internet services. Unlike private key approaches, which requires each Internet service to establish a shared secret between the user and the respective server, the PKI approach avoids practical issues concerning the difficulty of pre-arranging shared secret keys. In addition, it is obvious that the user authentication phase can easily be used in conjunction with a traditional username and password to produce a two factor authentication solution; something that the user knows (i.e. the password) and something that the user possesses (i.e. the mobile device).

In practice, a reasonable value for l_{otp} and l_{tan} should be between 6 to 8 characters. Ideally, for security purposes the full hash value should be transmitted to the server. However, there is a trade-off between security and usability, as it would be impractical to require the user to input more than 10 characters. Therefore, we adopt a method similar to the approach in Starnberger [27] of converting the hash value into an alphanumeric form and only requiring the user to enter the first few characters. In our approach, we convert the hash value into base-64 characters. The base-64 representation of a hash consists of upper and lower case alphabets, the numbers 0–9, and two additional printable characters that can be decided by the system. This will result in 64 possible values for a character and each of them represents 6 bits of the hash.

5.2   User and Transaction Authentication

We show that without the active involvement of a legitimate user and the device, an attacker who controls the untrusted computer cannot successfully impersonate the user or perform an online transaction on behalf of the user.

Brute-Force Attack. Let l be the OTP or TAN length (i.e. l can represent l_{otp} or l_{tan}). Furthermore, let the values of l range between l_{min} and l_{max}. Hence the total number of possible values for the OTP or TAN, denoted by N_{bf}, is

$$N_{bf} = \sum_{i=0}^{l_{max}-l_{min}} 2^{6(l_{min}+i)}$$

and the probability of success of a random guess will be $\frac{1}{N_{bf}}$. If we consider the simple (and less secure) setting where $l_{min} = l_{max} = 8$, then the probability of success of a random guess is at most $1/2^{48}$. As with most password/TAN mechanisms, there should be a limit to the number of incorrect password/TAN entry attempts, which can effectively defeat the brute-force attack.

Password Stealing and Replay Attacks. Unlike traditional username and password login approaches which are vulnerable to password stealing attacks like key-loggers, shoulder surfing, or replay attacks, our approach employs an OTP method. Hence, any attempt to reuse the OTP will fail. In addition, unlike other approaches like SMS approaches that require an active cellular or Internet connection between the server and the mobile phone to transmit an OTP, in our approach, the OTP is sent via the untrusted computer and communicated to the mobile device through the visual channel. This approach also prevents password phishing, because the user does not even know the password until he/she initiates the user authentication phase.

To measure the success probability of a replay attack, first of all we should note that both the session key, k_s, and transaction key, k_t, are single use keys randomly chosen by the server in each session/transaction, which guarantees the uniqueness of input to the hash function in each session/transaction. However, since we use only the first few characters of the hash output as an OTP or TAN, there is a chance of hash collision even when the hash inputs in two sessions are different. According to the Birthday attack, for an OTP or TAN of length l (i.e., l base-64 characters or $6l$ bits), the chance (denoted by $P(l,q)$) of a collision among q different sessions is bounded by

$$P(l,q) \leq \frac{q(q-1)}{2^{6l+1}}.$$

5.3   Transaction Integrity

Man-in-the-Middle and Man-in-the-Browser. Man-in-the-Middle (MitM) and Man-in-the-Browser (MitB) attacks can come in a variety of forms, for example, phishing websites or Trojans on an untrusted computer. In an MitM attack, an attacker may create a spoofed website and lure the user into using this website, while relaying and attempting to modify messages between the user and the actual transaction server. In MitB attacks, an attacker essentially hijacks a session, and it has to be assumed that the attacker has full control of the untrusted computer. These attacks are difficult to defend against because it can happen after the user has already logged in and been authenticated by the server. For the scheme proposed in this paper, MitM and MitB attacks are addressed in the transaction verification phase. In general, an attacker can perform two malicious activities; in particular, an attacker can attempt to perform an unauthorized transaction, or alter the transaction information sent to the server and/or to the user.

To combat against such attacks, our approach requires important transactions to be verified with a TAN. Our analysis in Sect. 5.2 has demonstrated that the probability of success for an attacker to launch an unauthorized transaction is negligible. If the attacker attempts to alter transaction information sent from the server to the user, the computation of $h'_t = \mathsf{H}(T\|user_{ID}\|c_t)$ on the mobile device will be able to detect if changes were made to the transaction information, T, as the resulting value will be different from h_t. Similarly, if the attacker attempts to alter transaction information sent from the user to the server, the value of h_{tan} computed by the mobile device and the value of h'_{tan} computed on the server will be different with an overwhelming probability. It is worth noting that here the chance of a collision is nearly negligible (close to $1/2^{6l_{tan}}$) since the target T is fixed. Hence, transaction integrity is ensured as any attempt to alter transaction information will be detected.

5.4   Drawbacks

The security of the proposed approach relies heavily on the availability and integrity of a trusted mobile device. If the security of the mobile device is compromised and an attacker can steal the user's private key or hijack the mobile device, then the security of the proposed authentication and verification scheme will be compromised. This also applies if the user loses the mobile device or if it is stolen. Moreover, without the mobile device the user will not be able to use Internet services that are based solely on this scheme.

The proposed approach also assumes the trustworthiness, integrity and security of the PKI. It should be noted that if a PKI is by a user to secure multiple Internet services, so that a mobile device is only required to store one private key, the PKI will probably become the focus of attacks. Since once the security of the PKI is breached, an attacker will be able to gain access to the multiple Internet services employed by the user.

Another drawback of the scheme is that users might feel that it is tedious to have use the mobile device to scan a QR code and to enter a TAN for important transactions, despite having already been logged in and authenticated using the OTP. However, this may be a small price to pay to secure important online transactions, such as banking activities and financial transfers. Also, while our approach prevents MitM and MitB attacks from performing unauthorized transactions or altering transaction information, it only prevents attacks against transactions protected by the TAN. It does not defend against Denial-of-Service attacks or eavesdropping attacks.

6   Conclusion

This paper investigates the problem of authentication and the verification of online transactions performed on an untrusted computer or device. To address this problem, we proposed a user authentication and transaction verification approach using QR codes and a trusted mobile device, equipped with a camera. Our approach works via the visual channel and does not require an active connection. In this paper, we analyze the security of our scheme and discuss the mechanisms in the scheme for circumventing a variety of security threats including password stealing, man-in-the-middle and man-in-the-browser attacks.

References

1. Barkan, E., Biham, E.: Conditional estimators: an effective attack on A5/1. In: Preneel, B., Tavares, S. (eds.) SAC 2005. LNCS, vol. 3897, pp. 1–19. Springer, Heidelberg (2006). doi:10.1007/11693383_1
2. Bonneau, J., Herley, C., van Oorschot, P.C., Stajano, F.: The quest to replace passwords: a framework for comparative evaluation of web authentication schemes. In: IEEE Symposium on Security and Privacy, pp. 553–567. IEEE Computer Society (2012)
3. Bonneau, J., Herley, C., van Oorschot, P.C., Stajano, F.: The quest to replace passwords: a framework for comparative evaluation of web authentication schemes. Technical report 817, University of Cambridge Computer Laboratory (2012)
4. Chow, Y.-W., Susilo, W., Au, M.H., Barmawi, A.M.: A visual one-time password authentication scheme using mobile devices. In: Hui, L.C.K., Qing, S.H., Shi, E., Yiu, S.M. (eds.) ICICS 2014. LNCS, vol. 8958, pp. 243–257. Springer, Heidelberg (2015). doi:10.1007/978-3-319-21966-0_18
5. Chow, Y.-W., Susilo, W., Yang, G., Phillips, J.G., Pranata, I., Barmawi, A.M.: Exploiting the error correction mechanism in QR codes for secret sharing. In: Liu, J.K.K., Steinfeld, R. (eds.) ACISP 2016. LNCS, vol. 9722, pp. 409–425. Springer, Heidelberg (2016). doi:10.1007/978-3-319-40253-6_25
6. Clarke, D., Gassend, B., Kotwal, T., Burnside, M., Dijk, M., Devadas, S., Rivest, R.: The untrusted computer problem and camera-based authentication. In: Mattern, F., Naghshineh, M. (eds.) Pervasive 2002. LNCS, vol. 2414, pp. 114–124. Springer, Heidelberg (2002). doi:10.1007/3-540-45866-2_10
7. Cronto Limited, Cronto. http://www.cronto.com/

8. DeFigueiredo, D.: The case for mobile two-factor authentication. IEEE Secur. Priv. **9**(5), 81–85 (2011)

9. Denso Wave Incorporated. http://www.QRcode.com, http://www.qrcode.com/en/

10. Dmitrienko, A., Liebchen, C., Rossow, C., Sadeghi, A.-R.: Security analysis of mobile two-factor authentication schemes. Intel Technol. J., ITJ66 Identity, Biometrics, Authentication Ed., **18**, 138–161 (2014)

11. Dodson, B., Sengupta, D., Boneh, D., Lam, M.S.: Secure, Consumer-friendly Web Authentication and Payments with a Phone, pp. 17–38. Springer, Heidelberg (2012)

12. Dunkelman, O., Keller, N., Shamir, A.: A practical-time related-key attack on the Kasumi cryptosystem used in GSM and 3G telephony. J. Cryptol. **27**(4), 824–849 (2014)

13. Grosse, E., Upadhyay, M.: Authentication at scale. IEEE Secur. Priv. **11**(1), 15–22 (2013)

14. Huang, C.-Y., Ma, S.-P., Chen, K.-T.: Using one-time passwords to prevent password phishing attacks. J. Netw. Comput. Appl. **34**(4), 1292–1301 (2011)

15. Jeun, I., Kim, M., Won, D.: Enhanced password-based user authentication using smart phone. In: Li, R., Cao, J., Bourgeois, J. (eds.) GPC 2012. LNCS, vol. 7296, pp. 350–360. Springer, Heidelberg (2012). doi:10.1007/978-3-642-30767-6_30

16. Lee, H.-C., Dong, C.-R., Lin, T.-M.: Digital watermarking based on JND model and QR code features. In: Pan, J.-S., Yang, C.-N., Lin, C.-C. (eds.) Advances in Intelligent Systems and Applications, vol. 2, pp. 141–148. Springer, Heidelberg (2013)

17. Li, S., Sadeghi, A.-R., Heisrath, S., Schmitz, R., Ahmad, J.J.: hPIN/hTAN: a lightweight and low-cost e-banking solution against untrusted computers. In: Danezis, G. (ed.) FC 2011. LNCS, vol. 7035, pp. 235–249. Springer, Heidelberg (2012). doi:10.1007/978-3-642-27576-0_19

18. Liao, K.-C., Lee, W.-H.: A novel user authentication scheme based on QR-code. JNW **5**(8), 937–941 (2010)

19. Lu, J., Li, Z., Henricksen, M.: Time-Memory Trade-Off Attack on the GSM A5/1 Stream Cipher Using Commodity GPGPU, pp. 350–369. Springer, Cham (2015)

20. Mannan, M., Oorschot, P.C.: Using a personal device to strengthen password authentication from an untrusted computer. In: Dietrich, S., Dhamija, R. (eds.) FC 2007. LNCS, vol. 4886, pp. 88–103. Springer, Heidelberg (2007). doi:10.1007/978-3-540-77366-5_11

21. McCune, J.M., Perrig, A., Reiter, M.K.: Seeing-is-believing: using camera phones for human-verifiable authentication. In: IEEE Symposium on Security and Privacy, pp. 110–124. IEEE Computer Society (2005)

22. Mulliner, C., Borgaonkar, R., Stewin, P., Seifert, J.-P.: SMS-based one-time passwords: attacks and defense. In: Rieck, K., Stewin, P., Seifert, J.-P. (eds.) DIMVA 2013. LNCS, vol. 7967, pp. 150–159. Springer, Heidelberg (2013). doi:10.1007/978-3-642-39235-1_9

23. Parno, B., Kuo, C., Perrig, A.: Phoolproof phishing prevention. In: Crescenzo, G., Rubin, A. (eds.) FC 2006. LNCS, vol. 4107, pp. 1–19. Springer, Heidelberg (2006). doi:10.1007/11889663_1

24. Pohlmann, N., Hertlein, M., Manaras, P.: Bring your own device for authentication (BYOD4A) - the Xign-system. In: Reimer, H., Pohlmann, N., Schneider, W. (eds.) ISSE 2015, pp. 240–250. Springer Fachmedien Wiesbaden, Wiesbaden (2015)

25. RSA Security, RSA SecurID. https://www.rsa.com/en-us/products-services/identity-access-management/securid

26. Schneier, B.: Two-factor authentication: too little, too late. Commun. ACM **48**(4), 136 (2005)
27. Starnberger, G., Froihofer, L., Goeschka, K.M.: QR-TAN: secure mobile transaction authentication. In: International Conference on Availability, Reliability and Security, ARES 2009, pp. 578–583, March 2009
28. Subpratatsavee, P., Kuacharoen, P.: Transaction authentication using HMAC-based one-time password and QR code. In: Park, J.J., Stojmenovic, I., Jeong, H.Y., Yi, G. (eds.) Computer Science and its Applications, pp. 93–98. Springer, Heidelberg (2015)
29. Sun, H.-M., Chen, Y.-H., Lin, Y.-H.: oPass: a user authentication protocol resistant to password stealing and password reuse attacks. IEEE Trans. Inf. Forensics Secur. **7**(2), 651–663 (2012)
30. Vapen, A., Byers, D., Shahmehri, N.: 2-clickAuth optical challenge-response authentication. In: International Conference on Availability, Reliability, and Security, ARES 2010, pp. 79–86, February 2010

Secure and Efficient Mobile Payment Using QR Code in an Environment with Dishonest Authority

Xiaoling Zhu$^{(\boxtimes)}$, Zhengfeng Hou, Donghui Hu, and Jing Zhang

School of Computer and Information,
Hefei University of Technology, Hefei 230009, China
{zhuxl,houzf,hudh,zhangjing}@hfut.edu.cn

Abstract. Quick response (QR) code payment has become the mainstream of mobile payment in China. However, severe security threat greatly influences consumer confidence. Unifying security and convenience of QR code is a difficult issue. The paper proposes a secure and efficient mobile payment (SEMP) solution where signed and encrypted payment data are embedded into QR code. Since private keys are issued by fully distributed private key generators (PKGs), no matter malicious user, dishonest third party payment platform (TPP), or dishonest PKG, can not impersonate a legal person to authorize a payment or eavesdrop on the communication to obtain privacy information. The scheme has confidentiality and unforgeability. Especially, it can resist against authority attacks. Since no public key certificate is required, it has clear advantage over existing PKI schemes. The comparisons with related schemes show our SEMP scheme maintains less communication cost, while it provides higher security level. So it can better meet security and convenient requirements of mobile payment and it can apply in the QR code payment environment with dishonest authority.

Keywords: Mobile payment · QR code · Security · Signcryption · Authority attacks

1 Introduction

As smartphone is becoming prevalent, mobile payment steps into daily life and brings more convenient services to people. Since quick response (QR) code has the characters of convenient generation, easy publication and quick reading [1], it has been used in payment, advertisement, access control, etc. In China, QR code payment is vigorously promoted by WeChat [2] and Alipay [3], and it has become a mainstream way of mobile payment.

However, when an illegal person embeds malicious URLs into QR code, an ordinary user lacks the ability of detecting malicious URLs, Trojan and virus. If he continues to visit the websites, malicious software will be downloaded and installed quietly. What's worse, if his smartphone infects some payment virus, his money account will suffer serious threats. By modifying color of specific blocks of QR code,

G. Wang et al. (Eds.): SpaCCS 2016, LNCS 10066, pp. 452–465, 2016.
DOI: 10.1007/978-3-319-49148-6_37

literature [4] launched a tampering attack. Data leak is also a hidden danger when QR code is plaintext.

Figure 1 shows the application scenario of QR payment. Entities in a QR payment system may include smart phones, payment terminals and third pay platform (TPP). Private key generator (PKG) may be included due to the use of cryptographic techniques. The communication between users and terminals uses QR code and other communications use wireless or wired network. is shown in. When a user scans a QR code from a payment terminal, he has no idea whether the code really comes from a legitimate store; he wishes that the content of the code is not known by attackers. When TPP receives a request for payment, he needs to decide whether it is an authorize payment. Furthermore, a user and a shop both wish that PKG does not leak their secrets. How do they prevent PKG from leaking? In order to solve the upper issues, we propose a secure and efficient mobile payment (SEMP) scheme using QR code. The scheme can ensure confidentiality and integrity of payment data, authentication of payer identity, convenience and non-repudiation of payment operation. Especially, it can resist authority attacks.

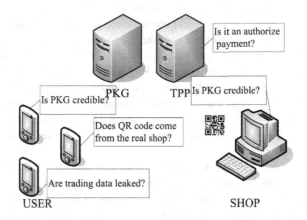

Fig. 1. A scenario of SEMP service

The remainder of this paper is organized as follows. Firstly, we introduce related works in Sect. 2, which will emphasize the motivation of our work. We then describe the framework of our solution in Sect. 3 and the proposed SEMP scheme in details in Sect. 4. We analyze security and performance of our scheme in Sects. 5 and 6, respectively. Finally, we conclude the paper in Sect. 7.

2   Related Works

There exist two patterns in QR application. Active scanning means that a user scans QR code, which is generated by a shop. Otherwise, it is called passive scanning.

For active scanning, checking QR code credibility is an idea. Yao et al. [5] proposed a SafeQR scheme for Andriod phone using Google Safe Browsing API and

Phishtank API; the system should frequently update phishing website list. Literature [6] introduced a third party to detect URL and the burden of the third party is heavy. Milburn et al. [16] presented an identity authentication system, which is based on the SQRL (secure quick reliable login) system by Steve Gibson [17]. In SQRL system, website address and master key are hashed together to create a private key for identity authentication; there are no usernames, passwords or keyboard interaction; if the master key is exposed, the identity unlock key can cancel the master key; however, after analysis, we find if someone steals the smartphone of some person, anyone in possession of the phone can impersonate the person; so complete withdrawal is difficult [16, 17]. Secure design of QR code is another research idea. Czuszynski et al. [7] proposed that the hospital check center encrypts patient data. Lee et al. [8] suggested that a user signs sensitive data with his private key; the communication between a shop and a user requires a payment gateway, which is the bottleneck of system performance. In [8], embedding a public certificate into QR code is a hidden issue due to limited capacity of QR code. How to unify convenience and security deserves attention. For passive scanning, it decreases phishing attacks. But it has the following security threats: (i) money for payment is decided by a shop, and it lacks user's confirmation. (ii) A malicious shop might forge QR code by violent searching for a collision.

Therefore, anti-forgery, anti-leak and convenience are the most concerned issues in mobile payment. In general PKI schemes, the user require obtaining public key certificate before encryption. In identity based encryption (IBE), the public key certificate is not required. IBE has clear advantage over PKI schemes in communication costs [9]. However, PKG in IBE generates all private keys, and he may leak all secrets if he is dishonest, which violates high security requirements of a payment. Some IBE schemes are accountable [10, 11], which eliminate key escrow by combining users and PKG to generate a private key. However, they cannot thoroughly prevent a dishonest PKG from impersonating users.

To solve the above issues, we propose a secure and efficient mobile payment scheme. The main contributions are: (i) Ensure confidentiality and integrity of payment data, authentication of payer identity, non-repudiation of payment operation; (ii) QR code is used to ensure convenience of mobile payment; (iii) The authority can neither forge a signature, nor leak private keys. Our scheme is security and effective when facing a dishonest authority.

3   Overview of the SEMP Scheme

The SEMP scheme supports QR code secure payment when users buy goods from shops. This section provides the system framework, the payment process and security requirements.

3.1   QR Code

QR code is two-dimensional bar code. It can store up to 4296 alphanumeric characters. In our scheme, QR code contains the signed and encrypted payment message.

The message is date || order id || shop id || goods description || total fee. A shop signs and encrypts it, then embeds it into QR code; a user scans and decrypts it. The communication between a user and a shop adopts near field communication; other communications use wireless or wired network. It means that TPP and PKG neither read QR nor generate QR.

3.2   Payment Process

The payment system consists of a user (U), a shop (S), third party payment platform (TPP) and private key generator (PKG).

- A user: A user is equipped with a smartphone, a PDA or a Laptop. He can access the Internet. He can generate and read QR code. His identity, public key and private key are denoted as ID_U, Q_U and D_U, respectively. His phone number or email address may be as ID_U.
- A shop: A shop is equipped with PC terminals. By terminals, he has ability of generating and reading QR code. The identity, public key and private key of the shop are denoted as ID_S, Q_S and D_S, respectively.
- TPP: TPP is an independent agency to protect the interests of both trading parties. If money accounts of trading parties are both on TPP, money is transferred directly from buyer account to seller account. Otherwise, TPP forwards message to a bank. The identity, public key and private key of TPP are denoted as ID_{TPP}, Q_{TPP} and D_{TPP}, respectively.
- PKG: Users, shops and TPP need to obtain their private keys from PKG. If only one authority acts as PKG, abuse occurs. We extend one authority to n authorities forming PKG group $\{P_1, P_2, ..., P_n\}$. The extension will increase some costs. The costs generally occur during system setup phase and user registration phase. Since setup occurs once and registration generally occurs once for users, the impact of increased costs is limited.

A user finishes purchasing goods and he comes to a counter for payment. If money accounts of buyers and sellers are on the same TPP, a payment process is as follows.

1. A shop signs and encrypts payment data, embeds them into QR code and shows QR code to a user.
2. The user scans the QR code, extracts data from the QR code, decrypts and verifies the data. If passed, he sends a signed and encrypted payment request to TPP.
3. TPP decrypts and verifies the message. If verification is passed, he transfers money from buyer account to seller account.
4. TPP notices the user money is paid and notices the shop money is received.

When money accounts of buyers and sellers are both on the banks, TPP leads the user to the interface with the bank. The communication between a user and a bank can adopt our proposed signcryption method.

3.3 Security Requirements

We assume that the user, the shop and PKG are all dishonest. They might eavesdrop on the communication to obtain trading information and launch a passive attack. They might forge a signature to obtain illegal money and launch an active attack. So the security requirements are as follows.

Definition 1 (Confidentiality). For attackers, it is computationally infeasible to obtain plaintext from ciphertext.

Definition 2 (Unforgeability). For attackers, it is computationally infeasible to forge a legitimate signature.

Definition 3 (Resistance against authority attacks). For a dishonest authority, it is computationally infeasible to impersonate other entity or leak secrets of others.

Definition 4 (IND-CCA2). A signcryption scheme is semantically secure against chosen ciphertext attack if no probabilistic polynomial time adversary has a non-negligible advantage in the following game.

1. The challenger C runs the setup algorithm and sends system public parameters to the adversary A.
2. In the first phase, A makes polynomial bounded number of queries to the following oracles.

   Extract Oracle: A produces an identity ID_i and queries for the private key. The challenger C returns the key.
   Signcrypt Oracle: A produces a message m, a sender identity ID_i and a receiver identity ID_j. C returns the signcrypted ciphertext.
   Unsigncrypt Oracle: A produces a sender identity ID_i, receiver identity ID_j, and a signcryption result. C returns the decrypted result.

3. A produces two messages m_0 and m_1 of equal length and an arbitrary sender identity ID_A. C randomly chooses a bit $u \in \{0,1\}$ and computes the signcryption σ^*, and returns σ^* to A as a challenge.
4. A is allowed to make polynomial bounded number of new queries as in Step 2 with the restrictions that it should not query Unsigncryption Oracle for σ^* and Extract Oracle for ID_B.
5. At the end of this game, outputs a bit u', A wins the game if $u = u'$.

4 Description of the SEMP Scheme

Since smartphone is a resource constrained device, it cannot bear much burden. Signcryption can complete digital signature and public key encryption at the same time, and its communication and computation costs might be lower. In the IBE, the public key is directly from the identity, and the user does not need to get public key certificate. So based on IBE, we design a signcryption scheme. It is derived from the IBE proposed by Boneh and Franklin [12] and Paterson [13] and a distributed structure proposed by Feldman [14]. In the scheme users need one time scan to complete the communication with payment terminal.

Definition 5 (Bilinear map). Let G_1 be a cyclic additive group with a generator P, whose order is a prime q, and G_2 be a cyclic multiplicative group with the same order q. A map $e : G_1 \times G_1 \rightarrow G_2$ is a bilinear map if following properties are satisfied: bilinearity, non-degeneracy and computability.

4.1 Setup

Let $H_1 : \{0,1\}^* \rightarrow G_1$, $H_2 : \{0,1\}^l \times \{0,1\}^* \rightarrow Z_q^*$, $H_3 : G_1 \rightarrow Z_q^*$ and $H_4 : G_2 \rightarrow \{0,1\}^l$ be collision-resistant functions.

1. Each member P_i $(1 \le i \le n)$ in PKGs randomly picks a secret $d_i \in Z_q^*$ as his member private key, computes and broadcasts his member public key $P_{pub_i} = d_i P$ and further computes the group public key $P_{pub} = \sum_{i=1}^{n} P_{pub_i}$. He chooses a random polynomial $f_i(x) = f_{i,0} + f_{i,1} x + f_{i,2} x^2 + \ldots + f_{i,t-1} x^{t-1}$ over Z_q^*, where $f_i(0) = d_i$.
2. P_i computes $s_{i,j} = f_i(ID_j) \bmod q (1 \le j \le n)$ and sends $s_{i,j}$ to P_j secretly. He broadcasts $F_{i,l} = f_{i,l} P (1 \le l \le t - 1)$.
3. P_j receives $s_{i,j}$ from other members and verifies $s_{i,j} P = \sum_{l=0}^{t-1} F_{i,l} \cdot ID_j^l$ If the validation passes, he computes the share $s_j = \sum_{i=1}^{n} s_{i,j} \bmod q$ and broadcasts $s_j P$. $s_j P$ will be accepted by other members if $s_j P = \sum_{l=0}^{t-1} F_l ID_j^l$, where $F_l = \sum_{i=1}^{n} F_{i,l}$. Otherwise, P_j will be complained. When the complaint number achieves a threshold value, P_j will be added to a blacklist.

After implementing the steps, each member obtains public parameters $\{P, P_{pub}, \{s_i P\}_{1 \le i \le n}\}$ and his secrets $\{s_i, d_i\}$. The group private key $d = \sum_{i=1}^{n} d_i$ is owned jointly by PKGs; any single member does not know d. The group public key P_{pub} satisfies $P_{pub} = dP$ since $P_{pub} = \sum_{i=1}^{n} P_{pub_i} = \sum_{i=1}^{n} d_i P = dP$. The two verification equations in Step 3 are clearly established since $s_{i,j} P = f_i(ID_j) P = f_{i,0} P + f_{i,1} P \cdot ID_j + \ldots + f_{i,t-1} P \cdot$

$ID_j^{t-1} = \sum_{l=0}^{t-1} F_{i,l} \cdot ID_j^l$ and $s_j P = \sum_{i=1}^{n} s_{i,j} P = \sum_{i=1}^{n} \sum_{l=0}^{t-1} F_{i,l} \cdot ID_j^l = \sum_{l=0}^{t-1} \sum_{i=1}^{n} F_{i,l} \cdot ID_j^l = \sum_{l=0}^{t-1} F_l \cdot ID_j^l$.

The protocol is implemented among PKGs. It increases the burden of PKG. Since the setup protocol occurs once, the impact of the increased costs is limited.

4.2   Registration

A user, a shop or TPP needs to obtain his private key from t participating members of PKGs, namely, P_1, P_2,..., P_t. First, the applicant sends his identification ID to t participating members.

1. Each participating member P_i $(1 \le i \le t)$ computes $s_i Q_{ID}$ and sends it to the applicant secretly. Here, $Q_{ID} = H_1(ID)$.
2. Assume the applican has obtained member public key $s_i P$, and he verifies $e(s_i Q_{ID}, P) = e(Q_{ID}, s_i P)$. If passed, he computess the private key

$$D_{ID} = \sum_{i=1}^{t} l_i(0) s_i Q_{ID}, \quad \text{where} \quad l_i(0) = \prod_{\substack{j=1 \\ j \ne i}}^{t} \frac{j}{j-i} \quad \text{and} \quad D_{ID} = \sum_{i=1}^{t} (\sum_{j=1}^{n} s_{j,i}) l_i(0) Q_{ID} =$$

$$(\sum_{j=1}^{n} (\sum_{i=1}^{t} s_{j,i} l_i(0))) Q_{ID} = (\sum_{j=1}^{n} d_j) Q_{ID} = d Q_{ID}.$$

After interaction between the applicant and t participating members of PKGs, the applicant obtains his private key D_{ID}, i.e., the user obtains D_U, the shop obtains D_S or TPP obtains D_{TPP}. In the above process, even if m participating members $(m < t)$ launch collusion attack, they cannot obtain a legitimate D_{ID}. Our registration protocol maintains good property of security in the presence of dishonest authorities.

4.3   Bill Generation

When a user comes to a counter for payment, a shop generates a payment list and signs it. The payment list is denoted by m, where m = date || order id || shop id || goods description || total fee. Their byte length is 2, 16, 10, 100 and 8, respectively.

1. A shop picks a random number $r \in Z_q^*$, computes $R = rP$ and makes a signature

$$S = \frac{H_2(m, ID_S)P + H_3(R)D_S}{r + H_2(m, ID_S)} \tag{1}$$

where ID_S and D_S are the identity and the private key of the shop, respectively.

2. The shop computes $w = e(Q_U, P_{pub})^r$, where $Q_U = H_1(ID_U)$, ID_U and Q_U is the identity and the public key of the user respectively. Then, the shop encrypts m and obtains the cipher

$$c = H_4(w) \oplus m \tag{2}$$

He further embeds the results (c, R, S) into QR code and shows QR code to the user.

4.4   Bill Payment

1. The user scans QR code and obtain (c, R, S).
2. He computes $w = e(D_U, R)$, where D_U is his private key. Then he makes a decryption $m = H_4(w) \oplus c$.
3. The user verifies

$$e(S, R + H_2(m, ID_S)P) = e(P, P)^{H_2(m, ID_S)} e(Q_S, P_{pub})^{H_3(R)} \tag{3}$$

where $Q_S = H_1(ID_S)$.

4. If verification passes, the user generates the payment request $m' =$ date $\|$ order id $\|$ shop id $\|$ user id $\|$ total fee.
5. He picks a random number $r' \in Z_q^*$, computes $R' = r'P$ and makes a signature $S' = \frac{H_2(m', ID_U)P + H_3(R')D_U}{r + H_2(m', ID_U)}$. He computes $w' = e(Q_{TTP}, P_{pub})^{r'}$ and $c' = H_4(w') \oplus m'$ and submits a payment request (c', R', S') to TPP.
6. TPP receives (c', R', S'), computes $w' = e(D_{TTP}, R')$ and $m' = H_4(w') \oplus c'$, further verifies $e(S', R' + H_2(m', ID_U)P) = e(P, P)^{H_2(m', ID_U)} e(Q_U, P_{pub})^{H_3(R')}$, where D_{TTP} is his private key. If passed, TPP transfer money from the user account to the shop account.

Equation (3)   is   correct   since $e(S, R + H_2(m, ID_S)P) = e(\frac{H_2(m, ID_S)P + H_3(R)D_S}{r + H_2(m, ID_S)},$
$(r + H_2(m, ID_S))P) = e(H_2(m, ID_S)P, P) \, e(H_3(R)D_S, P) = e(P, P)^{H_2(m, ID_S)} e(Q_S, P_{pub})^{H_3(R)}$.

5   Security Analysis

Definition 6 (Computational bilinear Diffie-Hellman (CBDH) problem). Given $P \in G_1$, aP, bP, cP for some unknowns $a, b, c \in Z_p^*$, find $e(P, P)^{abc}$.

Definition 7 (CBDH assumptions) The advantage of any probabilistic polynomial time algorithm in solving the CBDH problem is negligibly small, i.e., CBDH problem is assumed to be hard.

Proposition 1. *Our scheme is secure against any IND-CCA2 adversary under the random oracle model and CBDH assumption.*

Proof. The challenger $\mathcal{C}$ receives an instance (P, aP, bP, cP) of the CBDH problem. His goal is to compute $e(P, P)^{abc}$. We expect that $\mathcal{C}$ can use an IND-CCA2 adversary $\mathcal{A}$ to solve the CBDH problem. $\mathcal{C}$ gives $\mathcal{A}$ public parameters $\{P, P_{pub} = cP\}$. The descriptions of some oracles are as follows.

- $H_1(ID_i)$: $\mathcal{C}$ checks whether there is a tuple (ID_i, Q_i) in list L_1. If it exists, $\mathcal{C}$ returns Q_i to $\mathcal{A}$. Otherwise, $\mathcal{C}$ does the following: If $ID_i = ID_B$, $\mathcal{C}$ returns $Q_i = bP$; else chooses a random number $x \in Z_q^*$ and returns $Q_i = xP$. Then, add (ID_i, Q_i) to L_1.
- $H_2(m, ID_i)$: $\mathcal{C}$ checks whether there is a tuple (m, ID_i, h_2) in L_2. If it exists, $\mathcal{C}$ returns h_2. Otherwise, C chooses a random number h_2, adds (m, ID_i, h_2) to L_2 and returns h_2.

- $H_3(R)$: C checks whether there is a tuple (R, h_3) in L_3. If it exists, C returns h_3. Otherwise, C chooses a random number h_3, adds (R, h_3) to L_3 and returns h_3.
- $H_4(w)$: C checks whether there is (w, h_4) in L_4. If it exists, C returns h_4. Otherwise, C chooses randomly a l -bit integer h_4, adds (R, h_4) to L_4 and returns h_4.
- Extract (ID_i): If $ID_i = ID_B$, return stop simulation. Otherwise, get (ID_i, Q_i) through H_1 and return $D_i = cQ_i$.
- Signcrypt (m, ID_i, ID_j):
  - $ID_i \neq ID_B$. Get the private key D_i by running Extract Oracle. Choose a random number r. Compute $R = rP$. Get a tuple (m, ID_i, h_2) through H_2 and (R, h_3) through H_3. Compute $S = \frac{h_2 P + h_3 D_i}{r + h_2}$. Get (ID_j, Q_j) through H_1. Compute $w = e(Q_j, P_{pub})^r$. Get (w, h_4) through H_4. Compute $c = h_4 \oplus m$. Finally, return signcryption results (c, R, S).
  - $ID_i = ID_B$. Choose random numbers r and k. Compute $R = rP$ and $S = kP$. Get (ID_j, Q_j) through H_1. Compute $w = e(Q_j, P_{pub})^r$. Get (w, h_4) through H_4. Compute $c = h_4 \oplus m$. Return signcryption results (c, R, S).
- Unsigncrypt(c, R, S, ID_i, ID_j):
  - $ID_j \neq ID_B$. Get D_j through Extraction oracle. Compute $w = e(D_j, R)$. Get (w, h_4) through H_4. Compute $m = h_4 \oplus c$. Get (ID_i, Q_i) through H_1, (m, ID_i, h_2) through H_2 and (R, h_3) through H_3. Verify $e(S, R + h_2 P) = e(P, P)^{h_2} e(Q_i, P_{pub})^{h_3}$. If verification does not pass, C stops simulation. Otherwise, C returns m.
  - $ID_j = ID_B$. Traverse each tuple (w, h_4) in L_4 and compute $m = h_4 \oplus c$. Get (ID_i, Q_i) through H_1, (m, ID_i, h_2) through H_2 and (R, h_3) through H_3. Verify $e(S, R + h_2 P) = e(P, P)^{h_2} e(Q_i, P_{pub})^{h_3}$. If the above equation holds for a certain tuple, then C returns related m. If not passed for all tuples in L_4, C stops simulation.

After the first stage, A outputs two plaintexts m_0 and m_1, C chooses $u \in \{0,1\}$ and signcrypts m_u. Assume $R^* = aP$ and $w = h$, then C return $\sigma^* = (c^*, R^*, S^*)$ to A. A performs a second series of queries which is treated in the same way as the first one. At the end of the simulation, A returns a bit u' to C for which he believes the relation $\sigma^* = $ Signcrypt $(m_u' ID_i, ID_j)$ holds. If $u = u'$, C outputs $h = e(R^*, D_B) = e(aP, cbP) = e(P, P)^{abc}$ as a solution of the CBDH problem, otherwise C stops.

If there is an adversary who can succeed in such a CCA2 attack with non-negligible advantage, that means there is an algorithm to solve the CBDH problem with non-negligible advantage. The scheme is secure against any IND-CCA2 attack under CBDH assumption.

Proposition 2. *Our scheme has the existential unforgeability against adaptive chosen messages attacks under the random oracle model and CBDH assumption.*

Proof. The scheme is based on Paterson's scheme [13] and Paterson's scheme can resist existential forgery against adaptive chosen messages attacks.

Proposition 3. *Our scheme can resist authority attacks under CBDH assumption.*

Proof. Since the hardness of the discrete logarithm problem, $s_i Q_{ID}$ cannot leak out s_i and P_{pub} cannot leak out d. For a given identity ID, at least t members are needed to issue a valid private key. Therefore, any entity, even including PKG and TPP, cannot impersonate others to forgery valid signature.

We compare our scheme with similar works that are intended to ensure security of

Table 1. Secutity features comparisons

	Confidentiality	Resist forgery	Resist authority attacks
Czuszynski et al.'s scheme [7]	Yes	No	No
Lee et al.'s scheme [8]	No	Yes	No
Milburn et al.'s scheme [16]	Yes	Yes	No
Our scheme	Yes	Yes	Yes

QR code. The results of comparisons of security features are shown in Table 1. Czuszynski et al. [7] used AES algorithm to encrypt data for confidentiality. Lee et al. [8] made a digital signature on a payment list, which is unforgeability. However, a trust center exists in the two schemes: the check center for encryption in [7] and CA in [8]. The schemes are suffered attacks from a trust center. Milburn et al. [16] used AES encryption and ECDSA signature, which achieves confidentiality and unforgeability. In [16], a user issues private key and public key by himself and no third party knows the private key. It seems secure. But a server can also issue private key and public key, and then claims that the keys are issued by the user. For any assessment institution, he cannot distinguish the keys issued by the user from the keys issued by the server. So the method is still unable to resist this kind of authority attacks. In our scheme, the payment list is signed and encrypted. Private keys are generated by distributed PKGs. The collusion of less than n members cannot know the private key and further forge a valid signature. Therefore, our scheme has confidentiality, unforgeability and resistance against authority attacks.

6 Performance Analysis

For convenience to evaluate the computation costs of the scheme, we ignore some operations such as a hash function and a multiplication operation since they are quite lighter in terms of load. We focused on some time-consuming operations defined in the following notations. T_P denotes the time of executing a bilinear map operation. All exponentiations in G_2 can be transformed into scalar multiplications in G_1 to get a fast implementation of a bilinear map. So we use T_{G1} to represent the time of executing a scalar multiplication or an exponentiation operation. To evaluate the communication costs, $|q|$, $|G_1|$, $|c|$ and $|c'|$ denote the length of the order of G_1, the element in G_1, the cipher c and c', respectively.

6.1 Performance of the SEMP Scheme

Table 2 shows computation and communication costs of SEMP scheme during four different phases, i.e., setup, registration, bill generation and bill payment. In the table, n is the number of total members in PKGs and t is the number of members participating to issue private keys.

Table 2. Computation and communication costs of the SEMP scheme

	Setup	Registration	Bill generation	Bill payment
Computation costs	$((n-1)$ $(2t+1)+t+1)T_{G1}$	$2tT_P + 2tT_{G1}$	$T_P + 4T_{G1}$	$9T_P + 11T_{G1}$
Communication costs	$(t+1)|G_1| + (n-1)|q|$	$2t|G_1|$	$|c| + 2|G_1|$	$|c'| + 2|G_1|$

6.2 Performance Comparisons with Our Schemes

To achieve the similar security level of 1024 bits RSA signature, Literature [15] proposed $|q| = 160$ bits $= 20$ bytes and $|G_1| = 161$ bits ≈ 20 bytes; it requires 4.5 ms to perform a bilinear map and 0.6 ms to perform a scalar multiplication in G_1. For elliptic curve digital signature algorithm (ECDSA), if the key is 28 bytes, then ECDSA signature is 53 bytes; the point on the elliptic curve is 29 bytes; public certificate is 84 bytes. It requires 0.8 ms to perform a signature and 4.2 ms to perform a verification [18]. For AES algorithm, it requires 94 µs to perform encryption, the same with decryption [19]. Raya proposed that when HMAC is based on SHA-224, the output is 28 bytes and the operation time is 28 µs [18]. From the definition of the bill list in Sect. 4.3 and the payment list in Sect. 4.4, we obtain $|m| = 2 + 10 + 16 + 200 + 8 = 236$ (bytes) and $|m'| = 2 + 16 + 10 + 10 + 8 = 46$ (bytes). Since $c = H_4(w) \oplus m$, $|c| = 236$ bytes. Similarly, $|c'| = 46$ bytes.

In the following, we shall mainly compare our SEMP scheme with Lee et al.'s scheme [8] and Milburn et al.'s scheme [16]. The framework of Lee et al.'s scheme is similar to ours. Though Milburn et al.'s scheme is mainly used in identify authentication environment and the system framework is not similar to ours, we extend it to a QR payment environment.

In Lee et al.'s scheme [8], both a user and a shop have to obtain their public certificates from CA during the initialization. Then they register themselves to payment gateway (PG) using certificate. When finishing shopping, payment information and digital signature are transmitted to PG. After verification, the shop shows shop number, payment number and digital signature value in the form of QR to users. Then the user downloads payment information from PG. During payment, he signs payment data and transmits them to PG. In Milburn et al.'s scheme [16], the SQRL app hashes the website address and master key together to create a private key. The identity of the user is proved by the digital signature with the private key. There is no third party

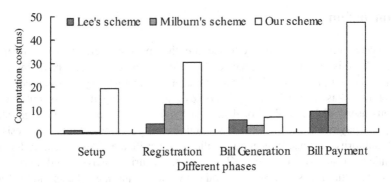

Fig. 2. The computation cost comparisons in different phases

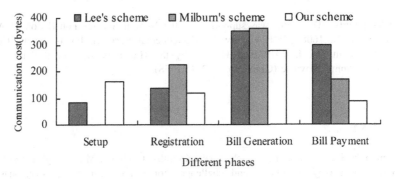

Fig. 3. The communication cost comparisons in different phases

involvement in the authentication process. When master key leaks, SQRL identity lock uses Diffie-Hellman key agreement to revoke it.

Figures 2 and 3 show communication and computation cost comparisons during different phases, respectively. Here, $n = 5$ and $t = 3$ in our scheme. We observe that setup phase in our scheme requires more computation and communication costs, compared with the existing solutions [8, 16]. It is because we adopt a distributed key generator structure to resist authority attacks and a detection method to find dishonest authority nodes. Considering the setup protocol generally performs one time in the system, its influence is limited. In addition, bill payment phase in our scheme requires more computation cost. It is because the phase requires 9 bilinear map operations, which is time-consuming. For communication cost, our SEMP scheme has better performance to the existing solutions [8, 16] during registration, bill generation and bill payment, while providing higher security level, especially in the aspect of resisting authority attacks.

7   Conclusion

Anti-forgery, anti-leak and convenience are the most concerned issues in mobile payment. In this paper, we formalized the definition and secure payment model. Subsequently, we proposed a SEMP scheme. In the scheme, payment data are signed and encrypted based on IBE and private keys are issued by fully distributed PKGs. Malicious users, dishonest TPP or dishonest PKG cannot impersonate a legal user to authorize a payment. Our scheme has confidentiality, unforgeability and resistance against authority attacks. Since no public key certificate is required, it has clear communication advantage over PKI schemes. Security analysis and performance analysis show that it has high security and convenience and it can be applied in mobile payment efficiently.

For future research, we will discuss how to put the scheme into a practical system to satisfy specific security and application requirements of mobile payment.

Acknowledgments. This work was supported by the Natural Science Foundation of Anhui Province (Grant No.1608085MF141), by the Fundamental Research Funds for the Central Universities (Grant No. J2014HGBZ0131) and by the Humanity and Social Science Key Foundation of Anhui Province (Grant No. SK2015A578).

References

1. Krombholz, K., Frühwirt, P., Kieseberg, P., Kapsalis, I., Huber, M., Weippl, E.: QR code security: a survey of attacks and challenges for usable security. In: Tryfonas, T., Askoxylakis, I. (eds.) HAS 2014. LNCS, vol. 8533, pp. 79–90. Springer, Heidelberg (2014). doi:10.1007/978-3-319-07620-1_8
2. Tencent Inc. (2016). https://wx.qq.com/
3. Alibaba Group (2016). https://www.alipay.com/
4. Shah, D., Shah, Y.: QR code and its security issues. Int. J. Comput. Sci. **2**(11), 22–26 (2014)
5. Yao, H., Shin, D.: Towards preventing qr code based attacks on android phone using security warnings. In: Proceedings of the 8th ACM SIGSAC Symposium on Information, Computer and Communications Security, pp. 341–346 (2013)
6. Wang, C.D., Feng, C.R., Gao, S.M.: Research on the security of two-dimension code used in the mobile payment. J. Tian Jin Univ. Technol. **30**(3), 15–20 (2014)
7. Czuszynski, K., Ruminski, J.: Interaction with medical data using QR-codes. In: Human System Interactions (HSI), pp. 182–187 (2014)
8. Lee, J., Cho, C.H., Jun, M.S.: Secure quick response-payment (QR-Pay) system using mobile device. In: Advanced Communication Technology (ICACT), pp. 1424–1427 (2011)
9. Han, J., Yang, Y., Huang, X., Yuen, T.H., Li, J., Cao, J.: Accountable mobile E-commerce scheme via identity-based plaintext-checkable encryption. Inf. Sci. **345**, 143–155 (2016)
10. Goyal, V.: Reducing trust in the PKG in identity based cryptosystems. In: Menezes, A. (ed.) CRYPTO 2007. LNCS, vol. 4622, pp. 430–447. Springer, Heidelberg (2007). doi:10.1007/978-3-540-74143-5_24
11. Libert, B., Vergnaud, D.: Towards practical black-box accountable authority IBE: weak black-box traceability with short ciphertexts and private keys. IEEE Trans. Inf. Theor. **57**(10), 7189–7204 (2011)

12. Boneh, D., Franklin, M.: Identity-based encryption from the weil pairing. In: Kilian, J. (ed.) CRYPTO 2001. LNCS, vol. 2139, pp. 213–229. Springer, Heidelberg (2001). doi:10.1007/3-540-44647-8_13

13. Paterson, K.G.: ID-based signatures from pairings on elliptic curve. Electron. Lett. **38**(18), 1025–1026 (2002)

14. Feldman, P.: A practical scheme for non-interactive verifiable secret sharing. In: Foundations of Computer Science, pp. 427–438 (1987)

15. Chen, L., Ng, S.L., Wang, G.: Threshold anonymous announcement in VANETs. Sel. Areas Commun. **29**(3), 605–615 (2011)

16. Milburn, J., Lee, H.: FassKey: a secure and convenient authentication system. In: IEEE Netsoft Conference and Workshops, pp. 489–495 (2016)

17. Steve, G.: SQRL–Secure Quick Reliable Login (2013). https://www.grc.com/sqrl/sqrl.htm

18. Raya, M., Hubaux, J.P.: Securing vehicular ad hoc networks. J. Comput. Secur. **15**(1), 39–68 (2007)

19. Calandriello, G., Papadimitratos, P., Hubaux, J.P., Lioy, A.: On the performance of secure vehicular communication systems. IEEE Trans. Dependable Secure Comput. **8**(6), 898–912 (2011)

User Preference-Based Spamming Detection with Coupled Behavioral Analysis

Frank Jiang[1], Mingdong Tang[2(✉)], and Quang Anh Tran[3]

[1] Faculty of Engineer of IT, University of Technology Sydney, Sydney 2007, Australia
Frank.Jiang@uts.edu.au
[2] School of Computer Science, Hunan University Science and Technology,
Hunan 411201, China
814100501@qq.com
[3] Posts and Telecommunications Institute of Technology, Hanoi 10000, Vietnam
tqanh@ptit.edu.vn

Abstract. Nowadays, the explosive growth of unsolicited emails on Internet has been challenging the spam filtering systems when at the presence of big data. Current spam filters suffer from the following problems: (1) Not personalised; (2) Comparatively static association rules defined in the firewalls, or gateways; (3) Cannot identify the extremely hidden information that mixed in the syntax or semantics. To overcome these problems, we develop and implement a new email spamming system leveraged by coupled text similarity analysis on user preference and a virtual meta-layer user-based email network, we take the social networks or campus LANs as the spam social network scenario. Fewer current practices exploit social networking initiatives to assist in spam filtering. Social network has essentially a large number of accounts features to be considered.

We construct a new model called meta-layer email network which can reduce these features by only considering individual user's actions i.e., replying network, reading network and deleting network. For the first time, these common user actions are considered to construct a social behavior-based email network. Further, a coupled selection model is developed for this email network, we are able to consider all relevant factors/features in a whole and recommend the emails practically to the user individually. The experiment data comes from the Enron email dataset, which has been recognized as a representative dataset for testing and validation. The experimental results show the new approach can achieve higher precision and accuracy with better email ranking in favor of personalised preference.

Keywords: PageRank · Multi-class classification · Support vector machines · Spam detection · Behavioral analysis

1 Introduction

Email spams are unsolicited emails which are sent massively to many other recipients from one user [1]. According to the 2010 Annual Security Report from Symantec Message Labs Intelligence, approximately 89 % of all emails are spam; resulting in an

© Springer International Publishing AG 2016
G. Wang et al. (Eds.): SpaCCS 2016, LNCS 10066, pp. 466–477, 2016.
DOI: 10.1007/978-3-319-49148-6_38

estimated 260 billion spam emails every single day [2]. Spam e-mails may contain either text or images or both text and images, which expose many challenges to the current spam filtering techniques.

The specific issues for the new spam system include: (1) Not personalised; (2) Comparatively static association rules defined in the firewalls, or gateways; (3) Cannot identify the extremely hidden information that mixed in the syntax or semantics.

Moreover, the conventional i.i.d. ness-based learning methods do not scale well and nor do they perform well under highly unstructured, unpredictable conditions (data volume, data variety, data categories etc.).

The most recent approaches [3–7] for email spam can be generally grouped into two categories: (1) based on email content, (2) based on email header. The first approach has low error but high computational cost. The second approach has lower computational cost but with higher error rate. In the first category, statistical methods such as Bayesian Classification or Support Vector Machines (SVM) are used to filter emails Bayesian Classification. It was introduced by Paul Graham in 1998 [8], and further addressed by Androutsopoulos [9]. The second category of techniques often have higher performance but also higher error rate.

There is a great need to develop the new spam learning and classification techniques to meet the new data challenges and requirements. Conventionally, email spamming is a two-class text classification problem that divides emails as SPAM or HAM. By so doing, it reduces the number of email sending to users. However, this may not be suitable for anyone. Personalised emails recommender becomes more and more important nowadays as we receive the increasing amount of emails everyday. People's preferences are different. The spam emails for person A might NOT mean to be spam emails for person B. For instance, a person is in favor of sporting, the emails with the keywords "sports game", "soccer" or "tennis" may not be spam for this particular person, while when a person dislikes shopping, the emails with "shopping" will be the spam. The advertisements or news related to these keywords might be filtered out by the spam filter governed by the static spam rules. Therefore, it is necessary to define the user-oriented spam system without the constraints from static rules.

In this paper, we propose a new framework of email recommender system using user actions and statistical methods. Instead of labeling emails as SPAM or HAM, we label emails with the personalized importance ranking based on user actions and preferences. The possible number of user's actions may vary but mainly falls into the following general categories: (a) reply, (b) read, (c) forward, (d) delete or mark as spam. By using this approach, we can not only filter spam, but also suggest the action for users and prioritize emails by different actions based on user preferences. In summary, the contributions of the paper are threefold:

(1) Propose a new definition for spam focusing on personal preferences;
(2) For the first time, the user actions are employed to construct a new meta-email network inspired by social networking behaviors to reduce the amount of data processed;
(3) Seamlessly combine the user preferences and content-based analysis in a new email recommender system for multi-class spam problem on the basis of personal profiles.

This paper is organized as follows: Sect. 2 introduces the preliminaries of four spam filtering algorithms including our own algorithm. Section 3 further presents the prioritisation theory and its experiment validation. A description of the dataset is also included. Section 4 investigate the classification problem in our new user-action based meta-email network, the classifiers are considered by use of Naïve Bayesian Classifier and Support Vector Machines. Experimental results show the promising performance of the new meta-email network by these two classifiers. Section 5 concludes and discusses future work of this research.

2   Preliminaries

In this section, we review new methods to detect spams via the theory of the complex networks. Each method as reviewed, has advantages and disadvantages. Firstly, we introduce three popular spam filtering methods and one improved spam detection algorithm developed by authors in the past [24–26]. In the next theory section of this paper, this improved filtering scheme is integrated in part with the meta-email network for user ranking particularly. Secondly, we summarize the current text mining methods.

2.1   Method Based on Clustering Coefficient

Boykin and Roychowdhury [15] propose a solution to detect spam based on the clustering coefficient. The authors collect emails from their own personal mailbox to build an email network, in which email addresses are nodes and links on the sender-receiver nodes are considered as edges. In this method, the email exchanges between the set of users are modeled as a social network. Based on the two specific characteristics of the social network (and the email network), the free-scale degree [20] and the small-world degree [21], the clustering coefficient of node i in the email network is calculated by the following formula:

$$C_i = \frac{2 * E_i}{k_i(k_i - 1)} \tag{1}$$

Where Ci is the clustering coefficient; ki is the number of nodes that link to node i; Ei is the number of edges between neighboring vertices of node i. According to the experimental result in [15], Boykin uses the personal email as the dataset. Based on the incoming and outgoing mail from the author's address, he builds the personal email network. On that basis, Boykin calculates the clustering of network nodes and distinguishes who is the real sender and who is sending spam. The achieved result is 53 % of emails being correctly classified as true or spam email, the remaining 47 % of emails not identified. Hence, it is really necessary to evaluate the clustering coefficient of the nodes with a fully-featured dataset supplied by an email server, instead of personal mailbox, to gain more promising achievements.

2.2   Method Based on PageRank Algorithm

Both the WWW network and email network have the same properties from the complex network such as small-world degree and scale-free degree. Thus, the major findings of the WWW network have enormous significance in the study of email network.

The WWW network is a kind of complex network in which the nodes are webpages and the edges are the links from this webpage to others. Brin and Page, in 1998, proposed the PageRank algorithm [17] used to rank the webpage. The remarkable idea of the algorithm is that a webpage is considered as "important" if there are plenty of "important" webpage links to it. Here is the PageRank formula:

Assume that webpages T1 to Tn have links to the webpage A. C(A) is defined as the number of link-outs from the webpage A; then the page rank of webpage A can be calculated by the formula:

$$PR(A) = (1 - d) + d\left(\frac{PR(T1)}{C(T1)} + \ldots + \frac{PR(Tn)}{C(Tn)} \right) \tag{2}$$

d is the damping which is the probability that a user clicks on a link available on the site. According to Brin and Page's calculations, this damping is set equal to 0.85.

2.3   Method Based on Weighted PageRank Algorithm

Xing and Ghorbani [18] proposed the Weighted PageRank algorithm in 2004. The ranking score of a webpage (rank) is divided for webpages having link-in(s) from that page with different weights, instead of equally sharing as in the original PageRank algorithm [17].

The weighted PageRank algorithm offers two values $W^{in}_{(v, u)} = \dfrac{I_u}{\sum_{p\in R(v)} I_p}$ and $W^{out}_{(v, u)} = \dfrac{O_u}{\sum_{p\in R(v)} O_p}$, in which Iu and Ip are respectively the number of link-in(s) to webpage u and p; Ou and Op are respectively the number of link-out(s) from the webpage u and p. R(v) is the set of webpages with links from webpage v. Here is the formula for the Weighted PageRank:

$$PR(u) = (1 - d) + d \sum_{v\in B(u)} PR(v)W^{in}_{(v, u)} W^{out}_{(v, u)} \tag{3}$$

In particular, the damping index d has the same meaning as the formula (4).

The literatures on the author's Web data show that weighted PageRank algorithm is better than the original PageRank algorithm. However, there is not any review on the application of weighted PageRank algorithm on spam data set. It is very important to use the same dataset to test weighted PageRank algorithm.

2.4 Method Based-on Extended Clustering Coefficient

In order to overcome the shortcoming of the original Clustering Coefficient formula (1), the authors have made the modifications on the formula of Boykin [15] to compute the clustering coefficient of the nodes [5] termed as Extended Clustering Coefficient as follows:

$$C_i = \frac{2 * (E_i + 1)}{k_i(k_i - 1) + 1} \tag{4}$$

As a result, the email network in the view of directed graph with weighted edges can be considered. Under such description, the clustering coefficient is further modified as:

$$C_i = \frac{2 * (E_i + 1)}{S_i(S_i - 1) + 1} + 0.2 * R_i \tag{5}$$

In particular, Ei has the same meaning in the formula (1), namely the number of edges. Si is the number of nodes, which receives at least one email from i, Ri is the number of nodes, which sends at least one email to i. The details of the justification of this equation can be referred to the authors' work [24–26].

3 Theoretical Framework - New Spam-Filtering Methods Based on Meta-Email Networks

Unlike the two classes spam and ham classifications, the problem is therefore transformed into a multi-class classification problem for the email network. The overall email recommender system produces a ranking list denoted as Rank (E, P), that is defined for the purpose of email prioritisation. It considers both the global ranking and the personalised ranking, where the global rank is calculated by using the Extended Coefficient Clustering [22, 23], and the personalised rank is calculated independently on the individual user's preferences. We adopt the top - k selection as the way to generate the final important email lists for individual users. It is denoted in a general form as follows.

$$Rank(E, P) = C1 * G(s) + C2 * P(c, p) \tag{6}$$

where "E" represents "email", "P" stands for "person", "s" is "sender", "c" is the content of the email", and C1 and C2 are two constant weight numbers. G(s) represents the Global rank(s), and P(c, p) represents Personalized rank (c,p).

Rank (E,P) is the rank (or prioritization) of an email E to a person P, this is the rank we would like to compute as describe in the objective). We compute the overall rank by considering two components: Global rank (s) and Personalized rank (c,p) C1 and C2 are adjustment weights.

The global rank evaluates the importance of the emails sender(s) via the calculated ranks, while the personalised rank identifies the content of this email is of the email recipients' interest or not according to the users' actions.

As shown in the Table 1, the higher global rank usually indicates the email is more important. Moreover, the higher personalized rank indicates this email is much of user's individual interest, therefore, more likely this email is important to the user. A high overall Rank (E, P) is to be achieved in this case.

Table 1. Global rank and Personalised rank

Rank (E, P)	Global rank	Personalised rank
High	High	High
Medium high	Low	High
Medium high	High	Low
Low	Low	Low

Figure 1 shows the social behavior-based meta-email network. The user actions to email such as replying, reading and deleting build up replying network, reading network and deleting network. For instance, when User E receives email from A, E replies to A, there is one arc from A to E, and the other reply arc occurs from E to A. The replying, forwarding and deletion actions can be observed. The following section focuses on the personalised ranking, which is done by the coupled behavioural analysis on personal interests/preference.

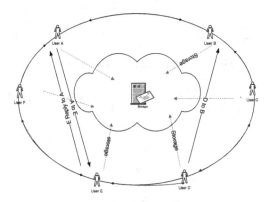

Fig. 1. Meta-email network

3.1   Coupled Content Classification

The most general form of text data is string, and the most common representation for texts is the vector-space representation. The vector-space model represents the texts for each document as a "bag-of-words". Though the vector-space representation is very simple and efficient, it loses information about the structural information of the words in the document, especially when the text is short.

Unlike the TF-IDF model that ignores the sequence of the word, this work use neural network to maintain more sequential information of the words by the following definition:

$$f(w_t, \ldots, w_{t-n+1}) = P(w_t | w_1^{t-1}) \tag{7}$$

Where $w_1, w_2, \ldots, w_t$ is the sequence of words, and $w_t \in V$ where V is vocabulary set, the function f could be any format, in neural network it often use energy function to compute the probabilities. However, the input's dimension still very high, it is not suitable for large date set. Consequently, it was developed the continuous Bag-of-words model (CBOW) and continuous Skip-gram (SG) model respectively. Formally define as follows:

$$P_\theta(w|h) = \frac{exp(s_\theta(w,h))}{\sum_{w'} exp(s_\theta(w',h))} \tag{8}$$

Where $s_\theta(w,h)$ is the function to compute the relation between given word w and its context h, the θ is the parameter which quantifies the relation of the w and h (Figs. 2 and 3).

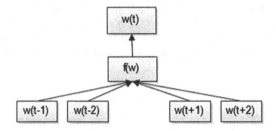

Fig. 2. Continuous Bag-of-words model

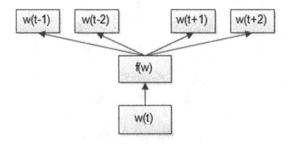

Fig. 3. Continuous Skip-gram model

Maximum Likelihood Learning. Though those methods restricted the range of surrounding context to reduce the computational cost, computing the gradient of log-likelihood related the vocabulary size which is always large. The optimization can be given by:

$$\frac{\partial}{\partial \theta} \log P_\theta(w|h) = \frac{\partial}{\partial \theta} s_\theta(w,h) - \sum_{w'} P(w'|h) \frac{\partial}{\partial \theta} s_\theta(w',h) \tag{9}$$

The computation $s_\theta(w, h)$ require all words in the vocabulary, hence the learning could be very slow.

Recently introduced a noise-contrastive estimation which can perform a more stable and efficient importance sampling for training. Applied this method to build a new model which can train the vector representation of the words by using the formula:

$$\frac{\partial}{\partial\theta}J^{h,w}(\theta) = \frac{kP_n(w)}{P_\theta(w|h) + kP_n(w)}\frac{\partial}{\partial\theta}logP_\theta(w|h) - \sum_{i=1}^{k}[\frac{kP_n(x_i)}{P_\theta(x_i|h) + kP_n(x_i)}\frac{\partial}{\partial\theta}logP_\theta(x_i|h)] \qquad (10)$$

where $x_1, \ldots, x_k$ are the k noise samples.

By doing this, the computation of $s_\theta(w, h)$ is unnecessary and reduce the computation cost enormously.

Finally, we compute the vector representation of the words and we can obtain the intra relation similarity (CS) between two words straightforwardly:

$$RS^{Intra}(w_\alpha, w_\beta) = \frac{V_\alpha \cdot V_\beta}{\|V_\alpha\|\|V_\beta\|} \qquad (11)$$

Where V_n is the vector representation for the word w_n.

Document similarity by using Word to word Coupled relations $IDN(w_\alpha, w_\beta|w_\gamma) = $ True if $DN(w_\alpha, w_\gamma) = $ True and $DN(w_\beta, w_\gamma) = $ True (Fig. 4).

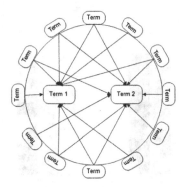

Fig. 4. Illustration of the indirect neighbors in texts

4   Experiment and Evaluation

The experiments are based on the Enron email dataset. The Enron Corpus is a large database of over 600,000 emails generated by 158 employees of the Enron Corporation and acquired by the Federal Energy Regulatory Commission during its investigation after the company's collapse. We use the proposed model to do the email classification task. When a new email came, based on the proposed model, this experiment predicts the actual mailbox it should belong to. More precisely, this experiment the experiment decides whether the incoming mail belongs to the deleted folder or the inbox folder.

First, this experiment calculates the user preference score UP for each user, based on the aforementioned definition. For the computation efficiency, this experiment sets the maximum neighbors amount for each user to 100. Secondly, for the text content pre-process, this experiment set the minimum term frequency to 10 and ignored the top 50 highest frequent terms when calculating the TFIDF values.

The experiment runs on the entire Enron data set in the first stage, and focuses separately on each user. Due to the limitation of the space, we only select 34 representative users' results.

Figure 5 shows the classification accuracy on the whole data set, comparing the two most widely used classifiers. In all the following figures, we use NB to represent naïve Bayesian classifier, and use SVM to represent the Support Vector Machines classifier, and use CS to represent the Coupled Similarity classifier, and use UP to represent the User preference score. Figure 5 shows the user preference score that can significantly enhance the accuracy performance of the classification task by merging it with the classic classification method. Meanwhile, the proposed coupled similarity classifier also outperforms the traditional classification method. Finally, when combined the coupled similarity classifier with the user preference score, it get the best performance of all the experiment tasks. Figure 6 is the F-measure comparison of the proposed method with the classic method. The result confirmed the advantage of the performance of the proposed method.

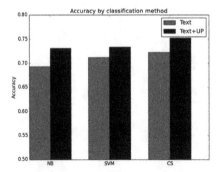
Fig. 5. The accuracy comparison

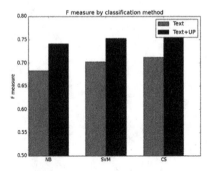
Fig. 6. The F-measure comparison

Figures 7 and 8 are the comparisons of the recall and precession which proved the performance of the proposed method comprehensively.

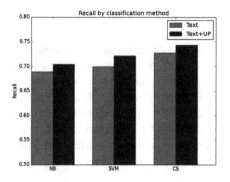

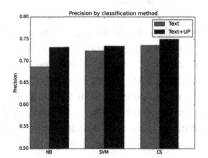

Fig. 7. The recall comparison   **Fig. 8.** The precision comparison

The next section of the experiment is the evaluation of the weight when merge the classifier and the user preference scores. Figure 9 demonstrate the variation of the weight when merge the classifier possibility and user preference score. It is clear that for all the classifier merge with the user preference score, the peak value of the accuracy all appeared at the weight equals 0.4. When the weight equals 0, the result 100 % completely comes from the classic classifier, when the weight equals 1, it means the result only come from the user preference score. Hence every classifier achieves the same classification accuracy at the weight of 1. The experiment demonstrates the classification accuracy on each individual user, it shows that for most of the users, when the user preference score is merged with the classic classifier, the improvement of the performance is significant.

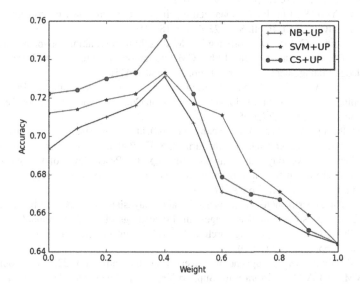

Fig. 9. The weights comparison

5   Conclusions

In this paper, we develop and implement a new email spamming system leveraged by coupled text similarity analysis on user preference and a virtual meta-layer user-based email network, we take the social networks as the spam social network scenario. A coupled selection model is developed for this email network, we are able to consider all relevant factors/features in a whole and recommend the emails practically to the user individually. Enron data has been recognized as a representative dataset for testing and validation. The experimental results show the new approach can achieve higher precision and accuracy with better email ranking in favor of personalised preference.

References

1. Steve, W.: Email overload: exploring personal information management of email. In: Proceedings of the SIGCHI Conference on Human Factors in Computing Systems: Common Ground, vol. 96, no. 1, pp. 276–283 (1996)
2. Nicholas, K.: Automated email activity management: an unsupervised learning approach. In: Proceedings of the 10th International Conference on Intelligent User Interfaces, vol. 5, no. 1, pp. 67–74 (2005)
3. Anirban, D.: Enhanced email spam filtering through combining similarity graphs. In: Proceedings of the Fourth ACM International Conference on Web Search and Data Mining, vol. 11, no. 1, pp. 785–794 (2011)
4. Khurum, N.J.: Automatic Personalized spam filtering through significant word modeling. In: ICTAI 2007, Proceedings of the 19th IEEE International Conference on Tools with Artificial Intelligence, vol. 2, no. 1, pp. 291–298 (2007)
5. Yang, Y., Yoo, S., Lin, F.: Personalized email prioritization based on content and social network analysis. IEEE Intell. Syst. **25**(4), 12–18 (2010)
6. Paul-Alexandru, C, Jörg, D, Wolfgang, N.: MailRank: using ranking for spam detection. In: CIKM 2005, Proceedings of the 14th ACM International Conference on Information and Knowledge Management, vol. 5, no. 1, pp. 373–380 (2005)
7. Mingjun, L., Wanlei, Z.: Spam filtering based on preference ranking. In: CIT 2005 Proceedings of the Fifth International Conference on Computer and Information Technology, vol. 5, no. 1, pp. 223–227 (2005)
8. Graham, P.: A plan for spam. Web document (2002). http://www.paulgraham.com/spam.html
9. Androutsopoulos, I., Koutsias, J., Chandrinos, K.V., Paliouras, G., Spyropoulos, C.D.: An evaluation of Naive Bayesian anti-spam filtering. In: Proceedings of the Workshop on Machine Learning in the New Information Age, 11th European Conference on Machine Learning, Barcelona, Spain, pp. 9–17 (2000)
10. Ion, A.: An experimental comparison of naive Bayesian and keyword-based anti-spam filtering with personal e-mail messages. In: Proceedings of the 23rd Annual International ACM SIGIR Conference on Research and Development in Information Retrieval, SIGIR 2000, no. 1, pp. 160–167 (2000)
11. Manu, K: Building Search Applications: Lucene, LingPipe, and Gate, p. 22. MustruPublising, US
12. LIBSVM: LIBSVM - A Library for Support Vector Machines. http://www.csie.ntu.edu.tw/~cjlin/libsvm/. Accessed 10 July 2012
13. Chih-Wei, H.: A comparison of methods for multiclass support vector machines. IEEE Trans. Neural Netw. **2**(13), 415–425 (2002)

14. Thorsten J.: Text Categorization with support vector machines: learning with many relevant features. In: Kunstliche Intelligenz 1997 (2008). Manning, C.D

15. Boykin, P.O., Roychowdhury, V.: Leveraging social networks to fight spam. IEEE Comput. **38**(4), 61–68 (2004). Sorting e-mail friends from foes. Nature news (2005)

16. Hanoi University website. http://www.hanu.edu.vn

17. Brin, S., Page, L.: The anatomy of a large-scale hypertextual web search engine. In: Proceedings of the 7th International Conference on World Wide Web (WWW), Brisbane, Australia, pp. 107–117 (1998)

18. Xing W., Ghorbani A.: Weighted PageRank algorithm. In: Proceedings of the Second Annual Conference on Communication Networks and Services Research, pp. 305–314 (2004)

19. Bui, N.L., Tran, Q.A., Ha, Q.T.: User's authentic rating based on email networks, In: Proceedings of the First International Conference on Mobile Computing, Communications and Applications (ICMOCCA 2006), pp. 144–148 (2006)

20. Ebel, H., Mielsch, L.I., Bornholdt, S.: Scale-free topology of email networks. Phys. Rev. E **66**, 035103(R) (2002)

21. Newman, M.E.J., Watts, D.J.: Renormalization group analysis of the small-world network model. Phys. Lett. A **263**, 341–346 (1999)

22. Hromada, D.: Quantitative intercultural comparison by means of parallel page ranking of diverse national wikipedias. In: Proceedings of JADT (2010)

23. Chirita, P., Diederich, J., Nejdl, W.: MailRank: using ranking for spam detection, In: Proceedings of the 14th ACM International Conference on Information and Knowledge Management, pp. 373–380 (2005)

24. Tran, Q.A., Vu, M.T., Jiang, F.: Email user ranking based on email networks. In: American Institute of Physics, Conference Proceedings, vol. 1479, pp. 1512–1517. ICNAAM (2012). doi:10.1063/1.4756451

25. Ha, Q.M., Phung, V.D., Jiang, F. Nguyen, Q.L.: Image spam filtering based on maximum entropy segmentation method. In: Proceeding of 7th International Conference on Broadband Communications and Biomedical Applications (IB2COM 2012), pp. 147–151 (2012)

26. Vu, M.T., Tran, Q.A., Jiang, F., Tran, V.Q.: Multilingual rules for spam detection. In: Proceeding of 7th International Conference on Broadband Communications and Biomedical Applications, pp. 106–110 (2012)

Analysis of SIFT Method Based on Swarm Intelligent Algorithms for Copy-Move Forgery Detection

Fei Zhao, Wenchang Shi[(✉)], Bo Qin, and Bin Liang

School of Information, Renmin University of China,
Beijing 100872, China
wenchang@ruc.edu.cn

Abstract. Scale Invariant Features Transform (SIFT) method has proven effective for detecting the images with the copy-move forgery in digital forensics field. However, by a great number of tests and practicalities, it is certificated that the detection results highly depend on the presetting of the multiple thresholds. The exhaustive manual searched for the preset thresholds, based on a wise guess, must cause a high computational cost and inefficiency. In this paper, a SIFT method based on swarm intelligent algorithm for copy-move forgery detection is proposed. Three canonical swarm intelligent algorithms (particle swarm optimization-PSO, differential evolution-DE and artificial bee colony-ABC) are applied to find the optimal multiple thresholds for SIFT-based method. Experimental results against various test images with different sizes of duplicated regions show that no algorithm is always more excellent than others. For most cases, PSO algorithm is more adept at finding optimal multiple thresholds for SIFT-based copy-move forgery detection.

Keywords: Copy-move forgery detection · Differential evolution · Artificial bee colony · Particle swarm optimization · SIFT

1 Introduction

Copy-move forgery (CMF) detection is an important and common technique in digital forensics. For typical CMF, at least one part of an image is copied and pasted into a different location in the same image [1]. Researchers presented many methods to identify whether the image is a CMF one or not and even to point out the duplicated regions. Keypoint-based methods, as robust and effective technologies, have been widely used for CMF detection [2]. These methods involve first extracting keypoints from the test image, building a descriptor for each keypoint, and matching keypoints based on descriptors. In accordance with the matched keypoints, duplicated regions in the image are revealed. However, the detection effects depend heavily on multiple threshold values determined by experience. Due to various combinations of thresholds adopted by different researchers, CMF image detection without a unified standard results in a lack of authority. Moreover, an insufficient number of matched keypoints declines the credibility of estimating duplicated regions. These two issues limit the applications of keypoint-based methods.

G. Wang et al. (Eds.): SpaCCS 2016, LNCS 10066, pp. 478–490, 2016.
DOI: 10.1007/978-3-319-49148-6_39

To solve these problems, swarm intelligent (SI) methods are employed to automatically generate customized threshold values for each image, which can detect as large number as possible of true matched keypoints. Compare with the traditional exhaustive methods, heuristic methods for finding optimal thresholds gained the attention of researchers on account of the computational inefficiency. There are many canonical works, such as ant colony optimization (ACO) [15], particle swarm optimization (PSO) [6–11], differential evolution (DE) [4, 5], bacterial foraging (BF) [16], honey bee mating optimization (HBMO) and artificial bee colony (ABC) [12–14].

Compared to many other heuristics algorithms, DE, PSO and ABC algorithms are simple but efficient models and easy to implement. The purpose of this paper is to investigate the search abilities of DE, PSO and ABC algorithms against thresholds estimation of SIFT-based copy-move forgery detection. Meanwhile, the attempt to find out which algorithm is suitable for threshold values optimization of SIFT-based method is presented.

The remainder of this paper is organized as follows. Section 2 briefly introduces the SIFT&SI-based CMF detection method. A brief overview of DE, PSO and ABC algorithms are provided in Sect. 3. Section 4 presents the experimental results, and Sect. 5 concludes.

2   Brief Explanations of SIFT&SI-Based CMF Detection Method

In this section, the common SIFT-based detection methods for copy-move forgery detection are described first. Then, a new copy-move forgery detection method benefited from swarm intelligent approaches can automatically generate customized threshold values for images.

2.1   The Typical Detection Flow of SIFT-Based Methods

Most existing SIFT-based methods have a common detection flow. The keypoints are first detected from the test image and the features for these keypoints are extracted. Then keypoints with similar feature will be matched. After that, there may be some false matched keypoints, which should be eliminated. At last the affine transforms between the original region and target region are estimated according to these matched keypoints. The detail above will be shown in the following four subsections.

SIFT-based methods present two main problems. Firstly, the detection results depend heavily on multiple threshold values. Existing SIFT-based methods often preset one group of threshold values according to experience. With such empirical values, SIFT-based methods may generate unsatisfactory detection results or even error ones. Otherwise, because different individuals adopt various preset thresholds, CMF image detection methods do not adhere to unified standards, which results in a lack of authority. Secondly, as often happens in CMF detection, an insufficient number of matched keypoints found by these methods inevitably decreases detection accuracy. These two issues extremely limit the applications of SIFT-based methods.

2.2   SIFT&SI-Based CMF Detection Method

A new copy-move forgery detection method is proposed to solve the two issues of SIFT-based methods, which is benefited from swarm intelligent approaches. The detection method involves the following two stages: Elemental Detection and Threshold Estimation. Firstly, Elemental Detection detects the test image by using given threshold values, which are widely used in existing detection methods. Secondly, new detection threshold values are produced by Threshold Estimation according to the detection results of Elemental Detection. Then repeat the above two steps N times. Last, the best result is found from these N results. The best result has high degree of precision and large number of true matched keypoints. The specific processes are shown as following.

2.2.1   Elemental Detection

The goal of Elemental Detection is to detect whether an image is CMF, which is similar to the keypoint-based methods (introduced in Sect. 2.1). The only difference is the detection threshold values. Elemental Detection involves Keypoint Detection and Feature Extraction, Matching, Filtering and the Estimation of Affine Transformations.

The task of Keypoint Detection and Feature Extraction is to detect keypoints from test image and build descriptors for each keypoint. SIFT algorithm is used to do this work. Then these keypoints will be matched according to their descriptors. The best-bin-first algorithm is used to match keypoints in Matching. After Matching, the false match keypoints should be eliminated in Filtering. If the distance between two matched keypoints is too small, these keypoints may constitute a false match. Because the descriptors of such paired matched keypoints may be very similar, but they are not in forgery regions. In [17], if the distance between two paired keypoints is smaller than a preset value, they these keypoints are removed. At last, RANSAC algorithm is used to estimate the affine transform according to the matched keypoints.

2.2.2   Threshold Estimation

Threshold Estimation is to automatically create customized threshold values for each test image, which can increase the number of true matched keypoints. At this stage, new groups of threshold values are selected based on the detection results, which are generated during Elemental Detection, and these threshold values are used in subsequent test image elemental detection. The threshold values that must be determined automatically and their domains are listed in Table 1.

The values of these threshold values are various in different literatures.

We turn parameter value estimation into an issue of optimal solution. The parameter value estimation issue can be expressed as (1). The optimal solution of (1) within the range of each parameter can be found out by SI algorithm.

$$D = f(X), \quad X = (x_1, x_2, x_3, x_4 \ldots) \tag{1}$$

where X is a group of input parameters, $f(x)$ is a detection process. D is the detection result. By adjusting the values of X, D can converge to the extreme value.

Table 1. Optimization threshold values (threshold values of the SIFT-based method)

Threshold values	Meaning	Lower bound	Upper bound
S	The number of blurred images in each octave	3	6
σ	The Gaussian kernel of the initial width	1.00	2.00
τ	Keypoint matching threshold	0.01	1.00
R	Maximum inlier distance in RANSAC	1	10
Dismin	The minimum distance	10	50
Thresh	The threshold used to reject unstable keypoints	0.0001	0.1000

In order to choose the result with high level of precision and large number of true matched keypoints, we define D as the ratio of true matched keypoints and the sum of true matched keypoints and the false match coefficient φ. The value of D is used to measure the detection results, which is similar to the precision as shown in (2). Higher D values denote better detection results. D values are associated with the number of matched keypoints.

$$D = \frac{TMK}{TMK + \varphi}, \quad \varphi = \begin{cases} FMK, FMK > 10 \\ 10, FMK \leq 10 \end{cases} \tag{2}$$

where TMK denotes the number of keypoints that meet the affine transformation (defined in Sect. 2.1), and the number of other keypoints is denoted by FMK. The φ is the false match coefficient that generates a default minimum value for FMK. The φ ensures that larger TMK detection results are chosen as the best results.

In this paper, PSO, DE and ABC algorithm are used to find the customized threshold values for each image. And then the most suitable algorithm from them for this work will be found. We use the number of true matched keypoints, the precision of matched keypoints and the value of D to measure which algorithm can find the most suitable threshold values.

3 Canonical Swarm Intelligent Optimizers

Many swarm algorithms have been presented and have been successfully applied to a large number of optimal thresholds problems.

In this study, we have three reasons to use DE, PSO and ABC algorithms. Firstly, they employ less control threshold values, which make them have low complexity in addition to high performance. Secondly, they based on simple models, which make them easy to implement. Last, their computation times are low, which make them preferable in real-time implementation of signal processing applications.

A brief description of the DE, the PSO and the ABC algorithms are given in the following subsections.

3.1 Differential Evolution (DE)

The DE algorithm is one comparatively simple variant of an evolutionary algorithm that is developed in 1997 by Kenneth Price and Rainer Storn. DE algorithm has only three or four operational threshold values, and can be coded in about 20 lines of pseudo-code. With its ease of implementation and proven efficiency, DE is ideally suited to both novice and experienced users wishing to optimize their simulation models. DE is a method that optimizes a problem by iteratively trying to improve a candidate solution with regard to a given measure of quality. Such methods are commonly known as metaheuristics as they make few or no assumptions about the problem being optimized and can search very large spaces of candidate solutions. However, metaheuristics such as DE do not guarantee an optimal solution is ever found. DE works as follows:

(1) All individuals are randomly initialized and evaluated using the fitness function provided;
(2) For each individual in the population, an offspring is created using the weighted difference of parent solutions;
(3) The offspring replaces the parent if it is fitter. Otherwise, the parent survives and is passed on to the next iteration of the algorithm;
(4) Repeating the steps, which are from (2) to (3), until meeting the requirements.

3.2 Particle Swarm Optimization (PSO)

The PSO algorithm was developed by Eberhart and Kennedy in 1995, models the social behavior of bird flocking or fish schooling. In PSO, a swarm is a collection of the particles moving in search space. The particles change their positions depending on their previous experience and the best experience of the swarm to find the global optimum. Each particle keeps track of its coordinates in the problem space which is associated with the best solution it has achieved so far. The algorithm starts to iterate the following steps:

(1) Initializing the population;
(2) Calculating the fitness values of the particles;
(3) Updating the best experience of each particle;
(4) Choosing the best particle;
(5) Calculating the velocities of the particles;
(6) Updating the positions of the particles;
(7) Repeating the steps, which are from (2) to (6), until meeting the requirements

3.3 Artificial Bee Colony (ABC)

The ABC algorithm is a swarm based meta-heuristic algorithm that was introduced by Karaboga in 2005. The ABC algorithm has shown super performance on numerical optimization and has been widely used in different research areas. In nature, there is a division of labor in the hive, and the forager bees work collectively without a central control mechanism to maximize the amount of nectar loaded into the hive. The behavior of real bees and a detailed analogy can be found in [12]. There are three types of bees in the foraging process: employed bees associated with specific food sources, onlooker bees watching the dance of employed bees within the hive to choose a food source, and scout bees searching for food sources randomly. The bees are classified according to how they select the food source to exploit. It is assumed that there is only one artificial employed bee for each food source. The main steps of the algorithm are given below:

(1) Initial food sources are produced for all employed bees;
(2) Each employed bee goes to a food source in her memory and determines a neighbor source, then evaluates its nectar amount and dances in the hive;
(3) Each onlooker watches the dance of employed bees and chooses one of their sources depending on the dances, and then goes to that source. After choosing a neighbor around that, she evaluates its nectar amount;
(4) Abandoned food sources are determined and are replaced with the new food sources discovered by scouts;
(5) The best food source found so far is registered;
(6) Repeating the steps, which are from (2) to (5), until meeting the requirements.

4   Experiments and Results

4.1   Experimental Setup

All of the test images are from Christlein et al.'s database [1]. Forty-eight CMF images are included in the database. In our experiment, we use 40 of them. The images are 3000 * 2300 pixels in size on average. To shorten detection periods and to simplify the detection process, all images are first roughly resized to 1024 * 700 pixels, and then multiple copied forgery images are changed to individual copied forgery images. The test CMF images have not undergone any additional post-processing.

A group of initialization detection threshold values is set for each algorithm, when they detect an image first time. This group of threshold values is set according to existing literatures, which is widely used to CMF detection. The initialization detection threshold values can make the detection results more satisfactory.

In the DE algorithm, the classical DE was used and the same parameter settings are adopted as in [4]. We set zoom factor as $F = 0.9$ and crossover rate as $CR = 0.9$.

In the PSO algorithm, the inertia weight w is changed from 1.2 to 0.8 in searching process. Both of the cognitive and social learning coefficients c1 and c2 are set as 0.729. The population size is 20 and the maximum number of fitness evaluations is 100.

In the ABC algorithm, the classical ABC was used and the same parameter settings are adopted as in [12]. We set Max reset-limitation as $limit = 200$.

We not only compare the detection results among the detection methods based the three SI algorithms, but also compare with the detection method, which is not using any

SI algorithms and uses a group of fixed detection parameters. We defined this method as original method and the detection parameters are set as [1].

4.2 Metrics

In order to make comparison detection results clearly, two variables are introduced first.

$$SR = \frac{The\ pixels\ in\ duplicated\ regions}{The\ pixels\ in\ the\ whole\ tested\ image} \tag{3}$$

$$KR = \frac{The\ true\ matched\ keypoints}{The\ pixels\ in\ duplicated\ regions} \times 100 \tag{4}$$

SR is the ratio of duplicated region to the whole image. KR is the ratio of true matched keypoints to the pixels of duplicated region. The true matched keypoints mean that one of the matched keypoints is in the copied original region and the other one is in the pasted target region. The remainders of matched keypoints are regarded as the false matched keypoints.

Here, the precision of true matched keypoints can be described as the ratio of true matched keypoints and all matched keypoints, as shown in (5):

$$P = \frac{TMK}{TMK + FMK} \tag{5}$$

where TMK is the number of the true matched keypoints and FMK is the number of the false matched keypoints. We also use the value of D to measure the accuracy of detection results, which is introduced in formula (1) of Sect. 2.2.2. In the same number of cycles, the algorithm, which is able to generate the greatest value of D, is identified as the most suitable one for estimating threshold values of CMF detection.

4.3 Results

Nine examples of detection results are shown in Fig. 1. Figure 1(a–i) are the CMF images, which are from Christlein et al.'s database. Figure 1(a1–i1), (a2–i2) and (a3–i3) are the detection results of DE, PSO and ABC, respectively. SR in the Fig. 1(a–c) is less than 1 %, in the Fig. 1(d–f) is between 1 % and 5 % and in the Fig. 1(g–i) is greater than 5 %. It is obvious that both of PSO and DE obtain better results than ABC and the performance of PSO is relatively best. In Fig. 1(i), the detection result of PSO is better than that of ABC and they are all better than DE. In Fig. 1(a3) and (i1), no matched keypoints is detected, because the SIFT-based detection technology is difficult to detect the CMF image, in which the duplicated region is too small or too smooth. The duplicated region in Fig. 1(a) is too small and in Fig. 1(i) is too smooth. If the threshold values are not suitable for such image, the SIFT-based detection technology may be useless. In Fig. 1(d–h), it is difficult to visually compare the detection results of

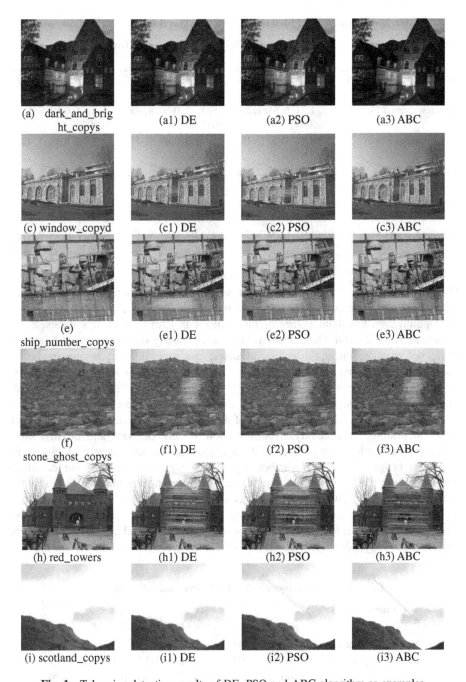

Fig. 1. Take nine detection results of DE, PSO and ABC algorithm as examples

Table 2. Optimization threshold values are determined by the three algorithms

Image name	Optimization threshold values (S, σ, τ, R, $Dismin$, $Thresh$)		
	DE	PSO	ABC
dark_and_bright_copys	5, 1.26, 0.53, 5, 20, 0.01	5, 1.14, 0.42, 5, 31, 0.0064	6, 1.89, 0.57, 5, 24, 0.0034
window_copyd	6, 1.31, 0.34, 3, 39, 0.0099	5, 1.32, 0.50, 4, 43, 0.0100	4, 1.74, 0.59, 9, 16, 0.0062
ship_number_copys	5, 1.16, 0.6, 7, 45, 0.006	6, 1.10, 0.49, 9, 47, 0.0054	5, 1.02, 0.38, 3, 43, 0.0076
stone_ghost_copys	4, 1.39, 0.64, 2, 40, 0.0065	3, 1.10, 0.74, 3, 44, 0.0015	4, 1.39, 0.64, 3, 40, 0.0065
red_towers	4, 1.4, 0.48, 7, 19, 0.0008	6, 1.21, 0.38, 3, 43, 0.0097	4, 1.64, 0.5, 4, 20, 0.0001
scotland_copys	5, 1.93, 0.79, 7, 31, 0.0051	4, 1.07, 0.57, 9, 17, 0.0066	4, 1.37, 0.73, 9, 41, 0.0032

three SI algorithms, because they seem similar. Further comparisons need detail information of the detection results, which is listed in Table 3.

Optimization threshold values of nine images in Christlein et al.'s database are shown in Table 2. And Table 3 shows the corresponding detection results based on these optimization threshold values to detect the nine images. In the image of dark_and_bright_copys, mask_copys and window_copyd, SR is less than 1 %. SR of christmas_hedge_copys, ship_number_copys and stone_ghost_copys are between 1 % and 5 %. SR of hedge_copys, red_towers and scotland_copys are greater than 5 %.

Table 3 shows the detail information of detection results obtained by DE, PSO and ABC algorithms, respectively. The detection results of dark_and_bright_copys, mask_copys, window_copyd and scotland_copys can be seen clearly in Fig. 1. In christmas_hedge_copys, ship_number_copys and stone_ghost_copys, the detection results of three SI algorithms are very similar. The detection result of PSO is slightly better than DE and ABC in stone_ghost_copys, because its TMK is the greatest. Similarly, the detection result of ABC is the best in christmas_hedge_copys and the detection result of DE is the best in ship_number_copys. In hedge_copys, red_towers and scotland_copys, the best SI algorithm is PSO, the second is ABC and DE is the last.

Table 3. The detection results of DE, PSO and ABC algorithm

Image name	DE			PSO			ABC		
	TMK	P	D	TMK	P	D	TMK	P	D
dark_and_bright_copys	104	0.58	0.58	100	0.79	0.79	0	0	0
window_copyd	90	1	0.9	190	1	0.95	70	0.87	0.87
ship_number_copys	1060	1	0.99	1054	1	0.99	1049	1	0.99
stone_ghost_copys	1872	1	0.99	1890	1	0.99	1874	1	0.99
red_towers	600	1	0.98	1142	1	0.99	898	1	0.98
scotland_copys	0	0	0	18	0.9	0.64	8	0.36	0.36

Three measurements (*KR, P* and *D*) are used to measure the detection results, which are shown in Fig. 2. As a contrast, the original SIFT method is listed in Fig. 2. The original method detects the image using a group of fixed threshold values, which is determined by the experience of researchers. In Fig. 2, it is clear that the PSO algorithm can create greater *KR* at most time. The only exception is that when *SR* is around 4 %, ABC algorithm obtains a slightly better result than PSO algorithm.

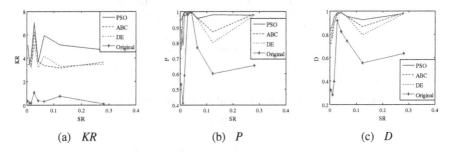

(a) *KR*   (b) *P*   (c) *D*

Fig. 2. *KR, P, D* of the detection results

When *SR* is less than 1 % and between 5.2 % and 20 %, DE algorithm is better than ABC algorithm. Otherwise, *KR* of ABC algorithm is greater than that of DE algorithm. All of the three SI algorithms have much greater *KR* than original method.

Figure 2(b) shows the precision of each algorithm. PSO algorithm has the best detection results in any *SR*. When *SR* is less 1 %, DE algorithm has a greater precision than ABC algorithm. Three SI algorithms have exactly similar precision, when *SR* is near 28 % and between 1 % and 6 %. Otherwise, ABC algorithm is better than DE algorithm. The original method is similar with three SI algorithms, when *SR* is between 3 % and 5 %. Otherwise, the precision of original method is fall far below three SI algorithms.

Figure 2(c) shows *D* of each algorithm. *D* is a comprehensive measure, which directly reveals the detection effect. Though selecting the false match coefficient φ as a constant, *D* can directly reveal the detection effect with a good balance between *KR* and *P*. In this paper, we set $\varphi = 10$. Figure 2(c) seems similarly to Fig. 2(a). The PSO algorithm is also creating the best detection result. When *SR* is near 28 % and between 1 % and 5 %, three SI algorithms show the similar performance. DE algorithm is better than ABC algorithm, when *SR* is less than 1 %. When *SR* is greater than 5 %, ABC algorithm has a greater *D* than DE algorithm. *D* of original method is far below three SI algorithms.

Table 2 shows the mean values of *TMK, P* and *D* among three SI algorithms and original method. The PSO algorithm is the best. The ABC and DE algorithms have similar performance. All of them are much better than original method.

SR can be divided into three sections: less than 1 %, between 1 % and 5 %, and greater than 5 %. The mean values of *TMK, P* and *D* in each section are shown in Table 5. In the three sections, PSO algorithm shows the best performance and the original method is the worst one. When *SR* is less than 1 %, DE algorithm is better than ABC algorithm. It gets the opposite result, when *SR* is greater than 5 %. PSO, DE and ABC algorithms have similar performance in the section, which *SR* is between 1 % and 5 % (Table 4).

Table 4. Compare the mean values of *TMK*, *P* and *D* among the three SI algorithms

	PSO	ABC	DE	Original
TMK	2527.425	1854.1	1858.275	178.5
P	0.978	0.940	0.924	0.692
D	0.939	0.904	0.899	0.661

Table 5. Compare three SI algorithms in the three section of *SR*

	Less than 1 %			Between 1 % and 5 %			Greater than 5 %		
	TMK	*P*	*D*	*TMK*	*P*	*D*	*TMK*	*P*	*D*
PSO	229	0.968	0.885	1073	0.995	0.974	5626	0.971	0.952
ABC	186	0.881	0.806	997	0.996	0.960	3932	0.938	0.935
DE	216	0.863	0.825	869	0.996	0.956	4030	0.911	0.907
Original	11	0.477	0.334	129	0.910	0.225	355	0.674	0.365

From the experimental results, no algorithm is always better than the other two. The detection results of three SI algorithms are various in different SR. The results suggest that in SIFT-based detection technique, PSO algorithm outperforms ABC and DE while SR is less than 1 % and more than 5 %. They show similar performance when SR is between 1 % and 5 %. In this range, there is no obvious difference among three SI algorithms. When SR is less than 1 %, DE is better than ABC. ABC is better than DE, when SR is greater than 5 %. Experiments based on SIFT-based detection technique indicate that the PSO algorithm can be efficiently used to find optimal thresholds for CMF detection. All of the three SI algorithms can get much better detection results than original method.

5   Concluding

The classical scale invariant features transform (SIFT) methods for copy-move forgery (CMF) detection suffer from the selection of multiple threshold values with a lack of authority and an insufficient number of matched keypoints with a low credibility of duplicated regions estimation.

In this study, the canonical swarm intelligent algorithms (differential evolution - DE, particle swarm optimization - PSO and artificial bee colony - ABC) have been employed to search the optimal combinations of multilevel thresholds for SIFT-based CMF detection. The ratio of true matched keypoints to the pixels of duplicated region

(KR), the ratio of true matched keypoints and all matched keypoints (P) and the ratio of true matched keypoints and the sum of true matched keypoints and the false match coefficient $\varphi(D)$ are selected as the essential measurements of these SIFT&SI-based CMF detection. The test against forty images of Christlein et al.'s database reveals that PSO is the best choice if SR is less than 1 % or more than 5 %. When SR is between 1 % and 5 %, all swarm intelligent (SI) algorithms have nearly the same performance. On the whole, PSO algorithm is relatively suitable for searching optimal combination of multilevel thresholds for SIFT&SI-based CMF detection.

In our future work, we will try to improve the detection speed of SIFT&SI-based CMF detection method by means of adjusting SI algorithm and parallel programming. At the same time, we will also consider several approaches to improve the detection performance for the CMF images with small or smooth duplicated regions.

Acknowledgments. This work was supported in part by the National Natural Science Foundation of China under grant No. (61472429, 61070192, 91018008, 61303074, 61170240), Beijing Natural Science Foundation under grant No. 4122041, National High-Tech Research Development Program of China under grant No. 2007AA01Z414, and National Science and Technology Major Project of China under grant No. 2012ZX01039-004.

References

1. Pan, X.Y., Lyu, S.W.: Detecting image region duplication using SIFT features. In: IEEE International Conference on Acoustics Speech and Signal Processing (ICASSP), pp. 1706–1709 (2010)
2. Christlein, V., Riess, C., Jordan, J., Riess, C., Angelopoulou, E.: An evaluation of popular copy-move forgery detection approaches. IEEE Trans. Inf. Forensics Secur. **7**(6), 1841–1854 (2012)
3. Li, J., Li, X., Yang, B., Sun, X.: Segmentation-based image copy-move forgery detection scheme. IEEE Trans. Inf. Forensics Secur. **10**(3), 507–518 (2015)
4. Storn, R., Price, K.: Differential evolution–a simple and efficient heuristic for global optimization over continuous spaces. J. Global Optim. **11**, 341–359 (1997)
5. Storn, R.: On the usage of differential evolution for function optimization. In: North American Fuzzy Information, NAFIPS 1996, pp. 519–523 (1996)
6. Kennedy, J., Eberhart, R.: Particle swarm optimization. In: IEEE International Conference on Neural Networks, pp. 1942–1948 (1995)
7. Eberhart, R., Kennedy, J.: A new optimizer using particle swarm theory. In: Sixth International Symposium on Micro Machine and Human Science, MHS 1995, pp. 39–43 (1995)
8. Yin, P.Y.: A fast scheme for multilevel thresholding using genetic algorithms. Sig. Proc. **72**, 85–95 (1999)
9. Yin, P.Y.: Multilevel minimum cross entropy threshold selection based on particle swarm optimization. Appl. Math. Comput. **184**(2), 503–513 (2007)
10. Maitra, M., Chatterjee, A.: A hybrid cooperative–comprehensive learning based PSO algorithm for image segmentation using multilevel thresholding. Expert Syst. Appl. **34**, 1341–1350 (2008)

11. Guo, C., Li, H.: Multilevel thresholding method for image segmentation based on an adaptive particle swarm optimization algorithm. In: Orgun, M.A., Thornton, J. (eds.) AI 2007. LNCS, vol. 4830, pp. 654–658. Springer, Heidelberg (2007). doi:10.1007/978-3-540-76928-6_70

12. Karaboga, D., Basturk, B.: On the performance of artificial bee colony (ABC) algorithm. Appl. Soft Comput. **8**, 687–697 (2008)

13. Horng, M.-H., Jiang, T.-W.: Multilevel image thresholding selection using the artificial bee colony algorithm. In: Wang, F.L., Deng, H., Gao, Y., Lei, J. (eds.) AICI 2010. LNCS, vol. 6320, pp. 318–325. Springer, Heidelberg (2010). doi:10.1007/978-3-642-16527-6_40

14. Zhang, Y., Wu, L.: Optimal multi-level thresholding based on maximum Tsallis entropy via an artificial bee colony approach. Entropy **13**, 841–859 (2011)

15. Ye, Z.W., Zheng, Z.B., Xin, Y., Ning, X.G.: Automatic threshold selection based on ant colony optimization algorithm. In: The International Conference on Neural Networks and Brain, pp. 728–732 (2006)

16. Sathya, P.D., Kayalvizhi, R.: Modified bacterial foraging algorithm based multilevel thresholding for image segmentation. Expert Syst. Appl. **24**, 595–615 (2011)

17. Shi, W.C., Zhao, F., Qin, B., Liang, B.: Improving image copy-move forgery detection with particle swarm optimization techniques. China Commun. **13**(1), 139–149 (2016)

Encryption Scheme Based on Hyperelliptic Curve Cryptography

Asha Liza John[✉] and Sabu M. Thampi

Indian Institute of Information Technology and Management-Kerala,
Technopark Campus, Trivandrum 695581, India
{asha.mphilcs3,sabu.thampi}@iiitmk.ac.in

Abstract. In modern times, common man uses small computing devices like mobile phones, RFID systems and embedded systems. Such devices are resource constrained. Hence, algorithms used in such devices must consume less power and should have minimal memory requirements. But, several existing cryptosystems like RSA require more memory and other resources for operation. So, in the proposed work an optimized and secure encryption scheme is developed to ensure confidentiality in communication. This algorithm is developed with reference to Elliptic Curve Integrated Encryption Scheme (ECIES) included in standards from ANSI, IEEE, and also ISO/IEC and is integrated with the concept of hyperelliptic curve cryptography (HECC). The proposed encryption scheme based on HECC makes use of three cryptographic functions viz. *key agreement, encryption/decryption algorithms* and *message authentication code (MAC)*. The key agreement function generates a l-bit secret key. For this, the existing Diffie Hellman Key Agreement Algorithm is improved suitably so as to defend Man-in-the-Middle (MitM) attack. The encryption/decryption mechanism is developed by improving the RC4 algorithm. The proposed scheme integrates the concept of hyperelliptic curves with the key stream generation process. Finally, the paper presents a proposal for MAC based on HECC.

Keywords: Cryptography · Encryption · Message authentication code · Key agreement · Hyperelliptic curve cryptography

1 Introduction

The advent of transistors and microprocessors led to smaller size devices, more efficient computation, lower cost especially in small-signal circuits, lower power and voltage consumption, less waste heat, and higher efficiency. So, in modern times, smaller computing devices like mobile phones, RFID systems and embedded systems which use transistors and microprocessors in its construction are more popular and common. But, such devices are resource constrained. Hence, algorithms used in such devices must consume less power and should have minimal memory requirements.

The existing cryptosystems like RSA require more memory and other resources for operation [1]. Hence, they are not widely used in resource constrained devices. "The security gap between the systems grows as the key size grows" [2]. As algorithms for integer factorization have become more and more efficient, the RSA based methods

© Springer International Publishing AG 2016
G. Wang et al. (Eds.): SpaCCS 2016, LNCS 10066, pp. 491–506, 2016.
DOI: 10.1007/978-3-319-49148-6_40

have had to resort to longer and longer keys. The Elliptic curve cryptography (ECC) has evolved as a vast field for public key cryptography systems. ECC has comparatively the highest strength-per-bit compared to other public key cryptosystems [3]. The ECC can thus provide the same level and type of security as RSA but with much shorter keys. Moreover, the shorter keys reduce storage space for keys and faster computation speed [2].

The security of Public Key Cryptosystem is essentially based on three mathematical problems that are believed to be both secure and practical after years of intensive studying viz. Integer Factorization Problem, Finite Field Discrete Logarithm Problem (FFDLP), and the Elliptic Curve Discrete Logarithm Problem (ECDLP). Among these, Elliptic Curve Discrete Logarithm Problem (ECDLP) which is the Discrete Logarithm Problem (DLP) in a group defined by points on an elliptic curve over a finite field is very hard to solve. The security of ECC based schemes depends on ECDLP.

The first encryption schemes based on elliptic curves were the equivalent versions of the Massey-Omura [4] and ElGamal [5] cryptosystems, both presented by Koblitz in 1985 (and published in 1987), and the Menezes-Vanstone cryptosystem [6]. The main disadvantage of the Massey-Omura and El-Gamal versions adapted for elliptic curves is that plaintexts and encrypted messages must be represented as points of an elliptic curve E. The Menezes-Vanstone cryptosystem for elliptic curves was designed precisely to overcome this limitation, as instead of matching each message with a point of the curve E, it represents the plaintexts as ordered pairs of $F^* * F^*$. But the disadvantage of this procedure is that, instead of transforming each clear message into a single point of the curve, the size of the encrypted message depends directly on the length of the plaintext.

However, the discovery of the limitations of these early cryptosystems paved way for the development of hybrid schemes that use elliptic curves such as Elliptic Curve Integrated Encryption Scheme (ECIES) [7], PSEC (Provably Secure Elliptic Curve encryption scheme) [8, 9], and ACE (Advanced Cryptographic Engine) [9, 10]. Of the three schemes, ECIES is available in a greater number of standards (ANSI X9.63, IEEE 1363rd, ISO/IEC 18033-2, and SECG SEC 1). Hence, the ECIES is considered to be more suitable for application in resource constrained devices, because ECC uses shorter keys which results in faster execution and less memory utilization. Although, ECIES is performing better than its predecessors, still there is scope for improvement. This is mainly because; the key size of existing ECC based cryptosystems is very large even though ECC use significantly smaller key sizes than their non elliptic curve equivalents. This larger key size leads to difficulty in data management, increased hardware and bandwidth requirements while transmitting keys via network and low battery life. Such disadvantages are not desirable for resource constrained systems.

In 1988 Koblitz suggested for the first time the generalization of EC to curves of higher genus, namely hyperelliptic curves (HEC) [11]. "Hyperelliptic curves are a special class of algebraic curves which can be viewed as a generalization of elliptic curves. It is widely accepted that for most cryptographic applications based on elliptic curves or HEC, one needs a group order of size at least $\approx 2^{160}$. For hyperelliptic curve cryptography (HECC) over Fq we will need at least $g \cdot \log_2 q \approx 2^{160}$, where g is the genus of the curve. In particular for a curve of genus two, we will need a field Fq with | Fq| $\approx 2^{80}$, i.e., 80-bit long operands" [12]. In short, the security achieved by an 80 bit hyperelliptic curve cryptosystem is equivalent to that of a 160 bit elliptic curve cryptosystem. The HECC provides greater efficiency in terms of computational overheads, key sizes, and bandwidth. Hyperelliptic Curve cryptosystem can acquire the same security level as ECC with shorter operating parameters. At present, the attack algorithms against hyperelliptic curve cryptosystem with low genus prove to be inapplicable with exponent complexity [12].

This paper introduces an efficient cryptosystem based on the concept of HECC for operating in resource constrained environments. Our scheme consists of a key agreement function, and encryption/decryption algorithms. The proposed algorithms are developed with reference to Elliptic Curve Integrated Encryption Scheme (ECIES) and are integrated with the concept of HECC. Hence, the scheme is called Hyperelliptic Curve Integrated Encryption Scheme (HECIES). The key agreement function is an improvement over the well-known Diffie-Hellman (DH) algorithm. The key agreement scheme overcomes few limitations of the DH. The encryption based on HECC modifies the RC4 scheme to reduce the key size and provide more security. The theoretical proof and experimental results are presented. Finally, the paper provides a proposal for a new message authentication code (MAC) as an alternative to hash based MAC.

The remainder of this paper is organized as follows: Section 1 provides an overview of related work and literature. Section 2 presents the proposed Scheme. Sections 3, 4, 5, 6 and 7 provide comprehensive security and computational performance analysis of the scheme. Section 8 discusses a proposal for message authentication code using HECC. Finally, Sect. 9 concludes the paper.

2 Proposed Scheme

The proposed encryption scheme requires the use of a few global parameters which are publicly available. The global parameters introduced are all based on the concept of HECC. Among the chosen global parameters, we have prime numbers, prime fields, a hyperelliptic curve and its divisor. The detailed list of global parameters is given in Table 1:

Table 1. List of global parameters

F_p	Finite prime field
C	Hyperelliptic curve of genus 2 over prime field Fp
D	Unique Reduced Divisor over Hyperelliptic curve C

The following steps are used to find the parameters:

i. Choose finite prime field F_p with elements of order n
ii. Choose a random hyperelliptic curve C of genus 2 over F_p
iii. Compute unique reduced divisor D represented in Mumford form as D = <u(x), v(x)> over hyperelliptic curve C (using Harley's Algorithm or Cantor's Algorithm [16]) such that points $(x_i, v(x_i))$ lies on C.

The two algorithms - Harley's or Cantor's are used to compute reduced divisors. The Cantor's algorithm can be used for finding the unique reduced divisor of hyperelliptic curves of any genus g. This algorithm is a universal algorithm. However, the algorithm is slow because it involves polynomial arithmetic computations. In Harley's algorithm, polynomial operations are transformed to field operations through explicit formulae. Field arithmetic is faster, which may even lead up to an 80 % decrease in computational cost. But Harley's algorithm is very poor in dealing with exceptional cases (although it appears with less probability $\approx 1 - O\left(\frac{1}{q}\right)$ in the case of genus 2 curves). So, for such exceptions, Cantor's algorithm is used. This replacement of Cantor's with Harley's for cases other than exceptions, also improves the performance to a great extent.

In the proposed cryptosystem, both the sender and the receiver require the use of a permanent private key and a public key each. The public keys are generated using the corresponding permanent private key and divisor value, D for sender and receiver (Table 2).

Table 2. Permanent private and public keys

Sender
Let senders permanent private key be S_{PR}
Let senders permanent Public Key be S_{PU} such that $S_{PU} = S_{PR} * D$
Receiver
Let receivers permanent private key be R_{PR}
Let receivers permanent Public Key be R_{PU} such that $R_{PU} = R_{PR} * D$

2.1   Key Agreement

The key agreement function is used for the generation and agreement of shared secret by two parties. The key agreement scheme is an improved version of existing Diffie Hellman Key Agreement Scheme. The Diffie Hellman algorithm is prone to man-in-the-middle attack, the key size obtained is larger and the key generation process requires primality testing [13]. Hence, the existing Diffie Hellman algorithm is improved by employing HECC. In the proposed improved Diffie Hellman Scheme (Fig. 1), two parameters S_s and S_r are computed each for the sender and the receiver side respectively. S_s and S_r are values calculated using the permanent and temporary private key parameters of the corresponding parties in communication.

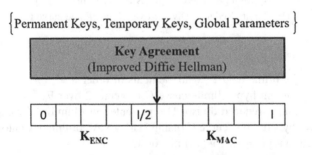

Fig. 1. Improved Diffie Hellman Key Agreement Scheme

The key agreement at the sender side is explained in Algorithm 1. The scheme first chooses a private key 'a' which is less than 'p'. Using 'a' and divisor value D, a temporary public key A is computed. The first L bits of sum of coefficients of u(x) of A, value of 'a' and the permanent private key S_{PR} are used to compute S_s. The secret key K_1 is computed using S_s, temporary public key B, L_2 and receivers permanent public key R_{PU}. Finally, the shared secret key K will be the hash of K_1. The same process has been applied at the receiver side to generate the shared secret key. This is discussed in Algorithm 2.

Algorithm 1: Key Agreement- At the Sender Side

> **Input**: Permanent keys, Temporary Keys and Global Parameters
> **Output**: Shared Secret Key
>
> 1) Choose temporary private key $a < p$
> 2) Compute temporary public key as $A = aD$ where D=<u(x), v(x)> is the divisor on hyper-elliptic curve C
> 3) Let L_1= first L bits of sum of coeff. of u(x) of A
> 4) Receive public keys of receiver (R_{PU}, B) and compute L_2 from B
> 5) Compute $S_s = a + [L_1 * S_{PR}]$
> 6) Compute secret key $K_1 = S_s [B + L_2 * R_{PU}]$
> 7) Shared secret key $K = Hash (K_1)$

Algorithm 2: Key Agreement- At the Receiver Side

> **Input**: Permanent keys, Temporary Keys and Global Parameters
> **Output**: Shared Secret Key
>
> 1) Choose temporary private key $b < p$
> 2) Compute temporary public key as $B = bD$ where D=<u(x),v(x)> is the divisor on Hyper-elliptic curve C
> 3) Let L_2= first L bits of sum of coeff of u(x) of A
> 4) Receive public keys of sender (S_{PU}, A) and compute L_1 from A
> 5) Compute $S_r = b + [L_2 * R_{PR}]$
> 6) Compute secret key $K_2 = S_r [A + L_1 * S_{PU}]$
> 7) Shared secret key $K = Hash (K_2)$

The 1-bit shared secret key K, thus generated both at the sender and receiver side will be equal. The first half (l/2 bits) of K is used by the preceding encryption/decryption algorithm and the last (l/2 bits) of K is used by the preceding MAC algorithm.

2.1.1 Theoretical Proof of Correctness

$$K_1 = S_s[B + L_2 * R_{PU}]$$
$$= S_s[bD + L_2 * R_{PR}.D]$$
$$= S_s[b + L_2 * R_{PR}]D \qquad (1)$$
$$= S_s.S_r.D$$

$$K_2 = S_r[A + L_1 * S_{PU}]$$
$$= S_r[aD + L_1 * S_{PR}.D]$$
$$= S_r[a + L_1 * S_{PR}]D \qquad (2)$$
$$= S_r.S_s.D$$

From (1) and (2) we get $K_1 = K_2$; thus, the shared secret calculated by both parties is equal.

2.1.2 Man in the Middle Attack (MitM)

The two values S_s and S_r transform the existing Diffie Hellman Key Agreement process to a signed key agreement process there by defending Man-in-the-Middle Attack (MitM). This section illustrates how the improved Diffie Hell-man Key Agreement Algorithm defends the MitM Attack effectively. First, the traditional Diffie Hellman Key Agreement scheme is analysed for MitM attack. Figure 2 illustrates the man in the middle attack. Here, Alice is the sender, Bob is the receiver and Mallory is the adversary in the middle.

(1) Alice chooses a as its private key and computes key as g^a
(2) Alice sends the public key to Bob. But Mallory intercepts this message
(3) Mallory chooses m as its private key and computes its own public key as g^m
(4) Mallory then sends its own public key instead of that of Alice's public key
(5) On receiving this, Bob chooses its private key b and computes its public key g^b
(6) Bob sends this public key to Alice

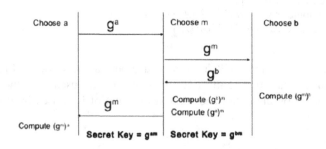

Fig. 2. Man in the middle attack against DH

(7) Mallory intercepts this message and sends its public key to Alice instead of that of Bob's

(8) Now, both Alice and Bob along with adversary Mallory calculate the shared secret key.

The improved Diffie Hellman Key Agreement Algorithm uses a pair of ephemeral keys in addition to a pair of permanent keys. Along with the computation of the shared secret key, both Alice and Bob also compute two additional parameters S_s and S_r respectively. S_s and S_r are computed using the permanent and ephemeral private keys of the corresponding parties. These S_s and S_r parameters are then used in the calculation of the shared secret key. Hence, it is difficult for the adversary Mallory to calculate the shared secret key although he may intercept the message by both the communicating parties. Figure 3 illustrates this scenario. The public keys of Alice, Mallory and Bob are A, M and B respectively.

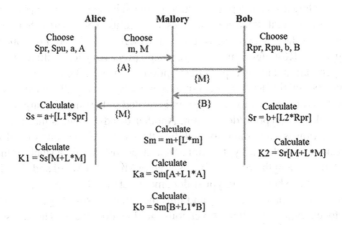

Fig. 3. Proposed improved Diffie Hellman Scheme and MitM attack

Theoretical Security Analysis for MitM Attack on Proposed Improved Diffie Hellman Key Agreement Mechanism is shown below:

$$
\begin{aligned}
K_1 &= S_s\big[M + L * M_{pu}\big] \\
&= S_s\big[mD + L * M_{pr}.D\big] \\
&= S_s\big[m + L * M_{pr}\big]D \\
&= S_s.S_mD
\end{aligned}
\tag{i}
$$

$$
\begin{aligned}
K_2 &= S_r\big[M + L * M_{pu}\big] \\
&= S_rS_mD
\end{aligned}
\tag{ii}
$$

$$
K_a = S_m[A + L * A]
\tag{iii}
$$

$$K_b = S_m[B + L * B] \tag{iv}$$

From (i), (ii), (iii) and (iv) we get $K_1 \neq K_a \neq K_b \neq K_2$. Hence, it is proved theoretically that the adversary Mallory can never obtain the shared secret key by intercepting the messages of Alice and Bob.

For the proposed key agreement scheme, given level of security can be attained with smaller key size. The key generation requires no prime number generation or primality testing. The entire key agreement process is authenticated to avoid man-in-the-middle attack. Since the proposed scheme exchanges smaller public keys between sender and receiver, the process requires less message size. Moreover, no known algorithm is available to break HCDLP.

2.2 Proposed Encryption Scheme

RC4 [14] is a widely used encryption technique due to its speed and simplicity in design. It is used in commercial software packages like Lotus Notes and MS Office, and in network protocols like Secure Socket Layer (SSL), and Wired Equivalent Privacy (WEP). In general, RC4 algorithm is a three stage process which includes initialization, key stream generation and encryption/decryption. However, the key stream generation process involved in the RC4 algorithm is generally weak and hence vulnerable to attacks. The speed of encryption/decryption is related to key size i.e. larger the key size lesser the speed of encryption/decryption. Another disadvantage is that the key stream generation function is vulnerable to analytic attacks. Moreover, one out of every 256 keys is a weak key i.e. the encrypted cipher text depends on only a small number of key bits. "RC4 with key length up to 128 bits is used in Microsoft Word and Excel to protect the documents. But when an encrypted document gets modified and saved, the initialization vector (IV) remains the same and thus the same keystream generated from RC4 is applied to encrypt the different versions of that document. The consequence is catastrophic since a lot of information of the document could be recovered easily" [15].

In the proposed RC4 algorithm, the first two stages of RC4 i.e. initialization and key stream generation are improvised to include the concept of HECC so that the existing weakness of the key stream generation process is resolved. Figure 4 shows the process of encryption with the proposed scheme.

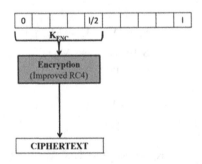

Fig. 4. Improved RC4 encryption algorithm

Algorithm 3 explains three stages of the improved RC4 encryption algorithm proposed in this work viz. initialization, key stream generation and encryption. The initialization process is done using hyper-elliptic curve of genus 2 over prime field F_p. The key stream generation involves computation of initial key value and transformation to key stream K_s of length n bits. The initial key value uses the shared secret key, a constant value and a variable r which denotes the left shift positions. The third step is the encryption process in which the n bits of keystream K_s is divided into m words of b-bits each followed by dividing the plaintext to streams of length b-bits each. Finally, XOR the b-bits of K_s with b-bits of plaintext to form b-bits of cipher text.

Algorithm 3: Improved RC4 Encryption Algorithm

Input: Plain text, Secret key K
Output: Cipher text

1. **Initialization**
   1.1. Let C be a hyper-elliptic curve of genus 2 over prime field Fp
   1.2. Compute divisor $D_1 =< u_1(x), v_1(x) >$ of curve C
2. **Key Stream Generation**
   2.1. Compute initial key value
       2.1.1. $K_i = (u_i (K) \, const) << r$, where const - a constant value « r - left shift
             by r positions
       2.1.2. r - variable value
       2.1.3. K - shared secret key
   2.2. Compute $D_{i+1} = K_i * D_i$
   2.3. Transform D_{i+1} to key stream K_s of length n bits.
3. **Encryption**
   3.1. Divide the n bits of keystream K_s to m words of b-bits each
   3.2. Divide the plaintext to streams of length b-bits each
   3.3. XOR the b-bits of K_s with b-bits of plaintext to form b-bits of cipher text
   3.4. Check if there is still more plaintext to be encrypted if so, use the keystream
         generator to generate more keystreams.

The decryption process is same as that of the encryption process. The obtained cipher text is XORed with the key stream derived at the receiver end. For this, the constant value *const*, the variable value *r*, and the shared secret key K are all known by both the parties in communication.

The modified RC4 algorithm requires smaller key size. The proposed algorithm replaced the simple logical operations with the hard to solve HCDLP for increasing the level of security. Moreover, the method of encryption is simple.

3   Hyperelliptic Curve Discrete Logarithm Problem (HCDLP)

Security depends on the difficulty of solving the Hyperelliptic Curve Discrete Logarithm Problem (HCDLP) stated as follows: Given a hyperelliptic curve C of genus g over a finite field Fq, a point $P \in J(C)$ of order n, a point $Q \in <P>$, the Discrete

Logarithm Problem is to find an integer $I \epsilon [0, n-1]$ such that $Q = IP$. The integer I is called the discrete logarithm of Q to the base P, denoted by $I = \log_P Q$.

4 Hyperelliptic Curve vs. Elliptic Curve

The effort required by the best algorithms to solve the Discrete Logarithm Problem, in the worst case, is $O(\sqrt{|G|})$ group operations. For curves of genus g over a finite field Fq, $|G| \approx q^g$ as $q \to \infty$. As per standards, the lowest level of security recommended is 80 bits. i.e. $\sqrt{(q^g)} \approx 2^{80}$ elliptic curves are hyperelliptic curves of genus g = 1.

Therefore,

$$O\left(\sqrt{|G|}\right) = O\left(\sqrt{|q^g|}\right)$$
$$= O\left(\sqrt{|q^1|}\right) \qquad (3)$$
$$= O\left(\sqrt{|q^1|}\right)O(2^{80})$$

$q = 2^{80*2} = 2^{160}$.

Therefore, number of Group Operations for ECC = $|G| \approx q^1 = 2^{160}$.

For Hyperelliptic Curves of genus g = 2 (Used)

$$O\left(\sqrt{|G|}\right) = O\left(\sqrt{|q^g|}\right)$$
$$= O\left(\sqrt{|q^2|}\right) \qquad (4)$$
$$= O\left(\sqrt{|q^2|}\right)O(2^{80})$$

$$q = 2^{80}.$$

Therefore, number of Group Operations for HECC of genus 2 = $|G| \approx q^2 = 2^{160}$.

From the above analysis, it is evident that the hardness of solving an 80 bit HCDLP is equal to the hardness of solving a 160 bit ECDLP. Hence, the proposed work used hyperelliptic curves instead of elliptic curves to improve the performance.

5 Comparison of Proposed Scheme with Elliptic Curve Integrated Encryption Scheme (ECIES)

The proposed scheme is theoretically compared with ECIES. Table 3 compares the effect of key size on security level of the schemes. The proposed scheme can attain a security level of 80 bits with a lower key size of 80–111 bits while ECIES requires 160–223 bits for the same.

Table 3. Comparison of proposed scheme with ECIES

Security level (bits)	Key length (bits)	
	ECIES	Proposed scheme
80	160–223	80–111
112	224–255	112–127
128	256–283	128–191
192	384–511	192–255
256	512–571	256–286

6 Other Advantages of the Proposed Scheme

- *Availability:* DoS attack is possible only if adversary knows the secret key value K. This is impossible because man-in-the-middle attack is prevented by calculating values S_r and S_s. So, availability is ensured.
- *Forward security:* The key K used for communication is recalculated after each session by changing the temporary keys. Also, obtaining the first key from the second communication requires a solution to the HCDLP. So, forward security is ensured.
- *Unauthorized tracking:* Each communication between the parties involves the use of values S_s and S_r for calculating key K. So, unauthorized tracking is not possible.
- *Replay attack:* Replay attack is not possible since secret key involved changes after each session.
- *Known plain text attack:* Even if the intruder has some knowledge of (plaintext (PT), ciphertext (CT)) pairs, it is impossible to find out the key from the statistical relationship between those pairs. It is not possible, apart from a brute force search over all possible keys. Instead, he/she should solve HCDLP to find out the key value.
- *Chosen cipher text attack:* Even if the intruder knows the algorithm that produces PT for the CT messages chosen by intruder using a secret key, unless he solves the HCDLP, he cannot find the secret key.
- For the same reason stated above *Cipher text only attack* and *Chosen plaintext attacks* are also impossible.

7 Experimental Results and Discussion

The proposed Hyperelliptic Curve Integrated Encryption Scheme (ECIES) is implemented in Java using the HECCinJava package. This GNU GPL v3 licensed project was developed as a library for allowing HECC over both PRIME and BINARY Finite Fields. It is a step towards the practical use of HECC by narrowing the performance gap between ECC and HECC. It is a practical library available that allows users to do HECC in Java like that of Bountsy Castle ECC library. There is a single library for doing hyperelliptic curve cryptography namely, jSaluki 0.82. This library is an Open Source Java Hyperelliptic Curve Cryptography Library and only recommended for research and educational purposes. It is also too slow and didn't include the recent advancement in area of HECC, like use of explicit formula for group operations and point counting. The Heccin-Java package resolves these shortcomings of jSaluki.

The implementation of the proposed scheme in Java is tested over various field order values for assessing its performance. From Table 4, it is clear that the execution time of all the two algorithms of the new scheme decreases as field order value increases.

Table 4. Prime order vs. execution time

Field order	Execution time (ms)	
	Key agreement	Encryption
F_{1087}	7	67
F_{1151}	11	16
F_{1283}	9	17
F_{1381}	8	14
F_{1423}	9	14
F_{1571}	9	15
F_{1619}	8	15
F_{1789}	8	15
F_{1877}	7	14

The RC4 encryption algorithm is used by standards such as IEEE 802.11 within Wired Equivalent Privacy using 40 and 128-bit keys. This standard has shown several security vulnerabilities such as "passive attacks to decrypt traffic based on statistical analysis; active attack to inject new traffic from unauthorized mobile stations, based on known plaintext; active attacks to decrypt traffic, based on tricking the access point, and dictionary-building attack that allows real-time automated decryption of all traffic" [17]. IEEE 802.11i is an IEEE 802.11 amendment used to facilitate secure end-to-end communication for wireless local area networks (WLAN). It makes use of the famous Advanced Encryption Standard (AES) block cipher. Hence, the performance of the proposed scheme is also compared with AES.

The execution time of the proposed improvised encryption scheme is compared with two existing schemes AES and RC4 for different data sizes. The execution time of the proposed encryption scheme is found to be almost equal to that of existing RC4 encryption scheme (Table 5).

Table 5. Execution time comparison

Data size	Execution time (ms)		
	AES	RC4	Proposed scheme
100 KB	32.0	15.2	15
500 KB	90.0	54.4	50.3
1 MB	345.3	229.0	218.0
2 MB	626.0	550.8	500.7
5 MB	2433.0	1743.7	1755.0

Another important parameter is memory utilization based on different data sizes. The memory utilization defines how much memory is being consumed while doing the encryption. By analyzing the data given in Table 6, it is found that the memory utilization of the proposed encryption scheme is less than that of the other two encryption schemes viz. AES and RC4.

Table 6. Comparison of memory utilization

Data size	Memory utilization (MB)		
	AES	RC4	Proposed scheme
100 KB	1	0.70	0.40
500 KB	2.4	1.5	0.90
1 MB	4	2.7	2
2 MB	7.2	5.2	4
5 MB	13.5	9.3	7

Throughput of an encryption scheme specifies the speed of encryption. Throughput is calculated as total plaintext in Kilobytes encrypted divided by the time consumed for encryption (KB/ms). As the throughput increases, power consumption decreases. The proposed scheme is found to have high throughput compared to existing schemes like AES and RC4 (Table 7). So, obviously the power consumption of the proposed scheme will be less compared to that of the other two schemes.

Table 7. Comparison of throughput

Data size	Throughput (KB/ms)		
	AES	RC4	Proposed scheme
100 KB	3.125	6.67	6.57
500 KB	5.56	9.94	9.19
1 MB	6.60	10.58	9.34
2 MB	5.93	9.39	8.94
5 MB	8.17	10.22	9.29

8   A Proposal for Message Authentication Code (MAC) Using HECC

HMAC (keyed-hash message authentication code) is a derivative of nested MAC which is standardized by NIST. But HMAC has several drawbacks which makes it vulnerable to several attacks. HMAC uses SHA-1 Hashing algorithm as part of the algorithm. SHA-1 hashing has been proved to be a weak hashing mechanism. Collision attack on SHA-1's compression function requires only 2^{57} SHA-1 evaluations (this attack was termed as SHAppening). Structural complexity of HMAC is high since HMAC

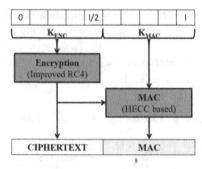

Fig. 5. New MAC algorithm based on hyperelliptic curve cryptography

generates 160-bits MAC which consumes more bandwidth while transmitting through network. Hence, a proposal based on HECC has been presented (Fig. 5 and Algorithm 4) for computing the MAC value of the cipher text generated by the improved RC4 algorithm used for encryption, so as to ensure that the received cipher text has not been altered while in transit from the sender to the receiver.

Algorithm 4: New MAC Algorithm based on HECC

Input: Ciphertext, Second half of shared secret key K
Output: MAC Value

1) Let CT be the cipher text obtained after encryption
2) Divide the cipher text CT to several groups of characters
3) Convert each group of characters to its ASCII equivalent
4) Find the sum of ASCII values in each group
5) Find the binary equivalent of these sum
6) Convert binary equivalent to a polynomial CT(x)
7) Divide CT(x) by U and V to obtain r_1 and r_2 as residues and
8) Compute $r = r_1 + r_2$ where D=<U,V> is the divisor on C
9) Compute $R_1 = r_1(r) * K$ and $R_2 = r_2(r) * K$
10) Find $R_1 + R_2$ to get the MAC

In the proposed MAC, the cipher text obtained after the encryption process (modified RC4) is divided into several groups of characters. Each group of characters is then converted into ASCII equivalent. As the next step, the sum of ASCII values in each group is computed and the binary equivalent is generated. The binary equivalent is converted to a polynomial CT(x). The polynomial is divided to obtain two residues r_1 and r_2. The sum of the residues are computed which is followed by computation of R_1 and R_2. The MAC is obtained by summing together R_1 and R_2. The advantages of proposed MAC compared to existing MAC algorithm are smaller key size, free from hash functions for generating MAC, less complexity, size of MAC is very less, and low bandwidth requirement for transmission.

9   Conclusion and Future Scope

An encryption algorithm integrated with the concept of hyperelliptic curve cryptography is developed with reference to Elliptic Curve Integrated Encryption Scheme (ECIES). The algorithm has three phases viz. key agreement, encryption/decryption and message authentication code. Proposed key agreement and encryption/decryption algorithms were theoretically proved and analyzed for security and performance. A proposal for new MAC was also presented.

A rough implementation of the algorithm was done in Java using HECCinJava package. The implementation was simulated for a range of field orders. Also, a comparison of this work was evaluated against ECIES and was found to perform better. Also, the proposed scheme was evaluated for metric parameters like execution time, memory usage and throughput and was found to be efficient.

The scope of this work may be extended to mobile environments with similar requirement for confidentiality. Proposed work can also be optimized further for providing lightweight cryptographic services that can perform on ultra-low power devices. The proposed encryption scheme can be combined with a light weight digital signature scheme so as to provide authentication to the messages transferred between both the parties in communication. By integrating this with a digital signature scheme it can be developed into a fully equipped cryptographic system.

References

1. Bafandehkar, M., Md Yasin, S., Mahmod, R.: Comparison of ECC and RSA algorithm in resource constrained devices. In: 2013 International Conference on IT Convergence and Security, pp. 1–3 (2013)
2. Hosseinzadeh, N.A.: Elliptic curve cryptography, University of Windsor, 31 July 2016. www.vlsi.uwindsor.ca/presentations/hossei1.pdf
3. Gajbhiye, S., Karmakar, S.: Application of elliptic curve method in cryptography: a literature review. Int. J. Comput. Sci. Inf. Technol. **3**, 4499–4503 (2012)
4. Massey, J., Omura, J.K.: Method and apparatus for maintaining the privacy of digital messages conveyed by public transmission. US Patent 4,567,600, 28 January 1986
5. ElGamal, T.: A public key cryptosystem and a signature scheme based on discrete logarithms. IEEE Trans. Inf. Theor. **IT-31**(4), 469–472 (1984)
6. Menezes, A.J., Vanstone, S.A.: Elliptic curve cryptosystems and their implementation. J. Cryptol. **6**, 209–224 (1993)
7. Brown, D.: Standards for Efficient Cryptography 1 (SEC-1). Standards for Efficient Cryptography, 1 (2009). http://www.secg.org/sec1-v2.pdf. Accessed 10 June 2016
8. Roy, D.B., Mukhopadhyay, D., Izumi, M., Takahashi, J.: Tile before multiplication: an efficient strategy to optimize DSP multiplier for accelerating prime field ECC for NIST curves. In: 51st Annual Design Automation Conference, pp. 1–6, IEEE Press, New York (2014). doi:10.1145/2593069.2593234
9. Shoup, V.: A proposal for an ISO standard for public key encryption (v. 2.1), 15 June 2016. http://www.shoup.net/papers/iso-2_1.pdf
10. Cramer, R., Shoup, V.: Design and analysis of practical public-key encryption schemes secure against adaptive chosen ciphertext attack. SIAM J. Comput. **33**(1), 167–226 (2003)

11. Koblitz, N.: A family of Jacobians suitable for discrete log cryptosystems. In: Goldwasser, S. (ed.) CRYPTO 1988. LNCS, vol. 403, pp. 94–99. Springer, Heidelberg (1990). doi:10.1007/0-387-34799-2_8

12. Pelzl, J., Wollinger, T., Guajardo, J., Paar, C.: Hyperelliptic curve cryptosystems: closing the performance gap to elliptic curves. In: Walter, C.D., Koç, Ç.K., Paar, C. (eds.) CHES 2003. LNCS, vol. 2779, pp. 351–365. Springer, Heidelberg (2003). doi:10.1007/978-3-540-45238-6_28

13. Raymond, J.F., Stiglic, A.: Security issues in the Diffie-Hellman key agreement protocol. IEEE Trans. Inf. Theor. **22**, 1–17 (2002)

14. Rivest, R.L.: The RC4 Encryption Algorithm, RSA Data Security, 12 March 1992

15. Wu, H.: The Misuse of RC4 in Microsoft Word and Excel. IACR Cryptology ePrint Archive (2005)

16. Sugizaki, H., Matsuo, K., Chao, J., Tsujii, S.: A generalized Harley algorithm for genus two hyperelliptic curves. In: Proceeding of SCIS 2003, IEICE Japan, pp. 917–921 (2003)

17. (In) Security of the WEP algorithm (2016). Isaac.cs.berkeley.edu, http://www.isaac.cs.berkeley.edu/isaac/wep-faq.html. Accessed 30 June 2016

Author Index

Printed in the United States
By Bookmasters